About the Author

Whilst working for Royal Mail for the last 27 years, Ray Bostock completed an Open University degree in history (2.1 Hons) and wrote his first book. He is currently taking time out to work on his next book. He lives in Stone in Staffordshire with his wife and two children.

Dedication

To the three Bostocks: Judith my long suffering history widow, without whom this book would not be, and to Toria and Jack, my two patient history orphans.

Ray Bostock

EMPIRE DAYS:
BRITAIN AND THE EMPIRE IN A YEAR

AUSTIN MACAULEY
PUBLISHERS LTD.

A CIP catalogue record for this title is available from the British Library.

ISBN 9781785546105 (Paperback)
ISBN 9781785546112 (Hardback)
ISBN 9781785546129 (E-Book)

www.austinmacauley.com

First Published (2016)
Austin Macauley Publishers Ltd.
25 Canada Square
Canary Wharf
London
E14 5LQ

Acknowledgments

There are a number of people who I would like to thank for their help in the writing of this book. Mr Graham Finlay, my history teacher at my secondary school and an inspiration to everyone in his class. He was the one who always emphasised that every historian, despite what they may say are biased in some little way or other and that when reading any historical account, the reader should always 'take sides' and try to 'get involved' with the events. This makes the history personal and come alive. He has been proven correct time after time.

My Grandfather Bostock. He passed away before my thirteenth birthday but he spoke to me in a way during the 1970s that made me imagine that the British Empire was still expanding and would always expand and whose style of speech I have attempted to reflect in this book. It was he who always used to say 'Happy Empire Day' and 'remember, remember Empire Day the 24th May'.

My daughter Victoria and my son Jack who managed to remind me on a regular basis that constant talk of historical events isn't necessarily what everyone would like to listen to?

In particular Tom Haynes, Vinh Tran and Alex Cracknell as well as all the others in the Austin Macaulay team for their expertise, suggestions and advice and who have proved that no one can write a book on their own.

The many people who suggested to me so many events and people that should perhaps appear in this book, but sadly, despite wanting to, nowhere near all of them could ever hope to be included.

I would especially like to thank my wife Judith, who encouraged me to turn my pet project and hobby into a book and allowed me the opportunities I would not otherwise have had. Her patience and tolerance of me has been nothing short of a miracle.

Finally, despite our collective best efforts to the contrary, any mistakes within this book are entirely of my own doing.

Contents

Chapter 1

Introduction

"The Empire which has grown up around these islands is essentially commercial and marine. The whole course of our history, the geography of the country, all the evidences of the present situation, proclaim beyond a doubt that our power and prosperity alike and together depend on the economic command of markets and the naval command of the sea; and from the highest sentimental reasons, not less than from the most ordinary practical considerations, we must avoid a servile imitation of the clanking military empires of the European continent, by which we cannot obtain the military predominance and security which is desired, but only impair and vitiate the natural sources of our strength and vigour."

Winston Spencer Churchill.
13ᵗʰ May 1901
Winston Churchill's Speeches. (Ed. Winston S Churchill 2006)

Those words, uttered by our greatest leader and probably the greatest ever Briton, were the words that he used to describe the largest and most powerful empire in world history, the British Empire; our Empire. This Empire of ours was a unique, worldwide phenomenon that has never and will never be equalled. Still a subject of much discussion and much more controversy, at its height, towards the end of the nineteenth century and into the early twentieth, it had a direct influence over a quarter of the earth's population. It controlled a fifth of the land mass and was a power that was both respected and feared around the globe. As the world's first industrial nation, Britain was in effect the first true Super Power. What is even more surprising, and is often forgotten or ignored, is that from its earliest beginnings the Empire was primarily a commercial endeavour and not an aggressive military exercise, which sets it apart from all other empires in history. That commercial enterprise was the product of a single private company, the Honourable East India Company. In the year 1600, the East India Company received its Royal Charter from Elizabeth I, permitting it to own the monopoly of trade with India, the Far East and the new Colonies in the Americas. The early years of the Company were supported by private finance and by men who were eager entrepreneurs and who wanted to better themselves and make their fortune. Though the Crown and the government invested in the Company, it was still a private enterprise and therefore a huge financial gamble. It was from those early beginnings that the Empire began to spread out across the globe. In fact, it was some seventeen years before The East India Company received its Charter that Humphrey Gilbert, on his second attempt in 1583, had claimed Newfoundland for Elizabeth I and England. This was to become the first imperial stepping stone for England and later Great Britain.

Due to the East India Company's monopoly on trade, the Empire's formation was in actuality an unintended consequence of its commercial endeavour. Unlike any other Empire in world history, it had no real design or course; no one sat down and devised an empire with an all conquering objective to rule the world. No one planned military expeditions with the sole purpose of seizing land and territory to create an empire. In fact, throughout its existence, many members of the successive British Governments had grave doubts about an empire, claiming it was an unnecessary financial burden on the country. In many cases, it was indeed a burden. With so many differing individuals and organisations often working independently of the British Government and each other, making the most of the commercial opportunities as they appeared, the Empire began to form as these endeavours began to acquire territory through trade and agreements. Gradually, over time, through trade and the hard work of its supporters, this economic empire spread around the world: seeking out ever more commercial and business opportunities, using the possibility of military force usually only when its interests were threatened. Starting in the early seventeenth century, England began the settlement of the east coast of America and the Caribbean islands. These would eventually total thirteen colonies. During this period, England (and Britain from 1707) was constantly in a struggle with her main challengers for trade: Spain in the Americas, the Netherlands in India and the Pacific and primarily France almost everywhere for both territory and trade. Throughout the latter part of the seventeenth and well into the eighteenth century, Britain steadily gained the upper hand. Establishing ever more colonies and opportunities for trade around the world, we rose to become a world power at the expense of the Spanish and Dutch Empires. Unfortunately, despite this success, all was not well and in 1776 the colonists in America rebelled and were ultimately granted their independence in 1783. Though the newly independent colonies and their ally France attempted to wrest the remaining Northern America possessions from our influence, Britain managed to secure these territories, later to become the Dominion of Canada.

Despite the initial shock that followed the loss of the thirteen North American colonies, Britain's attention continued to focus on other areas of opportunity for trade around the world. Although we had had a presence in India for many years, the East India Company increased its efforts and over a relatively short period of time, came to influence and rule India economically on behalf of Great Britain. In effect, the whole of India was ruled by a private company. From here, we accelerated our expansion further into the pacific, in particular Australia and New Zealand. Though the threats from the Spanish and Dutch had long since disappeared, the French were a constant and troublesome nuisance. Throughout the French Revolutionary Wars (1792-1802) and the Napoleonic Wars (1803–1815), Britain and France were constantly in conflict with an almost constant chain of British victories, eventually culminating with the victory over France at the Battle of Waterloo in 1815. France had perhaps the second largest and second most powerful empire of all time. However, with this total defeat, any hope France had of a world Empire even remotely to challenge ours was finally crushed. The world now had a dominant, democratic nation that gave birth to the industrial revolution. Instead of choosing a tyrannical and aggressive dominance, Britain began the spread of its technological achievements around the globe improving the infrastructure and economies of its many possessions as well as inculcating the democratic values of the nation.

With the overpowering and restraint of France and its empire, the world now entered a period, often referred to by some historians as the 'Pax Britannica' or British Peace. There was now no other power in the world that could contemplate defying successfully our great nation. For a century from 1815, virtually all of the earth's sea-going trade routes were controlled and patrolled by the Royal Navy, making Great Britain the first unchallenged world power. The Royal Navy became, in effect, a worldwide police force, enforcing the ban on slavery that our country championed and protecting our nation's vital trade routes and interests. Part of the reason for the Empire's success was the gradual adoption of the 'policy' of 'splendid isolation'. Following over two hundred years of bloody involvement in European conflicts, Britain pursued a policy of non-involvement in European affairs. Having experienced the huge cost of large-scale involvement in European disagreements and wars, Britain was unwilling to enter into alliances with allies on the continent. Alliances had all too often dragged our country into conflicts that it didn't really want. Britain's overriding interest in Europe was the balance of power between states, thus ensuring it wasn't drawn into costly drawn-out conflicts, that would drain man power and resources that could be used to strengthen trade and Empire. It is interesting to note that due to the Empire's spread around the globe to all corners of the world, it meant that no matter whether those in the mother country were sound asleep in their beds or up and at work, somewhere in the world the Sun was always shining on a part of our Empire. It was this phenomenon that gave rise to the saying that the British Empire was 'the Empire on which the sun never set'. This Empire achieved its zenith, its greatest extent between the world wars, in particular the 1920s.

It was during the second half of the twentieth century that the majority of our colonial possessions had gained their independence. The majority, once disparate, often tribal areas, had been unified into democratic entities that carried with them the benefits of the British parliamentary system, its laws, language and economic models. Some chose democracy and order whilst others, though allowed to go their own way, could not manage their responsibilities and descended into dictatorships, poverty, conflicts and civil war, thus unravelling all the benefits accrued under our governance.

Throughout its history, the Empire consisted of many ethnic groups, languages, customs, traditions and religious beliefs. Though there were missionary attempts, unlike its contemporary and rival empires, our empire never earnestly attempted to impose a uniform appearance, belief system or culture upon its subjects. In many instances, the local ways and customs were encouraged to continue while at home in Britain, the ever-increasing population was ever desirous of newer and more exotic items from far-flung corners of the Empire. Whether it was materials, foods, fashions, ideas or even words, they were all absorbed into the lives of Britons at home, thus fuelling the need for an ever-expanding Empire.

Great Britain, our mother country, has been formed from three differing Kingdoms and a Principality, so, although the beginning of the Empire was English, it did not remain an English endeavour for long but became a British Empire. The indigenous peoples from all three Kingdoms and the Principality have taken a full share in the progress of the Empire and thus the greater good of the world. All of these countries, England, Ireland, Scotland and Wales, have their own unique history but have all contributed to the success of Great Britain and the Empire in their own way. As these indigenous inhabitants spread out across the colonised world, their descendents in their new homes began in turn to contribute to the glories of the Empire.

Unfortunately, since the time of the independence of most of our Empire's territories, there is a sad aspect to the glorious story of our Empire that has come to prominence over the past few years. In the Britain of today, our history is taught in such a way that those now leaving school are not fully aware, if at all, of their proud shared heritage, culture and history. In general, when our history is taught, the time is used to dwell on the perceived negative aspects as a whole and at the centre of this is our Empire. Either in part or in its entirety, the Empire is used unjustifiably as the personification of evil and heartless exploitation of weak and defenceless peoples. A one-sided, blinkered perception is all that is taught and perpetrated. This means that today there is a whole generation of citizens that have only a negative, poisoned and unbalanced view of their history, cultural heritage and the Empire.

Sadly, the use of the word Empire today triggers a whole variety of emotions, usually a mixture of contempt, shame and, with others, a perceived need for an outward display of guilt. There have always been the detractors of the Empire: they were present even at its height and even more so in modern times, more than willing to denigrate our Empire and refusing to contemplate the good that it brought. They are the 'Empire deniers'. These apologists bewail what they see as the savagery, the brutality and the oppression perpetrated by the Empire. So often they seem ashamed of our shared history and heritage and see taking a pride in our past as a mark of racism and bigotry. Very often, they express embarrassment by anything predating the year 1947 and grumble about most that has followed since. They imagine that to be accepted and noticed within today's society, they need to demonstrate publicly the impression they are wracked with guilt over our shared cultural past. Whilst there have undoubtedly been periods and events in our long history that were wrong and should not be something we are proud of, slavery being the most often quoted subject, there is one thing the apologists fail to realise. We today should never judge those of previous generations by our present day morals and standards. What we believe today to be wrong, in the past may have been perfectly acceptable and commonplace.

So, instead of being ashamed of who we are; our history, our culture and what are ancestors achieved, let us concentrate on the greatness of our history, the many benefits of the Empire both to ourselves and those around the world. Within this can be seen so many benefits, including the model for democracy that has remained the model and jealous ideal for the majority of countries to this day, and not just those that were former colonies. Democracy and the long held desire for freedom was begun in the modern world by Great Britain and taken up by our former colonies with one or two sad exceptions. Our Laws, hand in hand with democracy, are very often copied exactly or used as a basis for their own laws by many other countries. Free and fair trade, the basic building block for national and global economic growth and prosperity, was a creation that was spread worldwide by our Empire. Many of our former Colonies saw more prosperity and economic stability during the days of Empire and the decades following independence than they do at present. The greatest influence and gift that our forbears left for us to inherit and supplied the rest of the world with was the English language. English has today become the international language, the language of commerce, the language of entertainment, the language of the Internet and the language that is more often employed when two differing foreigners meet and need to converse.

By means of comparison, a previous empire that lasted for just as long as our Empire is the Roman Empire. It too brought much to the world, much of which we still feel the benefits of today. However, there is one glaring contradiction between the apologists approach to the Roman and British

Empires. Despite the Roman Empire's brutal oppression of its conquered peoples and its ruthless approach to conflict and savage suppression of discontent, nowhere do we read and hear people denounce it and vilify it to the extent that our Empire has suffered from the tongues of the apologists.

Throughout our Empire's existence there have been countless numbers of people who have helped to shape and mould its course and to provide us with the Great Britain we know today. Behind all those famous individuals have been the ordinary, everyday people, much like ourselves today, who contributed and left their mark on a culture and history that is the pride of the world. This book is about the great and the good, the large and small, the famous and the anonymous who have contributed knowingly or unknowingly to our history, Britain's history.

Sadly, as a direct result of our leading part in bringing an end to two world wars against brutal systems, our country became broken and debt-ridden, our Empire gradually eroded and broke apart in the years following the Second World War. It finally came to an end at some little noticed and long forgotten point in the late 1960's. For those who continue to feel ashamed of their history and what great works and deeds our forbears have achieved, then please read no further. However, for those who are proud to be sharers in a rich and glorious history, who revel in the achievements of our ancestors, who are proud of their identity and culture and who are proud to be British, then this book is for you.

Notes:

Brackets: Dates in brackets e.g. (see 24th May). This is pointing the reader towards another date that is connected to the subject of a particular date entry.

Sport and entertainment: Unfortunately for some, there are almost no dates relating to sporting events or people, songs and events from popular music, television or the cinema, primarily from the twentieth century. These are far too numerous and diverse to ever be complete and fit into this publication.

Dates: Wherever possible, all dates prior to September 1752 are given in the form of the Julian calendar, as they were before our present Gregorian calendar was adopted in that same year. This has been done as the dates of all those events are the dates that the individuals of those times would recognise. All dates following 1752 are given according to the present day Gregorian calendar.

Opinions: This book is written from the point of view of a patriotic Briton or member of the Empire, writing prior to the sad end of the Empire in the 1960's. There has been no intention to cause offense to the modern sensitivities of the reader. If it should cause offence, then stop reading this book and any other history book. It must be remembered that those of previous generations thought quite differently from us today and held different values, values that in themselves changed over the course of the Empire. These values were correct for the time in which they were held and are not necessarily wrong today. Therefore, if you should continue with the book, stop and think before judging our forebears.

Chapter 2

The 366 days of the Year

JANUARY

1st January: the Act of Union between Great Britain and Ireland

1651 Charles II (see 6th February and 29th May) is crowned King of Scotland at Scone in Scotland by the Marquis of Argyll. This was after lengthy and detailed discussions with the Covenanters. This would prove to be the last time that a monarch was crowned in Scotland (see 23rd April).

1660 Samuel Pepys starts his now world famous diary (see 23rd February and 26th May). He kept the diary, in a form of shorthand, for almost ten years and recorded everything from public and national events as well as minute details about his own personal life and relationships.

1729 The birth of Edmund Burke in Dublin (see 9th July). He was to become a leading Whig MP, writer, philosopher and an arch opponent of William Pitt the Younger (see 23rd January and 28th May), although they were originally good friends and political allies.

1753 This day becomes the first New Year's Day celebration on this date as the calendar is brought in line with most of Europe in readiness for the adoption of the Gregorian calendar on 3rd September (see 14th September). Prior to today, New Year's Day had been celebrated on the 25th March, the final occasion being in 1752.

1766 The death of James Francis Edward Stewart, the Jacobite James III and the 'Old Pretender', at the Palazzo Muti in Rome (see 10th June). He was the son of James VI (James II of England, see 16th September and 14th October) and his second wife, Mary of Modena and he was the father of the Jacobite heir to the throne Charles Edward Stewart ('Bonnie Prince Charlie', see 31st January and 31st December). On his father's death in 1701 (see 16th September), he declared himself James VII (James III of England). In 1708 he attempted an invasion of Britain to regain the throne (see 23rd March), but was driven back by the Royal Navy. Again in 1715 he attempted another invasion, actually setting foot on Scottish soil (see 22nd December). Following the indecisive Battle of Sheriffmuir that same year (see 13th November) and with the failure to decisively win the battle and with poor support, he returned to France. Following the death of the French King Louis XIV, he was not welcome in France and was offered the Palazzo Muti in Rome by Pope Innocent XIII where he ended his days. He is buried in the crypt of St. Peter's Basilica in the Vatican.

1801 The union of the Kingdom of Great Britain and the Kingdom of Ireland to form the United Kingdom of Great Britain and Ireland as a result of the two Acts of Union being passed the previous year (see 2nd July and 1st August). The flag of the Union is also first authorised by Royal Proclamation as a result of the union on this day, in the form as it is now recognised. The current flag of the union was constructed from the flags of the Kingdoms of Scotland and England and the Irish Flag bearing St. Patrick's Cross was added with this union of Ireland (see 12th April and 1st May).

1877 Her Britannic Majesty, Queen Victoria, is proclaimed Queen Empress of India at the Delhi Durbar in India (see 22nd January, 27th April, 1st May, 22nd June and 24th May). Although she was not in attendance, she was represented by the Viceroy, the 1st Earl of Lytton.

1901 Edmund Barton is sworn in as the first Prime Minister of the Dominion of Australia (see 7th January and 18th January). On this day, the six colonies of Australia; New South Wales, Queensland, South Australia, Tasmania, Victoria and Western Australia federated and became the Commonwealth of Australia, a Dominion within the Empire.

1903 Edward VII is proclaimed Emperor of India at the Coronation Durbar in Delhi (see 6th May, 9th August and 9th November). The celebrations actually began on the 29th December 1902 and would continue for two weeks but the proclamation and the Durbar took place today. The event was organised by the Viceroy of India, Lord Curzon (see 11th January and 20th March). However, Edward VII did not attend but sent his brother, the Duke of Connaught as his representative. There were over 40,000 troops involved in the ceremonies under the command of Lord Herbert Kitchener (see 5th June and 24th June).

1909 Passed the previous October, today saw the introduction day of the 1908 Old Age Pensions Act or 'Pension Day' as it was then called. Half a million people receive the first ever non-contributory old age pension. The payments range between one shilling and five shillings a week to people over 70 years old with an income of less than £31 per year (see 27th October).

1944 The death of Sir Edwin Landseer Lutyens (see 29th March) from cancer. One of the greatest of twentieth-century architects, he is known for many designs that are thought of as being traditional designs of the Empire. These designs include the Cenotaph in London (amongst many cenotaphs and memorials across Britain and the Empire), India Gate in Delhi (see 15th

December), the Viceroy's House in New Delhi, the Thiepval Memorial on the Somme and numerous buildings across Britain.

1947 The entire coal mining industry in this country is nationalised under the Labour Government (see 26th July) and is run by the National Coal Board (see 12th July) on behalf of the government.

1948 The entire British railway network is nationalised by the Labour Government (see 26th July).

1960 The Farthing, worth one quarter of a penny, ceases to be legal tender from midnight on the 31st December. The Royal Mint had stopped minting the coins in 1956.

1973 Great Britain joins the European Economic Community on the third attempt. Two previous attempts had been rejected in 1963 and 1967, primarily because of strong objections by the French under the leadership of a bitter De Gaulle (see 30th January, 23rd June,28th October and 27th November) who had died in 1970, thus allowing the French nation to finally decide for itself (see 7th February).

1974 New Year's Day becomes an official Bank Holiday (see 1st May and 26th December).

1999 The Euro becomes the currency of eleven of the States in Europe. Great Britain retains the pound (see 1973 above and 16th September).

2nd January:

1757 Sir Robert Clive (see 29th September and 22nd November) and his army recapture the fort and town of Calcutta with relative ease and with minimal casualties. The town was a key economic investment for the East India Company (see 31st December) and its loss was extremely costly. The city had been taken when the Nawab of Bengal rebelled and took the city. The Nawab's uncivilised, brutal and savage treatment of the prisoners led to the infamous 'Black Hole of Calcutta' (see 20th June) and his fellow barbarous rebels were swiftly punished.

1833 Two British ships, HMS Clio and HMS Tyne under the command of Captain James Onslow, arrive at Port Louis on East Falkland to re-establish British sovereignty over the islands following attempted settlement by the United Provinces of the Rio de la Plata (see 22nd January, 2nd April, 25th April, 14th June and 9th August). The operation was successful and peaceful and the forces from the United Provinces left without any resistance.

1896 Doctor Leander Starr Jameson (see 9th February and 26th November) and around 600 of his raiders surrender near Doornkop in the Boar Republic of the Transvaal (see 29th December) bringing an end to his so-called 'Jameson raid'. Without the hoped-for rising of the local Uitlanders in support and having met stiff resistance from the Boers, the force surrendered after losing 16 men.

1947 Silver coins cease being produced and are replaced by cupro-nickel coins, to help repay the war debt owed by this country to our supposed allies, the United States (see 31st December).

3rd January:

1670 The death of General George Monck, 1st Duke of Albemarle (see 6th December). A career soldier who saw service with the Dutch during the Thirty Years War, he later joined the army of Charles I (see 30th January and 19th November). He was captured during the first Civil War (see 25th January) and imprisoned but then changed sides, thereafter serving the Commonwealth where he was appointed General at Sea, despite having no experience at sea. Following he death of Oliver Cromwell (see 25th April and 3rd September), he entered into secret talks with the representatives of Charles II (see 6th February and 29th May) and was instrumental in the restoration of 1660. He was appointed Captain General of the army and created a Duke for his services. He is buried in Westminster Abbey.

1741 The birth of Benedict Arnold (see 14th June) in Norwich in the Colony of Connecticut.

1795 The death of Josiah Wedgwood (see 12th July). He was one of the leading and probably most famous figures in the Pottery Industry. As a young man he contracted smallpox. Though he survived the effects of the illness, it necessitated the amputation of his leg. Despite this, he went on to open a number of businesses in the Burslem area, including his Etruria works in 1789. Through his work he greatly improved the quality and durability of crockery. His designs and products were sold around the world and were owned by most of the European Royal Houses. He also took a keen interest in the development of the canal and road systems to enable the easier transport of his wares. He was elected to the Royal Society in 1783 and was the Grandfather of Charles Darwin (see 12th February and 19th April).

1883 The birth of Clement Richard Attlee (see 8th October) in Putney, London.

1911 The Siege of Sidney Street in London. Four Bolshevik revolutionaries are besieged by Police and a detachment of Scots Guards at 100 Sidney Street after attempting to rob a nearby jewellers shop and then killing a Police Officer and wounding others, two of whom would die later. The Home Secretary Winston Churchill (see 24th January and 30th November) was present and armed with his shot gun, for which he was heavily criticised afterwards.

1946 William Joyce, traitor, Fascist and one time friend of Sir Oswald Mosley and known during the war as Lord Haw Haw, is hanged for treason in Wandsworth prison (see 24th April). Born in New York City to Irish parents, he moved to Ireland as a young child. The family, despite being Roman Catholic, were Unionist and suffered during the Irish Rebellion. After the creation of the Irish Free State in 1921 (see 6th December), he moved to

England. He had joined the British Fascists in 1923 and had steadily become more extreme. In 1933 he joined the British Union of Fascists lead by Oswald Mosley (see 16th November and 3rd December) but after becoming more racist, he was sacked by Oswald Mosley and went on to help form the Nationalist Socialist League. In 1939 he left Britain for Germany, where he started broadcasting on German radio in English and soon acquired the name Lord Haw Haw in the British press. He was captured on the 28th May 1945 and eventually tried and convicted for treason at the Old Bailey.

4th January:

1642 Charles I (see 30th January and 19th November), along with a guard of soldiers, enters the Houses of Parliament to arrest five Members of Parliament, thus beginning the slide into civil war. They were John Pym, John Hampden, Denzil Holles, William Strode and Arthur Haselrig. Informed in advance of the impending arrests, the five MPs had slipped out of the Commons and escaped before Charles and his troops managed to enter the House of Commons.

1761 The death of Stephen Hales (see 17th September). A Botanist and Chemist, he worked on the physiology of plants and animals and later studied the role that air and water had in the physiology of both plants and animals. He was the first to recognise the movement of water within plants and was also credited with the invention of surgical forceps.

1813 The birth of Isaac Pitman (see 12th January) in Trowbridge in Wiltshire.

1832 The birth of George Tryon in Northamptonshire (see 22nd June).

1906 The foundation stone for the Victoria Memorial Hall in Calcutta, India, designed by Sir William Emerson, is laid by the Prince of Wales, the future George V (see 20th January and 3rd June).

1944 The beginning of Operation Carpet Bagger. The United States Air Force, in liaison with the Special Operations Executive (SOE), begin dropping arms and other supplies to the Resistance in France and also to the resistance in Belgium and Holland in anticipation of the invasion of Europe by allied forces (see 6th June).

1948 Independence is granted to the Colony of Burma. However, it sadly chose not to join the British Commonwealth. The area had come under British protection in 1824 (see 24th February and 5th March) and in January 1886 it came under the authority of British India.

1967 Donald Campbell (see 23rd March) dies attempting to break his own world water speed record in his boat the Bluebird K7 on Coniston Water. His body was recovered in 2001 (see 3rd September and 10th November). Born in Kingston upon Thames, he was the son of Sir Malcolm Campbell, also a land and water speed record holder. Donald is the only person to simultaneously hold both the land and water speed records.

1985 The death of Lieutenant-General Sir Brian Horrocks (see 7th September) in Chichester. He was commissioned into the Middlesex Regiment in 1914 but was captured in the October and spent the rest of the war as a prisoner. He attempted numerous times to escape but failed. After the war, he served in the force sent to Russia and fought with the White Russian forces. However, in 1919 he was captured by the Red Army and spent just under a year in captivity. In the Second World War he served under General Montgomery in France and was evacuated at Dunkirk. He later served in North Africa. In 1943 he was badly wounded and took well over a year to recover. He returned to Command XXX Corps and was involved with them in Operation Market Garden (see 17th September). In 1945 he was also involved in the crossing of the Rhine into Germany. On retirement, he became the Gentleman Usher of the Black Rod for a number of years and enjoyed a brief television and writing career.

5th January:

1066 The death of Edward the Confessor (see 6th January, 3rd April and 13th October). The penultimate Anglo-Saxon King, he was responsible for the founding and then the consecration twenty years later of Westminster Abbey in 1065 (see 28th December). He was known as the confessor due to his famed piety. His remains would later be buried in the Abbey and become the focal point of pilgrimages for many centuries.

1834 The birth of William John Wills in Totnes, Devon (see 29th June).

1922 The death from a heart attack of Sir Ernest Henry Shackleton (see 15th February) on board the ship *Quest* off the coast of South Georgia, the island on which he was then buried. He was the leader of the famous Imperial Trans-Antarctic Expedition of 1914. Born in Ireland, the family moved to London when he was very young. When he was 16 he joined the merchant navy and travelled around the world. In 1901 he went on the Antarctic expedition led by Robert Falcon Scott. Though not reaching the South Pole, he, Scott and one other travelled the closest to the Pole than anyone previously. He led his own expedition to the South Pole in 1908 and was knighted upon his return. It was in 1914 that he made his third attempt on the South Pole. The Endurance became stuck in ice and the crew made it to Elephant Island from where Shackleton and five others set off in a small boat, travelling 800 nautical miles across the ocean to South Georgia, in storms and a hurricane, to get help. Not one member of the expedition died. It was on his fourth expedition that he died.

1941 The death of Amy Johnson C.B.E. (see 1st July). She was the first woman to fly solo from Britain to Australia; her journey lasted from the 5th May to the 24th May 1930 and covered 11,000 miles. Along with her husband and co-pilot, she held a number of world records including being the first person to fly from London to Moscow in one day. She died when the plane she was flying, an Airspeed Oxford, as a member of the Air Transport

Auxiliary, ran out of fuel after she became lost in bad weather. She bailed out over the Thames Estuary and is believed to have drowned. Her body was never found.

6th January:

1066 Harold Godwinson is crowned King of England at Westminster Abbey the day after the death of Edward the Confessor (see 5th January and 14th October). He was to be the last Anglo-Saxon King of England.

1367 The birth of the future Richard II in Bordeaux in the English possession of the Principality of Aquitaine. He was the son of Edward (see 8th June and 15th June), (later known as the Black Prince) the eldest son of Edward III (see 21st June and 13th November). In 1377 he acceded to the throne on his Grandfather's death. He increasingly surrounded himself with unpopular favourites. Following action by some of his leading nobles against him in 1388, he took his revenge and arrested many and confiscated vast swathes of their land. In 1399 he was deposed by Henry Bolingbroke, son of John of Gaunt, who had lost his lands. Richard was imprisoned and at some point during February 1400, or in the months following, he died.

1540 The Marriage of Henry VIII (see 28th January and 28th June) and his fourth wife, Anne of Cleves, at the Palace of Placentia in Greenwich (see 9th July, 16th July and 22nd September).

1705 The birth of Benjamin Franklin in Boston in the Province of Massachusetts Bay (see 17th April).

1781 The battle of Jersey is fought on the Channel Island of Jersey. The French attempted to invade the island to prevent its continuing role as a base for British privateers and the Royal Navy's disruption to American shipping on its way to the French port of Brest during the American colonial rebellion (see 3rd September). The local troops suffered around 30 killed, including their commanding Officer, Major Francis Peirson, who, despite repeated French attacks, led his men on, only to be killed at the moment of triumph. The French suffered a similar number of casualties. However, the French lost around 600 taken as prisoners out of a force of around 1,000 men.

1840 The death of Fanny Burney (see 13th June) in Bath. She was a novelist and married a Frenchman, Alexander d'Arblay, in 1793. She wrote four existing novels, 'Evelina', 'Cecilia', 'Camilla' and 'The Wanderer', as well as journals, letters and a couple of works of non-fiction. In 1801 she followed her husband to France to work for Napoleon's government but, due to the outbreak of war (see 18th May), stayed for around ten years. In 1811, after experiencing pains in her breast, she underwent a mastectomy whilst fully conscious. She wrote up a detailed account of the operation and sent it to her sister.

1842 The ill-fated retreat from Kabul begins during the First Afghan War, 1839-1842. Around 16,000 British and Indian troops, families and camp followers leave the fortress of Kabul to march the ninety miles to Jellalabad after surrendering to the Afghan leader on generous terms. Unfortunately, the force was harassed and repeatedly attacked on its journey until the majority of the force, except its leader General Elphinstone, was massacred (see 13th January).

7th January:

1536 The death of Catherine of Aragon at Kimbolton Castle (see 16th December). The first wife of Henry VIII (see 28th January and 28th June), she was the widow of his older brother Arthur. She was born in Madrid in 1485 and was the daughter of King Ferdinand and Queen Isabella. In 1501, at the age of 16, she married Prince Arthur but shortly afterwards he contracted a disease and died (see 2nd April and 14th November). Henry became King in 1509 and shortly afterwards they were married (see 11th June). Unfortunately, of the six children she bore Henry, only one, the future Mary I (see 18th February and 17th November) survived. After Henry began his pursuit of Anne Boleyn, he attempted to have the marriage annulled but failed and Catherine fought against his plans constantly. She was banished from court and was denied access to her daughter.

1558 Calais, our last possession in Europe, is lost for the final time to France. Francis, Duke of Guise, attacked and took the defensively weakened and neglected town. Calais had been an integral and legal part of England's possessions for centuries (see 21st May), so much so that its representatives had sat in the English Parliament (see 17th July).

1758 The death of Allan Ramsey in Edinburgh (see 15th October), a poet and playwright. Born in Lanarkshire, he was apprenticed to a wig maker and eventually set up in business as such in Edinburgh. From about 1718, he became a prolific poet and subsequently became a book seller, publishing his own books, plays and collections of songs and poems. Due to his ability and large volume of work, he was recognised by Robert Burns as a major influence upon his own works. He was the father of Allan Ramsay (see 10th August and 2nd October) the painter and is buried in Greyfriars Kirk yard in Edinburgh.

1827 The birth of Sandford Fleming (see 22nd July) in Kirkcaldy, Fife.

1841 The second battle of Chuenpee at the Bocca Tigris in China during the First Opium War 1839-1842. A joint land and Naval assault on Chinese forces led to the British and East India Company forces capturing a number of Chinese forts and destroying several Chinese junks. The result of the action led to the inclusion of Hong Kong into the Empire (see 20th January).

1920 The death of Sir Edmund Barton (see 1st January and 18th January) in New South Wales, Australia. A politician, he became the first Prime Minister of a federated Australia as leader of his Protectionist Party. Born in Sydney, he was a Barrister with a career in law, becoming an MP in 1879, Speaker in 1883 and then Australia's Attorney-General before becoming Prime Minister. He was an ardent and leading federalist.

1976 HMS Andromeda a Royal Navy Leander-class Type 121 frigate is involved in a collision with the Icelandic gunboat Thor during the Third Cod War (1975-1976). The Thor had been sailing far too close to the frigate and, despite being warned, deliberately rammed the frigate. Although Andromeda was dented, the Thor holed her hull and was badly damaged (see 11th December). This was the third and most serious occasion in which the ship was attacked by Icelandic vessels.

8th January:

871 The Battle of Ashdown. King Ethelred's army of West Saxons led by his younger brother, the future King Alfred the Great (see 26th October), defeat the Danes in a pyrrhic victory. Though it showed Anglo-Saxon strength and determination, it still did not bring an end to the Danish threat.

1697 Thomas Aikenhead is hanged in Edinburgh, becoming the last person executed in the British Isles for blasphemy. At only twenty years of age, he was a student at Edinburgh University and had been accused and tried on the testimony of so-called friends, being sentenced on Christmas Eve.

1815 The Battle of New Orleans. Our forces, led by General Sir Edward Pakenham, are defeated by rebel American colonial forces now fighting for the new so-called 'republic'. Two main attacks were made upon the American positions but were repulsed with great losses to our forces; including the loss of many Officers compared with the minimal losses on the American side (see 18th June and 24th December).

1823 The birth of Alfred Russell Wallace in Monmouthshire (see 7th November).

1921 Chequers is officially handed over to Prime Minister David Lloyd-George (see 17th January and 26th March) by its owners. The house, situated just to the south of Aylesbury in Buckinghamshire was donated as a weekend residence for the incumbent Prime Minister.

1940 Rationing and the use of ration books are introduced due to the effects of the Second World War. Bacon, butter and sugar are the first commodities restricted (see 9th February, 4th July, 9th July, 9th September and 3rd October).

1941 The death of Robert Stephenson Smyth Baden-Powell, 1st Baron Baden-Powell (see 22nd February) in Nyeri, in the Colony of Kenya (see 12th December). He was the successful leader of the occupants of Mafeking during the siege of 1899-1900 by Boer forces (see 17th May and 12th October). Though he was a Victorian hero and the successful outcome of the siege gave way to great rejoicing throughout the Empire, he is sometimes criticised for some of his actions. He is most famous as the founder of the Scouting Movement (see 1st August).

9th January:

1735 The birth of John Jervis (see 14th March) at Meaford Hall, near Stone in Staffordshire.

1799 Prime Minister William Pitt (see 23rd January and 28th May) introduces Income Tax on a sliding scale at 2d in the £ for incomes over £60 rising to 2s in the £ on annual income over £200. This was to raise money to finance our participation in the Napoleonic Wars and to pay for weapons, men and equipment.

1806 The state funeral of Admiral Horatio Nelson takes place (see 29th September and 21st October). His body had lain in state at Greenwich for three days before being taken up the Thames to the Admiralty, where it lay for one more night. On the day, the funeral procession made its way from the Admiralty to St. Pauls Cathedral (see 2nd December), where he was interred.

1813 The execution of three Luddites takes place in York. They were hanged for the murder of a mill owner, William Horsfall, on the 28th April 1812.

1863 The Metropolitan Railway, the first line to open on the London Underground and the oldest in the world is officially opened between Paddington and Farringdon (see 14th December and 15th December).

1957 Sir Anthony Eden resigns as Prime Minister (see 14th January and 12th June) due to ill health which had been aggravated by the Suez Crisis (see 31st October and 5th November) and Harold Macmillan (see 10th February and 29th December) becomes the new Prime Minister. This was a direct result of the betrayal by our so-called closest ally, America. May we never forget!

10th January:

1645 The execution of Archbishop William Laud (see 7th October) at Tower Hill. Born in Reading to a wealthy cloth merchant, he later became a long-standing and vocal High Churchman whose opposition to reforms of the Church and dislike of Puritanism were well-known. His desire for complete uniformity within the Church of England as well as in Scotland and Ireland and his support for Charles I (see 30th January and 19th November) during the Civil Wars contributed towards his impeachment, trial and eventual death by beheading.

1761 The death of Admiral Edward Boscawen (see 19th August). He joined the Royal Navy at the age of 12 and rose rapidly. He served during the War of Jenkins' Ear (1739-1748), the War of the Austrian Succession (1740-1748) and the Seven Years War (1756-1763), taking part in or leading numerous actions within these conflicts. He signed the death warrant for Admiral Byng following his courts martial in 1757 (see 14th March). His most famous action was during the Battle of Lagos Bay in 1759 (see 18th August) where he took three French prizes and burnt another two ships, thus preventing the French Navy from covering their planned invasion of Britain.

1775 The death of Stringer Lawrence (see 6th March), regarded as the 'Father of the Indian Army'. Having served in the British army and fought at the Battle of Culloden in 1746 (see 16th April), he went to India to command the East India Company's troops (see 31st December). Whilst in India, he became a good friend of Robert Clive (see 29th September and 22nd November) and took part in a number of actions and in the 1760s he presided over the re-arranging of the Company's Madras army before retiring and returning to Britain.

1776 The birth of George Birkbeck (see 1st December) in Yorkshire.

1806 Cape Town, the capital of the Dutch Colony of the Cape of Good Hope, surrenders to our forces following the battle of Blaauwberg. The battle which involved over 5,000 of our troops against over 3,000 Dutch colonists was part of the greater Napoleonic Wars and the victory secured the town's future as part of the future Cape Colony for Great Britain (see 13th August and 31st May).

1840 Sir Rowland Hill (see 27th August and 3rd December) introduces the Penny Black, the first standardised universal tariff for postage. There were over 112,000 letters posted on this day in London (see 16th September).

1992 The first 'Margaret Thatcher Day' in the Falkland Islands is celebrated and has been celebrated each subsequent year. Today is the anniversary of Margaret Thatcher's (see 8th April and 13th October) first visit in 1983 to the islands following the Falklands War with Argentina (see 2nd April and 14th June) and in recognition of her determination and success in defending the islands and liberating them from Argentinean occupation (see 2nd January).

11th January:

1569 The first National lottery is held in England. There were 40,000 lots sold at 10s each and they were sold at St. Paul's Cathedral (see 2nd December), with the first winning tickets being drawn outside the cathedral.

1753 The death of Sir Hans Sloane (see and 16th April) in Chelsea, London. A physician, he is famous for bequeathing his vast and varied private collection to the nation, thus forming the nucleus of the British Museum (see 15th January). He married a widow from the colony of Jamaica (see 6th August) and encountered cocoa which was drunk with water. Disliking this, he mixed it with milk and invented drinking chocolate milk.

1815 The birth of John Alexander Macdonald in Glasgow (see 6th June), later to become the first Prime Minister of Canada (see 1st July).

1859 The birth of George Nathanial Curzon in Kedleston, Derbyshire (see 20th March).

1928 The death of Thomas Hardy in Dorset (see 2nd June). When he left school, he became apprenticed to an architect and in 1862 travelled to London where he attended King's College. He began to get his novels published in the early 1870s and it was in 1898 that his first works of poetry were published. His ashes were interred in Westminster Abbey. His works included the 'Greenwood Tree', 'Far from the Madding Crowd', 'Return of the Native' and 'Tess of the d'Urbervilles'.

1973 The Open University, Britain's world-renowned distance learning University awards its first degrees.

12th January:

1834 The death of William Wyndham Grenville in Buckinghamshire (see 25th October). He was a Whig Prime Minister and succeeded William Pitt the Younger (see 23rd January and 28th May) following the latter's death. His term as Prime Minister (1806-1807) was notable as being referred to as the 'Ministry of all the Talents'. His father was George Wyndham, a previous Prime Minister. Elected as a MP in 1782, he served under William Pitt the Younger and was Home Secretary and Foreign Secretary. He didn't serve in Pitt's next administration but succeeded him as Prime Minister on his death. His 'Ministry of all the Talents' was a broad coalition of differing parties and factions. Achieving little during his term, he was able to bring about the abolition of the slave trade in 1807 (see 25th March).

1879 The beginning of the Zulu war. Our Imperial forces, numbering around 5,000 in the main column and Commanded by Lord Chelmsford, crossed the Buffalo River into Zululand following the murder of British subjects and the perpetrators then being sheltered by the Zulu chief (see 22nd January, 23rd January, 29th March, 2nd April, 4th July, 28th August and 1st September).

1895 The Foundation of the National Trust, a charity originally intended for the preservation of open areas of outstanding beauty and historic interest as well as historical buildings that required protection.

1897 The death of Sir Isaac Pitman (see 4th January) in Somerset. The inventor of Pitman Shorthand, he was a religious man and had an interest in phonetics and their use in the English language. He was a vegetarian, did not drink alcohol and was a teacher before starting his own private school.

13th January:

1842 The famous 'Last stand at Gandamak' during the First Afghan War 1839-1842. In the morning, a total of 20 Officers and 45 soldiers of the 44th Foot are surrounded and massacred by Afghan tribesmen after refusing to surrender. As the Afghans attacked, the gallant men stood firm and fought to the last man. Later, in the afternoon, William Brydon, the reputed sole survivor of over 16,000 men from the army (originally led by Major General William Elphinstone that had entered Afghanistan and then evacuated Kabul), reaches Jalalabad on horseback (see 6th January).

1849 The Battle of Chillianwala in the Punjab, during the Second Sikh War (1848-1849). Our forces were led by General Hugh Gough (see 2nd March and 3rd November), who ordered the commencement of the battle at

3pm. A hard-fought and savage battle, there was no outright and clear victor. However, the battle was the prelude to the victory at the Battle of Goojerat (see 21st February) and ultimately the annexing of the Punjab to British India.

1893 The Independent Labour Party is formed under the influence of, amongst others, James Keir Hardie (see 15th August and 26th September) and William Henry Drew. At the Conference that established the 'Labour' party, Keir Hardie was elected as the organisation's first chairman.

1906 The first day of the General Election. The Liberal Party ultimately wins with a majority of 132 seats under Sir Henry Campbell-Bannerman (see 22nd April and 7th September), who becomes Prime Minister.

2013 An RAF C-17 transport plane landed at a French military airbase near Paris at the beginning of an operation involving two RAF aircraft to support French troops fighting Islamist rebels in the former French Colony of Mali (see 2nd November).

14th January:

1742 The death of Edmond Halley, mathematician and astronomer (see 29th October), in Greenwich, now part of London. He was the first to calculate the orbit of the comet that was to be named after him. In 1678 he was elected a Fellow of the Royal Society. He also played a major role in the publication of Newton's *Principia*. Later, in 1720, he became the Astronomer Royal at Greenwich.

1814 The Treaty of Kiel is signed between Great Britain and the Kingdom of Sweden on one side and the Kingdom of Denmark-Norway on the other. The Kingdom of Denmark-Norway had allied itself with Napoleonic France and the treaty ended hostilities between the signatories (see 18th May).

1943 The Casablanca Conference begins in the Anfa Hotel, Casablanca, Morocco. It was attended by Winston Churchill (see 24th January and 30th November) and the American President, Franklin D Roosevelt, as well as the Chiefs of Staff of the respective governments and lasted until 24th January 1943. Generals Henri Giraud and Charles de Gaulle were also in attendance, representing the Free French. However, they were intense rivals for leadership of the Free French and agreed, eventually, to jointly lead the French Committee for National Liberation. The Conference discussed the future aims of the allies during the war, agreeing that Germany, Italy and Japan should surrender unconditionally whilst a dual bombing campaign on Germany should be launched by the British and Americans (see 4th February, 17th July and 28th November).

1977 The death of Sir Anthony Eden (see 9th January, 7th April and 12th June), former Prime Minister. He served in the King's Royal Rifle Corps during the First World War and won the Military Cross during the battle of the Somme in 1916 (see 1st July and 18th November). He entered Parliament in the 1923 General Election as a Conservative MP. He served in various

Offices in Government and opposition, becoming Foreign Secretary in 1951 when Winston Churchill (see 24th January and 30th November) was re-elected Prime Minister. In 1955 he replaced Churchill as Prime Minister and was in power during the Suez Crisis in 1956, initially triggered by the United States cancelling a loan to Egypt because of that country's relationship with the Soviet Union (see 31st October, 5th November, 6th November, 25th November and 23rd December). Following pressure on Britain by her so-called ally, Britain withdrew her troops and, due to ill health, he resigned as Prime Minister. He was created Earl Avon in 1961.

1994 The Duchess of Kent becomes the First member of the Royal family to convert to Catholicism in over 300 years and in particular since the Act of Settlement in 1701 (see 29th March and 12th June).

15th January:

1559 Sunday: the Coronation of Queen Elizabeth I (see 24th March and 7th September) at Westminster Abbey. The Coronation is carried out by the Bishop of Carlisle, Owen Oglethorpe, as most of the senior Bishops were either too old or too infirm to perform such an honour.

1759 The British Museum in London opens to the public at Montagu House in Bloomsbury. The British Museum was initially founded in 1753 (see 11th January) when Sir Hans Sloane died (see 11th January and 16th April) and his vast and varied private collection was bequeathed to the nation, thus forming the nucleus of the museum's displays.

1761 The French city of Pondicherry in India, under the command of the Count de Lally, surrenders to British forces, under the command of Sir Eyre Coote, after a six month siege, thus ending any French hope of influence in India (see 22nd June, 18th July and 15th August).

1815 In an action during the War of 1812, the American 44-gun large frigate and Flag Ship, USS President, is captured off the coast of New York by the smaller 40-gun frigate HMS Endymion, part of a Royal Navy squadron of four Frigates that pursued the American, the others being HMS Tenedos, HMS Majestic and HMS Pomone. The ship had been attempting to escape from New York, which had been successfully blockaded by the Royal Navy. After a chase and a fight in which HMS Endymion inflicted the vast majority of the damage, the USS President struck her colours. She was commissioned into the Royal Navy as HMS President and reclassified as a 50-gunner. The USS President had interfered with British shipping as far away as the Channel, but only with very limited success, capturing a number of merchant vessels as well as the schooner HMS Highflyer. She was found to be poorly-made and was eventually broken up just three years later in 1818 (see 18th June and 24th December).

1918 The birth of Diana Barnato (see 28th April and 26th August) in London. She was the daughter of Woolf Barnato, a Chairman of Bentley Motors and a racing car driver.

16th January:

1707 The Scottish Act of Union, uniting the Kingdoms of England and Scotland is signed by MPs in the Scottish Parliament (see 4th March, 6th March, 1st May and 22nd July) after some lengthy debates. This paves the way for the creation of the United Kingdom of Great Britain.

1780 The first Battle of Cape St. Vincent (see 14th February). Admiral Sir George Rodney (see 24th May) leads his fleet of twenty ships against a Spanish squadron of ten ships during the American colonial rebellion (see 3rd September). Admiral Rodney was en route to supply besieged Gibraltar, escorting a supply convoy when he came across a Spanish squadron under the Spanish naval officer, Juan de Langara. Upon seeing that they were outnumbered, the Spanish attempted to evade our fleet. A general chase was commenced and the running battle continued into the night. Though fighting bravely, the Spanish lost four ships captured and one destroyed, with minimal casualties by the Royal Navy. The battle is rare in that the majority of the battle was conducted at night (see 12th April).

1809 The Battle of Coruna and the death of General Sir John Moore (see 13th November) and the wounding five times of General Sir Charles Napier, leading his forces to victory. General Sir John Moore led 16,000 men against an equally sized French force under Marshal Soult. Our forces lost 900 men and the French lost about 1,500 killed and wounded. The Royal Navy pounded the French positions, allowing our forces to abandon the town in good order. Though the town was captured by the French, our forces under General Moore successfully evacuated and were able to continue the war. When the French took the town, Marshal Soult had a memorial built over General Moore's grave to his honour. General Moore served in the suppression of the Irish rebellion in 1798 and was instrumental in the formation of Light Infantry units as well as his effective training regimes.

1839 Aden became part of British India when it was occupied by Marines of the East India Company (see 31st December) under the command of Captain Stafford Haines in order to prevent pirate attacks on British shipping bound for India (see 1st April).

1894 Elizabeth Yates (see 6th September) becomes the first woman across the British Empire to hold the office of Mayor when she is sworn in as the Mayor of Onehunga in New Zealand (see 1st July and 26th September) following the general election in 1893 (see 19th September and 28th November).

17th January:

1746 The battle of Falkirk; when the Jacobite troops, led by Prince Charles (see 31st January and 31st December) and General Lord George Murray (see 4th October and 11th October), stand against the government forces led by General Henry Hawley. Both sides were even in their numbers and the government troops lined up prior to any conflict. The government troops charged first but were mown down by the Highlanders firing a volley of shots before throwing down their weapons and charging. The panicking government troops fled, although some Regiments remained steadfast in the face of the Highlanders. Around fifty Jacobites were killed but around 350 Hanoverians were also killed (see 16th April and 19th August).

1773 Commander James Cook (see 14th February and 27th October), on his second voyage and on board the HMS Resolution in company with HMS Adventure, possibly become the first people to cross the Antarctic circle as he circumnavigates the globe (see 18th January).

1781 The Battle of Cowpens in South Carolina. Our forces, of regulars and Loyalists led by Lieutenant Colonel Banastre Tarleton are defeated by General Daniel Morgan's rebel forces. Although both sides had barely over 1,000 men, the engagement is believed to have been a turning point in the American rebellion, in particular in the Carolinas (see 3rd September).

1863 The birth of David Lloyd-George in Manchester (see 26th March).

1871 The birth of David Beatty in Nantwich, Cheshire (see 11th March).

1885 The battle of Abu Klea in the Sudan occurs between the Desert Column of less than 1,500 men under Major General Herbert Stewart and Mahdist forces. The Desert Column was on its way to relieve Khartoum that was under siege by the Mahdists. At Abu Klea, the Mahdists set upon the column with over 10,000 men. Forming into squares to confront them, our forces were hard-pressed at first but with the use of the Gardner machine gun, the Mahdists were quickly repelled with great loss. It was about this battle that Sir Henry Newbolt wrote his famous poem 'Vitai Lampada' (see 19th April and 6th June).

1911 The death of Sir Francis Galton in Halemere in Surrey (see 16th February). A half cousin of Charles Darwin (see 12th February and 19th April), he was one of the great Victorian scientists and was an explorer, meteorologist, eugenicist and anthropologist and is credited with the invention of fingerprint testing into criminal investigation. He is most well known for his leading work on eugenics and a method for the classification of fingerprints.

1912 Sir Robert Falcon Scott (see 29th March and 6th June) and his team reached the South Pole, the first Britons to do so. Sadly, they had been beaten to the Pole by Roald Amundsen just a month earlier.

1991 Operation Desert Storm, often referred to as the First Gulf War, is launched with missile and air attacks on targets within Iraq and Kuwait by British and American forces. The initial goals were the destruction of Iraqi aircraft and anti-aircraft missiles before moving onto the military and civilian infrastructure.

18th January:

1671 Captain Henry Morgan (see 25th August) and around 1,500 fellow pirates attack and capture the Spanish city of Panama which was defended by around 2,000 Spanish troops and cavalry. In a pitched battle, the Spanish suffered heavy casualties amongst the cavalry, resulting in the infantry line faltering then fleeing. The city was plundered and large parts put to the torch. Captain Henry Morgan returned to Jamaica a hero but the Godolphin Treaty between England and Spain was in tatters (see 8th July).

1752 The birth of John Nash in London (see 13th May).

1778 Captain James Cook, on his third voyage, becomes the first European to discover the Hawaiian Islands (see 17th January, 14th February and 27th October) as he makes sight of the island of Kauai.

1779 The birth of Peter Mark Roget in London (see 12th September).

1788 HMS Supply, the first ship from the First Fleet, commanded by Captain Arthur Philip, arrives in Botany Bay. Despite setting up camp, it was decided that the position was not ideal and, after the remainder of the fleet had arrived, they moved north to Port Jackson and established Australia's first permanent settlement to be named Sydney after the Home Secretary, Lord Sydney, who was responsible for the programme of colonisation (see 26th January and 7th February).

1849 The birth of Edmund Barton (see 1st January and 7th January) in Sydney, New South Wales in Australia.

1873 The death of Edward George Earle Bulwer-Lytton (see 25th May) in Torquay. A Politician, playwright, poet and novelist, he also coined some of the more well-known phrases in the English Language. He served first as a Whig MP in 1831 and then eleven years later as a Conservative MP from 1852 to 1866. He had a very unpleasant relationship with his wife due to his unfaithfulness, which resulted in a legal separation. He wrote for a number of well known magazines and wrote numerous essays.

1936 The death of Rudyard Kipling, poet, writer and novelist (see 30th December) in London. A celebrated and proud imperialist, he was a keen champion of all things British and of the Empire. He is remembered for a wide variety of literary works, including *If, Kim, the Jungle book, the Man Who Would be King, Gunga Din* and *Mandalay*. In 1907 he was awarded the Nobel Prize for Literature. A great patriot and supporter of the Empire, his only son John 'Jack', a Lieutenant in the 2nd Battalion Irish Guards, was killed in September 1915 at the battle of Loos during the First World War. He was cremated and his ashes were laid to rest in Poets' Corner in Westminster Abbey.

19th January:

1419 The French city of Rouen in Normandy is captured by English forces under Henry V (see 31st August) during the Hundred Years War (1337-1453) and returned to English control. The city was the capital of English

France for thirty years until recaptured by French forces in 1449 (see 30th May).

1736 The birth of James Watt in Greenock, Scotland (see 19th August).

1764 The MP John Wilkes is tried in his absence, expelled from the House of Commons and declared an outlaw (see 17th October and 29th December) over his writing and then publication of an alleged blasphemous and seditious poem.

1812 British and Portuguese forces, commanded by General Wellington (see 1st May and 14th September), storm and capture the besieged city of Ciudad Rodrigo in Spain. Unfortunately, following the taking of the city, the troops went on a violent rampage. However, the fall of the city allowed General Wellington to focus his campaign on the city of Badajoz (see 16th March and 6th April).

1813 The birth of Henry Bessemer in Hertfordshire (see 15th March).

1839 The city and port of Aden is stormed and taken by troops from the East India Company (see 31st December). The city was of strategic importance for the replenishment and security of vessels travelling to and from the colonies and possessions in Africa and India (see 20th June, 5th July and 10th December).

1848 Matthew Webb, later the first man to swim the Channel, is born in Dawley in Shropshire (see 24th July and 25th August).

1909 A three man team, Douglas Mawson, Edgeworth David and Alistair Mackay, become the first people to reach the Magnetic South Pole. The team took photos and then raised the Union Flag and claimed it for Great Britain (see 17th January).

1915 The first Zeppelin raid on Britain, with Great Yarmouth and Kings Lynn becoming the first targets, resulting in the death of four people and the wounding of 16 others (see 31st May, 7th June and 24th December).

20th January:

1265 The first meeting of Parliament at Westminster Hall. The meeting was headed by Simon de Montfort (see 14th May and 4th August) and was attended by Knights and elected Burgesses. It lasted until March and discussed taxes and legal matters affecting those present.

1327 Edward II is deposed. He was brutally murdered in September 1327, the exact date being unknown (see 25th February, 25th April and 21st September). He was the fourth son of Edward I and the first English prince to hold the title Prince of Wales (see 7th February). He was unpopular with his nobles almost immediately for his bad choice in 'favourites' and there was open hostility to his rule. His wife, Isabella of France, eventually became the mistress of Roger Mortimer, an exiled opponent of Edward's. They invaded the country in 1326 and met with relatively little resistance. Edward was deposed in favour of his and Isabella's son, who became Edward III (see 21st June and 13th November).

1649 The illegal trial of King Charles I on charges of High Treason and other crimes against the country and its people begins in Whitehall (see 30th January and 19th November).

1779 The death of David Garrick (see 19th February) in London. An actor, theatre manager, playwright and producer, he was a former pupil and very good friend of Doctor Samuel Johnson (see 7th September and 13th December) and influenced all aspects of theatre life throughout the 18th Century. He was given an expensive funeral and is buried in Poets' Corner in Westminster Abbey.

1841 Hong Kong Island is seized during the First Opium War 1839-1842 (see 7th January, 9th June, 1st July and 29th August) with the idea of using it as a base for the East India Company (see 31st December).

1900 The death of John Ruskin (see 8th February). A writer, he is best remembered as the leading art critic of his time and an early advocate of Christian Socialism, arguing that the State should intervene in the economic and social aspects of society. He was a friend of J M W Turner, the painter, and campaigned for his public recognition. Believing that being rich and socialism were not compatible, he gave much of his inherited wealth away to charitable organisations.

1936 The death of George V at Sandringham House (see 6th May, 3rd June, 22nd June and 17th July). As the second son, he wasn't expected to ascend to the throne until the premature death of his elder brother Albert Victor. He was King throughout the Great War and, in 1917, as a result of intense anti-German feelings during the war, he changed the family name to Windsor. As a Grandson of Queen Victoria (see 22nd January and 24th May), he was the cousin of Kaiser Wilhelm II of Germany as well as Tsar Nicholas II of Russia. He is the Grandfather of Queen Elizabeth II (see 21st April).

21st January:

1846 The first edition of 'The Daily News', edited by Charles Dickens (see 7th February and 9th June), is published. It was intended to extol the 'principles of progress and improvement; of education, civil and religious liberty and equal legislation' as Dickens himself wrote. The paper, though not successful to begin with, did indeed become extremely successful.

1919 The birth of Captain Eric Melrose 'Winkle' Brown in Leith. He joined the Royal Naval Volunteer Reserves as a Fleet Air Arm Test pilot in 1939. During his career as a test pilot, he has flown more different types of aircraft than any other pilot. He is also the Fleet Air Arms most decorated pilot. On the 3rd December 1945 he became the first pilot to take off and land his jet aircraft, a De Havilland Sea Vampire on an Aircraft Carrier, HMS Ocean.

1919 Members of Sinn Fein, refusing to recognise the Westminster government, met together at what they called the Dail Eiraan. The Dail illegally declared itself the Republican government of Ireland and also declared itself independent of the true Government in London (see 24th April, 29th April, 6th December and 8th December). Parliament did not recognise the Dail and declared it illegal. The declaration by Sinn Fein instigated a terrorist campaign against the government.

1919 Two Royal Irish Constabulary officers are ambushed and murdered by members of the IRA as they were escorting workers carrying explosives in County Tipperary in Ireland. The attack is regarded as the beginning of the so-called Irish War of Independence (see 24th April, 29th April, 5th December, 6th December and 8th December).

1935 Snowdonia becomes Britain's first National Park. It covers an area of around 838 square miles and contains Wales' highest Mountain, Snowdon, at 3560 feet.

1950 The death of George Orwell from Chronic Tuberculosis in London. His real name was Eric Arthur Blair (see 25th June). After leaving Eton, he joined the Indian Imperial Police in the colony of Burma. He later resigned his position with the aim of becoming a writer. In 1936 he went to fight in the Spanish Civil War and fought for the Republicans against Franco. In 1937 he wrote 'The Road to Wigan Pier' and during the war he worked on propaganda for the BBC before writing his two most well-known books, 'Animal Farm' in 1945 and then '1984' in 1949.

1976 Concorde's first scheduled commercial flights take off simultaneously from London to Bahrain and from Paris to Rio. There were no immediate transatlantic flights to America due to the US Congress initially banning such flights due to supposed fears over sonic booms and noise pollution (see 24th October).

22nd January:

1561 The birth of Sir Francis Bacon (see 9th April) in London.

1760 The Battle of Wandiwash in India during the Seven Years' War (1756-1763). The Fort at Wandiwash, in the South East of the Continent, had been besieged by French troops under the Count de Lally. However, on this day Colonel Eyre Coote arrived with a relieving force and after a preliminary artillery bombardment, our troops defeat the French. The remnants of the French force are forced to retire to Pondicherry (see 15th January). The battle was such a decisive victory for our forces from the East India Company (see 31st December) that it contributed to our imminent control over India.

1771 Spain cedes Port Egmont and the Falkland Islands to Great Britain. Port Egmont on the east of the islands was the possession that had been established in 1765 with the settlement being created a year later (see 2nd January, 2nd April and 14th June).

1788 The birth of George Lord Byron in London (see 19th April).

1879 The Battle of Isandlwana in Zululand and the massacre of 1,200 British soldiers by around 12,000 Zulu warriors. Our forces were led by Lieutenant Colonel Pulleine of the 24th Regiment of Foot and Colonel

Durnford of the Royal Engineers. The Zulu armies approached our camp in their traditional chest and horn formation, attempting to encircle the camp. The battle lasted from around 8am until the late afternoon. The Zulus showed no mercy to wounded soldiers and mutilated many of the bodies of those killed and dying (see 12th January and 23rd January).

1879 The beginning of the defence of the mission station at Rorke's Drift from an attack by Zulu forces fresh from the massacre at Isandlwana (see 12th January and 23rd January) earlier the same day. Our forces were led by Lieutenant John Chard of the Royal Engineers and Lieutenant Gonville Bromhead of the 24th Regiment of Foot.

1887 The death of Sir Joseph Whitworth (see 21st December), inventor and engineer, in Monte Carlo. Born in Stockport, he was an apprentice to his uncle and later worked as a machine mechanic in Manchester and London. In the 1830s he started his own business in tool making. A year later he patented a screw cutting machine and went on to produced numerous machine tools and parts. It was in the 1850s that he championed the cause of standardised screw threads across the engineering industry. During the Crimean War (1853-1856) he supplied weapons and equipment to the army and in the late 1850s he developed the 'Whitworth rifle' which was ultimately not adopted by the Ordinance Board.

1901 The death of Queen Victoria, Queen of Great Britain and Ireland and Empress of India, at Osborne House on the Isle of White (see 24th May). She was the longest reigning monarch and the Empress of the world's largest and greatest Empire (see 2nd February, 20th June and 28th June). Born in Kensington Palace, she was the daughter of Edward Duke of Kent and Victoria Maria Louisa of Saxe-Coburg and the niece of William IV (see 20th June and 21st August), whom she succeeded when she was eighteen years old. She married Prince Albert in 1840 (see 10th February), had nine children of whom most married into the monarchies of Europe and became Empress of India in 1876 (see 1st January and 1st May). During her reign, the Empire grew even bigger and British influence spread far across the globe.

1924 James Ramsay McDonald (see 12th October and 9th November) goes to Buckingham Palace to see George V (see 20th January and 3rd June) and becomes the Labour Party's first Prime Minister, leading a minority government after the resignation of the Conservative Prime Minister Stanley Baldwin (see 3rd August and 14th December) earlier in the day. The Conservative government had lost a vote of no confidence and Labour, with the help of the Liberals, formed a minority government.

23rd January:

1745 The birth of William Jessop in Devonport, Devon (see 18th November).

1806 The death of William Pitt the Younger at the age of 46 (see 28th May) at Putney Heath in London. The son of the former Prime Minister,

William Pitt the Elder, Lord Chatham (see 11th May and 15th November), he entered parliament at the age of 21 and soon became a champion of parliamentary reform. He became Prime Minister at the age of 24, the youngest ever, and led the country through some of the most momentous events in our history: the French Revolutionary and Napoleonic wars (see 9th June and 20th November), brought economic stability to the country following the American colonial rebellion (see 3rd September) and also unification with Ireland. He served two terms as Prime Minister; the first ended when he resigned following the failure of his attempts at Catholic emancipation (see 5th February). He served the second time due to the threat from Napoleonic France and died whilst in office (see 9th January, 10th May and 19th December).

1833 The death of Admiral Edward Pellew, 1st Viscount Exmouth (see 19th April) in Teigmouth. Born in Dover, he entered the Royal Navy in 1770 and saw extensive service across the globe. He saw active service in the American Colonial rebellion (during which he was taken prisoner), the French Revolutionary Wars and the Napoleonic Wars and saw action during a diplomatic mission helping to end the Second Barbary Wars in 1816 (see 27th August).

1879 The conclusion to the heroic defence of Rorke's Drift (see 12th January and 22nd January). Despite the ferocious fighting, much of it hand to hand, the 139 troops, British regulars and Colonial troops in the fort suffered only 15 killed in action and another two died of their wounds later. The Zulus had a force of around 4,000 warriors, of whom at least 350 were killed (see 29th March, 2nd April, 4th July, 28th August and 1st September).

24th January:

1749 The birth of Charles James Fox (see 13th September), Whig MP and former friend of William Pitt the Younger (see 23rd January and 28th May).

1759 The Battle of Guadeloupe, during the Seven Years' War (1756-1764), begins. After two days of bombardment by the Royal Navy on the islands capital, our forces come ashore on the French Colony to begin the battle for the island (see 1st May).

1857 Fires, probably the result of arson, break out near Calcutta, marking the beginning of unrest that would lead to the start of the Indian Mutiny (see 26th February and 10th May).

1901 The Battle of Spion Kop in Natal, South Africa, during the Boer War (1899-1902), which results in very heavy losses for our forces, concludes. Winston Churchill (see 24th January and 30th November) is present as a war correspondent for the London paper, The Morning Post. Britain wins but with high casualties. Our forces, under General Redvers Buller (see 2nd June and 7th December), suffered 1,500 casualties, 243 of which were in the trench on the summit of Spion Kop, and the Boers suffered just 335 casualties (see 31st May and 11th October).

1915 The Battle of Dogger Bank in the North Sea between the Grand Fleet under Admiral Beatty and the German High Seas Fleet under Admiral Franz von Hipper. After an initial chase of the German fleet, there was a hard-fought battle with our fleet gaining a tactical victory. One German cruiser was sunk and another battle ship was very badly damaged. None of our ships were sunk though some received damage (see 1st November and 8th December).

1916 A bill is introduced into Parliament by the Prime Minister Herbert Henry Asquith (see 15th February and 12th September) that would lead to the Military Service Act being passed to allow the conscription of single men between the ages of 19 and 41. Up until this time, our country had relied entirely upon voluntary enlistment (see 27th January and 2nd March).

1965 Sunday: The death of Winston Leonard Spencer Churchill (see 30th November and 30th January). Our wartime leader, saviour of this country and the Greatest Prime Minister and Briton the country has known. Despite the rapid fall of Europe, he led the country in our solitary stand against Nazi Germany, determined that we would not surrender but would fight to the bitter end. A former soldier himself, he saw action at the Battle of Omdurman 1898 (see 2nd September), during the Boer War (1899-1902), both as a soldier and a reporter, during which he was captured and made his famous escape. He also saw action as a battalion commander of the Royal Scots Fusiliers in the Western Front during the Great War in 1916. He held several Governmental positions, especially in the 1920s. During the 1930s he went into relative obscurity, being one of the few to speak up about the growing threat of Nazi Germany and in open criticism of the policy of appeasement. Knighted in 1953, he remained in Parliament until 1964 (see 10th May and 26th October).

25th January:

1533 Henry VIII (see 28th January and 28th June) and Anne Boleyn (see 19th May) are married lawfully and for the second time by the Bishop of Lichfield in London.

1627 The birth of Robert Boyle (see 31st December) in County Waterford, Ireland.

1644 The Battle of Nantwich during the Civil War (see 3rd September). The town was occupied by a Parliamentarian garrison of around 2,000 men and was besieged by the Royalists, commanded by Lord John Byron, in the predominantly royalist county of Cheshire. A Parliamentarian relief force under Sir Thomas Fairfax broke through into the town, effectively ending Royalist control over Cheshire. A large portion of the Royalist army surrendered and amongst the Royalist officers captured was Colonel George Monck (see 3rd January and 6th December).

1759 The birth of Robert Burns in Alloway, Ayrshire in Scotland (see 21st July).

1841 The birth of John Arbuthnot 'Jackie' Fisher in the Colony of Ceylon (see 10th July).

1859 The first 'Burns Night' at its inauguration in Scotland on the Centenary of Robert Burns birth (see 21st July).

1884 The Ilbert Bill (formally the Criminal Procedure Code Amendment Act) is passed by Parliament (see 1st May). A controversial bill proposed by the Viceroy Lord Rippon, it made provision for senior Indian Judges to preside over cases that involved British subjects. However, this caused great consternation in the European population and an amendment was agreed where a British subject could call for trial by jury which would contain half its members as European.

1981 The 'Gang of Four', David Owen, Roy Jenkins, Shirley Williams and Bill Rodgers, leave the Labour Party to form the Social Democratic Party (SDP).

26th January:

1788 The first consignment of convicts arrives at Port Jackson, Sydney Cove in Australia, with the First Fleet Commanded by Captain Arthur Philip. Phillip and some marines and sailors rowed ashore and, hoisting the flag of the Union, declared the formal possession of the land in the name of the King. This was to become the first permanent European Colony on the continent and was known as New South Wales (see 18th January and 7th February). It was quickly celebrated across most of the colonies of what would later become Australia as 'Anniversary Day'.

1823 The death of Edward Jenner in Berkeley, Gloucestershire (see 6th May). He was the pioneer of vaccination and immunology. In 1796 he carried out his now famous experiment on eight-year-old James Phipps by infecting him with cowpox and then exposing him to the smallpox virus (see 14th May). As a result of the experiment, James had become immune to the smallpox virus and Jenner had created the first vaccination. In appreciation, Parliament awarded him £10,000 in 1802 and a further £20,000 in 1807.

1828 Arthur Wellesley, The Duke of Wellington, becomes Prime Minister leading a Conservative government (see 1st May and 14th September).

1878 The death of Kirkpatrick MacMillan (see 2nd September) in Keir, Dumfries and Galloway. A Blacksmith by trade, he is credited with inventing the first pedal-driven bicycle in 1839. He had seen a pedal-less 'hobbyhorse' style cycle and decided they would be far better with the rider's feet off the ground. In 1842 he famously rode his invention the 68-mile trip from his home to Glasgow.

1879 The death of Julia Margaret Cameron (see 11th June) in Ceylon. Given a camera as a present in middle age, she took up photography. Probably one of the best known of early photographers, she was influenced by the Pre-Raphaelites but introduced her own distinctive style as she photographed her friends and family. Amongst this group were many famous Victorians such as Charles Dickens (see 7th February and 9th June), Robert Browning (see 7th May and 12th December), Alfred Lord Tennyson (see 6th August and 6th October), George Frederic Watts and Thomas Carlyle (see 5th February and 4th December). In 1875 she moved with her husband to Ceylon (see 4th February) to die just five years later.

1885 Major-General Charles George Gordon, Imperial Victorian hero, is killed at Khartoum (see 28th January) in the Sudan as the city falls to Mahdist rebels. All the Garrison of 8,000 loyal Egyptian and Sudanese soldiers and their British Officers are killed. Commissioned into the Royal Engineers, he served in the Crimean War (1853-1856) and the Arrow War against the Chinese in 1860. In 1873 he was appointed as Governor of the Sudan but returned to England in 1880. In 1884 he returned with the instruction to evacuate the Egyptian and European forces from the Sudan due to the rebel Sudanese forces. Unfortunately, the city was surrounded and overwhelmed. The relief force arrived just two days later. In Britain there was national anger at the government, who they believed failed to do enough to rescue Gordon, who they viewed as an Imperial Martyr (see 2nd September).

1905 The discovery of the Cullinan Diamond by Frederick Wells, Surface Manager for the Premier Diamond Mining Company in Cullinan, South Africa. It was the largest rough gem-quality diamond ever discovered. It was cut and the two largest diamonds from this are in the Crown Jewels (see 9th November). The largest is worth around £200 million.

1926 John Logie Baird gives his first public demonstration of his new invention, the television (see 14th June and 14th August).

27th January:

1596 The death of Sir Francis Drake from dysentery off the coast of Portobello, Panama. Born in Tavistock around 1540, he was the cousin of John Hawkins (see 12th November) and joined the navy when very young. In 1567, along with John Hawkins, he was engaged in early slave trading to the 'New World'. In 1572 he became involved in the profitable Privateering against the Spanish and was richly rewarded. In 1578 in the Golden Hind he became the first Englishman to navigate the Straits of Magellan. He then continued his plundering of Spanish ports and settlements and returned to England in 1580 as the first Englishman to circumnavigate the world. For this historic and very profitable achievement, he was knighted by Elizabeth I (see 24th March and 7th September) aboard the Golden Hind (see 4th April). In 1587 he led a pre-emptive raid on the port of Cadiz, destroying thirty Spanish ships preparing to attack England. The following year in 1588 he was Vice-Admiral of the fleet that faced and ultimately destroyed the Spanish Armada (see 29th July).

1801 The birth of Henry Moule (see 3rd February) in Wiltshire.

1816 The death of Admiral Samuel Viscount Hood (see 12th December), Lord Hood, famous Admiral and influence on Lord Nelson (see 29th September and 21st October). Born in Somerset, he entered the navy in 1741 and saw service during the Seven Years' War (1754-1763), the American Colonial rebellion, where he fought at the battle of Chesapeake in 1781 (see 5th September), the Battle of the Saintes in 1782 (see 12th April) and the defence of Toulon in 1783. He was Nelson's Commanding Officer at the Battle of the Nile in 1798 (see 1st August). He was created a Baron in 1778 and a Viscount in 1796. In 1784 he was elected to Parliament and he lived long enough to be the Chief Mourner at Nelson's funeral (see 9th January).

1916 Conscription is introduced for the first time with the Military Service Act (see 24th January) receiving Royal Assent, to come into effect on the 2nd March 1916 for all males between 19 and 41 years of age.

28th January:

1457 The birth of the future Henry VII at Pembroke Castle (see 21st April and 30th October), the son of Edmund Tudor, the first Earl of Richmond.

1547 The death of Henry VIII, King of England, France and Ireland and founder of the Church of England at Whitehall Palace (see 24th June and 28th June) and the accession of his son as Edward VI (see 6th July and 12th October). One of England's greatest monarchs, he was the father of three future monarchs, Mary I (see 18th February and 17th November), Edward VI and Elizabeth I (see 24th March and 7th September). He married six times in his quest for a male heir and was responsible for this country's break with Rome and the adoption of a Protestant religious tradition (see 17th December). Under his influence, England and Wales were united, he became King of Ireland (see 18th June) and the Royal Navy began to become more important and effective. His six wives were Catherine of Aragon (see 7th January and 16th December), Anne Boleyn (see 19th May), Jane Seymour (see 24th October), Anne of Cleves (see 16th July), Catherine Howard (see 13th February) and Catherine Parr (see 5th September).

1807 The birth of Robert John Le Mesurier McClure (see 17th October) in Wexford, Ireland.

1829 William Burke is hanged on the Lawnmarket in Edinburgh in front of a huge crowd. An Irish immigrant and serial murderer, his accomplice, also an Irish immigrant, was William Hare. They committed their crimes during the years 1827 and 1828. They were responsible for the murder of 17 people and then the selling of the corpses onto a Doctor Robert Knox for medical dissection. Following their capture, Hare turned King's evidences against him and was not executed.

1833 The birth of Charles George Gordon (see 26th January) in Woolwich.

1841 The birth of Henry Morton Stanley in (see 10th May) in Denbigh, Wales as John Rowlands.

1846 The battle of Aliwal in the Punjab, India, during the First Anglo-Sikh War (1845-1846). The Sikh army, the Khalsa, had earlier crossed the border into British territory. Their forces numbered up to around 30,000. The British troops and troops of the Bengal Presidency under General Harry Smith numbered around 12,000 and met the Sikhs at the village of Aliwal. Our troops secured the village and after a heavy bombardment of the enemy positions, proceeded to enfilade the Sikhs with support from British and Indian cavalry. Very quickly the Sikhs lines faltered and began to retreat before turning into a rout for the humiliated Sikh army (see 10th February, 9th March, 18th December and 21st December).

1881 The Battle of Laing's Nek during the First Boar War. The Boers held the ridge called Laing's Nek and outnumbered our troops. Unfortunately, despite brave charges by our mounted troops and attacks by Infantry it was a defeat for our forces and they had to retire. Besides being a defeat, this battle was notable as being the last time a British Regiment took its colours into battle (see 3rd August and 11th October).

1909 The birth of Lionel 'Buster' Crabb (see 19th April) in Streatham, London.

1928 The death of Field Marshal Sir Douglas Haig (see 19th June) in London. A career soldier, he was Chief of the General Staff and commanded the British Expeditionary Force (BEF) during the Great War from 1915 after replacing General Sir John French. Born in Edinburgh, he studied at Oxford University and then Sandhurst Military Academy. He served in the Cavalry in India before taking part in the Sudan Campaign (1897-1898) and the Boer War (1899-1902). He was then given command of preparing the BEF in preparation for possible war with Imperial Germany. Though heavily criticised from the 1960s onwards by revisionist historians for his role in the Great War, he has quite rightly received better assessments from more modern and better educated historians. He is also remembered for being instrumental in the foundation of the Royal British Legion (see 15th May and 29th May).

29th January:

1689 Parliament (illegally) declares that James VII (James II of England see 16th September and 14th October) had abdicated. James had in fact fled the country after William's arrival (see 8th March and 4th November), as large sections of his forces began to melt away and defect to the Prince of Orange.

1737 The birth of Thomas Paine in Thetford, Norfolk (see 8th June).

1803 The birth of James Outram (see 11th March) in Butterley, Derbyshire.

1820 The death of George III at Windsor Castle (see 24th May). He reigned for almost 60 years and was the first of the Hanoverian Kings to be born in this country with English as his first language. He also never visited Hanover. During his reign, Britain fought the Seven Years' War (1756-1763), saw the 13 American Colonies rebel (see 3rd September) and took part in wars with Revolutionary as well as Napoleonic France. From 1810 he became very ill and suffered from increasing bouts of ill health and dementia. This allowed for the Regency Act to be passed in 1811 and his son, later George IV (see 26th June and 12th August), acted as Regent until his father's death. He was succeeded on his death by his son, George Augustus Frederick, as George IV (see 26th June and 12th August).

1856 The Victoria Cross, the highest award for valour, is founded when Queen Victoria (see 22nd January and 24th May) signs the Royal Warrant bringing the Victoria Cross into being (see 26th June).

1860 The birth of William Robert Robertson (see 12th February) in Welbourne, Lincolnshire.

1888 The death of Edward Lear (see 12th May) in Italy from heart disease. An artist, author and poet, he is widely known for his nonsense poetry and limericks, the most famous of his works being 'The Owl and the Pussycat', published in 1867. He suffered from epilepsy, bronchitis and asthma and because of this in the 1870s he settled in Sanremo on the northern Mediterranean coast of Italy. It was here that he died.

30th January:

1606 Sir Everard Digby, Thomas Winter, John Grant and Thomas Bates are executed by being hung, drawn and quartered for their part in the Gunpowder Plot (see 31st January, 5th November and 8th November).

1649 The death, execution and murder of Charles I (see 20th January, 2nd February, 18th June and 19th November) outside the Banqueting Hall of Whitehall Palace and the accession of his son Charles II (see 6th February and 29th May). He was beheaded on scaffolding purposely built for the execution. The King wore two white shirts so that it would prevent any shivering in the cold that may have been interpreted as nerves by the spectators. After giving a brief speech on the scaffold, the King placed his head on the block, gave a short prayer and then signalled to the executioner. He was beheaded with one clean stroke. The son of James VI (see 27th March and 19th June) of Scotland and Anne of Denmark, he became King of England and Scotland on the death of his father in 1625. Shortly afterwards, he married the Catholic Henrietta Maria of France. A devout High Anglican, his reign was marked by his increased suppression of Puritans and Catholics, his introduction of a new prayer book and his arguments with Parliament and Scotland about religion and his ability to raise taxes, all of which lead ultimately to Civil War in 1642 (see 22nd August). The King and the Royalists lost and in January 1649 he was tried and executed.

1891 The death of Charles Bradlaugh (see 26th September). A radical politician, he was elected to Parliament in 1880 as the MP for Northampton. An open atheist, he refuted the need to take the oath in the House of Commons, claiming the right to affirm his allegiance instead. He was re-elected three times before taking his seat as the Commons had repeatedly denied him the opportunity to sit. In 1866 he helped in the formation of the National Secular Society. In 1877, along with his friend Annie Besant, he published a book advocating birth control. Tried and convicted of publishing material likely to corrupt, they were both sentenced to six months imprisonment, which was later quashed on appeal.

1902 The Anglo-Japanese Alliance is signed in London by the Foreign Secretary, Lord Lansdowne. The alliance involved both countries agreeing to remain neutral when one or other was attacked but coming to the other's aid should the aggressors be more than one country. The alliance was in fact designed as a warning to the Russians about their Imperial expansion. It also marked the end of the informal policy of 'splendid isolation' (see 15th August and 8th December).

1963 Britain's first attempt at entry into The European Economic Community was refused by the member states after France, led by De Gaulle vetoed the attempt. France and De Gaulle in particular were afraid of our country's links with our colonies, dependencies and the Commonwealth, despite Frances' own overseas territories and possessions (see 1st January, 7th February, 23rd June, 28th October and 27th November).

1965 The State funeral of Sir Winston Leonard Spencer Churchill (see 24th January and 30th November), the Greatest leader this country has ever known. For three days prior to the funeral, his body lay in state in Westminster Hall and the state funeral service was conducted in St. Paul's Cathedral (see 2nd December). His body passed down the Thames on the launch Havengore from Tower Pier to Festival Pier and as it passed the docks, the Dockers lowered their cranes in his honour. The coffin was then taken to Waterloo Station to a specially prepared train for it's finally journey to the family plot at St. Martin's Church in Bladon. Along the way, in stations and in fields next to the track, thousands of people lined the route in silence to pay their respects.

1972 During a civil rights march in Londonderry, Paratroopers of 1st battalion the Parachute Regiment open fire on some of the marchers in the Bogside area of the city, killing thirteen, believing that they had come under fire themselves (see 9th March, 31st July, 12th August and 14th August).

31st January:

1606 Guy Fawkes is executed for his part in the Gun Powder plot. He is hung, drawn and quartered in the Old Palace Yard in Westminster along with three fellow conspirators, Thomas Wintour, Ambrose Rockwood and Robert Keyes. It was an extra ordeal for him as he had been severely weakened by his torture and had to be helped by his executioners to the scaffold (see 30th January, 5th November and 8th November).

1788 The death of Charles Edward Louis John Casimir Severino Maria Stuart (known as 'Bonnie Prince Charlie', the Jacobite King Charles III) in the Palazzo Muti in Rome and with him the hopes of all Jacobites (see 31st December). He was the eldest son of Prince James Francis Edward Stewart, the Jacobite James III and the 'Old Pretender' (see 1st January and 10th June). In 1745, in the name of his father, he led the most successful Jacobite rising and came very close to securing the throne for the Stuarts (see 19th August). He led his troops across Scotland and then advanced into England, getting as far as Derby before mistakenly turning back and to ultimate defeat. Following the Battle of Culloden in 1746 (see 16th April), he escaped to France whilst the Highlands were brutally cleared of all supposed rebels. Following the death of his father, he styled himself Charles III and although he married later in life, he remained childless and steadily sank into depression and alcoholism.

1858 The launch of Isambard Kingdom Brunel's ship the 'SS Great Eastern', the largest ship of her time, designed to carry up to 4,000 passengers around the world before refuelling. She was the first ship to feature a double-skinned hull and though this did not become common place for another 100 years, it is now mandatory for safety reasons (see 19th July). On her maiden voyage she suffered an explosion and was offered for sale in 1864. Later, after some major conversion work, she was fitted out to lay telegraph cables and in 1865 she was one of two ships that laid the first Trans-Atlantic telegraph cable (see 9th April and 15th September).

1919 Friday: The Battle of George Square in Glasgow referred to as 'Black Friday', one of Scotland's worst riots. Over 10,000 workers converged on George Square to demonstrate for a 40 hour working week instead of the then 54 hour week due to large-scale unemployment. The Government, fearing that Bolsheviks may agitate for revolution, decided to try and disperse the crowd, who eventually rioted with the use of English troops, in case Scottish troops sided with the rioters. Scottish troops from the Highland Light Infantry were effectively locked in their Barracks in Marryhill.

1941 The last British and Commonwealth troops leave the Malay Peninsula in an organised withdrawal as Imperial Japanese troops overrun the Colony of Malaya (see 31st January). Royal Engineers destroy the causeway linking Malaya with the Colony of Singapore and prepare its defence (see 15th February). Around 50,000 British and Commonwealth troops had been taken prisoner as Japanese forces advanced along the Malayan Peninsula.

1966 The death of Lieutenant General Arthur Ernest Percival. He was the Officer in charge of the defence of the Colony of Singapore against the Japanese during the Second World War. He is remembered for signing the articles of surrender and was therefore the Commanding Officer of the biggest British defeat and surrender in history. A total of around 80,000 Commonwealth forces were taken into captivity to join around 50,000 men already in captivity from the Malayan Campaign (see 1941 above, 15th February and 26th December).

1983 The wearing of seat-belts for the drivers and front seat passengers of cars became law at midnight (see 18th March and 22nd December).

FEBRUARY

1st February:

1587 Queen Elizabeth I (see 24th March and 7th September) signs the authorisation for the warrant for the execution of Mary Queen of Scots (see 18th February and 17th November).

1793 The newly formed Republic of France declares war on Great Britain, beginning the French Revolutionary Wars that would spread French revolutionary fervour across Europe and would last until the Treaty of Amiens in 1802 (see 25th March).

1851 The death of Mary Shelley (see 30th August) in London. She was the daughter of Mary Wollstonecraft (see 27th April and 10th September) and William Godwin (see 3rd March and 7th April) and is best remembered for her Gothic novel *Frankenstein* which was published in 1818. A prolific novelist and writer, she had an intense relationship that caused some scandal with the poet Percy Bysshe Shelley (see 8th July and 4th August) whom she later married in 1816.

1884 The first publication of the prototype Oxford English Dictionary (OED) under the editor James Murray. Work on the dictionary began in the 1850s by a group of academics in London and since its publication has been the largest dictionary of the English language (see 15th April).

1910 The first Labour Exchange (later called Job Centres) is opened.

1921 The Chattri, a War Memorial to the courageous Indian soldiers, is unveiled by Edward, Prince of Wales (see 28th May and 23rd June), on the South Downs, above the city of Brighton. It is a Memorial to the glorious and heroic Indian soldiers who died nearby from their wounds and illnesses received whilst serving the Empire during the Great War. The memorial is situated on the site of the funeral pyre used to cremate the Hindu soldiers in accordance with their religious practices (see 6th November).

1949 The Women's Auxiliary Air Force is renamed the Women's Royal Air Force (see 28th June).

2006 The launch of HMS Daring, the first of the Type 45 destroyer class. It was also the first destroyer class ship launched since the 1970s. All six ships in the class are the most advanced ever built for the Royal Navy at a cost of over one billion pounds each (see 4th July).

2nd February:

1626 The Coronation of Charles I in Westminster Abbey (see 30th January, 18th June and 19th November). His wife, Henrietta Maria of France, was not present as she was Catholic and there was already much controversy over their marriage

1650 The birth of Eleanor 'Nell' Gwynne in Pipewell Lane, Hereford, London or Oxford (see 14th November). Evidence for any of these locations is scarce.

1709 Alexander Selkirk is rescued after a four year and four months stay on the uninhabited island of Mas a Tierra, off the coast of Chile (see 13th December). He had elected to be left on the island after the ship he was on the 'Cinque Ports' became so unstable he correctly thought it would sink.

1901 Saturday: The State funeral of Queen Empress Victoria, Queen of Great Britain and Ireland and Empress of India and our second longest reigning Monarch (see 22nd January, 24th May, 20th June and 28th June). She had lain in state for the two days before. She was interred in the Royal Mausoleum at Frogmore House, in the gardens adjoining Windsor Castle next to her husband Prince Albert (see 26th August and 14th December). Becoming Queen at the age of 18 after the death of her Uncle, William IV (see 20th June and 21st August), she is one of our best remembered Monarchs. In 1840 she married her first cousin, Prince Albert. She became Empress of India in 1877 (see 1st January and 1st May).

3rd February:

1807 The battle of Montevideo in the Spanish Viceroyalty of the Rio de la Plata where 3,000 of our troops under General Sir Samuel Auchmuty attacked the city which was defended by around 5,000 Spanish soldiers. With approximately 150 soldiers killed, the city was carried later that morning despite a brave resistance by the Spanish garrison (see 27th June).

1830 The birth of Robert Arthur Talbot Gascoyne Cecil (see 22nd August) at Hatfield in Hertfordshire.

1873 The birth of Hugh Montague Trenchard (see 10th February) in Taunton in Somerset.

1880 The death of Henry Moule (see 27th January) in Fordington vicarage. A priest in the Church of England, he is remembered for being the inventor of the dry earth closet, or toilet, for which he was granted the patent in 1860. Born in 1801 in Wiltshire, he became the vicar at Fordington in 1829, where he was to remain for the remainder of his life. His work on the dry earth closet was motivated by cholera epidemics in the country during the 1840s and 1850s.

1960 Prime Minister Harold Macmillan (see 10th February and 29th December) delivers his famous 'Wind of Change' speech to the South African Parliament in Cape Town (see 31st May). The speech was significant as it signalled to the Empire, the Commonwealth (see 28th April) and the world that the Conservative government was preparing to grant independence to many of its colonies and territories, primarily in Africa.

4th February:

211 Roman Emperor Septimius Severus dies at Eboracum (modern day York). As Emperor, he had launched several campaigns, strengthened Hadrian's Wall and reoccupied the Antonine Wall before beginning to wage war in Caledonia in the year 210 (see 27th August).

1555 The first known Protestant Martyr in England, John Rogers, is executed by being burned at the stake for 'heresy'. He was the first victim of Mary I (see 18th February and 17th November) and her attempt to restore the Roman Catholic faith to her Kingdom (see 29th February).

1945 The start of the Yalta Conference in Livadia in the Crimea, between Great Britain, the United States of America and the Soviet Union. The leaders of the 'Big Three' countries, Winston Churchill (see 24th January and 30th November), Franklin D Roosevelt and Joseph Stalin met to discuss the organisation and spheres of influence in post-war Europe (see 17th July and 28th November).

1948 The Colony of Ceylon is granted Dominion status within the Commonwealth (see 28th April).

2012 The death of Florence Green in King's Lynn, Norfolk. She was the last surviving service member of the Great War (see 25th July). Born in 1901, she had joined the Women's Royal Air Force on 13th September 1918, just two months before the Armistice.

2013 Human bones, discovered under a car park in Leicester in August 2012, are formerly identified as those of Richard III (see 22nd August and 2nd October). Following his death at the battle of Bosworth in 1485, he was hurriedly buried at the Church of Greyfriars in Leicester, the position of which was lost during the reformation when the church was destroyed following its dissolution (see 26th March).

5th February:

1649 The Scottish Parliament declares Charles II (see 6th February and 29th May) King of Great Britain, France and Ireland. Following the execution of his father, Charles I (see 30th January and 19th November), the personal Union of the two Kingdoms under the same Monarch had been ended. The Scottish Parliament, reacting in opposition to the events in England, chose to declare Charles II as King (see 3rd September).

1788 The birth of Robert Peel (see 2nd July and 18th December) in Bury, Lancashire.

1801 William Pitt the Younger (see 23rd January and 28th May) resigns as Prime Minister over the King's refusal to accept Catholic Emancipation. His resignation is accepted by George III (see 29th January and 24th May) prior to his informing Parliament a few days later.

1811 The Regency Act is passed in Parliament (see 6th February). This allowed the Prince of Wales (the future George IV see 26th June and 17th August) to assume the responsibility of Regent whilst his father, George III (see 29th January and 24th May), was suffering incapacitation due to his mental and physical illness.

1840 The birth of John Boyd Dunlop (see 23rd October) in Ayrshire, Scotland.

1881 The death of Thomas Carlyle (see 4th December) in London. He was a successful Victorian essayist and historian, his first success being 'The French Revolution, a History', published in 1837. He started his career as a teacher before writing articles for the Edinburgh Review. He translated the German writers such as Goethe and Schiller. He married in 1826 and moved to London and became a close friend of John Stuart Mill (see 8th May and 20th May). An inspiration for many social reformers, he became increasingly right-wing and conservative as he grew older, becoming an influence on the more radically right-wing thinkers and politicians of the twentieth century.

1894 The birth of Frederick Edgeworth Morgan in Kent (see 19th March).

1924 The BBC broadcasts the first six-pip Greenwich Time Signal on radio. Broadcast on the hour with the sixth pip signalling the start of the hourly minute, they were the idea of the Astronomer Royal, Sir Frank Dyson (see 19th December).

1953 Sweet rationing finally comes to an end. Sweets had been rationed since 1942, with a maximum of 16oz per person a month (see 8th January, 9th February, 4th July, 9th July, 9th September and 3rd October).

6th February: Accession Day for Elizabeth II

1665 The birth of the future Queen Anne at St. James Palace (see 23rd April and 1st August). Her parents were James VII (James II of England, see 16th September and 14th October) and Anne Hyde.

1685 The death of Charles II in Whitehall Palace (see 1st January and 29th May). During the Civil War, he was appointed as Commander in Chief of Western England when only fourteen years old. Although forced into exile, he was crowned King at Scone in 1650 (see 1st January) and invaded England with a Scots army, only to be defeated at the battle of Worcester in 1651 (see 3rd September and 6th September). Following another period of exile, he returned to England for the Restoration (see 29th May). His reign saw the Plague in 1665, the Great Fire of London in 1666 (see 2nd September and 6th September) and two wars with the Dutch and a strengthening of the Royal Navy. It is claimed he converted to Roman Catholicism on his death bed. However, the extent to which he was conscious and aware of what was happening and whether it was what he intended is unclear.

1802 The birth of Charles Wheatstone in Gloucester (see 19th October).

1804 The death of Joseph Priestly (see 13th March and 14th July) in Pennsylvania, America. A scientist, clergyman and political theorist, he sided with the rebellious American Colonists in their rebellion against their mother country. He is generally credited with the discovery of oxygen and was a founder member of the Lunar Society and leading figure within the Midlands

Enlightenment. In 1772 he published 'On Different Kinds of Air' to the Royal Society and in 1774 he identified what he called 'dephlogisticated air' (oxygen). In 1791, in support of the French revolution, he published a response to Edmund Burke's 'Reflections' (see 1st January and 9th July) which was a criticism of the French revolution. After this outspoken support for the revolution, a mob attacked and burned his Birmingham home to the ground. Following this, he moved to London. Two years later he moved to Pennsylvania, built a home and laboratory and became involved in the politics of the new nation.

1806 The Battle of San Domingo in the Caribbean Sea is fought. The British squadron under Vice-Admiral John Duckworth attacked the French squadron off the Island of Hispanola. After an intense two hour battle, our forces were victorious. Three French ships were captured and two others ran aground and were burnt. This would be the last great fleet action in open water of the Napoleonic Wars (see 11th April).

1811 George, Prince of Wales (the future George IV), is sworn in as Prince Regent following the passing by Parliament of the Regency Act (see 5th February, 26th June and 12th August) whilst his father, George III (see 29th January and 24th May), was suffering incapacitation due to his mental and physical illness.

1819 Sir Thomas Stamford Bingley Raffles declares the foundation of the city of Singapore (see 5th July and 6th July).

1840 The signing of the Treaty of Waitangi by a Confederation of Maori Chiefs allowing New Zealand to become a British Colony. The Treaty, provided for a British Governor, recognised Maori rights over their land and gave all Maoris' rights as British subjects. It is often considered the founding document for the nation of New Zealand but has been the subject of much heated debate ever since (see 7th May, 1st July and 26th September).

1918 The Representation of the People Act receives Royal Assent, giving all men over 21 and all women over 30 the right to vote in the United Kingdom. It trebled the amount of people eligible to vote to 21 million (see 12th May, 19th September and 14th December).

1952 The death of George VI at Sandringham House (see 14th December) and the accession to the throne of his daughter, Queen Elisabeth II (see 21st April and 2nd June). The brother of Edward VIII (see 28th May, 23rd June and 11th December), he had not expected to become King but following his brother's abdication, became King as well as the last Emperor of the British Empire. He served in the Great War and saw action at the battle of Jutland in 1916 (see 31st May). He was King throughout the Second World War and refused to leave the country, in particular when the Germans began bombing the major cities.

1975 The death of Air Chief Marshall Sir Keith Rodney Park MC and Bar in Auckland, New Zealand (see 15th June). After having served in the Gallipoli Campaign during the Great War, he volunteered for the Royal Air Force and later became Commander of 11 Group RAF. As Commander, he was responsible for the defence of London and South East England and was one of the main characters responsible for the success of the Battle of Britain. Referred to by the Germans as 'The Defender of London', he is a hero of the war that is all too often forgotten.

2012 The Diamond Jubilee of Queen Elizabeth II (see 21st April and 1952 above). Only the second diamond jubilee in our history (see 20th June), the rest of the year will see a River Pageant (see 3rd June) on the Thames, a music concert outside of Buckingham Palace (see 4th June), a service of thanksgiving in St. Pauls Cathedral (see 2nd December) and a Royal Parade to Buckingham Palace and a fly by, as well as a special trooping of the colour in June.

7th February:

1301 Edward of Carnarvon, the future Edward II (see 25th April and 21st September) and son of Edward I (see 17th June and 7th July), is made Prince of Wales, the first holder of the title to cover all of Wales (see 20th January).

1478 The birth of Thomas More (see 6th July) in London.

1783 The unsuccessful great siege of the British territory of Gibraltar is finally lifted by the French and Spanish after three years and seven months. French and Spanish forces had blockaded Gibraltar (see 16th January) after they sided with the thirteen rebellious colonies in North America. Despite the long siege and several engagements, the inhabitants and troops on Gibraltar held out and the territory has remained British ever since (see 31st March, 24th July, 10th September and 7th November).

1788 The Botany Bay penal colony is established on the East coast of Australia with the proclamation of the establishment of the colony and the official commencement of Arthur Phillip's governorship (see 18th January and 26th January).

1812 The birth of Charles Dickens in Landport (see 9th June) in Portsmouth.

1823 The death of Ann Radcliffe (née Ward). An author, she is known as a pioneer of the Gothic novel (see 9th July). Shy and reclusive later in life, she had married at the age of twenty-two. She published a number of novels, her first being 'The Castles of Athlin and Dunbayne' in 1789.

1906 The General Election and the Liberals, under their current leader and Prime Minister, Henry Campbell-Bannerman (see 22nd April and 7th September) win a landslide victory.

1992 The Maastricht Treaty is signed between 12 of the nations of Europe, including Britain, forming the European Union. The treaty allowed for the European Union to come into existence with the inclusion of justice and home affairs as well as a common foreign and security policy (see 1st January, 30th January, 23rd June, 28th October and 27th November).

8th February:

1587 Mary Queen of Scots, aged 44, is beheaded in the Great Hall at Fotheringhay Castle (see 8th December) in Northamptonshire. She was buried first in Peterborough Cathedral. However, when her son James VI (see 27th March and 19th June) came to the English throne as James I (see 24th March), he had her exhumed and reburied in Westminster Abbey. The daughter of James V of Scotland (see 10th April and 14th December), she was the great grand-daughter of Henry VII of England (see 28th January and 21st April) and therefore her claim to the throne of both England and Scotland was extremely strong. She became Queen when she was six days old with the premature death of her father James V. In 1558 she married the Dauphin of France and became Queen of France (1559-1560). Following his death, she returned to Scotland and in 1566 married her cousin Henry, Lord Darnley (see 29th July), by whom she had a son, who would later become James VI of Scotland and James I of England. Following one intrigue after another, Darnley was murdered and she married the Earl of Bothwell in 1567 (see 15th May). By now, the ascending Protestant Lords of Scotland had had enough and they rose against her. Imprisoned and then escaping, she suffered defeat at the Battle of Langside (see 13th May) and fled to England. Imprisoned for almost two decades, she was put on trial following accusations of a series of Catholic plots and intrigues (see 9th March, 13th May, 24th July and 9th September).

1819 The birth of John Ruskin (see 20th January) in London.

1872 Richard Bourke, Earl of Mayo, Viceroy of India, is assassinated by Sher Ali, an Indian convict whilst visiting the Andaman Islands penal colony at Port Blair (see 21st February). Born in Dublin, he became MP for Kildare in 1847, becoming Viceroy of India in 1869. Until his death, he did much to improve the infrastructure of India and worked hard at helping to improve the day-to-day lives of Indians whenever he could.

1884 The birth of John Theodore Cuthbert Moore-Brabazon in London (see 30th April, 2nd May, 17th May and 30th October).

1952 Queen Elizabeth II is proclaimed Queen at St. James's Palace (see 6th February 21st April and 2nd June).

1998 The death of Enoch Powell (see 20th April and 16th June) in London. At the start of the Second World War, he enlisted as a Private but by the end of the War he had become one of the youngest Brigadiers in the army at the age of 32. He was elected as a Conservative MP in 1950 for Wolverhampton South West, which he held for 24 years. He resigned from the Treasury in 1958 in protest over the party's plans for increased expenditure. On the eve of the 1974 General Election, he quit the Party because of its leader's plans to join the European Common Market. Barely six months later, he was returned to Parliament as a Unionist MP for South Down. He was a true patriot and one of the very few Political Heroes of this country who was greatly misunderstood and reviled for attempting to start debates on sensitive and emotional subjects.

9th February:

1674 The Treaty of Westminster is signed bringing an end to the Third Anglo-Dutch War 1672-1674 (see 5th April and 19th May). It provided for the return of New Netherland to England and Suriname was granted to the Dutch Republic of the United Netherlands.

1853 The birth of Leander Starr Jamieson (see 2nd January, 26th November and 29th December) in Edinburgh.

1854 The birth of Edward Henry Carson (see 22nd October) in Dublin.

1942 Soap rationing begins (see 9th September). The average ration was four coupons, allowing 16oz of hard soap or 24oz of soft soap a month (see 8th January, 5th February, 4th July, 9th July and 3rd October).

1945 HMS Venturer sinks the German U-boat U-864 off the coast of Norway. It is the only time a submarine has sank another submarine whilst they were both submerged (see 2nd May). The U-Boat was taking a consignment of weapons grade mercury along with German and Japanese Scientists to Japan along with German jet engines parts in what was called by the Germans 'Operation Caesar'.

10th February:

1567 The death of Henry Stuart, Lord Darnley, following an explosion where he was sleeping at Kirk o' Field in Edinburgh. The husband of Mary Stuart (see 8th February and 8th December) and father of James Stewart, the future James VI (James I of England and see 27th March and 19th June), he had become unpopular with almost everyone. An arrogant individual, he craved more power as Mary's husband. He was responsible for the murder of Mary's private secretary David Rizzio (see 9th March) in 1566.

1763 The Treaty of Paris is signed between Britain, France and Spain. This brought to an end what has since been called the 'first' World War, the Seven Years' War (1756-1763). Britain returned Cuba and Manila to Spain and Guadeloupe, Martinique, Saint Lucia and other possessions to France. However, as a result, the French ceded the northern parts of what it called 'New France', the future Canada, Dominica, Grenada, Saint Vincent and the Grenadines, Tobago as well as parts of Louisiana. Spain ceded its colony of La Florida (see 24th January, 1st May, 30th May, 3rd September and 18th September). The treaty was made possible due to the defeat of this country's two greatest enemies, France and Spain. However, in Parliament there was much opposition to the Treaty by MPs, who refused to accept the return of hard-won gains to an enemy. They could, quite correctly, see our country fighting again.

1840 The Marriage of Queen Victoria (see 22nd January and 24th May) to Prince Albert of Saxe-Coburg and Gotha (see 28th August and 14th December) in the Chapel Royal of St. James's Palace.

1841 The British North America Act 1840, known as the Act of Union, is proclaimed in the city of Montreal. The act united the two colonies of Lower Canada and Upper Canada into one colony, the Province of Canada (see 1st July and 31st December)

1846 The Battle of Sobraon in India results in a glorious victory by the forces of the British East India Company over the Sikh army of the kingdom of Punjab during the First Anglo-Sikh War (1845-1846). Our forces were led by General Sir Hugh Gough (see 2nd March and 3rd November) and General Sir Henry Hardinge and numbered 20,000 against 30,000 Sikhs. After a brutal, no quarter given battle, much of which was hand to hand, Gough's men were victorious. Our forces suffered 230 men killed and 2063 wounded whilst the Sikhs suffered around 10,000 killed. The result of this battle led ultimately to the Punjab coming under the rule and protection of British India (see 28th January, 9th March, 18th December and 21st December).

1894 The birth of Harold Macmillan in London (see 29th December).

1906 The launch of HMS Dreadnought in Portsmouth. The most powerful battleship of its type, it was the first capital ship to be powered by steam turbines and to have a uniform main battery. The ship was so technologically advanced that it made all pre-dreadnoughts look dated and caused an arms race that would continue until the Great War. Due to its superiority, all subsequent battleships were termed as 'dreadnoughts' and those that came before as 'pre-dreadnoughts' (see 11th February, 18th March and 7th November).

1912 The death of Joseph Lister (see 5th April) in Walmer, Kent. Born in 1827 in Upton in Essex, he is best known for pioneering the sterilization of medical instruments and equipment. Whilst working at Glasgow University in the 1860s, he successfully introduced the use of Carbolic acid as a means to sterilize both the instruments he used, the surgeon's hands, the wounds he treated and even, for a period, the air in the operating theatre.

1941 Operation Colossus commences. This is the very first operational use of British Paratroopers in action, dropping into Italy. Of the thirty-eight participants, one was killed in action and another eventually escaped, all the others were captured. However, the raid was successful and it paved the way for future and very successful operations (See 17th September and 5th November).

1956 The death of Marshal of the Royal Air Force, Viscount Hugh Montague Trenchard (see 3rd February) in London. A career soldier, he was commissioned into the Army in 1893 and served in India and Africa, being badly wounded during the Boer War 1899-1902. He learned to fly at the age of 39 in 1912 and after only about one hour of flying, he flew solo for the first time. In 1915, as a Major-General, he transferred to the Royal Flying Corps. He was appointed Chief of the Air Staff in 1918 and oversaw the formation of the Royal Air Force (see 1st April). He remained in the Air Force until his retirement in 1929. He was amongst the first and a key exponent of strategic bombing, taking the war to the enemies' homeland. As a result of his hard work and foresight, he is remembered as the 'Father of the Royal Air Force.' He was appointed Commissioner of the Metropolitan Police Force and served in that capacity during the 1930s.

11th February:

1531 Henry VIII declares himself Head of the Church of England (see 28th January and 28th June) and is recognised as its Supreme Head.

1731 The birth of George Washington (see 14th December) in Virginia Colony. A descendent of English colonists, he would later rebel and become a traitor.

1800 The birth of William Henry Fox Talbot (see 11th September) in Melbury, Dorset.

1815 The Battle of Fort Bowyer. This is the last battle in the British and American War. General Lambert led a force against the heavily defended Fort in present day Alabama. Very slight casualties were caused to our forces in the initial attack. However, siege guns were brought up in preparation for the final bombardment the following day (see 27th February, 18th June and 24th December).

1931 The death of Charles Algernon Parsons in Cambridge (see 13th June). Born in London, the son of the Earl of Rosse, he was an engineer; he is most well known as the inventor of the steam turbine. In 1877 he designed his reciprocating engine whilst apprenticed before turning his attention to steam power. During the 1880s his company developed the turbine engine and in 1901 the TS King Edward was launched, the first turbine-powered passenger ship. In 1906 HMS Dreadnought was launched (see 10th February), the first turbine-powered battleship and therefore the fastest ship afloat.

1975 Margaret Thatcher becomes the first woman to lead a political party, becoming leader of the Conservative Party (see 8th April, 4th May, 13th October and 22nd November) in opposition, defeating William Whitelaw in the second ballot.

12th February:

1554 The execution of Lady Jane Grey, 'Queen Jane', by beheading on Tower Green (see 10th July and 19th July). She was born in October 1537 in Leicestershire; she was the great-granddaughter of Henry VII (see 28th January and 21st April) and was introduced at court at an early age. As Edward VI was dying (see 6th July and 12th October), her father in law, the Duke of Northumberland, was desperate to prevent Catholic Mary Tudor (see 18th February and 17th November) attaining the throne and persuaded Edward VI to declare his half sisters as illegitimate. Once she was proclaimed Queen, the Privy Council and other important figures switched their allegiance in favour of Mary Tudor. Jane was imprisoned in the Tower of London, tried and then convicted of treason.

1809 The birth of Charles Darwin in Shrewsbury (see 19th April). His mother was the daughter of Josiah Wedgwood (see 24th November and 27th December).

1815 The surrender of Fort Bowyer in present day Alabama, America. The Fort was attacked the previous day and siege guns were brought up. Under a flag of truce, General Lambert called on the American garrison to surrender and the American Commander, Major Lawrence, reluctantly complied (see 18th June and 24th December).

1933 The death of Field Marshall Sir William Robert Robertson (see 29th January). He enlisted in 1877 as a Private in the 16th (The Queens) Lancers and in 1919 was promoted to Field Marshall, becoming the first person in the army to rise from the lowest rank to the highest. He served in the Boer War 1899-1902 and during the Great War and later commanded the British Army in the Rhineland after the armistice in 1918.

13th February:

1542 Catherine Howard is executed by beheading at the Tower after being found guilty of adultery, after less than two years of marriage (see 28th July). The fifth wife of Henry VIII (see 28th January and 28th June), and a first cousin of Anne Boleyn (see 19th May), she was born in County Durham; the exact date though remains unknown. She married Henry in 1540 but within a year there were rumours followed by accusations that she had committed adultery with a favourite of Henry's, Thomas Culpeper. She was imprisoned, tried, convicted and then executed by beheading at the Tower of London.

1689 William III (see 8th March and 4th November) is proclaimed King by Parliament by the Declaration of Right. Parliament declared that James VII (James II of England see 16th September and 14th October) had in effect abdicated when he fled the country (see 5th November).

1692 The Massacre of Glencoe in the Lochaber area of the Highlands. About 120 men from the Earl of Argyll's Regiment were billeted on the people of Glencoe for up to two weeks before the massacre. Then in the early hours of the morning, 38 Glencoe MacDonald men were butchered and another 40 women and children died from exposure as a result of their homes being burnt. The attack was authorised as a punishment for the MacDonald's opposition to William III (see 8th March and 4th November).

1743 The birth of Joseph Banks (see 19th June) in London.

1766 The birth of Thomas Robert Malthus (see 23rd December) in Surrey.

1958 The death of Christabel Pankhurst in California, America (see 22nd September). The eldest daughter of Dr Richard Pankhurst and Emmeline Goulden, she joined the National Union of Women's Suffrage Societies (NUWSS) in 1901. However, in 1903, disappointed with the Union, Christabel, along with her mother and sister Sylvia, formed the Women's Social and Political Union (WSPU) whilst studying for a Law degree at Owens College in Manchester. From 1910, she began to advocate a more active and violent approach to protest and began to support stone throwing, smashing of windows and the destruction of property. She fled to France in 1912 as prominent members were being arrested. However, at the outbreak of the Great War she returned to Britain and was an enthusiastic supporter of the Government's war effort. In 1921 she went to live in America and became a member of the Second Adventist Movement and toured the country lecturing ad writing religious publications. She returned to Britain in the late 1920s but returned to America where she died from a heart attack.

2007 The last of the military watchtowers in Northern Ireland is removed as part of the culmination of Operation Banner. Situated in Crossmaglen in County Armagh, the tower stood twenty feet above the Army-supported Police station in the town (see 31st July).

14th February:

1649 Following the execution of Charles I (see 30th January), the Rump Parliament appoints the English Council of State to run the Commonwealth of England, in particular foreign and domestic policy and the general security of the state (see 20th April, 19th May, 3rd September, 6th December and 16th December).

1779 The death of Captain James Cook in Hawaii (see 27th October). One of our country's most famous explorers, he was a very skilled cartographer and produced finely detailed maps of Newfoundland, discovered the Hawaiian Islands, the eastern coast of Australia and became the first person to circumnavigate New Zealand (see 6th February, 1st July and 26th September). In 1746 he joined the Merchant Navy and then in 1755 he joined the Royal Navy, serving during the Seven Years' War 1756-1763, taking part in the siege of Quebec City and the Battle of the Plains of Abraham in 1759 (see 13th September). An accomplished and skilled surveyor, his first voyage of discovery after the war was during the years 1768 to 1771, sailing to Tahiti, New Zealand and the first landing on Australia (see 29th April). His second voyage was between the years 1772 and 1775 which took him to the south Atlantic, becoming the first person to circumnavigate the Antarctic Circle (see 17th January). He also took possession of South Georgia and the South Sandwich Islands for Britain. His third and final voyage was during the years 1776 to 1779. Its purpose was to discover the North West Passage. It was during this trip that he discovered the Hawaiian Islands. It was on a return trip to these islands later in the voyage that Cook met his death. He was clubbed about the head and then stabbed to death as he collapsed. He was helping one of his launches to get back into the sea in an attempt to get away from the on-coming natives.

1797 The Second Battle of Cape St. Vincent (see 16th January) and the destruction of the Spanish Fleet by our Fleet, led by Admiral Sir John Jervis (see 9th January and 14th March). We lost 73 men killed, 227 men badly wounded and around 100 lightly wounded. The Spanish losses were four ships taken as prizes and about 1,000 men killed or wounded. It was a glorious victory for the Royal Navy, despite being greatly outnumbered by the Spanish. It was in this battle that Horatio Nelson (see 29th September and 21st October) first displayed his heroism and style in his ship the *Captain*.

1831 The death of Henry Maudslay (see 22nd August). Born in 1771, he was an engineer and was a leading inventor and pioneer of machine tool making. He learned his profession in the Woolwich arsenal in London. Around 1800, he introduced his pioneering screw cutting lathe that allowed all screw thread sizes for nuts and bolts to be standardised. This was a major advancement as it allowed any bolt to be used with any nut of the same size. This was a major advancement in machine technology.

15th February:

1748 The birth of Jeremy Bentham (see 6th June) in London.

1834 The birth of William Henry Preece in Caernarvon (see 6th November).

1844 The death of Henry Addington, 1st Viscount Sidmouth in London (see 17th March and 30th May). He became Prime Minister after his predecessor, William Pitt the Younger (see 23rd January and 28th May) resigned after George III (see 29th January and 4th June) rejected his bill for Catholic Emancipation. He was born in London, studied Law and was a close friend of William Pitt. His Premiership was noticeable for the controversial 1802 Treaty of Amiens (see 25th March).

1874 The birth of Ernest Henry Shackleton in Kilkea, County Kildare in Ireland, the future Antarctic Expedition leader (see 5th January).

1886 The death of Edward Cardwell, 1st Viscount Cardwell (see 24th July), in Torquay. Elected to Parliament in 1842 and became a follower of Sir Robert Peel (see 5th February and 2nd July) and later one of his Peelite faction, only to become a Liberal when the Peelites finally dissolved. He served under Prime Minister William Gladstone (see 19th May and 29th December) as his Secretary of State for War (1868-1874). It was during this period that he enacted the Cardwell Reforms that modernised the army. He abolished flogging, proposed the abolition of the purchase of commissions, reformed the militia, shortened the term of enlistment and created a larger pool of reservists.

1900 The relief of the besieged town of Kimberley in Cape Colony during the Boer War, 1899-1902. The town had been under siege by Boer forces for 124 days and was ably led by Colonel Kekewich with the aid of Cecil Rhodes (see 26th March and 5th July). The town was reached by the cavalry column under General Sir John French (see 14th October).

1901 Winston Spencer Churchill (see 24th January and 30th November), newly elected Member of Parliament for Oldham, enters Parliament for the first time (see 18th February).

1922 The death of Herbert Henry Asquith (see 12th September) in Sutton Courtney in Oxfordshire. He was Prime Minister from 1908 until 1916 (see 5th April and 5th December). He was a Liberal and was in office at the start of the Great War. In 1909, along with the Chancellor David Lloyd George (see 17th January and 26th March), he attempted to introduce a radical budget that was rejected by the House of Lords. In turn, he introduced the Parliament Act, passed in 1911 (see 18th August), that ended the Lord's veto on financial legislation. In 1912, against fierce opposition, he attempted to introduce Irish Home Rule, only to be defeated by the start of the Great War. The Liberal government fell in 1915 and he formed a coalition government. Pressure continued to mount with the Gallipoli campaign failing and the Irish Easter rebellion until, in December 1916, he resigned. He became the Earl of Oxford in 1925.

1942 The besieged Colony of Singapore surrenders to the Japanese who had attacked the Colony across land from the Malay Peninsula. Following negotiations, forces of around 80,000 British, Australian and Indian troops led by Lieutenant General Arthur Percival (see 31st January and 26th December) surrender Singapore. The surrender was unconditional as the Japanese refused to grant terms (see 15th August and 2nd September). This is the largest surrender of British led forces in history and was nothing short of humiliating at the time. The PoW's were led into captivity to join around 50,000 Imperial and Commonwealth soldiers already captured during the Malayan Campaign (see 10th December).

1970 The death of Air Chief Marshall Sir Hugh Caswell Tremenheere Dowding in Royal Tunbridge Wells (see 24th April). He transferred to the Royal Flying Corps (RFC) in 1913 after serving with the Royal Garrison Artillery in a number of places, including India. He went on to command the RAF Fighter Command during the Battle of Britain and is credited with masterminding the success of the Battle and the ultimate salvation from German invasion.

1971 Monday: Decimalization Day as Britain officially adopts the new Decimal currency. The currency of pounds, shillings and pence, the currency we had known for centuries, was done away with and the new system of decimal coinage was adopted. Understandable confusion was common as people and shops everywhere struggled to get to grips with the European style of foreign currency (see 23rd April and 14th October).

16th February:

1646 the Battle of Torrington in Devon was one of the last major clashes of the Civil War (see 3rd September). The Parliamentarians, under Lord Thomas Fairfax, attacked the town which was defended by the Royalists under Lord Hopton. During the course of the hard fought battle, sparks from cannon ignited the Royalist magazine in Torrington Church and caused a huge explosion, killing many Royalists and their prisoners. This was effectively the end of the battle and defeat for the Royalist army as it withdrew into Cornwall.

1759 The relief of Madras during the Seven Years' War, 1756-1763 (see 10th February), after two months of siege. The city of Madras, occupied by French troops under the command of Thomas Arthur Comte de Lally, is evacuated by the French as a relief fleet of six ships of the Royal Navy arrived. However, Fort St. George within the city had held out defiantly against the French for the whole period of siege (see 15th January and 22nd January).

1822 The birth of Francis Galton (see 17th January) in Sparkbrook, Birmingham.

1957 The death of Leslie Hore-Belisha in Reims, France (see 7th September). Born in Plymouth, he served during the First World War. A Liberal Politician, it was as Minister for Transport that he introduced his Road Traffic Act in 1934 (see 26th March) that reintroduced 30 mph speed limits and introduced the driving test. He also rewrote the Highway Code and introduced the pedestrian crossing that bears his name, the Belisha beacon. In 1937 he was appointed Secretary of State for War, until his dismissal in 1940. Following the General Election of 1945, he left the Liberal Party and joined the Conservatives.

2011 Parliament finally passes the bill allowing for a referendum to take place about whether or not to change the voting process for future General Elections to the Alternative Vote system (see 5th May).

17th February:

1461 The second Battle of St. Albans. Lancastrian forces, led by Margaret of Anjou, wife of the captured King Henry VI (see 21st May and 6th December), heading towards London, were blocked by a Yorkist force led by the Earl of Warwick. However, the Lancastrians outflanked their opponents and surprised them, leading to a brief battle and the Yorkists retreating to Oxfordshire. This allowed their prisoner King Henry VI to be released (see 22nd May).

1720 The Treaty of The Hague is signed by Great Britain and our allies Austria, France and the Dutch Republic on one side and their Spanish enemies under Philip V of Spain on the other. The treaty brought a formal end to the War of the Quadruple Alliance, 1718-1720 (see 10th May and 10th June).

1815 The end of the British American War of 1812-1815 with the formal exchange of ratification papers of the Treaty of Ghent (see 18th June and 24th December), between our diplomat in Washington and the American President.

1843 The Battle of Miani in Sindh, India. A British force of around 2,800, under the command of General Sir Charles Napier, fought a force of around 20,000 troops of the Amir's armies from the province of Sindh. Our casualties were a little over 200 whereas the Amir's troop suffered well over 5,000 dead. The resultant victory allowed the Province of Sindh to come under the authority of British India (see 15th August).

1854 The death of John Martin (see 19th July) on the Isle of Man. Born in Northumberland, he was one of the famous Victorian Romantic painters. He was well-known for his striking, biblical orientated paintings and later engravings. Some of his more well-known works are *The Great Day of his Wrath*, *The Destruction of Sodom and Gomorrah* and *The Seventh Plague of Egypt*.

1912 The death of Petty Officer Edgar Evans (see 7th March and 29th March) somewhere in the South Pole. He enlisted in the Royal Navy in 1891 and was on Captain Scott's first expedition. As a Petty Officer, he was on the Terra Nova Expedition with Captain Scott. On the previous day he had collapsed and had to be left behind whilst the other four in the party pressed on to the next supply post. On reaching the post, they returned for him but he died later this day.

2003 A congestion charge of £5 is introduced in central London for all vehicles.

18th February:

1516 The birth of Mary I at Greenwich Palace (see 17th November), the daughter and only child to Catherine of Aragon and Henry VIII (see 28th January and 28th June).

1678 John Bunyan's 'Pilgrims Progress' is published (see 31st August and 30th November). He is believed to have begun writing the book whilst in prison.

1900 The Battle of Paardeberg during the Boer War (1899-1902) begins. Our forces of around 6,000 men of the 6th Division, led by Lieutenant General Kelly-Kenny, were ordered to carry out a frontal assault on the Boer defences by Lord Kitchener. Members of the Highland Brigade and the Canadian Regiment took the main role. Although after several days our forces were victorious, the particular attack failed at great cost and became known as 'Bloody Sunday' (see 27th February). Both the Highland Brigade and the Canadian Regiment behaved with the utmost heroism and were the reason for the eventual success. This was the first time in Canadian history that Canadian troops were engaged in battle outside of Canada (see 29th November).

1901 Winston Churchill (see 24th January and 30th November) delivers his maiden speech in the House of Commons as MP for Oldham (see 15th February), immediately after a speech from David Lloyd George (see 17th January and 26th March).

1922 The 'Black and Tans', units of Temporary Constables employed by the Royal Irish Constabulary since January 1920, are officially disbanded following the signing of the Anglo-Irish Treaty (see 6th December). Their nickname was derived from their mix of khaki and dark green uniforms and most of the recruits were former British soldiers with experience during the Great War. From their formation, many of the Tans were involved in brutal reprisals in retribution for atrocities carried out by Republican terrorists. However, they often involved civilians with only suspected sympathies with the terrorists and this led to public outcries in both Ireland and mainland Britain.

1930 The United Empire Party (UEP) is formed by Lord Rothermere. It eventually joined with the Empire Free Trade Crusade. Its purpose was to press for the British Empire to become a global free trading bloc.

1944 Operation Jericho, a low level bombing raid by the RAF is carried out. Altogether, nine Mosquito bombers and twelve Typhoon fighters in escort attack Amiens prison in the German-occupied town of Amiens in Northern France. The objective was to damage the buildings and breach the wall to allow surviving captured resistance fighters who were sentenced to death the opportunity of escape. Flying as low as thirty feet above sea level, the RAF crews showed exceptional skill and courage in the run up and execution of the mission. The mission was a success as over 250 prisoners escaped. However, over 150 were recaptured and three Mosquitos and two Typhoons were lost (see 25th November).

1968 British 'Standard' Time is introduced to bring our country in line with Europe. The same time is maintained throughout the following two years. It is abandoned in 1971 after an overwhelming vote against its continuation in Parliament.

2005 The Hunting Act 2004, banning hunting with dogs came into effect in England and Wales amongst much controversy and two years after a similar ban in Scotland (see 1st August).

19th February:

1717 The birth of David Garrick (see 20th January), the future actor, theatre manager and friend of Doctor Samuel Johnson (see 7th September and 13th December) in Hereford. Shortly after his birth, the family moved to Lichfield.

1845 The death of Sir Thomas Buxton (see 7th April). A social reformer, he married the sister of Elizabeth Fry and was elected as MP for Weymouth in 1818. He supported prison reform, opposed capital punishment and supported the abolition of slavery. In 1823 he helped found the Anti-Slavery Society and in 1825 took over as leader of the abolition of slavery movement following the retirement of William Wilberforce. In 1833 his efforts proved successful when slavery was abolished.

1901 The birth of Florence Green in London (see 4th February).

1915 British and French ships begin the preliminary bombardment of Turkish military positions along the coast in the Dardanelles area in preparation for the Gallipoli landings in April of that year (see 25th April).

1942 The port city of Darwin in Northern Territory of Australia is bombed for the first time by the Japanese (see 15th February). The city, a major military base and port, was attacked by surprise and indiscriminately bombed by almost 200 Japanese aircraft at about 10am in the morning. Darwin was totally unprepared and suffered around 250 deaths, with ten ships sunk, including an American Destroyer, 25 damaged and over 20 aircraft destroyed. The Japanese lost less than ten aircraft in the attack (see 15th August, 8th December and 25th December). Just a couple of hours later, the Japanese returned for a second attack with heavy bombers, initially attacking the RAAF base on the edge of the town.

20th February:

1472 By an Act of the Scottish Parliament, the Orkney Islands and Shetland Islands became part of Scotland after the King of Norway defaulted on dowry payments. The Norwegian King had pledged the islands as security against the dowry for his daughter Margaret who had married the future James III (see 11th June).

1929 The death of General Sir John Grenfell Maxwell in Cape Town, South Africa (see 12th July). A long-serving Army Officer, he served at the battle of Tel El Kabir in 1882, the Nile Expedition in 1884, led Egyptian forces at the battle of Omdurman in 1898 (see 2nd September) and led the defence of the Suez Canal during the Great War. He is best remembered for his success in the suppression of the traitorous Irish rebels and restoring order following the Eater Rising in 1916 (see 24th April and 29th April). Appointed Commander in Chief and Military Governor following the start of the rebellion, he used Martial Law to re-impose law and order and to process many of the terrorists through Courts Martial, with some being executed. Unfortunately, he faced criticism from some in the House of Commons because of his robust approach, despite the fact that he had restored that part of our country to law and order following a violent and brutal rebellion (see 24th April and 3rd May) by traitors whilst the country was involved in the Great War.

1947 Lord Louis Mountbatten becomes the last Viceroy of India (see 25th June and 27th August). Appointed by the Labour Government under Prime Minister Clement Attlee (see 3rd January and 8th October), his role was to oversee the transition of India from British rule to independence no later than 1948 (see 15th August).

21st February:

1437 The death of James I of Scotland as he is stabbed to death in the Dominican Monastery in Perth (see 25th July). Born in 1394, he succeeded his father to the throne whilst an eleven-year-old prisoner of the English. He was released in 1423 and set about reforming the monarchy and introduced social and economic change and was a strong monarch. Following much discontent amongst his nobles, he was assassinated by supporters of his uncle, Walter Stewart, the Duke of Atholl.

1705 The birth of Edward Hawke (see 16th October) in London.

1741 The death of Jethro Tull in Hungerford, Berkshire. Born in 1674, very little is known of his early life. In 1701 he invented the horse-drawn seed drill that allowed a far more efficient sowing of seed which was instrumental in the Agricultural Revolution. He is also known for inventing the horse-drawn hoe in 1714. In 1734 he published the book 'The New Horse Hoeing Husbandry' which caused great controversy.

1801 The birth of John Henry Newman (see 11th August) in London.

1804 The first self-propelled locomotive on rails, designed by Richard Trevithic (see 13th April and 22nd April) runs at Penydaren, Glamorgan reaching a speed of almost five miles an hour. The machine pulled a ten ton load of iron, several coaches and around seventy people along a distance of 9 miles from Penydaren to Abercyon in just over five hours.

1822 The birth of Richard Bourke in Dublin (see 8th February), the son of the 5th Earl of Mayo.

1848 The Communist Party Manifesto, written by Karl Marx with contributions from Friedrich Engels, is published in London.

1849 The battle of Goojerat takes place in the Punjab in the North West of India, effectively bringing an end to the Second Sikh War 1848-1849 (see 13th January). The British Indian army, numbering around 20,000 advanced against the rebellious Sikh army, entrenched in the town of Goojerat. General Sir Hugh Gough (see 2nd March and 3rd November) opened up with an artillery bombardment and once the Sikhs were silenced, the infantry advanced and after savage hand to hand fighting, the Sikhs withdrew. It became a rout as our cavalry pursued them for many miles. Less than two months later, the Punjab was annexed to British India (see 2nd April).

1910 The birth of Douglas Robert Steuart Bader in London (see 9th August and 5th September).

1952 The Government, under Prime Minister Winston Churchill (see 24th January and 30th November), brings an end to the use of Identity Cards that were introduced during of the war.

2010 The explorative drilling for oil off the coast of the Falkland Islands begins, despite unjustified protests from the Argentinean government (see 2nd April and 14th June).

22nd February:

1371 Robert Stewart accedes to the throne of Scotland as Robert II on the death of his uncle, King David II. The grandson of Robert Bruce (see 7th June and 11th July), he was the son of Walter Stewart, High Steward of Scotland and the first Stewart Monarch of Scotland (see 24th March and 1st August).

1797 Between 1,200 and 1,400 French troops, led by Irish-American General William Tate, attempt an invasion of Britain, coming ashore around three miles west of Fishguard in Pembrokeshire on the Welsh coast (see 24th February). Their force had been spotted off the coast long before landing and, despite moving about two miles inland after coming ashore, many locals flocked to the local Militias to aid the resistance to the French.

1806 The funeral of William Pitt the Younger. He was buried in Westminster Abbey after he had lain in state for two days at the Palace of Westminster (see 23rd January and 28th May).

1857 The birth of Robert Stephenson Smyth Baden-Powell (see 8th January) in Paddington, London (see 1st August).

1942 Air Chief Marshall Arthur 'Bomber' Harris takes over as Air Officer Commanding Bomber Command (see 5th April and 13th April).

23rd February:

1633 The birth of Samuel Pepys in Salisbury Court off Fleet Street (see 1st January and 26th May).

1792 The death of Joshua Reynolds in Leicester Fields in London (see 16th July). He is probably the best known 18th Century English painter, most well known for his portraits. He was also one of the earliest members of the Royal Society of Arts and was known to Samuel Johnson (see 7th September and 13th December).

1820 The conspirators in the Cato Street Conspiracy are arrested by members of the Bow Street Runners with the support of soldiers. During the arrest which turned violent, a Bow Street Runner was killed but a number of the conspirators were apprehended and the remainder a few days later. The conspirators had planned to blow up and murder the Prime Minister Lord Liverpool and his Cabinet (see 1st May).

1821 The death of John Keats from Tuberculosis in Rome, Italy (see 31st October). One of the leading romantic poets of the nineteenth century, he did not receive popular acclaim until after his death at the age of only twenty-five. He initially studied medicine in London but eventually developed Tuberculosis and was advised to move to a warmer climate and so left for Rome in 1820, where he died five months later.

1934 The death of the great Sir Edward Elgar (see 2nd June) in Worcester from cancer. One of the most famous of our composers, he favoured large orchestras featuring choral works. A great Imperialist, his best known works were 'Nimrod' of the 'Enigma Variations' (1899), which won him his first recognition and the 'Pomp and Circumstance Marches' (1901-1930). A Roman Catholic, his musical skill and ability were largely self-taught, although he did not achieve any noticeable success until well into his forties.

24th February:

1722 The birth of John Burgoyne, future General in the American Revolution (see 4th June) in Sutton in Bedfordshire.

1797 Between 1,200 and 1,400, French troops, led by Irish-American General William Tate, surrender to British forces (see 22nd February), led by John Campbell, 1st Baron Cawdor, after landing three miles west of Fishguard two days before. This was to be the last time foreign troops would land on British soil until the invasion of the Channel Islands by German forces in 1940.

1810 The death of Henry Cavendish in London, the aristocratic and eccentric scientist credited for the discovery of Hydrogen, which he called 'inflammable air' (see 10th October). He also discovered that water is a combination of two gasses, conducted early research into electricity and is known for 'the Cavendish experiment'. In this experiment, he was the first to be able to measure the force of gravity between masses in his laboratory and also the first to calculate accurately the density of the earth. A shy and eccentric man, he was nervous around women and is known to have communicated with his female assistants with written notes.

1826 The Treaty of Yandaboo is signed between the General Sir Archibald Campbell for our Country and the Burmese representative, bringing an end to the First Burmese War, 1824-1826 (see 5th March). The treaty imposed reparations on the Burmese for the cost to Britain of the war as well as ceding important parts of the country to British Indian control, including Assam. The war had broken out over Burmese incursions into North East India and the desire to prevent French influence within Burma (see 4th January).

1955 The Baghdad Treaty, formally creating the Middle East Treaty Organisation (METO), is signed by the United Kingdom, Iran, Iraq, Pakistan and Turkey. The pact provided for mutual defence and co-operation between the signatory countries. The Soviet Union saw the pact as a threat to its southern borders and opposed it.

25th February:

1308 The coronation of Edward II in Westminster Abbey (see 20th January, 25th April and 21st September). This was the first occasion in which the Coronation Chair or 'King Edwards Chair' was first used for a coronation. All subsequent coronations have taken place upon the chair and the Stone of Scone underneath.

1570 Queen Elizabeth I (see 24th March and 7th September), England's first Protestant queen is declared a heretic and excommunicated by Pope Pius V. He announced in a Papal Bull that her subjects are released from any allegiance to her. The Pope's action transforms all Catholics in the country from people who were quietly tolerated into potential enemy agents in the eyes of the State and Protestants.

1723 The death of Sir Christopher Wren, architect and scientist aged 90 (see 20th October). In 1657 he was appointed Professor of Astronomy at Gresham College in London and in 1662 he became a founding member of the Royal Society. In 1664 and 1665 he designed his first building but his career and fame as an architect got its opportunity when the Great Fire of London destroyed so much of the city (see 2nd September). Although, his initial plans for the rebuilding of the city were rejected. He designed fifty-one new churches as well as St. Paul's Cathedral (see 2nd December). In 1669 he was appointed Surveyor of the Royal Works and was knighted in 1673. In the following years he was responsible for designing the Royal Observatory at Greenwich, the Chelsea Hospital for soldiers and Trinity College Library in Cambridge as well as the facade at Hampton Court Palace. He is buried in St. Paul's Cathedral.

1857 The birth of Robert Bond in St. John's, in the colony of Newfoundland (see 16th March).

26th February:

1564 The baptism of Christopher Marlowe, the future dramatist, poet and suspected spy in Canterbury (see 30th May).

1852 The troop ship H.M.S. Birkenhead sinks after striking an unchartered rock off the coast of South Africa, near Cape Town. This event marks the start of the 'Women and Children first' tradition as troops of a number of Regiments, but mainly from the 73rd Regiment of Foot, later the Highland Light Infantry, following orders from their Officers, stand fast as the ship sinks, allowing the women and children more time to escape in the few life boats available. Once the women and children were well clear, the troops were then given the order to take to the water and make for shore. None of the Senior Officers survived.

1857 The 19th Bengal Native Infantry refuse to use the new cartridges for their new Lee Enfield Rifles, thus becoming the first known demonstration of outright rebellion against British rule in India (see 24th January and 10th May).

1903 The birth of Orde Wingate in British India (see 24th March).

1952 The Prime Minister Winston Churchill (see 24th January and 30th November) announces that Great Britain has an atomic bomb, making Britain the third country to posses such a weapon (see 15th May and 3rd October).

2002 The British Overseas Territories Act 2002 receives Royal Assent. The Act, which came into force on 21st May 2002, renamed all previous British Dependant Territories as British Overseas Territories. The key change was that from May, all people who were citizens of the British Overseas Territories prior to that date automatically became full British Citizens.

27th February:

1706 The death of John Evelyn (see 31st October) in his house in Dover Street, London. He was a writer, gardener, diarist and a contemporary of Samuel Pepys (see 23rd February and 26th May). At the time of his death, he had a huge personal library of at least 3,859 books and 822 pamphlets. An ardent Royalist, he went into exile following the execution of Charles I (see 30th January and 19th November), returning to England in 1652.

1765 The Stamp Act Bill, presented by the Chancellor of the Exchequer, is passed by the House of Commons (see 22nd March).

1829 The death of Lieutenant Colonel Charles-Michel de Salaberry in Chambly, Lower Canada (see 26th October and 19th November). He is famous as the French Canadian hero who defended Canada from American invasion during the war of 1812 against the United States (see 26th October and 11th November). Born in Beauport, near Quebec City in Lower Canada, he joined the British army aged 14 and served in both Europe and the West Indies before returning to Canada and contributing towards its defence and the ultimate withdrawal of the American forces.

1881 The Battle of Majuba Hill where our forces are humiliatingly defeated by the Boers. Our forces numbered around 650 men, of which 283 were killed during the engagement, including General Sir George Pomeroy Colley who led our troops. The Boers attacked up hill in the morning, engaging our forces, who became surrounded at the top of the hill. For many years until the Second Boer War (1899-1902), the battle would be a matter of deep shame for the army (see 28th January) and the phrase 'remember Majuba' would become a rallying cry for our troops (see 1900 below and 28th January and 3rd August).

1900 The end of the Battle of Paardeberg during the Boer War (1899-1902) comes to an end with British victory which saw the surrender of Boer forces under General Cronje (see 18th February). Around 15,000 of our troops attacked around 7,000 Boers who were entrenched on the other side of the Modder River. General Cronje, without any hope of relief from other Boer forces, surrendered with around 4,000 of his men. It was a fitting victory for our forces and a deserved humiliation for the Boers, coming on the anniversary of the Battle of Majuba Hill in 1881 (see 1881 above).

1900 The Labour Representation Committee is formed at the Memorial Hall in Farringdon Street, London, the predecessor of the future Labour Party (see 22nd January). After much debate at the Trades Union Congress, it was agreed upon that though not a political party as such, its role was to coordinate the support of MPs who represented the working class. It had no leader but Ramsay McDonald (see 12th October and 9th November) was elected as its secretary.

2002 The death of Terence Alan Patrick Sean 'Spike' Milligan (see 16th April) in Rye, East Sussex. The greatest comedian and comedy writer, he was the brains and creative genius behind *The Goon Show* (see 28th May).

28th February:

1638 In Greyfriars Kirk in Edinburgh, a meeting of nobles, clergy and burgesses met and signed the National Covenant. The covenant was the expression of the Scottish rejection of the religious innovations of William Laud, Arch Bishop of Canterbury and supported by Charles I (see 30th January and 19th November). In particular, the covenant opposed the imposition of the Book of Common Prayer.

1900 The relief of Ladysmith (see 2nd November) after a 118 day siege. Major Hubert Gough's party were the first of the relief column to get through and were greeted by Lieutenant General Stuart White who had commanded the garrison throughout the siege.

1931 Oswald Mosley (see 16th November and 3rd December) resigns from the Labour Party (see 29th February) after it had rejected his principles outlined in his 'Mosley Memorandum' of 1930 on how to deal with the increasing problem of unemployment.

1943 Operation Gunnerside is carried out in occupied Norway. It was a raid by British-trained Norwegian Commandoes in Norway to destroy the German nuclear heavy water programme so vital for their nuclear development plans. The raid was a complete success and resulted in the destruction of all the heavy water and all the important equipment necessary for its production. All of the commandos were able to either escape or remain to aid further resistance efforts (see 4th March).

1948 The last British troops leave India. The 1st Battalion the Somerset Light Infantry embark at Bombay for the journey home after marching through the city and under the famous Gateway to India (see 15th August and 4th December).

29th February:

1528 Patrick Hamilton becomes the first Protestant martyr when he is burned at the stake in St. Andrews for heresy. A Scottish churchman, he had travelled to Europe as a young man and probably met some of the reformers before returning to Scotland (see 4th February).

1796 The Jay Treaty officially takes effect when the respective ratified documents are exchanged between the British Government and the government of the United States (see 19th November).

1868 Benjamin Disraeli becomes Prime Minister for the first time (see 19th April and 21st December). He is the only Prime Minister of Jewish decent, although he himself had converted to Christianity at the age of 12.

1884 The battle of El Teb during the Sudan Campaign. Our forces were commanded by General Sir Gerald Graham and totalled about 4,500 men. They approached the Mahdist forces, led by Osman Digna, on the hill at El Teb. Our troops formed up in a square and advanced, seeing of repeated attacks by large groups of rebels. Eventually, after much fighting, the rebels broke and fled. Casualties for our forces were less than fifty killed but around 2,000 Mahdist troops lay dead.

1931 Oswald Mosley (see 16th November and 3rd December) forms the 'New Party' after resigning from the Labour Party the previous day (see 28th February, 10th March and 20th May). Seventeen Labour MPs signed his Manifesto of whom six joined the party. The party's purpose was the implementation of his proposals on the solving of unemployment and fielded twenty four candidates in the general election later in the year, all of whom were defeated (see 1st October).

MARCH

1st March: St. David's day, Patron Saint of Wales.

1812 The birth of Augustus Welby Northmore Pugin (see 14th September) in London.

1901 The Australian Army is officially formed (see 9th October, 2nd November and 22nd November), just two months after the federation of the six colonies into the Commonwealth of Australia, a Dominion within the Empire (see 1st January).

1950 Klaus Fuchs, a German-born Communist spy, is jailed for 14 years for betraying his adopted country by spying for the Soviet Union. Involved in the development of the nuclear bomb in both Britain (see 26th February, 15th May and 3rd October) and the USA, he returned to Great Britain and was arrested in 1949 and tried and convicted of passing secrets to the Soviet Union.

1979 The people of both Scotland and Wales vote against devolution in separate referendums. In Scotland, just over 51% of the turnout voted yes but this was only 63% of the electorate, thus falling below the minimum 40% of the electorate required to trigger devolution (see 6th May, 7th May and 11th September). In Wales there was an overwhelming no vote as over 79% voted no, meaning about 12% of the electorate voted in favour (see 18th September).

2nd March:

1791 The death of John Wesley (see 17th June) in London. The son of a Church of England Rector and himself an Anglican cleric, he is credited along with his brother Charles, as the founder of the Methodist movement. Educated in London, he attended Oxford and in 1725 he was ordained as a Deacon in the Church of England and then a parish priest three years later. He started to give open air sermons to the people and championed education for all and prison reform.

1869 The death of Field Marshall Sir Hugh Gough (see 3rd November) in Ireland. A leading British Officer of the early Victorian era, he is believed to have taken part in more actions than any other officer, except the Duke of

Wellington (see 1st May and 14th September). He served from 1809 in the Peninsular War, being wounded at the battle of Talavera in 1809 (see 28th July), was present at the battle of Barrosa 1811 (see 5th March), the Battle of Vitoria 1813 (see 21st June) and was again wounded at the battle of Nivelle in 1813 (see 10th November). He later served Commanding British forces during the First Opium War (1839-1842). In 1843 he became Commander of British forces in India and served in numerous conflicts and incidents during his time there, including the Battle of Sobraon in 1846 (see 10th February), the Battle of Chillianwala in 1849 (see 13th January) and the Battle of Goojerat in 1849 (see 21st February). For his services he was awarded a Viscountcy by a grateful nation upon his return to Britain.

1882 Queen Victoria survives an assassination attempt when she is shot at as she boarded a train at Windsor by a disgruntled poet Roderick Maclean (see 22nd January and 24th May).

1916 Conscription, as authorised by the Military Service Act 1916 (see 24th January and 27th January), begins. Initially it was for single men between 19 and 41 years old but this was extended to include married men in June 1916 and later still, men up to the age of 51 years old.

1939 The death of Howard Carter (see 9th May) in London. A world-famous Egyptologist, he is known for being the main discoverer of Tutankhamen's tomb in Egypt (see 26th November). From his teenage years he had been involved in Egyptology and in 1907 was employed by Lord Carnarvon to work on excavations which lasted continually until after Tutankhamen's discovery.

3rd March:

1284 Edward I (see 17th June and 17th July) issued the Statute of Wales at Rhuddlan Castle (see 19th August). The statute brought Wales into line with England and introduced legislation allowing Wales to be administered in the same manner as England and thus ended any serious further attempt at Welsh rebellion (see 11th December). The Principality was divided into counties and it was annexed to the Crown of England. The statute also created the Office of Sheriff and applied English laws and courts as well as applying English common laws and the application of the laws on inheritance, preventing illegitimacy from inheriting, as was the possibility under old Welsh law.

1703 The death of Robert Hooke in London (see 18th July). A physicist, he is perhaps one of this country's greatest scientists. He had a huge variety of scientific interests and worked with individuals such as Robert Boyle (see 25th January and 31st December). He composed the law of elasticity, known still as 'Hooke's Law' today. In 1663 he was elected Fellow of the Royal Society.

1756 The birth of William Godwin in Wisbech, Cambridgeshire (see 7th April).

1765 The death of William Stukeley (see 7th November) in London. A notable antiquarian, he studied medicine at Cambridge, becoming a doctor. He pioneered early archaeology and is remembered for his investigations of Stonehenge and Avebury. He was also a good friend of Isaac Newton (see 20th March and 25th December), going on to write his biography. In 1730 he became an ordained minister.

1792 The death of Robert Adam in London (see 3rd July). A leading architect and designer of his time, he worked for some of the leading members of society. Born in Kirkcaldy, he was the son of William Adam, who was the leading architect for his generation. After attending school, he worked under the tutelage of his father in the family business. In 1758 he set up business with his brother and they designed country houses as well as their decorations and furnishings.

1847 The birth of Alexander Graham Bell in Edinburgh, future inventor of the telephone (see 5th June and 2nd August).

1902 The birth of Claude Stanley Choules (see 5th May) in Pershore in Worcestershire.

1985 The year-long Miners' Strike ends in defeat for the Miners and their leader, Arthur Scargill (see 12th March). The members of the NUM narrowly vote in favour of a return to work, thus ending Britain's longest running industrial dispute. The unofficial strike was originally started in Yorkshire in protest at planned pit closures but quickly spread across the country.

1991 The death of William Penney in Oxfordshire (see 24th June). Born in Gibraltar and educated in England, he was a Mathematician. He led the British delegation that worked on the Manhattan Project and subsequently on Operation Hurricane, the first test of a British Nuclear device (see 3rd October). During the war, he worked with his American counterparts but, following the withdrawal of American technical and scientific support in an attempt to prevent our acquisition of the deterrent, Prime Minister Clement Atlee (see 3rd January and 8th October) decided that we would manufacture our own, despite repeated American obstruction (see 26th February).

4th March:

1133 The birth of Henry II 'Curtmantle' at Le Mans (see 6th July and 19th December), the eldest child of Geoffrey the Fair and the Empress Matilda.

1665 Charles II (see 6th February and 29th May) declares war on the Dutch Republic, starting the Second Anglo-Dutch War (1665-1667 and see 21st July). The two countries had come into conflict as a result of the competition over trade routes and control of the seas.

1681 The Colony of Pennsylvania institutes its colonial government following Charles II (see 6th February and 29th May) granting William Penn (see 30th July and 14th October) a charter to establish a Proprietary Colony in North America.

1706 The English Parliament passes the Act of Union between England and Scotland after relatively little debate (see 16th January, 6th March, 1st May and 22nd July) thus paving the way for the creation of the United Kingdom of Great Britain.

1756 The birth of Henry Raeburn (see 8th July) in Stockbridge, now part of Edinburgh.

1857 The Treaty of Paris is signed between Britain and Persia, bringing an end to the Anglo-Persian War (1856-1857). The war had begun in November 1856 (see 1st November), when Britain declared war on Persia for their occupation of the city of Herat and their possible alliance with Russia.

1890 The Forth Bridge, measuring 1,720 feet in length is opened in Scotland by the Prince of Wales, the future Edward VII (see 6th May and 9th November).

1941 Royal Marine, loyal Norwegian Commandoes and Royal Engineers, with Royal Naval support, take part in a daring raid called Operation Claymore which was an attack on the Lofoten Islands in German-occupied Norway (see 28th February). Although not the objective of the operation, the most important outcome from the raid was the capture of the wheels from an Enigma machine and the accompanying code books.

1945 The death of General Sir Henry 'Harry' George Chauvel in Melbourne, Australia (see 16th April). Born in New South Wales, he served in the local militia before seeing active service during the Boer War 1899-1902. At the outbreak of the Great War, he was a Colonel and Australia's representative on the Imperial General Staff before taking command of the 1st Light Horse Brigade in Gallipoli. In 1916 he was in command of the AIF in Egypt and prevented the Turks from reaching Suez. He was in command when Gaza was eventually taken on the third attempt which opened the way for an advance through Palestine leading to the Ottoman surrender. In November 1929 he became the first Australian to reach the rank of General.

1947 The Treaty of Dunkirk is signed between Great Britain and France in Dunkirk, France. The treaty was an agreement of mutual assistance between the two countries in the event of further German aggression following the conclusion of Second World War.

5th March: St. Piran's day, Patron Saint of Cornwall

1770 The Boston Riot takes place in Boston in the Province of Massachusetts Bay. Throughout the day, a crowd had gathered outside the Boston Customs House and continually harangued and abused the British sentries in protest against the Townsend Acts that were passed to raise revenue to pay for colonial administration. Eventually, the situation became extremely tense as the small detachment was surrounded. In the ensuing melee, a gun was discharged followed by a uniformed volley of fire into the increasingly hostile crowd. The shots killed five colonial protestors (one dying a couple of weeks afterwards from his wounds). In the subsequent trial, the soldiers charged with murder were acquitted as they were shown to have been provoked and had been in understandable fear of their lives (see 19th April).

1811 The battle of Barossa near Cadiz in southern Spain. A combined British and Portuguese force, led by General Thomas Graham, attack the much superior French division laying siege to the town of Cadiz. The French deployed to prevent our troops from reaching the city and a single British Division attacked and defeated two French Divisions and captured an eagle of the French 8th Ligne, the first to be captured in the Peninsular War. Throughout the battle, the Spanish contingent in the allied army refused to come to the aid of their British and Portuguese allies (see 30th May).

1824 War is declared on the Burmese in what became the First Burmese War, 1824-1826, and a struggle for control of north-east India. The Kingdom of Burma had expanded militarily right up to the borders of British India and had begun to attack British bases and areas under British control and protection (see 4th January, 24th February and 5th March).

1850 The Britannia (Menai) Bridge, a rail bridge built by Robert Stephenson, between Wales and Anglesey, is opened.

1879 The birth of William Beveridge in Bengal, India (see 16th March). An economist and social reformer, he was responsible for the Beveridge Report in 1942 which would form the basis for our modern welfare state and in particular the National Health Service. His main proposal was that all working people should pay a national insurance contribution that would enable the state to help them in time of need, in particular when sick, unemployed, widowed or retired.

1895 The death of Sir Henry Creswicke Rawlinson (see 11th April) in London. An Officer in the Army and a leading Orientalist, he succeeded in deciphering the cuneiform of Darius I at Bisitun in Iran. Because of his work, much more inscriptions were deciphered and contributed to the understanding of ancient Persia and the Middle East. In 1827 he went to India for the East India Company (see 31st December) and eventually was sent to train the Shah of Iran's army, developing a keen interest in the history of the country. In 1843 he became consul in Baghdad. He was knighted and then became a director of the East India Company before becoming a Member of Parliament.

1936 The first flight of the 'Spitfire' aircraft. Designed by Reginald Joseph Mitchell (see 20th May and 11th June), it has become the most iconic of British and world aircraft. It was the prototype that flew and it was flown by Captain Joseph 'Mutt' Summers, reaching a speed of 350mph at Eastleigh Aerodrome.

1943 The maiden flight of the Gloster Whittle 'Meteor', Britain's and the Allies' first Jet aircraft (see 27th July). Flying from RAF Cranwell, the prototype was powered by De Havilland jet engines due to technical difficulties with the intended turbojet engines designed by Frank Whittle's own company.

1946 Winston Churchill delivers his 'Sinews of Peace' speech, now famously referred to as his 'Iron Curtain' speech in Westminster College in Fulton, Missouri U.S.A. (see 24th January and 30th November). During the course of the speech, he uses the term 'Iron Curtain' to refer to the Soviet Union's sphere of influence in Eastern Europe

6th March:

1697 The birth of Stringer Lawrence (see 10th January) in Hereford.

1706 The birth of George Pocock (see 3rd April).

1706 The Act of Union between England and Scotland, passed by the English Parliament (see 4th March) receives Royal Assent from Queen Anne (see 16th January, 1st May and 22nd July).

1725 The birth of Henry Benedict Stewart in Frascati, in the Palazzo Muti in Rome in the Papal States (see 13th July). He was the younger brother of Charles Edward Stewart ('Bonnie Prince Charlie', see 31st January and 31st December) and the youngest son of James III (James VII of England, see 1st January and 10th June) 'The Old Pretender', as he was known by his Jacobite supporters.

1759 The Siege of Masulipatam in Eastern India begins during the Seven Years' War, 1756-1763. Our forces are commanded by Colonel Francis Foorde against the French forces under the Comte de Lally. The siege would last for a month and result in the capture of the city, thus greatly increasing Britain's area of influence in India.

1806 The birth of Elizabeth Barrett (later Browning) in Coxhoe Hall in County Durham (see 29th June).

1988 Three known IRA terrorists are shot dead by the SAS in Gibraltar during 'Operation Flavius'. The three were later shown to be unarmed when challenged but reacted as if they were armed. They were also proven to be about to activate a bomb attack on the island and this was prevented by the swift and courageous actions of the SAS teams.

7th March:

1671 The birth of Rob Roy MacGregor (see 28th December).

1792 The birth of John Frederick William Herschel in Slough, Berkshire (see 11th May).

1804 The Horticultural Society of London, the forerunner of the Royal Horticultural Society, is founded by Josiah Wedgewood (see 3rd January and 12th July) and six friends as they meet in Piccadilly in London.

1810 The death of Cuthbert Collingwood, 1st Baron Collingwood (see 26th September), from cancer aboard HMS Ville de Paris off Port Mahon, Minorca. He was one of our greatest Admirals and a veteran of battles such as The Glorious First of June in 1794 (see 1st June), Cape St. Vincent in 1797 (see 14th February) and Trafalgar in 1805 (see 21st October). He joined the

Navy when he was eleven years old and later served in North America during the American colonial rebellion. He was a good friend of Horatio Nelson and led one of the two Royal Navy Squadrons during the glorious Battle of Trafalgar. He was buried in St. Paul's Cathedral (see 2nd December).

1876 The birth of Edgar Evans (see 17th February) in Rhossili, Wales.

8th March:

1702 The death of William III, 'William of Orange'. "To the gentleman in black velvet" (see 13th February and 4th November) in Kensington Palace and the ascension to the throne of his sister in law, Queen Anne (see 6th February and 1st August). The nephew and son in law of James VII (James II of England, see 16th September and 14th October), he was the Prince of Orange by birth in the Dutch Republic as well as Stadtholder over the same Dutch Republic from 1672. A Protestant, he led the joint English and Dutch forces across the Channel in 1688 against his uncle in what became known as the 'Glorious Revolution' (see 5th November). Following his invasion, he led his troops successfully at the Battle of the Boyne in 1690 (see 1st July) and in 1694 he was instrumental in the establishment of the Bank of England to help finance the war against Louis XIV of France. His death was much celebrated amongst Jacobites, as this gave new hope to the cause of the Stewart Restoration.

1717 The death of Abraham Darby in Madeley in Shropshire (see 14th April). A Quaker, he is remembered for the development of a method to produce pig iron in a blast furnace, fuelled by coke instead of charcoal. He moved to Coalbrookdale in 1708 and it was in the same year that he made the discovery that coal can be used to smelt iron on a mass-produced scale. This was one of the key moments in the start of the Industrial Revolution.

1726 The birth of Richard Howe, later an Admiral in the Royal Navy (see 5th August), in London.

1803 The death of Francis Egerton, 3rd Duke of Bridgewater in London (see 21st May). A wealthy man, he is recognised as the founder of British inland navigation with his ardent support for canal construction. He commissioned the Bridgewater Canal and employed James Brindley (see 30th September) to construct the canal from his estates to the River Mersey.

1916 The battle of Dujaila in Mesopotamia. British forces, led by Lieutenant General Sir Fenton John Aylmer, attempt, unsuccessfully, to relieve the besieged forces in the city of Kut. Surrounded by Ottoman troops, the city had been under siege since December 1915 (see 30th October and 29th April).

1944 The beginning of the ferocious dual battle of Kohima-Imphal, during the Burma Campaign, to drive the Japanese invaders from the occupied territory. The city of Imphal, the capital city of Manipur, is situated in North-eastern India and the Japanese, supported by treacherous Indian National Army Units, crossed the Chindwin River in attempt to take the city and thus open up the road deep into India (see 4th April). The British and Indian Army units in the city clung onto their positions and along with the battle of Kohima proved to be one of the pivotal battles in the Far East (see 22nd June and 3rd July).

9th March:

1566 David Rizzo, Secretary and advisor to Mary Queen of Scots (see 8th February and 8th December) is murdered in the Palace of Holyrood in Edinburgh. Born in Turin, he became the advisor and close friend of Mary. Rumours began to circulate that he was Mary's lover, and that the unborn child (the future James VI, see 27th March and 19th June) was his. He was stabbed to death in front of Mary in her bedchamber by rebels who were believed to be supported by Mary's jealous husband, Henry Stewart, Lord Darnley (see 13th May, 9th September and 14th December).

1763 The birth of William Cobbett (see 18th June) in Farnham in Surrey.

1846 the Treaty of Lahore is signed ending the First Sikh War (1845-1846). The Treaty, signed for Britain by the Governor-General of India Viscount Hardinge and members of the East India Company (see 2nd August and 31st December), ensured that large areas of the Punjab and neighbouring areas were entrusted to British control and that the Sikh army was greatly reduced in size (see 10th February and 18th December).

1859 The death of Thomas Attwood in Malvern (see 6th October). He was an economist and radical politician. Born in Halesowen, he served as MP for Birmingham from 1832 until 1839. As an economist he promoted his idea that the government should use a paper currency that was not tied to gold, a theory that was popular in his area but was rejected by parliament. He founded the Birmingham Political Union and campaigned against the East India Company's (see 31st December) monopoly on trade as it was affecting the economy and the employment situation around Birmingham. In 1839 he presented the first Chartist petition to parliament but after it was rejected he resigned from parliament and took no further part in politics.

1884 The birth of John Lorimer in Stirling (see 18th November). He was the son of William Lorimer and Catherine Reid Lorimer (nee Meikle).

1973 The people of Northern Ireland vote overwhelmingly to remain part of the United Kingdom, despite a boycott by the Roman Catholic part of the population. A total of 98.9% of those that voted opted for Proposal 1, which was to remain part of the United Kingdom (see 31st July and 14th August).

10th March:

1629 Charles I (see 30th January and 19th November) dissolves parliament and rules alone, beginning an eleven year period of personal rule, often referred to later on as the "Eleven Years of Tyranny".

1653 The birth of John Benbow in Shrewsbury in Shropshire (see 4th November).

1792 The death of John Stuart, 3rd Earl of Bute (see 25th May), in London. A Conservative politician and a relative of the Campbell Clan, in 1762 he became the first Scottish Prime Minister of Great Britain following the Act of Union (see 1st May), ending the Whig dominance of Parliament. In 1755 he became the tutor of the Prince of Wales, the future George III (see 29th January and 24th May). He became Prime Minister for a short period of eleven months from 1762 to 1763 during which he brought the Seven Years' War (1756-1763) to a successful conclusion before resigning after losing favour with the king.

1922 Mohandas Karamchand Gandhi, the Indian Nationalist leader, is arrested for sedition. Shortly afterwards he was put on trial, found guilty and imprisoned for six years. Though supposedly an advocate of peaceful noncooperation, he in fact contradicted himself many times and many of his displays of civil disobedience actually resulted in acts of violence by his followers (see 15th August).

1931 Oswald Mosley (see 16th November and 3rd December) is expelled from the Labour Party (see 27th March and 20th May).

1943 The death of Laurence Binyon (see 10th August) in Reading. An acclaimed poet and dramatist, he worked for the British Museum before and after the Great War. He is most well known for his 'For the Fallen', written in September 1914 in Cornwall, an excerpt of which is used as the Exhortation and Citation on Remembrance Day (see 11th November) and Remembrance Sunday across Britain and the Commonwealth.

2013 The first day of the Falklands Islands referendum on whether the Islands should remain a British Overseas Territory (see 11th March). The Islanders decided to hold the vote due to the constant claims by Argentina that the Falkland Islands belongs to them, despite an overwhelming defeat in 1982 Falklands War (see 2nd April, 21st May and 14th June) and the refusal of the British Government to hold talks over the Islands' British sovereignty.

11th March:

1845 The start of the First Maori War (1845-1846) in the Colony of New Zealand (see 1st July). Up to 700 Maoris attack the settlement at Russell with the intention of hacking down the flagstaff flying the flag of the union. Almost overwhelmed, the garrison held off the Maoris long enough for the town's inhabitants to be evacuated to ships waiting in the bay. The settlement was then bombarded from the Royal Navy ship HMS Hazard and most of the town destroyed.

1863 The death of General Sir James Outram (see 29th January), 1st Baronet Outram and the 'Bayard of India' in Pau, France. He took part in the First Afghan War, 1839-1842, and later heroically defended the residency of Hyderabad. As Resident at Lucknow, he carried out the annexation of the

Province of Oudh in 1856. He was a hero of the Indian Mutiny of 1857 (see 10th May), during which he led his men in the capture of Lucknow and fittingly he is buried in Westminster Abbey, a true hero of the Empire.

1916 The birth of James Harold Wilson in Huddersfield in Yorkshire (see 16th March and 24th May).

1936 The death of Admiral of the Fleet David Beatty, 1st Earl Beatty (see 17th January) in London. The son of an Army Officer, he served in the Sudan Campaign in 1896-1899 and then during the Boxer Rebellion, after which he rose swiftly through the ranks. In 1913 he was appointed commander of the First Battle Cruiser Squadron and shortly after the commencement of the First World War was promoted up to Vice Admiral. He led during the battle of Heligoland Bight in 1914 (see 28th August), the Battle of Dogger Bank in 1915 (see 24th January) and at the Battle of Jutland in 1916 (see 31st May). After the war, in 1919, he was appointed Admiral of the Fleet and then First Sea Lord before being granted a peerage.

1955 The death of Alexander Fleming (see 6th August and 30th September) in London. A Biologist, he discovered the antibiotic benefits of penicillin after identifying the effects of mould on bacteria in 1928. Though he did not continue his research, it was through his early work that we now have penicillin. He served during the Great War in the Army Medical Corps and afterwards continued his work at St. Mary's Hospital Medical School in London. He was elected a fellow of the Royal Society in 1943, knighted in 1944 and in 1945 he won the Nobel Prize in Medicine. He was buried in St. Paul's Cathedral (see 2nd December).

2013 The second and final day of the Falklands Islands referendum on whether the Islands should remain a British Overseas Territory (see 10th March). The Islanders decided to hold the vote due to the constant claims by Argentina that the Falkland Islands belong to them, despite an overwhelming defeat in 1982 Falklands War (see 14th June) and the refusal of the British Government to hold talks over the Islands' British sovereignty. With the result declared the following day, there was a turnout of over 90%. There were 1,517 votes in favour of remaining a British Overseas Territory with only three votes against giving a 99.8% vote in favour.

12th March:

1655 The beginning of Penruddock's rising in Wiltshire led by Colonel John Penruddock. The rebels, numbering around 400 men, after proclaiming Charles II as King (see 9th February and 29th May) rode out of Salisbury and headed westward (see 14th March).

1795 The birth of William Lyon Mackenzie in Dundee (see 28th August).

1820 The death of Sir Alexander Mackenzie in Dunkeld, Scotland. Born in 1764 in Stornoway on the Isle of Lewis, he moved with his family to New York in 1774. In 1776 the family moved to Montreal due to the American rebellion and later began work for the North West Company. For the

Company he was to conduct several expeditions looking for the North West passage and finding new supplies of furs. In 1793 he and his team became the first to cross British North America from one coast to the other across land when he reached the Pacific Ocean (see 20th July and 22nd July). In 1799 he returned to Britain and was knighted in 1802

1879 The Battle of Intombe in Zululand. A small force of about 100 is attacked by around 500 Zulus in a surprise attack on their laager. A total of one Officer and 62 Other Ranks are killed. About forty men made it across the river under the command of Corporal Anthony Clarke Booth and escaped, fighting a courageous rearguard action with the pursuing Zulus. For his heroism, Corporal Booth was later awarded the Victoria Cross for his gallant leadership (see 12th January and 28th August).

1913 The foundation stone for the city of Canberra, the purpose built capital city of the Dominion of Australia (see 1st January and 26th January), is laid by Lady Denman, the wife of the Governor-General.

1984 The President of the National Union of Mineworkers, Arthur Scargill, declares a national coal miners strike. Up until then two pits had been on strike but Mr Scargill declared that the other pits should join in the unofficial strike (see 3rd March) and become a national dispute over proposed pit closures.

2009 Dorothy Hughes, aged 85, and Winifred Phillips, aged 82, become the first female Chelsea Pensioners.

13th March:

1733 The birth of Joseph Priestly in West Yorkshire (see 6th February and 14th July).

1764 The birth of Charles Grey (see 17th July) in Northumberland.

1781 Astronomer Frederick William Herschel discovers the planet Uranus (see 25th August and 15th November).

1842 The death of Henry Shrapnel in Southampton (see 3rd June). Commissioned as an Officer in the Royal Artillery, he developed a form of case shot for the artillery. A distinguished soldier who saw action in several campaigns, his invention bears his name to this day; the Shrapnel shell. However, he spent much of his own money on inventions and ideas. He invented the exploding shell and he was also instrumental in the Royal Navy moving from wooden battle ships to the ironclads.

1900 The town of Bloemfontein is captured by General Lord Frederick Roberts (see 30th September and 14th November) from the Boers following the Battle of Paardeberg (see 27th February) during the South African War, 1899-1902 (see 31st May and 11th October).

1940 The assassination of Sir Michael Francis O'Dwyer in Caxton Hall in London. He was murdered by Udham Singh who blamed him for the so-called Amritsar Massacre (see 13th April) in 1919 at which he was wounded. Sir O'Dwyer had been the Governor of the Punjab region of British India when the deaths at Amritsar had occurred and had supported General Dyer in his actions to restore order to the region.

1941 The first night of the Clydebank Blitz as almost 450 German bombers dropped around 1,000 bombs on the industrial heart of Britain and the Empire's second city (see 14th March). Clydebank was the centre of ship building and munitions production and was vital to the war effort (see 30th March, 7th September, 14th November and 29th December).

14th March:

1655 The Battle of Molton bringing an end to the so-called Penruddock's rising. Around 400 men, led by Colonel John Penruddock, had proclaimed Charles II as King (see 9th February, 12th March and 29th May) and had rode out of Salisbury. As they reached Molton, a force of Government Cavalry caught them up and a after a brief exchange of fire, the rebels force dissolved and they fled. The ring leaders, including Penruddock, were arrested and executed (see 16th May).

1748 The death of Field Marshal (General) George Wade. Commander in Chief of the Army, he served at the Battle of Dettingen in 1743 (see 16th June) and in the campaigns against the Jacobites in 1715 and 1745. He is best remembered for his work between 1725 and 1737 in which he built over 250 miles of roads across the Highlands as well as over 40 bridges. He was born in Westmeath in Ireland in 1673 and was elected as a Member of Parliament. He also served in the War of the Spanish Succession and War of the Austrian Succession (1701-1714). He is buried in Westminster Abbey.

1757 The execution of Admiral John Byng on the deck of the HMS Monarch (see 29th October). He signalled the firing squad with the drop of a handkerchief. He is the only Royal Navy Officer executed. He was held responsible for the loss of Minorca in 1756, despite being given command of a badly prepared fleet. He was court-martialled and found guilty of 'failing to do his utmost' to prevent the French from taking the island during and after the battle of Minorca in 1756 (see 20th May). He had been Governor of Newfoundland in 1756.

1823 The death of Admiral Sir John Jervis (see 9th January). At the age of 13 he left home and joined the Royal Navy. He rose steadily through the ranks and saw service across the Empire in many ships. One of this country's greatest naval heroes, he saw action in the siege of Quebec and the Battle of the Plains of Abraham in 1759 (see 13th September) with General James Wolfe, the first battle of Ushant in 1778 (see 27th July). He was present at the siege of Gibraltar in 1782 during which, in a related engagement, he was wounded. For his service he was subsequently invested as a Knight of the Bath. He then saw service in the French Revolutionary and Napoleonic wars, taking part in the glorious victory of the battle of Cape Saint Vincent in 1797 (see 14th February) for which he was made Earl St. Vincent. He was appointed First Lord of the Admiralty and Admiral of the Fleet in 1821. He was laid to rest in the family mausoleum in St. Michaels Church yard in Stone, Staffordshire.

1941 The second night of the Clydebank Blitz as almost 450 German bombers dropped around 1,000 bombs on Britain and the Empire's second city. Clydebank was the centre of ship building and munitions production and was vital to the war effort. Altogether, 528 people died, over 600 were seriously injured and almost all the buildings were destroyed but the Glaswegian spirit and morale was strengthened by the attack (see 13th March, 30th March, 7th September, 14th November and 29th December)

1943 HMS Thunderbolt, a T-class submarine and formerly known as HMS Thetis (see 1st June), is sunk off the coast of Sicily by an Italian corvette with the loss of all hands.

2012 The latest towns to be granted city status are announced as part of the celebrations for the Queen's Diamond Jubilee (see 6th February, 2nd June, 3rd June and 4th June). They are Chelmsford, Perth and St. Asaph.

15th March:

1779 The birth of William Lamb, later Viscount Lord Melbourne, in London (see 24th November).

1781 The Battle of Guilford Court House and defeat for the Colonial rebels in North Carolina. Around 1,900 of our troops, under the Command of Lord Cornwallis (see 5th October and 31st December) defeat around 4,000 rebels. The rebels were commanded by the so-called General Nathanael Greene, forcing them to retreat. It was a glorious but Pyrrhic victory as the casualties from his Majesty's forces could not be replaced (see 3rd September).

1813 The birth of John Snow in York (see 16th June).

1891 The death of Joseph Bazalgette (see 28th March) in Wimbledon, London. Born in London, he was originally a railway engineer before setting up his own engineering practice in the 1840s. A leading civil engineer, he was appointed the Chief Engineer of London for the Metropolitan Board of Works and was the man responsible for the sewage network for central London.

1898 The death of Henry Bessemer in London (see 19th January). A businessman, civil engineer and inventor, he is known for inventing the Bessemer process for manufacturing steel cheaply and efficiently and was used for the general manufacture of steel iron. The process gave a major boost to the iron and steel industry. He was knighted in 1879 but received very little other recognition.

1949 The end of clothes rationing after almost eight years.

16 March:

1774 The birth of Matthew Flinders (see 19th July) in Donnington in Lincolnshire.

1812 The beginning of the siege of the Spanish town of Badajoz (see 19th January and 6th April) during the Peninsular War. British and Portuguese forces, commanded by General Wellington (see 1st May and 14th September), invested the city, garrisoned by around 5,000 French soldiers.

1912 The death of Captain Lawrence Edward Grace 'Titus' Oates in the Antarctic (see 17th March). Captain 'Titus' Oates as he was known, joined the army in 1900, being posted to the 6th (Inniskilling) Dragoons during the Boer War, 1899-1902, where he was injured in 1901. In 1910 he joined the Terra Nova Expedition led by Captain Scott (see 29th March and 6th June). It was on the team's return journey from the South Pole, having been beaten by Amundsen, that he became weakened until he could continue no further. He made a heroic attempt to save the others of the expedition by sacrificing himself and going out into the snow, knowing he was to die. His body was never recovered (see 29th March).

1927 The death of Sir Robert Bond (see 25th February) in the Dominion of Newfoundland. Born in St. John's, Newfoundland, and educated in England, he returned to Newfoundland and in 1882 he entered politics for the first time. In 1900 he became the last Premier of the Colony of Newfoundland and when Newfoundland became a Dominion in 1907 (see 26th September), he became the first Prime Minister of the new Dominion of Newfoundland.

1963 The death of William Henry Beveridge (See 5th March) in Oxford. An economist, he is best known for his 1942 report 'Social Insurance and Allied Services', known as the 'Beveridge Report' (see 1st December), that formed the basis for the Welfare State, in particular the National Health Service (see 5th July). Prior to the Great War, David Lloyd-George (see 17th January and 26th March) asked him to advise on national insurance and pensions. He became involved in the controlling of manpower during the Great War and during the Second World War he was asked to examine how Britain could be rebuilt once the war was over. The 1942 report was the result. When Clement Attlee (see 3rd January and 8th October) became Prime Minister in 1945, he announced that he would introduce the welfare state as Beveridge had outlined. The NHS was established in 1948 with a policy of care, 'from the cradle to the grave'.

1976 Prime Minister Harold Wilson announces his resignation to the cabinet (see 11th March and 24th May). Taking effect on the 5th April 1976, the resignation was a surprise to most people.

2011 The Prime Minister, David Cameron, announces that Wotton Bassett in Wiltshire, will receive the title 'Royal', making it one of only three towns to bear the title Royal and the first since 1909. The other two towns are Royal Leamington Spa and Royal Tunbridge Wells. The honour is in recognition of the town's magnificent record in honouring the repatriation of our fallen troops during the Afghan War (see 26th October).

17th March: St. Patrick's Day, Patron Saint of Ireland.

1473 The birth of James Stuart, the future James IV of Scotland, probably in Stirling Castle (see 11th June, 8th August and 9th September). He was the son of James III (see 11th June) and Margaret of Denmark.

1649 The Monarchy is abolished and two months later England is declared a 'Commonwealth and Free State' Republic by the Rump Parliament (see 19th March and 19th May).

1766 The Stamp Act is repealed by Parliament (see 22nd March, 5th September and 1st November). Having been enacted the previous year, the Act provided for the imposition of a stamp on all official documents as well as pamphlets, papers and other items in the colonies of North America, with the idea of helping to pay for the military protection from foreign forces.

1778 Great Britain declares war on France over the help they were giving to the rebels in the thirteen American Colonies (see 19th April and 3rd September).

1801 Henry Addington (see 15th February and 30th May) becomes Prime Minister after his predecessor, William Pitt the Younger (see 23rd January and 28th May) resigns after George III (see 29th January and 24th May) rejects his Emancipation of Catholic's Bill.

1824 The Anglo-Dutch Treaty is signed (see 13th August) in London between Great Britain and the Netherlands. The treaty resolved some long-lasting issues regarding trade between the two countries and recognised 'most favoured trading status' in many colonies and possessions in the east that were owned by either nation.

1845 Stephen Perry, a businessman and inventor of rubber-based products, patents the rubber band.

1880 The birth of Lawrence Edward Grace Oates (see 16th March) in Putney, London.

18th March:

1745 the death of Sir Robert Walpole, 1st Earl of Orford, a Whig and the first Prime Minister (see 26th August and 22nd September) at Arlington Street, London. He was also the first Prime Minister to occupy 10 Downing Street. He was born in Norfolk where he became a Member of Parliament. In 1721 he was appointed as First Lord of the Treasury, which traditionally was the name of what would become Prime Minister. His administration is noted for pursuing peace and economic stability. In 1735 he was presented with 10 Downing Street by George II (see 25th October and 30th October). In 1739 he declared war on Spain in what would became the War of Jenkins's Ear, 1739-1748, and ultimately led to his resignation in 1742.

1834 The six 'Tolpuddle Martyrs', from Tolpuddle in Dorset are each sentenced to seven years transportation to the penal Colony of New South Wales in Australia for attempting to form a Union (see 22nd January and 27th February).

1869 The birth of Arthur Neville Chamberlain (see 9th November) in Edgbaston, Birmingham, the son of Joseph Chamberlain (see 2nd July and 8th July).

1893 The birth of Wilfred Edward Salter Owen in Oswestry, Shropshire (see 4th November).

1915 HMS Dreadnought rams and sinks the German submarine U-29 in the Pentland Firth with the loss of the entire submarine's crew. The submarine had fired a torpedo at HMS Neptune and had then surfaced ahead of Dreadnought, who chased her down and rammed her. She is the only Battleship to have sunk a submarine (see 10th February).

1935 Driving tests are introduced under the Road Traffic Act (1934) as well as the reintroduction of a speed limit of 30 miles per hour in urban built up areas. The Act was introduced by the Minister of Transport, Leslie Hore-Belisha (see 16th February and 7th September).

1967 The Oil Tanker 'Torrey Canyon' runs aground off Lands End. It struck Pollard's Rock and caused the first ever major oil spill and the ship at the time was carrying around 120,000 tons of crude oil. The Fleet Air Arm and the Royal Air Force (see 1st April) were used to bomb the slick in a partially-successful attempt to burn the slick off the sea. Around 120 miles of the Cornish coast was affected by the 240 square mile slick as it came ashore.

19th March:

1286 The death of Alexander III, King of the Scots (see 4th September). Born in Roxburgh, the son of Alexander II (see 6th July and 24th August) and the grandson of William the Lion (see 4th December), he was probably one of the Greatest of Scottish kings under whose reign Scotland enjoyed a long period of peace and prosperity. In 1251 he married Margaret, the daughter of King Henry III (see 1st October and 16th November), the English King. In 1266 he signed the Treaty of Perth (see 2nd July), ridding the Western Isles and the Isle of Man of Norse control. He died when his horse, carrying him home at night and in bad weather, stumbled and pitched him over a cliff (see 13th July and 4th September). He was buried in Dunfermline Abbey.

1643 The Battle of Hopton Heath. The Parliamentarians, under Sir John Gell, attempted to capture the town of Stafford. The Royalist army, under the command of the Earl of Northampton, had arrived in Stafford the day before to strengthen the town's garrison and had moved forward to confront the enemy. There was no overall victor: the Parliamentarians slipping away under cover of the night and the Royalists losing their commander, the Earl of Northampton, who was killed during the battle (see 14th June and 3rd September).

1649 The House of Lords is abolished and two months later England is declared a 'Commonwealth and Free State' Republic by the Rump Parliament (see 17th March and 19th May).

1721 The birth of Tobias George Smollett (see 17th September) in Dalquhurn, Scotland.

1792 The Treaty of Seringapatam is signed in Seringapatam, the capital of Mysore, bringing an end to the Third Mysore War (1789-1792). It was signed by Lord Cornwallis on behalf of the East India Company (see 31st December) and its allies and Tipu Sultan, the ruler of Mysore. Under the terms of the treaty, Mysore ceded over half of its territory, including an extensive coastal are to the East India Company and its allies.

1813 The birth of David Livingstone in Blantyre, South Lanarkshire (see 1st May).

1821 The birth of Richard Francis Burton (see 20th October) in Torquay, Devon.

1930 The death of Arthur James Balfour, 1st Earl of Balfour in Surrey (see 25th July). He entered Parliament as a Conservative in 1874 and served as Prime Minister from 1902 to 1905 (see 12th July). However, during his term, his cabinet was split over the issue of free trade. During the First World War, he served in the coalition government as First Lord of the Admiralty and then Foreign Secretary. It was in this role that in 1917 he wrote a letter that became known as the famous Balfour Declaration, which promised the creation of a Jewish homeland in Palestine.

1967 The death of General Frederick Edgeworth Morgan in Northwood, Middlesex (see 5th February). He is remembered for conceiving the plan for Operation Overlord (see 6th May). Born in Kent, he was commissioned into the Royal Artillery in 1913 and served throughout the war on the Western Front. Between the wars he served in India and at the outbreak of the Second World War he was in France, eventually being evacuated from Dunkirk. Later, he was appointed as Chief of Staff to the Supreme Allied Commander and conceived the idea and began planning for Operation Overlord.

2011 In the evening British Tornado GR4 fighter aircraft from the RAF flying from Britain and tomahawk missiles launched from a submarine attack targets in Libya, a few hours after French aircraft begin air cover over Benghazi. At the same time, tomahawk missiles from US submarines are also launched against the Libyan military targets (see 21st March and 3rd August).

20th March:

1413 The death of Henry IV in Westminster, London (see 4th April and 13th October) and the accession of his son Henry V (see 31st August). The first King from the House of Lancaster, his father was John of Gaunt, the third surviving son of Edward III (see 21st June and 13th November). In 1377 his cousin became Richard II (see 6th January). Some years later, Henry joined opposition forces to the King and following quarrels, Henry was banished. On the death of John of Gaunt, Richard seized his lands and caused Henry to invade to safeguard his inheritance in 1399, meeting little resistance. He was crowned in October 1399. However, over the successive years, Henry had to suppress a number of rebellions and conflict with France in order to secure his rule.

1726 The death of Sir Isaac Newton (see 25th December) in Kensington, London. Born in Lincolnshire, as a physicist, mathematician, alchemist and astronomer, he is best remembered for his description and understanding of the laws of gravitation and the three laws of motion, supposedly triggered by his witnessing the fall from a tree of an apple. In 1688 his reflecting telescope made his name and he was made a Fellow of the Royal Society in 1672. It was in 1687 that he published his work on gravity, for which he is best remembered. In 1692 he was appointed warden of the Royal Mint and worked tirelessly to fight the problem of corruption and counterfeiting.

1914 The so-called Curragh Mutiny occurs in County Kildare. A total of 57 out of 70 Army Officers resign their commissions rather than fight to suppress the Ulster Unionists in their campaign against Irish Home Rule. In 1912, the proposed Home Rule Bill had sought to establish a semi-autonomous government in Dublin (see 28th September). A large section of the Unionist community, opposed to any rule from Dublin, had created the Ulster Volunteers, a paramilitary force that would fight any British government enforcing the Bill or any Dublin government should the Bill get passed. In 1914 the government, fearful of a Unionist uprising, ordered the Commander in Chief, Ireland, Sir Arthur Paget, to mobilise the Army in Ireland in preparation to enforce Home Rule and fight if necessary any Ulster Volunteers. Paget gave his officers the choice of resigning their Commissions if they did not wish to participate in any possible imposition of Home Rule on Ireland. It was then that 57 out of 70 officers chose to resign. Upon hearing this news, the government, under Prime Minister Herbert Asquith, immediately climbed down, insisting that it was all a misunderstanding (see 25th May, 6th December and 8th December).

1925 The death of George Nathanial Curzon, 1st Marquess Curzon of Keddleston (see 11th January), in London. A staunch Imperialist, he had a long and extensive career in Foreign Service. He was Under Secretary for India (1891–1892) and worked at the Foreign Office for three years after that and then he was appointed Viceroy of India in 1898. Personally committed to the Imperialist preservation of India, he helped create the North West Frontier Province and was deeply suspicious of Imperial Russia. Because of this, he was responsible for the expedition to Tibet in 1903 and the partition of Bengal in 1905 to safeguard the borders of British India. After resigning in 1905, he served in a number of posts including Foreign Secretary from 1919.

2003 Operation Telic, commonly known as the Iraq War or Second Gulf War, begins as British, American and Allied ground forces cross the border into Iraq (see 22nd May) following initial air and missile strikes.

21st March:

1556 Thomas Cranmer, the first Protestant Archbishop of Canterbury and the major leader of the English reformation, is burnt at the stake on the orders of the Catholic Queen Mary (see 2nd July). Educated in Cambridge, he came to the notice of Henry VIII (see 28th January and 28th June) and travelled to Rome in 1530 to argue the case for Henry's divorce to the Pope. In 1532 he became Henry's ambassador to the holy Roman Emperor Charles V. In 1533 he was appointed Archbishop of Canterbury. Following the death of Edward VI (see 6th July and 12th October), he supported Lady Jane Grey (see 12th February) as successor to the throne. After her fall from power, he was tried for treason by Mary I (see 18th February and 17th November) and despite a public recanting of his Protestant faith, was burnt at the stake, publicly sticking his right hand with which he had signed his recantation into the fire first.

1918 The German Spring Offensive, masterminded by General Erich Ludendorff, begins on the Somme with a heavy artillery bombardment at 4.40am. The Offensive was initially a great success, forcing the British Army back miles in many places and causing heavy casualties. The plan was to have four different attacks, codenamed Michael, Georgette, Gneisenau and Blucher-Yorck, begin simultaneously. The main one, Michael, was intended to smash through the British lines, outflank them and then destroy and capture them. The other three arms of the attack were designed as diversions to draw Allied forces away from the main thrust. However, despite the initial success, the Allies kept a controlled withdrawal ahead of the Germans and were able to regroup as the German advance tired, slowed and then stopped.

2011 RAF Typhoon fighter jets, having flown in from RAF Coningsby and RAF Leuchars the previous day, take off from Gioia del Colle in Italy to take part in enforcing the no-fly zone over Libya. This is the first time that Typhoons have been involved in combat (see 19th March and 3rd August).

2013 The Scottish First Minister, Alex Salmond, announces to the Scottish Parliament that the independence referendum will be held on the 18th September 2014.

22nd March:

1765 The Stamp Act receives Royal Assent (see 27th February, 17th March, 5th September and 1st November) following its successful passage through the House of Commons and the House of Lords. It was the idea of the Prime Minister Lord George Grenville. It imposed a relatively small tax on every item of printed paper used by the American Colonists and would bear a revenue stamp. The tax was also to be paid in British currency and not in the colonial currency. It was designed to raise money to help pay a contribution towards the defence of the colonies by around 10,000 British troops as well as recuperate some of the cost of victory in the Seven Years' War, 1756-1764, that Britain and the colonies had won. However, the tax was viewed as a direct attempt by Parliament to raise revenue without the approval of the colonial legislature.

1808 The birth of Caroline Norton (née Sheridan, see 15th June) in London.

1979 Sir Richard Sykes, British Ambassador to the Netherlands, is shot dead as he leaves his residence in The Hague on the way to the embassy by IRA terrorists. His driver is also shot and killed. Both men were shot in the head.

23rd March:

1708 James Francis Edward Stuart, the 'Old Pretender' (see 1st January and 10th June), arrived in the Firth of Forth in Scotland in a vain attempt to start a rising against the Hanoverian Government. Unable to land, his French ships are repulsed by Admiral Sir George Byng and are forced to return to France.

1769 The birth of William Smith (see 28th August) in Churchill, Oxfordshire.

1921 The birth of Donald Campbell (see 4th January) in Kingston-upon-Thames in Surrey (see 17th July and 3rd September). He was the son of Sir Malcolm Campbell, who also held the land and water speed records (see 19th August and 3rd September).

1981 The death of Claude Auchinleck (see 21st June). Born in Aldershot into a military family, he joined the Indian Army in 1903 and was steadily promoted. During the Great War he served in the Indian army, mostly in the Mesopotamian Campaign. Between the wars he again served in India and at the outbreak of the Second World War he was appointed as head of Middle East Command based in Cairo. As Commander in Chief of our troops in the Middle East, he had initial success pushing east and took Tobruk. However, Rommel regrouped and counter attacked and in August 1942 he was replaced by General Alexander. It was in June 1943 that he became Commander in Chief of the British Army in India. After the war and disagreeing with the policy of Indian partition, he resigned his command in 1947.

1985 The death of Doctor Richard Beeching in East Grinstead (see 27th March and 21st April). Born in Sheerness, he became a physicist and worked through the Second World War in the design of armaments. In 1948 he joined ICI and in 1961 he became Chairman of the British Railways Board. It was in 1963 that he published his report entitled "The Reshaping of British Railways" in which he advocated the closure of a third of the over 7,000 Railway Stations and the withdrawal of services from around 5,000 miles of track.

2007 Fifteen Royal Navy personnel, eight sailors and seven Royal Marines in two boats are seized by troops from the Iranian Revolutionary Guard forces in Iraqi waters. The personnel were from the Type-22 frigate HMS Cornwall and were held for thirteen days.

24th March:

1603 The death of Queen Elizabeth I 'Gloriana' at Richmond Palace (see 7th September and 17th November). She died at 3 O'clock in the morning. The last of the Tudor Monarchs, she is rightly remembered as one of the Greatest Monarchs and leaders of this country, referred to as 'Gloriana' and 'Good Queen Bess'. She was the daughter of Henry VIII (see 28th January and 28th June) and Anne Boleyn. During the reign of her Catholic sister Mary (see 18th February and 17th November) she had been imprisoned on suspicion of being involved in Protestant plotting. In 1568 she had her only real rival, Mary Queen of Scots (see 8th February and 8th December), imprisoned and then executed in 1587. Viewed as religiously tolerant compared to her father and sister, her greatest and most praised achievement was during the war with Spain which saw the glorious defeat of the Spanish Armada in 1588 (see 29th July). The death of Elizabeth also saw the accession of the Scottish James VI to the throne as King James I of England (see 27th March and 19th June) and the union of the crowns of England and Scotland.

1693 The birth of John Harrison (see 1776 below).

1776 The death of John Harrison (see 1693 above). A self-taught clock maker, he is famous for inventing a marine chronometer, the device used for establishing longitude (the East-West position), thus revolutionising the age of sail and exploration. A long-standing problem with mariners, an easy way of establishing a ship's longitude was critical to better sea faring as well as the survival of shipping. The Admiralty offered £20,000 to whoever could devise a device for measuring Longitude. Despite his pioneering work, Harrison would only receive a part payment for his work just three years before his death.

1829 The Catholic Relief Act was passed by Parliament (see 13th April). It would allow Catholics to take their elected seats in the House of Commons for the first time.

1944 A total of 79 allied prisoners of war escape from the German prison camp Stalag Luft III in what is now modern day Poland. All but three were eventually recaptured. Unfortunately, 50 of those later captured were then murdered under orders from the Gestapo. The story of their escape and murder would form the inspiration for the film 'The Great Escape'. The nationalities of those involved were diverse and came from Britain, the Commonwealth and Europe.

1944 The death of Major General Orde Wingate near Imphal, Manipur in British India (see 26th February). He was commissioned into the army in 1923 and in 1936 was sent to the Mandated Territory of Palestine where he established Special Night Squads of British and Jewish volunteers to fight the Arab terrorists. At the outbreak of the Second World War he went to the Sudan and Ethiopia, formed the Gideon Force and later, with only a couple of hundred men, tricked around 12,000 Italians into surrendering. After spending time in a Cairo hospital, he went to India and formed the Chindits, crossing into Burma in 1943. His 3,000-strong force disrupted Japanese communications and destroyed Japanese bridges and infrastructure before returning. In March 1944 he launched Operation Thursday with the aim of destroying more Japanese communications with their forces fighting at Imphal. It was shortly after launching Operation Thursday that his plane crashed into a hillside near Imphal, killing all ten people on board.

1976 The death of Field Marshall Bernard Montgomery D.S.O. 'Monty', Viscount Montgomery of Alamein (see 17th November). He joined the Royal Warwickshire Regiment in 1908 and then served in India before being sent to France at the start of the Great War in 1914. In October 1914 he was badly wounded. He returned to the Front in 1916 and in 1918 became Chief of Staff in the 47th Division. He remained in the Army between the wars and in 1938 was sent to Palestine. When war broke out, he was sent again to France with the BEF. He was rescued from the beaches of Dunkirk in 1940. Then in 1942 he was placed in Command of the 8th Army in North Africa. After some initially difficult times, the 8th Army was able to take on Rommel's Afrika Korps and defeat the Germans at El Alamein in 1942 (see 23rd October and 4th November). From there he led the 8th Army during the Sicily landings in 1943 (see 10th July 1943) and then on into Italy in 1943 (see 3rd September). He was later appointed to the Command of the 2nd Army for the D-Day landings and it was Monty who proposed Operation Market Garden in 1944 (see 17th September) and though it ultimately failed, it was a bold and daring action designed to accelerate the end of the war that had become bogged down after the D-Day landings. After the war he served as Commander in Chief of the British Army of Occupation in Germany. For seven years he was Deputy Commander of Supreme Headquarters of NATO.

25th March:
Lady Day and until 1st January 1752, New Years Day
(see 2nd September and 14th September).

1306 Robert the Bruce is crowned King of Scotland at Scone (see 7th June and 11th July). Bishop William de Lamberton officiated and crowned the King, who was dressed in the royal robes that had been hidden from the invading English.

1707 The Scottish Parliament meets for the last time (see 16th January and 1st May). The session was adjourned with the intention of meeting a month later but that event never took place.

1802 The Treaty of Amiens between France and Great Britain is signed, bringing an end to war between the two countries (see 1st February). However, the peace would last only one year (see 18th May). Under the treaty, Britain ceded most of its gains from the conflict, including much of the West Indies and the Cape Colony, retaining only Gibraltar in the Mediterranean, but acquiring Trinidad and Tobago and the Island of Ceylon. The treaty was met with a great deal of derision within Britain due to the amount of concessions agreed by the government.

1807 The Slave Trade Act of 1807 received Royal Assent today, abolishing the slave trade. All trade in slaves was abolished throughout the Empire and the Royal Navy was used to enforce this act on all shipping across the world. Slave ships were viewed by the Navy as Privateers and so open to immediate attack if they refused to surrender (see 28th August).

1913 The death of Field Marshall Garnet Joseph Wolseley, 1st Baron Wolseley (see 4th June), in Mentone, France. A leading Victorian General, he was probably one of the most successful and greatest of British Army Officers. Born in Dublin into a Military family, he was commissioned into the army in 1852. He saw much active service in Burma, being wounded in 1853 before taking part in the Crimean War (1853-1856), where he was wounded again, this time losing his left eye. He went on to serve, leading troops during the Indian Mutiny (1857), in China during the Second Opium War (1860), in Canada on the Red River Expedition (1870) and he led the Ashanti Campaign (1873-1874). He went on to become Governor and High Commissioner of Natal Colony following the Zulu victory at Isandlwana (see 22nd January). He also served as High Commissioner of the new Colony of Cyprus and Commander in Chief in Ireland. He was a noted enthusiastic reformer of the army and wrote a number of military hand books.

26th March:

1797 The death of James Hutton in Edinburgh (see 3rd June). Born in Edinburgh, he is recognised as the father of modern Geology. He is best known for expanding our knowledge and understanding of the age of the Earth and the formation of rocks. He was also a leading influence in the Scottish Enlightenment and a founding member of the Oyster Club in Edinburgh with Adam Smith (see 5th June and 17th July), David Hume (see 26th April and 25th August) and his friend Joseph Black (see 16th April and 6th December).

1902 The death of Cecil John Rhodes in Cape Colony (see 5th July). He was a South African politician, a firm believer in the Empire and founder of the Colony of Rhodesia (see 18th April, 11th November and 11th December). Born in Hertfordshre, he was asthmatic as a child and was taken out of Grammar School and sent to Natal as his parents believed that the climate would be good for his health. Later, he attended Oxford University but retained business interests in South Africa, returning there after he graduated. He created the British South African Company and later the De Beers Diamond Company. Following the Matabele War, the various tribal areas were grouped together and named Rhodesia in his honour. Viewed by many as a racist and Imperialist, Cecil Rhodes was a truly Great Briton and ardent supporter of our Great Empire.

1945 The death of David Lloyd-George in Ty Newydd, Llanystumdwy in Wales (see 17th January). Born in Manchester, his father died when he was young so his mother took him to Wales to be brought up. He became a solicitor and in 1890 was elected to parliament as a Liberal. He caused much resentment for his opposition to the Boer War (1899-1902). In 1908 he became Chancellor of the Exchequer and in 1909 his budget became known as 'the people's budget' as it made provision for social insurance and pensions. He remained Chancellor until 1916 when he replaced Herbert Asquith (see 15th February and 12th September) as Prime Minister. In 1921 he was the motivating force behind the establishment of the Irish Free State and after a scandal over the selling of peerages, he resigned as Prime Minister.

2005 The death of James Callaghan (see 27th March) in Ringmer, East Sussex. He is the only Prime Minister to have held all four offices of State: Chancellor of the Exchequer, Home Secretary, Foreign Secretary and Prime Minister. Born in Portsmouth, he grew up in poverty before joining the Inland Revenue. He served in the Royal Navy in the Second World War and was elected to Parliament in 1945. In 1976 he succeeded Harold Wilson as Prime Minister (see 11th March, 5th April and 24th May) at a time of worsening economic problems in the country. He made cuts in expenditure but delayed the general election until 1979 just as the 1978/79 'winter of discontent' began, dooming his chances of another term as Prime Minister. He resigned as party leader after the election defeat.

2006 Smoking is banned in Scotland in all public buildings and areas, such as work places and pubs (see 2nd April, 30th April and 1st July).

2013 The Department of Transport announces that the American company 'Bristow' is to take over the Helicopter Search and Rescue Service from both the Royal Navy and the RAF from 2015, ending seventy years of involvement from the services.

2015 The remains of Richard III (see 22nd August and 2nd October), killed at the Battle of Bosworth (see 22nd August) and the last King of Britain to die in battle, are buried in Leicester Cathedral (see 4th February).

27th March:

1625 The death of James VI of Scotland and I of England at Theobald's Park in Herts (see 24th March, 19th June, 25th July and 29th July). Born in Edinburgh Castle, his mother was Mary Queen of Scots (see 8th February and 8th December) and his father, Henry Stuart, Lord Darnley (see 10th February). In 1567 his mother was forced to abdicate in his favour. In 1586 he concluded the Treaty of Berwick (see 6th July) with Elizabeth I of England (see 24th March and 7th September) and in 1589 he married Anne of Denmark and they had three children. Upon the death of Elizabeth I (see 24th March) he became King of England. He was famously called the 'wisest fool in Christendom' by Henri IV of France. In 1605, a plot by Catholic rebels to blow him and his parliament up was foiled at the last minute (see 5th November). A deeply religious man, in 1611 he had published the Authorized King James Bible that would remain the standard biblical text for over 250 years. After he gained the throne of England, he only returned to Scotland once, in 1617. He was buried in Westminster Abbey.

1869 The launch of HMS Captain, the Royal Navy's first turreted warship. Built in Merseyside, it was constructed to a pioneering design. Though still a masted ship, she was experimental and her guns were mounted upon the deck and not within the ship's hull (see 7th September).

1871 The first ever Rugby Union International match takes place at Raeburn Place in Edinburgh between Scotland and England. The game resulted in a win for Scotland who scored two tries and a goal to England's one try.

1883 The death of John Brown in Windsor Castle (see 8th December). Born in Crathie, Aberdeenshire, he was a ghillie to the Royal family on the Balmoral Estate and later became the controversial companion to Queen Victoria (see 22nd January and 24th May) following the death of Prince Albert (see 14th December). He is buried in Crathie Kirk in Crathie.

1912 The birth of James Callaghan in Portsmouth (see 26th March).

1924 Oswald Mosley (see 16th November and 3rd December) joins the Independent Labour Party (see 10th March and 20th May).

1963 The Beeching Report (properly known as 'The Reshaping of British Railways') is published. Written by Richard Beeching (see 23rd March and 21st April) it proposed the closure of over 2,000 Railway stations and 5,000 miles of track. Despite a public outcry and protests, the vast majority of the report was implemented.

28th March:

1760 The birth of Thomas Clarkson in Wisbech in Cambridgeshire (see 26th September).

1814 A classic Frigate against Frigate action of the War of 1812. HMS Phoebe (Captained by James Hillyar) and HMS Cherub had blockaded the American USS Essex (Captain David Porter) and its tender, the USS Essex Junior in Valparaiso, a neutral port in the new Republic of Chile. After weeks of waiting, both American ships attempted to escape but were quickly engaged by the British. The Phoebe and Cherub both engaged the Essex whilst the Essex Junior remained apart from the action. Within a short time, the Essex was overwhelmed and struck her colours and both American ships, with the Essex suffering terrible casualties, became prizes for the British.

1819 The birth of Joseph Bazalgette (see 15th March) in Enfield, London.

1854 Britain and the Second French Empire declare war on Russia following an ultimatum for Russia to withdraw from the Danubian Principalities along the Black Sea and the Mediterranean Sea, including Moldavia and Wallachia, then part of the Turkish Ottoman Empire. This was to be the beginning of the Crimean War (see 9th September).

1868 The death of James Brudenell, 7th Earl of Cardigan (see 16th October), in Northamptonshire. As Commander of the Light Brigade, it was he who led its famous charge during the Crimean War in 1854 (see 25th October). Born in Buckinghamshire, he received a varied education and in 1818 entered Parliament and in 1824 he joined the Hussars and steadily rose through purchase of commissions. The Charge of the Light Brigade was perhaps his only real participation in active military service. Following the Battle of Inkerman in 1854 (see 5th November), in which he took minimal part, he returned to Britain and ultimate retirement.

1879 The Battle of Hlobane and a defeat for our forces against the Zulus in Zulu teritory. However, during the battle, following typically gallant action by our forces, six Victoria Crosses were won by both Officers and men. Our forces suffered around 15 Officers and 100 men killed, 8 wounded and around 100 native soldiers killed. The Zulu casualties are not known (see 12th January, 22nd January, 23rd January, 28th August and 1st September).

1942 Operation Chariot, the raid on the dry dock at St. Nazaire in France, is carried out by members of the Royal Navy and Royal Marine Commandos. In one of the greatest Commando raids of all time, an obsolete destroyer, HMS Cambletown, full of timed explosives is sailed up the Loire and rammed into the dry dock art St. Nazaire. The plan was to prevent the docks being used by Germany, and in particular for the SS Tirpitz. At the same time, survivors from Cambletown and a force of Commandos went ashore from supporting motor launches to destroy machinery and equipment on the dock with the intention of escaping on the accompanying motor launches. Most of the shore parties were trapped on land and in the ensuing intense fire, fights continued the attack despite knowing all hope of escape had been lost. When the shore parties had completed their mission, they either surrendered or attempted to make their way to Spain. From this heroic mission, our troops lost 169 killed and 200 taken prisoner from a joint force of 622 men. Later at around noon, as the ship and dock were swarming with enemy personnel, the explosives aboard the ship detonated and destroyed the dock, killing upwards of 400 German officers and men. The dock was put out of action for the rest of the war (see 8th May).

29th March:

1461 The Battle of Townton in Yorkshire during what would later be called the Wars of the Roses. The Yorkist forces of Edward IV (see 9th April and 28th April) defeat those of the Lancastrian Henry VI (see 21st May and 6th December) who flees to Scotland. In perhaps one of the biggest battles ever fought on British soil, the defeat of the Lancastrians turned into a general route as survivors were chased from the battlefield and slaughtered. The result of the battle was significant in that the monarchical dynasty of the country changed forever (see 28th June).

1673 Royal Assent is given to the Test Act thereby excluding all Catholics from Public offices, both Military and Civil. All prospective holders of office were required to swear an oath of supremacy and allegiance to the Crown whilst denying any belief in transubstantiation. By such an oath, all Catholics were denied office (see 14th January).

1799 The birth of Edward Smith-Stanley (see 23rd October) in Lancashire.

1867 The British North America Act receives Royal Assent allowing for the union of three North American Colonies of New Brunswick, Nova Scotia and the Province of Canada (which was divided, upon union, into the Provinces of Ontario and Quebec) into the Dominion of Canada (see 1982 below and 1st July).

1869 The birth of Edwin Landseer Lutyens (see 1st January) in London.

1879 The battle of Khambula in Zululand. Around 20,000 Zulu forces surround the British camp but are defeated by a British force of 2,000 led by Colonel Evelyn Wood and his second in command Colonel Sir Redvers Buller (see 12th January, 2nd January, 23rd January, 2nd April and 4th July).

1912 The death of Captain Robert Falcon Scott CVO, RN, (see 17th January, 17th February and 6th June) and the last two of the five man party who were Lieutenant Henry Robinson (Birdie) Bowers (see 29th July) and Doctor Edward Adrian Wilson (see 23rd July). Scott became a naval cadet when he was thirteen years old and after an extensive naval career was appointed by the Royal Geographical Society to lead their National Antarctic Expedition during 1901–1904. The expedition reached further than anyone previously had managed and Scott and his team, which included Ernest Shackleton (see 5th January), returned heroes. In 1910, he set off from Cardiff in his attempt to reach the South Pole in his now famous race with Amundsen. Facing increasingly harsh conditions, most of the team had to turn back, leaving only Scott, Bowers, Wilson, Evans and Oates to press on. They reached the Pole to find Amundsen had beaten them there and disconsolate, the team headed back on their 1,500 mile journey. Evans, who had been ill for some time following a series of accidents deteriorated and he died first (see 17th February), followed by Oates (see 16th March). Suffering from starvation, frost bite and exposure, the three remaining heroes perished in the icy weather. Their bodies were discovered eight months later and buried beneath their tent.

1982 The Canada Act 1982 receives Royal assent. The act was passed by the Westminster Parliament in response to the Canadian Federal Government's request to 'patriate' the Constitution of Canada, thereby removing the final rights of the Westminster parliament to legislate for Canada. The act, in both English and French, is the only legislation in Britain to be passed in any language other than English since the Middle Ages (see 1867 above and 1st July).

30th March:

1603 The Nine Years' War in Ireland, which began in 1594 and was fought between English forces and Irish rebels, ends with the surrender of the rebels (see 31st March). The rebels were led by two Irish chieftains, Hugh O'Neill and Hugh Roe O'Donnell and they fought throughout Ireland but predominately in Ulster. Finally, though holding out in Tyrone the last of the rebels surrendered on good terms with the English. The long term result was the 'Flight of the Earls' which ultimately allowed for the Plantation of Ulster by Scottish and English Protestant settlers.

1840 The death of George 'Beau' Brummell in Caen, France (see 7th June). An icon of fashion, he was the leading champion of men's fashion in Regency London. In 1794 he was left £30,000 upon the death of his father. A good friend of the Prince Regent (see 26th June and 12th August), he transformed many aspects of men's clothing simply by wearing new designs and items in public. However, always a gambler, he retired in 1818 to France after falling out with the Prince and becoming burdened with debts. In 1835 he was imprisoned for his debts and died penniless in an asylum five years later.

1856 The Treaty of Paris, bringing an end to the Crimean War, 1854-1856, is signed by the alliance of Britain, France, the Kingdom of Sardinia and the Ottoman Empire on one side and Imperial Russia on the other (see 28th March and 9th September). Russia lost some territory, renounced its claim to be the protector of Christians within the Ottoman Empire and the Black Sea became demilitarized (see 20th September, 25th October and 5th November).

1944 RAF Bomber Command suffers its heaviest loss in one raid with the loss of 95 aircraft out of 795 bombers that had taken off on a bombing raid on Nuremberg. The raid began on this night and ended the following day (see 13th March, 14th March, 7th September and 29th December).

1972 Direct Rule from Westminster is introduced immediately in Northern Ireland and at the same time suspending the Parliament of Northern Ireland from Stormont Castle as the Northern Ireland (Temporary Provisions Act) 1972 received Royal Assent. The act allowed direct rule of Northern Ireland from Stormont Castle to be temporary suspended (see 31st July, 12th August, 14th August and 8th December).

1979 Airey Neave, former soldier, Conservative MP and one of the few to escape from Colditz during World War II, is murdered by an IRA car bomb as he leaves the car park of the Houses of Parliament.

31st March:

1603 The Treaty of Mellifont is signed in Ireland between the Lord Deputy of Ireland for the Crown and the rebels, led by the Earl of Tyrone (see 30th March). The treaty formally ended the Tyrone Rebellion or 'Nine Years'

War' that had culminated in the surrender of the rebel leaders the previous day.

1631 The death of John Donne (born in 1572 in London), a Jacobean preacher and a leading influential metaphysical poet. During the 1590s he studied law in London. He publicly renounced his Catholicism in 1610 with the publication of two anti-Catholic pamphlets. He was later appointed the Dean of St. Paul's Cathedral in 1621 by James I, despite his reluctance.

1657 Parliament offers Oliver Cromwell (see 25th April and 3rd September), the self-styled Lord Protector of the Commonwealth, the title of 'King'. He declines the offer (see 16th December).

1713 The main treaty of the Treaty of Utrecht is signed today. It was actually a series of treaties that were mainly agreed and signed during March and April 1713. It ceded many territories in North America and the West Indies to Britain as well as Gibraltar (see 7th February and 7th November) and Minorca (see 13th July).

1809 The birth of Edward Marlborough FitzGerald in Suffolk (see 14th June).

1837 The death of John Constable, a leading scenic painter (see 11th June) who is remembered mainly for his paintings of landscapes, especially of Dedham Vale in Suffolk which was the area around his family home. In 1816 he married Maria Bicknell, who suffered from tuberculosis and because of this they moved to London and frequently visited Brighton for her health. He made hundreds of sketches and oil paintings, with much emphasis on skies and the forces of nature. Popular on the continent, he did not achieve wide popularity in Britain until after his death.

1855 The death of Charlotte Bronte (see 21st April) at Haworth in Yorkshire from tuberculosis. Born in Yorkshire, she was one of five sisters, two of whom died in infancy, and a brother. She is best known for her world famous novel 'Jane Eyre' (written under her pen name Currer Bell), as well as 'Agness Grey' (both published in 1847). In 1854 she married a curate, Arthur Nicholls, but died the following year whilst pregnant.

1890 The birth of William Lawrence Bragg in Adelaide, Australia (see 1st July).

1949 The Dominion of Newfoundland joins the Canadian Confederation after a national referendum (see 1st July, 5th August and 26th September) resulting in a 52% vote in favour of confederation.

2010 The first trial without a jury for over 350 years concludes at the Old Bailey in London with a guilty verdict.

APRIL

1st April:

1867 Singapore becomes a Crown Colony as part of the Straits Settlements and is governed from Colonial House in London (see 31st August).

1918 The Royal Air Force (R.A.F.) is founded. It is the amalgamation of the Royal Flying Corps (see 13th April) and the Royal Naval Air Service (see 1st July) that both saw active service in the Great War.

1937 Aden becomes a Crown Colony after having been governed as the Aden Settlement from British India (see 16th January).

1947 The Electricity Industry is nationalised under the Labour Government (see 1st January and 26th July).

1973 Value Added Tax (VAT) is introduced, replacing Purchase Tax as a result of the United Kingdom joining the European Economic Community (see 1st January).

1974 The Local Government Act (1972) for England and Wales comes into force. The Act abolished the existing local government structure of administrative counties.

1999 The minimum wage is introduced in Great Britain by the Labour government (see 1st May) being set at £3.60 an hour for an adult.

2nd April:

1502 The death of Arthur Tudor (see 20th September), Prince of Wales and eldest son of Henry VII (see 28th January and 21st April) and Elizabeth of York and the elder brother of the future Henry VIII (see 28th January and 28th June). Born in Winchester, he was married to Catherine of Aragon in 1501 at St. Paul's Cathedral after much negotiation between the respective parents. Unfortunately, less than a year later he contracted some sort of disease, described as a 'sweating disease' in the March and died shortly afterwards. He was buried in Worcester Cathedral.

1801 The Battle of Copenhagen. The British Fleet, under Admiral Sir Hyde Parker but led into the main battle by Admiral Horatio Nelson (see 29th September and 21st October), defeats the Danish Fleet, who, despite being neutral were supporters of the French. This was Nelson's 'hardest fought battle' and it was here that he placed his telescope against his blind eye and famously said 'I really do not see the signal'. Less than 300 of our sailors were killed. However, over 2,200 of the Danish fleet were killed or wounded and 3 ships were destroyed and 12 captured in a decisive and glorious victory for our forces.

1807 The birth of Charles Edward Trevelyan in Taunton (see 19th June).

1849 The province of Punjab in northern India is brought under British rule following the Battle of Goojurat (see 21st February) and is initially governed by the East India Company (see 31st December).

1865 The death of Richard Cobden (see 3rd June). A Radical and Whig MP for Stockport then Rochdale, he was the leading figure in the defence of Free Trade and was instrumental in the repeal of the Corn Laws by helping to form the Anti-Corn Law League. He was also in favour of Parliamentary reform and state education. He died from a severe attack of Bronchitis.

1879 The Battle of Gingindlovu in Zululand. A Zulu army, trying to encircle the British laager and camp, under the command of Lieutenant General Lord Chelmsford, is defeated and eventually withdrawn. Following their retreat, Lord Chelmsford unleashed his mounted troops, killing many more natives. Throughout the short engagement, the foot soldiers had maintained their discipline. We lost around a dozen killed and about 40 wounded and the Zulus lost around 1,000 warriors (see 12th January, 22nd January, 23rd January, 4th July, 28th August and 1st September).

1982 An Argentinean invasion force land on the Falkland Islands but are met with stiff and gallant resistance from a detachment of Royal Marines before the Marines are ordered to surrender by the Governor of the Islands, Sir Rex Hunt. He ordered the surrender when he realised the small force was totally outnumbered and faced certain destruction along with many of the Islanders if they persisted with their heroic defence. Two of the invaders were killed and several others badly injured during the defence of British sovereign territory (see 22nd January, 25th April, 2nd May, 10th June and 14th June).

2007 Smoking is banned in Wales in all public buildings and areas, such as work places and pubs (see 26th March, 30th April and 1st July).

3rd April:

1043 (Easter Sunday) Edward the Confessor is crowned at Winchester Cathedral (see 5th January).

1721 Robert Walpole becomes the first Prime Minister (see 18th March and 26th August). The term 'Prime Minister' was at first a derogatory one, not officially recognised as a title until 1905.

1792 The death of Admiral George Pocock (see 6th March) in London. An experienced naval officer, he joined the Royal Navy in 1718 and served during the Seven Years' War, 1756-1764, fighting the French around the coast of India. He is best remembered for his command of the siege of Havana in 1762 resulting in the city's capitulation (see 13th August). Though most of his engagements with the French were indecisive, he was an experienced and energetic Commander. He is remembered in Westminster Abbey.

1811 The Battle of Sabugal in Portugal during the Peninsular War. A joint Anglo-Portuguese force, commanded by Arthur Wellesley (see 1st May and 14th September), repeatedly attacked a stronger French force under Marshall Andre Massena. Despite initially standing firm, the French were dislodged from their positions and our troops pursued the retreating French forces once they began to retreat. It was a resounding victory for our troops.

1862 The death of Sir John Clark Ross (see 15th April) in Aylesbury. He joined the Royal Navy in 1812 and after an extensive career he became famous for his Arctic voyages of exploration and navigation and his detailed observations from the voyages between 1839 and 1843, during which he made many notable discoveries. In 1848 he went on one of the expeditions attempting to locate Sir John Franklin (see 16th April and 11th June) who had disappeared the previous year.

1933 The first flight over Mount Everest. The first aeroplane was a specially adapted Westland PV-3 piloted by Douglas Hamilton, Lord Clydesdale and later 14th Duke of Hamilton and closely behind him flew David MacIntyre in a Westland-Wallace.

4th April:

1366 The birth of Henry IV in Bolingbroke Castle (see 20th March and 13th October).

1581 Sir Frances Drake is knighted by Elizabeth I aboard his ship, the Golden Hind, at Deptford (see 27th January), for his heroic and very profitable circumnavigation of the world, the first Englishman to do so.

1660 The proclamation of the Treaty of Breda by Charles II (see 6th February and 29th May). The treaty sets out Charles II's terms in accepting the crown and was issued in response to a secret letter received from General George Monck (see 3rd January and 6th December), who was effectively in control of England. In it he promised a general pardon for crimes committed against the Crown during the Civil War and the interregnum, that current owners of property purchased during that period could retain such property and that there would be religious tolerance. It is this date that is generally understood to be the end interregnum of the Commonwealth of England (see 19th May and 29th May).

1887 The first Colonial Conference opens in London (see 19th October). In attendance throughout the conference were representatives from the United Kingdom, Canada, Cape of Good Hope, Natal, Newfoundland, New South Wales, New Zealand, Queensland, South Australia, Tasmania, Victoria and Western Australia. There were representatives present from numerous other colonies and territories but only as observers. The Imperial Federation League (see 18th November) had proposed the conference with the aim of promoting Imperial Federation across the Empire and in particular between the Dominions, in a similar way to Canadian Confederation in 1867 (see 1st July). An Imperial Parliament in London was also proposed with responsibility for Foreign Affairs and defence with the local parliaments handling home affairs fostering ever closer ties between the colonies of the Empire. One suggestion approved was the laying of a telegraph cable between Australia and Vancouver in the United Colonies of Vancouver Island and British Columbia to speed up communications across the Empire (see 11th December).

1944 The beginning of the battle and siege of Kohima in north-eastern India, part of the dual battle of Kohima-Imphal, during the Burma Campaign to drive the Japanese invaders from the occupied territory (see 8th March). The Japanese had besieged the city and had blocked the Kohima-Imphal

Road. If Kohima had been taken, then the city of Imphal would have been completely cut off (see 22nd June).

1949 Great Britain and eleven other nations sign the North Atlantic Treaty in Washington DC in the USA. These countries formed the core of the North Atlantic Treaty Organisation or NATO as a result of the treaty. The agreement recognised that an attack against any one of the signature countries would constitute an act of aggression against them all.

5th April:

1654 The Treaty of Westminster is signed in London bringing an end to the First Anglo-Dutch War of 1652-1654 (see 9th February, 19th May, 2nd June and 31st July). The Lord Protector, Oliver Cromwell (see 25th April and 3rd September) was the chief negotiator and the treaty was relatively lenient towards the Dutch Republic of the United Netherlands.

1795 The birth of Henry Havelock in Bishopwearmouth in modern Sunderland (see 24th November).

1827 The birth of Joseph Lister (see 10th February) in Upton in Essex.

1908 Herbert Henry Asquith becomes Prime Minister (see 15th February, 12th September and 5th December), succeeding Henry Campbell-Bannerman (see 22nd April and 7th September).

1923 The death of George Edward Stanhope Molyneux Herbert, 5th Earl Carnarvon (see 26th June) in Cairo, Egypt. Born at Highclere Castle in Hampshire, he is best known as the financial backer of Howard Carter's successful search for Tutankhamen's tomb, which he and Carter opened together (see 26th November) in 1922. He suffered a mosquito bite aggravated by a razor cut which became infected and which was the cause of his death.

1955 Prime Minister Sir Winston Spencer Churchill resigns from office, thus ending the political career of our Greatest Prime Minister (see 24th January, 10th May, 26th October and 30th November).

1976 Prime Minister Harold Wilson resigns from office (see 11th March, 16th March and 24th May) to be succeeded by James Callaghan (see 26th March and 27th March).

1984 The death of Air Marshall Sir Arthur 'Bomber' Harris, mastermind of Bomber Command and war hero (see 13th April) who was later unjustly vilified by some and has never received the proper recognition and honour that he truly deserved. He lived in Rhodesia from the age of seventeen and served in the Great War. In 1915 he joined the Royal Flying Corps and later became Squadron leader in the Royal Air Force. In 1942 he became leader of Bomber Command and led the policy of Area Bombing of German Cities. After the war he was shamefully criticised for his efficient execution of the bombing policies of the government by ungrateful members of the public and members of Parliament. Partly as a result of this, he moved to South Africa.

6th April:

1199 The death of Richard the Lion Heart or 'Coeur De Lion' (see 8th September). While he was besieging the castle of Chalus in France, he was fatally wounded when he was struck by a cross-bow bolt fired from the castle walls. Richard is believed to have been about 6'4" tall and had red hair. He was devoutly religious and is remembered for leading the Crusades in the Holy Land.

1320 The Declaration of Arbroath is proclaimed. It is believed to have been drawn up at Arbroath Abbey and was a declaration of Scottish Independence. It was signed by 38 Scottish Lords and was actually in the form of a letter to Pope John XXII. It was sealed by fifty-one Scottish Nobles and Magnates (see 4th December).

1590 The death of Francis Walsingham, Spymaster and Principle Secretary to the Court of Queen Elizabeth I (see 24th March and 7th September). He is probably the first practitioner of the art of modern espionage and infiltrated Spanish intelligence prior to the Armada of 1588. Born in London around 1530 he appears to have studied law abroad before returning to England after the accession of Elizabeth I and was elected to Parliament in 1559. He had a deep-seated and almost zealous hatred and distrust of Catholics and Catholic countries. He began working for Lord Burghley in 1568 and he began to monitor foreigners in England and particular London as well as to discover and counteract plots against Elizabeth I. In 1573 he was made Principle Secretary and was knighted in 1577. He had a major part in the exposing of plots to free Mary Queen of Scots and her subsequent execution (see 8th February and 8th December). He was without doubt the most loyal servant to both his Queen and England.

1812 The culmination to the Battle of Badajoz during the Peninsular War (see 16th March). The Spanish City was besieged and stormed by the Anglo-Portuguese Armies under the command of General Lord Wellington (see 1st May and 14th September). Over 3,000 Allied soldiers were killed in the last few hours of the siege as they repeatedly stormed the walls of the town. The resultant slaughter, as British soldiers went on a 72-hour drunken rampage, is one of the darkest hours of the history of the British Army and is a rare example of a lack of discipline within our forces.

7th April:

1739 Richard 'Dick' Turpin, infamous Highwayman, poacher and murderer is hanged in York for the murder of an Inn Keeper. Born in Essex in 1705, he was a member of the Gregory Gang and became a highwayman upon the gang's breakup. Having killed the Innkeeper, he fled to York where he stole horses and attempted to sell them. It was after being detained for these offences that his identity was discovered and he was tried and convicted for the murder. At his execution, he hired five mourners and is reputed to have shown no fear or anxiety at the ordeal awaiting him. He is alleged to be buried in St. George's Church Yard in York.

1770 The birth of William Wordsworth in Cockermouth (see 23rd April).

1786 The birth of Thomas Buxton in Essex (see 19th February).

1836 The death of William Godwin (see 3rd March) in London. The husband of Mary Wollstonecraft (see 27th April and 10th September), he was a journalist and novelist and he is often regarded as one of the earliest proponents of political anarchism. In 1793 he published 'Enquiry into Political Justice' where he championed the idea that as long as people lived and acted rationally then it was possible to live without laws and structured society.

1853 Queen Victoria (see 22nd January and 24th May) uses chloroform during the birth of her son Prince Leopold. The chloroform was administered by Doctor John Snow (see 15th March and 16th June) and its use by Queen Victoria was the catalyst for its wide usage from then on.

1955 Sir Anthony Eden (see 14th January, 5th April and 12th June) becomes Prime Minister, following the resignation due to ill health of Winston Churchill (see 24th January and 30th November). He immediately called a General Election and increased his party's number of seats from seventeen to sixty as a result.

8th April:

1857 The execution of the disgraced sepoy Mangal Pandey by hanging. A sepoy in the 34th Bengal Native Infantry of the East India Company, he had disobeyed orders and mutinied, attempting to kill a number of officers (see 10th May) before being detained. He was subsequently tried and convicted for his disgraceful actions. His actions may well have been the catalyst for the beginning of the Indian Mutiny (see 24th January).

1898 The battle of Atbara in Sudan. This short-lived battle between the Anglo-Egyptian force led by Major-General Horatio Herbert Kitchener and the Sudanese Dervish rebels effectively brought an end to the Mahdist Revolt 1881-1899. The battle began early in the morning with an artillery bombardment of the Mahdist camp. This was followed by an advance into the rebel camp by the British and Egyptian troops involving close quarter hand to hand fighting. The battle lasted around 45 minutes before the rebels withdrew. Around 25 of our troops were killed and around 100 injured with the Sudanese losing about 3,000 killed and 2,000 captured.

1902 The birth of Andrew Irvine in Birkenhead, Cheshire (see 8th June).

1904 The Entente Cordial is signed by Britain and the French Third Republic in London. The Treaty in effect ended centuries of warfare and a certain amount of animosity between the two countries. The Treaty was a declaration regarding many colonial issues, with both Empires formally recognising and respecting each others spheres of influence around the world (see 18th September).

1919 The birth of Ian Douglas Smith in Selukwe in Southern Rhodesia (see 20th November), the son of British settlers.

2013 The death of Margaret Thatcher, the greatest peace time Prime Minister and the saviour of this country (see 13th October). Elected in 1979, she was the first female leader of a main political party, the first female Prime Minister and the longest serving twentieth century Prime Minister. Born Margaret Roberts in Grantham, Lincolnshire, she was the daughter of a grocer and attended the local schools before winning a place at Oxford. In 1951 she married Dennis Thatcher and in 1959 was elected to Parliament as the MP for Finchley (see 11th February, 4th May and 22nd November). Following defeat in the general election in 1974, she challenged Ted Heath to the leadership and won. A proponent of privatisation, she defended the Falkland Islands following Argentinean aggression in 1982. In 1984 in Brighton she narrowly escaped death or injury when the IRA bombed the hotel she was in. In 1987 she won a third term as Prime Minister but unfortunately she was betrayed by her own party in a leadership challenge which she lost.

9th April:

1413 Henry V is crowned at Westminster Abbey (see 9th August and 31st August).

1483 The death of Edward IV in the Palace of Westminster (see 28th April and 28th June).

1483 The future King Richard III is declared Lord Protector (see 22nd August and 2nd October) of Edward IV's son, Edward V who was only 12 and also Richard's nephew.

1626 The death of Sir Francis Bacon (see 22nd January) in Highgate, London. A philosopher, statesman, author, essayist and a pioneer of scientific thought. In 1620 he published 'Novum Organum', treaties on how to acquire natural knowledge and challenging the accepted method of scientific thought, stating that knowledge came from evidence. He was appointed Lord Chancellor in 1618 and created Viscount St. Albans in 1621.However, he was charged by Parliament with taking bribes which he admitted. He was fined, imprisoned and banished from court. Despite being pardoned by the King, his public and political life was over. He is one of the greatest pioneers of scientific thought and knowledge, contributing hugely to our country's cultural heritage.

1649 The birth of James Scott, the future Duke of Monmouth, in Rotterdam in the Republic of the United Netherlands (see 11th June, 6th July and 15th July). He was the illegitimate son of Charles II and Lucy Walters and was raised by Lord Crofts, taking his wife's surname Scott on their marriage.

1747 The execution of Simon Fraser, 11th Lord Lovatt, on Tower Hill in London. Born around 1670, he was not the direct heir to the Clan Chieftainship at his birth. He was educated in Aberdeen and studied law in Edinburgh. A ruthless individual, although allegedly supporting William (see

8th March and 4th November) and Mary (see 30th April and 28th December), he was an ardent Jacobite and supported James VII (James II of England see 5th September and 14th October) and his heirs. However, this did not prevent his back and forth contacts with both sides in an act of possible self-preservation. He went into exile in France but in the Jacobite rising of 1745 (see 19th August) he came out for Charles Edward Stewart ('Bonnie Prince Charlie' see 31st January and 31st December) and the Jacobite cause. Following the battle of Culloden in 1746 (see 16th April), he was captured and taken to London where he was tried by his peers and convicted. He was the last man to be publicly beheaded in Britain.

1806 The birth of Isambard Kingdom Brunel in Portsmouth (see 15th September).

1830 The birth of Edward James Muggeridge (later Eadweard James Muybridge) in Kingston upon Thames (see 8th May).

1917 The Battle of Vimy Ridge, part of the Battle of Arras begins as troops of the Canadian Corps (see 12th April and 26th July) attacked the German line following heavy bombardment and the detonation of mines under the enemy strong points.

10th April:

1512 The birth of James Stuart, the future James V of Scotland, in Linlithgow Palace (see 24th November and 14th December). He was the son of James IV (see 17th March and 9th September) and Margaret Tudor, the sister of Henry VIII (see 28th January and 28th June) of England.

1606 The Virginia Company of London and the Plymouth Company, both joint stock companies, are founded by Royal Charter from James VI (James I of England see 27th March and 19th June) with the purpose of establishing permanent settlements and colonies in the New World.

1778 The birth of William Hazlitt (see 18th September) in Maidstone, Kent.

1829 The birth of William Booth (see 20th August) in Sneinton, Nottingham.

1868 (Good Friday) A force of around 13,000 soldiers from the Bombay Army, led by General Sir Robert Napier attack and decisively beat an army of around 9,000 Abyssinian soldiers outside the city of Magdala, in the only real battle of the Abyssinian Expedition. The Expedition repelled a massive attack by the Abyssinians in a brief two-hour battle that became a rout. The Abyssinian Emperor had imprisoned the British Consul and numerous other Britons as hostages the year before over his demand for weapons and support from Britain (see 11th April). General Napier and his force were despatched by the newly-elected government to release the captives and prevent further aggressive action by the Abyssinians.

1912 The RMS Titanic sets off on her maiden voyage from Southampton to New York (see 15th April).

11th April:

1689 William III 'of Orange' (see 8th March and 4th November) and his wife Mary II (see 30th April and 28th December) are jointly crowned in Westminster Abbey.

1770 The birth of George Canning, friend of William Pitt the Younger and later Prime Minister. He fought a dual with Lord Castlereagh on the 21st September 1809 (see 12th April and 8th August).

1805 The Saint Petersburg Pact is signed between Great Britain and the Russian Empire, forming an alliance against Napoleonic France. Austria and Sweden joined the pact later in the year (see 9th June).

1809 The battle of the Basque Roads begins. Captain Thomas Cochrane (see 31st October and 14th December) leads a Royal Naval fire ship attack against the French fleet anchored in the Basque Roads in the Bay of Biscay in France. It was a very daring and successful attack, causing all but two of the French ships to be run ashore. However, Admiral James Gambier failed to press home the advantage and totally destroy the French fleet. Though a great success, the battle caused controversy for years afterward and ended the career of Thomas Cochrane in the Royal Navy.

1810 The birth of Henry Crewicke Rawlinson in Oxfordshire (see 5th March).

1868 Forces from the Bombay Army, led by General Sir Robert Napier, and fresh from their victory against an Abyssinia army the previous day (see 10th April) storm the Abyssinian capital city, Magdala, and succeed in capturing it in the face of weak resistance.

1906 The birth of James Power Carne (see 19th April, 22nd April and 25th April) in Falmouth.

2001 The death of Sir Harry Donald Secombe (see 28th May and 8th September) in Shamley Green, Surrey. An all round entertainer with a noted tenors singing voice, he was one of the legendary Goons.

12th April:

1606 A Royal Proclamation from James VI (James I of England see 27th March and 19th June) describes the Union Flag. This is the first known reference to a British flag of the Union and the first time the flag we know today was raised (see 1st January).

1665 The first burial of a Great Plague victim, Margaret Porteous.

1782 The Battle of the Saintes, a group of islands between Guadeloupe and Dominica. Fought during the American colonial rebellion (see 3rd September), the Royal Navy fleet of 36 ships, led by Admiral Sir George Rodney (see 24th May), beat the French Fleet of 33 ships under the Comte de Grasse. Our losses were 243 dead and 816 wounded but no ships were lost.

The French lost 2,000 dead and wounded and lost 5 ships, one of which blew up later.

1827 George Canning becomes Conservative Prime Minister (see 11th April and 8th August) following the resignation of Lord Liverpool due to ill health. Following his appointment by the King, the Duke of Wellington (see 1st May and 14th September) and Robert Peel (see 5th February and 2nd July) and a number of leading Tories resigned from his administration.

1917 The Battle of Vimy Ridge, part of the Battle of Arras concludes as troops of the Canadian Corps (see 9th April and 26th July) achieve their objective and take control of the ridge. The Canadians suffered over 3,500 killed and 7,000 wounded. Following the battle, four Victoria Crosses were awarded to participants for their valiant and brave actions on behalf of their country and the Empire.

1927 The Royal and Parliamentary Titles Act 1927 gains Royal Assent. The main part of the act authorised the alteration of the monarch's style and titles and the name of the British parliament from 'The United Kingdom of Great Britain and Ireland' to 'The United Kingdom of Great Britain and Northern Ireland' (see 1st January, 18th April, 25th May, 2nd July, 1st August, 6th December and 8th December).

13th April:

1423 The Treaty of Amiens is signed between John of Lancaster, the 1st Duke of Bedford, Philip the Good, the Duke of Burgundy and Arthur II, the Earl of Richmond and the Duke of Brittany. The treaty was formed following the deaths of Henry V of England (see 31st August) and Charles VI of France after their signing the Treaty of Troyes in 1420 (see 21st May) which agreed that Henry V and his heirs were the true Kings of France, following the Death of Charles VI. The Treaty of Amiens confirmed the Treaty of Troyes and recognised Henry VI (see 21st May and 6th December) as the rightful King of both England and France (see 16th December).

1748 The birth of Joseph Bramah (see 9th December).

1771 The birth of Richard Trevithic in Cornwall (see 21st February and 22nd April).

1829 The Catholic Emancipation Act receives Royal Assent (see 24th March). The long awaited act provided a new Oath of Allegiance so that Catholics could enter Parliament. It also meant that Catholics could hold government and Judicial positions previously denied them. The campaign for Catholic Emancipation was driven by Daniel O'Connell (see 15th May and 6th August) and was supported by prominent figures such as the Prime Minister, the Duke of Wellington (see 1st May and 14th September) as well as the two political parties.

1880 The death of Robert Fortune (see 16th September) in London. Born in Scotland in 1812 he was a botanist and traveller. He worked for the Horticultural Society of London and after the Treaty of Nanking in 1842 (see

29th August) he was sent to China to collect tea plants on behalf of the East India Company (see 31st December), a task he had to conduct in secrecy. He is most well-known for becoming the first person (in 1848) to introduce the tea plant from China to India. In his travels he made numerous trips inland from the treaty ports in China and, at great risk to himself, he smuggled plants out of the country and it was due to his tireless work that the Indian tea trade became so successful.

1892 The birth of Sir Arthur 'Bomber' Harris (see 5th April) in Cheltenham.

1892 The birth of Robert Alexander Watson-Watt (see 5th December) in Brechin, Angus.

1907 The launch of HMS Invincible, the world's first battle cruiser. The battle cruiser was a mixture of the armoured cruiser and the battleship, combining speed with lighter armament. She had a crew of up to one thousand in war time. She took part in the battle of Heligoland Bight in 1914 (see 28th August) and the battle of the Falklands in 1914 (see 8th December). At the battle of Jutland in 1916 where she was the flagship of the 3rd Battlecruiser Squadron, she was destroyed after being hit on her Q turret by a salvo from SMS Derfflinger with the loss of all but six of her crew (see 31st May). The other two ships in the Invincible class of battle cruisers and the sister ships of HMS Invincible were HMS Inflexible and HMS Indomitable.

1912 The creation of the Royal Flying Corps (see 1st April) after George V (see 20th January and 3rd June) signs a Royal Warrant creating the Corps which was established a month later (see 13th May). It was originally led by Brigadier Sir David Henderson.

1919 The so-called Amritsar 'Massacre' in Amritsar, Punjab, India. Around 90 British Indian Army troops, led by Brigadier-General Reginald Dyer (see 23rd July and 9th October) open fire for up to ten minutes on a large crowd of several thousand Hindu and Sikh demonstrators who had refused to disperse. Some 379 people were killed and over 1000 were wounded. The incident followed weeks of violence, three days of rioting and attacks on and the murders of Europeans and the destruction of their property in which telegraph cables were cut and government buildings destroyed. Fearing a violent insurrection by differing organisations, the government placed the Punjab under martial law in an effort to restore order. The restrictions included restrictions on freedom of assembly, which the gathering at Amritsar blatantly flouted.

1937 HMS Ark Royal is launched in Birkenhead, Liverpool. The first Aircraft Carrier of her kind, with her hangars (of which she had two) and the flight deck as integral elements to the ship and not constructed as add-ons (see 13th November, 14th November and 2nd December) as with all previous aircraft carriers.

14th April:

1471 The Battle of Barnet during what would later be called the War of the Roses (1455-1485). Though it did not end the war, it was one of the most important battles of the conflict. It was fought between forces loyal to Edward IV (see 9th April and 28th April) and Richard Neville, Earl of Warwick. It was a decisive Yorkist victory for Edward IV, restoring him to the throne as he defeated and killed Warwick.

1678 The birth of Abraham Darby in Staffordshire (see 8Th March).

1827 The birth of Augustus Henry Lane Fox at Hope Hall in Yorkshire (see 4th May).

1912 The RMS Titanic, on her maiden voyage hits an iceberg in the North Atlantic at 11.40pm (see 10th April, 15th April and 31st May). Despite being seen by the lookouts and veering to port side, the Titanic struck the iceberg and opened a gash in the starboard side, almost 300 feet long.

1983 The launch of HMS Edinburgh built by Cammell Laird on Merseyside. A Type 42 Destroyer, she is the last operational ship of her type. Although not launched until after the Falklands War, the Type 42s were the mainstay of the War with two of the class, HMS Sheffield (see 4th May) and HMS Coventry (see 25th May) being sunk during the conflict (see 2nd April, 2nd May and 14th June) in 1982.

15th April:

1599 Robert Devereux, 2nd Earl of Essex and Lord Lieutenant of Ireland, lands in Ireland in an attempt to put down the rebellion of the Earl of Tyrone, commonly referred to as the Nine Years War (1594-1603).

1755 Samuel Johnson's 'A Dictionary of the English Language' is finally published (see 7th September and 13th December) after taking nine years to write.

1793 due to a serious shortage of gold coin, the Bank of England issues its first five pound notes, a black on white design that would remain until the middle of the twentieth century.

1800 The birth of John Clark Ross (see 3rd April) in London.

1912 The RMS Titanic, the largest ship of her time sinks in the early hours of the morning with the loss of over 1,500 passengers and crew after striking an iceberg the previous evening. Only around 700 passengers and some crew survive. The exact figures for survivors and casualties are still unknown (see 10th April, 14th April and 31st May).

1921 Black Friday when the leaders of the rail and transport unions controversially announced that they had decided against calling for strike action by their members in support of the miners.

1942 The Colony of Malta (see 21st September) is collectively awarded the George Cross by George VI (see 6th February and 14th December) for their heroic resistance against relentless German and Italian attacks during the Second World War, especially the intense bombing inflicted by the Luftwaffe.

1945 The Bergen-Belsen concentration camp, situated 45 miles south of Hamburg, is the first camp to be liberated by British forces. Over 38,000 prisoners are freed. However, due to the barbaric and inhuman treatment meted out by the Germans, 13,000 died from disease soon after liberation. Typhus had become rampant within the camp and to prevent its spread outside of the camp environment, the camp was burnt to the ground once the last survivors had been relocated.

16th April:

1660 The birth of Hans Sloane (see 11th January and 15th January) in County Down, Ireland.

1728 The birth of Joseph Black in Bordeaux, France (see 6th December).

1746 The Battle of Culloden on Drummossie Muir. Hanoverian government forces, led by the Duke of Cumberland, inflict a crushing defeat on the Jacobite forces under Bonnie Prince Charlie, thus forever ending the hopes of a Stuart restoration to the throne of Great Britain (see 19th August and 28th September). The Highland army numbered around 7,000 at the time of the battle, though it had been bigger earlier in the campaign. It faced a government force of around 8,000 under the Duke of Cumberland. This was the last battle fought on Scottish soil as well as on the British mainland. The Highland army was tired and cold from foraging late into the night whereas the government troops were rested, well-fed and well-drilled.

1786 The birth of John Franklin (see 11th June) in Spilsbury in Lincolnshire.

1797 The Channel Fleet at Spithead mutinied by refusing orders to put to sea (see 15th May). The crews of sixteen ships from the Channel Fleet refused to obey orders as part of a protest against their living conditions and the poor rate of pay (see 12th May and 30th June).

1865 The birth of Henry 'Harry' George Chauvel (see 4th March) Tabulam, New South Wales, Dominion of Australia.

1918 The birth of Terence Alan Patrick Sean 'Spike' Milligan (see 27th February and 28th May) in Ahmednagar, British India.

17th April:

1790 The death of Benjamin Franklin (see 6th January). A writer, scientist, inventor and statesman, he was one of the traitorous colonial officials that instigated the rebellion in the British American colonies. He was born in Boston, the son of an English immigrant. After a brief education, he eventually became a printer, working for his brother and then himself. He travelled to London after which he settled in Pennsylvania. In 1748 he retired from printing to devote more time to his interest in science and inventing. Following many contributions to Pennsylvanian civic society, he lived mostly in London from 1757 to 1774 as the Colonial Representative of several

Colonies. When the Colonial rebellion broke out (see 19th April), as he was in Britain, he made attempts to reconcile the Government to the rebel's demands but failed. He then returned to America and treasonably supported the rebellion. He contributed to the drafting of the 'Declaration of Independence' and as the rebel Ambassador to France, signed the Treaty of Paris (see 3rd September) ending the rebellion.

1882 The death of George Jennings (see 10th November) in London. An engineer and plumber, he is known as the inventor of the first public flush toilets which first appeared at the Great exhibition of 1851. He charged one penny a time for their use, giving rise to the saying 'to spend a penny'.

1951 The Peak District National Park becomes our country's first National Park. Most of the park is situated in Derbyshire but contains elements of the counties of Cheshire, Staffordshire and Yorkshire.

1956 Premium Bonds are introduced by the Conservative Chancellor of the Exchequer, Harold Macmillan (see 10th February and 29th December).

1984 WPC Yvonne Fletcher is shot dead outside the Libyan People's Bureau in London by gunmen from within the Libyan Embassy.

2013 The Ceremonial Funeral of Margaret Thatcher (see 8th April and 13th October). At 10am her coffin, draped in the flag of the union, was taken from the crypt Chapel of St. Mary Undercroft at the Palace of Westminster to the RAF Chapel at St Clement Danes on the Strand. From there it was taken by military procession to St Paul's Cathedral. It was carried on a gun carriage and with a guard of honour made up from the Welsh Guards, Royal Air Force, Scots Guards, Royal Navy, Royal Marines, Royal Gurkha Rifles, Parachute Regiment and the Royal Artillery. Representatives from 170 foreign countries, veterans of the Falklands war and the three surviving former Prime Ministers and the current Prime Minister David Cameron were present.

18th April:

1674 The birth of Charles Townshend (see 21st June) at Raynham Hall in Norfolk, the eldest son of Horatio Townshend, 3rd Baronet Townshend.

1689 The death of George Jeffreys (see 15th May), 1st Baron Jeffrey's in 'protective custody' in the Tower of London. He was better known as 'Judge Jeffreys' or the "Hanging Judge". He rose to prominence as the Lord Chancellor under James VII (James II of England see 16th September and 14th October).

1802 The death of Erasmus Darwin (see 12th December) in Beardsley, Derby. A physician, he was a philosopher and thinker and a leading intellectual of his time as well as a founding member of the Lunar Society and leading figure in the Midlands Enlightenment. A Grandfather of Charles Darwin (see 12th February and 19th April), his writings on life and zoology foreshadow much of his grandson's work on evolution.

1949 The Ireland Act 1949 comes into force, allowing the Republic of Ireland to come into being and at the same time it leaves the Commonwealth. However, the six Northern Counties of Antrim, Armagh, Down, Fermanagh, Londonderry and Tyrone remain a loyal part of the United Kingdom as Ulster or Northern Ireland (see 18th June, 6th December and 8th December).

1980 Following its return to British rule the previous year, the Colony of Southern Rhodesia is granted its independence and is called Zimbabwe (see 11th November and 11th December).

19th April:

1587 Sir Francis Drake (see 27th January) raids the Spanish Port of Cadiz, sinking at least 30 of the Spanish fighting fleet which were being assembled for an attack on England. Initially in the port, the Spanish fleet sailed out to meet Drake's fleet but were repulsed due to the English superiority. Following the mostly ineffectual shelling of our fleet from the shore, Drake's forces moved in and wreaked havoc and devastation on the port and on the Spanish vessels within.

1757 The birth of Edward Pellew in Devon (see 23rd January).

1775 The Battle of Concord and Lexington in the Colony of Massachusetts. Our troops in Boston attempted to seize ammunition stored in Concord. On route they entered Lexington where they were fired upon from the village green. Returning fire, they killed eighteen of the rebels. Moving on to Concord they came across more rebels and were attacked whilst in the village and on the subsequent return to Boston. Our forces lost 19 officers and 250 men out of a force of 18,000 men and the rebels lost about 90 men. This was where the first shots were fired in the American Revolution in the colonies of British North America. Our Expeditionary force attempted to seize weapons that had been stored by would-be rebels. As the fighting intensified, our forces found it necessary to make a tactical withdrawal to Boston (see 17th March, 4th July and 3rd September).

1824 The death of George Lord Byron of Marsh Fever in Missolonghi, Greece (see 22nd January). He was one of the leading romantic poets of his time and is remembered for works such as 'Childe Harold's Pilgrimage' and 'Don Juan'. An ardent supporter of Greek independence, travelled to Greece in 1823 where he helped to lead and finance part of the Greek army in their battle for independence against the Ottoman Empire.

1839 Britain signs the Treaty of London along with Austria, France, Prussia and Russia on the one side and the Kingdom of the Netherlands on the other. The treaty recognized Belgium's independence and guaranteed her perpetual neutrality. It was this treaty that bound Britain to the defence of Belgium that brought our country into the First World War in 1914 (see 4th August).

1850 The Clayton-Bulwer Treaty is signed between by Sir Henry Lytton Bulwer for the United Kingdom and John M Clapton for the United Sates of

America. The United States had considered building a canal through Nicaragua linking the Atlantic and Pacific Oceans. This canal would have affected British interests in the area, in particular British Honduras. Therefore both countries agreed to show restraint and not to make any territorial claims in the area.

1881 The death of Benjamin Disraeli, Lord Beaconsfield, former Conservative Prime Minister and member of 'Young England' (see 21st December) in London. Known affectionately as 'Dizzy', he was the first and only Jewish Prime Minister. His most famous quote was "there are three kinds of lies: lies, damn lies and statistics". He was instrumental in arranging for Queen Victoria (see 22nd January and 24th May) to become Empress of India and in Britain buying the controlling stock of shares in the Suez Canal in Egypt.

1882 The death of Charles Darwin at Down House in Kent (see 12th February). One of the leading scientists of his time, he is recognised as the foremost champion and father of natural selection. Born in Shrewsbury, his paternal grandfather was Erasmus Darwin (see 18th April and 12th December) and his maternal grandfather was Josiah Wedgwood (see 3rd January and 12th July). He studied at Edinburgh University and Cambridge University. It took him around 20 years to develop his ideas on evolution following his voyage on HMS Beagle between the years 1831 and 1836. However, at the time of its publication and for many years afterwards the ideas within his book 'On the Origin of Species by Means of Natural Selection' caused great controversy. He was buried in Westminster Abbey (see 24th November and 27th December).

1938 The death of Sir Henry John Newbolt in Kensington, London. He was a novelist, Poet, Playwright and true patriot (see 6th June). He was knighted in 1915 and awarded the Companion of Honour in 1922. His best known poem is 'Vitai Lampada' (1897) and its famous line 'Play up! Play up! and play the game!' has become symbolic of his ideas of chivalry and gentlemanly behaviour in time of war that Sir Henry so espoused (see 17th January).

1956 The death of Lieutenant Commander Lionel 'Buster' Crabb, OBE, in Portsmouth Harbour whilst investigating the visiting Soviet ship Ordzhonikidze for MI6 (see 28th January). A frogman for the Royal Navy he had served during the Second World War. He was recruited as a civilian to spy on the Soviet ships and to this day, the circumstances surrounding his death remain a mystery.

1986 The death of Colonel James Power Carne VC (see 11th April). When serving as a Lieutenant Colonel of the 1st battalion Gloucestershire Regiment he commanded 700 men of the regiment at the battle of the Imjin River during the Korean War (1950-1953 see 25th June, 27th July and 29th August). In the action, for which he received his VC, he seriously delayed over 11,000 Korean and Chinese soldiers in what became desperate hand to hand fighting. He personally led two assaults on enemy positions before his position was overrun and he became a Prisoner of War (see 22nd April and 25th April). Due to the regiment's heroic stand, they became known as the 'Glorious Glosters'.

20th April:

1653 Oliver Cromwell (see 25th April and 3rd September) enters the Houses of Parliament and dissolves the Rump Parliament, which had sat since 1640. Using soldiers under his command to clear the chamber, he had the doors locked preventing the MPs from returning (see 16th December).

1657 The Battle of Santa Cruz on the island of Tenerife. General-at-Sea Sir Robert Blake (see 7th August) totally destroys the Spanish fleet, sinking 16 enemy ships with just one of his fleet badly damaged and around 200 sailors killed. He sailed his ships into the harbour, showing contempt for the Spanish shore defences and set about bombarding the ships and buildings. The defeat, the worst since the destruction of the Armada in 1588 (see 29th July), devastated Spain's economy and finances for years following the humiliation.

1912 The death of Abraham 'Bram' Stoker (see 8th November) in London following a series of strokes. The manager of the Lyceum Theatre in London, he was also secretary to the actor Sir Henry Irving. He was also a writer who is best known for his Gothic novel 'Dracula', which he wrote in 1897 although he wrote for a London newspaper and did write other horror novels.

1968 Enoch Powell MP (see 8th February and 16th June) delivers a speech to the local Conservative Party in Birmingham that would later be referred to as his 'Rivers of Blood' speech. In his speech he called for the cessation of immigration into this country and foresaw cultural segregation because of the so-called 'multi cultural society' that all parties at the time were appearing to advocate. Giving this speech would ultimately lead to the end his political career.

21st April:

1509 The death of Henry VII at Richmond Palace following recurrent attacks of gout and asthma (see 28th January). Born in Pembroke, his father Edmund Tudor died two months before his birth. He became the leading Lancastrian claimant to the throne of England. However, he did not become king until after the decisive Battle of Bosworth Field in 1485 and the death in that battle of the then king, Richard III (see 22nd August and 2nd October). It was this battle that brought an end to the Wars of the Roses, 1455-1485. He spent his reign avoiding further war and building up the Royal finances and leaving a country to his son free from civil and military strife. His second son Henry succeeded to the throne immediately on his father's death as Henry VIII (see 28th January and 28th June).

1652 At the Mercat Cross in Edinburgh, Commissioners from England declared that the 'Tender of Union', an Act of Union between England and Scotland passed by the English Parliament, was now enforced and that the two Kingdoms were now one under the Commonwealth. General George Monck, one of the Commissioners, was the military Governor of Scotland (see 1st May, 7th May, 3rd September and 16th December).

1816 The birth of Charlotte Bronte (see 31st March) at Thornton in Yorkshire.

1838 The birth of John Muir in Dunbar (see 24th December).

1913 The birth of Richard Beeching in Sheerness (see 23rd March and 27th March).

1926 The birth of Elizabeth Alexandra Mary, later Queen Elizabeth II in Mayfair in London (see 6th February, 8th February, 2nd June and 9th September). The eldest daughter of Prince Albert, the Duke of York, the future George VI (see 6th February and 14th December) and Elizabeth, Duchess of York.

1946 The death of John Maynard Keynes, 1st Baron Keynes (see 5th June) in Tilton, East Sussex from myocardial infarction. He was the leading figure in modern economics and championed the cause of state interventionism in the economic affairs of state. During World War One he worked for the treasury and after the war was an outspoken critic of the huge reparations placed upon Germany and predicted that they would cause long term resentment by the German people and government. In 1936 he published his best known work 'The General Theory of Employment, Interest and Money', which earned him worldwide recognition as the leading economist of his time. During the Second World War he was instrumental in the negotiations to settle the post-war economic world and order. In 1944 he led the British delegation to the Breton Woods Conference in America and played a notable part in the formation of the International Monetary Fund and the World Bank.

22nd April:

1707 The birth of Henry Fielding in Sharpham near Glastonbury (see 8th October).

1772 The birth of George Cockburn (see 19th August and 24th August) in London, the son of Sir James Cockburn, 8th Baronet.

1778 The death of James Hargreaves (born in 1720). Born in Lancashire, he was a carpenter and weaver and he is known as the inventor of the 'Spinning Jenny' and one of the key figures in the start of the Industrial Revolution.

1833 The death of Richard Trevithick (see 21st February and 13th April), Railway locomotive inventor, at the Bull Inn in Dartford. Born at Tregajorran in Cornwall, he did not do well at school. In 1797 he was appointed as an engineer at the Ding Dong Mine near Penzance where he developed his vacuum engine. He then went on to develop several steam-powered locomotives to be used for the transport of goods and passengers. Despite being the pioneer of the forerunner of the modern Railway system, he died penniless.

1908 The death of Sir Henry Campbell-Bannerman in London (see 7th September). He entered Parliament as the Liberal MP for Stirling in 1868 and held his seat for forty years. He served in Gladstone's administrations and later, when the Liberal leader Lord Roseberry resigned, he became leader of the Party. In 1905, after Arthur Belfour's resignation, he was invited to form an administration which won the General Election the following year. He was a firm advocate of Irish Home Rule and died within a month after resigning due to ill health.

1915 The first ever poison gas attack, just north of the Belgian town of Ypres, during the Second Battle of Ypres. The Germans unleashed the chlorine gas onto unsuspecting Allied forces at around 5pm in the evening, allowing the breeze to blow the gas across no-man's land. Those most affected were the French and Algerian troops positioned between the British and Canadian forces, although British and Canadian troops did suffer heavy casualties (see 25th September).

1930 The London Naval Treaty (officially the 'Treaty for the Limitation and Reduction of Naval Armament') is signed between Great Britain, Japan, France, Italy and the United States. The treaty regulated the building of submarines and also restricted the building of new Capital Ships until 1937.

1951 The Battle of the Imjin River begins during the Korean War (1950-1953). Over 11,000 men from the North Korean and the Chinese armies eventually attack Hill 235 that is held by about 750 men of the Gloucestershire Regiment (see 25th April).

1969 Robin Knox-Johnston arrives in Falmouth harbour after becoming the first person to sail solo non-stop round the world, a voyage that took him only 312 days.

23rd April: St. George's day, Patron Saint of England.

1564 William Shakespeare (see 1616) is allegedly born on this date in Stratford upon Avon. He was definitely baptised on the 26th May. There has been much debate over the years by historians as to his exact date of birth. However, it can never be conclusively proven.

1616 The death of William Shakespeare (see 1564 above) in Stratford upon Avon. Possibly the greatest playwright and certainly the most famous this country has ever produced. Educated and raised in Stratford, he married Anne Hathaway in 1582. Sometime around 1592 he was in London appearing in theatre as an actor before acquiring a financial stake in the Globe Theatre. He had poetry published in 1593 and then as a playwright he had his first plays published around 1594 and then continued a prolific writing career for much of the rest of his life.

1661 Charles II (see 6th February and 29th May) is crowned in Westminster Abbey, publically and officially confirming the restoration of the monarchy and the end of eleven years of the Republic and Commonwealth (see 1st January and 4th April).

1685 James VII (James II of England) is crowned in Westminster Abbey (see 6th September and 14th October).

1697 The birth of George Anson in Shugborough near Stafford (see 6th June).

1702 Queen Anne is crowned at Westminster Abbey (see 6th February and 1st August). She was the last of the Stuart Monarchs.

1838 The SS Great Western and the Sirius become the first two vessels to cross the Atlantic under steam power (see 19th July). The Sirius crossed the Atlantic arriving the previous day. However, the Great Western left four days after the Sirius and made up three days, therefore beating the crossing of the Sirius by three days.

1850 The death of William Wordsworth in Ambleside, Cumbria (see 7th April); one of the most influential of the Romantic poets. In 1798 he worked with Samuel Taylor Coleridge on 'Lyrical ballads' which is often credited as marking the beginning of the Romantic Movement in British literature. In 1799 he moved to Dove Cottage in the Lake District and here in 1804 wrote the famous poem 'I Wandered Lonely as a cloud'. In 1802 he married but suffered much personal loss and tragedy in his personal life from then on. In 1813 he moved to Ambleside in the Lake District and in 1843 he was appointed the Poet Laureate.

1861 The birth of Edmund Henry Hynman Allenby (see 14th May) in Nottingham.

1915 The Zeebrugge Raid takes place with the intention of neutralising the port of Zeebrugge in Belgium, which was a key U-Boat base for the Germans. The 4th Battalion, Royal Marine Light Infantry, who went ashore supported by 200 volunteers from the Royal Navy, were targeted with destroying or putting out of action the harbour itself, thus making it unusable for the enemy. During the night of the 22nd April 1918, a force of over 70 boats and ships left for the Port of Zeebrugge. HMS Vindictive was the main assault ship and was accompanied by the *Daffodil* and the *Iris II*. These two ships were requisitioned ferries that were used to cross back and forth across the Mersey in Liverpool. Their principle role was to transfer the troops for the assault and to pick up survivors after the attack had been completed. At 00:01 the Vindictive and the accompanying force arrived of the coast of Belgium. Smoke boats had released a smoke screen and all was going well until the Vindictive was just 100 yards from the Mole. At this point the enemy opened fire with devastating accuracy. All the Officers were either killed or wounded leaving only Lieutenant Commander Adams to lead the assault. Further adding to the difficulties, the enemy also knocked out ten of the twelve landing planks to be used by the raiding party to go ashore. The result was that half the men on the Vindictive were either killed or wounded. The attackers had to fight every inch of the way to their objectives. It was perhaps one of the greatest commando raids of our history. All the participants acted with heroism and gallantry in the true spirit of the Royal Navy. A total of 161 men were killed in action, 75 in one shell blast that hit the Ferry *Iris*, with 439 wounded, 28 men died of their wounds and 16 men were reported missing and 13 men were taken prisoner when they were left behind on the Mole.

1924 The British Empire Exhibition is opened by George V (see 20th January and 3rd June) and Queen Mary at the Empire Stadium in Wembley, London. It was years in the planning and all but two members of the Empire took part. It was designed as a means to increase trade by showcasing Imperial industry and produce and ultimately to bring closer the members of the Empire with the Mother country. This was also the first time a Monarch was broadcast on radio and millions heard his voice (see 19th December and 25th December).

1968 The first decimal coins are released into circulation. They are the 5 New Pence piece, the 10 New Pence piece and are the same size and weight as the one and two shilling coins. The new coins are temporarily used as the shilling and Florin coins until Decimal Day in 1971 (see 15th February).

24th April:

1743 The birth of Edmund Cartwright (see 30th October) in Nottinghamshire.

1815 The birth of Anthony Trollope (see 6th December) in London.

1882 The birth of Hugh Caswell Tremenheere Dowding in Moffat (see 15th February).

1906 The birth of William Joyce in Brooklyn, New York City (see 3rd January).

1916 Monday: The Easter rebellion begins in Ireland (see 29th April and 3rd May). Taking advantage of the war with Germany and treacherously using weapons supplied by the enemy, around 1,000 traitorous Irish rebels and terrorists attack and capture key buildings in Dublin that were defended by around just 400 British troops. The buildings captured by the rebels were quickly taken and included the Four Courts and the General Post Office in Sackville Street, which was to serve as the rebels' nerve centre and headquarters until, in the fighting to regain order they were badly damaged by fire (see 4th May).

1942 The Baedeker Raids commence on key British cultural targets. The raids, from April into June, were in supposed retaliation for the RAF bombing the city of Lubeck on the Baltic Sea. The first target was the city of Exeter and it is believed that the raids were based on a German tourist guide, published by Baedeker, from which we gave the raids their collective name (see 13th March, 14th March, 7th September, 14th November and 29th December).

1954 The launch of Operation Anvil in the Colony of Kenya (see 12th December) during the Mau Mau rebellion (see 20th October). For two weeks, around 25,000 members of the security forces sealed off Nairobi, the suspected centre of the Mau Mau rebellion in a move to rid the city of rebels. All African residents were screened and those likely to be Mau Mau or their sympathisers were transferred to reserves and scattered.

25th April:

1284 The birth of Edward II at Caernarvon Castle (see 20th January, 7th February, 25th February and 21st September).

1599 The birth of Oliver Cromwell (see 3rd September) in Huntingdon.

1915 Australian, British and New Zealand troops begin their amphibious landings along the Dardanelles coast in Turkey, at the start of what was the Gallipoli Campaign. British and French troops come ashore at Cape Helles and the Australian and New Zealand troops land in the area of Ari Burnu, later to be called ANZAC Cove (see 19th February, 30th October and 1921 below).

1920 Britain is given a League of Nations mandate for governance of Mesopotamia and Palestine (see 14th May and 29th September) as part of a resolution during the San Remo Conference of the four Allied powers in Italy.

1921 And all subsequent years since is ANZAC day (see 1915 above). This is the day that the landings at Gallipoli commenced in 1915, and is a national day of commemoration for the people of Australia and New Zealand, when the tremendous sacrifice of those few months in 1915 is remembered and will never be forgotten (see 20th December and 28th December).

1951 The end of the Battle of the Imjin River in North Korea. The Chinese army finally overwhelm the survivors of the 1st battalion the Gloucestershire Regiment on Hill 235. They make a gallant and heroic last stand, led by Colonel James Power Carne (see 11th April and 19th April), holding up the Chinese forces long enough for the UN forces to regroup. After attempting to fight their way out, only 39 men finally make it back. The rest were either killed or taken prisoner. Hill 235 becomes known as Gloster Hill and the Regiment is known as the 'Glorious Glosters' for their collective bravery and heroism (see 22nd April).

1953 The geneticists James Watson and Francis Crick publish their discovery of the structure of Deoxyribonucleic Acid (DNA).

1982 The Island of South Georgia is recaptured from Argentinean forces following their invasion of the island and the Falklands a few weeks earlier (see 2nd April and 14th June). The reclaiming of the islands took place as Operation Paraquet and involved Royal Marine Commandos, SAS and SBS forces. During the retaking of the islands the Argentinean submarine Santa Fe was damaged and prevented from diving then subsequently captured. During the operation there were no British casualties.

2013 The Succession to the Crown Act 2013 receives Royal Assent. The Act altered the laws of succession to the throne by allowing for the eldest child of the heir to the throne to succeed upon the monarchs death, regardless of gender. The Act did not change the line of succession of the heirs then living at the time of the acts Royal Assent. The Act still barred any Roman Catholic from inheriting the throne (see 6th February).

26th April:

1326 The Auld Alliance between Robert I (see 7th June and 11th July), King of Scotland and France is renewed (see 23rd October).

1607 Members of a fleet from England make landfall at Cape Henry in Virginia before moving along the coast to form the first settlement on the North American mainland (see 10th April, 13th May, 14th May and 21st December).

1710 The birth of Thomas Reid in Kincardineshire (see 7th October).

1711 The birth of David Hume, writer and philosopher of the Scottish enlightenment, in Edinburgh (see 25th August).

1731 The death of Daniel Defoe in Moorfields in London. He was born in 1660 and took part in the Monmouth Rebellion of 1685 and sided with William III (see 8th March and 4th November) during the Glorious Revolution of 1689. He is best remembered for his book, *Robinson Crusoe* (published in 1719) as well as others such as *Moll Flanders*. He was at first a Whig and was well known for his political writings and was eventually employed by the State as a spy.

1915 The Treaty of London is signed in London by Great Britain, France and Russia and the Kingdom of Italy. By signing the treaty, which was initially kept secret, Italy was agreeing to leave the Triple Alliance and Join the Triple Entente and at the same time declare war on Germany and the Austro-Hungarian Empire (see 11th November).

27th April:

1296 The Battle of Dunbar. The Scots, led by John Balliol (see 25th November and 30th November), are defeated by the English, who are led by John de Warenne, 7th Earl of Surrey under Edward I (see 7th June and 11th July). Edward had ordered his troops into Scotland in a move to punish the Scots for failing to support him and to provide troops for his army against France. When the belligerents met near the town of Dunbar, both armies appear to have been comprised of mounted cavalry and the numbers on either side are unknown (see 10th July).

1737 The birth of Edward Gibbon (see 16th January) in Putney.

1759 The birth of Mary Wollstonecraft (see 10th September) in Spitalfields in London.

1794 The death of James Bruce in Larbert near Stirling (see 14th November and 14th December). A leading explorer of Africa, he is credited with discovering the headstream of the blue Nile in Ethiopia, then believed to be the river's source. His travels were published in 'Travels to Discover the Source of the Nile' in 1790. Prior to this he had spent many years travelling across North Africa, in particular the Mediterranean coast of the continent and wrote about his travels.

1813 The battle of York (modern Toronto) in Upper Canada. American forces attack the town of York and force its capitulation. Following its agreed surrender, the Americans, apparently without any attempt by their officers to restore order, carried out numerous acts of robbery and arson and then burned down the Parliament buildings and loot the town over the next five days (see 18th June and 24th August).

1820 The birth of Herbert Spencer in Derby (see 8th December).

1840 The foundation stone for the new Palace of Westminster (see 16th October), also known as the Houses of Parliament, is officially laid by the wife of the architect of the project Sir Charles Barry (see 12th May and 23rd May).

1876 Following an acrimonious debate in Parliament, The Royal Titles Act 1876 was passed and received Royal Assent. The passing of the act enabled Queen Victoria (see 22nd January and 24th May) to assume the title Empress of India (see 1st January, 1st May and 22nd June).

1896 The death of Sir Henry Parkes (see 27th May) in Sydney, New South Wales. A journalist and politician, he is regarded as the leading proponent of Australian Federation. Born in Warwickshire, he and his wife emigrated to Australia in 1839. Despite a life of debt and failing businesses, he was elected to the New South Wales Legislative Assembly and in 1872 became Premier of the Colony of New South Wales until 1875. He served as Premier on four further occasions and was knighted in 1877. During his final Premiership he did much to outline the basis for the future Commonwealth of Australia. In 1891 he resigned his office after a defeat in parliament and was never to see Federation (see 1st January).

1908 London hosts the Olympic Games for the first time at the White City Stadium after the original preference, Rome, drops out. Britain won 56 Gold, 51 silver and 39 bronze medals (see 27th July and 29th July).

1968 The Abortion Act (1967) comes into effect (see 27th October) in Great Britain, except in Northern Ireland. The act legalised abortions up to 28 weeks gestation by registered practitioners and allowed the service to be carried out free under the National Health Service.

28th April:

1442 The birth of Edward IV in Rouen, France (see 9th April and 28th June), the son of the Duke of York, Richard Plantagenet.

1770 Captain James Cook discovers Botany Bay in what later becomes known as Australia. He makes landfall the following day (see 29th April).

1789 Lieutenant (later Captain) William Bligh (see 9th September and 7th December) and 18 of his loyal crew are set adrift in a twenty-three foot launch after a successful mutiny led by Fletcher Christian on the ship HMS Bounty. Eighteen of the 42 crew mutinied. Lieutenant Bligh navigated the boat for 47 days across 3,618 nautical miles of the southern Pacific Ocean (see 28th August).

1827 The birth of William Edward Hall (see 25th August) in Nova Scotia. He was the son of American slave refugees who had escaped America during the war of 1812 with the aid of the Royal Navy.

1944 the Slapton Sands disaster occurs at Slapton Sands in Devon. Over 750 US soldiers, part of a much larger force, training for the D-Day landings (see 6th June) are killed when a number of German E-Boats attacked and destroyed some of the landing craft taking part in the training exercise, called Operation Tiger. The troops were pat of a formation comprising one escort Corvette, HMS Azalea and eight American LSTs carrying the troops and tanks to shore. Two of the landing craft were sunk and others damaged before the German boats escaped.

1949 At the 1949 Commonwealth Prime Minister's Conference in London, The London Declaration is issued by the Heads of Government of the eight members of the Commonwealth. It stated that members of the Commonwealth could be states other than those that were former Dominions (see 11th December) and colonies, including republics and monarchies of indigenous peoples; it also changed the name of the organisation from the British Commonwealth to the Commonwealth of Nations thus formally creating the Commonwealth of Nations. The eight original member states were the United Kingdom, Australia (see 1st January), Canada (see 1st July), Ceylon (see 4th February), India (see 15th August), New Zealand (see 26th September), Pakistan (see 15th August) and South Africa (see 31st May).

2008 The death of Diana Barnato Walker (see 15th January). One of the greatest of female aviators, she was the first British woman to break the sound barrier. Born in London, she decided to become a pilot when she was twenty. During the Second World War she served in the Air Transport Auxiliary (ATA) and delivered hundreds of fighter aircraft to RAF bases across the country including Spitfires, Hurricanes, Tempests and Mustangs. After the war she continued to fly and in 1963, flying an English Electric Lightening XM996, she reached Mach 1.65 (1,262 mph, see 26th August). She was appointed MBE in 1965 for services to aviation.

29th April:

1770 Captain James Cook (see 14th February and 27th October), aboard the Endeavour, comes ashore at Botany Bay in what was later to be called the colony of New South Wales (see 26th January, 28th April and 6th October).

1909 The People's Budget is presented by the Chancellor of the Exchequer, David Lloyd George (see 17th January and 26th March), under the Prime Minister Herbert Henry Asquith (see 15th February and 12th September). The budget raised significantly the taxes on the rich and wealthy in order to pay for proposed welfare reforms.

1910 The People's Budget is passed by the House of Lords (see 1909 above).

1916 Saturday: The end of the Easter rebellion in Dublin (see 24th April) as the rebels surrender unconditionally to Government forces. The rebel casualties were 64 killed with 15 being tried and found guilty of treason in court and then subsequently executed (see 3rd May). Our forces lost 116 killed and 368 wounded and the police lost 17 killed. Even worse, the innocent Irish civilian population lost 254 killed and around 600 wounded because of the traitors' actions (see 4th May).

1916 The 8,000-strong Indian Expeditionary Force, mainly the 6th (Poona) Division of the British Indian Army, besieged in the city of Kut in Mesopotamia, surrender after a lengthy siege by German-led Ottoman forces. Our forces garrisoning the city were led by General Charles Townshend, who arranged a ceasefire but surrendered just days later (see 8th March).

1949 The death of General Sir Fabian Arthur Goulstone Ware in Amberley in Gloucestershire (see 17th June). Born in Bristol in 1869, he is remembered as the creator of the Imperil War Graves Commission in 1917 (see 21st May). When the First World War broke out he volunteered for active service but was deemed too old, however, he was able to take command of an ambulance unit. As the war progressed he became ever more concerned with lack of an official and structured way of recording the graves of those fallen in the service of their country and the Empire. He set about changing this and set up a commission which, with the help of Edward, Prince of Wales (see 28th May and 23rd June), became the Imperil War Graves Commission.

30th April:

1662 The birth of Princess Mary (see 28th December) in St. James's Palace in London. She was the eldest daughter of James Duke of York, the future James VII (James II of England see 5th September and 14th October) and Lady Anne Hyde.

1865 The death of Vice Admiral Robert FitzRoy (see 5th July) in Upper Norwood. An officer in the Royal Navy, he was famous for being the Captain of HMS Beagle during Charles Darwin's (see 12th February and 19th April) famous voyage. He was also a noted meteorologist who pioneered accurate weather forecasting. He joined the Royal Navy at the age of thirteen. From 1831 to 1836 he commanded HMS Beagle on its famous second voyage. Following the successful voyage and friendship with Charles Darwin, he became the Governor of New Zealand in 1843. A keen meteorologist, after retiring in 1851 he was elected to the Royal Society. In 1854 he was appointed to a new department that was the forerunner of the future Meteorological Society. He was also instrumental in the production of weather charts that allowed early weather forecasting.

1909 John Theodore Cuthbert Moore-Brabazon, later Lord Brabazon of Tara, is accredited with being the first Englishman to make an aeroplane flight in England, of about 450 feet (see 8th February, 2nd May, 17th May and 30th October).

1943 The start of Operation Mincemeat as a Royal Navy submarine surfaces off the coast of Spain to set adrift a dead body in the guise of an Army officer with false Allied invasion plans inside an accompanying brief case. The misinformation plan was successful in convincing the German and Italian command that Allied forces would invade Greece instead of the actual target, Sicily (see 10th July).

1945 Adolf Hitler commits suicide in his bunker in Berlin (see 8th May and 3rd September).

1980 The Iranian Embassy in London is seized by several Iranian terrorists (see 5th May) and the Police Officer on duty, PC Trevor Locke, is taken hostage.

1982 Operation Black Buck begins as two Vulcan Bombers, XM598 and XM607, take off from Ascension Island and were supported by eleven Victor Tankers for refuelling. Shortly after take off, XM598 developed a technical problem and had to return to base (see 1st May) leaving XM607 to carry out the mission alone.

2007 Smoking is banned in Northern Ireland in all public buildings and areas, such as work places and pubs (see 26th March, 2nd April and 1st July).

MAY

1st May: the Act of Union between England and Scotland

1650 The Treaty of Breda between Charles II (see 6th February and 29th May) and the Scottish Covenanters is signed. Although opposed to the terms, which included the Royal house adopting Presbyterianism as their religion, he signed it as a means to gaining Scottish help in regaining his thrown.

1672 The birth of Joseph Addison (see 17th June) in London.

1707 The Official proclamation and enactment of the Union of the two Kingdoms of England and Scotland and with this the United Kingdom came into being (see 21st April, 22nd July and 25th September). The Act of Union was in effect two acts, one from each of the English (see 4th March) and Scottish Parliaments (see 16th January and 25th March). Church bells throughout Scotland played the tune, 'Why am I so sad on my Wedding day?' Queen Anne (see 6th February and 1st August) becomes the first Monarch of the United Kingdom of Great Britain. From this moment onwards, the Great

Britain we know today began to form and grow economically and ultimately led to the Greatest Empire in world history (see 1st January).

1745 The Battle of Fontenoy in the south west of the Austrian Netherlands, during the War of the Austrian Succession (1740-1748). The British, Hanoverians, Austrians and Dutch, led by the Duke of Cumberland, came as a relief force for the town of Tournai against the French, who were led by Marshal Maurice de Saxe on behalf of Louis XIV. The allies lost the Battle with well over 7,000 killed, including 1,237 British killed and 2,425 wounded, the Hanoverians losing 1,412 killed and wounded to the French 7,137 killed and wounded. The Battle was a total failure with the Pragmatic Army leaving the field of battle to the French and retreating at night. However, there was no pursuit as our forces retired in good order thus avoiding a total route. Despite being a French victory, the British and Hanoverians were disciplined and orderly in the retreat, in particular in the rear guard. This allowed the honour of the British Regiments to remain.

1759 The French colony of Guadeloupe surrenders after three months of resistance to our forces. However, despite the victory, the troops garrisoning the islands quickly fall victim to the intense heat and disease (see 24th January and 10th February).

1769 The birth of Arthur Wellesley in Dublin, Ireland (see 26th January and 14th September). He was the son of the Earl of Mornington.

1775 The Quebec Act becomes effective (see 22nd June). From today, the Provence of Quebec was greatly enlarged and the colony was governed by a Governor and a council of between seventeen and twenty-three members. More importantly, the Act guaranteed the freedom of the Roman Catholic majority and a simplified Test Oath which enabled Catholics to hold public office.

1820 Five members of the Cato Street Conspiracy are hanged at Newgate Prison for attempting to blow up and murder the Prime Minister Lord Liverpool and his Cabinet. Other conspirators were transported for life (see 23rd February).

1851 The opening of the Great Exhibition in Hyde Park, London, by Queen Victoria (see 22nd January and 24th May). The exhibition was organised by Henry Cole and Prince Albert. The exhibition was a magnificent display of innovation and British technological advances as well as numerous displays from across the Empire and the rest of the world. There were displays of photography, kitchen appliances, voting machines and the world's first public toilets.

1873 The death of the explorer David Livingstone (see 19th March) from malaria near Lake Bangweulu in Northern Rhodesia. He studied medicine and Theology to become a missionary Doctor. He believed it was his mission to introduce the peoples of the interior of Africa to Christianity. During the 1850's and 1860's he undertook detailed explorations of Africa. In 1856 he became the first European to cross the entire southern part of Africa. He discovered and named the Victoria Falls. In 1871, on his last expedition, he was found by Henry Morton Stanley in their now famous meeting (see 10th November). His death occurred whilst he was still attempting to trace the source of the River Nile. Eventually his body and all his personal papers were returned back to Britain and he was buried in Westminster Abbey.

1876 Queen Victoria (see 22nd January and 24th May) is proclaimed Empress of India in Great Britain (see 1st January) following the passing of the Royal Titles Act of 1876 (see 27th April). She was the first British Monarch to become an Empress or Emperor (see 22nd June).

1884 The Ilbert Bill (see 25th January) comes into force amid much controversy. Proposed by the Viceroy Lord Rippon, it made provision for senior Indian Judges to preside over cases that involved British subjects. However, an amendment was agreed whereby a British subject could call for trial by jury which would contain half its members as European.

1933 The Roca-Runciman Treaty is signed in London between Argentina and Great Britain. The treaty, signed by Sir Walter Runciman, British envoy and Julio Argentino Roca for Argentina, gave Argentina a fixed share of the meat market in Great Britain and gave Britain generous trade concessions in Argentina.

1978 Monday: It becomes Britain's first May Day Bank Holiday when the first Monday in May is declared as the May Day Bank Holiday (see 1st January and 26th December).

1982 The culmination of Operation Black Buck as a lone Vulcan Bomber XM607 drops twenty-one, 1,000-lb bombs on Port Stanley runway scoring a direct hit, thus disabling the runway for fighter aircraft use. The crew had flown 8,000 nautical miles from Ascension Island and were refuelled by Victor Tankers along the way. This was the longest bombing raid in history up to that point (see 2nd April, 30th April and 14th June).

1997 The General Election takes place with the results confirmed in the early hours of the following morning (see 2nd May).

2nd May:

1670 the Hudson Bay Company is given its Royal Charter by Charles II (see 6th February and 29th May). It was given the monopoly over and effectively owned vast swathes of land in the northern and inner regions stretching inland from Hudson Bay in an area known as Prince Rupert's Land (see 22nd June and 1st July). The Company was intended to wrestle the very lucrative fur trade from the French traders already well-established in some of the areas. The formation of the Company was supported by Prince Rupert (see 29th November and 17th December).

1750 The birth of John André (see 2nd October) in London.

1909 Lord Brabazon of Tara becomes the first Briton to make an officially recognized aeroplane flight, taking off and landing on the Isle of Sheppey (see 8th February, 30th April, 17th May and 30th October).

1952 The De Havilland DH 106 Comet, the world's first commercial jet airliner, takes off from London on its maiden voyage with 36 fare paying passengers to Johannesburg in South Africa. Designed, developed and built by de Havilland, it had four built-in engines within its wings and its overall appearance was the most innovative for the time.

1964 The death of Lady Nancy Astor, Viscountess Astor (see 19th May) in Grimsthorpe Castle. Born in Virginia in the United States into a wealthy family, she married her first husband when she was eighteen but it lasted just four years. She travelled to Britain after her divorce and loved the country so much she moved here, encouraged by her father, in 1905. She met and married her second husband Waldorf Astor who, prior to becoming the 2nd Viscount Astor, had been in Parliament. She campaigned herself and in 1919 was elected to parliament (see 28th November and 1st December), becoming the first women MP. She supported many social reforms and initially Neville Chamberlain's (see 18th March and 9th November) appeasement of Germany. However, she supported Churchill's wartime government (see 10th May), despite openly stating during the 1930s that she was against another world war. She did not stand for e-election in the general election of 1945 (see 26th July).

1982 The Argentine cruiser General Belgrano is sunk by the submarine HMS Conqueror, just outside the 200 mile Total Exclusion Zone around the Falkland Islands. This is the only occasion where a nuclear-powered submarine has attacked and sunk another vessel in combat (see 9th February). Though the attack was criticised in the years following the contact, both countries were involved in a war and there were legitimate fears of a possible three-pronged Argentinean attack on our forces (see 2nd April and 14th June).

1997 'New' Labour, under the leadership of Tony Blair, win the General Election after 18 years of Conservative government (see 1st May). Tony Blair visits the Queen (see 21st April) and forms a government with himself as Prime Minister.

3rd May:

1747 The First battle of Finisterre, during the War of the Austrian Succession (1740-1748), where Admiral Lord George Anson (see 23rd April and 6th June) and 14 ships of the Royal Navy defeat a French convoy of 30 ships. As a result of courageous action, the French lost 4 ships of the line, 2 Frigates and 7 merchantmen were captured. The Royal Navy lost no ships in the battle.

1768 The birth of Charles Tennant in Alloway in Ayrshire (see 1st October).

1841 William Hobson is sworn in as the Governor of the new Colony of New Zealand as well as the Commander in Chief (see 10th September and 26th September).

1916 The first of the Irish Rebels involved in the treasonous Irish Rebellion earlier in the year are executed by firing squad following their courts martial (see 24th April and 29th April). A total of 15 traitors were eventually executed between the 3rd May and the 12th May 1916. Though controversy has raged over the executions ever since, the fact remains that whilst Britain was at war, the rebels had risen against their country, communicated with the enemy and even sought and received support and weapons from Germany, allying themselves against the democratic forces.

1951 George VI (see 6th February and 14th December) opens the 'Festival of Britain' on London's South Bank on the centenary of the Great Exhibition. The majority of the exhibition was in London although there were travelling exhibitions around the country at places such as Glasgow, Cardiff, York and Bournemouth. The brainchild of the post-war Labour government, it was intended to instil in people a feeling of recovery after the war and encourage new and better designs in housing.

4th May:

1806 The birth of William Fothergill Cooke in Ealing in Middlesex (see 25th June).

1825 The birth of Thomas Henry Huxley (see 29th June) in Middlesex.

1827 The birth of John Hanning Speke (see 3rd August and 15th September) in Bideford, Devon.

1843 The birth of Clementina Trentholm Fessenden (see 14th September) in Kingsey Township, Lower Canada (see 24th May).

1900 The death of Augustus Henry Lane Fox (Pitt Rivers see 14th April). He served in the army, seeing action in the Crimean War 1853-1856. He changed his name to Pitt Rivers as part of an inheritance. An amateur archaeologist, he started his interest whilst in the army. However, in 1889, he inherited a large estate in Devon that contained already existing archaeological sites. Here he developed detailed techniques; he was meticulous in the recording of finds, no matter how large or small and the recording of the item's context within the site. He became the first Inspector of Ancient Monuments.

1911 The National Health Insurance Scheme, offering sickness and unemployment benefits, was introduced by Lloyd George (see 17th January and 26th March). People receiving benefits referred to it as getting their 'Lloyd George'.

1926 The start of the General Strike (see 11th May and 12th May) which was an attempt to bring the country to a halt. Called out by the Trades Union Congress (TUC) the miners are the first to go but are quickly supported by workers in other industries. This was to be the only national strike in our history.

1979 The General Election and a Conservative victory. Margaret Thatcher is elected Prime Minister for the first time, becoming our first and only female Prime Minister (see 11th February, 8th April, 13th October and 22nd November). The Conservatives under Margaret Thatcher defeated the incumbent government of the Labour Prime Minister James Callaghan (see 26th March and 27th March) with a majority of 43 seats.

1982 HMS Sheffield, a Type 42 Destroyer, is struck by an Exocet missile fired by an Argentinean aircraft with the loss of twenty of the crew and another twenty four badly injured. The ship was abandoned later in the day and sank six days later (see 10th May).

5th May:

1646 King Charles I surrenders to the Scottish Presbyterian Army at Newark after he is given assurances about his safety and that his conscience and beliefs would be respected (see 30th January and 19th November).

1760 Laurence Shirley, 4th Earl of Ferrers, becomes the last aristocrat to be hanged in this country (see 18th August). He was executed using a silk cord instead of rope for the murder of his Steward.

1864 The birth of Henry Hughes Wilson in County Longford, Ireland (see 22nd June).

1882 The birth of Sylvia Pankhurst (see 27th September) in Manchester. Her parents were Dr Richard Pankhurst and Emmaline Goulden, both committed supporters of women's suffrage and socialism.

1883 The birth of Archibald Percival Wavell (see 24th May) in Colchester.

1980 Operation Nimrod begins as the S.A.S. (Special Air Service) storm the Iranian Embassy in London and releases the hostages that had been taken by the Iranian terrorists. All but one of the terrorists is killed in the operation and thankfully, none of our Special Forces were killed, although one was injured (see 30th April).

2011 Thursday: the death of Claude Stanley Choules in Australia (see 3rd March). Born in Pershore in Worcestershire, he was the last First World War veteran in the world. He joined the Royal Navy in October 1916 and witnessed the surrender of the Imperial German Navy and then the subsequent scuttling of the same fleet in Scapa Flow, both in 1918. He was also the last surviving serviceman to have served in both World Wars.

2011 For only the second time, the country goes to the polls for a national referendum. The choice is whether to change the way the country votes in the general election to an Alternative Voting system (AV) or remain with the present 'first past the post' system. In a 42% turn out the 'No to AV' campaign wins with a 68% to 32% share of the vote (see 16th February and 5th June).

6th May:

1749 The birth of Edward Jenner (see 26th January and 14th May) in Berkeley, Gloucestershire.

1754 The birth of Thomas Coke (see 30th June) in London, the son of the MP for Derby.

1820 The birth of Robert O'Hara Burke in County Galway, Ireland (see 28th June).

1870 The death of Professor Sir James Young Simpson (see 7th June) in Edinburgh. He discovered and pioneered the use of anaesthetics, in particular the properties of chloroform which he developed and introduced into general medical application. Born in Bathgate in West Lothian, he attended Edinburgh University and was later appointed as Professor of Midwifery at the University aged just 28. In 1847 he demonstrated on a woman in labour that chloroform could be successfully administered to relieve the pains of childbirth. This was after numerous experiments where he administered the drug on himself. However, it wasn't until chloroform was administered at the birth of Queen Victoria's (see 22nd January and 24th May) son Prince Leopold that its application became generally accepted (see 7th April). In 1866 he became the first person knighted for services to medicine. His funeral in Edinburgh was attended by around 1,700 colleagues, friends and admirers.

1882 The Phoenix Park murders are committed. Lord Frederick Cavendish, Chief Secretary of State for Ireland and Thomas Burke, his under Secretary, are murdered in Phoenix Park in Dublin by a Republican terrorist group called 'The Invincibles'. Five terrorists were eventually tried, convicted and then hanged for the murders.

1910 The death of Edward VII at Buckingham Palace (see 9th August and 9th November) and the accession of his second son, George V (see 20th January and 3rd June) to the throne. He was the longest heir apparent to the throne and during his early life was notorious as a playboy and arbiter of fashion around the world. Excluded from public roles by his mother Queen Victoria (see 22nd January and 24th May), many viewed him as totally unfit for Monarchy before his succession. However, soon after he became King his popularity soared and he was widely known as the 'Uncle of Europe' as his nephews were Kaiser Wilhelm II of Germany and Tsar Nicholas II of Imperial Russia.

1919 Britain declares war on the Afghan leader Amir Amanullah and his military leaders, after they cross the border into India and attack British positions. This conflict was to be called the Third Afghan War. It lasted little more than a month following heavy aerial bombing of towns by the R.A.F. (see 3rd June and 8th August).

1954 Roger Bannister breaks the four minute mile. His time was 3 minutes and 59.4 seconds and was completed in Oxford in front of over 3,000 spectators.

1994 Queen Elizabeth II (see 6th February and 21st April) officiates at the opening of the Channel Tunnel. Also present is the French President Francois Mitterrand.

1999 The first elections for the devolved Scottish Parliament take place. The Labour Party under the leadership of Donald Dewar wins the most seats but does not have an overall majority (see 11th September).

2010 The General Election takes place. With a prediction of a Hung Parliament, there is chaos in some places as people are locked out off Polling Stations at exactly 10pm and some Polling Stations run out of Ballot papers (see 7th May and 10th May).

7th May:

1659 Parliament reassembles and votes to abolish the Protectorate and the position of Lord Protector, held by Richard Cromwell (see 12th July and 4th October), son of Oliver Cromwell (see 25th April and 3rd September). Richard Cromwell's renunciation as Lord Protector is read to Parliament later in the month (see 25th May). This then allowed Parliament the opportunity to instigate proceedings for the restoration of the Monarchy the following year (see 29th May).

1718 The death of Mary Beatrice of Modena in the Château of St. Germain-en-Laye in France (see 25th September). She was the second and Catholic wife and Queen Consort of James VII (James II of England see 5th September and 14th October) and mother of the Jacobite James VIII, the 'Old Pretender' (see 1st January and 10th June). During the revolution of 1688 she fled to France with her son James and remained in exile there. Throughout the rest of her life she was an active supporter of the Jacobite attempts for the regaining of the British throne. Unfortunately her tomb was destroyed during the French Revolution.

1765 HMS Victory is launched at Chatham Dockyard where she was built. Designed by Sir Thomas Slade, she was a three-deck, 100-gun, First-Rate Line of Battle Ship and was commissioned in 1778. She took part in both the First and Second battles of Ushant in 1778 and 1781 (see 27th July and 12th December respectively) and the battle of Cape Saint Vincent in 1797 (see 14th February) where she was the Flag Ship of Admiral Sir John Jervis (see 9th January and 14th March). In 1812 she became a Depot ship and from 1889 until 1904 she served as the Naval School of Telegraphy. In 1922 she was moved to a dry dock in Portsmouth and work finally began on the restoration of the ship. She is currently a museum ship and the oldest Commissioned ship in the world.

1791 William Moorcroft becomes Britain's first qualified veterinary surgeon after qualifying in Lyons, France (see 27th August).

1812 The birth of Robert Browning in Camberwell, now part of London (see 12th December).

1856 Henry Sewell (see 7th September and 14th May) is asked by the Governor of New Zealand to form an administration after the general election and so becomes the Colonial Secretary, or what is generally regarded as the first Prime Minister of New Zealand (see 6th February, 1st July and 26th September).

1890 The death of James Nasmyth (see 19th August). An engineer and inventor, he is remembered for his invention of the steel hammer in 1839. The steel hammer, designed for the forging of wrought iron paddle shaft, assisted in the manufacture of steam engines. The hammer was adopted by the Admiralty in 1843. Born in Edinburgh, his hobby as a small boy was mechanics and this interest stayed with him all his life.

1915 At 2.28pm the R.M.S. Lusitania sinks 8 miles off the Old Head of Kinsale, in Ireland after being torpedoed by a German U-boat, U-20, just 18 minutes before with the loss of 1,198 people, including many women and children. There were 1,989 passengers and crew on this trip. Controversy still rages over the precise details about her sinking: primarily whether or not she was sunk with just one torpedo and whether she was carrying explosives and heavy ammunition for the war effort.

1945 German forces formally surrender at Reims in France. The act of military surrender was signed by General Alfred Jodl representing the new German President, Admiral Donitz and then ratified in Berlin the following day which is when it became effective (see 8th May).

1999 Donald Dewar becomes the First Minister of the new devolved Scottish Parliament following elections the previous day (see 6th May). The Labour Party won the most seats but did not have an overall majority (see 11th September, 18th September and 19th September).

2010 The General Election results come in, indicating a Hung Parliament, the first since 1974. The Conservatives are the largest party with 306 seats, the labour Party with 258 seats and the Liberals with 57 seats and other parties with a total of 29 (see 6th May, 10th May and 27th June). The Green Party of England and Wales returns its first Member of Parliament, Caroline Lucas.

2015 The General Election takes place with a widely predicted result of a hung Parlament expected but there is a shock as David Cameron continues as Prime Minister following a Conservative victory (see 2010 above), ending the Conservative and Liberal coalition (see 6th May). The Conservatives have a majority with 331 seats, Labour has 232 seats, the SNP has 56 seats and the Liberal Democrats are almost wiped out, receiving only 8 seats.

8th May: Victory in Europe Day.

1360 The Treaty of Bretigny is signed by Edward III (see 21st June and 13th November) and King John II of France (see 24th October), ending the first phase of the Hundred Years' War 1337-1453. The treaty is a result of the glorious English victory at the Battle of Poitiers (see 19th September) in 1356 and gave huge swathes of France to the English King in return for very little.

1660 Parliament proclaims Charles II as King of England (see 6th February and 29th May), officially restoring the Monarchy after more than ten years of a Commonwealth Republic (see 1st January and 23rd April).

1873 The death of John Stuart Mill in Avignon, France (see 20th May). He was a Philosopher, political economist and thinker, MP and advocate of Women's rights. He was a great believer in and a champion of individual liberty and opposed the meddling of the state in people's lives. In 1851 he married Harriet Taylor who was an early supporter of women's suffrage, and he supported her. She died in 1858 and the following year his most famous work 'On Liberty' was published. He continued his support for individual liberty, women's suffrage, Irish land reform and compulsory education.

1904 The death of Eadweard James Muybridge in Kingston upon Thames in London (see 9th April). Born Edward James Muggeridge, changing his name later in the United States, he was an early photographer and is credited with being the first person to invent a device to project moving pictures. He is most well known for his work with animal locomotion photography and thus discovering and demonstrating, using photography that horse's legs, when in full gallop, leave the ground.

1923 Stanley Baldwin becomes Prime Minister for the first of three times after Andrew Bonar Law resigns (see 3rd August and 14th December).

1945 Victory in Europe (V.E.) Day and the end of the European campaigns of the Second World War after Germany formally surrenders. However, the war in the East would continue (see 15th August), only to be constantly forgotten by many and to be known as the Forgotten War by its veterans. The German surrender was signed at Reims in France the previous day (see 7th May) by General Alfred Jodl representing Admiral Donitz and then ratified in Berlin, enacting the act of surrender (see 3rd September).

2007 The Northern Ireland Assembly is inaugurated at Stormont Castle. Ian Paisley is the First Minister and Martin McGuiness becomes the Second Minister with no swearing on the bible at the swearing in. This is the culmination of years of negotiation involving the Government, Loyalist Parties and Republican Parties (see 31st July, 12th August and 14th August).

9th May:

1386 The Treaty of Windsor is signed and Portugal becomes England's then Britain's oldest ally, as England supported John I of Portugal as the rightful King of Portugal. It is now the oldest alliance in Europe that is still in force.

1671 Colonel Thomas Blood, an Irish adventurer, briefly steals the Crown Jewels (see 24th August) but is pursued and captured whilst still in the proximity of the Tower.

1874 The birth of Howard Carter in London (see 2nd March).

1941 The Royal Navy Captures the German submarine U-110 after its initial attack on an allied convoy. Following depth charges being fired, U-110 was damaged and had to surface. After a brief exchange of fire with HMS Bulldog (see 1945 below) and HMS Broadway, the submarine crew surrendered. After the crew failed to scupper the submarine, she was boarded and an enigma machine and code books were retrieved and taken ultimately to Bletchley Park.

1945 'Liberation Day' in the Channel Islands, which has been celebrated each year since 1945 to mark the end their occupation by the German forces. The Channel Islands were the only part of Great Britain to be invaded and occupied during the Second World War. The article of surrender was signed aboard the B-Class Destroyer HMS Bulldog (see 1941 above) in St. Peter Port in Guernsey (see 30th June).

2007 The European Commission finally 'rules' that it is not illegal, after all, for goods to be sold in this country with the Imperial Measures of pounds and ounces used alongside the metric measures.

10th May:

1719 The Spanish garrison in the Castle of Eileen Donan on the edge of Loch Duich, surrenders to government forces. The Spanish soldiers had been sent from Spain as a support for the Jacobite Rising and as a distraction during the War of the Quadruple Alliance 1718-1719. The Spanish seized the castle but a Royal Navy Squadron of three ships bombarded the castle and after being stormed, the remainder of the garrison surrendered (see 17th February and 10th June).

1768 The 'Massacre of St. Georges Fields' takes place in London next to the King's Bench Prison. Following the arrest and imprisonment of the radical MP John Wilkes (see 19th January, 17th October and 26th December), a huge crowd of around 15,000 had descended on the prison where he was being held. The authorities, fearing the crowd would attempt to free John Wilkes, ordered the troops to open fire, killing seven protestors.

1773 The Tea Act receives Royal assent with immediate implementation (see 16th December). The Act allowed the East India Company (see 31st December) to sell its tea stocks directly to the thirteen colonies in America and to transport the tea directly into the colonies on its own ships thus securing a monopoly.

1798 The death of George Vancouver (see 22nd June) in Petersham near London. He joined the Royal Navy in 1771 and later served on Captain James Cook's (see 14th February and 27th October) second (see 17th January) and third voyages (see 18th January). He served during the Nootka Crisis in 1789 and then between 1791 and 1795 he was in Command of a round-the-world voyage, whose purpose was the exploration of the Pacific Ocean. During this historic journey he was responsible for the charting of the North West Coast of North America, the Sandwich Islands and the South West Coast of Australia. He was one of this country's greatest explorers and Vancouver in

British Columbia and Vancouver Island, amongst others, are named in his honour.

1804 William Pitt the Younger (see 23rd January and 28th May) becomes Prime Minister for the second and final time (see 19th December).

1857 The start of the Indian Mutiny at Meerut near Delhi. Following unrest, arrests and courts martial in the days before (see 24th January and 8th April), large groups of civilians became restless and attacked and killed many Europeans in the town of Meerut. This initially led to some mutineers releasing some of those guilty of refusing to obey orders and the murder of a number of Europeans including women and children. This was followed by a rebellion of large sections of the British Indian Army and a real threat to the Honourable East India Company and our authority in India (see 26th February, 25th September, 16th November and 6th December).

1904 The death of Henry Morton Stanley in London (see 28th January). Born in Wales as John Rowlands, he moved to New Orleans in 1859. He fought for both sides in the American Civil War and later became a journalist, working for the New York Herald. It was for this paper that he was commissioned to look for Doctor David Livingstone in 1869 (see 19th March and 1st May). It was at Lake Tanganyika that he found him in 1871 (see 10th November). Following Livingstone's death in 1873, he continued with the Doctor's exploration of Africa, completing some epic journeys across the continent. He became deeply involved with the development of the Congo region with the support of King Leopold III of Belgium from 1879 onwards. Eventually returning to Britain, he became an MP in 1895 and was knighted in 1899.

1907 The birth of Frederick 'Freddie' Spencer Chapman (see 8th August) in London

1940 Winston Spencer Churchill (see 24th January and 30th November) becomes the greatest Prime Minister this country has had following the resignation of Neville Chamberlain (see 18th March and 9th November). He heads a coalition Government and the country through the Second World War and on to ultimate victory (see 8th May, 15th August and 26th October).

1982 HMS Sheffield, a Type 42 Destroyer, sinks after being hit by an Argentinean Exocet missile six days earlier (see 4th May). Twenty members of her crew were killed in the attack. She was the first Royal Navy ship sunk since the Second World War (see 2nd April and 14th June).

2010 Labour Prime Minister Gordon Brown announces that he will resign as head of the Labour Party and also as Prime Minister as discussions continue between the Liberal Democrats and Conservatives and between the Liberal Democrats and the Labour Party following the Hung Parliament result to the General Election (see 6th May, 7th May and 27th June).

11th May:

973 The Coronation of Edgar I at Bath Abbey, where he became the first English King to become anointed, until then only a Papal privilege.

1655 The surrender of the Spanish Fleet and the capture of Jamaica (see 8th July and 6th August) by Admirals Sir William Penn and Robert Venables and a small force of troops, thus securing the island as a Colony.

1778 The death of William Pitt the Elder, Earl of Chatham (see 15th November), at Bromley in Kent. One of the greatest Whig Prime Ministers, he was known as the 'Great Commoner' and was father of William Pitt the Younger (see 23rd January and 28th May). Often a critic of George II (see 25th October and 30th October), who wanted British troops and money to defend his interests in Hanover, he was always wary of war and favoured a greater use of the Royal Navy to secure the Empire. During his time in Parliament he saw the rapid expansion of the Empire and Britain's increased commercial dominance. He was only Prime Minister for two years but won great favour with the population.

1812 The Prime Minister, Spencer Perceval, is assassinated in the lobby of the House of Commons by John Bellingham (see 18th May and 1st November), who fired a single shot from his pistol. Born in London, he was the second son of the 2nd Earl of Egmont. He studied Law and entered parliament for the first time in 1796. At one point he was both the Solicitor General and the Attorney General. He was against Catholic emancipation and became Prime Minister in 1809, succeeding the Duke of Portland. His assassin had run up business debts in Russia and had failed to get compensation from the British government and therefore sought revenge, blaming the Prime Minister.

1871 The death of John Frederick William Herschel in Kent (see 7th March). Born in Berkshire and the son of Sir Frederick William Herschel (see 25th August and 15th November), he studied at Cambridge. He took up astronomy and is famous for naming moons of the planets Saturn and Uranus. In 1813 he was elected as a fellow to the Royal Society. He was a co-founder of the Royal Astronomical Society in 1820. Between 1833 and 1838 he and his wife moved to South Africa and engaged in several areas of science, including Botany, in which they both studied the local flora and fauna, using early forms of photography to aid in his wife's art work, thus contributing to the role and development of photography.

1926 Representatives of the Trades Union Congress (TUC) visit 10 Downing Street and call off the General Strike (see 3rd May), with many people returning to work the next day (see 12th May).

1940 The first alien residents (all German) are interned as a result of the state of war between our country and Germany. This first wave of internees is all men (see 8th May, 15th August and 3rd September).

2010 Gordon Brown resigns as Prime minister and shortly afterwards, David Cameron becomes Prime Minister of the first Coalition Government for 70 years, thus ending 13 years of Labour power. Nick Clegg, leader of the Liberal Democrats, becomes deputy Prime Minister. Altogether, five of the twenty Cabinet posts go to the Liberal Democrats (see 6th May, 7th May and 27th June).

12th May:

1588 The ill-fated Spanish Armada consisting of 130 ships and around 30,500 men sets sail for England and ultimate destruction at the hands of the English Navy and the weather (see 29th July).

1641 Thomas Wentworth, the Earl of Strafford, is executed by beheading on Tower Hill before a crowd of over 100,000. A key supporter of Charles I (see 30th January and 19th November), he was tried before Parliament in Westminster Hall. However, the trial was abandoned due to his stout defence. Thereafter, a bill of attainder was passed against him by Parliament and he was tried and condemned to death.

1706 The Battle of Ramillies in Flanders, in the Spanish Netherlands, during the War of the Spanish Succession, 1701-1714. The Duke of Marlborough, John Churchill (see 16th June), led an Allied force that was intercepted by a French and Bavarian Army under Marshall Villeroi. It was a total rout for the French army of Louis XIV in a battle that lasted no longer than an hour. The French army lost over 12,000 killed and wounded and 7,000 prisoners and around 70 guns taken, compared to the Allied 1,066 killed and 3,633 wounded. This victory allowed the Duke of Marlborough to gain control of the Spanish Netherlands (see 2nd August).

1780 The rebel-controlled city of Charleston in South Carolina surrenders to General Sir Henry Clinton after a six-week siege during the American colonial rebellion. Despite previous successful attempts to fight off attackers, the humiliating failure to resist and the capitulation resulted in the capture of this key city and the imprisonment of over 5,000 rebel troops. This allowed our forces to concentrate on removing the last remnants of the Continental rebel army from much of the southern colonies (see 29th May and 3rd September).

1797 The second Naval Mutiny at the Nore is led by Richard Parker (see 30th June) when the crew of HMS Sandwich seize control of the ship. However, the mutiny was not a strong united rebellion and many ships slipped away and abandoned the mutiny. Parker was eventually captured, tried and hanged from the yardarm of HMS Sandwich (see 16th April and 15th May).

1812 The birth of Edward Lear (see 29th January) in London.

1820 The birth of Florence Nightingale in Florence in the Grand Duchy of Tuscany (see 13th August).

1860 The death of Charles Barry (see 23rd May) at 'The Elms' Clapham Common. A Victorian architect, he was responsible for many buildings, such as the emerging new clubs in London and Manchester as well as remodelling of large country houses for the wealthy. However, he is most well-known for his work in redesigning the Houses of Parliament. In this he worked closely with Augustus Pugin who worked primarily on the interior.

1911 The Festival of Empire is opened at Crystal Palace in London (see 30th November). The Exhibition was designed to celebrate the Coronation of George V. Part of the Exhibition involved a sports championship, the Inter-Empire Championships between four teams from Australasia (Australia and New Zealand were combined), Canada, South Africa and the United Kingdom (see 16th August).

1918 The Ocean liner RMS Olympic, sister ship to the RMS Titanic (see 15th April), spots the German submarine U-103 and attempts to ram the vessel. The submarine responded by attempting to dive but was successfully struck by the Olympic. With the submarine badly damaged, the crew had no option but to scuttle the boat and then abandoned ship. This is the only time a merchant vessel sank a military ship during the First World War.

1926 The General Strike comes to an end (see 3rd May). After 10 days of unsuccessful striking, the Trades Union Congress (TUC) called off the strike on the 11th May, with many people returning to work the following day. Despite this however, the miners carried on with their strike until November 1926.

1937 The Coronation of George VI at Westminster Abbey (see 6th February and 14th December). This was also the day that had been scheduled for the coronation of his brother Edward VIII (see 28th May, 23rd June and 11th December).

1969 The minimum voting age in the United Kingdom is lowered from 21 to 18 years of age (see 6th February and 14th December).

13th May:

1568 Mary Queen of Scots (see 8th February and 8th December) is defeated at the Battle of Langside in Glasgow by an army led by Protestant Lords and the Regent Moray. The battle lasted for only about 45 minutes before Mary's forces broke and fled, with Mary heading towards England (see 15th May and 9th September).

1607 The first settlers from England arrive at a site that will become the first permanent settlement in 'The New World', later to be called Jamestown (see 10th April, 26th April, 14th May, 3rd September and 21st December).

1835 The death of John Nash (see 18th January) on the Isle of Wight. He was the architect responsible for the Regent Street and the Regents Park areas of London, the Haymarket Theatre as well as remodelling Brighton Pavilion and designing the basis for Trafalgar Square.

1861 Queen Victoria (see 22nd January and 24th May) issues Britain's Declaration of Neutrality over the American Civil War, which at the same time also recognised the Confederate States as co-belligerents. This bestowed upon the ships of the Confederate States the same standing as Union shipping with the Royal Navy. This allowed them to use foreign ports and gave them the opportunity to engage US shipping around the world.

1912 The formal establishment of the Royal Flying Corps (see 1st April) after George V (see 20th January and 3rd June) signed a Royal warrant creating the Corps a month earlier (see 13th April). It was originally led by Brigadier Sir David Henderson.

1940 Winston Churchill (see 24th January and 30th November) gives his famous 'blood, toil, tears and sweat' speech to the House of Commons. This was his first speech to the Commons as Prime Minister (see 10th May).

14th May:

1219 The death of Sir William Marshal, First Earl of Pembroke, one of the greatest of English Knights and the greatest of his own time. Known as an accomplished tournament champion, he came to the attention of Henry II (see 4th March and 6th July) in 1186. He remained loyal to each of his Kings and was rewarded by Richard I (see 6th April and 8th September). He became a leading figure and a safe choice as Regent during the civil wars that marked Henry III's reign (see 1st October and 16th November). His reputation received true glory with his outstanding victories over the French forces of the future Louise VIII at the battles of Lincoln (see 20th May) and Sandwich (see 24th August) both in 1217.

1264 The Battle of Lewes in Sussex, one of the leading battles of the Second Baron's War (1264-1267). Henry III (see 1st October and 16th November) is defeated by Simon De Montfort, 6th Earl of Leicester (see 4th August), being captured along with his son, the future Edward I (see 17th June and 7th July).

1607 The first group of settlers from England make landfall at the site in the Chesapeake Bay chosen to be the first permanent settlement in 'The New World', called Jamestown. Initially it was a three-walled fort containing homes that was situated on an island in the Bay. This was the beginning of what was later to become the United States of America (see 10th April, 26th April, 13th May, 3rd September and 21st December). It was also the very first English, and later British, colony (see 31st December).

1727 The baptism of Thomas Gainsborough in Sudbury, Norfolk (see 2nd August). He was one of this country's greatest known painters.

1771 The birth of Robert Owen in Newtown, Montgomeryshire (see 17th November).

1796 Edward Jenner carries out the world's first vaccination. He inoculates eight year old James Phipps against smallpox (see 26th January and 6th May).

1818 The death of Matthew Lewis (see 9th July) at sea on his return home from Jamaica. A novelist, he is known for his most famous work 'the Monk' published in 1796 that earned him the nickname 'Monk Lewis'. Regarded as one of the early pioneers of the Gothic genre, 'The Monk' was widely criticised at the time for its graphic content.

1879 The death of Henry Sewell in Cambridge (see 7th May and 7th September), generally regarded as the first Prime Minister of New Zealand (see 1st July). Born in Newport on the Isle of Wight, he qualified as a Lawyer and in 1853 he moved to New Zealand, being elected to parliament that same year. Asked by the Governor to form a government following the 1856 general election, he thus became the first Prime Minister of New Zealand. In 1873 he retired from political life and returned to Britain a short time later.

1881 The death of Mary Seacole in London. Born Mary Jane Grant in Kingston, in the Colony of Jamaica in 1805, she was a widely-travelled individual. In 1854 she requested the War Office to send her as an army nurse to the Crimean War (1853-1856). They declined her request but undeterred she travelled to the Crimea using her own funds. There she established her own 'British Hotel' for sick and injured troops. She became known as 'Mother Seacole'. However, after the war she returned to Britain destitute and ill. In 1857 the British press heard about her plight and organised a campaign that raised money for her and later in that same year she published her own memoirs.

1925 The death of Sir Henry Rider Haggard (see 22nd June) in London. A writer of adventure novels, he is most well known for his novels, 'King Solomon's Mines', which was published in 1885, and 'She' in 1886 and 1887. He went on to write a series of novels that centred on the adventurer character of Africa, Allen Quatermain. Prior to becoming an author, he had worked in the Colonies of Natal and Transvaal before returning to Britain and studying law.

1936 The death of Field Marshall Edmund Henry Hynman Allenby (see 23rd April) in London. Commissioned in 1882 he served in Bechuanaland (1884-1885), Zululand (1888) and in the Boer War (1899-1902). At the outset of World War One he led the Cavalry Division in France and directed the Battle of Arras in 1917. Following this he was appointed to lead our forces in Palestine. He is famous as the General who led British forces in the conquest of Syria and Palestine during the First World War. He was responsible for the capture of Gaza in November 1917 and the liberation of Jerusalem in 1917 (see 9th December). In 1918 he led our forces and worked with the Arabs under T E Lawrence (see 19th May and 16th August) in capturing Damascus (see 1st October) and forcing the Turks to sign the Armistice (see 30th October). A strict disciplinarian, he was however popular with his troops. After the war he served as High Commissioner for Egypt.

1940 Anthony Eden (see 14th January and 12th June), Secretary of State for War, announces in a radio broadcast the formation of the Local Defence Volunteers (commonly called the Home Guard). Its purpose was for all men between the ages of 17 and 65 who were ineligible for active military service to volunteer to defend their country from invasion (see 3rd December).

1948 At midnight, the British United Nations Mandate for Palestine ended and the state of Israel declared its independence (see 25th April and 29th September).

15th May:

1567 Mary Queen of Scots marries the Earl of Bothwell, James Hepburn, at Holyrood Palace (see 8th February, 13th May and 8th December).

1645 The birth of George Jeffreys (see 18th April) at Acton Hall, near Wrexham.

1797 The end of the Spithead mutiny (see 16th April). The crew from sixteen ships of the Channel Fleet refused orders to put to sea. Following the break down of negotiations, Admiral Lord Howe intervened and the mutineers were pardoned and their demands for better pay and conditions were met (see 12th May and 30th June).

1800 A second attempt to assassinate King George III fails (see 29th January and 24th May). A deranged former soldier fires a shot at the King as he entered the Royal Box at the Drury Lane Theatre, narrowly missing him. He was applauded for calmly insisting the performance should continue and then falling asleep during the show.

1847 The death of Daniel O'Connell in Genoa, in the Kingdom of Sardinia (see 6th August). He was the leading campaigner for Catholic Emancipation (see 13th April) and the repeal of the Act of Union between Ireland and Great Britain (see 1st January) and was often referred to as 'the Liberator' or 'the Emancipator'. Born in County Kerry, he studied law in Dublin. In 1811 he founded the Catholic Board which campaigned for Catholics to enter parliament. In 1823 he set up the Catholic Association to campaign for better rights and conditions for Catholics. Once he gained Emancipation for Catholics, he unsuccessfully set about campaigning for the repeal of the Act of Union between Great Britain and Ireland (see 1st January). He died on a pilgrimage to Rome. His heart was buried in Rome and his body in Dublin.

1921 The British Legion (later to be known as the Royal British Legion, see 29th May) is founded with the support of Earl Haig, one of the co-founders and first President of the organisation until his death in 1928 (see 29th January and 19th June). It was originally the amalgamation of four different ex-servicemen's organisations that were formed after the Great War. The organisation's purpose was to help all ex-service men and their families.

1941 The first flight of Britain's first Jet Aircraft, the Gloster E28/39, piloted by Gerry Sayer. This aircraft led to the development of the Gloster Meteor, which was Britain's first active jet fighter.

1957 Britain's first H-Bomb (Hydrogen Bomb) is detonated over Christmas Island in the Pacific Ocean. The device was dropped by a Vickers Valiant of 49 Squadron under the code name Operation Grapple. The detonation allowed Britain to demonstrate to both the US and the USSR that we were able to design, build and develop our own independent nuclear deterrent (see 26th February and 3rd October).

16th May:

1152 Eleanor of Aquitaine, former Queen of King Louis VII of France, marries Henry of Anjou, the future King Henry II (see 4th March and 6th July). Through this marriage, Henry gains over half of France.

1620 The death of William Adams (see 24th September) in Hirado, Kyushu, Japan. A sailor and adventurer, he is believed to have been the first Briton to have reached Japan and eventually advised the Shogun on ship-building and contact with the West.

1655 The execution of Colonel John Penrudddock in Exeter (see 12th March and 14th March) by beheading. Along with Sir Joseph Wagstaffe, he organised the Royalist rising, working with the secret Royalist group the 'Sealed Knot'. Together, they took Salisbury and raised the standard for Charles II (see 6th February and 29th May). However, after leaving Salisbury the momentum was soon lost and after a fight lasting no more than three hours, the rising collapsed and he was taken prisoner.

1811 The Battle of Albuera in Spain near the Portuguese border. A British force of around 10,000 men along with 13,000 Spanish and 10,000 Portuguese faced an occupying French force of around 27,000. The Allies were led by Marshal Beresford and General Blake and the French were led by Marshal Soult. We suffered 4,200 casualties, the Portuguese 600 and the Spanish 2,000. The French suffered a total of 7,500 casualties before Marshal Soult was forced to withdraw. Tactically our forces won the battle but it was at great cost. However, it was a battle during which both sides suffered greatly.

1916 The signing of the Sykes-Picot Agreement. It was signed by Sir Mark Sykes and the French diplomat Francois Georges-Picot. This was an understanding between Britain and France over their respective areas of influence in the Middle East, primarily Mesopotamia, after the Great War.

1938 The Women's Voluntary Service (WVS) is founded by Stella Isaacs, the Marchioness of Reading. Its role was originally in civil defence, in particular with Air Raid Precautions and awareness. It also had a lead role in the evacuation of children from urban areas.

1943 Start of Operation 'Chastise', later referred to as 'The Dam Busters' raid of the now famous 617 Squadron. Nineteen Lancaster bombers led by Wing Commander Guy Gibson (see 12th August and 19th September) take off to attack three German dams on the rivers Mohne, Eder and Sorpe (see 17th May) with the objective of causing massive damage to the German industrial areas and their war effort.

17th May:

1220 The second Coronation of Henry III at Westminster Abbey (see 1st October and 16th November). The King had received permission for a second coronation from the Pope as the first one was quickly carried out to give authority to the then nine-year-old King following civil war (see 28th October).

1756 Britain declares war on France and her allies, starting the Seven Years' War (1756-1763), the first 'global' war that would last until 1763 (see 10th February). The two countries would fight each other around the globe in their various Colonies. The war would see our forces victorious, in particular at the battle of Plassey 1757 (see 23rd June) and in the 'annus mirabilis' of 1759, the battle of the Plains of Abraham (see 13th September), the battle of Minden (see 1st August), the battle Lagos (see 18th August and 19th August) and the battle of Quiberon Bay (see 20th November).

1900 The relief of Mafeking by Colonel Sir Bryan Thomas Mahon's Flying Column, consisting of the Imperial Light Horse and Royal Horse Artillery. Mahon's force had to fight their way into the town through the Boer lines but in the end they were too strong for the enemy. It is interesting that back home in Britain, news of the relief gave rise to feelings of incredible joy and celebration. This led to the phrase 'to Mafeking'; to be celebrating excessively (see 14th October). The forces in the town had been under siege for 215 days and were led very effectively by General Robert Baden-Powell (see 8th January and 22nd February).

1943 The conclusion to Operation 'Chastise', later referred to as 'The Dam Busters' raid of the now famous 617 Squadron (see 16th May). Nineteen Lancaster bombers led by Wing Commander Guy Gibson (see 12th August and 19th September) attacked three German dams on the rivers Mohne, Eder and Sorpe. Altogether, 53 of the 133 crew of the operation were killed and three captured and eight Lancaster Bombers were lost. However, two of the three Dams were destroyed which caused massive damage to the surrounding German industrial areas and setting their war effort back many months.

1964 The death of John Theodore Cuthbert Moore-Brabazon in Surrey (see 8th February). The son of an Army Officer, he became the first Englishman to fly a heavier than air machine (see 30th April, 2nd May and 30th October). At the outbreak of the First World War he joined the Royal Flying Corps and served throughout. After the war he was elected to parliament and served in Winston Churchill's (see 24th January and 30th November) wartime government (see 10th May). In 1942 he became Baron Brabazon of Tara.

2011 Elizabeth II (see 21st April) becomes the first British Monarch to visit Ireland since it was granted its independence and became a republic. At the start of the four-day state visit, she visited the Garden of Remembrance, where Ireland remembers those of their country who rebelled against the government (see 24th April, 29th April and 18th May).

18th May:

1795 The death of Robert Rogers in London (see 7th November). Born in the crown colony of the Province of Massachusetts Bay, he served during the Seven Years' War (1756-1763) against the French and their Indian allies. It was during the early part of the war that he raised the famous colonial company of troops that were later called 'Roger's Rangers' that specialised very successfully in reconnaissance and special operations. During the American Colonial rebellion he was suspected by the rebels of being a spy and offered his services as a loyalist, forming the 'Queen's Rangers' around 1776. After the rebellion he was evacuated to Britain in 1783 where he died in obscurity.

1803 Britain declares war on France and its Emperor Napoleon Bonaparte, thus revoking the Treaty of Amiens, signed a year earlier (see 25th March). France had broken a number of treaties with her European neighbours and this was taken as a pretext for war. This was the start of eleven years of war that ended with Napoleon's abdication in 1814.

1812 John Bellingham is executed for the murder of Spencer Percival the Prime Minister (see 11th May). He was publicly hanged outside of Newgate prison in London. Born in 1769 he had run up business debts in Russia for which he was imprisoned, spending a number of years there. Despite his efforts, he had failed to get compensation from the British government and therefore sought revenge, blaming the Prime Minister for his situation.

1927 The death of Private Edwin Hughes (13th Light Dragoons) in Blackpool. He was the last survivor of the Charge of the Light Brigade at Balaclava in 1854 (see 25th October), riding with the 13th Light Dragoons, having his horse shot from under him.

1991 Helen Sharman becomes the first Briton in space at the age of 27. She was a Cosmonaut on the Russian Soyuz TM-11 mission that was called 'Project Juno'. She was accompanied by two Russian Cosmonauts as they blasted off from the launch pad in the Soviet Republic of Kazakhstan.

2010 Parliament sits for the first time since the General Election (see 6th May) with David Cameron as Prime Minister of a Coalition government, the first in 70 years.

2011 On her visit to Ireland, Queen Elizabeth II (see 21st April) laid a wreath at the War Memorial Garden in Dublin, in memory of the 50,000 loyal Irish men who served King and Country against Germany during the Great War. The garden had remained totally neglected until the 1990s, shamefully dishonouring the sacrifice of so many loyal citizens (see 17th May).

19th May:

1536 Anne Boleyn, Henry VIII's (see 28th January and 28th June) second wife is beheaded on Tower Green. Born in Wiltshire, she was the mother of Elizabeth I (see 24th March and 7th September) and had met Henry VIII whilst she was a maid of Catherine of Aragon, Henry's first wife. It was following her marriage to Henry in 1533 (see 25th January) and the declaration of

Henry's first marriage as being null and void that Pope Clement VII excommunicated Henry and thus began the Church of England's break with Rome (see 11th July). She was charged with treason, adultery and incest and found guilty.

1649 The 'Rump' Parliament in Westminster declares England a 'Commonwealth and Free State' by issuing the 'Act Declaring England to be a Commonwealth' after having abolished the Monarchy two months before (see 17th March, 19th March and 6th December).

1652 The battle of Goodwin Sands (or the battle of Dover) in the First Anglo-Dutch War, 1652-1654 (see 31st July). This engagement actually took place before the official declaration of war. The British Fleet was commanded by General at Sea Robert Blake (see 7th August) against the Dutch Lieutenant Admiral Tromp. Refusing to lower his flag in conventional salute, Tromp provoked Blake to fire a warning shot at the Dutch, which in turn gave the Dutch fleet an excuse to engage the British fleet. The Dutch were beaten with the loss of one ship captured and another badly damaged (see 5th April and 2nd June).

1795 The death of James Boswell (see 29th October), writer, friend and biographer of Samuel Johnson (see 7th September and 13th December). In his early life he went to Glasgow University and was taught by Adam Smith (see 5th June and 17th July). Later he studied law at Edinburgh University and travelled to Europe, meeting the likes of Voltaire and John-Jacques Rousseau. He is best remembered for his travels with Doctor Johnson and his book 'Life of Johnson' about his friend.

1879 The birth Nancy Witcher Langhorne (see 2nd May, 28th November and 1st December) in Danville, Virginia in the United States.

1898 The death of Sir William Ewart Gladstone, four times Liberal Prime Minister (see 29th December), from cancer. He was the most dominant figure in late Victorian Politics and campaigned on a number of issues. He began his political life as a Conservative, serving under Sir Robert Peel (see 5th February and 2nd July) when he was Prime Minister. In 1859 he joined the Liberals and in 1867 became their leader. A year later in 1868 he became Prime Minister for the first time. In 1885, during the Mahdist Revolt, he and his government were blamed for the failure to save General Charles Gordon in Khartoum (see 26th January and 28th January) and he was forced to resign. He is well-remembered for his rivalry with the twice Conservative Prime Minister Benjamin Disraeli (see 19th April and 21st December). His latter two terms as Prime Minister are remembered for the contentious issue of Irish Home Rule and his campaign for the Home Rule bill. He is buried in Westminster Abbey.

1935 The death of Thomas Edward (T E) Lawrence in Dorset (see 16th August) as a result of a motorbike accident. A writer, scholar and eventually a soldier, he led Arab revolts and became known as 'Lawrence of Arabia'. Born in North Wales, he studied at Oxford and in 1909 he travelled to Syria and Palestine where he took part in archaeological digs and learned Arabic.

During the First World War he served in Intelligence in Cairo and supported the Aran revolt against Turkey, leading an effective band of irregulars. Despite some major success in 1917 and 1918, he lost faith in British support for Arab independence. He resigned in 1922 and joined the RAF but left in February 1935, just three months before his death.

20th May:

685 The battle of Dunnichen in Southern Scotland is fought between the Picts and Northumbrian Anglo-Saxons. The Anglo-Saxons, under Ecgfrith, advanced into the Pictish kingdom and were attacked in an ambush by Picts, led by Bridei, and destroyed. The Pictish victory freed the Picts, Gaels and Britons from the dominance of the northern Anglo-Saxons for many years.

1217 The Battle of Lincoln at Lincoln Castle between the forces of the young Henry III (1st November and 16th November), under the command of William Marshal (see 14th May) and the future King of France Louis VIII. It was a decisive English victory. The French Prince had landed in England following an invitation from some of the Barons who were resistant to King John (see 18th October and 24th December) and had started the Baron's War. The young King Henry III had, as the leader of his army, one of the greatest fighting men of his time. Marshall mustered a large force that attacked Louis and his forces, driving them from the city and ultimately back to France (see 24th August).

1756 The Battle of Minorca (see 14th March) between 17 ships of the Royal Navy under Admiral John Byng (see 14th March and 29th October) and a French fleet of 19 ships under Marquis de la Galissonniere during the Seven Years' War 1756-1763 (see 17th May). The French were engaged in an attempt to relieve the garrison that was under siege on the island. Unfortunately, despite no ships being lost or captured on either side, Admiral Byng, showing over caution, broke off the pursuit and made for Gibraltar. For his display of over caution, Admiral Byng faced a court martial and was found guilty, being executed by firing squad on board HMS Monarch (see 14th March and 29th October).

1806 The birth of John Stuart Mill in Pentonville (see 8th May), London.

1846 The birth of Sir George Goldie in Douglas on the Isle of Man (see 20th August).

1858 A combined force of allied British and French gun boats, under the command of Admiral Sir Michael Seymour attack and capture the five Taku mud forts at the mouth of the Peiho River in China, thus marking the beginning of the end of the Second Opium War, 1856-1860 (see 13th October, 18th October and 24th October).

1895 The birth of Reginald Joseph Mitchell (see 11th June) in Butt Lane, Kidsgrove in Stoke on Trent (see 5th March).

1930 Oswald Mosley (see 16th November and 3rd December) resigns from his position within the Labour government and is replaced by Clement Attlee (see 3rd January and 8th October). He resigned due to Prime Minister Ramsay MacDonald (see 12th October and 9th November) rejecting his economic plans based on Keynes's ideas on the market to help reduce unemployment (see 28th February, 29th February, 10th March, 27th March, 3rd December and 14th December).

2009 Michael Martin, the Speaker of the House of Commons, announces his resignation, effective on the 22nd June 2009 following controversy over the MP's expenses row. This is the first time this has happened in over 300 years.

21st May:

1421 The Treaty of Troyes is signed in the city of Troyes in France between Henry V of England (see 31st August) and Charles VI of France. The agreement allowed the marriage of Henry V to Charles' daughter Catherine of Valois and for their heirs to succeed to the French throne in preference to the Dauphin, Charles' own son (see 13th April, 21st October and 16th December). The agreement was reached following Henry V's success in his campaign for the control of France and in particular at the battle of Agincourt, 1415 (see 25th October).

1471 The death of Henry VI in the Tower of London (see 6th November and 6th December). He is believed to have been stabbed to death by the future Richard III (see 21st May and 2nd October). The only child of Henry V (see 31st August) and Catherine of Valois, he succeeded to the Throne of England when only nine months old, becoming the youngest monarch in our nation's history. Just two months later he became King of France upon the death of his grandfather Charles VI on 21st October 1422 (see 16th December).

1688 The birth of Alexander Pope in London (see 30th May).

1736 The birth of Francis Egerton (see 8th March), the future 3rd Duke of Bridgewater.

1780 The birth of Elizabeth (née Gurney) Fry in Norwich (see 13th October).

1894 The Manchester Ship Canal, designed by Edward Leader Williams, is officially opened by Queen Victoria (see 22nd January and 24th May).

1917 By Royal Charter from George V (see 20th January and 3rd June), the Imperial War Graves Commission is established, with Edward, Prince of Wales (see 28th May and 23rd June) as its President. The organisation was founded by Fabian Ware (see 29th April and 17th June) with the idea of recording and tending the graves and memorials of all British and Commonwealth soldiers who had died in the First World War in specially dedicated cemeteries. This was later extended to cover those who died in the Second World War. The Commission was renamed the Commonwealth War Graves Commission in 1960.

1982 4,000 British troops of 3 Commando Brigade and the Parachute Regiment carryout an amphibious landing on East Falkland around San

Carlos Water, called Operation Sutton and form a bridgehead to regain the Falkland Islands (see 2nd April, 25th April, 2nd May and 14th June).

1993 The death of Major General John 'Johnny' Dutton Frost (see 31st December) in West Sussex. One of the first to join the newly formed Parachute Regiment, he is best remembered as the leader of the 2nd Parachute Battalion during their heroic stand during the battle of Arnhem in 1944 (see 17th September). During the engagement he was badly wounded and spent the rest of the war as a POW. After the war he served in Malaya during the Emergency there in the 1950s (see 18th June and 31st August). He retired from the army in 1968. He is buried at Milland Cemetery in West Sussex.

2002 The British Overseas Territories Act 2002 is enacted (see 26th February). From today, all previous British Dependant Territories are reclassified as British Overseas Territories. The key change is that from today, all people who were born in any of the British Overseas Territories prior to that date automatically became full British Citizens.

22nd May:

1455 The first Battle of St. Albans starts the War of the Roses 1455-1585. The Yorkists, Richard, Duke of York and Richard, Earl of Warwick and a force of 3,000 captured King Henry VI (see 21st May and 6th December) and killed Edmund Beaufort 2nd Duke of Somerset defeating a force of around 2,000 men. Richard Duke of York then had himself appointed the Constable of England (see 17th February).

1670 The Treaty of Dover is signed secretly between England and France. The Treaty was designed to allow French help to England in an attempt to rejoin the Catholic Church and for the French to aid England in its war against the Dutch.

1794 The capitulation of Bastia to our forces on Corsica led by Admiral Horatio Nelson (see 29th September and 21st October) after a six week siege.

1859 The birth of Sir Arthur Ignatius Conan Doyle in Edinburgh (see 7th July).

1915 The Gretna Green train disaster involving three trains occurs, killing 227 people, the majority from the 6th Battalion of the Royal Scots Fusiliers on their way to sail to Turkey to take part in the Gallipoli campaign (see 19th February and 25th April). This was the worst train disaster in our country's history.

1923 The Prime Minister, Andrew Bonar Law, resigns the Premiership due to advance stages of throat cancer (see 16th September and 30th October) and is succeeded by Stanley Baldwin (see 3rd August and 14th December).

1940 The British Government announces the imposition of the Defence Regulation 18b. This act allowed the internment, at first in prisons and then in camps, such as on the Isle of Man, of anyone viewed as being sympathetic to the Nazis and anyone of German birth or descent who could pose a threat to national security. Perhaps the most famous detainee was Oswald Mosley (see 16th November and 3rd December).

2011 British involvement in Iraq officially comes to an end as the Royal Navy concludes its training of Iraqi naval personnel. The conflict in Iraq cost the lives of a total of 179 military personnel (see 20th March) since the invasion began in 2003.

23rd May:

1701 Captain William Kidd, Scottish privateer and alleged pirate is executed in London for Piracy. Born in Greenock, Scotland, in 1645, his family then moved to the colony at New York (see 27th August and 8th September). He went to sea as a young man and was engaged officially as a privateer to harass and engage French trading vessels on behalf of the colonies and Britain. Arrested in 1699 in Boston after returning from the Indian Ocean, he was brought to London for questioning before being tried in court and sentenced to death. He was blind drunk on rum as he went to the gallows. Following his death, his body was gibbeted over the River Thames as a warning against piracy. There has been some debate as to whether Captain Kidd was actually a pirate or simply a privateer working for the Whig Government at the time.

1795 The birth of Charles Barry (see 12th May), the future Architect of the new Victorian Houses of Parliament.

1800 The death of Henry Cort. Born in 1741 in Lancaster, he worked for the Royal Navy as a Pay Agent. In 1775, he set up a forge in Fareham where he perfected his technique of 'puddling and rolling', which allowed the use of coke to replace coal as a fuel to make bar and pig iron. This helped provide iron for the Navy. However, his over enthusiasm caused him to invest naval money in his control into his business which was discovered and he was ruined.

1873 The North West Mounted Rifles (NWMR), forerunners of the Royal Canadian Mounted Police, are formed by Canada's first Prime Minister, John A Macdonald (see 11th January, 6th June and 1st July).

24th May: Empire Day.

1153 The death of David I of Scotland at Carlisle. Born about 1080, he was the sixth son of Malcolm III and Margaret of Wessex. A pious man, he was the first Scottish monarch to issue coinage and also reformed civil institutions as well as founding Royal Burghs. He also improved relations with England, encouraging Anglo-Norman immigration to Scotland whilst expanding Scotland's borders by annexing Cumberland, Northumberland and Westmorland (see 25th November).

1738 The birth of George William Frederick, the future George III (see 29th January and 12th August) in Norfolk House, St. James's Square. He was the son of Frederick, Prince of Wales and Augusta of Saxe-Gotha and the grandson of George II (see 25th October and 30th October).

1792 The death of Admiral Sir George Brydges Rodney in Hanover Square, London. Born in February 1718 in Walton on Thames, he was a leading Naval Officer and later an MP. He joined the Royal Navy at the age of fourteen, serving in the Seven Years' War, 1756-1763, the American Rebellion 1776-1783 and leading Britain to victory in the battle of Cape St. Vincent in 1780 (see 16th January) and in his glorious victory over the French at the Battle of the Saintes in 1782 (see 12th April). Following this glorious victory he retired from naval service and led a quite life until his death.

1798 The outbreak of the Irish rebellion led by the 'United Irishmen' (see 22nd August). Despite initial confusion amongst the rebels in Dublin as government forces reinforce the city, the rebels rise up around Dublin and clashes take place with the government troops (see 21st June).

1819 The birth of Princess Alexandrina Victoria at Kensington Palace (see 22nd January and 1902 below). She was the daughter of Prince Edward, Duke of Kent, the fourth son of George III and Princess Victoria of Saxe-Coburg-Saalfeld.

1854 The first Parliament of New Zealand met for the first time in Auckland (see 6th February and 1st July) after the first elections the previous year.

1870 The birth of Jan Christiaan Smuts in Malmesbury, Cape Colony (see 11th September).

1902 And each subsequent year is Empire Day (see 1959 below). The date decided upon was Queen Victoria's birthday and was originally chosen as a celebration in the Dominion of Canada (see 1916 below). 1902 was the first time Empire Day was marked and this was after the tireless efforts of Clementina Trenholm Fessenden (see 4th May and 14th September). A celebration of the true greatness of our Glorious Empire and the good that has arisen throughout the history of our Great Country that many are nowadays so ashamed of for no real reason. The celebrations for Empire Day spread to the other Dominions and colonies and showed that the world would be far worse without the benefits of our Empire. As part of the celebrations, children were often let out of school early, there were parties and parades, bonfires and fire works were lit as a show of joy and pride in our Glorious Empire, the Mother country and their collective achievements. *"Remember, Remember Empire Day, the 24th of May"*.

1916 Having been celebrated since 1904, Empire Day is officially recognised in Britain by the government following much pressure and work by Reginald Brabazon, Lord Meath (see 31st July and 12th October) as well as the fine example of the celebration being set across the Empire itself.

1930 The aviator Amy Johnson, lands in Darwin, Australia, after flying solo in her aircraft *Gypsy Moth* from London in just 19 ½ days and covering 11,000 miles (see 5th January and 1st July).

1941 The Battle of Denmark Strait and the sinking of HMS Hood by the German Battleship Bismarck. There were only three survivors from a crew of 1,419. An Admiral Class battle cruiser, she was the pride of the Royal Navy and the nation and her freak sinking in combat with the Bismarck was a major shock to the population during the war. However, she was part of a four-ship attack on the Bismarck with the intention of destroying the German ship (see 27th May).

1950 The death of Field Marshal Archibald Percival Wavell (see 5th May) in London. He was one of the leading British Generals of the Second World War. Born in Colchester, he was educated at Sandhurst and received a commission in 1901. He was decorated in the Boer War (1899-1902) and later served in northern India. When the First World War broke out he went with the BEF to France where he was badly wounded, losing his left eye. During the Second World War he formed Middle East Command and, despite numerical inferiority with the Italians, drove them back over 500 miles and captured Tobruk in 1941. Later however, the Germans had more success and he was replaced by General Auchinleck. He then took command of our forces in India fighting the Japanese. It was here that, despite some initial difficulties, he supervised the liberation of Burma. In 1943 he was appointed Governor General and Viceroy of India which post he held until replaced by Lord Mountbatten in 1947.

1959 In a sad bow to what is now called political correctness; Empire Day becomes Commonwealth Day until 1996 when it is absorbed into the Queen's Official Birthday celebrations, celebrated on the 11th June.

1995 The death of James Harold Wilson in London (see 11th March). He was Labour Prime Minister twice from 1964 to 1970 and again 1974 to 1976. Born in Yorkshire he visited 10 Downing Street when he was eight years old. He studied at Oxford University and entered Parliament in 1945. After Hugh Gaitskell died, he won the leadership of the Labour party and in 1964 he won the general election (see 15th October) but he was Prime Minister of a minority government. During his terms in Office he devalued the pound in 1967, oversaw the withdrawal of our influence in the east, in particular Suez and Aden, and introduced many social reforms. Then in 1976 he surprised everyone with his announcement to resign (see 16th March), allowing James Callaghan to take over as Prime Minister.

25th May:

735 The death of the Venerable Bede in Jarrow. He entered the Monastery of St. Peter and St. Paul in Jarrow at the age of 7, around 680AD. He was a prolific writer and his most famous work was his 'Ecclesiastical History of the English People' completed in 731. He is also credited with popularising the use of the terms BC and AD with reference to the recording of time.

1659 Richard Cromwell's (see 12th July and 4th October) renunciation as the Lord Protector is read to Parliament, after the protectorate and the position of Lord Protector was abolished by Parliament earlier in the month (see 7th May). This then allowed Parliament the opportunity to instigate the restoration of the Monarchy (see 29th May).

1713 The birth of John Stuart, later the 3rd Earl of Bute (see 10th March) in Edinburgh.

1768 Captain James Cook (see 14th February and 27th October) sets off on his first voyage to explore the Antipodes.

1803 The birth of Edward George Earle Bulwer-Lytton (see 18th January) at 31 Baker Street in London.

1871 The Bank Holidays Act is passed. Four Bank Holidays were designated for England, Wales and Ireland and five for Scotland.

1914 The House of Commons passes the third Irish Home Rule bill by a majority of 77. The bill was intended to provide for a self-governing Ireland within the United Kingdom of Great Britain and Ireland (see 24th April, 29th April, 6th December and 8th December).

1982 HMS Coventry, a Type 42 Destroyer, is sunk to the North-West of Falkland Sound. Posted to her position with HMS Broadsword, they were to act as decoys to incoming enemy aircraft to protect other ships in San Carlos Bay. After repeated attacks by Argentinean Skyhawk aircraft (a number of which were successfully shot down), she was struck by three bombs, two of which exploded, and within twenty minutes she was abandoned and had capsized, sinking shortly thereafter. Nineteen of the crew were killed in the attack and thirty injured. However, one of the injured died of his wounds in 1983 (see 2nd April and 14th June).

26th May:

1650 The birth of John Churchill (see 16th June) at Ashe House in Devon.

1703 The death of Samuel Pepys (see 1st January and 23rd February) in Clapham and he was buried at St. Olaves Church. He was a famous diarist, Secretary to the Admiralty and, for a time, a Member of Parliament and was elected as a fellow of the Royal Society in 1665. He was a witness to the Great Plague and subsequent Fire of London in 1665 and 1666 respectively.

1733 The 'Flying Shuttle', which would revolutionise the Lancashire cotton industry, is patented by the Warrington clock maker, John Key, assistant to Richard Arkwright.

1840 The death of Admiral Sir William Sidney Smith (see 21st June) in Paris. He joined the Navy in 1777 and saw service during the American Colonial Rebellion. He later fought at the Battle of Cape St. Vincent in 1780 (see 16th January), the Battle of Chesapeake in 1781 (see 5th September). He then fought for the Swedes in the Russo-Swedish War. He then saw active service during the French revolutionary wars. In 1796 he was captured and spent two years in prison in Paris before mounting a daring escape with the aid of French Royalists. He went on to fight in the battle of the Nile in 1798 (see 1st August) and served extensively in the Mediterranean.

1879 The Treaty of Gandamak is signed in an army camp near the village, bringing an end to the Second Afghan War, 1878-1880 (see 27th July). It was signed by Sir Pierre Louis Napoleon Cavagnari for the British Government in India and by King Mohammed Yaqub Khan for the Afghans. The Afghans agreed to receive a permanent British resident and to conduct Afghan foreign policy in accordance with British advice. The Afghans also ceded areas to British control, agreed commercial contacts and allowed for a telegraph line between Kabul and India.

1940 The start of 'Operation Dynamo', the evacuation of Allied troops from Dunkirk when the Admiralty ordered ships to Dunkirk to begin the evacuation (see 4th June) and that all forces in France were, as Secretary of State for War, Sir Anthony Eden (see 14th January and 12th June) said, to prepare for evacuation. The first ships and troops to leave Dunkirk left the following day (see 27th May).

27th May:

1199 King John *'Lackland'* is crowned at Westminster Abbey (see 18th October and 24th December).

1679 The Habeas Corpus Act becomes law, forever after preventing anyone being held in prison without trial.

1774 The birth of Francis Beaufort (see 17th December) in Ireland.

1815 The birth of Henry Parkes (see 27th April) in Warwickshire.

1897 The birth of John Douglas Cockcroft in Todmorden in Yorkshire (see 18th September).

1914 The death of Sir Joseph Wilson Swann (see 31st October) in Surrey. A Chemist and physicist, he is famous for inventing the incandescent electric light bulb in 1878. His house was the first in the world to be lit by a bulb and three years later, in 1881, the Savoy Hotel in Westminster became the very first public building in the world to be lit with his bulbs.

1940 The second day of 'Operation Dynamo', as the first of the flotilla of ships leave British ports to cross the Channel to evacuate Allied troops from the beaches around Dunkirk (see 26th May and 4th June).

1941 10.39am: The German Battleship Bismarck is finally sunk after an intense battle, primarily with the Battleships HMS King George V and HMS Rodney. She had been attacked and torpedoed by Swordfish aircraft flown from HMS Ark Royal (see 13th November and 14th November) the previous day and badly damaged. There were only 110 survivors from a crew of around 2,200 (see 24th May).

28th May:

1660 The birth of George, Prince-elector of Hanover, the future George I, at Leineschloss in Hanover (see 11th June, 1st August and 20th October).

1672 The Battle of Solebay between British and Dutch Fleets and was the first battle in the Third Anglo-Dutch War (1672-1674). Our force of over 90 ships was commanded by James, Duke of York (see 5th September and 14th October), against about 75 Dutch ships. The outcome was inconclusive, with one English ship, the Royal James and one Dutch ship destroyed and one captured.

1759 The birth of William Pitt 'The Younger' (see 23rd January, 10th May and 19th December) in Hayes, Kent. He was the son of William Pitt 'the Elder' (see 11th May and 15th November).

1937 The Prime Minister Stanley Baldwin (see 3rd August and 14th December) retires from office and is succeeded by Neville Chamberlain (see 18th March and 9th November).

1951 The very first episode of the 'Goon Show' is broadcast on the BBC Home Service. It featured Spike Milligan (see 27th February and 16th April), Peter Sellers (see 24th July and 8th September), Harry Secombe (see 11th April and 8th September) and for the first two series, Michael Bentine. The Goons were the forerunners of all modern day comedy and through the scripts of Spike Milligan influenced comedy for the rest of the century.

1972 The death of Edward VIII, later the Duke of Windsor, after his abdication, in Paris (see 23rd June and 11th December). Well-known for his playboy lifestyle, very much like his Grandfather Edward VII (see 6th May and 9th November), he had to abdicate the throne due to his desire to marry the American divorcee Wallis Simpson. Later, during the 1930s and 1940s, he became infamous for his apparent sympathies towards Nazi Germany.

1982 The start of the Battle of Goose Green on the Falkland Islands. The 2nd Battalion the Parachute Regiment (2 Para) attack and take heavily-armed Argentinean positions during an intense 14-hour battle. During the assault on the Argentine positions, two V.C.'s are won in this action. The battalion lost 17 killed and 47 wounded whilst the Argentineans lost 47 killed, 120 wounded and around 1000 captured. During the battle, lieutenant-Colonel Herbert 'H' Jones was killed, earning a posthumous VC. This battle is generally recognised as the turning point in the battle for the Islands (see 2nd April and 14th June).

29th May: Oak Apple Day.

1630 The birth of Charles II at St. James Palace (see 6th February), the son of Charles I (see 30th January, 19th November and 1660 below) and Henrietta Maria, the daughter of Henry IV of France.

1660 Charles II (see 6th February) and the Monarchy are restored as Charles enters London on his thirtieth birthday after returning from exile in the Southern Netherlands. '*Oak Apple Day*' held annually on this date until well into Victorian times, celebrates this joyous occasion (see 4th April and 3rd

September) and was declared by Parliament in 1660 as a holiday to celebrate the end of tyranny and the restoration of the Monarchy.

1780 The Battle of Waxhaws during the colonial rebellion in the American colonies (see 3rd September). Regular and Loyalist forces, under the command of Lieutenant-Colonel Banastre Tarleton faced a much larger force of Virginian rebels under the command of Abraham Buford. Many of the rebels, when they were charged by the Loyalist cavalry, simply threw down their weapons and attempted to surrender (see 12th May).

1829 The death of Humphry Davy (see 17th December), renowned chemist and inventor, in Geneva, Switzerland. Born in Penzance in Cornwall in 1778, he studied science in Bristol. In 1803 he became a Fellow of the Royal Society and his lectures became very popular with London society. Over the following years he isolated numerous chemical substances and in 1812 was knighted by George III (see 29th January and 24th May). In 1813 he travelled across Europe and France in particular, receiving an award from Napoleon at the height of Britain's war with France. In October 1815 he invents and patents his Miners safety lamp (see 17th December) and in his later years he was helped by his assistant, Michael Faraday (see 25th August and 22nd September).

1904 Winston Spencer Churchill crosses the floor of the House of Commons from the Conservative benches to the Liberal benches (see 24th January and 30th November).

1953 Sir Edmund Hillary and the Sherpa Tenzing Norgay reach the summit of Mount Everest in Nepal (see 24th September). The first people to climb the Mountain, the pair spent about fifteen minutes on the summit, taking photographs as evidence.

1971 The British Legion is granted a Royal Charter to mark its fiftieth anniversary and is given the honour of bearing the prefix 'Royal' thus becoming the Royal British Legion (see 15th May).

30th May:

1381 The start of the Peasants' Revolt in the village of Fobbing in Essex. Villagers refused to pay the taxes they were charged with owing to a local collector who they sent away empty handed. Upon their refusal, there was an attempt to arrest their leader and immediately violence broke out, involving the deaths of several people. From this point the revolt quickly spread across the country, in particular in the south (see 15th June).

1431 Joan of Arc is executed by burning at the stake for heresy in the city of Rouen, the capital of English France. Born in 1412 she had received visions as a young girl and was convinced that she was to lead a rebellion and the French to victory against the English and their Allies to drive them out of English France. She was captured by the Burgundian allies of England and handed over to the English to face trial (see 19th January, 21st May and 25th October).

1536 The marriage of Henry VIII (see 28th January and 28th June) and Jane Seymour, his third wife, in the Palace of Whitehall (see 24th October).

1593 The death of Christopher Marlowe, playwright, dramatist, poet and alleged spy in an Inn in Deptford (see 26th February). He was born in 1564 in Canterbury where he was educated. Known as Kit, he was a contemporary of William Shakespeare (see 23rd April) and a prolific dramatist, his greatest works included 'Tamburlaine the Great' and 'Doctor Faustus'. Little is known about his personal life but rumours about his involvement as a government spy have persisted, possibly due to his murky connections he became embroiled in an argument and a fight with a friend, Ingram Frizer, who stabbed him in the eye killing him.

1744 The death of Alexander Pope (see 21st May) in Twickenham. He is often viewed as the greatest Poet of his time and one of the few to make a living from his work whilst still alive. He best known works are his translations of Homers the 'Iliad' and the 'Odyssey'. Born in London in 1688 to Catholic parents, he received little formal education. As a child he suffered severe headaches and illness, growing to only 4' 6 inches with a noticeable curved spine. In 1712 he produced his famous 'Rape of the Lock' which secured him fame and the beginning of an income. The following year he began his six-volume translation of Homer's 'Iliad' and after 1719 he translated Homer's 'Odyssey'. In response to severe criticism he published his controversial 'Dunciad' and later still in 1734 he published his 'Essay on Man'. After this his output slowed considerably due to his failing health.

1757 The birth of Henry Addington, in London (see 15th February and 17th March)

1814 The Treaty of Paris between the allies Britain, Austria, Russia and Prussia with France that brought an end to the first part of the Napoleonic Wars (see 10th February). It saw the reinstatement of the Bourbon Monarchy in France under Louis XVIII but it was widely considered to be extremely lenient towards France, in an effort to bolster the Monarchy (see 9th June, 18th June and 20th November).

1871 Whit Monday becomes Britain's first Bank Holiday. This lasts until 1967 when the bank holiday is replaced with the Spring Bank Holiday Monday at the end of May.

1929 The General Election. The result was a hung parliament, with the Labour Party's Ramsay MacDonald becoming Prime Minister (see 22nd January, 12th October and 9th November).

1942 RAF Bomber Command launches 'Operation Millennium', its first raid of a thousand bombers against the German targets, mainly the city of Cologne when it drops around 2,000 tons of bombs in the raid from a total starting force of 1,047 aircraft (see 28th June).

31st May:

1076 Waltheof, Earl of Northumbria, is executed for his part in the rebellion against William the Conqueror (see 9th September), known as the Revolt of the Earls. Having previously resisted William and then submitted himself, he finally took part in the Revolt in 1075, which was the last serious act of resistance against the Norman invader (see 28th September and 14th October). He was beheaded on St. Giles' Hill near Winchester.

1859 The Clock on the Clock Tower of the new Houses of Parliament began to display the time for the first time (see 11th July).

1863 The birth of Francis Younghusband in Muree, British India (see 31st July and 2nd August).

1889 The Naval Defence Act receives Royal Assent. The Act of Parliament was introduced by the government of Lord Salisbury (see 3rd February and 22nd August) and proposed the concept of the 'two-power standard' whereby the Royal Navy would be maintained at twice the size and strength of the nearest two navies combined, which at that time was France and Russia. To this end the Act provided over the following four years an extra £20 million pounds for another seventy vessels of different styles (see 11th December).

1902 The signing of the Treaty of Vereeniging in Pretoria ending the South African War (Boer War), 1899-1902, and ensuring British protection for the two Colonies of Natal and Cape Colony as well as the two new Colonies of the Orange River Colony and the Transvaal, both previously Boer Republics (see 11th October).

1910 The Union of South Africa comes into being as the four Colonies of Cape Colony, Natal Colony, Orange River Colony and Transvaal Colony unite to receive Dominion status within the Empire (see 1902 above, 13th August and 11th October). Louis Botha (see 27th August and 7th September) becomes the Dominion's first Prime Minister.

1911 The launch of the RMS Titanic in Belfast (see 15th April) at the Harland and Wolf Shipyard. It was only the hull that was launched and the construction and outfitting was complete by March 1912.

1915 The first Zeppelin raid on London is carried out by Zeppelin LZ38 with the loss of seven lives and thirty-five injured (see 19th January, 7th June and 24th December).

1916 The Battle of Jutland in the Great War begins. It was the greatest naval battle of the First World War and was between the German Imperial Navy's High Seas Fleet, Commanded by Vice-Admiral Reinhard Scheer and the Royal Navy's Grand Fleet commanded by Admiral Sir John Jellicoe near Denmark. Although the results were technically inconclusive, it resulted in the continued dominance of the North Sea by the Royal Navy. The Germans claimed victory due to the amount of tonnage lost and the greater number of casualties sustained by ourselves compared to the Germans. However, following the battle, the High Seas Fleet was never again able to even contemplate another confrontation with the Royal Navy and therefore the overall victory lay with the Royal Navy, as this was the Imperial German

Navy's only major naval engagement. We lost 14 ships (113,300 tonnes) and over 6,000 men killed. The Germans lost 11 ships (62,300) and over 2,500 killed. Those ships lost were HMS Indefatigable, HMS Invincible, HMS Queen Mary, HMS Black Prince, HMS Warrior, HMS Defence, HMS Tipperary, HMS Shark, HMS Sparrowhawk, HMS Turbulent, HMS Ardent, HMS Fortune, HMS Nestor and HMS Nomad. May the sacrifice of the crews and their contribution to the denial of freedom to the German Navy never be forgotten.

JUNE

1st June:

1679 The Battle of Drumclog in South Lanarkshire, between rebellious Covenanters attending an illegal Conventical conducted by the Reverend Thomas Douglas and Government Dragoons under John Graham of Claverhouse (see 27th July) occurs. The Covenanters force of around 200 men, under the command of William Cleland, some of whom were mounted, easily routed the troops but the victory was short lived as the battle of Bothwell Bridge in 1679 (see 22nd June) saw the rebels defeated by Government troops.

1740 The Plantation Act comes into effect within the North American colonies. The act allowed any non-British Protestant living in the colonies for seven years or more without a break of more than two months to be regarded as a natural born subject (see 4th July, 3rd September and 5th September) of the Kingdom. The act is notable in that it made provision for Jews and Quakers but not Catholics to become naturalised without the need for the previous Sacramental test.

1794 The 'Glorious First of June' or the Battle of Ushant, when the British Fleet under Admiral Howe (see 8th March and 5th August) defeated the French Navy. Although a series of intermittent clashes from the end of May, this was the first great naval battle of the French Revolutionary Wars and emphasised the greatness of the Royal Navy. Led by Admiral Earl Howe, our losses were 8 ships damaged, 287 men killed and 811 wounded. The French navy was severely mauled and never fully recovered, losing 7 ships and 13 damaged, 1,500 men killed, 2,000 wounded and 3,000 captured.

1813 In a stunning action during the War of 1812 (see 18th June and 24th December), HMS Shannon engages the much larger American frigate USS Chesapeake outside Boston harbour and takes her as a prize. HMS Shannon was commanded by the heroic Captain Broke and during the action the Chesapeake, with a much less professional crew and Captain was devastated and eventually boarded by a superior British crew (see 15th January). The Chesapeake was entered into service with the Royal Navy as HMS Chesapeake until she was broken up in 1820.

1935 The red learner or 'L' plates are made compulsory on motor vehicles driven by people who have not yet passed their driving test.

1939 The submarine HMS Thetis sinks in Liverpool Bay whilst on sea trials and its maiden voyage. A total of 99 men were lost, 53 were sailors, 9 naval officers, 26 were engineers from Cammell Laird (the builders of the submarine) and several others, whilst on sea trials. There were only four survivors. The loss was considered to be due to a design fault that then caused confusion on board. Later that year she was salvaged, refitted and re-launched as HMS Thunderbolt (see 14th March).

1943 BOAC Flight 777, from Portela Airport in Lisbon, Portugal to Whitchurch Airport in Bristol is shot down by German aircraft over the Bay of Biscay. There were no survivors. On board the Douglas DC-3 was the actor Leslie Howard and ever since there have been speculation and conspiracy theories about the reasons surrounding the attack. These include that Howard was a spy and that the Germans were under the impression that Winston Churchill (see 24th January and 30th November) was on board.

1946 The radio licence was increased from 10s to £1 per year. At the same time, at a cost of £2 for a year the first Television Licence was introduced.

1999 The death of Sir Christopher Sydney Cockerell (see 4th June and 25th July) in Hythe in Hampshire. An engineer, he is best known as the inventor of the modern hovercraft. During the war he worked on the radar system and began work on the hovercraft design in 1953. The prototype hovercraft SR-NI was launched in 1959 and crossed the Channel from Dover to Calais on 25th July 1959. He was knighted in 1969.

2nd June:

1653 The Battle of the Gabbard begins off the coast of Suffolk. This was a major engagement during the First Anglo-Dutch War (1652-1654) and the first battle to involve the complete fleets of both the English and Dutch (see 19th May). The English Navy had, under the Command of Generals at Sea George Monck (see 3rd January and 6th December) and Richard Deane, over one-hundred ships against the Dutch with almost one hundred under the command of Admiral Maarten Tromp. Attacking the Dutch under new guide lines and involving the 'line of battle' technique, the Dutch were out-fought and suffered heavy casualties, especially when General at Sea Robert Blake arrived (see 7th August).

1780 The Gordon Riots begin when a crowd of up to 50,000 people march to St. George's Fields in London. They were originally opposed to the Catholic Relief Act of 1778 which relieved some of the penalties on Catholics. Their leader, Lord George Gordon, had set up a Protestant association in 1780 to force the repeal of the Act. While he presented a petition to Parliament, the protesters outside became rowdy. It eventually got out of hand and it turned into a full blown anti-Catholic riot with the mob running riot for several days attacking and burning some Catholic homes and buildings (see 7th June).

1840 The birth of Thomas Hardy in Dorset (see 11th January).

1857 The birth of Edward Elgar in Broadheath, near Worcester (see 23rd February).

1908 The death at home in Crediton of Sir Redvers Henry Buller VC (see 7th December) a leading Victorian General who was blamed, unjustifiably, for the initial failures of the British campaign during the Second Boer War 1899-1902. During a long army career he took part in the Second Opium War (1856-1860), the Red River Expedition in Canada (1870), the Ashanti Campaign (1873-1874) and the Zulu War in 1879 where he won his Victoria Cross (see 26th June). This was followed by service during the First Boer War (1881) and the Sudan Campaign (1885-1899). His last role was in command during the Second Boer War (1899-1902) where he unfairly shouldered the blame for initial defeats and he was sacked in 1900, although he received huge public support and sympathy. However, upon his return to Britain he chose quiet retirement until his death.

1953 Queen Elizabeth II is crowned at Westminster Abbey (see 21st April) as Queen of the United Kingdom of Great Britain and Northern Ireland, the Commonwealth Realms and head of the Commonwealth of Nations (see 6th February). There were many dignitaries and Heads of State present amongst the 1,000 guests. Millions listened to it on the radio around the world as well as many watching on the very latest technology, the television (see 3rd June, 4th June and 9th September).

3rd June:

1657 The death of William Harvey, a Physician who described the circulation of the blood being pumped around the body. He studied at Caius College in Cambridge before studying medicine at the University of Padua in Italy. He returned to England and in 1607 became a fellow of the Royal College of Physicians and in 1618 he was appointed as 'Physician Extraordinary' to James VI (James I of England see 27th March and 19th June). In 1628 he published his theories on the heart and how it was responsible for the circulation of blood around the body.

1665 The Battle of Lowestoft during the Second Anglo-Dutch War (1665-1667) and the Dutch are defeated by the Royal Navy. The battle commenced at 4am. Our Fleet was commanded by James Duke of York as he led 109 ships against a Dutch Fleet of 103 ships. It was a resounding victory for our Fleet and a devastating and humiliating defeat for the Dutch. We lost only one ship and 283 men while the Dutch lost 32 ships and around 4,000 dead.

1726 The birth of James Hutton in Edinburgh, Scotland (see 26th March).

1761 The birth of Henry Shrapnel (see 13th March) in Bradford on Avon in Wiltshire.

1804 The birth of Richard Cobden (see 2nd April) in Midhurst in Sussex.

1865 The birth of the future George V (see 20th January, 23rd April and 22nd June) at Marlborough House, London. His full name was George Frederick Ernest Albert Saxe-Coburg and Gotha. He was the second son of Edward VII (6th May and 9th November) and Princess Alexandra of Denmark.

1900 The death of Mary Henrietta Kingsley in Islington in London (see 13th October). Born in London, she had a limited education. The year 1893 was her first visit to the west of Africa. She travelled extensively and lived with the native peoples and through her subsequent lectures and publications did much to improve the public's awareness of the African people and their customs as well as collecting many specimens for the British Museum. She volunteered as a nurse in the Boer War (1899-1902) where she contracted, and then died from, typhoid.

1919 An Armistice is granted between Afghan rebels and our forces bringing an end to the three months of conflict in the Third Afghan War (see 6th May and 8th August).

2012 Sunday: The Thames Jubilee River Pageant proceeds from Battersea to Tower Bridge at 3pm. The flotilla of vessels, made up of over a thousand boats, marks the Queen's Diamond Jubilee (see 6th February) and is the largest flotilla on the Thames for over three hundred years. The Queen leads the pageant on board 'The Spirit of Chartwell' and after leading the pageant under Tower Bridge, the Royal Barge stops at HMS President as the flotilla passes by in salute (see 4th June, 9th September and 18th December).

4th June:

1792 The death of General John Burgoyne, known as 'Gentleman Johnny' (see 24th February). He first saw active during the Seven Years' War 1756-1763. In 1777 during the American Colonial Rebellion he surrendered the town of Saratoga to the rebels along with his force of 5,500 men, a decision for which he was harshly criticised. In his later years he was the Commander in Chief of Ireland for a period and became a Member of Parliament and a noted playwright.

1833 The birth of Garnet Joseph Wolseley (see 25th March) in Golden Bridge, County Dublin, Ireland.

1910 The birth of Christopher Sydney Cockerell in Cambridge (see 1st June and 25th July).

1913 Derby day and the suffragette Emily Wilding Davison throws herself in front of the King's horse 'Anmer' and is mortally wounded (see 8th June and 11th October), dying four days later.

1940 The completion of 'Operation Dynamo', the evacuation of the Dunkirk beaches by hundreds of vessels, large and small. The last of the heroic rear guard of British and French units defending the immediate area around the beaches surrender after being surrounded and cut off by the advancing German forces (see 26th May, 27th May and 12th June). The last of the 338,000 rescued left the harbour at around 3.40am.

2012 Bank Holiday Monday: as part of the Queen's Diamond Jubilee (see 21st April), a concert is held outside Buckingham Palace around the Victoria Memorial. Some 10,000 ticket holders and 2,000 VIPs along with over 200,000 along the Mall and in the Parks celebrate the Jubilee with a huge line up of stars. Prior to the concert, the 10,000 ticket holders had a picnic in the Palace gardens and received a hamper for lunch as a souvenir (see 6th February, 3rd June, 9th September and 18th December).

5th June:

1723 The birth of Adam Smith in Kirkcaldy (see 17th July).

1875 Alexander Graham Bell (see 3rd March and 2nd August) and his assistant Thomas Watson produce the very first intelligible telephonic transmission in America after moving there from Canada after previously emigrating from Britain.

1883 The birth of John Maynard Keynes (see 21st April) in 6 Harvey Road, Cambridge.

1900 British troops capture Pretoria, Capital of the Orange Free State in South Africa, during the Boer War, 1899-1902 (see 31st May). Our forces, under the command of General Sir Frederick Roberts, approach the city and take it with no resistance from the Boers, who abandoned the city and melted away at the approach of our Imperial forces.

1916 HMS Hampshire sinks off the coast of Orkney after hitting a mine. All but 12 men on board are killed. Amongst the dead is Field Marshall Lord Horatio Herbert Kitchener (see 24th June). Kitchener was one of the great Victorian and Edwardian Generals. He saw service in Egypt, the Sudan (at Omdurman, see 2nd September), in India and in the Boer War, 1899-1902. At the start of the Great War, he was appointed Secretary of State for War by the Prime Minister Herbert Asquith (see 15th February and 12th September).

1964 The first launch of Britain's 'Blue Streak' ballistic missile at the Woomera test range in Australia (see 28th June and 5th November). The missile was designed and built primarily by de Havilland to replace the V Bomber and allow this country the capability to deliver a nuclear deterrent. Unfortunately due to increasing costs and a lack of determination by the government, the military aspect of the project was cancelled. The technology was then used to develop the 'Black Arrow' satellite launch system (see 28th October).

1975 The first ever Referendum is held nationally on whether Britain should remain within the Common Market (European Economic Community or EEC). Still only one of three referendums ever held (see 5th May), the result was 67% (from a 65% electorate turn out) in favour of remaining within the Common Market. The 'yes' campaign had been led by the Prime

Minister Harold Wilson (see 11th March and 24th May), but the parties had all been divided on the question.

6th June: D Day
The beginning of the Liberation of Europe

1762 The death of Admiral George Anson, 1st Baron Anson (see 23rd April). A wealthy and prominent individual, he is one of the best remembered Naval Commanders. He entered the Royal Navy in 1712 and in 1740 he was given command of a poorly-manned squadron to harass Spanish trade and territories in the Pacific Ocean. On this mission he lost so many men to disease that towards the end only his ship, the Centurion, remained. Despite this, he captured a Spanish Manila Galleon with huge amounts of gold aboard which made him immensely wealthy. In 1747 he commanded the fleet that defeated the French at the First Battle of Cape Finisterre (see 3rd May). In 1751 he was appointed First Lord of the Admiralty and introduced many reforms. He also successfully oversaw the Royal Navy during the Seven Years' War, 1756-1763, guiding it well enough for the war to be decisively won.

1813 The Battle of Stoney Creek in Ontario during the war with America, 1812-1815. British forces, with the element of surprise intact, attacked the American camp. Despite initial success, the Americans were forced to withdraw in the face of determined pressure. Though the casualties on both sides were not huge, they were nevertheless similar in size. Because of the victory, the Americans were prevented from getting any sort of useful foothold in Canada (see 24th June).

1829 The birth of Allan Octavian Hume in Kent (31st July and 28th December).

1832 The death of Jeremy Bentham (see 15th February) in London. A philosopher, jurist and social reformer, he is best known for his life-long attempts at reforming English law. He argued for equal rights for women, freedom of the individual, economic freedom and argued for the abolition of slavery. During the 1790s he made concerted efforts to engage the government in his idea for a new, model prison he called the 'Penopticon'. Following its failure, he was persuaded to engage in attempts at Parliamentary reform and he was an influence on many other social reformers, including John Stuart Mill (see 8th May and 20th May).

1862 The birth of Sir Henry Newbolt in Bilston, Staffordshire. He was to become one of the most well-known of patriotic poets (see 19th April).

1868 The birth of Captain Robert Falcon Scott, Royal Navy, the first Briton to the South Pole (see 17th January and 29th March).

1891 The death of Sir John Alexander Macdonald, the first Prime Minister of Canada, in Ottawa. He suffered a severe stroke on the 29th May from which he never recovered (see 11th January and 1st July). The son of a Glasgow merchant, the family emigrated to Canada in 1820 after his father's business ventures had failed. He trained as a lawyer and was a member of the Conservative party. He served two terms in office as Prime Minister, making a total of 18 years during which he played an integral role in the confederation of his country. For his loyalty and service he was knighted by Queen Victoria (see 22nd January and 24th May).

1944 Just after midnight, Gliders containing British Paratroopers of the 7th Parachute Battalion and men of the 2nd Oxfordshire and Buckinghamshire Regiment landed in German-occupied France at the start of Operation Deadstick. The objective was to drop behind German lines (about 5 miles from the coast) and capture and secure two bridges over the River Orme and the Caen Canal, the only way out for British troops landing on Sword Beach. They were to hold the bridges until advanced elements of Lord Lovat's 1st Commando Brigade reached the bridges and reinforced the Para's positions. Their objectives were gloriously achieved with the sad loss of around twenty dead.

1944 D-Day and the Normandy landings begin as the first day of Operation Overlord and the largest amphibious landing in history (Operation Neptune). British forces go ashore at Sword and Gold beaches with the Canadians landing at Juno beach. The Royal Navy gave support from the sea with suppressing fire and bombardment and also many naval personnel manned the Landing Craft that take the waves of American soldiers ashore on their assigned beaches of Omaha, Pointe du Hoc and Utah (see 8th May and 3rd September).

7th June:

1329 The death of Robert I, 'The Bruce', from Leprosy in Cardross near Dumbarton (see 11th July), one of Scotland's greatest monarchs. Descended from the Scots Royal family, he refused to recognise John Balliol as King and in 1296 supported Edward I (see 17th June and 7th July) of England's invasion of Scotland. However, he eventually supported William Wallace (see 23rd August) and rebelled against Edward I and the English and was crowned at Scone in 1306 (see 25th March). He had to flee to Ireland but returned to wage war against the English, eventually defeating them at Bannockburn in 1314 (see 23rd June and 24th June). In time, a peace was concluded with England and all English claims on the Scottish throne were renounced. He is buried at Dunfermline and his heart at Melrose Abbey.

1761 The birth of John Rennie (see 4th October) in East Lothian.

1778 The birth of George Brummell in London (see 30th March).

1780 The Gordon Riots (see 2nd June) are brought to a bloody end. A number of important buildings were attacked and damaged, including the Bank of England. Fearing for the city, the army is called out and fires upon the mob. It was reported later that some 285 of the rioters were killed, 173 wounded and 193 arrested. Lord George Gordon, who was the supposed leader of the rioters, was tried for treason but was not found guilty. However,

25 of the rioters were found to be guilty and were subsequently hanged for their crimes.

1811 The birth of James Young Simpson (see 6th May) in Bathgate, West Lothian.

1832 The Great Reform Act finally receives Royal Assent, thereby becoming law. Proposed by the administration of the Whig Prime Minister Earl Grey (see 13th March and 17th July), the act succeeded on its third attempt. The resulting Reform Act provided for the removal of a large number of 'rotten boroughs', created over 60 new constituencies and extended the franchise to individuals with land or leased land of £10 or more. This was the first truly modernising of the parliamentary system (see 15th August and 6th December).

1868 The birth of Charles Rennie Mackintosh (see 10th December) in Glasgow.

1915 Lieutenant Reginald 'Rex' Alexander John Warneford, 1 Squadron, of the Royal Naval Air Service, flying a Morane-Saulnier aeroplane, attacks and destroys a Zeppelin (LZ 37) over Ghent in Belgium. He had spotted the airship as it returned from a bombing mission over England. He followed it for some time before attacking and bombing it. One of his bombs caused the airship to explode. The explosion caused his aircraft to flip over and he had to make an emergency landing behind enemy lines, repair the craft and take off and return home. For this courageous act he received both the Victoria Cross and the Legion d'honneur (See 19th January, 31st May and 24th December).

1917 The battle of Messines Ridge begins. Following an initial bombardment of the German lines from 21st May by 2,300 heavy guns and 300 heavy mortars the detonation of 19 mines and almost 450 tons of explosives caused an explosion that was reportedly heard in London. Around 10,000 Germans were killed in the simultaneous explosions. Immediately following the explosions, nine divisions of the British Second Army moved forward behind a creeping barrage towards the remnants of the enemy lines. Within three hours, all the key objectives were taken. The attack was the precursor to the Third Battle of Ypres which was launched on the 31st July and was the biggest man made blast up until that point.

1935 Stanley Baldwin, Conservative, becomes the Prime Minister (see 3rd August and 14th December) for the third time after the resignation of James Ramsey MacDonald.

1954 The death of Alan Mathison Turing (see 23rd June) in Wilmslow, Cheshire by suicide. He is now recognised as the father of modern computing. During the Second World War he worked at Bletchley Park on code breaking and was instrumental in the war effort by his part in breaking the German codes from the enigma machine. He led a team that designed a machine that was known as a 'bombe' to decode German messages and signals. In 1949, he worked at Manchester University on what would later form the basics of artificial intelligence. He was elected as a Fellow of the Royal Society in 1951. Following his arrest for homosexuality, he elected to take a form of chemical castration. His security clearance was withdrawn following his arrest and he therefore could not work for GCHQ. With his life falling apart, he committed suicide.

1960 HMS Vanguard, the last Royal Navy Dreadnaught and the last battleship launched in the world is decommissioned from service (see 10th February and 30th November). Launched in 1946, she never saw action but took part in a number of NATO exercises.

8th June:

793 The first recorded substantial Viking raid on the British Isles takes place as the Monastery on the Island of Lindisfarne is attacked and pillaged as the Vikings kill many Monks and loot many of the Monastery's valuables (see 1st November and 13th November).

1376 The death of the Prince of Wales, Edward of Woodstock (see 15th June). Born in Woodstock in Oxfordshire, he was the son of Edward III (see 21st June and 13th November) and was created Prince of Wales in 1343. He was a brilliant leader and led his father's forces against the French at the glorious victory at Crecy in 1346 (see 26th August) and again at the Battle of Poitiers (see 19th September) in 1356. He was buried at Canterbury Cathedral. Although commonly known as the 'Black Prince', this sobriquet was never used by Edward or his contemporaries and wasn't used until well over one hundred years after his death.

1724 The birth of John Smeaton (see 28th October) near Leeds.

1758 The beginning of the siege of Louisbourg in the French Colony of Ile-Royale, now Nova Scotia. The capture of Louisbourg was critical as it was a key defence for the French along the Atlantic coast and ensured that inland French possessions such as Quebec could receive naval protection and supply lines (see 26th July).

1809 The death of Thomas Paine (see 29th January) in New York, America. A writer and radical politician, he was very outspoken about man's rights and is well-known for writing 'Common Sense'. Born in Thetford, he became an Excise Officer and after campaigning for better conditions, he was sacked. He later emigrated to the Colony of Philadelphia in 1774 on the advice of Benjamin Franklin. There he became editor of the Pennsylvania Magazine and in 1775 he wrote 'Common Sense' in defence of the American colonists call for independence and so becoming a traitor. He was elected to a Congressional Committee and went to France on behalf of the General Assembly of Pennsylvania before returning to London. In 1791 and 1792 he published 'Rights of Man'. He returned to France and was tried in his absence for seditious libel. Imprisoned in France, he was eventually released and supported Napoleon and helped him in his plans to invade Britain in 1801. He returned to New York the following year to spend the rest of his days descending into drunken obscurity. An outspoken republican, he was popular in some intellectual circles but often despised by the political elite and the patriotic crowds for his disloyalty and treachery.

1913 The death in hospital of Emily Wilding Davison (see 4th June and 11th October). Four days before she had thrown herself in front of the King's horse 'Anmer' at Tattenham Corner on Derby day at the Epsom Derby on 4th June. Born in London, she became involved with the Women's Social and Political Union in 1906. On her own initiative and without the WSPU sanction, she moved towards becoming a militant suffragist, being jailed eight times for activities such as breaking windows, pillar-box arson and assault. Whilst in prison she engaged in hunger strikes for which she was forcibly fed forty-nine times. On census night in 1911 she hid in a cupboard in the Palace of Westminster so she could claim that on that night her residence was at the Palace. The nature of her death has caused much controversy ever since. However it is generally accepted that she did not intend to commit suicide but rather she either pre-planned or acted on impulse on the day to disrupt the Derby to draw attention to the cause of female suffrage.

1924 The probable deaths of Andrew Irvine (see 8th April) and George Leigh Mallory (see 18th June) on Mount Everest, somewhere near the Summit. Both men were part of the British Mount Everest Expedition and there is much speculation on whether the two made it to the summit and then died after reaching the summit and were in the process of their descent.

1982 At Bluff Cove in East Falkland our ships are bombed by Argentinean planes whilst sheltering in the cove waiting to put troops ashore. RFA Sir Galahad was struck and destroyed and 50 Welsh Guardsmen are killed and many more badly injured during the attack and the subsequent fire that engulfed the ship (see 2nd April and 14th June). The RFA Sir Tristram was also attacked at the same time and two crewmen were killed and the ship very badly damaged.

9th June:

1667 The Dutch fleet, commanded by Admiral Willem Joseph Van Ghent, begin their attack up the Medway and land a raiding party at the start of what was to become the Battle of Medway (see 12th June and 14th June).

1781 The birth of George Stephenson in Wylam, near Newcastle upon Tyne (see 12th August and 27th September).

1815 The final act of the Congress of Vienna is signed by Great Britain, Austria, Russia and Prussia on one side and France on the other. Its purpose was the redrawing of the map of Europe with the political boundaries agreed upon by the signatories after the impending defeat of Napoleonic France (see 30th May, 18th June and 20th November).

1836 The birth of Elizabeth Garrett Anderson in Whitechapel, London. She was to become the first qualified female Doctor (see 28th September, 9th November and 17th December) in this country.

1840 Queen Victoria (see 22nd January and 24th May) and Prince Albert (see 26th August and 14th December) survive an assassination attempt by Edward Oxford. The Queen and Prince Albert were out on Constitution Hill when Oxford fired twice at the couple, missing both times. He was apprehended by onlookers, arrested and tried for treason. He was acquitted due to insanity and sentenced to Bethlehem Royal Hospital. Decades later he was released on condition that he left Britain, which he did, eventually living in Australia where he died.

1870 The death of Charles Dickens from a brain haemorrhage (see 7th February). He had collapsed the previous day with a stroke. Perhaps one of our country's greatest and best known authors, he worked as a young lad in a blacking firm before becoming a journalist. He married in 1836, just before the publication of 'The Pickwick Papers'. From this point on he became a prolific writer of books, short stories and travel books. He travelled extensively, lecturing in America and Europe. He had ten children and became estranged from his wife in 1858. He is buried in Westminster Abbey (see 21st January).

1898 Hong Kong is leased to Britain by China for 99 years (see 30th June and 1st July). A number of Islands were added to the British possession and became known as the New Territories (see 20th January and 29th August). Hong Kong was extremely important to the Empire and became a very successful port.

1975 The first live radio broadcasts from the House of Commons are transmitted by the BBC (see 27th April and 16th October).

10th June:

1551 The Treaty of Norham Castle is signed between representatives of the English and Scottish Kings. The treaty terms included English forces abandoning occupied lands in Scotland and the borders reverting to their previous lines, thus bringing an end to the last major conflict between the two kingdoms (see 10th September).

1683 The birth of James Francis Edward Stewart (the Jacobite James VIII or James III of England, the 'Old Pretender' and also known as the 'Warming Pan baby') at St. James's Palace (see 1st January). The son of James VIII (James II England see 5th September and 14th October) and the Catholic Mary of Modena, he had two sisters, Princess Mary (see 30th April and 28th December) and Princess Anne (see 6th February and 1st August). His birthday was celebrated as 'White Rose Day' by Jacobites at the time and for a long time thereafter.

1719 The Battle of Glen Shiel in the west of Scotland, near the Five Sisters Hills. Jacobite forces, including around 250 Spanish marines under William Murray, the Earl of Tullibardine had deployed for battle across a river on elevated ground. The Government forces were led by Major General Joseph Wightman and, despite being repulsed at first, fought gallantly up hill to dislodge the Jacobites, eventually forcing the Highlanders and their Spanish allies to retire in what is generally viewed as a victory by the government forces over the Jacobites. Participating in the action was Rob Roy McGregor (see 28th December) and this action was the only proper battle of the 1719 Jacobite rising, which was used by the Spanish as a distraction during the War of the Quadruple Alliance, 1718-1719 (see 10th May and 17th February).

1770 A Spanish force of five frigates and over a thousand marines arrive at Port Egmont on the Falkland Islands to commence their invasion. Against overwhelming odds, the commander of our small garrison, George Farmer, heroically exchanges fire but is then compelled to surrender honourably by the Spanish Commander (see 2nd April and 14th June) or face certain and pointless annihilation.

1940 Following Germany's invasion of France, Italy declared war on Great Britain and France (see 3rd September and 10th September) as Italian forces invade France.

11th June:

1488 The battle of Sauchieburn and the death of James III of Scotland. James III faced open rebellion by his nobles who supported his fifteen-year-old son, the future James IV (see 17th March and 9th September), as their champion and King. James is often viewed as Scotland's first enlightened King but his rule was marred by much discontent. His major achievement was the acquisition in 1472 of the Orkney and Shetland Islands (see 20th February). The opposing armies met near Stirling and it is believed that at some point in the battle, James was killed.

1509 The wedding of Henry VIII (see 28th January and 28th June) and Catherine of Aragon (see 7th January, 14th November and 16th December) is held at Greenwich Church.

1685 James Duke of Monmouth (see 6th July and 15th July) lands at Lyme Regis with a small force after crossing the Channel with three ships at the start of his short and ill-fated rebellion against his father, James II.

1696 The birth of James Francis Edward Keith (see 14th October) in Inverugie castle near Peterhead.

1720 The Bubble Act receives Royal assent. Though introduced and passed prior to the collapse of the South Sea Company in what is referred to as the 'South Sea Bubble' (see 10th September), it was intended to prevent joint-stock companies from forming without a Royal Charter.

1727 The death of George I at Osnabruck, Lower Saxony (see 28th May, 1st August and 20th October). He was the first monarch of the house of Hanover. His mother, Sophia, was the granddaughter of James VI of Scotland (James I of England, see 27th March and 19th June). Throughout most of his reign he was unpopular as it was believed he spoke little, if any English and was too German and was far too influenced by a succession of greedy mistresses. Whilst King he faced two Jacobite risings in 1715 and 1719 and the collapse of the so-called 'South Sea Bubble'.

1776 The birth of John Constable in East Bergholt, Suffolk (see 31st March).

1815 The birth of Julia Margaret Pattle (later Cameron) in Calcutta, India (see 26th January).

1847 The death of Sir John Franklin (see 16th April) near King William Island in Canada. An Officer in the Royal Navy, he had fought at the Battle of Trafalgar in 1805 (see 21st October) and had also been a Governor of Tasmania. However, he is most widely known for his four journeys to the Arctic and his attempts to find the North West Passage. It was on his last journey that he and all 129 of his crew disappeared. It was several years before their fate became known. It is now believed that they died from a mixture of exhaustion, hyperthermia, tuberculosis, starvation and lead poisoning.

1847 The birth of Millicent Garrett, later Fawcett, in Aldeburgh, Suffolk (see 5th August).

1937 The death of Reginald Joseph Mitchell C.B.E. (see 20th May) from cancer. Born in Kidsgrove, he was the inventor of the world famous Spitfire fighter plane. He died just twelve months after his creation made its maiden flight and so never saw how it performed in combat (see 5th March).

1959 The first flight of the SR-N1 Hovercraft at Cowes on the Isle of Wight. It was designed by Sir Christopher Cockerell (see 1st June, 4th June and 25th July) and built by the Sanders Roe Company on the Isle of Wight.

1982 The beginning of the Battle of Mount Longdon on the Falkland Islands between the 3rd Parachute Regiment and the occupying Argentinean forces. It was a brutal fight and was a British victory accomplished by the heroic determination of our troops. At the end of the battle the following day, 23 men were dead and 47 wounded. Of the Argentineans, 31 were dead, 120 wounded and 50 captured (see 2nd April, 2nd May, 21st May and 14th June).

1987 Margaret Thatcher wins her third General Election (see 11th February, 8th April and 13th October), with her Conservative Party gaining a 102 seat majority. This was the first time since 1820 that a Prime Minister had led their party to three consecutive electoral victories.

12th June: The official birthday of Queen Elizabeth II.

1667 The Dutch Fleet attack and raid Chatham Dockyard in a rare and humiliating raid for the Royal Navy. During the raid, the Dutch broke through a large chain barrier that had been stretched across the Thames and captured two ships and burnt many others. With little resistance, the Dutch attacked forts and defences on the Thames before running out of fire ships and withdrawing (see 14th June). As little resistance was offered to the Dutch, over a dozen ships had been sunk to prevent their capture (see 9th June).

1683 The discovery of the controversial Rye House Plot to assassinate Charles II (see 6th February and 29th May) and the Duke of York (see 16th September and 14th October) and possibly secure the City of London. Included amongst the alleged conspirators was James, Duke of Monmouth. The plot was named after Rye House in Hertfordshire, near to the spot where the King and the Duke were to be ambushed and killed. A number of the supposed Whig conspirators were arrested, tried and executed.

1701 The Act of Settlement was passed by Parliament following the signature of William III (see 8th March and 4th November). Amongst other provisions, the Act primarily ensured the succession of an Anglican Monarch to the throne of England and that no Catholic could succeed to the throne. The succession to the throne was passed to the Electress Sophia of Hanover and those of her Protestant heirs who had also not married a Catholic. She was the granddaughter of James VI of Scotland (see 27th March and 19th June) and the niece of Charles I of England (see 30th January and 19th November).

1798 The beginning of the battle of Ballynahinch in County Down in Ireland during the Irish Rebellion of that year. The town of Ballynahinch, held by the rebels, had been surrounded by Government forces on the two adjacent hills, led by General George Nugent. After an initial bombardment of the town, the rebels attempted to attack, which (after a brief period of success) was reversed and turned into a rout of the rebels who turned and fled. Pursued by the army, many were killed as they attempted to escape (see 24th May).

1851 The birth of Oliver Joseph Lodge (see 22nd August) in Penkhull, Stoke on Trent.

1897 The birth of Anthony Eden in Bishop Auckland (see 9th January and 14th January). He would be Prime Minister during the Suez Crisis in 1956 (see 31st October) when we were betrayed by our supposed ally, the United States of America.

1928 The Welsh National War Memorial is unveiled in Alexandra Gardens, Cathays Park in Cardiff by the Prince of Wales, the future Edward VIII (see 28th May and 23rd June). The memorial was designed by Sir Ninian Comper (see 4th August and 11th November).

1940 The battle of Saint-Valery-en-Caux ends with the surrender of the heroic 51st Highland Division under the command of General Fortune after becoming surrounded by German forces, despite holding out with the hope of possible evacuation. Around 13,000 men surrendered, including some from the French 9th Army Corps (most of whom had surrendered the previous night) to which it was attached, thus formally ending our country's role in the battle of France. They surrendered when it became known that there was no hope of evacuation and their continued resistance and sacrifice would serve no further purpose (see 4th June).

13th June:

1373 The Anglo-Portuguese Treaty of Alliance is signed in London by Edward III (see 21st June and 13th November) and King Ferdinand of Portugal. It is the world's oldest active alliance and established a treaty of 'perpetual friendship, unions and alliances'. Throughout history it has been reinforced numerous times to the benefit of both countries.

1381 Wat Tyler becomes the leader of the Peasants' Revolt (see 15th June).

1752 The birth of Fanny Burney in Lynn Regis, now King's Lynn (see 6th January).

1831 The birth of James Clerk Maxwell in Edinburgh (see 5th November).

1842 Queen Victoria (see 22nd January and 24th May) becomes the first Monarch to travel by train. With her on the journey were her Court, husband Prince Albert and the Prime Minister Lord Melbourne. The party travelled from Slough, near Windsor to Paddington in London.

1854 The birth of Charles Algernon Parsons (see 11th February) in London.

1944 Germany launches its V1 rocket for the first time against Britain, targeting London where 6 people are killed in Bethnal Green. It was commonly referred to as the 'doodle bug' (see 8th May, 15th August and 3rd September).

14th June:

1645 The Battle of Naseby in Northamptonshire takes place. It is a Parliamentarian victory and is one of the key British battles of the Civil War. The New Model Army of around 15,000 men under Lord Fairfax resoundingly defeated the Royalist army of around 12,000 men led by Prince Rupert of the Rhine (see 29th November and 17th December). As a result of the battle, the King's baggage train was captured and secret papers showing he had sought help from Irish Catholics and the Catholic nations of Europe (see 29th May, 14th June and 3rd September).

1667 The Dutch withdraw from the Medway, following the Battle of Medway, one of the most humiliating defeats for the Royal Navy, with the loss of thirteen ships destroyed and two captured (see 9th June and 12th June), HMS Royal Charles and HMS Unity. As the Dutch fleet headed for home, they took to raiding the villages and forts along the coast.

1801 The death of Benedict Arnold (see 3rd January) in London. Born in 1740, in Norwich in the Colony of Connecticut, he was a businessman before the American rebellion. He went on to become a much respected 'General' amongst the American colonial rebels who was involved in a number of actions during the colonial rebellion. He was injured at the Battle of Saratoga in 1777 (see 17th October) and later, showing a true Loyalist spirit, he reverted to the Government side and attempted to surrender West Point to our forces before being discovered (see 2nd October). He came to England afterwards and received a commission into the army as a Brigadier General.

Vilified in America for ultimately showing loyalty to the Crown, he was a true Loyalist and patriot of our country and the colonies.

1822 Charles Babbage (see 18th October and 26th December) first proposes his 'difference engine', the forerunner of today's computers.

1883 The death of Edward Marlborough FitzGerald (see 31st March), a writer most famous for his translation of the 'Rubaiyat of Omar Khayyam', released from 1859. Born in 1809 as Edward Purcell, he changed his name when his father took on Edward's mother's family name and arms. His first work was published in 1851.

1928 The death of Emmeline Pankhurst (see 14th July), leading women's rights campaigner and suffragette. In 1889 she founded the Women's Franchise League which campaigned for the right of married women to vote in local elections. In 1903 she helped form the Women's Social and Political Union, a more militant group that became known as suffragettes. The main period of her militancy came to an abrupt end in 1914 with the outbreak of war when she threw her energies into supporting the war effort against Germany.

1946 The death of John Logie Baird (see 26th January and 14th August) at Bexhill-on-Sea in Sussex. He is best remembered for being the inventor of the first true television which he demonstrated for the first time in 1926 (see 3rd July). Born in Helensburgh in 1888 he was rejected for military service in the Great War due to poor health. After the war, he moved to England with the goal of creating a television broadcasting system. In 1926 he demonstrated the first television images in an attic room at his house (see 26th January). Though he experimented with the mechanical devices for picture transmission, his systems lost out to the electronic devices being developed by Marconi.

1982 The occupying Argentinean Forces on the Falkland Islands surrender to our troops led by General Jeremy Moore. The letter of surrender is signed in Port Stanley by General Moore and General Menendez for the Argentineans and British sovereignty is re-established (see 2nd January). Our nation has once again defended her people, no matter where they are in the world (see 2nd April, 25th April and 21st May) and no matter who does or doesn't support us. A total of 255 service personnel were killed in the war and three brave Falklands islanders also lost their lives. May their sacrifice and achievements never be forgotten!

15th June:

1215 The Magna Carta (Great Charter) is sealed by King John (see 18th October) and the Barons at Runnymede. Although viewed with little seriousness by both sides at the time, it is in fact the first advocate of justice for freemen. It declared that no freeman could be detained without trial (see 27th July) and would become the most important document in English then British and Imperial law.

1330 The birth of Edward of Woodstock (see 8th June) in Woodstock in Oxfordshire. He was the son of Edward III (see 21st June and 13th November).

1381 The death of Wat Tyler and the end of the peasant's revolt. The peasants were persuaded to meet the Lord Mayor and dignitaries outside the city of London at Smithfield. At some point during the meeting Tyler was stabbed by the Mayor of London and then finished off by John Standwich (see 30th May). Richard II (see 6th February) also agreed to the peasants' demands and they dispersed. However, the King later reneged on all his promises, claiming they were made under duress and other leaders of the revolt were then arrested, tried and executed (see 13th June).

1846 The Oregon Treaty is signed between Great Britain and the United States in Washington DC. It permanently settled the boundary between British North America and the United States along the 49th parallel that had been initially agreed in 1818 in the London Treaty (see 20th October). It thus ended years of dispute between settlers from both countries over borders and settler rights.

1866 The death of John McDouall Stuart in London (see 7th September). Born in Scotland, he emigrated to Australia and became one of the most famous explorers of Australia. His greatest achievement was leading the first expedition to travel from the south of the country and return successfully via the same route in 1862. He led a total of six successful explorative expeditions.

1877 The death of Caroline Norton (née Sheridan, see 22nd March). A pioneering social reformer and author, her father died when she was eight and the family became impoverished. She was married to George Norton MP when she was only 16 years old. An unhappy marriage from the outset, she also endured brutal beatings from her husband. She turned to writing and after a few years became reasonably financially independent and left her husband. He however sued Lord Melbourne, with whom she was accused of committing adultery. He lost but her reputation was destroyed. He denied her access to their three children and her battle for access was instrumental in the passing of the 1839 Infant Custody Bill. Later, she played a key role in the passing of the Divorce Act of 1857. She married a close friend, William Stirling Maxwell, only three months before her death.

1892 The birth of Keith Rodney Park in Thames, New Zealand (see 6th February).

1919 Captain John William Alcock (see 5th November and 18th December) and Lieutenant Arthur Whitten Brown (see 23rd July and 4th October) become the first aviators to complete a non-stop transatlantic flight. They took off in their modified Vimy IV aeroplane the day before in Newfoundland and landed in Connemara, Ireland at about 8.40am having completed 1,980 miles in just over sixteen hours.

1998 The £2 coin is introduced into general circulation. Unlike the other coins in our currency, it was a two tone coin. It had a gold-coloured outer ring and a silver coloured inner disk. There had been a £2 coin minted since 1989 as a commemorative piece but not issued into general circulation.

16th June:

1487 The Battle of Stoke Field in Nottinghamshire, the last battle in the War of the Roses 1455-1587. The Yorkist rebel army, under the Earl of Lincoln and Lord Lovell possessed the high ground on the hill outside the village as the Royal army of Henry VII (see 28th January and 21st April) approached. The rebels advanced on the Royal army and at first seemed to be making progress. However, the experienced Royal troops turned the advantage and the rebels were defeated in a general rout. Lambert Simnel, who claimed to be Edward Plantagenet, is captured after rebelling against Henry VII.

1722 The death of John Churchill, 1st Duke of Marlborough (see 26th May) and ancestor of Winston Spencer Churchill (see 24th January and 30th November) from a stroke at Windsor Lodge. Arguably one of this country's greatest generals, he rose to prominence during the reign of the Stuarts. However, his greatest years were during the reign of Queen Anne (see 6th February and 1st August), during which time he achieved stunning victories at the Battle of Blenheim in 1704 (see 2nd August) for which he is best remembered. He also achieved glorious victories over the French army and their allies at the battles of Ramillies in 1706 (see 12th May), Oudenarde in 1708 (see 30th June) and Malplaquet in 1709 (see 11th September).

1743 The Battle of Dettingen is fought in the Electorate of Bavaria during the War of the Austrian Succession 1740-1748. This was the last battle where our troops were led into battle by a reigning British sovereign. The Pragmatic army, including our troops led by George II (see 25th October and 30th October), and Hanoverians and Austrians totalling around 50,000 men, beat the French army of around 70,000 men. The French were commanded by the Duc de Noailles and the Comte de Grammont and their forces blocked the Pragmatic army at Dettingen. After both armies had formed up, the French advanced on the allies and attempted to outflank them but, after some initial success were pushed back towards the river and broken.

1755 The brief siege of Fort Beausejour in the French colony of Acadia in New France ends when the French Commander surrenders to British forces under Lieutenant-General Robert Mockton. Though only a relatively minor military exercise, the Fort's capitulation ultimately led to the removal of the Acadian population, the end to French threats around the area and ultimately to the end of New France and French influence and presence in Canada (see 18th June and 1st July).

1858 The death of Doctor John Snow in London (see 15th March). Born in York, he became a surgeon and moved to London in 1836. In 1849 he published his work 'On the Mode of Communication of Cholera', dispelling the theory that Cholera was an airborne disease. He was also instrumental in identifying the source of the Cholera epidemic in Soho in 1854. Besides this discovery, he also worked in the field of anaesthetics. Through his continued experiments he made the application of the process much safer. In 1853 he gave chlorophorm to Queen Victoria (see 22nd January and 24th May) at the birth of her son Leopold (see 7th April). Later, in 1857 he conducted he same process when Queen Victoria gave birth to her daughter Beatrice.

1912 The birth of Enoch Powell in Strechford, Birmingham (see 8th February and 20th April).

1969 The death of General Harold Alexander (see 10th December). A leading Commander of the Second World War, he had served in the Great War, was wounded twice and was awarded the Military Cross. After the Great War, he volunteered to command the Baltic Landwehr, a force of ethnic Germans fighting against the Red Army during the Russian Civil War. At the outbreak of the Second World War he was part of the BEF and was given command of the rear guard at the evacuation from Dunkirk in 1940 (see 26th May and 4th June). In 1942 he was sent to India to take command of the fight against the Japanese and their invasion of Burma. He then commanded the successful operation in North Africa followed by the invasion of Sicily. In March 1946 he was created Viscount Alexander of Tunis. After the war he served as Governor General of Canada and in 1952 became Minister of Defence under Prime Minister Winston Churchill (see 24th January and 30th November). In 1952 he was created Earl Alexander of Tunis.

2012 In the Queen's Birthday Honours list, the British Empire Medal is reintroduced. The medal was left in abeyance by John Major and his government in 1997 in a misguided effort to make the honours system classless. Its reintroduction with 293 people receiving the award is to recognise the achievements and hard work of people for their communities and the country.

17th June:

1239 The birth of Edward I 'Longshanks', the 'Hammer of the Scots', at Westminster Palace (see 7th July). He was the son of Henry III (see 1st October and 16th November) and was named after his father's favourite Saint, the Anglo-Saxon King, Edward the Confessor (see 5th January).

1497 The battle of Blackheath (sometimes referred to as the battle of Deptford Bridge) near London. It was the culmination of the Cornish Rebellion against Henry VII (see 28th January and 21st April) and his raising of taxes to pay for his war with Scotland. Henry VII had a well-organised army of around 25,000 when he faced the rebels who had around 15,000 men. The rebels, lacking cavalry, initially took the bridge but, with little experience and cohesion, were no match for the King's forces. After a fierce battle, the Cornish lines broke and many were killed in the ensuing flight from the battle.

1703 The birth of John Wesley (see 2nd March) in Lincolnshire.

1719 The death of Joseph Addison in London (see 1st May). He was a leading writer, poet, dramatist, essayist and influential Whig politician of his time. Along with his friend Richard Steele, he founded the periodical magazine 'The Spectator' and contributed towards the 'Tatler' magazine. He was also a co-founder of the infamous Kit-Cat Club. His most well known play is 'Cato'. He is buried in Westminster Abbey.

1775 The Battle of Bunker Hill (Breeds Hill as it was known at the time) during the American Colonial rebellion (see 3rd September). Major-General Howe commanded around 2,400 of our troops against a rebel force of about 1,500. Two frontal attacks were made on the rebel positions on the hill and were driven back before a third and final advance forced the enemy positions and the rebels took flight. Our forces suffered 1,150 dead and wounded and the rebels about 450 casualties. However, despite our heavy losses, the traitorous rebels were driven out of the Charlestown Peninsula (see 23rd August). This was also the first action of the newly-formed Continental Army and, while individual rebel defenders fought with great determination and heroism, the Continental Army was shown to be entirely amateur in its performance.

1806 The death of Henry Holland (see 20th July), architect to the nobility and aristocracy who trained under Lancelot 'Capability' Brown. He worked on the Brooks' Club, St. James's, designed the Knightsbridge and Chelsea areas of London and also the marine Pavilion in Brighton for George IV (see 26th June and 12th August) and the remodelling of Carlton House in London.

1812 The birth of Charles John Canning, the future Viscount and 1st Earl Canning (see 1st November and 14th December) on his father's estate near London.

1869 The birth of Fabian Arthur Goulstone Ware in Clifton near Bristol (see 29th April and 21st May).

1898 The birth of Henry John 'Harry' Patch in Combe Down near Bath (see 25th July).

1940 The sinking of the R.M.S. Lancastria off the shores of Dunkirk whilst attempting to evacuate people during Operation Ariel. The ship was carrying between 6,000 and 9,000 passengers. Most of those on board were civilian refugees from the war but there were many Allied troops on board. The ship was hit three times by dive bombers. It took just twenty minutes to roll over and sink. The German aircraft then strafed those in the water. There were 2,477 survivors but the exact number killed will never be known as the ship was over crowded. Estimates of those killed vary between 4,000 and as many as 5,000 people. The news of the tragedy was suppressed by the government at the time using the special D-notices so as not to damage morale.

1963 The death of Field Marshall Alan Francis Brooke, 1st Viscount Alanbrooke (see 23rd July), at his home in Hampshire. He was one of our greatest twentieth-century generals. He served during the First World War in the Royal Artillery. During the Second World War, he commanded II Corps of the BEF and oversaw the retreat to Dunkirk in 1940 (see 26th May and 4th June). In 1941 he was appointed Chief of the Imperial General staff and, though disappointed at the appointment of Dwight D Eisenhower as commander of Operation Overlord (see 6th June), he worked closely with him, to the successful conclusion of the Invasion of Europe (see 8th May).

18th June: Waterloo Day.

1541 The Crown of Ireland Act is passed by the Irish Parliament in Dublin, recognising Henry VIII of England (see 28th January and 28th June) as the rightful King of Ireland (see 18th April, 6th December and 8th December).

1633 The coronation of Charles I as King of the Scots was held in St. Giles's Cathedral in Edinburgh (see 30th January, 2nd February and 19th November). The coronation was held according to the Anglican rite, which caused much anger and bitterness amongst the many Presbyterians in the country.

1812 The former American Colonies, now known as the United States of America, under the direction of their President James Madison, declared war on Great Britain and our Empire with the intention of expanding their nation by capturing our North American colonies in Canada (see 1st July). President Madison signed the declaration of war only after receiving a slim margin in favour in the Congressional vote (see 17th February and 24th December) as the Federalist Party mostly opposed the war. They declared war but their only hope of a victory was because Great Britain was engaged in a total war against Napoleonic France.

1815 The Battle of Waterloo near Brussels in Belgium and defeat for Napoleon and his forces. The Duke of Wellington (see 1st May and 14th September) commanded 67,000 men and 156 guns, along with Marshal Blucher whilst Napoleon commanded his Grand Armee of 80,000 men and 246 guns. The French began the battle with an artillery bombardment of the Hougoumont Farm. The French then advanced towards the allied lines. In a battle that lasted all day, the victory could have gone either way. In the end, with greater leadership, better communications and the arrival of the Prussians under Blucher, the Duke of Wellington was victorious. The French lost about 24,000 dead and around 8,000 taken as prisoners. Our forces lost 15,000 dead and the Prussians around 7,000 dead. With Waterloo came the culmination of almost 26 years of war with France, periods of which saw Britain standing alone against the European dictator. It virtually brought to an end the French Empire and power which went into rapid decline in the years following the battle. Waterloo is probably the greatest British battle fought on land. It also brought in three years of allied occupation of France, with Wellington as the Commander in Chief of the Army of Occupation (see 30th May, 9th June, and 20th November).

1835 The death of William Cobbett (see 9th March). A journalist and writer, he is best known for his campaigns for parliamentary reform. Born in

Farham, he was a farmer and journalist. He took up radical politics and campaigned for Catholic emancipation, the end of the rotten boroughs and was a founder of the newspaper, 'The Political Register'. He was charged with seditious libel three times and attempted to become an MP, succeeding on his third attempt in 1832 as the MP for Oldham.

1886 The birth of George Leigh Mallory (see 8th June) in Mobberely, Cheshire.

1948 A state of Emergency, known as the 'Malayan Emergency', is declared in the Federation of Malaya. This was declared after the Communist Party of Malaya, disgruntled at the formation of the Federation of Malaya, began a guerrilla insurgency, made up mainly of Chinese Communist immigrants who were determined to capture the rubber and tin producing areas of the country (see 31st August). Just two days before, the guerrillas had murdered three plantation managers which was the trigger for the emergency to be declared.

1970 The General Election is won unexpectedly by the Conservative Party under Edward Heath (see 9th July and 17th July). According to opinion polls, the Labour Party under the Prime Minister Harold Wilson (see 11th March and 24th May) was expected to win the election.

19th June:

1566 The birth of James VI (later James I of England) at Edinburgh Castle (see 27th March, 25th July and 29th July), the son of Mary Stuart, Queen of Scots, and Henry Stuart, Lord Darnley (see 10th February).

1754 The first day of the Albany Congress, meeting in Albany, New York (see 11th July). Organised by the British Board of Trade, delegates from seven colonies of the thirteen colonies of British North America met to discuss issues over Native American tribes and the threat posed by the French.

1820 The death of Sir Joseph Banks (see 13th February) in London. A naturalist and explorer he was on Captain Cook's first voyage to the pacific in 1768. The voyage went to South America, Australia, New Zealand and Tahiti. During the expedition he collected many species of plants which were returned to Britain and his account of the voyage caused great interest throughout Europe. He was President of the Royal Society as well as Director of the Royal Botanical Gardens at Kew. In 1793, a small group of Islands were named the Banks Islands in his honour by Captain Bligh (see 9th September and 7th December), who had captained the ship HMS Bounty on the infamous voyage that ended in mutiny (see 28th April). During his life time he amassed a large collection of specimens and a large library. He was also influential in selecting Australia as a penal colony.

1829 The Metropolitan Police Act receives Royal Assent. The Act established the first modern uniformed and paid Police service. It was only for the Metropolitan area of London, including the city and allowed for the recruitment of 1,000 new officers.

1861 The birth of Douglas Haig in Edinburgh (see 28th January).

1886 The death of Charles Edward Trevelyan (see 2nd April). In 1826 he went to work in Bengal for the East India Company. He worked hard for a number of years to improve the lives of the local populations. In 1840 he returned to London and worked for the Treasury. Whilst there he became a contentious figure as he was responsible for relief during the famine in Ireland. In the 1850's he became linked with Sir Stafford Northcote's improvements in the British Civil Service, raising standards and introducing an entrance examination. In his final years he became actively involved with and supported the reorganisation of the army.

20th June:

1549 The start of the Norfolk rising (see 7th July) as peasants in the village of Attleborough tear down hedges and fences erected by the local Lord of the Manor to enclose common land (see 27th August and 7th December).

1756 The night of the 'Black Hole of Calcutta'. A total of 146 British subjects were captured when the Newab of Bengal, Siraj ud-Daulah, occupied the city of Calcutta following its surrender earlier in the day. The prisoners were herded into a tiny guard room about 14 feet by 18 feet in Fort William. It was extremely hot and without any form of ventilation. In the morning, following the barbaric and uncivilised treatment and neglect, only 23 emerged alive (see 2nd January), the majority of the cruel deaths being from suffocation, exhaustion and crushing.

1763 The birth of Theobald Wolfe Tone in Dublin (see 19th November).

1837 The death of William IV at Windsor Castle (see 21st August) and his niece, Princess Victoria becomes Queen Victoria (see 22nd January, 24th May and 28th June). Born in 1765, he was the third son of George II (see 29th January and 24th May) and was in later life known as 'Sailor Billy', joining the Royal Navy at the age of 13. He became King in 1830 and his reign is notable for his support for and the passing of the Reform Act of 1832 (see 7th June).

1897 The Empress Queen Victoria's Diamond Jubilee (see 22nd January and 24th May). Throughout the country and the Empire there are parties and celebrations to mark the first ever diamond jubilee (see 6th February) of any monarch. The Prime Ministers of the Dominions were invited to London and the Queen's Jubilee procession passed through London to St. Paul's Cathedral with Victoria in an open carriage escorted by many Imperial Troops from across the Empire.

1900 The Boxer rebellion enters its final stage as the siege of the International legations area of Peking begins with the Chinese Imperial Army and Boxer rebels firing on the Foreign Legation following an ultimatum demanding the foreigners' departure which was delivered on the previous day (see 14th August).

1967 The start of the Battle of Crater in Aden Colony. Members of the local Police force mutiny and attack and kill some British soldiers (see 19th January, 5th July and 10th December).

1984 O Level and CSE examinations are replaced by GCSE examinations in one of the biggest changes to the education system and one of the biggest made by a Conservative government.

21st June:

1377 The death of Edward III (see 13th November) at Sheen Palace in Richmond. He was one of the most successful Medieval Monarchs and did much to restore Royal authority after the pathetic and disastrous reign of his father Edward II (see 25th April and 21st September). He was responsible for making England one of the most efficient and formidable powers in Europe. He reign lasted over 50 years, one of the longest reigning Monarchs of Britain.

1652 The death of Inigo Jones (see 15th July) in Somerset House, London. He was the first architect of any note in England. In 1615 he was appointed Surveyor General to the King. His first work was the Queens House at Greenwich for the wife of James VI (James I of England see 27th March and 19th June). He later built the Banqueting House at Whitehall Palace after the original burnt down. He designed Covent Garden Square and was responsible for the renovation and work on St. Paul's Cathedral. He suffered for his Royal connections during the civil war and had his property confiscated, although it was later returned.

1738 The death of Charles Townshend, 2nd Viscount Townshend (see 18th April). A leading Whig, he entered the Lords in 1697. He was a friend and brother-in law of Robert Walpole (see 18th March and 26th August). In 1716 he became Lord Lieutenant of Ireland, later becoming Secretary of State and influencing the League of Hanover in 1725. He was known as 'Turnip Townshend', due to his interest in agriculture and agricultural reform and in particular the use of turnips in crop rotation.

1764 The birth of William Sidney Smith (see 26th May) in London.

1798 The Battle of Vinegar Hill in County Wexford during the Irish Rebellion (see 24th May). General Gerard Lake led a force of around 20,000 men against the rebel camp in a battle that lasted for about two hours. The rebels put up stiff resistance but were beaten, many escaping through a gap in the lines to be charged down by the cavalry. They made their way to the town of Enniscorthy where brutal fighting took place, much of it from street to street. It was in the town that there were many casualties on both sides until the rebels were either slaughtered or escaped (see 8th September).

184

1813 The Battle of Vitoria in Spain. Lieutenant General, the Marques of Wellington (see 1st May and 14th September) led an army of British, Spanish and Portuguese against Joseph Bonaparte, King of Spain. Our forces lost 3,675 men, the Portuguese lost 921 and the Spanish 567. The French lost 8,000. The battle was of vast significance for the people of Europe as it not only effectively ended the Peninsular War by virtually liberating Spain but it also signalled the end of Napoleons control over the continent.

1884 The birth of Claude John Eyre Auchinleck (see 23rd March) in Ulster, the son of a colonel in the army.

22nd June:

1611 Henry Hudson, his young son and seven of his crew are set adrift by the mutinous crew of his ship the Discovery after months trapped in the ice. They were never seen again. Some of the mutinous crew were later killed by Eskimos but the others eventually made it back to England to recount their adventures. Hudson had made several voyages looking for a north-west passage to Asia and explored the area around what would later become New York City (see 21st July and 27th August). The River Hudson was named after him (see 2nd May).

1679 The Battle of Bothwell Bridge (see 1st June) by the River Clyde near Bothwell in Lanarkshire where over 5,000 Government troops under the Duke of Monmouth (see 9th April and 15th July) defeated the rebel Covenanters. With the rebels on the south bank of the River Clyde, the Government troops eventually forced themselves across the bridge following which the rebel force collapsed and were quickly routed.

1757 The birth of George Vancouver (see 10th May) in King's Lynn.

1774 The Quebec Act receives Royal Assent (see 1st May). The Act provided for alteration to the governing of and the size of the Province of Quebec. It also provided for the free practice of Roman Catholicism and restored French Civil Law and customs unless it contravened certain British Laws.

1856 The birth of Henry Rider Haggard (see 14th May) in Norfolk.

1893 HMS Victoria, flagship of Admiral Tryon and the Mediterranean Fleet collides with HMS Camperdown off the coast of Tripoli and sinks, killing 358 of her crew, including Admiral Tryon (see 4th January). Admiral Tryon had given an order for both ships to take part in a difficult manoeuvre, despite reservations of other commanders present. Following a courts martial, Admiral Tyron was held responsible for the chain of events leading to the collision and the collision itself. He had joined the navy as a cadet in 1848 and served in the Mediterranean from 1851. He served during the Crimean War, 1853-1856, getting wounded in the trenches fighting in the Naval Brigade. He went on to have a successful career and was promoted steadily before commanding numerous ships and being promoted to Rear Admiral in 1884.

1911 The Coronation of George V (see 20th January and 3rd June) and Mary of Teck at Westminster Abbey.

1922 The murder of Sir Henry Hughes Wilson by two Irish terrorists of the IRA on the steps of his London home (see 5th May). Born in Ireland in 1864, he served during the Boer War and later served as a Field Marshal during the Great War. He was also to become a Conservative MP and he was appointed Chief of the Imperial General Staff in 1918.

1944 British troops of the 2nd Division and Indian troops of the 5th Infantry Division meet at Milestone 109, ending the Japanese advance and attempted occupation of both Kohima and Imphal in North East India. This meeting signalled the end of the battle of Kohima, one of the bloodiest battles in World War Two that changed the course of the War in the East and saved India from invasion (see 8th March and 4th April).

1948 The SS Empire Windrush docks in London, marking the start of post war immigration to Britain from across the Commonwealth (see 28th April). Nearly 500 immigrants, mainly Jamaican, had boarded the ship with the hope of work in the Mother country.

1948 George VI (see 6th February and 14th December), by Order-in-Council, officially removes the title Emperor from the titles of the Monarchy. He therefore becomes our last Emperor (see 1st January, 27th April, 1st May, 18th July and 15th August).

1972 The Sterling Zone or area comes to an end. In existence since the outbreak of World War Two, it was a group of countries with their currencies tied to the pound sterling. This was done due to Britain's anticipation of entry into the EEC and French concerns over British advantage in trade due to the Commonwealth. This was, however, despite France's ongoing agreements with its former colonies and territories.

23rd June:

1314 The first day and start of the Battle of Bannockburn (see 24th June). The English knight, Henry de Bohun, leading the cavalry, sees Robert the Bruce (see 7th June), lowers his lance and charges. Bruce, seeing the oncoming knight, moves to the side, stands up in his stirrups and strikes the English knight with his axe, splitting his head in two.

1650 Charles II lands in Scotland in an attempt to reclaim the throne. In doing so, he had to agree to the terms of Solemn League and Covenant in order to gain Scottish support (see 6th February and 29th May)

1757 The Battle of Plassey in Bengal, India, led by Sir Robert Clive (see 29th September and 22nd November). Clive led an army of 3,000 of whom 2,000 were Indian troops or Sepoys. The Nabob, Suraja Dowla had an army of 50,000 men and some French Artillery and had attacked the East India Company's Bengal settlements, seizing Calcutta. Sir Robert Clive soon regained the city and marched on to meet the Nabob. In the ensuing battle, our losses were between 20 and 70 men and a truly great victory against overwhelming odds was gained. This one event more than any other, led ultimately to British control over the much divided kingdoms of India. Through this battle, the North East of India came under British rule (see 1st January, 1st May, 18th July and 15th August).

1894 The birth of Prince Edward Albert Christian George Andrew Patrick David, Prince of Wales and the future Edward VIII in Richmond in Surrey (see 28th May). Known as David to his family, he was the eldest son (see 11th December) of George V (see 20th January and 3rd June) and Queen Mary of Teck.

1912 The birth of Alan Mathison Turing (see 7th June) in London.

2016 The United Kingdom holds the EU referendum on whether to remain or leave the EU. The nation votes 51.9% to leave and 47.1% to remain. This day is Britain's Independence Day (see 1st January, 30th January, 7th February, 28th October and 27th November)

24th June:

1314 The second and main day of the battle of Bannockburn and defeat for the English at the hands of a Scottish army led by Robert the Bruce (see 7th June). The army of Edward II (see 25th April and 21st September) numbered around 30,000 men and the Bruce's numbered only about 13,000. The Scottish troops fought in schiltroms and resisted the English cavalry. The English archers, though deployed quickly, were swiftly disrupted by the Scottish cavalry early on (see 23rd June) and the English began to flee. Many were drowned in the River Forth. Edward made it to Dunbar Castle and from there took a ship to England.

1340 The Battle of Sluys, just off the coast between Zeeland and West Flanders. The English Fleet led by Edward III (see 21st June and 13th November) fought the combined fleet of the French, Castilians and Genoese. It was a resounding victory for our forces that destroyed the French fleet, the effect of which would last for years and allowed Edward III (see 21st June and 13th November) to land our armies on the north coast of France with little resistance.

1497 John Cabot lands in what is believed to be Newfoundland and claims the land for King Henry VII (see 28th January and 21st April). Probably born in Genoa, he moved to England in about 1490 and with support from Henry VII (see 28th January and 21st April) he sailed across the Atlantic in his ship the 'Matthew' with the idea of discovering a route to Asia. The following year he made another voyage with five ships but was never seen again. It is believed he may have reached the North American coast but either wasn't able to make or didn't survive the return journey (see 5th August).

1509 Henry VIII is crowned at Westminster Abbey (see 28th January and 28th June). The ceremony was performed by the Archbishop of Canterbury, William Warham. The ceremony was followed by a huge banquet and feast in Westminster Hall.

1701 The Act of Settlement received Royal Assent today. This Act prevents any Catholic from inheriting the throne of this country and also prevents the reigning monarch from marrying a Catholic. It settled the succession to the British throne on the heirs of the Electress Sophia of Hanover, a Granddaughter of James VI (James I of England see 27th March and 19th June) and the mother of the future George I (see 28th May and 11th June).

1813 The Battle of Beavers Dams in Canada (see 1st July). American soldiers, attempting a surprise attack on the British Fort at Beavers Dams are ambushed by Native Forces as they attempt advance on our positions. Savagely out fought by our Indian allies, the Americans attempt to make it to open ground in order to use their artillery but fail. Surrounded and under danger of total slaughter, the American leader Colonel Charles Boerstler is forced to surrender to British Officers (see 6th June, 18th June, 17th October and 24th December).

1850 The birth of Horatio Herbert Kitchener, later Lord Kitchener, in County Kerry, Ireland (see 5th June).

1909 The birth of William Penney in Gibraltar (see 3rd March).

2016 The Prime Minister David Cameron announces he will resign after leading the failed remain campaign leading up to the EU referendum (see 7th May and 23rd June).

25th June:

1487 Edward V is deposed and imprisoned in the Tower of London (see 4thNovember). He disappears with his younger brother and is commonly believed to have been murdered by order of their uncle Richard III (see 22nd August and 2nd October).

1646 The Royalist city of Oxford is surrendered to Parliamentary forces who are led by General Sir Thomas Fairfax. The Royalist garrison, as part of the agreed treaty, were allowed to leave the city unmolested over a period of days and the city was therefore saved from attack (see 30th January).

1879 The death of Sir William Fothergill Cooke in Farnham (see 4th May). Born in Ealing, he entered the Indian Army and served for around five years. He then studied medicine in Paris and in 1836 he saw an example of experimental telegraphy. From here on he worked on developing his own electric telegraph. In 1837 he approached Charles Wheatstone with the idea of forming a partnership to develop a telegraph. One year later they had the first working commercial telegraph for the Great Western Railway. In 1846, along with John Lewis Ricardo, he created the Electric Telegraph Company, the first commercial public telegraph company (see 2nd September). He was knighted in 1869.

1900 The birth of Louis Francis Albert Victor Nicholas Mountbatten in Frogmore House in Windsor (see 20th February and 27th August). He was the son of Prince Louis of Battenberg and Princess Victoria of Hesse.

1903 The birth of Eric Arthur Blair (later known as George Orwell) in India (see 21ˢᵗ January).

1950 Communist North Korean troops, supported by China, cross the 38ᵗʰ Parallel into South Korea starting the Korean War (see 27ᵗʰ July and 29ᵗʰ August).

1971 The death of Lord John Boyd Orr in Angus (see 23ʳᵈ September). The leading expert on nutrition of his time, he is well known for his published report *Food, Health and Income* in 1936. In it he highlighted the dietary deficiencies in over half the population. Because of his approach to vitamins, proteins and calories, he was the leading influence on rationing during the Second World War. In 1949 he was awarded the Nobel Peace Prize.

26ᵗʰ June:

1793 The death of Gilbert White in Selborne in Hampshire (see 18ᵗʰ July). Born in 1720, he was educated in Oxford and later he became the Curate of Selborne but was famous for also being a pioneering naturalist and ornithologist. He is regarded by many as the father of ecology. His most famous work is *The Natural History of Antiquities of Selborne*, published in 1789. He kept a journal and in it he recorded his observation s of the local flora and fauna of his home in Selborne.

1824 The birth of William Thompson (see 17ᵗʰ December) in Belfast, Ireland.

1830 The death of George IV (see 12ᵗʰ August) at Windsor Castle. The eldest son of George III (see 29ᵗʰ January and 24ᵗʰ May), he had served as Prince Regent (see 5ᵗʰ February and 6ᵗʰ February) from 1811 until his father's death in 1820 when he became King due to his father's continued insanity (see 19ᵗʰ July). In 1821 he visited Scotland, the first Monarch since 1650 to do so. He involved himself greatly in politics and, despite his own reluctance, agreed to Catholic Emancipation in 1829. He was a patron of the arts and was responsible for the development of Brighton Pavilion. He was succeeded by his brother as William IV (see 20ᵗʰ June and 21ˢᵗ August).

1857 The very first investiture of the Victoria Cross takes place in Hyde Park. Sixty-two service men out of one hundred and eleven who were awarded the VC on this day are honoured for their bravery by Queen Victoria (see 22ⁿᵈ January and 24ᵗʰ May) who personally presented them with the medal (see 29ᵗʰ January).

1866 The birth of George Edward Stanhope Molyneux Herbert, 5ᵗʰ Earl Carnarvon (see 5ᵗʰ April and 26ᵗʰ November) at High Clare Castle in Hampshire.

1960 British Somaliland, a Protectorate since 1888 but with no resources other than serving as an area to help supply Aden, gains its independence.

27ᵗʰ June:

189

1806 Our forces, under General Sir William Beresford and numbering slightly over 1,500 men, finally capture the city of Buenos Aires in the Spanish colony of the Viceroyalty of the Rio de la Plata. The city would be held heroically for 46 days (see 3rd February).

1829 The death of James Smithson in Genoa. A Chemist, he is remembered for leaving a bequest in his will to the United States of America for the founding of an establishment of learning in America, which eventually became the Smithsonian Institute. Born in Paris in 1764, little is known of his early life. When he died, he was buried in Genoa but his remains were later moved to Washington DC in the United States.

1846 The birth of Charles Stewart Parnell (see 6th October) in County Wicklow, Ireland.

1865 The birth of John Monash in Melbourne, Australia (see 8th October).

1898 The birth of Henry Lovell Goldsworthy Gurney in Cornwall (see 6th October).

2006 The first Veterans Day takes place. Its inauguration was announced earlier in 2006 by the Labour Government. It would continue until 2009, to be replaced by Armed Forces Day.

2007 Tony Blair resigns as Prime Minister and Gordon Brown becomes Prime Minister after his visit to the Queen (see 21st April) at Buckingham Palace (see 6th May, 7th May, 10th May and 11th May).

2009 Is the first Armed Forces Day celebration. This day replaced the Veterans Day that was begun on this date in 2006. Celebrations are held around the country, with the celebrations for 2009 being centred in Edinburgh with the Queen (see 21st April) leading them.

28th June:

1461 Edward IV is crowned in Westminster Abbey (see 29th March, 9th April and 28th April) following the overthrow of Henry VI (see 6th December).

1491 The birth of Henry VIII at Greenwich Palace (see 28th January), the second son and third child of Henry VII (see 28th January and 21st April) and Elizabeth of York.

1838 The Coronation of Queen Victoria at the age of 18 in Westminster Abbey (see 22nd January, 24th May and 20th June).

1861 The supposed date of death of Robert O'Hara Burke at Cooper Creek in Australia (see 6th May). Born in County Galway, Ireland, he joined the Austrian Army where he served for a number of years. On his return to Ireland he became a Police Officer. He emigrated to Australia in 1853, serving as a Police Officer, ultimately becoming a Police Superintendent. In 1860 he was appointed to lead what would become known as the 'Burke and Wills Expedition', to cross Australia from Melbourne to the Gulf of Carpentaria. However, in part due to poor decision-making and planning as well as inexperience, the expedition split, with Burke in one group and his second in command, William John Wills (see 5th January and 29th June), leading the other. After supplies ran out, the expedition members became week and both Wills and Burke were unable to continue. Both men were to die within days if not hours of one another (see 29th June).

1919 The signing of the Treaty of Versailles in the Palace of Versailles in Paris, formally ending World War One. The most controversial aspect of the treaty were the 440 Articles that specified the punishments for Germany and calling for Germany to accept total responsibility for the start of the war and be held responsible for causing all the damage (Article 231). The treaty also compelled Germany to make territorial concessions and to make reparations to the nations that formed the Allied powers (see 4th August, 10th August and 11th November).

1922 The Irish Civil War begins as pro-Anglo-Irish Treaty Dominion troops of the Irish Free State commence an artillery bombardment of the Four Courts buildings in Dublin after it had been occupied since April by members of the IRA. Supported by Britain with a supply of artillery pieces, troops of the Irish Free State ultimately won, but the Four Courts building and much of its contents were destroyed in an explosion (see 24th April, 29th April, 6th December and 8th December).

1939 The Women's Auxiliary Air Force is founded (see 1st February). Their roles were extensive and of vital importance to the war effort but did not involve them directly in combat. However, by the nature of their work they were equally exposed to the same dangers as anyone working at military sites throughout the country.

1969 The first launch of the British designed and built Black Arrow (R0) satellite carrier rocket at Woomera in Australia, though there was no pay load on board. On its fourth and final launch (R3) in 1971 it placed the British satellite 'Prospero' (built by the British Aircraft Corporation) into orbit (see 28th October). In 1971 the program was cancelled by the short-sighted government of the time, giving economic problems as the reason.

2012 Queen Elizabeth II (see 21st April and 2nd June) unveils a Memorial to Bomber Command in Green Park, London. A long overdue memorial, it commemorates the 55,573 heroes of bomber command who, despite paying the ultimate sacrifice for their country, had been shamefully ignored and forgotten by many in post-war Britain without even the dignity of a campaign medal (see 14th July). At a cost of only £2 million pounds, it features seven aircrew figures made of bronze around nine feet high. May they never be forgotten!

29th June:

1613 The Globe Theatre is destroyed by fire. The fire had started following the discharge of cannon as part of the performance of a play and quickly spread through the building.

1801 The first census is carried out, revealing a national population for Great Britain of 8,800,000 people.

1861 The death of Elizabeth Barrett Browning (née Barrett) in Florence, Italy (see 6th March). She was one of the leading Victorian poets of her time. Born in County Durham, she was an invalid and in 1838 her family moved to London from where she wrote her first volumes of poetry. She corresponded with Robert Browning whom she eventually married in 1846 and in 1849 she had a son, Robert Weidman Barrett Browning. She experienced immense popularity during her life time. Her health began to fade until her death and she was buried in Florence.

1861 The death of William John Wills at Cooper's Creek in South Australia (see 5th January). Born in Devon, he came to Australia in 1853 aged eighteen and eventually studied surveying and was employed as a surveyor, in time moving to Melbourne. In 1860 he was employed in the 'Burke and Wills Expedition' led by Robert O'Hara Burke (see 6th May and 28th June) to cross Australia from Melbourne to the Gulf of Carpentaria. However, in part due to poor decision making and planning as well as inexperience, the expedition split with Burke in one group and Wills leading the other. After supplies ran out, the expedition members became week and both Wills and Burke were unable to continue. Both men were to die within days if not hours of one another (see 28th June).

1882 The death of Joseph Hansom (see 26th October). An architect of the Gothic Revival style, he is known as the designer of the Hansom Cab, a carriage designed to be pulled by one horse, carrying two passengers with a driver sitting behind them. His building designs include Birmingham Town Hall, Plymouth Cathedral and Victoria Terrace in Beaumaris on Anglesey.

1890 The death of Alexander Parkes in West Dulwich, London (see 29th December). Born in Birmingham, he was a prolific inventor; he had over 80 patents to his name and is famous for the development of 'Parksine', the first form of celluloid, the original plastic in 1856.

1895 The death of Sir Thomas Henry Huxley (see 4th May) in Eastbourne. A Biologist, he was the key advocate of Darwin's theory on evolution. The son of a maths teacher, at the age of 21 he was assigned to HMS Rattlesnake on its voyage to chart the seas and coast around Australia and New Guinea. He met Charles Darwin (see 12th February and 19th April) in 1856 and was eventually persuaded about his theory of evolution. Because of his advocacy of Darwin, he became known as 'Darwin's Bulldog'. In 1860 in Oxford he took part in the famous debate on evolution with Samuel Wilberforce, the Bishop of Oxford. He wrote his own works on evolution and was president of the Royal Society from 1881 to 1885.

2007 Two car bombs are discovered in London and defused. One is in the Haymarket area and the other is in Park Lane (see 30th June).

30th June:

1685 The birth of John Gay in Barnstable (see 4th December).

1708 The Battle of Oudenarde in Flanders. The Duke of Marlborough (see 16th June), leading the armies of Britain, the Dutch, Hanoverians and the Prussians, overwhelmingly defeats the French and her mixed armies of allies in the War of the Spanish Succession (1701-1714). The French were led by the Duke of Burgundy and Marshal Vendome and number around 90,000 men and 130 guns against our allied forces of 80,000 and over 110 guns. Despite the decisive victory, the French were only saved from total annihilation by the onset of darkness. The future King George II (see 25th October and 30th October) fought with the Hanoverian Cavalry and had his horse shot from under him.

1797 Richard Parker, Naval mutineer and elected mutiny ring-leader is executed. He is hung from the Yardarm of HMS Sandwich (see 12th May) following his court-martial.

1842 The death of Thomas Coke, the 1st Earl of Leicester (see 6th May), in Derbyshire. He inherited his father's large Norfolk estate at Holkham Hall and in 1776 he was elected to Parliament. At his estate, between 1778 and 1821 he held annual meetings where he would enthusiastically demonstrate new farming methods and encourage their adoption by his tenant farmers. Well-known for his care of his tenants, he provided security and stability by offering long leases on farms and houses, an unusual approach in his time.

1917 The death of Dadabhai Naorowji in Bombay (see 4th September). Born in 1825 in Bombay, he travelled to London in 1855 to open the first Indian company in Britain as a Partner. In 1885 he was a moderate founder member of the Indian National Congress (see 28th December) which was, for its first few decades, loyal to the Crown. He later became the first Asian Member of Parliament in 1892, representing Finsbury Central until 1895.

1940 German forces from the Luftwaffe land on British soil at Guernsey Airfield to begin the invasion and occupation of the Channel Islands (see 9th May).

1997 At just before midnight, the ceremony begins to handover the Colony of Hong Kong to the Republic of China, attended by many dignitaries including Prince Charles and the last Governor of the Colony, Chris Patten (1st July).

2007 An attempted suicide car bombing of Glasgow Airport fails and the two Muslim terrorists are captured, one is badly burned whilst attempting to murder people at the airport and dies of his injuries later in hospital (see 29th June).

JULY

1st July:

1690 The Battle of the Boyne, near the town of Drogheda in Ireland. The forces of William of Orange (see 8th March and 4th November), numbering around 35,000 men defeat those of James VII (James II of England and see 16th September and 14th October), whose forces were around 25,000-strong. The Jacobites suffered around 1,500 killed and the Williamite's suffered around 500 to 750 casualties. The battle is traditionally celebrated on the 12th July due to the modern use of the Gregorian calendar (see 2nd September and 14th September).

1731 The birth of Adam Duncan in Lundie, Angus in Scotland (see 4th August).

1841 New Zealand, originally part of the Colony of New South Wales (see 1st January), becomes a separate colony (see 6th February, 26th July and 26th September).

1867 Sir John Maxwell Alexander Macdonald (see 11th January and 6th June), Conservative, is sworn in as the first Prime Minister of Canada as the Canadian Confederation is formed when the British North America Act takes effect (see 29th March). Nova Scotia, New Brunswick and the Province of Canada (see 10th February) unite to form the Dominion of Canada. At the same time, the Province of Canada ceases to exist and becomes the two separate Provinces of Quebec and Ontario. This date is subsequently celebrated as Dominion Day in Canada, though not officially until 1879 as Canadians thought of themselves as being primarily British until well into the twentieth century (see 31st March).

1890 The Heligoland-Zanzibar Treaty is signed between Great Britain and the German Empire. The treaty allowed Britain to extend the Railway from Lake Victoria and to consolidate territories in East Africa, including the area later to become the Colony of Kenya (see 12th December), whilst ceding the islands of Heligoland to Germany. Germany agreed not to interfere in British interests in Africa, and Britain gained the opportunity to create the Zanzibar Protectorate.

1895 The British East Africa Protectorate (later Kenya Colony) is formed after the Imperial British East Africa Company transfers its territories to the Crown (see 12th December).

1903 The birth of Amy Johnson in Kingston upon Hull (see 5th January).

1912 The Royal Naval Air Service (see 1st April) is officially recognised by the First Lord of the Admiralty, Sir Winston Spencer Churchill (see 24th January and 30th November).

1916 The first day of the Battle of the Somme. On a glorious sunny morning at zero hour (7.30am), thirteen divisions of the British Army positioned north of the Somme River and eleven French divisions to the south advanced from their forward trenches towards the Germans following seven days of artillery bombardment to 'soften up' the German lines. Our forces suffer over 60,000 casualties, with almost 20,000 of those killed. By the end of the campaign in November 1916, there would be over 420,000 casualties from across the Empire. This day would become the costliest single battle in our military history (see 18th November).

1971 The death of Sir William Lawrence Bragg in Ipswich (see 31st March). A Physicist, he was born in Australia, coming to Britain in 1909. He is remembered for 'Bragg's Law', the diffraction of x-rays by crystals. With this he worked with his father and their results were published in the publication 'X-rays and Crystal structure' in 1915, for which they jointly received the Nobel Prize for Physics. From 1915 until the end of the First World War he worked on perfecting sound raging for locating the positions of enemy artillery guns and was awarded the Military Cross.

1997 The Colony of Hong Kong is granted to the People's Republic of China, having been ceded in to Britain 1841 (see 20th January, 9th June, 30th June and 29th August). In a formal ceremony beginning the previous evening, over 150 years of British administration came to an end.

1999 The Scottish Parliament in Edinburgh is officially opened by Queen Elizabeth II (see 21st April and 2nd June) and elements of power are transferred from Westminster to the newly devolved parliament (see 18th September and 19th September).

2007 At 6am smoking is banned in England in all public buildings and areas, such as work places, theatres, restaurants and pubs (see 2nd April and 30th April).

2009 The Elizabeth Cross is instituted. This is an award to the next of kin of those members of Her Majesty's Armed forces who have given their lives in service of our country. The award is also given retrospectively to the families of all those who have died since the end of World War Two (see 12th October). The award is a large silver cross and a miniature version designed to be worn as a brooch.

2nd July:

1266 The Treaty of Perth is signed between the Kingdom of Scotland under Alexander III (see 19th March and 4th September) and Norway under Magnus VI reaching agreement on Scottish sovereignty of the Hebrides and the Isle of Mann (see 13th July) in return for a payment and Norwegian sovereignty over Shetland and the Orkneys.

1489 The birth of Thomas Cranmer (born see 21st March) in Nottinghamshire.

1644 The Battle of Marston Moor. The battle took place near Long Marston in Yorkshire during the Civil War and is believed to be the largest battle to have been fought on English soil. The Royalists, under Prince Rupert (see 29th November and 17th December), were decisively beaten by a combined army of English Parliamentarians and Scottish Covenanters led by the Earl of Leven in a battle that lasted around two hours. Less than 500 Parliamentarians were killed but around 1,500 Royalists were killed and

4,000 taken prisoner. The result for the Royalists of losing the battle was that they lost control of the North of England to Parliament and its army.

1800 The Union with Ireland Act (1800) is passed by Parliament. As one of the two Acts of Union with the United Kingdom of Great Britain, the act was one of two that came into force in Ireland once the Act of Union (Ireland) Act 1800 was passed by the Irish Parliament (see 1st January, 12th April and 1st August).

1850 The death of Sir Robert Peel (see 5th February) in Whitehall Gardens, London. His most enduring and well-known legacy was whilst he was Home Secretary under the then Prime Minister, the Duke of Wellington (see 1st May and 14th September), when he became responsible for the creation of the Metropolitan Police Force in 1829. He served as Prime Minister twice and published the 'Tamworth Manifesto' in 1834 (see 18th December), generally believed to be the foundation of the modern Conservative Party.

1862 The birth of Christopher George Francis Maurice Craddock (see 1st November) in Yorkshire.

1914 The death of Joseph Chamberlain (see 8th July) a Liberal Unionist MP and one of the leading political figures of the late 19th Century. He was the father of the future Conservative Prime Minister, Neville Chamberlain (see 18th March and 9th November). Though he was never to become Prime Minister, he was nevertheless one of the greatest influences on late nineteenth and early twentieth-century politics. Whilst serving as Secretary of State for the Colonies (1895-1903), he played a key role in the events leading up to the outbreak of the South African War in 1899 (see 12th October). An opponent of Free Trade, he favoured a policy of Imperial Preference for colonies within the Empire (and in particular Imperial Federation) and imposing tariffs on foreign imports, a stance that would ultimately lead to his political demise.

1919 The airship R34 departs from Britain in its quest to become the first return flight across the Atlantic Ocean (see 6th July).

1928 The Representation of the People (Equal Franchise) Act 1928 is given Royal Assent and thereby allowing for the voting age of women to be reduced from 30 years to 21 years.

3rd July:

1728 The birth of Robert Adam in Kirkcaldy, Fife (see 3rd March).

1760 The start of the battle of Restigouche off the coast of New France (see 8th July) as a Squadron of Royal Navy vessels intercept a French flotilla of merchant vessels and their escorts. As a direct result of this battle, most French ships were prevented from docking (see 8th September).

1858 The signing of the Treaty of Tientsin. It was signed between the Chinese and Lord Elgin on behalf of Great Britain. It allowed Christian missionaries entry into China and opened up eleven ports to trade with the Europeans as well as a permanent British Ambassador in Peking. More importantly, it also brought to an end the Second Opium War, 1856-1860 (see 8th October and 23rd October).

1928 The first colour television transmission is broadcast in London by John Logie Baird (see 14th June and 14th August).

1938 The A4 Class steam train 4468 Mallard becomes the fastest steam locomotive of all time. At Stoke Bank near Grantham, on a section of the East Coast Main Line the train reached a speed of 125.88 miles per hour setting a world steam train speed record that has not been broken (see 11th August).

1940 Our Warships destroy the French Fleet in the French Algerian port of Mers el Kabir during Operation Catapult. The purpose of the attack was to prevent the fleet from falling into German hands via the Vichy regime. Our Mediterranean fleet was commanded by Admiral James Somerville. Following the failure of the French fleet to submit to the terms of a generous ultimatum, and with no guarantee of the willingness of the French to persevere with the war, the Royal Navy opened fire upon the French ships in port. The French fleet did return fire, but quite ineffectually. At the same time, Swordfish fighters from HMS Ark Royal attacked the ship and those that had managed to escape into the sea. Over 1,000 French sailors were killed, 1 Battleship was destroyed and 2 Battleships and 4 destroyers were badly damaged.

1944 The battle and siege of Imphal, part of the Burma Campaign to drive the Japanese invaders from the occupied territory, ends as mauled and demoralised Japanese end their siege of the city and withdraw, completely beaten (see 8th March). The city of Imphal, the capital city of Manipur, is situated in North-eastern India and the Japanese, supported by treacherous Indian National Army Units, crossed the Chindwin River in attempt to take the city, thus opening up the road deep into India (see 4th April). The courageous and determined British and Indian Army units in the city had refused to give up and the battle of Kohima proved to be one of the pivotal battles in the Far East.

4th July:

1761 The death of Samuel Richardson in Parsons Green, London (see 19th August). He was a successful printer and published the first successful modern novel, *Clarissa*. It is the longest novel in the English language.

1776 A so-called 'Declaration of Independence' from Great Britain is signed by most of the traitorous rebel leaders of the 13 British colonies of North America (see 5th September). Though many mistakenly believe and celebrate the colonies becoming independent from this moment, independence was not formally granted until 1783 at the Treaty of Paris and then only after its ratification by King and Parliament in 1784 (see 19th April and 3rd September).

1837 The opening of the Grand Junction Railway. Designed to connect Birmingham with the Liverpool and Manchester Railway, it initially had

Joseph Locke (see 18th September) and George Stephenson (see 12th August) as joint Chief Engineers, though Stephenson later resigned.

1879 The Battle of Ulundi in Central Zululand where 17,000 British and native troops engaged a large Zulu army of around 24,000 warriors. Commanded by Lieutenant General Lord Chelmsford, our forces crossed the river and approached the Zulu Kraal in a hollow square formation. The Zulus attacked our troops and surrounded them, but after around thirty minutes their attack faded and faltered in the face of consistent and heavy rifle fire. As the attack failed, the Zulus turned and they fled, pursued by the 17th Lancers. Our troops lost 3 Officers and 79 men and the Zulus are said to have lost around 1,500 warriors. The victory at Ulundi effectively ended the Zulu War (see 12th January and 28th August).

1886 The first passenger train on the Canadian Pacific Railway, the first to cross Canada arrives in Port Moody at midday. The railway, designed by Sir Sandford Fleming (see 7th January and 22nd July), was the first transcontinental railway to cross the Dominion of Canada (see 1st July) from east to west.

1954 All remaining food rationing finally comes to an end at midnight (see 8th January, 5th February, 9th February, 9th July, 9th September and 3rd October).

2014 Her Majesty Queen Elizabeth II (see 6th February, 21st April and 6th June) names and launches HMS Queen Elizabeth, the largest ever Royal Navy ship from the Rosyth Dockyard in Fife. An aircraft carrier, it is the first aircraft carrier to have two island superstructures, the front to navigate the ship and the rear to control aircraft flights. The ship is capable of carrying up to forty aircraft and is the sister ship of the next carrier, HMS Prince of Wales.

5th July:

1805 The birth of Robert FitzRoy (see 30th April) in Suffolk.

1820 The birth of William John Maquorn Rankine in Edinburgh (see 24th December).

1826 The death of Sir Thomas Stamford Bingley Raffles in London from apoplexy (see 6th July). He is known as the founder of Singapore and was one of the greatest expansionists of our Empire (see 6th February). He started his working life as a clerk in the London offices of the East India Company (see 31st December). Later, in 1805, he was sent to work as an assistant to the Territories Resident in Penang. On the way he taught himself the Malay language and became a translator. In 1811 he became governor of Java following a brief military operation and in 1819 he founded the colony of Singapore. He was knighted in 1816 for his work for the Empire.

1853 The birth of Cecil Rhodes, businessman, explorer and founder of the Colonies of Rhodesia (see 26th March) in Bishops Stortford in Hertfordshire.

1948 The introduction of the National Insurance Act of 1946. Today the Government takes over responsibility of all health and medical care with the introduction of the National Health Service (see 1st December).

1967 The 1st Battalion the Argyll and Sutherland Highlanders, led by Lieutenant Colonel Colin Campbell Mitchell (see 20th July and 17th November), enter the rebellious Crater area of Aden Colony and restore order (see 19th January, 20th June and 10th December) by implementing the controversial but highly effective 'Argyll Law'.

2012 The Government announces its controversial plans to reduce the army by around 20,000 personnel or a fifth of its strength by the year 2015 from 102,000 to 82,000. Seventeen units are to go but the number of reservists is to double from 15,000 to 30,000 (see 5th July, 2nd November and 24th November).

6th July:

1189 The death of Henry II *Curtmantle* at Chinon in France (see 4th March). The son of the Count of Anjou and Matilda, he was the grandson of Henry I of England (see 1st December) through his mother. In 1152 he married Eleanor of Aquitaine and in 1153 he crossed to England to pursue his claim to the English throne. Although Matilda had been named as Henry's successor, her cousin Stephen had taken the throne on his death. However, he succeeded Stephen upon his death in 1154 (see 25th October). He restored order and improved the judicial system. In 1164 he attempted to assert control over the church which led to conflict with Thomas Beckett and ultimately to the murder of the Archbishop (see 29th December). In 1169 an Anglo-Norman army landed in Ireland to support Irish kings. Fearing a powerful Norman state on his doorstep, he travelled to Ireland to assert his control over the country, thus beginning English influence in Ireland forever more (see 18th October). In his latter years, his own sons, jealous of his power and distrustful of one another, argued and came to conflict, the stress of which hastened Henry's own demise.

1249 The death of Alexander II of Scotland (see 24th August) on the isle of Kerrera in the Inner Hebrides. The son of William the Lion (see 4th December) he was the father of Alexander III (see 19th March and 4th September). In 1215, the year after his succession, he led his army into England in support of the Barons revolt against King John (see 19th October and 24th December) and with his army reached the south coast of England at Dover, the only Scottish King to advance so far. His first wife was Joan of England, the sister of Henry III of England (see 1st October and 16th November). In 1237 he signed the Treaty of York (see 25th September) with Henry III settling a dispute between the two and indirectly established the limit of the Scottish border. In his final years he attempted negotiations on the Western Isles but with only limited success.

1483 The coronation of Richard III at Westminster Abbey (see 4th February, 22nd August and 2nd October)

1535 The execution of Sir Thomas More, lawyer, writer and former Lord Chancellor to Henry VIII (see 28th January and 28th June), for treason (see 7th February). Born in London, he was the writer of the book 'Utopia', thus creating a new word for the language. He opposed Henry VIII's self-appointment as Governor of the Church of England and therefore Henry's opposition to and stance against Rome.

1553 The death of Edward VI at Greenwich Palace (see 12th October) at the age of 15. The only son of Henry VIII (see 28th January and 28th June), his mother was Jane Seymour (see 24th October). Physically weak and continually ill, he succeeded to the throne before his older sisters, the future Queens Mary (see 18th February and 17th November) and Elizabeth (see 24th March and 7th September) at the age of 9 in 1547. At first, his uncle Edward Seymour assumed the role of Protector and in an effort to ensure England was a Protestant state, an English Prayer book was introduced and legislation to enforce it in 1549. A rebellion broke out against the Prayer Book in the West Country which was put down and led to the fall of Somerset. When it became clear that Edward was terminally ill, he was persuaded to change the succession from his Catholic sister Mary to Lady Jane Grey (see 12th February, 10th July and 19th July), a Protestant and a distant relative. He was buried in Westminster Abbey.

1586 The Treaty of Berwick is signed between representatives of Queen Elizabeth I (see 24th March and 7th September) of England and James VI of Scotland (see 27th March and 19th June). The treaty was a mutual defensive pact between the two countries guaranteeing aid to one another if either country should be attacked by an invading foreign army.

1685 The Battle of Sedgemoor and the conclusion to the short lived Monmouth Rebellion (see 11th June). Cornered in the town of Bridgewater, the Duke of Monmouth (see 9th April and 15th July) led his rebel army in an attempted surprise attack against government troops. However, the element of surprise was lost and the government forces were able to rally and the inferior numbers of rebel troops were easily routed and fled from the battlefield with government forces in pursuit. The rebels lost around 13,000 killed and another 500 captured in the following pursuit. The government forces lost around 200 men.

1747 The birth of John Paul (later 'Jones') in Scotland (see 18th July).

1781 The birth on board the ship *Ann* off the coast of Jamaica of Thomas Stamford Bingley Raffles (see 5th July), who would later found the city of Singapore (see 6th February).

1813 The death of Granville Sharp in London (see 10th November). He was a leading abolitionist and had a major role in the creation of the first settlement of freed black slaves in Sierra Leone. Born in Durham, he worked as a Civil Servant, becoming interested in the abolition of slavery after meeting Jonathan Strong, an abused slave, in 1765. He successfully fought for Strong's freedom and prevented him returning to the Colonies. He was instrumental in the 1772 ruling preventing slaves from being compelled to return to the Colonies once they had arrived in Britain. He supported the creation of Sierra Leone for freed slaves from Britain and Canada. Along with Thomas Clarkson, he was key in the formation of the Society for the Abolition of the Slave Trade. The Society was successful, with the slave trade abolished in the British Empire in 1807 (see 25th March), though he continued until his death campaigning for the complete abolition of slavery.

1827 The Treaty of London is signed by Great Britain, France and Russia. The agreement between the three countries called upon the Greeks and the Ottoman Empire to end the conflict and called for an independent Greek Republic. The treaty also enabled all three to enter the Greek War of Independence (1821-1832) on behalf of the Greeks who had recently rebelled against the Ottoman Empire (see 20th October).

1919 The British airship R34 lands in New York, becoming the first airship to cross the Atlantic Ocean (see 2nd July, 10th July and 13 July).

1960 The death of Aneurin 'Nye' Bevan in Chesham (see 15th November). A socialist and former miner and union official, he was a long-time Member of Parliament and Deputy Leader of the Labour Party. As Minister for Health and Housing under Prime Minister Clement Attlee (see 3rd January and 8th October), he was instrumental in the formation and introduction of the National Health Service in 1948 (see 5th July).

7th July:

1307 The death of Edward I '*Longshanks*' the 'Hammer of the Scots' at Burgh on the Sands near Carlisle from dysentery (see 17th June) whilst on his way to Scotland for another war against the Scots, under Robert the Bruce. Probably the most outstanding English monarch of the middle ages, he initiated reforms and he laid the foundations for what would later become a parliamentary system of government. He was the king that began England's and ultimately Britain's steady march to greatness. He conquered Wales and was responsible for the building of a network of castles throughout north Wales, which still stand today.

1549 Robert Kett, a yeoman farmer, who had enclosed some common land around his manor at Wymondham, is confronted by protesters against enclosure and decides to lead the rebels and takes charge, leading the Norfolk rising (see 20th June, 27th August and 7th December).

1742 The Battle of Bloody Marsh on St. Simon's Island in the Province of Georgia. A Spanish force of around 5,000, under Don Manuel de Montiano, attempted to invade the Province of Georgia. General James Oglethorpe led less than 1,000 regulars, local militia and local settlers and Indians in the defence of the island. The defenders bravely repulsed two main Spanish attempts to attack the British positions. Despite being greatly outnumbered, the defenders caused the Spanish to retreat and abandon the invasion (see 18th October).

1896 The death of Sir John Pender (see 10th September), the leading submarine telegraph cable pioneer. Born in the Vale of Leven in Scotland, he entered Parliament for the first time in 1862. He became a successful textile merchant in both Glasgow and Manchester and invested his money in trans-Atlantic telegraph cable laying and despite initial failure succeeded in the first successful trans-Atlantic telegraph being sent between Britain and America (see 16th August).

1930 The death of Sir Arthur Conan Doyle (see 22nd May). Though a prolific writer, he is best remembered for his stories about the adventures of Sherlock Holmes, the first of which, 'A Study in Scarlet' appeared in 1887. He was a fervent defender of the Empire and wrote a book about Britain's role in the Boer War (1899-1902), entitled 'The Great Boer War', explaining the reasons for the conflict. He wrote numerous other fictional stories and later in life developed a deep interest in spiritualism following the deaths of his first wife, one of his sons and other close relatives. He served as a soldier through most of the Great War, despite being in his 50s.

2005 Four London suicide bombings occur. Four British-born traitorous Muslim terrorists blow themselves up on three Tube trains and a bus, murdering 52 people innocent people from different countries and religions.

8th July:

1647 The birth of Frances Theresa Stuart (see 15th October) in exile in Paris.

1670 The Godolphin Treaty between England and Spain is signed in Madrid. As part of the Treaty, Spain formally recognised the English sphere of influence in the West Indies, in particular English control of Jamaica and the Cayman Islands (see 18th January and 6th August) and to limit trading to each nation's respective territories.

1760 The conclusion to the battle of Restigouch off the coast of New France (see 3rd July) as a Squadron of Royal Navy vessels intercept a French flotilla of merchant vessels and their escorts attempting to bring supplies into New France. The French vessels scattered but were no match for British ships and sailing skills and a number were scuttled with the loss of their cargo, thus preventing the re-supply of French territories. The battle was instrumental in the ultimate loss by the French of their colonies in New France (see 10th February, 8th September and 13th September).

1822 The death of Percy Bysshe Shelley off the coast of the Grand Duchy of Tuscany (see 4th August). A leading Romantic poet of his time, he is known for his unconventional lifestyle. Expelled from Oxford University for making contributions towards radical pamphlets, he became romantically attached to two successive 16 year old girls. The second of these being Mary Godwin (see 1st February and 30th August) and they eventually married after travelling Europe and settling in Italy. Italy was where he wrote his more well-known poems. It was whilst he was returning from visiting his friends Lord Byron and James Leigh Hunt that the boat he was travelling in capsized and he was drowned.

1823 The death of Henry Raeburn (see 4th March) in Stockbridge, now part of Edinburgh. He was the earliest portrait painter of distinction to emerge from Scotland and his works include paintings of Sir Walter Scott and many other notable figures from across Scotland. He was apprenticed to a goldsmith in 1771 and when he started his own work, he began with miniatures. In 1812 he was elected as president of the Edinburgh Society of Arts which was followed by knighthood in 1822.

1836 The birth of Joseph Chamberlain, the future statesman and Whig MP (see 2nd July and 3rd September) in Camberwell, London. His father was a successful shoemaker and manufacturer who provided well for his children's education.

9th July:

1540 The marriage of Henry VIII (see 28th January and 28th June) and Anne of Cleves (see 16th July and 22nd September) is annulled after only six months of marriage. The marriage was never consummated but she received a generous settlement (see 6th January).

1755 Braddock's expedition of over 2,000 men and led by General Edward Braddock is attacked and after an initial brief success is savagely defeated at the Battle of Monongahela by French militia and irregulars and their Indian allies. The force was part of a greater offensive against the French presence in North America and designed to capture a series of French forts and positions. General Braddock was mortally wounded in the battle and died of his wounds four days later (see 13th July). On the expedition with him was a volunteer officer, George Washington (see 11th February and 14th December), who rallied the rear guard, allowing the British to withdraw following the battle.

1764 The birth of Ann Radcliffe (nee Ward) in London (see 7th February).

1775 The birth of Matthew Lewis in London (see 14th May).

1795 The death of General Henry Seymour Conway (born 1721). A cousin of Horace Walpole, he participated in the War of the Austrian Succession (1740-1748) where he served on the staff of General George Wade (see 14th March) at the battle of Dettingen in 1743 (see 16th June). He was on the staff of the Duke of Cumberland at the battle of Fontenoy 1745 (see 1st May) and was at the battle of Culloden (see 16th April) in 1746. He was elected to Parliament in 1741 and later served in the Seven Years' War (1756-1763), fighting in numerous major engagements. He had a turbulent political career following the end of the war until shortly before his death.

1797 The death of Edmund Burke, Whig MP, at Beaconsfield in Buckinghamshire. Born in Dublin to a solicitor (see 1st January), he studied law in London. He was elected to Parliament in 1765 and became involved in the debates over the power of the Monarch and the increased power of Parliament. He expressed interest in the governing of India and attempted to introduce a Bill to this effect that was defeated in Parliament. He opposed British policy in the American colonies, believing it to be too harsh and inflexible. However, he openly opposed the French revolution, warning against the dangers of 'mob rule' and the violent upheaval of tradition.

1864 The Admiralty decreed that from this day, the White Ensign would be the Royal Navy's only standard, distinguishing it from the red ensign of the merchant service. It is flown from all Royal Navy vessels, shore establishments, bases and buildings both at home and abroad (see 10th February, 4th July and 21st October).

1877 The first Wimbledon Championship opens at the All England Lawn Tennis and Croquet Club in Wimbledon, London. There were ten matches held on the first day, with a total of twenty-two competitors and it was a men-only completion.

1900 Her Britannic Majesty, Queen Victoria, gives Royal assent to the Australian Federation Bill that allows for the creation of the Commonwealth of Australia (see 1st January and 26th January).

1919 The birth of Edward Richard George Heath in Broadstairs in Kent (see 17th July and 28th July).

1940 Tea rationing is introduced and for most of the war and to the end of rationing (see 3rd October); it was set at 2oz per person (those over nine years old) per week (see 8th January, 5th February, 9th February, 4th July and 9th September).

10th July:

1296 John Balliol (see 25th November), King of Scotland, surrenders to Edward I (see 17th June and 7th July) of England in the churchyard at Stracathro in Angus and is then forced to abdicate. He and his forces had been defeated at the Battle of Dunbar (see 27th April). Following his abdication he was taken as a prisoner to the Tower of London before being released into the custody of the Pope and being sent into exile to Picardy (see 17th November and 30th November).

1460 The Battle of Northampton in the Wars of the Roses (1455-1585). Henry VI (see 21st May and 6th December) is captured by the Yorkist army under Edward, Earl of March, as many of his retinue are slaughtered attempting to fight off the enemy.

1553 Lady Jane Grey is proclaimed Queen (see 12th February and 19th July). The great granddaughter of Henry VII, she was also cousin to Edward VI, who proclaimed her as his successor whilst he was dying and again on his death bed, although in contravention of the Act of Succession proclaimed by his father, Henry VIII (see 28th January and 28th June).

1919 The British built airship R34 takes off on the return trip across the Atlantic from Minneola, Long Island, in America (see 2nd July, 6th July and 13th July).

1920 The death of Admiral of the Fleet John Arbuthnot 'Jackie' Fisher (see 25th January) in Norfolk. A one-time First Sea Lord, he was probably the most influential and innovative Admiral after Nelson. Born in Ceylon in 1841, he joined the Royal Navy in 1854. Though not widely known as an active Admiral, his influence is undoubted, especially with naval reform and development of new weapons and tactics that brought the Royal Navy into a league of its own.

1943 British and American airborne forces begin the invasion of Italy and land on Sicily under the command of General Montgomery. In what was codenamed 'Operation Husky', British and American paratroopers land just after midnight and, despite some initial setbacks, they begin to take up positions. Despite being in small, unconnected groups, the troops continue to attack and destroy key objectives as the land forces begin to come ashore and progress inland (see 30th April).

11th July:

1274 The birth of the future Robert I, or 'The Bruce' (see 7th June, 23rd June and 24th June).

1509 The marriage of Henry VIII (see 28th January and 28th June) and Catherine of Aragon (see 7th January and 16th December), his first wife. She was his sister-in-law and he married Catherine after her first husband, Henry's older brother Arthur, Prince of Wales (see 2nd April) had died.

1533 Pope Clement VII announces that King Henry VIII (see 28th January and 28th June) and the Archbishop of Canterbury, Thomas Cranmer (see 21st March), had been excommunicated from the Catholic Church. He also announced that Henry's second marriage to Anne Boleyn (see 19th May) was null and void.

1754 The concluding day of the Albany Congress meets in Albany, New York (see 19th June). Organised by the British Board of Trade, delegates from the seven northern colonies of the thirteen colonies of British North America met to discuss relations with the Native American tribes and a more common defence strategy against the French threat (see 17th March, 22nd March and 3rd September).

1859 Big Ben, the bell in Saint Stephen's Clock Tower at the Houses of Parliament, is rung for the first time to mark time (see 31st May).

1882 Following the Egyptians' failure to comply with an ultimatum, a Royal Navy Squadron under the command of Admiral Beauchamp Seymour bombards the defences of the port of Alexandria in Egypt following a revolt by elements of the Egyptian Army (see 13th September).

12th July:

1543 Henry VIII (see 28th January and 28th June) marries the widow Catherine Parr at Hampton Court Palace, the last of his six wives (see 5th September).

1691 The battle of Aughrim in County Galway. One of the bloodiest battles in Ireland, it effectively brought an end to Jacobite hopes in Ireland. At first, the Jacobite forces under Marquis de St. Ruth were on the point of dominance when he was killed. At this point, the Jacobite forces folded and fled the field. Many leading Irish Catholic noblemen were killed and following the battle, the remaining Jacobite Catholic areas capitulated to William's forces (see 1st July).

1712 The death of Richard Cromwell, the Lord Protector (see 4th October). Born in Huntingdon, he was the third son of Oliver Cromwell (see 25th April and 3rd September). Following his father becoming Lord Protector, he became more involved in politics and in 1654 he was elected as an MP. He was proclaimed Lord Protector on his father's death and enjoyed much initial support. His reign as Lord Protector lasted for just a year but the army became more discontented with his rule. After coming under house arrest for his own protection, Parliament voted in 1659 (see 7th May and 25th May) to abolish the Protectorate. By succeeding his father he was the second of only two Republican heads of state this country has had.

1730 The birth of Josiah Wedgwood (see 3rd January) in Burslem in Staffordshire.

1794 Horatio Nelson is injured and loses the sight of his right eye at the siege of Calvi on the island of Corsica (see 29th September and 21st October). Standing in a forward artillery position, a shot hit the protective sand bag nearby causing debris to strike him in the eye.

1859 The birth of John Grenfell Maxwell (see 20th February).

1871 The launch of HMS Devastation at Portsmouth Dockyard, the first mastless capital warship and the first to carry all her main armaments mounted on top of the hull instead of within. She was the first 'modern' looking warship and this two-ship class (the other being HMS Thunderer) was the most powerful of her time (see 10th February).

1902 Arthur Balfour (see 19th March and 25th July) becomes Conservative Prime Minister after the resignation on the same day of his uncle, Robert Gascoyne-Cecil, Lord Salisbury (see 3rd February and 22nd August).

1926 The death of Gertrude Margaret Lowthian Bell in Baghdad (see 14th July). She was an archaeologist, traveller, writer and administrator. Born in County Durham, she travelled extensively throughout Arabia in the years leading up to the Great War, her first journey being to Persia in 1892. Following the outbreak of war, her knowledge and mapping work and skills became invaluable to the government in its campaigns in the area. Following

British victory in Mesopotamia, she was the most influential figure in the founding of the state of Iraq.

1946 The Coal Industry Nationalisation Act receives Royal assent (see 1st January). The act allowed the Labour government under Prime Minister Clement Attlee (see 3rd January and 8th October) to nationalise the coal industry with over 200 companies being taken under government control.

13th July:

1249 The coronation of Alexander III King of Scotland at Scone Abbey (see 19th March, 2nd July and 4th September).

1713 The part of the Treaty of Utrecht between Great Britain and Spain is signed, bringing an end to the War of the Spanish Succession, 1701-1714. Spain ceded Gibraltar and Minorca to Great Britain (see 31st March) as well as the Asiento.

1755 The death of General Edward Braddock in Great Meadows, Pennsylvania. Born in Perthshire about 1695 he was commissioned originally into the Coldstream Guards. He served as the Commander in Chief of Colonial forces in North America at the start of the American part of the Seven Years' War (1756-1763). He is remembered for commanding the unsuccessful and disastrous Braddock Expedition that was savagely defeated at the Battle of Monongahela in 1755 (see 9th July). During the attack on his expedition by French militia and Indian natives he became mortally wounded managed to escape as a volunteer officer, George Washington (see 14th December) commanded and maintained a disciplined and effective rear guard.

1794 The death of James Lind in Gosport in Hampshire (see 4th October). A surgeon, he is famous for proving that citrus fruit was a cure for scurvy. Born in Edinburgh in 1716 he attended Edinburgh University and studied medicine and qualified as a Physician. In 1739 he joined the Navy as a surgeon's mate. Although the treatment of scurvy by using fruit was already known, he was the first person to conduct tests on patients with the objective of providing a cure for scurvy. In 1747 he fed twelve patients with different food stuffs and discovered that those who ate citrus fruits recovered the quickest of all the test subjects. He also took a close interest in the general hygiene and cleanliness of the ships of the Royal Navy and the sailors aboard. In 1764 he published a work on typhus aboard ships and the methods required to avoid the infection.

1807 The death of Cardinal Henry Benedict Stewart in Frascati, Rome (see 6th March). Born in Rome in 1725, he was the brother of Charles Edward Stewart ('Bonnie Prince Charlie', see 31st January and 31st December) and the youngest son of James III (James VII of England see 1st January and 10th June) 'The Old Pretender'. He spent his life in the Papal States and became a Cardinal. He was known by Jacobites, after his brother's death as Henry IX but he only referred to himself as Cardinal Duke of York but later accepted an annuity of £4,000 from George III (see 29th January and 24th May).

1919 The British built airship R34 arrives back in Britain at Pulham St. Mary in Norfolk after completing the first return Atlantic crossing of an airship from Minneola, Long Island, in America. The flight had taken 75 hours (see 2nd July, 6th July and 10th July).

1955 Ruth Ellis becomes the last woman to be executed in this country when she is hanged at Holloway prison for the murder of David Blakely (see 13th August).

1962 The Prime Minister Harold Macmillan (see 10th February and 29th December) announces that he is sacking seven members of his Cabinet in what would become known as the 'Night of the Long Knives'. The Lord Chancellor, Chancellor of the Exchequer (Selwyn Lloyd), Minister of Education, Minister of Defence, Minister of Housing and Local Government, the Secretary of State for Scotland and another Minister without Portfolio were all sacked. The Conservatives were being beaten in by-elections and took a severe dip in the opinion polls after the 1959 General Election. It was this pressure which pushed the Prime Minister to act in this major reshuffle.

2016 David Cameron visits Queen Elizabeth II (see 21st April and 9th September) and steps down as Prime Minister. Shortly afterwards, Theresa May visits the Queen and becomes Prime Minister (see 23rd June and 24th June)

14th July:

1791 In a display of patriotic fervour that quickly gets out of control, the Priestley Riots take place in Birmingham and drive Joseph Priestley (see 6th February and 13th March) from the city due to his support for the French Revolution. His house and all the family's possessions were destroyed.

1858 The birth of Emmiline Pankhurst (née Goulden, see 14th June) in Stretford, Manchester.

1868 The birth of Gertrude Margaret Lowthian Bell in County Durham (see 12th July).

1927 The Scottish National War Memorial is officially opened by the Prince of Wales, the future Edward VIII (see 28th May and 23rd June). Designed by Sir Robert Lorimer it is housed in a redeveloped barracks within Edinburgh castle and contains the names of those Scots who have given their lives for Great Britain during the Great War and subsequent conflicts (see 4th August and 11th November).

1936 RAF Bomber Command is formed. Its role was to conduct all the Bombing activity by the RAF. Its greatest period was under Air Marshall Arthur 'Bomber' Harris (see 5th April and 13th April) between 1942 and 1945 when it carried out the controversial but necessary strategic bombing of targets in Germany. Though criticised by some, the sacrifice of its personnel, with over 55,000 killed and over 8,300 aircraft lost, helped take the war to the enemy, to the eternal gratitude of our nation. A vast number of the crews were made up of officers and men from the Dominions and Colonies within the Empire. However, despite the heroic sacrifice of all Bomber Command's personnel, in particular those that paid the ultimate sacrifice for their country, their contribution to the success of World War Two had been shamefully ignored and forgotten by many in post-war Britain without even the dignity of a campaign medal (see 28th June).

1948 Six de Havilland Vampire jets from No. 54 Squadron become the first jet aircraft to cross the Atlantic Ocean. They travelled via Stornoway and landed in Labrador (see 3rd December).

2014 The Royal 22nd Regiment of Canadian Guards (The Van Doos) became the ceremonial guard at Buckingham Palace for the first time since 1940. Of note is that this was the first time that Palace Guards have received their orders in French.

15th July:

1573 The birth of Inigo Jones (see 21st June) in Smithfield, London.

1685 James Scott, the Duke of Monmouth, is executed at Tower Hill for treason (see 9th April, 11th June and 6th July) over his attempt to take the throne from his uncle James VII (James II of England see 16th September and 14th October). The illegitimate son of Charles II (see 6th February and 29th May) and Lucy Walters, he was raised by Lord Crofts and was created the Duke of Monmouth in 1663, shortly after which he married. During the Second Anglo-Dutch War (1665-1667) he served under his uncle, the future James VII. Due to his popularity amongst the Protestant masses, he was forced into exile in the Netherlands in 1679. In 1683 he became linked to the so-called Rye House Plot to assassinate Charles II and his brother the Duke of York. His dying father declared his own brother and James' uncle as King on his death. In the belief that he should have succeeded to the throne, he launched the Monmouth Rebellion in an attempt to depose his Catholic uncle from the throne.

1815 Off the coast of Rochefort, Napoleon Bonaparte, the defeated former Emperor of France surrenders to Captain Maitland aboard HMS Bellerophon. The Bellerophon was a third-rate ship of the line that had fought at Trafalgar in 1815 (see 21st October) and as Napoleon came aboard he requested political asylum in Britain (see 18th June and 15th October).

1857 During the Indian Mutiny and with animal-like savagery, the Indian rebels brutally murder their British prisoners in the city of Cawnpore, the majority of who were defenceless women and children, as a British relief column approaches. Some are shot but the majority are hacked to death. Their bodies were then thrown down a large well and when that became full, the rest of the bodies were thrown into the River Ganges (see 10th May and 16th July).

16th July:

1557 The death of Anne of Cleaves in Chelsea Manor (see 22nd September). Born in Dusseldorf in the Duchy of Berg in the Rhineland the daughter of John II, she had a limited education and was never described in anything more than average terms. Her marriage to Henry VIII (see 28th January and 28th June) was never consummated and (see 6th January and 9th July) the King took an instant dislike to her. However, she always stated that the King was kind and considerate towards her.

1723 The birth of Joshua Reynolds in Plympton in Devon (see 23rd February).

1857 The city of Cawnpore is bravely retaken by British forces, the day after savage Indian rebels massacred their British prisoners in what was called the Satichaura Ghat massacre and the Bibighar massacre (see 15th July). In the Bibighar massacre, all the surviving women and children were cold-bloodedly murdered by the savages and some were then thrown down the well whilst still alive to have the dead bodies of other victims thrown on top off them. In understandable revulsion for the savagery meted out to innocent women and children, the soldiers rampaged through the town and local area seeking revenge on the perpetrators and those who had done nothing to help the victims in their plight (see 10th May, 25th September, 16th November and 6th December).

1970 Edward Heath (see 9th July and 17th July) declares a state of emergency during the Dock Strike, the first State of emergency since the General Strike of 1926 (see 4th May and 12th May).

17th July:

1453 The Battle of Castillon and the defeat of English forces under John Talbot, 1st Earl of Shrewsbury, marking the end of the Hundred Years' War, 1337-1453. As a result of the French victory, England lost all of its possessions in France, including Aquitaine and Gascony, except the town of Calais (see 7th January and 21st May).

1790 The death of Adam Smith in Canongate, Edinburgh (see 5th June). He is recognised as the father of modern economic thought and pioneer of the free market. He studied at Glasgow University and in 1751 was appointed Professor of Logic there. He moved to London in 1776 and published his most well-known work, 'The Wealth of Nations'. This work was the first of its kind in political economics. He argued against any sort of trade regulation and was an early pioneer of the free market economy to produce individual and national wealth. He became a founding member of the Royal Society of Edinburgh in 1783.

1845 The death of Charles Grey, second Earl Grey (see 13th March), at home at Howick, Northumberland. A leading Whig Politician and Statesman, he succeeded the Duke of Wellington (see 1st May and 14th September) as Prime Minster between 1830 and 1834 and played a leading role in the passing of the Reform Bill of 1832 (see 7th June). He was elected to

Parliament in 1786 and was known for his ideas on Parliamentary reform and Catholic emancipation. He gave his name to the famous Earl Grey blend of aromatic tea.

1892 The birth of Edwin Harris Dunning in (see 2nd August and 7th August).

1917 King George V (see 20th January and 3rd June) delivers his proclamation that from today, all his male descendants are to have the surname Windsor and that they are no longer of the name Saxe-Coburg and Gotha. This is in response to understandable anti-German feelings across the country (see 4th August and 11th November).

1945 The Potsdam Conference begins in the German town of Potsdam. The final conference of the war, in attendance were Winston Churchill (replaced midway by Clement Attlee and see 24th January and 30th November), President Truman for the United States and Joseph Stalin for the Soviet Union. The conference agreed the future surrender terms of Japan, the future of Poland and the disarmament of Germany and its level of reparations as well as the frame work for a war crimes trial (see 14th January, 4th February and 28th November).

1964 Donald Campbell (see 4th January and 23rd March) sets a new land speed record at 429 mph in his Bluebird CN7 on Lake Eyre in South Australia (see 3rd September). In setting this record, he was half way to achieving the 'double', holding both the Land speed record and the water speed record in the same year, which he would finally achieve on the last day of the year (see 31st December).

2005 The death of Edward Richard George 'Ted' Heath in Salisbury in Wiltshire (see 9th July). A Conservative politician, he served as leader of the Conservative Party from 1965 until 1975 (see 28th July) and as Prime Minister from 1970 until 1974. The son of a builder, he studied at Oxford and served in the Second World War. He was elected to parliament in 1950 and was openly in favour of the European Union. He became Conservative Party leader in 1965 and in 1970 he won the General Election (see 18th June), becoming Prime Minister. His term in office had only one notable achievement and that was taking the country into the European Union in 1973 (see 1st January). The rest of his term was marked by increasing amounts of industrial unrest and strikes. The 1974 General election was undecided and he resigned as Prime Minister. In 1975, he was replaced by Margaret Thatcher as Party Leader (see 11th February, 8th April and 13th October).

2006 A total of 69 of our nationals are evacuated from Beirut by Royal Navy helicopters to HMS Gloucester, a Type 42 Destroyer at the beginning of an evacuation of up to 10,000 Britons following increased hostilities between Israel and the Lebanese and Hezbollah (see 18th July).

18th July:

1290 Edward I (see 17th June and 7th July) issues the Edict of Expulsion, ordering all Jews to leave England, eventually leading to the flight of possibly up to 17,000 people. Edward and England were in great debt and Edward planned to levy taxes upon his knights and nobles and to make the taxes more palatable he offered to expel all Jews, seizing their wealth and assets.

1635 The birth of Robert Hooke in Freshwater, Isle of Wight (see 3rd March).

1720 The birth of Gilbert White at Selborne in Hampshire (see 26th June).

1792 The death of the pirate John Paul 'Jones' in Paris. A colonial traitor and rebel, he joined the navy of the rebellious colonies of America but was in fact a pirate. Born in Scotland, he fled Britain to avoid facing a court over the death of one of his crew. Settling in Virginia, he joined the rebels and their navy in their rebellion against Britain. His naval career, whilst daring, was only marginally successful and was based on repeated acts of piracy. Following the independence of the colonies in 1783 (see 3rd September), he settled in France and joined the Russian navy in 1788 where he did serve with some distinction. He left the Russian navy in disgrace in 1789 and returned to Paris where he died.

1811 The birth of William Makepeace Thackeray (see 24th December) in Calcutta, India.

1817 The death of Jane Austen in Winchester (see 16th December). A novelist, her most famous works include 'Sense and Sensibility', 'Emma', 'Pride and Prejudice', 'Mansfield Park' and 'Northanger Abbey'. One of seven children, she wrote mostly about the people and social class around her in the countryside where she lived.

1872 The Secret Ballot Act is passed, receiving Royal Assent. The Act ensured that all subsequent elections are held in secret to reduce the influence of corrupt landlords and employers bribing or intimidating voters (see 15th August).

1919 The unveiling of the Cenotaph in Whitehall. This was a wooden version of the more permanent and identical stone Cenotaph to be unveiled the following year (see 11th November) and was designed for the Victory parade the following day (see 1st February, 19th July and 6th November).

1947 The Indian Independence Act receives Royal Assent when George VI (see 6th February and 14th December) signs the Bill. The Act partitioned India into the two separate Dominions of India and Pakistan, coming into force on 15th August 1947. Amongst a number of provisions was the eventual removal of the word Emperor from the titles of our Monarch (see 22nd June and 2nd August). Initially, however, the monarch would remain head of state and both countries would also enter the Commonwealth.

2006 A further 170 British nationals are taken aboard HMS Gloucester on route to Cyprus, as part of the evacuation of British nationals from the Lebanon (see 17th July).

19th July:

1333 The Battle of Halidon Hill where the English defeat the Scots near Berwick on Tweed. The Scots had been under siege in Berwick and a Scots army, under Sir Archibald Douglas was advancing in an attempt to relieve the town. The English, under Edward III (see 21st June and 13th November), took the high ground on Halidon Hill and the Scots, formed into Schiltrons, attempted to advance uphill but were hit by a heavy storm of English arrows. Though combat was eventually joined with the English, the Scots ranks began to falter then they turned and fled, being hit by arrows and pursued by cavalry.

1545 The 'Mary Rose', Flagship of Henry VIII, sinks in the Solent with the loss of 700 lives (see 11th October). Named after Mary Tudor, the sister of Henry VIII (see 28th January and 28th June), the ship was a key part of Henry's plan to build up the Royal Navy. In the evening, the English fleet set out of Portsmouth harbour to engage the French fleet. Advancing ahead of the rest of the Navy, she put about and was caught by a gust of wind and, with her opened gun ports now below the water line, sank very quickly.

1553 Lady Jane Grey is dethroned, ending her short nine-day reign (see 12th February and 10th July).

1789 The birth of John Martin at Haydon Bridge in Northumberland (see 17th February).

1814 The death of Captain Matthew Flinders (see 16th March). He was a great early cartographer and navigator of Australia. In 1798 he sailed round Tasmania, proving it to be an island. He also sailed with Captain Bligh. He sailed round Australia and mapped the Continent and also suggested that Terra Australis be called Australia.

1821 George IV is crowned at Westminster Abbey (see 26th June and 12th August).

1837 The launch of the SS Great Western in Bristol. The first ship designed by Isambard Kingdom Brunel (see 9th April, 23rd April and 15th September), it became the first steam ship to provide a regular trans-Atlantic service.

1843 The launch of the SS Great Britain, designed by Isambard Kingdom Brunel (see 9th April and 15th September) in Bristol. It was the largest passenger ship afloat and the first to have both an iron hull and a screw propeller. It was also the first steam ship purpose-built to cross the Atlantic Ocean. After a period as a passenger ship, she was used to transport convicts to Australia before she was retired to the Falkland Islands and eventually scuttled. Returned to Bristol in 1970, she is now a museum (see 31st January).

1919 The country celebrates a nationwide Peace Day to mark the end of the First Wold War (see 4th August). The central event was a victory parade through Whitehall by around 15,000 service men and the allied leaders as they marched past the original wooden Cenotaph unveiled the previous day (see 18th July and 11th November).

1972 The Battle of Mirbat in the Sultanate of Oman. In one of the greatest Special Forces battles, 9 SAS soldiers and a British Intelligence Officer defended their base from a force of over 300 Omani communist rebels. Following an intense 4-hour fire fight, 2 of the SAS were killed and one badly wounded. However, the number of rebels killed is unknown but is believed to have been well in excess of 80.

20th July:

1745 The birth of Henry Holland (see 17th June) in London.

1793 Alexander Mackenzie makes it to the Pacific Coast of British North America, becoming the first person to cross the North American continent (see 12th March and 22nd July).

1804 The birth of Richard Owen in Lancaster (see 18th December).

1922 The Summer Time Act received Royal Assent. This act provided for the first non-emergency implementation of British Summer Time, one hour ahead of Greenwich Mean Time (see 7th August).

1982 The Hyde Park and Regent's Park bomb attacks murder 8 soldiers and injure 47 others. The murdering terrorist group the IRA is responsible for both attacks.

1996 The death of Lieutenant Colonel Colin Campbell Mitchell (see 17th November). In 1967 he became famous for leading his Regiment the 1st Battalion Argyll and Sutherland Highlanders in an operation to regain control of the Crater area of the Colony of Aden. He carried this out with total efficiency and great success by imposing what he termed as 'Argyll Law' on the area effected (see 20th June and 5th July). It was completed with only one native casualty and no British. He had served in the Second World War, Palestine, the Korean War, Borneo and Cyprus. Though well received by the public, his actions were not supported by the week-willed government of the day. On his return to Britain, he was shamefully snubbed by the government and did not receive the recognition that was traditionally bestowed upon heroes of the nation's forces. He resigned shortly afterwards. Following his military career, he became a Conservative MP and then an active supporter of the Halo Trust, the organisation championing the de-mining of former war zones.

21st July:

1403 The Battle of Shrewsbury. The armies of Henry IV (see 20th March and 15th April) are drawn up against a rebel army under Henry 'Hotspur' Percy. Henry 'Hotspur', originally an ally of Henry IV, changed sides after the failure of the King to pay him money owed. The rebels had the advantage to begin with, but the Royal army slowly gained the upper hand until Percy was struck by an arrow and killed. From this moment the rebel forces collapsed and fled the field, being pursued by Royalist forces for up to three miles.

1667 The Treaty of Breda is signed between Britain, the Netherlands, France and Denmark. It brought an end to the Second Anglo-Dutch War, 1665-1667 (see 4th March). The treaty was a hasty conclusion to a disastrous war for England but allowed opposing sides to retain acquisitions resulting from the conflict, such as New Amsterdam that was taken by England (see 27th August and 8th September).

1796 The death of Robert Burns, famous poet, in Dumfries (see 25th January). Known as Scotland's national poet, he was famous for a number of poems, such as 'Tam O'Shanter', 'To a Mouse' and 'To a Louse'. The son of a farmer and a farmer himself, he tried to return to farming after his literary success but failed and also spent some time as an Exciseman in Dumfries. In the latter part of his life he held some rather revolutionary views and politics, especially those towards the rebellious America colonies which were suspect.

1897 The National Gallery of British Art (now called the Tate Gallery) in London is opened. It was built on the site of the former Millbank Prison and was funded by Sir Henry Tate while the government paid for the site as a national art collection. He then donated his own collection of art to the gallery.

1932 The British Empire Economic Conference begins in Ottawa, Canada. The Colonies and Dominions present met to discuss the Great Depression and its effects, the failure of the gold standard and the possible establishment of a zone of tariffs within the Empire (see 19th October).

1960 Sir Francis Chichester arrives in New York aboard his boat the Gypsy Moth II after setting a new record of 40 days for a solo crossing of the Atlantic Ocean.

1976 Our Ambassador to Ireland, Christopher Ewart-Biggs, is murdered by Irish terrorists in Dublin along with a colleague when a landmine detonates under his car (see 31st July, 14th August, 6th December and 8th December).

22nd July:

1298 The Battle of Falkirk. William Wallace (see 23rd August), the Guardian of Scotland and the rebel Scottish leader, led a force against the far superior forces of Edward I (see 17th June and 7th July). Facing one another, the battle was hard-fought with the Scots holding the high ground and formed into four schiltrons. Edward sent in his knights in waves against the Scottish schiltrons to no avail. Then, Edward decided to use his new weapon and the English unleashed their longbows with a devastating effect that destroyed the Scottish lines. Many Scots leaders were killed and those that remained surrendered to Edward I.

1706 The Treaty of Union is signed between representatives of both the English and Scottish Parliaments, agreeing to a Political Union between both countries and so creating the United Kingdom of Great Britain (see 16th January and 1st May). The Union would secure one Parliament, a single currency, the Protestant Succession and equal rights to all subjects of the new Kingdom and free access to trade throughout the now British Empire.

1793 Alexander Mackenzie makes it to the most westerly point in what was later to be called Canada as the culmination of the first east west crossing of the North American continent (see 12th March and 20th July).

1797 The beginning of the battle of Santa Cruz de Tenerife, as Royal Marines, led by Captain Thomas Troubridge under Admiral Horatio Nelson (see 29th September and 21st October) attempted to row ashore to begin an amphibious assault on the north-east of the city to capture that area and silence the shore batteries. Unfortunately, the swell prevented any artillery from being landed and after heavy resistance and heavy casualties, the troops were forced back to the boats and retired (see 24th July and 25th July).

1812 The battle of Salamanca, in Southern Spain during the Peninsular War. The Earl of Wellington (see 1st May and 14th September) led 50,000 British, Portuguese and Spanish troops against 52,000 French. Despite being led by experienced Generals, the French line became over-extended and Wellington seized the opportunity for an attack. In a decisive victory for Wellington, the Allies lost 5,000 killed and wounded and the French lost 7,000 killed and another 7,000 wounded. As a reward for his victory, the Earl of Wellington was made a Marquis, an honour for which he was not overly impressed.

1915 The death of Sir Sandford Fleming (see 7th January) in Halifax, Nova Scotia. Born in Scotland, he was a civil engineer and inventor who proposed the international time zones and was responsible for huge amounts of surveying in Canada as well as being involved in the engineering of both the Intercolonial Railway and the Canadian Pacific Railway (see 4th July).

1940 The Special Operations Executive (SOE) is officially formed by the Prime Minister Winston Churchill (see 24th January and 30th November) and the Minister of Economic Warfare, Sir Hugh Dalton. Its role when created was to conduct warfare by means other than direct military action. It was to encourage, facilitate and carry out acts of sabotage, espionage and guerrilla attacks behind enemy lines within the occupied countries of Europe.

1946 The bombing of the King David Hotel in Jerusalem by the Jewish terrorist group, Irgun. A total of 91 people, mainly British subjects but including about 15 Jewish workers, were murdered by the blast. The explosion caused the whole side of the building to collapse trapping many in the rubble.

2013 The Duchess of Cambridge, wife of the Duke of Cambridge, Prince William, gives birth to a son at St Mary's Hospital in London. At his birth, George Alexander Luis, the Prince of Cambridge is third in line to the throne.

23rd July:

1745 Prince Charles Edward Stewart, ('Bonnie Prince Charlie', see 31st January and 31st December) lands on Scottish and British soil for the first time on the Island of Eriskay (see 19th August). He came ashore from the French frigate Doutelle (le Du Teillay) along with his seven companions, known as the 'Seven Men of Moidart'. Prior to the landing, the Doutelle and its companion ship Elisabeth had been attacked by HMS Lion off the coast of Cornwall. In the engagement the Elisabeth was badly damaged and was forced to return to France, leaving the Doutelle to proceed alone (see 23rd September).

1839 The Battle of Ghuznee in Central Afghanistan during the First Afghan War (1839-1842). British and Indian forces storm the town of Ghuznee and defeat the Afghan rebels. Our forces suffered 200 casualties killed and wounded and the rebels lost 500 killed and 1,600 taken prisoner. The amount of Afghan wounded is not known (see 13th January).

1872 The birth of Edward Adrian Wilson (see 29th March) in Cheltenham.

1883 The birth of Alan Francis Brooke (see 17th June) in France.

1886 The birth of Arthur Whitten Brown (see 15th June and 4th October) in Glasgow.

1916 The death of William Ramsay (see 2nd October) in High Wycombe. He was a chemist who is well-known for his discovery of the noble gasses Argon, Neon, Krypton and Xenon as well as isolating and characterising Helium and Radon. He received the Nobel Prize in Chemistry in 1904 for his work in discovering the gasses.

1927 The death of Brigadier General Reginald Edward Harry Dyer (see 9th October) of a cerebral haemorrhage near Bristol. He was commissioned into the British Army in 1885 and in 1887 he was commissioned into the British Indian Army in which he served in numerous expeditions and campaigns before serving during the Great War. He was fluent in many of the Indian languages. In 1919 he was in the Punjab when there were rumours and threats of mutiny and rebellion. He was in command of nearly 100 soldiers, mainly Ghurkhas, at what became known as the Amritsar Massacre on the 13th April 1919. Following weeks of violence and rioting, culminating in three days of extreme violence and the sabotage of government buildings, the government had declared the Punjab region under martial law in order to restore order. Part of the conditions included the restriction on the freedom of assembly. A large group of illegally gathered civilians, in contravention of the restrictions, were then fired upon by Dryer's troops. At the time, his actions were widely supported at home and by politicians, including the Governor of the Punjab, Sir Michael O'Dwyer (see 13th March).

24th July:

1567 Mary Queen of Scots (see 8th February and 8th December) is forced to abdicate in favour of her son, James VI (later James I of England, see 27th March and 19th June), whilst imprisoned in Lochleven Castle.

1704 The island of Gibraltar is captured from the Spanish by Admiral Sir George Rooke, who led a combined fleet of British and Dutch ships and troops. Our sovereignty over the island was later recognised under the Treaty of Utrecht (see 31st March). Following the surrender of the Rock, the vast majority of the Spanish population left for Spain and settled there permanently (see 7th February, 10th September and 7th November).

1797 The second attempt to land British troops during the battle of Santa Cruz de Tenerife. After the first attempt (see 22nd July), Rear Admiral Horatio Nelson (see 29th September and 21st October) leads Royal Marines in an attempt to row ashore to begin an amphibious assault directly on the town. Leading the troops, Nelson is wounded in the arm, which would require amputation, and command went to Captain Troubridge, who, facing stiff resistance, was eventually surrounded and trapped (see 25th July) during the night.

1813 The birth of Edward Cardwell (see 15th February) the son of a Liverpool businessman.

1883 Captain Matthew Webb, the first man to swim the Channel, drowns trying to swim across and behind the foot of the Niagara Falls (see 19th January, 24th July and 25th August). His body was recovered four days later. Born in Shropshire, he joined the Merchant Navy at the age of twelve and served with the Cunard Line. After swimming the Channel, he embarked on a career as a professional swimmer.

1923 The Treaty of Lausanne is signed in Lausanne in Switzerland. A peace treaty, it officially ended the state of war between Britain, France, Italy, Greece, Japan and others on the one hand and Turkey on the other. The treaty defined the majority of the modern Turkish borders and Turkey agreed to end its claims on the territories of the old Ottoman Empire (see 30th October).

1980 The death of Richard Henry 'Peter' Sellers (see 8th September) in London. A classic comedian, he was famous for his film character of Inspector Clouseau and above all else his part in the legendary Goon Show (see 28th May).

25th July:

1394 The birth of James Stewart in Dunfermline Palace in Fife (see 21st February), the son of Robert III and Annabella Drummond.

1554 The marriage of Queen Mary I of England and Prince Philip of Spain at Winchester Cathedral (see 7th January, 18th February and 17th November).

1603 The Coronation of James VI of Scotland as King James I of England takes place at Westminster Abbey (see 27th March, 19th June and 29th July).

1666 The St. James' Day battle during the Second Anglo-Dutch War (1665-1667). The English Fleet, commanded by Prince Rupert (see 29th November and 17th December) and General Sir George Monck (see 3rd January and 6th December) and consisting of around 90 ships, attacked the Dutch fleet, commanded by Michiel de Ruyter, of slightly fewer ships. The Dutch, despite only losing two ships to the loss of one English ship, broke off the battle and fled back to port.

1779 The start of the Penobscot Expedition when the navy of the rebellious American colonials open fire on the British Forts in the Penobscot Bay along the coast of Maine and attempt to land a military force in an attempt to take the British fortifications at Fort George (see 12th August).

1797 Trapped and isolated in the town of Santa Cruz de Tenerife, with Rear Admiral Nelson wounded (see 22nd July and 24th July), Captain Troubridge, leading the Royal Marines, signs a truce with the Spanish General and is allowed to embark for the British fleet with their arms and full honours and accordingly did not burn the town.

1814 George Stephenson (see 9th June and 12th August) demonstrates his first steam engine, the 'Blucher'. It is the first Steam engine to use flanged wheels instead of rack and pinions.

1834 The death of Samuel Taylor Coleridge, author of 'Kubla Khan' and 'Chrsitabel' (see 21st October). Cambridge educated, he formed a lasting friendship with William Wordsworth and with him produced 'Lyrical Ballads' in 1798. In this publication was his most famous work, 'The Rime of the Ancient Mariner'. In 1804 he became the secretary to the governor of Malta for two years, returning to England to continue his publication of political essays.

1843 The death of Charles Macintosh (see 29th December). Born in Glasgow, he was a famous chemist and inventor, he is known for developing waterproof materials and the waterproof raincoat, the MacKintosh is named after him.

1848 The birth of Arthur James Balfour (see 19th March and 12th July) in East Lothian.

1959 The prototype hovercraft SR-NI, designed by Sir Christopher Sydney Cockerell (see 1st June, 4th June and 11th June), crosses the Channel for the first time. Built by Saunders-Roe on the Isle of Wight, it was the first practical hovercraft.

2009 Henry John 'Harry' Patch, last survivor of the Trenches of the Great War and the 'last fighting Tommy' dies (see 17th June). Born in 1898, he left school at 15 and became a plumber. The Great War broke out within a year and at the age of eighteen he was conscripted into the Duke of Cornwall's light Infantry. He arrived in France in 1917 and saw his first action at the Third Battle of Ypres or Passchendaele. On the 22nd September 1917 he was wounded by shrapnel and whilst convalescing, the Armistice was signed. During the Second World War he served as a fire-fighter in Bath. In 1999 he was awarded the Legion d'Honneur (see 8th November).

26th July:

1469 The Battle of Edgcote, North East of Banbury in Northamptonshire during the Wars of the Roses (1455-1585). The Earl of Pembroke, with a weakened force and without archers, withstood a strong enemy attack, under the command of Robin of Redesdale, involving ferocious hand to hand fighting. Pembroke's forces were on the brink of victory when the rebel reinforcements arrived. Believing these arrivals to be a much larger force, Pembroke's troops broke ranks and fled. A large number of Pembroke's men were killed in the ensuing route and Pembroke himself was captured, to be executed the following day.

1758 The end of the siege of Louisbourg in present day Nova Scotia, then part of the French colony of Ile-Royale (see 8th June). Our forces of British army and American Colonial troops landed from ships near to the fortress under intense bombardment from the French. They were under the Command of General Amherst and Brigadier James Wolfe (see 2nd January and 13th September). Following a heavy bombardment of the fort, the French were called upon to surrender, which they did. Our casualties were around 500 but the French casualties were unknown, although over 5,000 surrendered. The garrison, under the command of Chevalier de Drucour, was around 7,000-strong when the siege began and surrendered despite their initial terms of surrender being refused. The garrison surrendered all its weapons, equipment and their flags. The fall of Louisbourg signalled the end of the French presence along the Atlantic coast and deprived inland French possessions, such as Quebec, of naval protection and supply lines and marked the beginning of the end for 'New France' in North America.

1856 The birth of George Bernard Shaw in Dublin (see 2nd November).

1858 Lionel Rothschild takes his seat in the House of Commons becoming the first Jewish Member of Parliament.

1865 The city of Wellington becomes the capital of the colony of New Zealand, replacing Auckland when the colony's Parliament meets officially for the first time (see 1st July and 26th September).

1936 The Vimy Ridge Memorial is unveiled by Edward VIII (see 28th May and 23rd June). Designed and built by Walter Seymour Allward, it is a national memorial to the members of the Canadian Expeditionary Force who died in the battle for Vimy Ridge (see 9th April and 12th April), part of the bigger Battle of Arras in 1917. It is also a general memorial to commemorate all those Canadian soldiers who have no known grave and thus bears over 11,000 names.

1945 The General Election results are declared and the Labour Party wins with a landslide, ousting Winston Churchill (see 24th January and 30th November) as Prime Minister. Clement Attlee (see 3rd January and 8th October) becomes Prime Minister leading the first post-war Labour

Government. The majority of the voting took place on the 5th July 1945 but some areas were delayed, with the results being declared today.

27th July:

1214 The Battle of Bouvines in which England, as part of a coalition of forces led by Otto IV of Brunswick, is beaten by the French under Phillip II and as a result, King John (see 18th October) loses his French lands to King Phillip of France. A tight and hard-fought battle that could have gone either way, the French eventually closed their wings in on the coalition troops and their defeat was inevitable. The battle had long lasting consequences for both the English King (see 15th June) and the French King.

1689 The Battle of Killiecrankie and the death of Viscount John Graham of Claverhouse (Bonnie Dundee) as his Jacobite force claim victory over Major-General Hugh MacKay's Government forces. The Jacobite forces numbered between 1,800 and 2,000 men whilst the government forces numbered 3,500 (see 21st August).

1694 William III (see 8th March and 4th November) grants a Royal Charter thus establishing the Bank of England. It was founded by William Paterson, a Scotsman, as the English Government's banker. The subscribers and Paterson himself gave a loan to the Government of £1.2 million and its first Governor was John Houblon.

1778 The First Battle of Ushant in the Bay of Biscay between our Fleet of thirty ships under Admiral Augustus Keppel and the French Fleet of twenty-nine ships under Admiral the Comte d'Orvilliers. It was an indecisive battle as part of the American colonial rebellion (see 3rd September) with more or less equal losses on both sides. The lack of any real result led to political recriminations on both sides and the resignation of Admiral Keppel.

1844 The death of John Dalton in Manchester (see 6th September). Born in the Lake District, he became a Chemist. In 1794 he released his first paper in which he identified colour blindness, a condition that affected both him and his brother. Following this he published numerous papers on subjects such as the expansion of gasses by heat from which was formulated 'Dalton's Law'. He went on to publish the first table of atomic weights and his 'atomic theory' on the structure of matter is regarded as the basis for modern day chemistry.

1854 The birth of Clementina Black (see 19th December) in Brighton.

1880 The Battle of Maiwand in Afghanistan during the Second Afghan War (1878-1880). Brigadier General Burrows lead our forces. Unfortunately, our forces are totally defeated and the famous last stand of the 66th Foot takes place as a result just outside the village of Khig. Two officers and nine men fight to the death. Killing many Afghans whilst surrounded, when their ammunition ran out, they charged the enemy with bayonets fixed before becoming overwhelmed. Afghan rebels lost around 1,800 men and our forces just under 1,000 men killed and wounded (see 26th May).

1944 The first combat mission for the new Gloster Whittle 'Meteor', Britain's and the Allies first Jet aircraft (see 5th March). Three Meteors from 616 Squadron took to the skies, flying from RAF Manston to combat the threat from the V-1 Flying bomb.

1949 The prototype De Havilland DH106 Comet, the world's first jet airliner, makes its maiden flight in England from Hatfield airstrip.

1953 An armistice agreement agreeing a ceasefire is signed to end the Korean War in the abandoned village of Panmunjom. Great Britain, fighting as part of the United Nations Forces, suffered 1078 dead, 2674 wounded and 1060 missing or taken prisoner (see 25th June and 29th August) during the conflict.

2012 The 30th Olympic Games begins with the opening ceremony in London. This is the third time the games have been held in London (see 27th April and 29th July).

28th July:

1540 The execution of Thomas Cromwell, the 1st Earl of Essex on Tower Green. Born in 1485 he spent most of his early manhood in Europe as a soldier, merchant and accountant. He worked for Cardinal Wolsey and when he fell out of favour, Thomas took his place. He helped Henry VIII (see 28th January and 28th June) become Head of the Church of England and engineered his marriage to Anne of Cleves. This marriage was a disaster and because of this and other issues, Thomas was sent to the Tower of London. He was tried and condemned to death. It took three attempts by an inexperienced axe man to take off Cromwell's head which was then boiled and displayed on a spike outside the city of London.

1540 The Marriage of Henry VIII (see 28th January and 28th June) and Catherine Howard (see 13th February) at Oatlands Palace in Weybridge.

1809 The Battle of Talavera, south-west of Madrid. Lieutenant General Sir Arthur Wellesley (see 1st May and 14th September) led 20,000 British and 30,000 Spanish against King Joseph Bonaparte and 46,000 French. A victory for our forces, however the Allies were in danger of having their supply route to Portugal severed and so had to retire back towards the border. We suffered 5963 killed and wounded and the French suffered 7,268 casualties,

1833 The Emancipation Act is passed. This allows for the freeing of all slaves in Britain and her Empire from the 1st August 1834 (see 28th August).

1862 John Hanning Speke, travelling from Uganda, reaches a huge lake that he names Lake Victoria in the Queen's honour. Travelling round it he discovered the Nile River flowing from it at the also newly discovered Rippon Falls (see 4th May and 15th September).

1917 Under Royal Warrant, the Tank Corps is formed, becoming the first Tank Corps in the world. It was an amalgamation of units of Tanks that had originally been the Heavy Section of the Machine Gun Corps (see 15th September and 20th November).

1965 Edward Heath (see 9th July and 17th July) becomes leader of the Conservative Party and the Opposition after the resignation of Sir Alec Douglas-Home.

29th July:

1565 Mary Queen of Scots marries her first cousin, Henry Stuart, Lord Darnley (see 8th February and 8th December).

1567 The coronation of James VI (later James I of England) at the Church of the Holy Rude in Stirling (see 27th March, 19th June and 25th July) at the age of thirteen months. He was crowned by the Bishop of Orkney, Adam Bothell, and John Knox preached the sermon. It is notable as the first coronation in Scotland of a Protestant Monarch.

1588 The Battle of Gravelines off the coast of France and the Spanish Netherlands. The Spanish Armada, under the Duke of Parma and made up of 130 ships and 30,493 men, is defeated following an initial attack by English fire ships and the Fleet commanded by Admiral Sir Charles Howard and his second in Command Sir Francis Drake (see 27th January) along with Martin Frobisher (see 22nd November) and John Hawkins (see 12th November). The remaining ships had to retreat back to Spain around the coast of Scotland and Ireland. The Armada lost half its ships and about three-quarters of its men, mainly due to bad weather and poor navigation following the initial battle (see 12th May and 9th August).

1801 The birth of George Bradshaw (see 6th September) in Salford.

1833 The death of William Wilberforce, leading anti-slave trade campaigner (see 24th August). Educated at Cambridge, it was there that he became a friend of William Pitt the Younger (see 23rd January and 28th May). In 1780 he became a Member of Parliament. Whilst on a European tour in 1784 he began to study the bible and had a form of conversion. He was instrumental, along with Thomas Clarkson (see 28th March and 26th September) in the abolition of the slave trade in Britain and the Empire in 1807 and the rest of the world subsequently. He continued in his philanthropic ways, striving to improve the condition of the poor as well as the work of the Missionary Schools and the British and Foreign Bible Society. Despite wishing to be buried in a family plot, he was buried in Westminster Abbey on the 5th August.

1883 The birth of Henry Robertson Bowers in Greenock (see 29th March).

1948 The 14th Olympic Games opens at Wembley in London, the first games in twelve years, due to the Second World War (see 27th April and 27th July).

30th July:

1718 The death of William Penn in Berkshire (see 14th October). Born in London in 1633, he was a Quaker and the founder of the Colony of

Pennsylvania. He was expelled from Oxford for being a Dissenter and spent many years championing the Quaker cause. Charles II (see 6th February and 29th May) repaid a debt owed to his father and granted Penn a huge expanse of land in North America, later named Pennsylvania. He oversaw the construction of Philadelphia between 1682 and 1684 and returned to England. He returned in 1699 but due to financial problems returned again to England, selling his proprietary rights to his Colony.

1927 Stanley Baldwin (see 28th May and 7th June) becomes the first Prime Minister of Great Britain to visit a Dominion whilst still in office as he arrives in Quebec in the Dominion of Canada (see 1st July) along with Edward Prince of Wales (see 20th January and 11th December) and George Duke of Kent.

1935 Penguin paperbacks are launched with the goal of bringing cheap but high-quality books to the mass market.

1948 The British Nationality Act is passed in the Commons. The act gave nationals of the Empire (Commonwealth) the right to British Citizenship.

1949 HMS Amethyst begins her escape from China along the Yangtze River at the end of the 10 week long 'Yangtze incident'. The ship had been attacked by Chinese communist forces and her commanding officer and a large number of officers and crew had been killed or wounded during the long drawn-out battle. After 100 days, the ship slipped away under the cover of darkness after the British Naval Attaché in Shanghai, Lieutenant-Commander John Simon Kerans had assumed Command.

1966 In the football World Cup final at Wembley Stadium, England beat West Germany four goals to two. In the game, Geoff Hurst became the only player to score a hat trick of goals in a World Cup final.

31st July:

1653 The battle of Scheveningen off the Dutch coast between the Commonwealth Fleet and a fleet from the United Provinces of the Dutch Republic during the First Anglo-Dutch War, 1652-1654. Admiral at Sea, George Monck (see 3rd January and 6th December), engaged the Dutch fleet under Admiral Maarten Tromp causing at least twelve ships to be lost while the English Fleet lost only two. Admiral Tromp was killed in the action with numerous Captains and other officers (see 5th April and 19th May).

1841 The birth of Reginald Brabazon, the future 12th Earl of Meath (see 24th May and 11th October) in London.

1872 The Licensing Act is passed. It created the offence of being drunk in public, restricted the opening hours of Public Houses, regulated the content of beer and allowed local authorities more freedom in decisions over opening times. A very unpopular Act, it caused much anger and some riots.

1910 Dr Hawley Harvey Crippen is arrested aboard the SS Montrose in Quebec by Inspector Drew. Inspector Drew, who had sailed on the faster ship the SS Laurentic after receiving a telegram from the Captain of the SS

Montrose, arrested Crippen on board the ship after it had docked in Quebec (see 23rd November).

1912 The death of Allan Octavian Hume in London (see 6th June). Born in Kent, he joined the Indian Civil Service in 1849 in Bombay and held a number of positions within the administration of India until he retired in 1882. After his retirement, he became politically active and worked to give Indians more say in the running of India, becoming instrumental in setting up the Indian National Congress in 1885 (see 28th December). Whilst in India, he produced a number of works on ornithology and in time he became known as 'the Father of Indian ornithology'.

1917 The Third Battle of Ypres, commonly referred to as Passchaendale, begins. Led by our forces, it was an attempt to push through the German lines in Flanders in Belgium. For two weeks before, the artillery bombardment of the German lines used over four million shells from 3,000 artillery pieces to soften up the enemy; however, the ground over which they would advance was churned up and turned into a quagmire. The left wing achieved all its objectives but unfortunately the right wing of the advance failed (see 19th October).

1942 The death of Francis Younghusband in Dorset (see 31st May). Born in Muree, British India, he was commissioned into the army in 1882. In 1904, appointed by the Viceroy Lord Curzon (see 11th January and 20th March), he successfully led the Expedition to Tibet to counter the possible influence and presence of Russians within the country (see 2nd August). Following the expedition he became the Resident in Kashmir for a number of years and in 1936 he founded the World Congress of Faiths.

1970 Known as 'Black Tot Day' as the last daily rum ration (or 'tot') is issued throughout the Royal Navy. A tradition stretching back to 1655, it replaced the previous issue of beer as water and ultimately beer itself were difficult to preserve for long on voyages.

1992 The death of Group Captain Geoffrey Leonard Cheshire (see 7th September). Born in Chester, he joined the RAF in the 1930s and was a Second World War pilot and hero who won the V.C. In August 1945 he was the official British observer when the Japanese city of Nagasaki became the second target for a nuclear attack. After the war he and his wife Sue Ryder founded the Cheshire Foundation Home for the terminally ill in 1948.

2007: Midnight and the end of Operation Banner in Northern Ireland, the longest ever deployment of our forces. The Army was deployed onto the streets in Northern Ireland as a last resort in 1969 originally to protect and reassure the Catholics and as a result a total of 763 soldiers were murdered in the conflict (see 13th February, 8th May, 12th August and 14th August).

AUGUST

1st August:

1714 The death of Queen Anne at Kensington Palace aged 49 following a series of strokes (see 6th February and 23rd April) and the accession of George I (see 28th May and 11th June) the Elector of Hanover. The daughter of James VII (James II of England, see 5th September and 14th October) and his first wife Lady Anne Hyde, she was the last of the Stewart Monarchs. It was towards the end of her reign that the Act of Union came into affect (see 1st May) uniting the two politically independent states of England and Scotland into one country, Great Britain. With the accession of George I, Britain and Hanover were joined in a personal union until the accession of Queen Victoria in 1837 (see 22nd January, 24th May and 20th June).

1746 The Act of Proscription comes into effect. This act, part of the follow up to the '45 Jacobite rising (see 16th April and 19th August) made the wearing of a kilt or tartan illegal and redefined the Disarming Act of 1716 which forbade the carrying of all forms of weapons within certain designated areas of the Scottish Highlands and made outlaws of anyone carrying such weapons. The Act was not repealed until 1782.

1759 The Battle of Minden in Prussia during the Seven Years' War, 1756-1763. There were 41,000 British, Hanoverians, Hessians and Prussians under the German Prince Ferdinand, Duke of Brunswick against around 51,000 French and Saxons. The British suffered around half of the 2,600 allied casualties whilst the French lost around 10,000 to 11,000 casualties. A glorious victory in the true tradition of the British army, the French and Saxons were routed after a hard days fighting. The battle formed part of the 'Annus mirabilis' or 'year of victories' in which the year 1759 saw our great country strike one military success after another on France and her allies. This year saw the beginning of the end of France as a world power and its true eclipse by Great Britain (see 13th September).

1774 Joseph Priestly discovers oxygen (see 6th February and 13th March) in his laboratory in Bowood House in Wiltshire. At the time he called it 'Vital Air'.

1798 The Battle of the Nile at Aboukir Bay led by Lord Nelson (see 29th September and 21st October). The British Fleet of 13 Ships of the Line and one 50 gunner defeat the French Fleet of 13 Ships of the Line and 4 frigates in one of the most decisive naval battles of history. There were 895 British casualties and 5,225 French dead and 3,105 French captured. Four French ships were sunk and nine captured. Two of the nine French ships captured during the battle, the Spartiate and the Tonnant, later fought in the British fleet at the battle of Trafalgar in 1805 (see 21st October).

1800 The Act of Union (Ireland) Act 1800 is passed by the Irish Parliament. As one of the two Acts of Union with the United Kingdom of Great Britain, the passing of the act came into force in Ireland in 1801 (see 1st January) as the Union with Ireland Act 1800 had been passed by Parliament the month before (see 12th April and 2nd July).

1834 All slaves in Britain and our Empire are freed as the Emancipation Act of 1833 (see 28th July and 28th August) comes into force. The Act legislated for the former slaves to spend some time in apprenticeships to prepare them for freedom but this system was abolished in 1838.

1870 The Irish Land Act gives limited improved rights to the tenants of Irish landlords though in practice there was little benefit to the majority of tenants.

1907 The first Scout Camp opens in Brownsea Island on Poole Harbour. Twenty boys led by Lieutenant General Robert Baden-Powell (see 8th January and 22nd February) camp for seven days to test his ideas for his book, 'Scouting for Boys'.

1908 The Old Age Pensions Act receives Royal Assent, or 'Pension Day' as it was then called. Half a million people were to receive the first ever non-contributory old age pension. The payments range between one shilling and five shillings a week to people over 70 years old with an income of less than £31 per year (see 1st January).

2002 The Protection of Wild Animals (Scotland) Hunting Act 2002, banning hunting with dogs comes into effect in Scotland, two years ahead of a similar ban in England and Wales amongst much controversy (see 18th February).

2nd August:

1100 The death of William II 'Rufus' in the New Forest. The third son of William I (see 9th September), he was born in the Duchy of Normandy. A ruthless Monarch, he was little liked by his subjects. He was called Rufus probably due to his ruddy complexion. He was killed whilst out hunting when he was struck by an arrow; the exact cause of the accident remains a mystery.

1704 The Battle of Blenheim in Bavaria, during the War of the Spanish succession (1701-1714). It was won by the allied forces of the Grand Alliance under the command of John Churchill, the 1st Duke of Marlborough (see 26th May and 16th June) and the ancestor of Sir Winston Spencer Churchill (see 24th January and 30th November). The armies of the Grand Alliance of around 52,000 men engaged the French and Bavarian armies of around 56,000 men under the command of Marshall Tallard. The battle was hard-fought and was nothing less than a complete victory for the allies and Marlborough. The French lost over half their men as casualties and their army was destroyed (see 12th May, 30th June and 11th August).

1788 The death of Thomas Gainsborough from cancer (see 14th May). In 1769 he became a founding member of the Royal Academy. He was both a portrait painter as well as a landscape artist. His last words; 'We are all going to heaven and Van Dyke is of the company'.

1858 The Government of India Act receives Royal Assent. The act enabled the transferral of the administration of India from the Honourable East India Company (see 31st December) to the Crown. It also called for the termination of the East India Company, therefore beginning the era known as the British Raj. Following the suppressing of the Indian Mutiny the previous year (see 10th May and 18th July) and the growing costs and debts of the Company, the Government acted to safeguard the Colony and its people from further turmoil (see 15th August and 23rd December).

1894 The launch of the Turbinia, the first steam turbine-powered steam ship and at the time the fastest ship afloat. Designed and built by the company founded by Charles Parsons (see 11th February and 13th June), it was first demonstrated at the 1897 Spithead Navy Review.

1904 British troops, under Colonel Francis Younghusband (see 31st May and 31st July), Commander of the Expedition to Tibet, enter the city of Lhasa in Tibet. The expedition was the result of increasing rumours and concerns about suspected Russian influence in the country.

1917 Squadron Commander Edwin Harris Dunning (see 17th July and 7th August) becomes the first person to successfully land an aeroplane on a moving ship. He landed his Sopwith Pup on the deck of HMS Furious in Scapa Flow in the Orkneys.

1922 The death of Alexander Graham Bell in Nova Scotia, Canada (see 3rd March). A scientist and prolific inventor, he is credited with inventing the first proper workable telephone as well as many other inventions. He was born in Edinburgh in 1847. He moved to Canada in 1870 with his family, later moving to Boston in Massachusetts. In 1875 (see 5th June) he carried out the first telephone transmission and in 1876 he patented his telephone. In 1888 he was a founder member of the National Geographic Society.

3rd August:

1305 William Wallace is captured at Robroyston near Glasgow (see 23rd August and 11th September).

1792 The death of Richard Arkwright (see 23rd December) in Cromford, Derbyshire. The inventor of the Spinning Frame and the Carding Machine and a key individual in the start of the Industrial Revolution, that gave rise to Cotton Mills in the north of England. Born into a poor family, he was originally apprenticed to a barber and wig maker. In 1775 his Carding Machine was patented. He constructed a horse-powered mill in Preston and was the first to use James Watt's (see 19th January and 19th August) steam engine to help power his machinery. He established factories throughout the Midlands, the North and in Scotland and encouraged the swift expansion of mechanised cotton spinning, one of the motivating forces behind the Industrial Revolution.

1856 The birth of Alfred Deakin in Melbourne, in the Colony of Victoria, Australia (see 7th October).

1867 The birth of Stanley Baldwin (see 14th December) in Bewdley in Worcestershire.

1881 The signing of the Pretoria Convention, bringing an end to the First Boer War. The treaty was signed in Pretoria between and representatives of the Transvaal Boers and Great Britain. Its basic agreement was the recognition by Britain that the South African Republic would be self-governing (see 28th January and 11th October).

1916 Roger David Casement, rebel and traitor, is hanged in Pentonville Prison in London for acts of treason committed by him during the Easter rebellion in Dublin (see 1st September). He had served as British Consul in Africa but later developed Irish Republican leanings that led him into treasonable activities and his subsequent role in the rebellion of 1916 (see 24th April and 29th April). When the Great War broke out and when so many of his fellow country men were fighting and dying for their country, the traitorous Casement went to Germany and attempted to raise support and help from the German enemy for an Irish rebellion as well as raising an Irish Brigade from amongst British prisoners of war to fight against his own country and the Empire.

2014 HMS Enterprise, a Royal Navy survey ship, evacuates 110 people, mainly British nationals as well as a few other nationals from the Libyan town of Tripoli, and transports them safely to Malta. This followed advice from the Foreign and Commonwealth Office that all British nationals should leave the country due to increased fighting between the Libyan Army and rival militia groups (see 19th March and 21st March).

4th August:

1265 The Battle of Evesham in Worcestershire. The future Edward I (see 17th June and 7th July) defeats the rebellion led by Simon De Montfort (see 20th January), who was outnumbered about three to one and frees his father, Henry III (see 1st October and 16th November). In a brutal battle, most of the rebel leaders, including De Montfort, were killed either in the battle or during the pursuit of their defeated and fleeing forces.

1792 The birth of Percy Bysshe Shelley (see 8th July) in Horsham, West Sussex.

1804 The death of Admiral Adam Duncan, 1st Viscount Duncan in Cornhill, Northumberland (see 1st July). He entered the Royal Navy in 1746 and served in the Seven Years' War, 1756-1763, and later saw action in the Battle of Cape St. Vincent in 1780 (see 16th January). He is best remembered for his flare and leadership at the Battle of Camperdown in 1797 (see 11th October) which effectively destroyed the Dutch participation in the French Revolutionary Wars.

1914 Britain declares war on Germany following the German invasion of Belgium and thus the violation of the Treaty of London (see 19th April and 11th November). The government had issued an ultimatum to Germany to safeguard Belgian neutrality that expired at 11pm. Subsequent to this, His

Majesty's government issued a declaration of war against the German Empire.

1954 The first prototype of the English Electric Lightning Fighter aircraft, designated P.1, takes off for the first time. Powered by two Sapphire engines it became one of this country's greatest aircraft and one of the world's best fighters of the time. Introduced into service in 1959 and with over 330 that were built, it was never used in combat and was retired from service with the RAF in 1988 (see 26th August).

5th August:

1583 Sir Humphrey Gilbert comes ashore at present day St. Johns in Newfoundland (see 31st March and 26th September). He claimed this 'New Found Land' for Queen Elizabeth I and in so doing founded the first English and later British Colony and ultimately the British Empire (see 24th June, 9th September and 31st December).

1729 The death of Thomas Newcomen in London. Born in Dartmouth in February 1664, he is remembered for inventing the first practical steam engine for pumping water, the 'Newcomen Steam Engine', the first of which was built and developed in Dudley. Because of this, he is generally considered the forefather of the Industrial Revolution.

1799 The death of Admiral Richard Howe, 1st Earl Howe, known as 'Black Dick' to his crews and friends because of his swarthy complexion (see 8th March). He fought during the Seven Years' War, 1756-1763, in the Channel against the French and later also served during the early part of the American colonial rebellion (see 3rd September). He became First Lord of the Admiralty and during the French Revolution took command of the Channel Fleet again, leading the navy to victory in the 'Glorious First of June' in 1794.

1929 The death of Dame Millicent Fawcett (nee Garrett. See 11th June). A sister of Elizabeth Garrett Anderson, the first female doctor, Millicent was a leading Suffragist and in 1870 she published 'Political Economy for Beginners'. In 1871 she co-founded Newnham College in Cambridge and was a campaigner for University education for girls. For nearly twenty years she was the president of the National Union of Women's Suffrage. In 1901 she was appointed the head of a commission sent by the government to investigate the concentration camps in South Africa and the conditions therein during the Boer War, 1899-1902. A patriot, she favoured achieving equality by peaceful, law-abiding methods, such as through politics. At the outbreak of war she supported the government's position.

6th August:

1775 The birth of Daniel O'Connell in Cahersiveen in County Clare, Ireland (see 15th May).

1809 The birth of Alfred Tennyson (see 6th October) in Somersby, Lincolnshire.

1881 The birth of Alexander Fleming (see 11th March and 30th September) in Darvel, Ayrshire.

1891 The birth of William Joseph Slim (see 14th December) in Bishopton near Bristol.

1925 The death of Sir Surendranath Banerjee in Barrackpore, Bengal (see 10th November). Born in Calcutta, he entered the Indian Civil Service and travelled to England more than once. He was one of the earliest Indian political leaders and founded the Indian National Association. He opposed the extremist and violent ideas of many but also the ideas of civil disobedience as proposed by Mahatma Gandhi and in effect supported the Raj in many of its earliest reforms, accepted various positions within government and therefore became unpopular with many Indians (see 15th August). He was knighted in 1921 for his loyalty to the Crown and his sensible approach to the future of India.

1945 The city of Hiroshima in Japan is destroyed by a single nuclear bomb dropped by the American B29 bomber 'Enola Gay', thus contributing to the end of the Second World War and the saving of thousands of allied lives (see 15th August and 8th December).

1962 The colony of Jamaica is granted its independence. Originally a Spanish Colony, it was captured from them in 1655 and became the Empire's, and therefore the world's, leading sugar producer (see 8th July) with English and then British (see 1st May) sovereignty recognised by the Spanish.

7th August:

1574 The birth of Robert Dudley in (see 6th September) Richmond Palace. He was the illegitimate son of Sir Robert Dudley, 1st Earl of Leicester, and Lady Douglas Sheffield.

1657 The death of Admiral Robert Blake aboard his flagship, the George. He was born in 1599 in Bridgewater in Somerset. During the Civil Wars, he fought for the Parliamentarian forces and commanded the defence of Lyme Regis for three months then went on to capture Taunton and defend it for a year against three unsuccessful sieges until he was relieved. He was appointed General at Sea in 1649 and in 1651 was effective in destroying much of Prince Rupert's fleet. In 1652 he was successful against the Dutch fleet in the First Anglo-Dutch War, 1652-1654 (see 2nd June), during which he received a bad wound to his leg. He retired for a while but was back in action against the Spanish in 1655. In 1657 (see 20th April) he successfully attacked the Spanish port of Santa Cruz in a heroic and skilful operation. It was on his return to England after the battle that he died. He was given a State Funeral attended by the Lord Protector, Oliver Cromwell (see 25th April and 3rd September). He was initially buried in Westminster Abbey. However, after the restoration, Charles II (see 6th February and 29th May) had his body exhumed and buried in a common plot.

1795 The Battle of Muizenberg in the then Dutch Cape Colony between forces of the British East India Company and their Dutch equivalent. It was a victory for our forces that had attacked the town to prevent the Dutch Colony falling into Republican Dutch control, who were supporters of Napoleonic France. Though the battle is relatively insignificant on its own, the result ultimately led to the Dutch Colony becoming Britain's second African Colony (see 13th August).

1917 The death of Squadron Commander Edwin Harris Dunning (see 17th July and 2nd August) whilst attempting a second landing of his Sopwith Pup aeroplane onto the deck of a moving ship. He had become the first pilot to land on a moving ship five days before. On this attempt, the tyre of his aircraft burst on landing and his plane went overboard. Commander Dunning was knocked unconscious on hitting the water and he subsequently drowned.

1925 The Daylight Saving Act, requiring clocks to be altered by one hour twice a year to introduce and end British Summer Time at one hour ahead of Greenwich Mean Time, receives Royal Assent. This act made the changes introduced by the Summer Time Act 1922 permanent without the need for Parliament to renew it each year (see 20th July).

8th August:

1503 The marriage of James IV (see 17th March and 9th September) of Scotland and Margaret Tudor, daughter of Henry VII of England (see 28th January and 21st April). The 'marriage of the Thistle and the Rose' took place at Holyrood Abbey in Edinburgh and although it did not improve relations between England and Scotland, their grandson, the future James VI (James I of England see 27th March and 19th June), became King of both Kingdoms in 1603 (see 24th March).

1827 The death of George Canning, Conservative Prime Minister for only four months. He died in the home of the Duke of Devonshire, in the same room as Charles Fox had died twenty-one years previously (see 11th April). An able Foreign Minister and briefly Prime Minister, he is mostly remembered for his pistol duel with Lord Castlereagh in which he missed and Castlereagh hit him in the thigh. Unpopular in his own Party, upon his appointment following Lord Liverpool's resignation, the Duke of Wellington (see 1st May and 14th September) and Robert Peel (see 5th February and 2nd July) and several leading Tories resigned from his administration. This forced Canning to rely on Whigs to support him in exchange for positions within government. During his tenure as Prime Minister, he attempted reform of the Corn Laws, which was opposed by the Duke of Wellington. Though passed by the House of Commons, it was defeated by the House of Lords.

1914 The Defence of The Realm Act (DORA) is passed by Parliament without debate and received Royal Assent. The act gave the government far

232

reaching and increased powers throughout the period of the First World War to enable the country maintain its war effort (see 4th August and 11th November).

1919 The Treaty of Rawalpindi is signed, officially ending the Third Afghan War in 1919 (see 6th May and 3rd June). The treaty reaffirmed Afghan independence and allowed them to control their own foreign policy whilst bringing an end to subsidies from Britain (see 12th November).

1971 The death of Lieutenant Colonel Freddie Spencer Chapman (see 10th May) by his own hand. An army Officer during the Second World War, he is famous for his activities behind enemy line in Malaya between 1941 and 1945. He spent his time behind Japanese line committing acts of sabotage and, along with a few others, killed many of the enemy and destroyed trains and bridges. Captured by both the Japanese and Chinese Communist guerrillas, he escaped every time.

9th August:

1387 The birth of Henry V in Monmouth Castle (see 9th April and 31st August). He was the son of Henry Bolingbroke who would later become Henry IV (see 20th March and 4th April).

1588 Queen Elizabeth I (see 24th March and 7th September) delivered her famous speech to her troops at Tilbury. The Spanish Armada had been driven away at the battle of Gravelines (see 29th July) and had scattered around the coast and its remnants were limping home. However, there was still the strong possibility that Spanish troops might attempt an invasion from Dunkirk and so it was that Elizabeth delivered her great rallying cry to her forces.

1592 John Davis, Commander of HMS Desire, lands on the Falkland Islands, which would be known for a period after his landing as Davis Land (see 2nd April, 2nd May and 14th June).

1757 The birth of Thomas Telford in Westerkirk, Dumfriesshire (see 2nd September).

1805 The birth of Joseph Locke (see 18th September) in Attercliffe near Sheffield.

1842 The signing of the Webster-Ashburton Treaty between the British Colonies in present day Canada and the American government. The treaty resolved many long-standing disputes around the actual border between the Colonies and the United States. It was signed by Alexander Baring, 1st Baron Ashburton and the American Secretary of State, Daniel Webster.

1902 The coronation of Edward VII at Westminster Abbey (see 6th May and 9th November).

1941 Douglas Bader (see 21st February and 5th September) is shot down over northern France and captured by the Germans. He reports that he crashed his plane into a German aeroplane and destroyed it before bailing out.

10th August:

991 AD: The Battle of Maldon. A Viking army defeats an Anglo-Saxon force led by the Ealdorman Byrhtnoth during the reign of Aethelred the Unready in Essex. Following the defeat, Aethelred was advised to buy off the Vikings, which he did, this payment being the first example of Danegeld. Byrhtnoth was killed during the battle.

1585 The Treaty of Nonsuch is signed at the Royal Palace of Nonsuch in Surrey. The treaty was signed between Elizabeth I (see 24th March and 7th September) and Dutch rebels and provided for English support for Dutch forces in the provinces that were fighting for their independence against the Spanish Empire.

1782 The birth of the future General Sir Charles James Napier (see 16th January and 29th August) in London.

1784 The death of Allan Ramsay (see 2nd October) in Dover, the son of Allan Ramsay the poet (see 7th January and 15th October). A famous portrait painter, he is well-known for his paintings of David Hume (see 26th April and 25th August), Queen Charlotte, George III (see 29th January and 24th May) and many Scottish Lords and Gentlemen. He travelled extensively in Europe and to the Italian states several times. In 1767 he was appointed Principal Painter to the King and became an ardent supporter of his new patron. He was also a well-known supporter of abolitionism.

1794 The formal surrender of Calvi on Corsica to our forces led by Colonel Sir Charles Stuart and the future Admiral Horatio Nelson following a sustained bombardment during the French Revolutionary wars. It was during this siege that Nelson was injured and lost the use of his eye (see 12th July).

1869 The birth of Laurence Binyon (see 10th March) in Lancaster.

1911 The Parliament Act is passed in the House of Lords by a majority of 131 to 114. Introduced by the Liberal Government of Prime Minister Herbert Asquith (see 15th February and 12th September), the Act removed the ability of the Lords to veto any budget-related bill proposed by the House of Commons. The act also reduced the maximum time allowed between General Elections from seven years to five years.

1915 The death of Henry Gwyn Jeffreys Moseley in Gallipoli (see 23rd November). He was an outstanding physicist and contributed enormously to the advances in the chemical concept and understanding of atomic numbers, predicting missing elements and the application of x-rays. Born in Dorset, he studied at Oxford University and after graduation worked under Ernest Rutherford (see 30th August and 19th October) at Manchester University. At the outbreak of the First World War, he enlisted as an Officer in the Royal Engineers and was posted to Gallipoli where he was killed in action. He is commemorated on the Helles Memorial in Turkey.

1920 The signing of the Treaty of Sevres by Britain, France, Italy and Japan as well as representatives of the recently defeated Ottoman Empire (see 30th October). A peace treaty between the two sides, the treaty was in actual fact an agreement on the dividing up of the Ottoman Empire following their defeat in the Great War (see 4th August and 11th November).

11th August:

1718 The Battle of Cape Passero (see 14th March) off the coast of Sicily. A total of 22 ships of the Royal Navy, under Admiral George Byng, pursue and then attack around 30 ships of the Spanish fleet, taking thirteen as prizes and burning another three before the battle finished. The battle preceded a formal declaration of war that started the War of the Quadruple Alliance (1718-1720).

1890 The death of Cardinal John Henry Newman (see 21st February) in Birmingham. Educated at Trinity College in Oxford, he held a number of academic posts as an Anglican and he had an influence on the Oxford movement, which was started in 1833. After a few years, he began a steady move towards Catholicism and in 1845 he was received into the Church of Rome. A year later he was ordained as a Catholic Priest. He had a number of roles within the Church and was Rector of Ireland between 1854 and 1858. Then, in 1879, Pope Leo XIII appointed him to a place on the College of Cardinals.

1941 The Atlantic Charter is agreed by Winston Churchill (see 24th January and 30th November) and the American President Roosevelt to demonstrate solidarity between our country and the former colonies of the U.S.A. (see 14th August). The Prime Minister forwarded the text of the declaration to his cabinet on this day.

1968 The last steam locomotive passenger service is run by British Railways. The 'Fifteen Guinea Special', as the service was known, was hauled by four engines with the engine 'Oliver Cromwell' operating the final leg of the outward journey between Manchester and Carlisle (see 3rd July).

12th August:

1652 The Act for the Settlement of Ireland is passed by the Rump Parliament in response to the Irish rebellion of 1641. The Act imposed penalties upon all those who took part or did nothing to prevent or suppress the rebellion. Under the Act, the death penalty and the confiscation of land and assets were permitted (see 11th September and 22nd October).

1762 The birth of George Frederick Augustus, later George IV (see 26th June), at St. James's Palace. He was the eldest son of George III (see 29th January and 24th May) and Princess Charlotte of Mecklenburg- Strelitz.

1779 The conclusion of the Penobscot Expedition when the Navy of the rebellious American colonials open fire on the British Forts in the Penobscot Bay along the coast of Maine and attempt to land a military force. The intention was to take the British fortifications at Fort George (see 25th July) and then reclaim New Ireland. However, despite intense bombardment of the

Fort, the courageous garrison did not surrender and the rebels were driven away in humiliation following utter defeat at the hands of the Royal Navy.

1827 The death of William Blake (see 28th November), mystic, composer, poet, painter and writer of the famous 'Jerusalem'. A prolific artist, he sadly found no popularity when alive and sank into obscurity. His religious beliefs were often considered shocking for his time. His book, The Book of Thel (1789-1794), was the start of a number of works of a visionary and prophetic nature. When he died he was buried in an unmarked grave in Bunhill Fields, London. The site of his grave has subsequently been lost.

1848 The death of George Stephenson at Tapton House near Chesterfield (see 9th June and 27th September). Illiterate until his late teenage years, he became the pioneer of the steam locomotive, his most famous engines being the 'Blucher', the 'Locomotion' and the 'Rocket'. He worked on the Stockton and Darlington Railway and also the Liverpool and Manchester Railway whilst realising and promoting a standard gauge, which was later adopted across the Empire and most of the world.

1918 The birth of Guy Penrose Gibson in Simla, India (see 19th September).

1969 The Royal Ulster Constabulary (RUC) uses tear gas for the first time on British streets in the Bogside area of Londonderry (see 9th March, 31st July and 14th August).

13th August:

1762 The battle of Havana, including the two month siege, ends when the city surrenders to British forces commanded by Admiral Sir George Pocock (see 6th March and 3rd April) and General Sir George Keppel, third earl Albermarle. The city was the major port for the Spanish in the West Indies and so was a key target during the Seven Years' War (1756-1763). However, during the siege, our forces suffered around 2,700 casualties of war and around 4,700 from disease.

1814 The Anglo-Dutch Treaty between Great Britain and the Netherlands is signed in London. The Treaty confirmed our control over the previously Dutch Cape Colony in Africa whilst ceding some lesser acquisitions back to the Dutch (see 10th January, 17th March, 31st May and 7th August).

1910 The death of Florence Nightingale (see 12th May). Known famously for her work in Military Hospitals, especially Scutari during the Crimean War (1853-1856), she advanced nursing in Britain and made it a respectable profession for women. She returned to Britain and established Training Schools for Nurses and introduced many practices that are still used to this day.

1946 The death of Herbert George 'H. G' Wells (see 21st September) in London. Born 1866, he had a difficult childhood but graduated from London University in 1888 and became a teacher. He had his first book published in the early 1890s and this was followed by his most famous works, such as

'The Time Machine' in 1895, 'The Island of Doctor Moreau' in 1896, 'The Invisible Man' in 1897, 'War of the Worlds' in 1898 and 'The First Men in the Moon' in 1901. After his initial successes he moved away from the science fiction genre to more social based, real-life works. Later in life he became a socialist, joining the Fabian Society and wrote about social issues in society and highlighted the problems faced by the lower classes.

1964 Peter Allen in Liverpool and John Walby in Manchester are the last executions to be carried out in Britain (see 13th July).

14th August:

1834 The Poor Law Amendment Act receives Royal Assent, introducing workhouses for the poor who were healthy and able to work. The Act, the work of the government of the Prime Minister Earl Grey (see 13th March and 17th July), ensured that no able-bodied individual could obtain relief except in a workhouse and that conditions in these buildings were to be extremely harsh to discourage people from wanting to claim instead of working.

1850 The Libraries Act receives Royal Assent. The Act provided the local authorities with the power to establish free public libraries and enable people to get access to information and education (see 6th September).

1888 The birth of John Logie Baird (see 26th January and 14th June) in Helensburgh.

1900 The city of Peking is entered by British troops along with troops from allied nations thus lifting the siege of the International Legations and so ending the Boxer rebellion (see 20th June). The British troops were first into the city and the first to reach the beleaguered Foreign Legation area.

1914 The British Expeditionary Force (BEF) arrives in France. They ultimately number 120,000 men and are concentrated in Northern France and the very tip of Southern Belgium. Known as 'The Old Contemptibles' they form the backbone of resistance to the German Imperial Army's push into France and Belgium and make several heroic stands against their advances, sustaining very heavy losses in the process (see 4th August, 23rd August and 11th November).

1941 The Atlantic Charter, the forerunner of much of the United Nations, is issued and agreed between Great Britain and the United States. Later agreed by the Allies, it set forward goals for a post-war world and included national self-determination, freedom from fear and freedom of the seas amongst others (see 11th August).

1969 Troops are deployed on the streets of Northern Ireland to protect the Catholic members of the community from the possible threat of Protestant violence and intimidation (see 9th March, 31st July and 12th August).

15th August: Victory over Japan.

1649 Oliver Cromwell (see 25th April and 3rd September) lands in Ireland at the port of Rathmines south of Dublin to begin his conquest of Ireland following the Irish Rebellion of 1641 (see 12th August, 11th September and 22nd October).

1771 The birth of Sir Walter Scott in the Old Town of Edinburgh (see 21st September)

1856 The birth of James Keir Hardie, first leader of the Labour Party (see 25th September), in Lanarkshire.

1867 The Representation of the People's Act receives Royal Assent, doubling the number of men eligible to vote. The franchise for voting was set as any male householder with property worth £10 or more or a male lodger paying £10 per annum or more in rent. Also, constituencies and boroughs that had less than 10,000 inhabitants as voters were reduced to just one seat in Parliament (see 7th June and 6th December).

1872 The first Parliamentary election by secret ballot in Britain is held. The ballot was introduced in a ministerial by-election as a result of the Ballot Act 1872 (see 18th July).

1923 Eamon De Valera, a leading American born Irish rebel during the Easter Rebellion of 1916 (see 24th April and 29th April), is captured by troops of the Dominion of the Irish Free State in County Clare and is then interned (see 6th December and 8th December).

1945 Victory over Japan (V.J.) Day and the official end to the Second World War and victory over the Japanese (see 8th May and 8th December). The Japanese Emperor, in a radio broadcast to his nation, announces his country's surrender. Our Troops in the east, in the 'Forgotten Army' are victorious and can return home, proud conquerors of the Japanese Imperial Army and true heroes. May their sacrifice never be forgotten: 'When you go home, tell them of us and say, for their tomorrow, we gave our today' (the 'Kohima Epitaph' by John Maxwell Edmonds).

1947 The granting of independence to India with the partitioning of the country into two newly created Dominions within the Empire, the states of India and Pakistan (see 22nd June, 18th July and 17th August).

16th August:

1745 The Battle of High Bridge. The first of the battles of the Jacobite counter revolution, just south of present day Spean Bridge (see 19th August). A group of a dozen Highlanders, MacDonalds of Keppoch, were on their way to meet Prince Charles Edward Stewart ('Bonnie Prince Charlie', see 31st January and 31st December) at Glenfinnan, when they came across two companies of the Royal Scots under Captain Scott at the bridge crossing the Spean River. The Highlanders, using continuous movement, allowed the Government troops to believe they were surrounded. After a brief retreat, the soldiers, still believing they were surrounded, surrendered after losing a couple of their number. The Jacobites lost none of their men in the brief action.

1765 The Treaty of Allahabad is signed by the Mughal Emperor Shah Alam II and Lord Robert Clive (see 29th September and 22nd November) on behalf of the East India Company (see 31st December). This was as a direct result of the decisive victory of the East India Company at the Battle of Buxar in 1764 (see 22nd October). The treaty allowed British control over much of Bengal and awarded the rights to collect revenue from the native peoples to the new administration run by the Company (see 15th August).

1780 The Battle of Camden, South Carolina, during the American rebellion. Our forces, led by General Charles Cornwallis (see 5th October and 31st December), achieved a decisive victory over the American rebels led by so called major General Horatio Gates. Although the rebels had a larger force, their casualties were much greater; over a thousand killed and another thousand taken prisoner against just over 300 killed and wounded from our troops. The victory allowed our control over the South Carolinas to be strengthened.

1812 Fort Detroit is surrendered by the American Commander, General William Hull, to our forces commanded by Major General Isaac Brock (see 13th October) and his Shawnee allies under their leader, Tecumseh (see 5th October). The surrender cost the Americans control over the Michigan Territory for the rest of the war (see 18th June, 13th October and 24th December).

1819 The so-called 'Peterloo Massacre' takes place. In the area now known as St. Peter's Place, formerly St. Peter's Fields in Manchester, a crowd of upwards of 60,000 had gathered to demonstrate for parliamentary reform. Though the multitude was described as being orderly, the local magistrates were concerned that with so many radical reformers present and due to speak, the situation could have quickly descended into a riot. The Riot Act was read out and after an attempt to arrest some of the speakers partially failed, the cavalry were sent in to clear the fields and aid in the arrests. At least fifteen people were killed and over 500 were wounded.

1858 The first trans-Atlantic telegraph is sent when Queen Victoria (see 22nd January and 24th May) sends a message to the American President, James Buchannan. However, the cable proved very unreliable and it failed just one month later (see 25th June, 7th July and 19th October).

1888 The birth of Thomas Edward Lawrence in Tremadog in Carnarfonshire in Wales (see 19th May).

1930 The first British Empire Games (see 12th May) are opened in Hamilton, Ontario, Canada, by the Governor General Lord Willingdon. They were the forerunner of the modern Commonwealth Games, held every four years. Eleven teams competed from the empire: Australia, Bermuda, British Guiana, Canada, England, Ireland, Newfoundland, New Zealand, Scotland, South Africa and Wales.

1960 The colony of Cyprus is granted its independence. The colony had become a protectorate in 1878 from the Ottoman Sultan in gratitude for British support against Russian aggression. The island became a key strategic base for the Royal Navy due to its proximity to the Suez Canal. The Ottomans sided with Germany in the Great War so the island was formally annexed and became a formal Protectorate of Britain in 1914, becoming a Crown Colony in 1925 (see 10th August and 30th October). In 1955 terrorist attacks by Greek Cypriots and Turkish Cypriots began and this prompted a State of Emergency to be declared (see 26th November).

17th August:

1836 The Registration Act is introduced requiring all births, deaths and marriages to be registered beginning in 1837. The General Register Office and the post of Register General were created by means of the Act.

1896 Bridget Driscoll becomes the first traffic accident fatality caused by a car. The 44 year old woman was visiting Crystal Palace with her 16-year-old daughter when she was struck and killed by a Roger-Benz car that was travelling at around 4 mph.

1943 The first Quebec Conference begins in the city of Quebec with Winston Churchill (see 24th January and 30th November), Franklin D Roosevelt and the Prime Minister of Canada William Lyon Mackenzie King. They agreed, amongst other things, to begin discussing the future invasion of France (Operation Overlord), the build up of American forces prior to this, the continued bombing of Germany and the coordination of work towards the development of a nuclear bomb (see 19th August).

1947 The Radcliffe Line is announced (see 15th August). The line was named after Sir Cyril Radcliffe who was Chairman of the Board of Commissions, set up to demarcate the boundaries between the majority Hindu and Majority Muslim areas of India. In effect it would be the dividing line between the two independent states of the former British India now secular and Hindu India and Muslim Pakistan. Almost half of British India was actually governed as Princely States and these had to choose whether to join the newly independent countries.

18th August:

1587 Virginia Dare becomes the first child born of English parents in Colonial America (see 3rd September).

1720 The birth of Laurence Shirley, later to become the 4th Earl of Ferrers (see 5th May).

1759 The start of the Battle of Lagos Bay (see 19th August). The French, under Admiral de la Clue, left the port of Toulon and attempted to slip past Gibraltar. Spotted, our Fleet, led by Admiral Edward Boscawen (see 10th January and 19th August), gave chase and cornered the French off the

Portuguese coast at Lagos. Boscawen engaged the French and defeats their fleet and captures or destroys five French ships. The Battle ends the following day with our forces suffering 252 casualties but the French lost 500 killed and three ships taken as prizes and two ships were burnt (see 17th May and 20th November).

1809 The death of Matthew Boulton in Birmingham (see 3rd September). A leading manufacturer and a key figure in the industrial revolution, he was a partner with James Watt and their company, Bolton and Watt, made the steam engines from their Soho Manufactory near Handsworth, hundreds of which were used across the country and abroad. He also founded the Soho Mint and after receiving a contract in 1797, he used the latest steam-powered machinery to strike the copper coinage and the first large penny that was minted and was the basic design in use until decimalisation in 1971. He was a founding member of the Lunar Society in 1765, a group of Birmingham based thinkers, intellectuals, industrialists and business men. He was a supporter of the arts and civic activities of Birmingham for much of his life.

1911 The Parliament Act is given Royal Assent and comes into affect. The act was a landmark piece of legislation, defining the constitutional relationship between the Commons and the Lords. The act limited the power of the Lords over legislation from the Commons. The Lords could now only delay legislation on money bills for one month and for two months for all other public bills. The act also allowed for the reduction in time between general elections from seven years to five years.

1945 The death of Subhas Chandra Bose on Formosa. An Indian nationalist, he was a traitor and enemy of Great Britain, India and the Empire. Born in Cuttack, he became ever more extreme from his college days. He spent two years in England before returning to India in 1921. He joined the Indian National Congress (see 28th December) and was in and out of jail up until the Second World War for his often violent activities against British targets. In 1941 he left India and by 1943 he was in Japan and his treachery began. He restructured the Japanese supported 'Indian National Army', set up the 'Free India' provisional government and supported the attempted Japanese invasion of India. When Japan and the few treacherous Indians suffered heavy defeat he fled and was killed in a plane crash on the Japanese occupied island of Formosa (see 15th August and 2nd September).

19th August:

1274 The coronation of Edward I at Westminster Abbey (see 3rd March, 17th June and 7th July).

1689 The birth of Samuel Richardson in Mackworth, Derbyshire. He went on to publish the first successful novel, *Clarissa* (see 4th July).

1711 The birth Edward Boscawen (see 10th January) near Falmouth.

1745 The Royal Jacobite Standard is raised on the shores of Loch Shiel at Glenfinnan on the west coast of Scotland, marking the start of the Jacobite rising of 1745 (see 16th August). Prince Charles Edward Stewart, 'Bonnie Prince Charlie' and grandson of James VII (James II of England and see 5th September and 14th October), claims the thrones of England and Scotland on behalf of his father, the 'Old Pretender' James VIII (James III of England, see 1st January and 10th June).

1759 The conclusion to the Battle of Lagos Bay (see 18th August). The French, under Admiral de la Clue, left the port of Toulon and attempted to slip past Gibraltar. Spotted, our Fleet, led by Admiral Edward Boscawen (see 10th January and 19th August), gave chase and cornered the French off the Portuguese coast at Lagos. Boscawen engaged the French and defeats their fleet and captures or destroys five French ships. The Battle, fought over two days ends with our forces suffering 252 casualties but the French lost 500 killed and three ships taken as prizes and two ships were burnt. Though the battle did not end French plans of an invasion, they were nevertheless severely hindered (see 17th May and 20th November).

1808 The birth of James Nasmyth in Edinburgh (see 7th May).

1819 The death of James Watt at his home in Handsworth near Birmingham (see 19th January). A mechanical engineer, he was the first to develop an efficient and reliable steam engine, improving on the previous Newcomen engine that contributed to the rise of the Industrial Revolution. He developed his version of the Newcomen steam engine in 1769 and in 1774 went into partnership with Matthew Boulton (see 18th August and 3rd September) at the Soho Manufactory near Handsworth. A member of the Lunar Society, the SI unit of power, the 'watt', is named after him.

1853 The death of Admiral George Cockburn (see 22nd April) in Leamington Spa, a leading Naval officer and hero of the Revolutionary Wars, the Napoleonic Wars and the War with America in 1812. Born in London to Sir James Cockburn, 8th Baronet, he joined the Royal Navy in 1781. He went on to serve in the French Revolutionary Wars and the Napoleonic Wars and then during the War of 1812 with America. In 1814, along with General Robert Ross (see 12th September), he led an expedition of 4,000 men into the American mainland and entered the undefended city of Washington where the American President had fled just before in complete humiliation. He was then responsible for the order to burn Washington in 1814, along with General Ross (see 24th August), in retribution for the uncalled for American burning of the Canadian city of York the year before (see 27th April).

1939 Sir Malcolm Campbell takes the Water Speed Record for the last time. He achieves 141.74 mph in his Bluebird K4 on Coniston Water (see 3rd September).

1942 The Allied raid on Dieppe, France, goes disastrously wrong as the element of surprise is lost and heavy casualties are sustained. The initial plan was conceived by Admiral Lord Mountbatten (see 25th June and 27th August). The raid, designed to test the ability to frontally assault and hold an occupied port, commenced at 5am when mainly Canadian forces with British Commandos supported by the Royal Navy and the Royal Air Force came ashore at the German-occupied port and shore line. The Germans had been heavily reinforced and from the very start the heroic Canadians suffered heavy casualties. The withdrawal commenced at 11am and was completed by 2pm. The gallant Canadians suffered nearly 3,500 killed, wounded and taken prisoner. Some 275 Commandos became casualties and the Royal Navy and Royal Air Force lost over 600 personnel. The Americans lost three men.

1943 Winston Churchill (see 24th January and 30th November) and Franklin D Roosevelt of the United States sign the Quebec Agreement in Quebec City during the Quebec Conference (see 17th August). The secret Agreement formalised arrangements between both counties for the pooling of resources and the sharing of technology for the development and construction of a nuclear weapon in the Manhattan Project. However, after the war the Americans reneged on their word and refused to share their technology and secrets with their closest ally, despite Britain sharing all its advances and technology with America during the war and sending 50 scientists to America. The result was that Britain designed and built its own nuclear weapons, much to the annoyance of the Americans who were forced into another agreement with Britain (see 26th February, 15th May and 3rd October).

20th August:

1810 The start of the battle of Grand Port on Mauritius. This was our country's only naval defeat against Napoleonic France. A British squadron, under the then Captain Sir Samuel Pym, consisting of four ships attempted to storm Grand Port on the then French held Isle de France. Two ships were captured, HMS Sirius and HMS Magicienne, and two were destroyed, HMS Nereide and HMS Iphigenia, as our ships were cornered in the harbour and some ran ground under intense French fire.

1912 The death of William Booth, the founder of the Salvation Army in Hadley Wood, London (see 10th April). Born in Nottingham, he converted to Methodism in the 1840s. Initially with a close friend, he preached to the poor of Nottingham and then later in London, along with his wife. With his wife Catherine he formed the Salvation Army from their missionary work in London with their East London Christian Mission in 1865. In 1890 he published 'In Darkest England' highlighting the dire conditions of London's East End.

1925 The death of Sir George Goldie in London (see 20th May). A colonial administrator, he was responsible for the creation and success of the colony of Nigeria. Born on the Isle of Man, he served for a short period in the Royal Engineers before forming the Central African Trading Company in 1879. He united all the various commercial interests in Niger and in 1886 his company received a Royal Charter as the Royal Niger Company. In 1895 he became governor of the company and played an instrumental role in British colonial success in West Africa. The charter was withdrawn in 1900 after the company struggled to compete with state-sponsored territories owned by

France and Germany. The Colony's interests were transferred to government control in London.

21st August:

1689 The Battle of Dunkeld between the Jacobite forces, under Colonel Alexander Cannon, fresh from their victory at the battle of Killiecranckie (see 27th July) and the Cameronian Regiment of Covenanters under Colonel Cleland. After some extremely fierce and brutal fighting in which Colonel Cleland was killed, the Jacobites were routed, leaving some 300 of their dead in the streets of Dunkeld.

1740 Admiral Edward Vernon (see 30th October and 12th November), known as 'Old Grog' by many, ordered his men's rum ration to be diluted to prevent drunkenness.

1765 The birth of Prince William Henry, the future William IV, in Buckingham House (see 20th June and 26th June). His parents were George III (see 29th January and 24th May) and Queen Charlotte Mecklenburg-Strelitz.

1808 The Battle of Vimeiro in Portugal. Major General Arthur Wellesley (see 1st May and 14th September) beats the French under their leader Marshal Junot. In a magnificent display of his leadership, Wellesley sheltered his troops from the French Artillery by having them deployed behind the crest of the ridge before attacking the French downhill with infantry and the use of cannon. However, he was superseded in his command by a more senior officer who did not follow up the victory. In the following capitulation terms, Sir Harry Burrard and Sir Hew Dalrymple agreed to transport the French with their baggage and plunder back to France in British ships. Understandably, there was outrage in Britain and an enquiry ensued (see 30th August) in which Wellesley was exonerated.

22nd August:

1485 The Battle of Bosworth, originally called 'the Battle of Reed Moore', and the death of Richard III (see 4th February, 9th April, 6th July and 2nd October), the last of the Plantagenet kings. Henry Tudor (see 28th January and 21st April), a descendent of the House of Lancaster, returned from exile in France, landed at Milford Haven and marched inland to confront Richard's bigger force. However, many of Richard's supposed allies failed to rise in support and the Stanleys actually hesitated and defected to Henry. This is one of the great battles in English and Welsh history and a defining moment in this country's development.

1642 Following failed negotiations, Charles I (see 30th January and 19th November) decides to raise his standard at Nottingham and calls on all his loyal subjects to join him against the Parliamentary forces. In raising his standard he effectively declared war on his rebellious opponents and so started the Civil War.

1771 The birth of Henry Maudslay in Woolwich (see 14th February) near London.

1798 Around 1,000 French troops land in County Mayo under the leadership of General Jean Humbert as part of Frances support for the Irish Rebellion. They are joined by about 5,000 Irishmen and actually beat the British force sent to oppose them. They also declare a 'Republic' of Connaught and request extra troops from the French government (see 8th September).

1818 The death of Warren Hastings in Gloucestershire (see 6th December). Born in Churchill in Oxfordshire, he joined the East India Company in 1750 (see 31st December), leaving for India the same year. He was the first Governor-General of Bengal in 1771 and Governor of India from 1773. He was responsible for many reforms in the Indian administration and judiciary and was Governor during the First Maharatta Wars. Accused of corruption by his one time friend Edmund Burke MP (see 1st January and 9th July), he was impeached in 1787 followed by a trial that lasted until 1795 when he was acquitted.

1903 The death of Robert Arthur Talbot Gascoyne Cecil, Lord Salisbury (see 3rd February), at Hatfield in Hertfordshire. A leading Conservative statesman of his time, he served as Prime Minister three times for a total of thirteen years. The saying 'Bob's your uncle' is thought to originate from the fact that he appointed his nephew Arthur Balfour as Minister for Ireland. He was, during his third and final term in office, the Prime Minister throughout the Boer War, 1899-1902. In 1902 he resigned, leaving the Premiership to his nephew, Arthur Balfour (see 19th March, 12th July and 25th July).

1940 The death of Oliver Joseph Lodge in Wiltshire (see 12th June). A physicist, he originally had the idea of electromagnetic waves but due to teaching commitments could not further his work, which was over taken by Heinrich Hertz. He later worked on radio waves and he and his colleague sold their patents in 1912 to Marconi. With some of his sons, he developed a device for electrical spark ignition in combustion engine. This developed into the Lodge Spark Plug Company. A member of the Fabian Society, he became deeply interested in psychic phenomenon and life after death after the Great War, following his son's death in active service in 1915.

23rd August:

1305 The execution of William Wallace at Tyburn. He was hung, drawn and quartered. Wallace led an open rebellion against Edward I (see 17th June and 7th July) of England which began with his attack on Lanark in 1297, killing the Sheriff. In the September of 1297, he defeated a much larger English army at the battle of Stirling Bridge (see 11th September) and the following year began raids into the north of England. However, in July 1298 he was defeated at the Battle of Falkirk (see 22nd July) and his rebellion was effectively ended. He went to France and in his absence a truce was signed between Edward I and Robert the Bruce (see 7th June and 11th July) in 1308. Excluded from the truce, and with a reward on his head, Wallace was eventually captured near Glasgow (see 3rd August) and handed over to the English.

1775 George II (see 20th October and 25th October) issues 'A Proclamation for Suppressing Rebellion and Sedition', declaring parts of the American Colonies as being in a 'state of open and avowed rebellion' in response to the news of the Battle of Bunker Hill (see 17th June) and the savage resistance to government's authority and His Majesty's forces by the traitorous rebels (see 3rd September).

1914 The Battle of Mons and the first major battle of the Great War involving our forces, under the Command of Sir John French. The German First Army advanced towards the Mons Canal where our troops had taken up defensive positions on the opposite side. During this defence, just over 1,600 British Expeditionary Force (BEF) soldiers and just over 5,000 of the enemy became casualties. The BEF made a stout stand against the advancing Imperial German First Army, employing far superior musketry skills than their opponents and causing the momentum of the advance to falter and inflicting a disproportionate number of casualties on the numerically superior German troops. However, due to the overwhelming German numbers and the sudden retreat of the French Fifth Army, badly exposing the BEF's right flank, the BEF retired in an orderly and well-disciplined manner (see 4th August, 14th August and 11th November).

1921 The only rigid airship of the R-38 class, ZR-2, suffers structural failure whilst in flight as the frame crumpled and split into two, exploded then crashed into the Humber Estuary. Only 5 of the British and American crew of 49 survived. She had been sold to the Americans and was on her fifth and final test flight when the accident occurred.

24th August:

1198 The birth of Alexander II of Scotland (see 6th July) in Haddington in Lothian.

1217 The battle of Sandwich off the coast of Kent. In one of the greatest sea battles of English and British history, the French fleet was annihilated. The English fleet was led by Hubert de Burgh and the French by Eustace the Monk (see 20th May). The French were attacked as they passed the port of Sandwich and attempted to fight back but were quickly outmanoeuvred and were routed. Many supply vessels were taken and more were captured as the fleeing French were pursued. Eustace the Monk was summarily beheaded and most of the French sailors were despatched at the scene.

1680 The death of Thomas Blood in Westminster (born 1618). Born in Ireland to a family of English descent, he is famous for briefly stealing the Crown Jewels from the Tower of London in 1671 (see 9th May). Having been captured, he was pardoned by the King and granted land.

1759 The birth of William Wilberforce, the future MP and anti-slavery campaigner, in Hull (see 29th July). He was to become a leading figure in the freeing of British slaves throughout our Empire.

1787 The birth of James Weddell (see 9th September) in Ostend in the Southern Netherlands.

1814 The Battle of Blandensburg in Maryland and a resounding victory for our forces. General Robert Ross (see 12th September) led our troops against the Americans and after initial close quarter fighting, the ill-disciplined and badly-led Americans fled in what rapidly became a general rout. This humiliating display by the Americans on their own soil allowed our forces to enter the city of Washington later that day with little resistance (see 18th June and 24th December).

1814 Our troops, numbering only 4,000, led by General Robert Ross (see 12th September) and Rear Admiral Sir George Cockburn (see 22nd April and 19th August), enter the city of Washington without any resistance to the invasion of the capital city. General Ross and his officers dined in the White House on a meal prepared for President Madison before his humiliating flight as our forces approached. Once the meal was finished, our troops burn the White House (then called the Presidential Palace), the Capitol building, the Treasury and the navy yard as well as other important buildings. The following day our forces withdrew from the city. This destruction was in understandable retaliation for the despicable burning by completely undisciplined American forces of the town of York (modern day Toronto) during its five day occupation the previous year (see 27th April). The success of the operation and that our forces were able to act with total impunity revealed the feebleness of the American army and the ineptitude of their government (see 18th June and 24th December).

1875 Captain Matthew Webb (see 19th January and 24th July) sets off from Admiralty Pier in Dover on his attempt to become the first man to swim the English Channel (see 25th August).

25th August:

1688 Captain Henry Morgan, pirate and adventurer, dies in Port Royal, Jamaica (see 18th January). Born in Monmouthshire in 1635, he was the son of a farmer. He left for the West Indies when very young, heading first for Barbados but settling eventually in Jamaica. Much of his activities were directed towards the Spanish Main and shipping whilst acting in his capacity as a privateer. His most famous achievement was his plundering of the Spanish Main along the Caribbean coast of Panama. In 1671 he captured the city of Panama (see 18th January) for which he was viewed as a hero in England and especially Jamaica. He grew very wealthy and bought much land and slaves in Jamaica.

1778 The death of David Hume, philosopher of the Scottish enlightenment (see 26th April), historian and essayist in Edinburgh. Initially denounced by many of his contemporaries as a sceptic and because of his atheism, he wrote extensively on religion and morals and the relationship with the human mind. His major works include *Treatise of Human Nature* (1739-1740), *Enquiry Concerning Human Understanding* (1748) and the more successful *History of England* (1754-1762). He briefly served as Under Secretary of State for the Northern Department before settling in Edinburgh in 1768.

1822 The death of Sir Frederick William Herschel in Slough (see 15th November). A well-known astronomer, he is remembered for the discovery of the planet Uranus and two of its moons as well as two moons of Saturn. Born in Hanover, he came to Britain at the age of 19. He was an accomplished oboist and had served in the Hanover Military Band. He composed symphonies, travelling England as an organist and teacher of music. It was in 1781 that he discovered Uranus (see 13th March) and was elected a Fellow of the Royal Society. In 1782 he became George III's (see 29th January and 24th May) own private astronomer.

1867 The death of Michael Faraday at Hampton Court (see 22nd September). Apprenticed to a Bookbinder when he was fourteen years old, he then spent the next seven years educating himself by reading books. In 1813 he attended a lecture by Humphrey Davy and wrote to him for a job. Though unsuccessful, Davy later appointed him to a job in the Royal Institution. Over the next few years he worked closely with Davy and other scientists and in 1821 published work on electromagnetic rotation. In 1831 he discovered electromagnetic induction and in 1833 the laws of electrolysis. He spent the next few years developing his ideas and discoveries around electricity and developed the classical field theory. He held numerous official posts that allowed him to continue his research and gave his name to the 'farad', a unit of electrical charge.

1875 Captain Matthew Webb wades ashore in Calais after becoming the first man to swim the English Channel. He set off from Dover the previous day and took 21 hours and 45 minutes to cover about 50 miles (see 19th January and 24th July and 24th August). He had support boats with him and suffered jelly fish stings which delayed his arrival.

1904 The death of William Edward Hall (see 28th April) in Horton Bluff, Nova Scotia. An Able Seaman in the Royal Navy, he was the first black person to win the Victoria Cross. He was born in 1827 and was the son of two refugee American slaves who had escaped to Nova Scotia with the help of the Royal Navy. He joined the American Merchant Navy before joining the Royal Navy. He won the VC at Lucknow during the Indian Mutiny on the 16th November 1857 when he and an Officer were the only ones to survive from their gunnery crew. When only they were left, they gallantly kept up a constant fire upon the enemy despite the danger to themselves. He retired in 1876.

1940 The RAF (see 1st April) bomb Berlin for the first time in retaliation for the bombing of London a few nights earlier. Ninety-five bombers attack the airport in Berlin. Though little damage was inflicted in comparison with later raids, it is probable that the raid caused Hitler to change his focus from the beleaguered airfields in Britain to the cities, thus allowing Fighter Command time to recuperate (see 22nd February and 15th September).

26th August:

1346 The Battle of Crècy in France, during the Hundred Years' War, 1337-1453. A small English army of around 16,000 led by Edward III (see 21st June and 13th November) and his son the Prince of Wales (see 8th June), later to be known as the Black Prince, stand against the French army of Philip VI of between 50,000 to as high as 80,000 men. The English lost around 40 men whilst the enemy lost at least the king of Bohemia, 11 Princes, 1 Archbishop, around 1,200 Knights and between 10,000 and 30,000 other men, more than the total English army on the field. It was at this battle that the supremacy of the English Longbow over the enemy weapons was recognised for the first time. Tradition has it that the emblem of the King of Bohemia, three white feathers of the fleur de lis and the motto 'Ich Dien' (I serve), was taken by the Black Prince as his emblem, remaining the emblem of the Prince of Wales to this day.

1676 The birth of Sir Robert Walpole, a future Whig MP and our first Prime Minister (see 18th March and 22nd September) in Houghton, Suffolk.

1819 The birth of Francis Albert Augustus Emmanuel (later known as Prince Albert) at Schloss Rosenau, near Coburg in Bavaria (see 14th December).

1841 The battle of Amoy in China against forces of the Qing dynasty during the First Opium War. Following a relatively brief bombardment of the forts in Amoy and on Gulangyu Island, our forces were landed and took the forts with little resistance from the Chinese. Our forces suffered relatively minor casualties compared to the heavy losses of the Chinese (see 29th August).

1936 the Anglo-Egyptian Treaty is signed in Cairo, Egypt. The treaty required Britain to withdraw all our troops from Egypt, except those that were required to protect the Suez Canal Zone. Britain also agreed to provide training for the Egyptian army and to assist the country in the event that it was invaded or threatened (see 31st October, 5th November, 25th November and 23rd December).

1963 Diana Barnato Walker (see 15th January and 28th April) becomes the first British woman to break the sound barrier. Flying an English Electric Lightening XM996 (see 4th August) from RAF Middleton St. George, she reached Mach 1.65 (1,262 mph).

27th August:

249

55BC The official date for the landing in Britain of Roman Emperor Julius Caesar and 10,000 Romans soldiers as they begin their attempted occupation of our country and the subjugation of the native Britons by the Roman Empire until 410AD (see 4th February).

1549 The battle of Dissindale near Norwich brings the 'Norfolk Rising' or 'Kett's Rebellion' to an end (see 20th June and 7th July). The rebellion had broken out as a protest against the enclosure of common land. Robert Kett eventually led the rebellion and brought the mob into a disciplined force of around 16,000 men. They captured the city of Norwich but were enticed out of the city by the earl of Warwick. Faced by a professional army and mercenaries, the rebels were soon defeated and the leaders, including Kett, captured (see 7th December).

1652 The Battle of Monte Cristo in the First Anglo-Dutch War (1652-1654). This took place in the Mediterranean Sea and was a victory for our fleet, led by Admiral Richard Badiley, with the loss of only one of our ships, the Phoenix which was captured by the Dutch.

1664 New Amsterdam, capital of the Dutch colony of New Netherland, is cut off and the surrender of the Dutch is demanded (see 21st July). Four English ships, under the command of Richard Nicolls, sailed into the harbour and demanded New Netherland's surrender (see 8th September).

1776 The Battle of Long Island during the American Rebellion. In the first major battle in the rebellion, American Colonial rebels, led by George Washington (see 11th February and 14th December), are beaten back by our forces, led by Major General Lord William Howe. Our forces suffered around 400 casualties whilst the rebels suffered about 2,000 killed with the result that they were ultimately forced to abandon the city of New York (see 8th September).

1816 The city of Algiers is bombarded by a squadron of Royal Navy and some Dutch ships under the command of Admiral Pellew (see 23rd January and 19th April). Having failed to persuade the Dey of Algiers to release his Christian slaves, Admiral Pellew and his ships sailed into Algiers and after issuing an ultimatum, bombarded the city for around nine hours and destroyed the ships and shore batteries in the harbour. The bombardment persuaded the Dey of Algiers to sign a peace treaty and release his captives.

1825 The death of William Moorcroft in Northern Afghanistan. Born in Ormskirk in Lancashire in 1767, he trained as a veterinary surgeon in France, qualifying as Britain's first veterinary surgeon in 1791 (see 7th May). In the early 1800s he travelled to India for the East India Company (see 31st December) and spent the next twenty years exploring India and central Asia on trade and exploration expeditions. In 1825 he reached Bokhara in Central Asia. It was following his departure from the city that he became feverish and died.

1879 The death of Sir Rowland Hill in Hampstead (see 3rd December). Born in Kidderminster and the son of a school master, he was brought up in Birmingham and worked in his Father's school. He took an interest and participated in the organising of the colonisation of South Australia. In 1836, along with the MP Robert Wallace, he began taking an interest in Postal reforms and began to develop his idea of a pre-paid postage stamp as a means of payment which was finally introduced in 1840 (see 10th January). He was promoted to Secretary to the Postmaster-General in 1864. He was buried in Westminster Abbey.

1896 The 'Zanzibar War', which lasted less than 40 minutes, begins and concludes. On the death of the pro-British Sultan, an anti-British Sultan took over and took up defensive positions in the city of Zanzibar. According to a treaty of 1886, which recognised Zanzibar's own sovereignty, any successor was to be authorised by the British Consul, which the new Sultan had failed to do. The British sent in the Royal Navy and began bombarding positions in the city which quickly forced the defenders to capitulate.

1919 The death of Louis Botha (see 27th September), the first Prime Minister of the Dominion of South Africa (see 31st May). In 1897 he became a member of the parliament of the Boer Republic of Transvaal. During the Boer War (1899-1902) he fought against British troops, was a very successful and skilful General and was the man who captured Winston Churchill (see 24th January and 30th November) in an ambush on an armoured train. However, he was a signatory at the Treaty of Vereeniging in 1902 (see 31st May), recognised the benefits of closer association with Great Britain and worked tirelessly for the permanent entry of South Africa into the Empire as a Dominion. At the outbreak of the First World War he sent South African troops into the German colony of South West Africa, defeating them in July 1915. Because of his loyalty, he was viewed with hatred by some Afrikaners.

1979 Lord Louis Mountbatten, the last Viceroy of India, is murdered in a bomb blast by the terrorist group the IRA in Sligo, Southern Ireland (see 25th June). He was born at Windsor to Prince Louis of Battenberg and Princess Victoria of Hesse. His maternal Grandmother was Princess Alice, the daughter of Queen Victoria (see 22nd January and 24th May). He joined the Royal Navy and served during the First World War. Later during the Second World War he had a number of commands and took part in many operations. He was involved in the operations to recapture Burma as well as the Japanese surrender of Singapore. He was appointed Viceroy of India (see 20th February) by Clement Attlee (see 3rd January and 8th October) and was also the first Governor General of the Union of India. He was buried in Romsey Abbey in Hampshire.

28th August:

1640 The Battle of Newburn Ford. A victory for the Scottish forces led by Alexander Leslie, Earl of Leven, with 22,000 troops, against an English Royalist force, under Lord Conway and Lord Fairfax, of around 3,000 troops. The English troops were defending their positions south of the ford over the River Tyne and the Scots took up positions on higher ground to the north and commenced an artillery bombardment. The Scots then launched a swift attack that routed the English troops.

1791 HMS Pandora, a sixth rate, 24-gun Frigate, runs aground on the Great Barrier Reef off the Australian coast and sinks the following day. In 1790, captained by Edward Edwards, she was sent to pursue and capture the mutineers from HMS Bounty (see 28th April). Arriving in Tahiti in March 1791, with relative ease they captured fourteen of the Bounty's former crew. A further search of Tahiti and other Pacific islands was carried out to no further avail. It was whilst sailing for the Torres Strait that she foundered, claiming the lives of thirty one of the crew and four of the prisoners.

1793 The port of Toulon in southern France is willingly handed over to a combined force of predominantly British and Spanish troops (see 18th December) commanded by Vice Admiral Lord Hood (see 27th January and 12th December) and Admiral Juan de Langara with the support of some local Royalist French. The British-led Fleet also seized upwards of seventy French ships, about half the French Navy.

1833 The Slavery Abolition Act receives Royal Assent (see 25th March, 28th July and 1st August). The act abolished slavery throughout Great Britain and the Empire. Slaves were at first designated as apprentices to allow a phased abolition until 1840.

1839 The death of William Smith (see 23rd March). A renowned geologist, he is credited with creating the first geological map of most of Great Britain, published in 1815. Despite his excessive work, due to cheap copies of his work, he was reduced to poverty and served time in a debtor's prison. He is viewed by many as the 'father' of modern geology.

1861 The death of William Lyon Mackenzie in Toronto (see 12th March). Born in Dundee in Scotland, he emigrated to British North America in 1820 and eventually settled on York, Upper Canada, and in 1828 he was elected to the York County House of Assembly. In 1834, when York became Toronto, he was elected as the city's first Mayor. In 1837 he was a leading figure and supporter of the Upper Canada Rebellion (see 7th December). The rebellion failed and he went into exile in the United States, only returning to Canada in 1849 after a pardon. Later in life he advocated the incorporation of Canada into the United States.

1879 The Zulu Chief Chetewayo is captured by troops as he was hiding in a kraal (see 1st September). He was taken first to Cape Town and then sent into exile in London, returning in 1883 (see 12th January and 4th July).

1914 The battle of Heligoland Bight, the first naval battle of the Great War and a victory for the Royal Navy (see 1st November and 8th December). Our Fleet was commanded by Commodores Roger Keyes and Reginald Tyrwhitt, who despite requesting reinforcements, never the less engaged the German High Seas Fleet. We lost less than 40 men killed and one ship damaged whereas the enemy lost over 700 killed, over 300 captured and 6 ships sunk and another 6 damaged. Three of the six German ships sunk were the Light Cruisers SMS Mainz, SMS Koln and the SMS Ariadne.

29th August:

1350 The battle of Winchelsea takes place between an English Fleet of around fifty ships commanded by Edward III (see 21st June and 13th November) and the Prince of Wales, later known as the Black Prince (see 8th June) against a Castilian Fleet of around forty ships. A resounding victory for the English Navy, around half of the Castilian fleet were either sunk or captured with the probable loss of only two English ships.

1632 The birth of John Locke in Somerset (see 28th October).

1782 HMS Royal George, under the command of Rear-Admiral Richard Kempemfelt, keels over and sinks in the Solent with the loss of around 900 crew and visitors, including Kempemfelt. Launched in 1756, she was a 100 gun first-rate ship of the line, seeing action during the Seven Years' War (1756-1763). When she sank, she was anchored at Spithead and was heeled over for repairs and was taking in supplies. With the weight all on one side to allow her to be heeled over and the activity to take on provisions, she heeled further over, causing water to enter open gun ports. Within minutes she had sunk, with only 200 to 300 survivors.

1831 Michael Faraday demonstrates the first electrical transformer at the Royal Institute in London (see 25th August and 22nd September).

1833 The Factory Act is passed in Parliament. The Act, for the first time, regulated the hours that children could work in a day and also provided for their basic education (see 30th August).

1842 The Treaty of Nanking is signed in Nanking, China, between Great Britain and the Chinese Emperor. The treaty ended the First Opium War, 1839-1842, and also, more importantly, ceded Hong Kong to the Empire (see 20th January, 9th June, 1st July and 26th August).

1848 The Battle of Bloomplaats takes place in the Orange River Sovereignty. Our troops, numbering around 1200 and led by General Harry Smith, attacked and overwhelmingly defeated around 300 Boers led by Andries Pretorius, who disliked British control in the region.

1853 The death of General Sir Charles James Napier (see 10th August) in Portsmouth. A notable officer, he fought in the peninsular war, getting wounded five times and left for dead at the Battle of Coruna in 1809 (see 16th January) and is also notable for his magnificent conquering of the province of Sindh, despite his orders being only to suppress the rebels. Sometimes criticised for his apparent brutal but effective suppression of rebels, he served as Governor of the Bombay Presidency and also served as Commander in Chief of the forces in India.

1950 The first of our troops arrive in Pusan, Korea, to support the American-led and instigated United Nations war against the Communist North Korean invasion of South Korea. The initial force was made up of the Middlesex Regiment and the Argyll and Sutherland Highlanders (see 25th

June and 27th July) and these were later constituted into the 27th British Infantry Brigade.

30th August:

1797 The birth of Mary Shelley (nee Wollstonecraft Godwin) in London (see 1st February).

1808 The Convention of Cintra is signed, allowing the defeated French army, beaten at the battle of Vimeiro in 1808 (see 21st August), to leave Portugal with all their baggage, weapons and Portuguese plunder and be transported back to France aboard British ships. Sir Harry Burrard and Sir Hew Dalrymple arrived to take command of the army from Sir Arthur Wellesley (see 1st May and 14th September). Sir Dalrymple took charge of the disgraceful negotiations and although he was in disagreement with it, Sir Arthur Wellesley signed it. The Convention was seen in Britain as a complete disgrace and humiliation, allowing a defeated army to escape and fight again. All three were ordered back to Britain where Wellesley was exonerated and the other two were removed from command.

1871 The birth of Ernest Rutherford (see 19th October) in Brightwater, New Zealand.

1874 The Factory Act is passed. The Act extended previous Acts by ensuring that children under nine years old could not work in textile mills (see 29th August) and those over nine could work no more than twelve hours.

31st August:

1422 The death of Henry V at Bois de Vincennes in France, probably from the 'Bloody Flux', as dysentery was then called (see 9th April and 9th August). One of our greatest monarchs, he was born in Monmouth in 1386 or 1387 to the future Henry IV (see 20th March and 4th April) and was created Prince of Wales at the coronation of his father in 1399. On behalf of his father, he waged an aggressive and successful campaign against the Welsh rebel Owen Glendower. He became King in 1413 and was responsible for some of England's more outstanding and successful achievements on the continent. His success during the Hundred Years' War (1337-1453) brought England close to total control of France with notable victories such as the Battle of Agincourt in 1415 (see 25th October) in which the French armies of Charles VI were all but annihilated. He continued this success with the conquest of Normandy. He forced the French to agree the Treaty of Troyes in 1420 (see 21st May) where the French King recognised Henry as his heir and his descendents as Kings of France (see 21st October). Also, as part of the agreement, Henry married Charles' daughter Catherine.

1688 The death of John Bunyan, preacher, writer and author of 'Pilgrims Progress' (see 18th February), in London (see 12th November and 30th November). When a young man, he joined the Parliamentary army during the

Civil War. After leaving the army, he became a Puritan preacher and travelled around the country. After the Restoration of the monarchy, he was arrested for preaching more than once and at one time served five years in prison for preaching without a licence. It was in 1678 that he published 'Pilgrim's Progress' which became very popular.

1888 Mary Ann 'Polly' Nichols becomes the first known victim of Jack the Ripper. Aged 43, she had separated from her husband and had resorted to prostitution due to her poverty and drunkenness (see 8th September, 30th September and 9th November). Her body was found in Buck's Row in Whitechapel in London.

1939 The order to commence Operation Pied Piper, the evacuation of children from the major cities in anticipation of heavy enemy bombing raids is given. The children evacuated would be forever known as 'the evacuees' (see 8th May, 3rd September and 15th August). **1957** The Federation of Malaya is granted independence and our involvement in the Malayan Emergency officially ends (see 18th June). Altogether, almost 500 British military personnel, 39 Australians, 15 New Zealanders and 8 Southern Rhodesians were killed during what was called the 'Malaysian Emergency', the fight against Communist-backed insurgents attempting to overthrow the Malayan government.

1963 The colony of Singapore (see 1st April) is granted its independence.

SEPTEMBER

1st September:

1159 Pope Adrian IV, born Nicholas Breakspear, dies in Anagni in the Papal States. He was born around 1100 in Hertfordshire and was elected Pope in 1154. He is the only Englishman and Briton to have become Pope (see 4th December).

1864 The birth of Roger David Casement in Dublin. He would become a British Diplomat in Africa only to turn traitor. He was later captured, tried for treason, convicted and then executed (see 3rd August).

1864 The first day of the Charlottetown Conference begins in Charlottetown on Prince Edward Island. In attendance were representatives of New Brunswick, Nova Scotia, Prince Edward Island and the Province of Canada. The meeting was arranged to discuss a Maritime Union between the three Colonies, with the Province of Canada as observers (see 9th September).

1879 Zulu Chiefs sign a peace treaty with the British after the capture of the Zulu Chief Chetwayo (see 28th August), effectively bringing an end to the Zulu War.

1880 The battle of Kandahar in Afghanistan. Lieutenant General Sir Frederick Roberts led around 11,000 troops from the British, Bengal and

Bombay armies, of which around 2,500 were British and fought an Afghan army of around 12,000. After initial artillery bombardment of the Afghan positions, there followed a series of infantry attacks. Eventually, after some heavy fighting, the Afghans abandoned their positions and their flight turned into a rout. It was a resounding victory for our forces, our casualties being about 250 with the Afghan casualties being over ten times as much. It was the effective end to the Second Afghan War of 1878-1880 (see 21st November).

2nd September:

1666 The Great Fire of London breaks out, eventually destroying over 13,000 buildings (see 6th September).

1752 The last day under the Julian calendar as the Gregorian calendar is adopted in Britain with the loss of eleven days. The following day becomes the 14th September under the new Gregorian calendar, bringing our country in line with most of Europe (see 25th March and 14th September).

1807 The bombardment of Copenhagen by the Royal Navy under Admiral James Gambier begins (see 5th September and 7th September) after the Danish refuse to surrender their large fleet. The Danish town and fleet were in danger of falling into French hands and the seizure of the fleet was seen as a preventative measure in the war against Napoleonic France.

1812 The birth of Kirkpatrick Macmillan (see 26th January) in Keir in Dumfries and Galloway.

1834 The death of Thomas Telford in London (see 9th August). Stonemason, architect and civil engineer, he is most famous for his many innovative bridges that can still be seen around the country. Born in Dumfries, he was a stonemason's apprentice and intended to move to London to further his career. In 1787 he became Surveyor of Works in Shrewsbury. In 1793 he was responsible for the Ellesmere Canal and later worked on the Pontcysyllte Aqueduct (1795-1805), the Caledonian Canal (1804-1822), the Menai Suspension Bridge (1819-1826) and many other bridges, aqueducts and roads. He is buried in Westminster Abbey.

1845 The foundation of the Electric Telegraph Company, the first commercial public telegraph company. The company was created by William Fothergill Cooke (see 4th May and 25th June) and John Lewis Ricardo.

1898 The Battle of Omdurman led by Lord Kitchener (see 5th June and 24th June) and the subsequent occupation of Khartoum. Lord Herbert Kitchener led his force of 8,000 British and 17,000 Sudanese and Egyptian soldiers against the Mahdist army of about 50,000 that had killed General 'Chinese' Gordon ten years earlier at Khartoum in 1888 (see 26th January and 28th January). Lord Kitchener organised his forces in an arc around the village of Egegia almost against the River Nile with a flotilla of Gunboats in support. During the battle, Winston Churchill (see 24th January and 30th November) was involved in a cavalry charge against the Dervishes with his Regiment, the 21st Lancers. The British casualties were 28 Officers and men killed and 434 wounded. The Mahdist army lost approximately 9,700 killed, 13,000 wounded and 5,000 captured.

1945 The Japanese Instrument of Surrender is signed aboard the USS Missouri in Tokyo Bay by representatives of the Japanese government, the United Kingdom of Great Britain and Northern Ireland, Canada, Australia, New Zealand, the United States, the Republic of China, the Soviet Union, the Provisional Government of France and the Kingdom of the Netherlands (see 15th February and 25th December). The document formally ended hostilities with Japan and also officially brought to an end the Second World War. Hostilities had already ceased in August with the Japanese Emperor's radio broadcast of his acceptance of surrender (see 15th August and 8th December).

3rd September:

1189 Richard the Lion Heart is crowned king in Westminster Abbey (see 6th April and 8th September).

1650 The Battle of Dunbar is fought. The battle was a two-hour battle launched just before dawn, when the English Parliamentarian Army under Oliver Cromwell (see 25th April and 3rd September) defeated the Scots covenanters under General David Leslie in a resounding victory. Around 3,000 Scots were killed and over 10,000 taken prisoner and officially only around 30 of the English were killed (see 27th April).

1651 The Battle of Worcester and defeat for the Royalists followed by the escape of Charles II (see 6th February and 29th May). This was the final conflict in the English Civil War (see 21st April). The battle commenced outside of the city with the Royalist thrust against the Parliamentarians meeting much initial success. However, just as the Parliamentary forces were beginning to falter, Oliver Cromwell personally rallied his troops and the Royalists were pushed back into Worcester. As the Parliamentarians shelled the city, the Royalist lines collapsed and they were pursued through the city streets and the battle was lost. Most of the Royalist commanders were killed in the battle and Charles II narrowly escaped (see 6th September).

1658 The death of the dictator and regicide, Oliver Cromwell, in Whitehall; God save the King! His son Richard Cromwell is declared 'Lord Protector' (see 25th April and 25th May) upon his death. Born in Huntingdon in Cambridgeshire, he first became a Member of Parliament in 1628 for Huntingdon and became known as a radical puritan. During the Civil War, he created a force of cavalry that were later called the 'Ironsides' and rose swiftly from Captain to Lieutenant General in only three years. He was instrumental in the formation of the professional 'New Model Army' that was responsible for the increasing number of Parliamentary victories. In 1653 he was declared Lord Protector of the Commonwealth of England, Scotland and Ireland 1653 (see 16th December) and in 1657 was offered the Crown which he declined. Following the restoration of the Monarchy (see 29th May) his body was dug up and hanged.

1728 The birth of Matthew Bolton (see 18th August) in Birmingham, engineer and pioneer of the steam engine.

1783 At the signing of the Treaty of Paris, Britain officially grants independence to its 13 rebellious colonies, now known as the United States of America (see 10th February and 4th July).

1916 The first ever Zeppelin to be shot down crashed in Hertfordshire while it was on a raid over England. Captain Leefe Robinson of the Royal Flying Corps (see 1st April and 13th April) won the V.C. for shooting it down (see 19th January).

1935 Sir Malcolm Campbell in his 'Bluebird' Rolls-Royce car breaks the Land speed record for the third and final time at Bonneville Salt Flats in Utah, U.S.A., travelling at 301.13 mph. He was the first man to exceed 300mph (see 4th January and 19th August).

1939 Following Germany's failure to respond to our ultimatum to withdraw from Poland, war is declared on Germany. The Prime Minister, Neville Chamberlain (see 18th March and 9th November), announces the declaration of war to the nation in his famous wireless Broadcast (see 8th May and 15th August). At the same time, the Dominion of Australia, the Dominion of New Zealand and British India declare war on Germany.

1939 Just hours after Britain declares war on Germany, the British liner SS Athenia is torpedoed and sunk by the German submarine U-30 off the North West coast of Scotland. Of the 1,400 passengers and crew aboard, around 120 were killed. This marked the beginning of the battle for the Atlantic and the ship became the first British ship lost in the Second World War (see 17thSeptember).

1943 British 8th Army forces of XIII Corps, consisting of British and Canadian troops, land on the 'toe' of Italy at Reggio di Calabria to begin the allied invasion of mainland Italy under the codename 'Operation Baytown' (see 10th June and 10th September).

1943 Generals representing the new Italian government sign an unconditional Armistice with the Allies on board HMS Nelson off the coast of Cassabile in Sicily. Italian General Giuseppe Castellano signed for Italy and the American General Bedell Smith for the allies. However, the Germans in mainland Italy and some Italian units fight on against the Allies (see 10th June and 10th September).

2007 Moira Cameron becomes the first female Yeoman of the Guard at the Tower of London after spending 22 years in the army.

4th September:

1241 The birth of Alexander III, the future King of Scots, in Roxburgh (see 19th March and 13th July). He was the only son of Alexander II (see 6th July and 24th August) and his second wife, Marie de Coucy.

1607 From the shores of Lough Swilly in Ireland, the Earl of Tyrone and the Earl of Tyrconnel and about 100 of their family and followers left for

Spain in what would be known as 'The Flight of the Earls'. Allegedly in fear of their lives and to avoid arrest, the Earls looked to Spain for shelter and possible support for an invasion of Ireland.

1800 Malta is surrendered to Britain by the French under General Vaubois who are besieged in Valletta following a blockade and bombardment by Admiral Lord Nelson. Shortly afterwards it became a Protectorate and then a Crown Colony at the Treaty of Amiens (see 25th March).

1825 The birth of Dadabhai Naorowji in Bombay (see 30th June).

1912 Twenty-two people are injured when two trains collide on the Piccadilly line, becoming casualties of this country's first London Underground accident.

1964 Elizabeth II (see 21st April) opens the Forth Road Bridge, at the time Europe's longest bridge. It replaced a centuries old ferry service and was, until 2008, a toll bridge.

1981 The start of the Greenham Common protests against the future presence of Nuclear Cruise missiles in Britain. Started outside RAF Greenham Common, a number of women arrived and encamped outside of the base, forming a Peace Camp in protest at the Government's decision to allow Cruise Missiles to be based at the site.

5th September:

1548 The death of Catherine Parr, the sixth and final wife of Henry VIII (see 28th January, 28th June and 12th July). She had been married twice before marrying Henry and had a close relationship with her three step-children, in particular Edward (see 6th July and 12th October) and Elizabeth (see 24th March and 7th September), whom she helped in their education. After Henry's death, she was married for a fourth time to Sir Thomas Seymour but died from complications following childbirth. She was buried at Sudeley Castle in Gloucestershire.

1701 The death of James VII (James II of England) at St. Germain-en-Laye, France (see 23rd April and 14th October), from a brain haemorrhage. The son of Charles I (see 30th January and 19th November), both he and his brother went into exile following their father's murder and served under Marshal of France, Turenne, in the French Army. Later he would serve in the Spanish Army and become acquainted with Irish Catholics in Spanish service. Though raised a Protestant, he later converted to Catholicism sometime after his first marriage to Anne Hyde, possibly as early as 1668. He faced open rebellion by the Duke of Monmouth in 1685 (see 9th April, 6th July and 15th July) which was swiftly put down. Following the birth of a son and successor, James Francis Edward Stuart in 1688 (see 1st January and 10th June), Protestant nobles appealed to William of Orange (see 8th March and 4th November), who landed with a force in November and the 'Glorious Revolution' had begun. James fled to France but in 1690 he landed in Ireland with an army but was defeated at the battle of the Boyne (see 1st July). After that defeat he fled into exile. The last Catholic monarch of this country, he was buried in the Church of the English Benedictines in Paris and later moved to the Parish Church of St. Germain. Sadly, his tomb was despoiled during the French Revolution and his remains were destroyed.

1750 The birth of Robert Fergusson (see 16th October) in Edinburgh.

1774 The first Continental Congress of twelve of the thirteen colonies in North America convenes in Carpenter's Hall, Philadelphia, in Pennsylvania. The Congress lasted until the end of October but had no clear objectives at the beginning. Following much discussion, the fifty-six delegates discussed what was at the time referred to as the 'Intolerable Acts' or the 'Coercive Acts' set by Parliament under Lord North's Premiership. They discussed an economic boycott of British goods and various complaints and grievances (see 22nd March and 1st November) as well as petitioning George III for help (see 29th January and 24th May).

1781 The Battle of Chesapeake and a rare defeat for the Royal Navy. Tactically it was inconclusive but strategically it prevented the supply and reinforcement of Lord Cornwallis at Yorktown, thus contributing to his eventual surrender (see 19th October). Our Fleet of nineteen ships was commanded by Rear Admiral Sir Thomas Graves and the French Fleet of twenty-three ships was commanded by Rear Admiral François Joseph Paul, the Comte de Grasse. Though relatively equal in numbers, the French managed to prevent the British from gaining the advantage and thus a complete victory (see 3rd September).

1807 The bombardment of Copenhagen in the Kingdom of Denmark by the Royal Navy under Admiral James Gambier ceases (see 2nd September). The Danish, under Ernst Peymann, sued for peace, realising that after the death of 2,000 inhabitants, the city could not hold out much longer (see 7th September).

1808 The death of John Home (see 22nd September) near Edinburgh. A poet and dramatist, his best known works included 'Douglas', 'Agis: a tragedy', 'The Siege of Aquileia' and his 'History of the Rebellion of 1745'. In 1758 he became private secretary to Lord Bute, then Secretary of State and was appointed as tutor to the then Prince of Wales.

1982 The death of Group Captain Douglas Robert Steuart Bader from a heart attack (see 21st February and 9th August). He was one of the most famous fighter pilots of the Second World War. He joined the RAF in 1930 but some 18 months later the plane he was flying crashed and, though he survived, he lost both legs. However, during the Second World War he flew in many sorties and was shot down and captured by the Germans and spent time at Colditz Castle. After the war he worked for the Shell Oil Company.

6th September:

1649 The death of Sir Robert Dudley in Italy (see 7th August). He was an explorer and cartographer. The illegitimate son of Sir Robert Dudley, 1st Earl of Leicester, he was born in Richmond Palace. In 1594 he led an expedition to the West Indies and captured a number of Spanish ships. After failing in his attempt at establishing his birth as legitimate, he left England in 1605, never to return. He settled in the Grand Duchy of Tuscany. There he designed and built ships for the Grand Duke. It was here that he produced the 'Del'Arcano del Mare', published in 1645, and the first known atlas of the entire world as it was understood at the time. He died outside Florence in the Grand Duchy of Tuscany.

1651 Charles II (see 6th February and 29th May) spends a night in an Oak tree at Boscobel Hall following defeat at the battle of Worcester (see 3rd September). Having made his way to Boscobel House after the battle, it was deemed too unsafe for him to evade capture in the house. He therefore spent the night in the tree with an assistant before making his escape the following day.

1666 The Fire of London ends (see 2nd September) with only five deaths in total. Over 13,000 houses, 87 churches as well as most of the major buildings in the city were destroyed and thousands were left homeless.

1715 John Erskine, the Earl of Mar and ardent Jacobite, proclaimed James Frances Edward Stewart as James VIII (James III in England see 1st January and 10th June) King of Scotland, England, Ireland and France and raised the old Scottish standard at Braemar, thus beginning the Jacobite rising of 1715 (see 19th August, 13th November and 22nd December).

1766 The birth of John Dalton (see 27th July) in Cumberland.

1852 The country's first free-lending library opens in Campfield in Manchester (see 14th August). In attendance for the opening were Charles Dickens (see 7th February and 9th June), who championed the cause of free public libraries, and fellow author William Makepeace Thackeray (see 18th July and 24th December).

1853 The death of George Bradshaw (see 29th July) from cholera whilst in Oslo, Norway. Moving to Manchester whilst in his teens, George obtained work as an engraver producing maps of canals, railways and rivers. Whilst engaged in this work, he had the idea to form a company to produce the first railway timetables, which he began doing 1838.

1918 The death of Elizabeth Yates (née Oman) in Auckland, New Zealand (see 1st July and 26th September). She was born in Caithness in Scotland sometime after 1840 and moved to New Zealand in 1853. She is known for becoming the first woman across the British Empire to hold the office of Mayor which she achieved in 1893, being sworn in during 1894 (see 16th January).

7th September:

1191 The battle of Arsuf between the Crusader forces led by Richard I (see 6th April) and the armies of Saladin. The Crusaders, who were marching between Acre and Jerusalem, won and though it was not a total victory, it proved that the invincible Saladin could at last be beaten.

1533 The birth of Queen Elizabeth I in the Riverside Palace at Greenwich (see 15th January and 24th March).

1709 The birth of Samuel Johnson in Lichfield (see 15th April and 13th December).

1807 The city of Copenhagen and its massive fleet surrender to our forces under General Lord Cathcart. The city and fleet had been besieged to prevent it falling into Napoleonic French hands (see 2nd September and 5th September). The city had been bombarded since 2nd September in the successful attempt to persuade it to surrender. The fleet that surrendered to the Royal Navy contained eighteen ships of the line, eleven frigates and several other smaller vessels.

1807 The birth of Henry Sewell in Newport on the Isle of Wight (see 7th May and 14th May).

1815 The birth of John McDouall Stuart in Dysart, Scotland (see 15th June).

1836 The birth of Henry Campbell-Bannerman in Glasgow (see 22nd April).

1838 Grace Darling, a lighthouse keeper's daughter, rows out and rescues four men and a woman from the ship 'Forfarshire' which had ran aground off the Northumberland coast.

1870 HMS Captain, the Royal Navy's first turreted warship, sinks. Though still a masted ship, her guns were mounted upon the deck and not within the ship's hull. Whilst cruising off Cape Finisterre with the Channel Squadron, she ran into a storm on the 6th September and in the early hours she became unstable and capsized, with the loss of almost 500 of the crew (see 27th March) including her Captain, Hugh Talbot Burgoyne VC.

1893 The birth of Leslie Hore-Belisha in Devonport in Plymouth (see 16th February).

1895 The birth of Brian Horrocks (see 4th January and 17th September) in Ranikhet in India.

1901 The signing of the Boxer Protocol between the eight powers and the Qing Empire of Imperial China, ending the Boxer Rebellion. The protocol was signed by representatives from Great Britain, Austria-Hungary, France, Germany, United States, Italy, Japan and Russia, known as the Eight-State Alliance (see 20th June and 14th August).

1917 The birth of Geoffrey Leonard Cheshire, the future Second World War fighter ace who won the V.C. (see 31st July) in Chester. He and his wife Sue Ryder founded the Cheshire Foundation Home for the terminally ill in 1948.

1940 The first night of the Blitz as the Luftwaffe begin bombing London as the first city targeted amongst many up and down the country (see 13th March, 14th March, 24th April, 14th November and 29th December). The bombing raids were aimed at strategic targets as well as being designed to break the British population's morale but met with utter failure.

8th September:

1157 The birth of Richard 'the Lion Heart' (Coeur de Lion see 6th April and 3rd September) in Oxford, the third son of Henry II (see 4th March and 6th July) and Eleanor of Aquitaine.

1664 New Amsterdam, capital of the Dutch colony of New Netherland, is formally surrendered to an English squadron of four ships under the command of Richard Nicolls (see 27th August).

1760 The city of Montreal surrenders to our forces under General Jeffrey Amherst. Following the battle of Restigouche (see 3rd July and 8th July) where the Royal Navy intercepted a flotilla of supply ships and prevented them from supplying their troops, and with the city surrounded by three British armies totalling 17,000 men, the Governor Marquis de Vaudreuil decided the position was hopeless and sought terms, then surrendered the city (see 10th February and 18th September).

1798 The battle of Ballinamuck in County Longford, the last large battle of the Irish rebellion results in final defeat for the French backed force (see 24th May). British forces were led by General Lake and Viceroy Lord Cornwallis. Following a brief artillery bombardment followed by a charge from the Dragoons, the Irish rebels and their French allies capitulated. The captured French soldiers, including their leader General Jean Humbert, were eventually repatriated in exchange for British prisoners. The Irish prisoners were in the main all executed for their treachery (see 21st June and 22nd August).

1888 The body of Annie Chapman is discovered in the yard of 29 Hanbury Street, in Whitechapel in London. She is believed to have been Jack the Ripper's second victim (see 31st August, 30th September and 9th November).

1921 The birth of Harry Donald Secombe (see 11th April and 28th May) in Swansea, Wales.

1925 The birth of Richard Henry 'Peter' Sellers (see 28th May and 24th July) in Portsmouth.

1944 The first German V2 rocket launched against Great Britain lands in London. It came down in Chiswick, killing three people (see 10th November).

9th September:

1087 The death of William I, Duke of Normandy (later known as 'The Conqueror', see 14th October), in Rouen, France, from injuries received following a fall from his horse. Born in Falaise in Normandy to Robert I, Duke of Normandy, and his mistress, he was often referred to as William the Bastard. He became Duke of Normandy on his father's death in 1035. In

1066, on the death of Edward the Confessor (see 5th January), William claimed he had been declared by Edward as his heir and that Harold had usurped his rightful position. He thus began invasion plans (see 28th September) and upon his successful invasion, was crowned in Westminster Abbey (see 25th December). Following his coronation, the first twenty years of his reign were spent crushing resistance, in particular in the north of England and also invading Scotland. In 1086 he ordered the survey of his Kingdom, later referred to as the 'Domesday Book'. The final fifteen years of his rule were spent in Normandy securing his possessions on the continent.

1513 The Battle of Flodden Field in Northumberland and the death of James IV of Scotland (see 17th March and 11th June). King James IV led the invading Scots army of around 30,000, including about 5,000 French, into England to honour the 'Auld Alliance'. The English army of around 25,000 led by Thomas Howard, the seventy-year-old Earl of Surrey, confronted the Scots and delivered a crushing defeat upon them. The Scottish king, James IV, was killed in the battle along with many of his Scottish Nobles. This was the largest battle fought between the two countries and the last time any British monarch was killed in battle. The English lost around 1,500 killed and the Scots about 10,000 in total. James' son acceded to the throne as James V (see 10th April and 14th December). James IV is regarded as the first true Renaissance King of Scotland and was a patron of the arts and sciences and under his rule brought peace and stability to his Kingdom, bringing an end to the influence of the Lords of the Isles. He married Margaret Tudor (see 8th August), the sister of Henry VIII of England (see 28th January and 28th June).

1543 Mary Queen of Scots is crowned in the chapel at Stirling Castle at the age of only 9 months (see 8th February, 13th May and 8th December).

1583 The death of Sir Humphrey Gilbert on his return to England after claiming Newfoundland for the Crown (see 5th August), England's first Colony and thus the start of our Empire. Born in Devon, he had a military career and financial interests in Ireland and later became a Member of Parliament. A champion of the search for the fabled North West passage, he set out to claim as much land for the Queen as possible. Due to a lack of supplies, no settlement was attempted in the New Found Land and on the return journey the ship he was commanding, the 'Squirrel', was lost with all hands.

1754 The birth of William Bligh (see 28th April and 7th December) in Plymouth.

1834 The death of James Weddell (see 24th August) in London. A Naval Officer, navigator, seal hunter and explorer he is famous for his voyages into the Antarctic, where in 1823 he travelled the furthest south anyone had travelled since Captain James Cook (see 14th February and 27th October). The Weddell Sea, part of the Southern Ocean, is named after him.

1855 The last remnants of the city of Sebastopol held by the Russians during the Crimean War (1853-1856) finally falls to British and French forces as the Russians abandon their positions and scuttle and burn the last of their

Black Sea fleet in their escape. The majority of the city had fallen the previous day (see 28th March and 30th March).

1864 The final day of the Charlottetown Conference ends in Charlottetown on Prince Edward Island (see 1st September). In attendance were representatives of New Brunswick, Nova Scotia, Prince Edward Island and the Province of Canada. The meeting was initially arranged to discuss a Maritime Union between the three Colonies, with the Province of Canada as observers. However, it quickly became a full discussion on British North American Union (see 1st July). When the conference was adjourned, it was agreed that the idea of a Union was viable and it was followed by more meetings across the Colonies.

1903 The Colonial Secretary, Joseph Chamberlain, submits a letter of resignation to the Prime Minister over the tariff reform debate (see 2nd July and 8th July) and his desire for Imperial Preference.

1907 The issuing of the Royal Proclamation of Edwards VII (see 6th May and 9th November), announcing Dominion status within the Empire to the colony of New Zealand which would take effect on 26th September of that year (see 6th February).

1950 The rationing of soap finally comes to an end (see 8th January, 9th February, 4th July, 9th July and 3rd October).

2015 at 5.30pm, Elizabeth II (see 6th February, 21st April and 2nd June) becomes the nation's, the Empire's and the Commonwealth's longest reigning monarch as she exceeds the reign of her great-great grandmother Queen Victoria (see 22nd January, 24th May, 20th June and 28th June).

10th September:

1547 The Battle of Pinkie Cleugh near Musselburgh and defeat for the Scots. It came as the culmination to a conflict that broke out as a result of Henry VIII (see 28th January and 28th June) attempting to force the Scots to accept a marriage alliance between his son, the future Edward VI (see 6th July and 12th October) and Mary, Queen of Scots (see 8th February and 8th December), in order to eventually unite the two kingdoms. The English had marched north under the Duke of Somerset up to the River Esk. The Scots, under the Earl of Arran, advanced to meet them but under sustained artillery and naval fire (from English ships nearby) they took heavy casualties and then broke and fled. Though suffering a complete rout, the Scottish government refused to submit to the English and Mary Queen of Scots was smuggled out to France. The English occupied much of southern Scotland until the Treaty of Norham in 1551 (see 10th June). This was the last battle between England and Scotland before the unification of the crowns in 1603.

1711 The South Sea Company is granted its charter. Designed primarily to reduce the national debt, the company was granted the monopoly of trade with South America. Company stock rose in such value that it was unable to maintain the rise and the company finally collapsed in what is referred to as the 'South Sea Bubble' (see 11th June).

1759 The Battle of Pondicherry during the Seven Years' War, 1756-1763. Vice-Admiral George Pocock defeats the French Admiral D'Ache. Our forces lost 569 killed and wounded against the French 886 killed and wounded. Our ships were too damaged to pursue the French but it was a victory for our Fleet nevertheless.

1797 The death of Mary Wollstonecraft (see 27th April) in London of septicaemia following the birth of her second child. An early advocate of women's education and liberty, she is known for her two best works 'A Vindication of the Rights of Men' published in 1790 and 'A Vindication of the Rights of Women' published in 1792. She railed against marriage, Monarchy and championed social equality between men and women, causing much controversy at the time. Following public criticism, she moved to France in 1793 and there had her first child. Eventually she returned to England and in 1797 she married William Godwin (see 3rd March and 7th April) and had her second child soon afterwards. Her child was healthy but the placenta remained in the womb and this caused the blood poisoning from which she died.

1814 The launch of HMS Saint Lawrence at the Royal Naval Kingston Dockyard in Kingston, Ontario in Upper Canada where it was built. A 100-gun first-rate three-decker capital ship of the line, it was the only ship of the line launched by the Royal Navy to operate entirely on fresh water. She served on Lake Ontario towards the end of the 1812 war with America. Control of the lake had passed between both sides until the launch of the ship from which time onwards control of the lake rested firmly with Britain (see 18th June and 24th December).

1816 The birth of John Pender in the Vale of Leven (see 7th July).

1842 The death of William Hobson, the first Governor of New Zealand (see 26th September) in Auckland, New Zealand, from a stroke. Born in Waterford, Ireland, he joined the Royal Navy in 1803 and saw service during the Napoleonic wars. In 1836 he arrived in Australia and helped survey areas of the coast. Hobson's Bay, now part of Melbourne, was named after him. In 1837 he went to New Zealand, eventually becoming the first Governor in 1841 (see 3rd May).

1943 Several ships of the Italian Fleet, the Regia Marina, surrender at Valetta in Malta as part of the agreement within the armistice signed between the Allied armed forces and Italy (see 3rd September).

1967 Gibraltar holds a referendum over the question of whether to pass to Spanish Sovereignty or to retain their link with Great Britain. The result was a massive majority of 99% voting to remain under British sovereignty, much to the annoyance of the Spanish (see 7th February, 31st March, 24th July and 7th November). This date has subsequently been celebrated as Gibraltar's 'National Day'.

2000 Operation Barras is carried out. Units of the SAS, SBS and members of the 1st Parachute Regiment rescue six British Soldiers of the Royal Irish Regiment who were being held by Sierra Leone rebels called the 'West Side Boys'. In a heroic attack, they were flown in by helicopter, extracted the captives and withdrew in less than two hours. Dozens of rebels were killed with unfortunately one British soldier killed and twelve injured.

11th September:

1297 The Battle of Stirling Bridge and William Wallace (see 3rd August and 23rd August) and Andrew Morray defeat the English. The Scots waited on the north side of the River Forth and as the English vanguard crossed, they attacked from high ground cutting them off. The Scots devastated the English spearhead and the rest of the English army, under John de Warenne, 7th Earl of Surrey, panicked and retreated. The Scots casualties are unknown but the English suffered around 5,000 infantry dead and around 100 cavalry dead as well as Hugh de Cressingham.

1649 The end of the siege of Drogheda by Parliamentarian forces under Oliver Cromwell (see 25th April and 3rd September) as the town is taken by force. Around 3,500 defenders and residents died in the assault and the subsequent destruction following the collapse of the defence. Around 150 Parliamentarian besiegers died after the garrison had refused terms offered by Cromwell (see 12th August, 15th August and 22nd October) and around 3,500 Royalists were killed in the massacre that followed the fall of the town, many of whom were prisoners.

1709 The Battle of Malplaquet in France during the War of the Spanish Succession, 1701-1714, where the Duke of Marlborough defeats the French (see 26th May and 16th June). This was his last battle. On the side of the Allies were the Hanoverians, Austrians, Dutch, Prussians and Danes against a combined force of French and Bavarians. The French and their Bavarian allies lost around 15,000 men and the Allies lost around 17,000 men.

1771 The birth of Mungo Park near Selkirk. One of the greatest Scottish explorers of Africa, he is believed to be the first westerner to have come across the Niger River. He led two expeditions to the Niger, discovering it on the first. It was on his second expedition in 1806 that, in an attempt to escape the hostility of a group of natives, he and the remainder of his party were drowned, the exact date being unknown.

1777 The Battle of Brandywine Creek, Pennsylvania, where George Washington (see 11th February and 14th December) and his traitorous rebel army is defeated. Around 6,000 British and Hessians led by Major General Sir William Howe faced 8,000 rebels led by the so-called General Washington. The rebels were driven off the field of battle with a loss of 1,000 men killed, wounded or captured. Our forces lost 550 men killed and wounded.

1877 The death of William Henry Fox Talbot (see 11th February) in Lacock in Wiltshire. A scientist, archaeologist, astronomer, mathematician and Member of Parliament, he is remembered for his pioneering work in photography. Born in Melbury in Dorset, he studied at Cambridge University and in 1932 he became an MP. In 1833 whilst on holiday, he began to think about a machine that would take images instead of an artist recording them. During his work he developed the three main areas of photography, developing, fixing and then printing. In 1839 he reported his discoveries to the Royal Society. He also realised that he could make several images from the one negative and in 1841 patented the process and idea he called 'calotype'.

1898 The birth of Gerald Walter Robert Templer in Colchester (see 25th October).

1950 The death of Field Marshal and former Prime Minister of South Africa, Jan Christiaan Smuts at Doornkloof, South Africa (see 24th May). Though he was a very successful Boer rebel leader against Britain in the Second Boer War (1899-1902), he recognised that the future for South Africa lay in closer co-operation with Britain. He later joined the army and fought for the Empire in the Great War, serving with distinction and became a Field Marshal. He was a signatory in the Peace Treaties of both the World Wars, becoming the only person to hold such a position.

1997 The Scottish people go to the polls to vote in Scotland's Devolution Referendum. Voters were asked two questions: whether here should be a Scottish Parliament and whether that Parliament should have tax-raising powers. The result was a 'yes' to both questions. The majority was 74.3% and 63.5% respectively to the questions (see 1st March, 6th May and 7th May).

12th September:

1609 Henry Hudson sails into New York harbour and then a further 150 miles up the river, later to be called the 'Hudson River', in his ship the 'Half Moon' (see 22nd June).

1814 The death of General Robert Ross from wounds received the same day during the battle of North Point, part of the larger battle of Baltimore. Born in 1766 in County Down in Ireland, he joined the army in 1789. He served during the Napoleonic Wars and in North America during the war with America, 1812-1815. He led our forces at the glorious capture and destruction of the American capital Washington (see 24th August) which met with no resistance from the ramshackle American army whose President had fled in panic. It was at the start of the battle of Baltimore that he was shot by a sniper and died from the wound. He was buried in Halifax, Nova Scotia.

1852 The birth of Herbert Henry Asquith (see 15th February) in Morley, Yorkshire.

1869 The death of Peter Mark Roget in West Malvern in Worcestershire (see 18th January). Born in London, he studied medicine and graduated in

1798, later being made a fellow of the Royal Society. He had a wide range of interests both medical and scientific and later began to compile a dictionary of synonyms for his own use, but which was later published in 1852 as 'Roget's Thesaurus of English Words and Phrases'.

1897 The battle of Saragarhi in the North West Frontier of British India during the Tirah Expedition (1897-1898). It was a heroic last stand by twenty-one members of the 36th Sikh Regiment against around 10,000 rebel Pushtuns. The Sepoys, led by Havildar Ishar Singh, were surrounded in the small square block-house piquet by the 10,000 tribesmen who repeatedly attacked and attempted to force their way in. With no hope of rescue, they stood firm but after six hours, the siege ended with each of the Sepoys having fought to the death, killing up to 600 tribesmen in the process. All twenty-one of those killed were posthumously awarded the Indian Order of Merit.

1942 The RMS Laconia, carrying civilians, British and Polish troops and Italian PoWs is torpedoed off the coast off West Africa by the German U-Boat U-156 with a heavy loss of life. Before the ship went down, the U-boat surfaced and began to rescue the survivors as other U-boats joined in the rescue. As the operation proceeded and despite signals from the U-Boat, American Liberator bombers began to attack the submarine, even though it was a Red Cross sanctioned rescue and the U-boats were displaying the Red Cross sign.

13th September:

1759 The Battle of the Plains of Abraham outside of the city of Quebec where General James Wolfe defeats the French under General Montcalm. Both Wolfe and Montcalm died in the battle (see 22nd December). The previous day, troops under General Wolfe had crossed the St Lawrence River and landed under cover of darkness. The troops scaled the cliffs and formed up at the top. The French under Montcalm approached from Quebec. They fired early but our forces were lying down to avoid the shot. As the enemy approached, our forces rose and fired two brief volleys into the French which took a heavy toll on the French forces. As our forces advanced, the French were forced to retire from the field. In the fray, Wolfe was injured and both he and Montcalm were mortally wounded. The battle led to the surrender of the city of Quebec and ultimately to Canada coming under the British Empire (see 10th February and 18th September). James Wolfe had joined the army at thirteen and went on to see service in the War of the Austrian Succession (1740-1748) at the battle of Dettingen in 1743 (see 16th June), and the Seven Years' War (1756-1763), as well being present at the battle of Culloden in 1745 (see 16th April).

1775 The birth of Laura Secord in Massachusetts (see 17th October).

1806 The death of Charles James Fox MP, in the Duke of Devonshire's house in London (24th January). In his early years he was a gambler running up huge debts. He entered Parliament in 1768 and in 1782 he became the country's first Foreign Secretary under Lord Rockingham as Prime Minister. He supported the American rebels in their revolt against British rule and was openly critical and hostile to George III (see 29th January and 24th May). He was buried in Westminster Abbey next to his arch political enemy, William Pitt the Younger (see 23rd January and 28th May).

1882 The battle of Tel el-Kabir in Egypt. A British force, led by Lieutenant General Garnet Wolseley (see 25th March and 4th June) and consisting of over 18,000 men, attacked an Egyptian force of around 15,000 men. The resulting battle, led by a Highland Brigade bayonet charge on the enemy lines cost us over 500 killed and about 340 wounded whilst the Egyptians lost about 1,300 killed and over 680 wounded. The result of the victory allowed British influence in Egypt to continue until 1956 (see 11th July).

1914 The start of the Battle of the Aisne. It was here that 'trench warfare' was started as the Germans retreated and 'dug in' to face the British Expeditionary Force (BEF) and the French Fifth and Sixth Armies who likewise dug in to form the early trench systems that quickly became such a symbol of the Great War. The Germans held their positions on the north side of the River Aisne as the BEF crossed and attempted to advance on the enemy (see 4th August, 23rd August and 11th November).

14th September:

1402 The battle of Homildon Hill in Northumbria. A Scottish Army led by the Earl of Douglas, returning from pillaging the North of England, is attacked and totally routed by an English army led by Henry 'Hotspur' Percy. Thousands of Scots were killed and many Nobles taken prisoner, including the Earl of Douglas.

1752 The first day of the Gregorian calendar in this country. The previous day was the 2nd September 1752 and the last day of the Julian calendar. The Gregorian calendar was at this point officially adopted throughout Great Britain and our Empire, some 200 years after most of Europe (see 25th March).

1852 The death of Augustus Welby Northmore Pugin (see 1st March) in Ramsgate. The recognised leader of the Gothic revival movement his most famous works were the new Houses of Parliament and St. Giles Church in Cheadle, Staffordshire.

1852 The death of the Field Marshal Arthur Wellesley aged 83 in Walmer in Kent (see 1st May). The 1st Duke of Wellington (Tory Prime Minister from 1828 to 1830) was one of our greatest military leaders, a national hero and the saviour of Europe. He led the British and Allied forces during the Napoleonic Wars and achieved some glorious victories at Talavera in 1809 (see 28th July), Salamanca in 1812 (see 22nd July), Vitoria in 1813 (see 21st June) and Waterloo in 1815 (see 18th June). After his illustrious military career, he turned to politics, becoming Prime Minister for two years in 1828. About his first cabinet meeting as Prime Minister he said 'an extraordinary affair, I gave them their orders and they wanted to stay and discuss them'.

1857 The assault on the city of Delhi to bring the siege to a culmination begins as our forces heroically attempt to capture the city from Indian rebels. The city had been under siege by British and East India Company troops led by Brigadier John Nicholson and for the assault, the force was divided into five columns that attacked the city simultaneously (see 10th May).

1918 The death of Clementina Trentholme Fessenden (see 4th May) in Hamilton, Ontario. As a life-long advocate of the Empire, she continually sought ways to maintain the Empire and Canada's connection to it. She modelled herself on Queen Victoria, including dressing in the formal black mourning attire following the death of her own husband as Victoria did following the death of Prince Albert. In 1898 she was responsible for the institution of the very first Empire Day (see 24th May) in Ontario on the last school day before the 24th May.

15th September: Battle of Britain Day.

1762 The battle of Signal Hill near St. John's, Newfoundland, the last battle of the Seven Years' War in North America (1756-1763). Our forces, commanded by Colonel William Amherst, climbed the hill at dawn and with complete surprise stormed the French positions and regained the hill after a swift action. The remnants of the French withdrew to St John's and surrendered three days later (see 10th February and 17th May).

1859 The death of Isambard Kingdom Brunel (see 9th April) aboard his steamship the 'Great Eastern' following a stroke. Born in Portsmouth to a French Father, he was educated in both England and France. He was the most famous of all engineers and is known for his tunnels, viaducts and bridges along many miles of railway, in particular the Great Western Railway as well as the Clifton suspension bridge and other numerous important bridges, and the redesigning and building of many docks around the country, thus revolutionising our transport system. He also excelled in ship design and construction with his three famous ships: the Great Western (1837), Great Britain (1843) and the Great Eastern (1859).

1864 The death of John Hanning Speke (see 4th May). Born in Devon, he was one of the leading African explorers of his day. He was an Army Officer, commissioned in 1844, and took part in three voyages to Africa and was a friend, colleague and later rival of Richard Burton (see 19th March and 20th October). He was wounded during an expedition exploring Somaliland and after recovering he served during the Crimean War (1853-1856). In 1862 he discovered and named Lake Victoria (see 28th July) and on the same expedition at Lake Victoria, he discovered the source of the River Nile, though for years it remained a source of much controversy. He died from a gunshot wound whilst out hunting. It is uncertain whether it was accidental or suicide.

1916 The first use of tanks in battle. Forty-nine MKI tanks were deployed during the Somme offensive (see 1ˢᵗ July and 18ᵗʰ November) at the battle of Flers-Courcelette. Originally referred to as 'land ships', their effectiveness was less than satisfactory. Of the forty-nine, thirty-two made it into the battle but seven of those failed to start. Tactically they were of limited benefit but psychologically their effect was tremendous. The enemy soldiers were terrified and some fled in panic at their first sight of the machines (see 28ᵗʰ July and 20ᵗʰ November).

1931 The Invergordon Mutiny in the Royal Navy begins over pay cuts. It is to be the last ever mutiny in the Royal Navy and concludes the following day. Over 1,000 ratings refused to put to sea. The disturbances were due the National Government's decision to impose a 10% pay cut on all public sector workers, including the armed services. Some new entrants would face a 25% cut in their wages (see 16ᵗʰ September).

1940 And all subsequent years is celebrated as 'Battle of Britain Day'. About the RAF, it was said that "Never in the field of human conflict was so much owed by so many to so few" (Winston Churchill, 20ᵗʰ August 1940). On this day the Royal Air Force declares an end to the Battle of Britain and provides a breathing space for our country. Despite an overwhelming numerical advantage in aircraft, the Luftwaffe was seen off by the fighters, pilots and personnel of the RAF in their heroic defence of our country. In all subsequent years, this day is one of commemoration as the day the RAF saved our Great Nation from German invasion.

16ᵗʰ September:

1400 Owain Glyndwr proclaims himself Prince of Wales, leading to the last Welsh rebellion against English rule, which would last until 1409. Born in the late 1350s in the Welsh Marches between England and Wales, as a young man he served the English King Richard II (see 6ᵗʰ January). Following the usurpation of Richard and the success of Henry IV (see 20ᵗʰ March and 4ᵗʰ April), Owain was proclaimed Prince of Wales and the revolt began.

1812 The birth of Robert Fortune in Berwickshire (see 13ᵗʰ April).

1858 The birth of Andrew Bonar Law in Rexton in the Colony of New Brunswick (see 22ⁿᵈ May and 30ᵗʰ October).

1931 The Invergordon Mutiny comes to an end, having started the previous day. The last ever mutiny in the Royal Navy, it was about pay cuts from between 10% and 25%, with those rated below Petty Officer receiving even greater cuts. The 'strike action' did not involve any other issue and involved members from the crews of a number of ships, totalling over 1,000 men (see 15ᵗʰ September).

1963 The Colonies of North Borneo and Sarawak are granted their independence as they become part of Malaysia (see 31ˢᵗ August). However, a native mob of 100,000 then riots and burns down the British Embassy in the

Indonesian capital Jakarta with little or no attempt to intervene by the incompetent local 'Police and Authorities'.

1968 The Post Office begins its two-tier postal system. First class post for delivery the next working days costs 5d and second class post costs 4d (see 10th January).

1992 'Black Wednesday': in political and economic terms when Britain withdraws from the European Exchange Rate Mechanism (ERM) under the Chancellor of the Exchequer Norman Lamont, abandoning steps towards European monetary union (see 1st January).

17th September:

1677 The birth of Stephen Hales in Kent (see 4th January).

1771 The death of Tobias George Smollett (see 19th March) in the Grand Duchy of Tuscany. A renowned Scottish author, he is most remembered for 'The Adventures of Roderick Random' and 'The Adventures of Peregrine Pickle'. He qualified as a surgeon at the University of Glasgow before he obtained a Commission in the Royal Navy as a ships Surgeon and served for a number of years before retiring. He set up a practice in Downing Street before becoming successful as an author.

1939 The aircraft carrier HMS Courageous is sunk by the German U-boat U-29 and becomes the first major Royal Navy ship to be sunk during the Second World War (see 3rd September, 14th October and 10th December). Courageous had been a battleship launched in 1916 and saw action in the Great War. In the 1920s she was converted to an Aircraft carrier.

1944 Operation 'Market Garden' begins, leading to the battle at Arnhem in Holland. Around 10,000 British and Polish troops land by parachute and glider around the town of Arnhem. By the end of the ultimately failed operation, only around 2,000 escape. Of the rest, the majority are either killed or captured by the enemy (see 26th September).

1993 The British National Party wins its first Council seat in a by-election in Milwall, East London.

18th September:

1759 The French city of Quebec, capital of 'New France' formally surrenders following the battle of the Plains of Abraham (see 13th September) and is handed over to British forces, controversially under very generous capitulation terms (see 10th February).

1830 The death of William Hazlitt (see 10th April) in London. A political essayist, he was a friend of many of the more famous literary writers and philosophers of his day. Considered a radical, he was an outspoken opponent of William Pitt (see 23rd January and 28th May), Britain's war with France and the taxation imposed to pay for it. He was also critical of political corruption and was an early exponent of reform of the voting system. His first book, 'An Essay on the Principles of Human Action' was published in 1830.

1860 The death of Joseph Locke (see 9th August). He was a civil engineer and one of the leading pioneers of the railways. He was responsible for the Manchester and Sheffield Railway as well as other major lines and numerous bridges. His early career saw him working with George Stephenson (see 9th June and 12th August) on a number of his projects and his most well-known achievement was the Grand Junction Railway. It was over eighty-two miles long and connected Birmingham to the Liverpool and Manchester line, opening in 1837 (4th July). He is buried in London.

1898 The 'Fashoda incident', at Fashoda on the banks of the Nile in the Sudan. Our troops, aboard a flotilla of gun boats under the command of Lord Herbert Kitchener (see 5th June and 24th June), arrive at the fort where French forces had already been in the town since July. Neither our forces nor the French, under Major Jean-Baptiste Marchand, would back down to begin with. However, Lord Kitchener defused the situation and the French eventually withdrew a few months later after the French government ordered Marchand to leave. However, the peaceable resolution between both the governments and military forces ultimately laid the foundations for the beginning of the Entente Cordial (see 4th November). This was the last major military incident between Great Britain and France (see 8th April).

1955 The island of Rockall, in the North Atlantic Ocean and 290 miles to Britain's west, is claimed for Great Britain. Three naval personnel, an officer, two NCOs and a civilian are put ashore by helicopter and raise the flag of the Union and affix a plaque claiming the island for this country.

1967 The death of Sir John Douglas Cockroft (see 27th May) in Cambridge. Along with Ernest Walton, he was the recipient of the Nobel Prize for Physics for his work on splitting the atom. His work was instrumental in the development of nuclear power. He had served during the Great War in the Royal Artillery after which he obtained a degree at Cambridge University. He went on to work under Ernest Rutherford (see 30th August and 19th October) and progressed to working on Britain's early atomic power programme.

1997 The Welsh people go to the polls to vote in the Welsh Devolution Referendum. Voters were asked one question: Should Wales have a devolved Assembly? The result was only just a 'yes' to the question with a 50.3% majority of those who voted in favour (see 1st March).

2014 The Scottish referendum on independence from the United Kingdom is held (see 1st May and 15th October). The question was 'Should Scotland be an independent country?' with a simple 'yes' or 'no' to decide. A total of 97% of the eligible population registered to vote with 16 and 17 year olds voting for the first time. The result was declared the following morning (see 19th September).

19th September:

1356 The Battle of Poitiers in France. Edward, Prince of Wales (later known as the 'Black Prince', see 8th June and 15th June), defeats the French in the second of the three great English victories of the Hundred Years' War, Crecy in 1346 (see 26th August), Poitiers and Agincourt, 1415 (see 25th October). Our English forces numbered up to 8,000 and the French well over 20,000. Taking a defensive position, the English used their archers well, destroying the first wave of French Cavalry. The next wave on foot was once again wiped out by the skill of the archers. As the third and final wave of French troops advanced into a hail of arrows, the French will was already broken and the survivors fled the field, now littered with the dead and dying French soldiers and nobility. By the time the battle was over, English casualties were minimal but the French suffered around 3,000 killed and many more wounded and the French king, John II, his son and many of his nobles were taken captive (see 8th May).

1893 The Colony of New Zealand becomes the first country in the world to grant women the vote when Lord Glasgow, the Governor, signs the Electoral Act, giving it Royal Assent and bringing it into law (see 6th February, 9th September, 26th September and 11th December).

1944 The death of Wing Commander Guy Penrose Gibson (see 12th August) and Squadron Leader James Warwick on active service as their De Havilland Mosquito crashes in the Netherlands. Gibson was famous for being the Commanding Officer of Operation Chastise (see 16th May), often referred to as the 'Dam Busters Raid'. Gibson was born in Simla, India, and joined the RAF in 1936. On the outbreak of war he joined Bomber Command but transferred to Fighter Command. A couple of years later he went back to Bomber Command and eventually took command of 617 Squadron. For his role in the Dam Busters Raid he was awarded the Victoria Cross. In June 1944 he returned to active service and flew with 627 Squadron when he was killed.

2014 The result of the Scottish referendum on independence from the United Kingdom is declared with 55% voting 'no' and to remain part of the United Kingdom and 45% voting 'yes' for independence (see 1st May, 1st July, 18th September and 15th October). The United Kingdom of Great Britain and Northern Ireland is saved.

20th September:

1502 The birth of Arthur Tudor (see 2nd April), Prince of Wales and eldest son of Henry VII (see 28th January and 21st April) and Elizabeth of York and the elder brother of the future Henry VIII (see 28th January and 28th June) at Winchester (see 11th June).

1643 The first battle of Newbury in Berkshire during the Civil Wars. The two armies, the Royalists under Charles I (see 30th January and 19th November) and Prince Rupert (see 29th November and 17th December) against the Parliamentarians under the Earl of Essex were fairly evenly matched. However, as night fell, King Charles decided not to continue the engagement the following day and withdrew to Oxford, leaving the road to London open, much to the surprise of the Parliamentarians. The casualties were large with an even amount on both sides totalling about 3,500 men.

1854 The Battle of Alma, the first battle during the Crimean War (1853-1856). The battle was between British, French and Turkish troops against the Imperial Russian Army. It was a resounding victory for the allies with the Russian casualties numbering around 5,700 and British casualties 2,000. However, the French did not follow up the victory when urged to do so, thus ensuring that it was not a decisive victory and so lengthening the Crimean War (see 28th March, 30th March, 25th October and 5th November).

1857 Following a lengthy siege by our forces of the city of Delhi, which was in the hands of treacherous Indian sepoy rebels, the city is overrun by our troops under the command of Brigadier John Nicholson (see 14th September) and the city finally relieved.

1933 The death of Annie Besant (nee Wood) in India (see 1st October). A socialist, women's rights activist and orator, she left her husband, co-edited the National Reformer and became Vice President of the National Secular Society. In 1875 Annie and a close friend published a treatise on birth control for which they were both convicted of obscenity. In 1885 she joined the Fabian Society and became involved in many union activities and strikes, including the match girl strikes of 1888. In 1889 she went to live in India and became an open critic of Imperialism and an advocate of Home Rule.

21st September:

1327 Edward II, known as Edward of Carnarvon, dies at Berkeley Castle (see 25th April). The son of Edward I, he became the Prince of Wales in 1301, the first holder of the title to cover all of Wales (see 7th February). His reign was marked by conflict with his nobles, primarily because of his reliance on his favourites. In 1314 he attempted to invade Scotland but was decisively beaten at Bannockburn by Robert the Bruce (see 23rd June and 24th June). Edward's wife, Isabella, became more politically ambitious, and after becoming the mistress of Edward's enemy, they invaded England in 1326 (see 24th September). There was little resistance and Edward was deposed in January 1327 (see 20th January) in favour of his wife and their son, Edward III (see 21st June and 13th November).

1745 The Battle of Prestonpans and victory for the Jacobite forces. The government forces of 2,300 faced the Highland army of 2,500. The Jacobites lost less than 30 killed and 70 wounded and the Government lost around 300 killed, 400 to 500 wounded and 1,400 to 1,500 taken as prisoners whilst the few left were completely routed. The government forces were commanded by Sir John Cope, the Commander in Chief of Scotland, and faced a ferocious

Highland Charge and it as at this point that the government troops turned and fled (see 16th April and 19th August).

1756 The birth of John Loudon McAdam (see 26th November) in Ayr, Scotland.

1832 The death of Sir Walter Scott, Scottish novelist and poet (see 15th August) in Abbotsford, Melrose. Perhaps one of the most well-known of Scottish writers, he is famous for a number of works, including 'Ivanhoe', 'Lady of the Lake', 'Rob Roy', 'Waverley', 'The Bride of Lammermoor' and 'The Heart of Midlothian'. His first success came with his poetry and later with his works of historical fiction. In 1809 he helped establish the Quarterly Review and in 1820 he was raised to a Baronet.

1857 The city of Delhi is finally declared to be captured from the Indian Mutineers who had taken it in May following a brief siege (see 10th May and 14th September) and a heroic storming of the city walls. Following the capture of the city, many rebels were executed in retribution for their savage and inhuman treatment of the Europeans that they had captured and then murdered.

1866 The birth of Herbert George Wells (see 13th August) in Bromley in Kent.

1964 The island of Malta gains its independence. The island had become part of the Empire as a result of the Treaty of Paris in 1814 (see 30th May). The island was collectively awarded the George Cross (see 15th April) by George VI (see 6th February and 14th December) for their heroic resistance against intense German and Italian attacks during the Second World War.

22nd September:

1515 The birth of Anne of Cleaves in Dusseldorf, Duchy of Berg in the Rhineland, the daughter of John II (see 6th January, 9th July and 16th July).

1722 The birth of John Home (see 5th September) in Leith near Edinburgh.

1735 Sir Robert Walpole becomes the First Prime Minister to reside at 10 Downing Street (see 18th March and 26th August).

1761 George III is crowned at Westminster Abbey (see 29th January and 24th May) aged 22 with his wife, Charlotte of Mecklenburg-Strelitz.

1791 The birth of Michael Faraday in Newington Butts (now the Elephant and Castle), London. He was appointed Chemical Assistant at the Royal Institution on 1st March 1813 (see 25th August).

1880 The birth of Christabel Pankhurst (future suffragist) in Manchester. She was the daughter of Emmeline Pankhurst, the leading suffragist of the time (see 13th February).

1914 Three Crecy-class armoured cruisers of the Royal Navy, the Flag Ship HMS Aboukir, HMS Hogue and HMS Crecy are attacked and sunk by the German Submarine U-9 in the North Sea, off the coast of the Netherlands. All three cruisers were part of the 7th Cruiser Squadron in the North Sea and were manned primarily by reservists. Around 1,450 sailors were killed in the attack and the reputation of the Royal Navy was badly damaged for sometime afterwards (see 31st May, 1st November and 8th December).

1943 In a heroically daring raid called Operation Source, six British midget submarines set out to attack the German Battle Ship Tirpitz in a heavily guarded Norwegian Fjord. Three submarines, X8, X9 and X10 did not make it to the target but three, X5, X6 and X7, did reach their objective and in the attack the Tirpitz was badly damaged (see 12th November).

23rd September:

1459 The Battle of Blore Heath in Staffordshire. This was the second major battle of the War of the Roses (1455-1487). The Lancastrian forces were commanded by Lords Audley and Dudley and the Yorkists were commanded by the Earl of Salisbury. An intense and bloody battle, it was a Yorkist victory, routing the Lancastrians shortly after the death of Lord Audley.

1746 Charles Edward Louis John Casimir Severino Maria Stuart (known as Bonnie Prince Charlie, see 31st January and 31st December) leaves Scotland for the last time from the banks of Loch Nan Uamh (see 16th April, 23rd July and 19th August).

1803 The Battle of Assaye (Assaye Day for the Highland Light Infantry Regiment) on the banks of the River Juah in Central India. Acting Major General Arthur Wellesley (see 1st May and 14th September) led an Army of 6,500 British and Madras Presidency Indian Troops against a Mahratta Army of at least 40,000 troops. The hard-fought battle was a resounding victory for our forces. We suffered 408 Officers and men killed and 1580 men wounded. The Mahratta army suffered over 5,000 casualties. This was an extremely decisive battle, securing British rule in central India until the middle of the twentieth Century.

1880 The birth of John Boyd Orr in Ayrshire (see 25th June).

24th September:

1326 Isabella of France, wife of Edward II (see 25th April and 21st September) and her lover Roger Mortimer land at Suffolk with the Future Edward III (see 21st June and 13th November). Despite having a very small force, they face little resistance as many nobles refuse to fight for Edward II (see 21st September) and London rises in support for the Queen.

1564 The birth of William Adams (see 16th May) in Gillingham, Kent.

1940 Both the George Cross and the George Medal are instituted at the same time by George VI (see 6th February and 14th December). The George Cross is the highest decoration for bravery and is awarded to both civilians and military personnel for acts of bravery whilst not actually engaged with an enemy. It is the highest civilian bravery award and is second in status with the military to the Victoria Cross. The George Medal is awarded for acts of bravery to civilians only.

1975 The first all-British team make it to the summit of Mount Everest, via the steep south-west face (see 29th May). Dougal Heston and Douglas Scott become the two climbers and the first Britons who make the summit from the expedition led by Chris Bonington.

25th September:

1237 The Treaty of York is signed between Henry III (see 1st October and 16th November) of England and Alexander II of Scotland (see 6th July and 24th August). The treaty indirectly began the process that culminated in the approximate future borders between the two Kingdoms (see 1st May).

1066 The Battle of Stamford Bridge, north of York, where King Harold defeated the forces of King Harald Hardrada of Norway (see 14th October). The Vikings force had forced the surrender of York and did not expect Harold to march north so quickly due to the threat from the Normans. The Vikings were taken by surprise and after a brief resistance completely destroyed by the English onslaught.

1658 The birth of Mary Beatrice of Modena, the future second wife of James VII (James II of England see 5th September and 14th October) in the Ducal Palace in Modena in the Duchy of Modena in Italy (see 7th May).

1818 The first blood transfusion using human blood is carried out at Guy's Hospital in London by Doctor James Blundell. He extracted a small quantity of blood from his patient's husband to use in the successful procedure.

1857 The first relief of Lucknow by forces under the command of General Henry Havelock (see 5th April and 24th November) and General Sir James Outram (see 29th January and 11th March) during the Indian Mutiny after a siege of nearly ninety days by rebel Indians. The relief force had to fight through the narrow lanes and streets and lost around a quarter of its 2,000-strong contingent. However, following the relief columns entry into the city, more rebel forces attacked the city and it was decided, due to losses incurred in the relief and the perilous state of the survivors, to remain and defend the Residency in anticipation of a second relief force (see 10th May, 16th November and 6th December).

1915 The first use of poison gas by Britain during the battle of Loos. Unfortunately, due to the changeable breeze, the chlorine gas either blew back onto our own lines or remained in no-mans land. This meant that our advancing troops were forced to pass through it to engage the enemy (see 22nd April) with resultant casualties.

26th September:

1580 Sir Francis Drake (see 27th January) returns to Plymouth in his ship the Golden Hind after becoming the first Briton to sail around the Earth. He set off in 1577 with five ships to seize Spanish gold and treasure and to raid Spanish colonies on the Pacific coast in the new world. Although only his ship the Golden Hind made it to the Pacific, he continued his raids on the Spanish and attempted in vain to find the Northeast Passage back to the Atlantic.

1748 The birth of Cuthbert Collingwood (see 7th March) in Newcastle upon Tyne.

1792 The birth of William Hobson (see 10th September) in Waterford, Ireland.

1833 The birth of Charles Bradlaugh in London (see 30th January).

1846 The death of Thomas Clarkson in Ipswich (see 28th March). He was a leading campaigner for the abolition of slavery. Born in Wisbech, he attended Cambridge University and in 1787 he was instrumental in the formation of the Committee for the Abolition of the African Slave Trade. He and the committee persuaded the MP William Wilberforce (see 29th July and 24th August) to champion the cause and he travelled Britain extensively collecting evidence against the vile trade. The slave trade was abolished in 1807 (see 25th March) and in 1833 legislation was passed freeing all slaves in Britain and the Empire (see 1st August and 28th August).

1887 The birth of Barnes Neville Wallis in Ripley, Derbyshire (see 30th October).

1907 Dominion Day in Newfoundland and New Zealand. On this day New Zealand becomes the Dominion of New Zealand (see 1st July, 26th July and 9th September) and Newfoundland becomes the Dominion of Newfoundland (see 31st March and 5th August) within the Empire following Edward VII's (see 6th May and 9th November) Royal Proclamation earlier in the month (see 6th February and 11th December).

1915 The death of James Keir Hardie (see 15th August) in hospital in Glasgow. Born in Lanarkshire, he went to work for a baker at the age of eight and then became a miner when he was eleven. He was elected as a Member of Parliament in 1892 as an Independent Labour candidate and in 1893 was instrumental in forming the Independent Labour Party. In 1899 he was prominent in the formation of the Labour Representative Committee, the forerunner of the Labour Party and became the leader of the party in the House of Commons. At the outbreak of the Great War in 1914, he openly declared himself a pacifist.

1938 With increased concerns over the possibility of war with Germany, gas masks begin to be issued to civilians (see 8th May and 3rd September).

1944 Operation Market Garden, the attempt to capture the bridges over the Rhine at Arnhem in Holland, comes to an end when the bridges are finally captured by the Germans and the remaining soldiers either escape or are taken captive (see 17th September). The operation was conceived by General Bernard Montgomery (see 24th March and 17th November) with the idea that

Paratroopers would land behind enemy lines and capture up to eight bridges over canals and rivers in and around Arnhem to allow our XXX Corps and their tanks to cross into Germany. Although the Operation failed to achieve its objectives, it was nonetheless a fine example of the courageous and determined spirit displayed by our armed forces, even when faced with seemingly impossible odds.

1953 The rationing of sugar is finally brought to an end across Britain (see 8th January, 4th July, 9th July and 3rd October).

1983 In Northern Ireland, 38 IRA terrorists escape from HM Prison Maze in the biggest escape from a British prison. Several Prison Officers were badly injured with one officer dying as a result of his injuries.

27th September:

1772 The death of James Brindley in Turnhrst in present day Stoke on Trent. An engineer and pioneer canal builder, in 1742 he set up as a millwright in Leek and later designed an engine for draining coal pits. In 1759 the 3rd Duke of Bridgewater commissioned the construction of the Bridgewater Canal in which Brindley was heavily involved and for which he is now famous. In 1766 he began work on constructing the Trent and Mersey Canal, with the company's headquarters based in Stone, Staffordshire. The canal was completed in 1777.

1825 The opening of the Stockton and Darlington Railway. George Stephenson (see 9th June and 12th August) drives his engine the 'Locomotion' along a 9-mile track pulling 36 wagons and reaching speeds of up to 15mph on some of the descents.

1862 The birth of Louis Botha in Greytown, Colony of Natal (see 27th August).

1938 The steam-powered ocean liner RMS Queen Elizabeth is launched from Clydebank, the largest ever passenger liner at the time. She served as a troop ship throughout the war before actually carrying paying passengers.

1960 The death of Sylvia Pankhurst (see 5th May) in Addis Ababa in Ethiopia. She was the daughter of Doctor Richard Pankhurst, an ardent socialist and Emmeline Pankhurst, also a socialist and suffragist. Sylvia was to become a leading women's rights activist and suffragette. A strong supporter of the Labour Party and a committed pacifist, she opposed the First World War but strangely supported the Russian Revolution of 1917. With her mother and three sisters, she formed the Women's Social and Political Union in 1903. Along with Annie Kenney, they were the first women to use violence in support of their goals. In 1908 the WSPU began a campaign of breaking the windows on government buildings. Later, she became an important individual in the Communist Party of Britain. Invited to live in Ethiopia by the Emperor Haile Selassie, she moved to Addis Ababa in 1956.

1964 The first flight of the British Aircraft Corporation TSR-2. A British-designed and built Tactical Strike and Reconnaissance aircraft (TSR) it was a state-of-the-art low-level attack aircraft that was the most advanced aircraft of its day. Unfortunately, the Government, under Prime Minister Harold Wilson (see 11th March and 24th May), incompetently decided to scrap its development in favour of a less effective American aircraft. Not long after, the Americans scrapped their own project and our forces were left without any equivalent aircraft.

28th September:

1066 William, Duke of Normandy (see 9th September) lands at Pevensey to begin his Conquest of England and bring an end to Anglo Saxon rule (see 14th October). This was the last time our Great Country would ever be invaded. The ruling elite were to be predominantly Norman from now on but the vast majority of the population remained Anglo-Saxon.

1652 The Battle of Kentish Knock takes place during the First Anglo-Dutch War, 1652-1654, in the Thames Estuary. Our Fleet, commanded by General at Sea Robert Blake (see 7th August and 27th September), at first struggled against the Dutch fleet, having had two large powerful ships run aground on the sandbanks. However, with light failing and the two ships pulled free, the Dutch were overwhelmed and were forced to withdraw, being pursued across the North sea. The Commonwealth Navy lost no ships but the Dutch suffered two losses.

1745 Our glorious National Anthem, 'God Save the King', is supposedly sung for the first time at the Theatre Royal in Drury Lane in support of King George II (see 20th October and 25th October) after the defeat of government forces by Jacobite troops at the battle of Prestonpans a week earlier (see 21st September) during the Jacobite rising of that year (see 19th August).

1865 Elizabeth Garrett Anderson (see 9th June and 17th December) becomes the first female Doctor after passing the Apothecaries examination (see 9th November).

1912 Thousands of Unionists in Northern Ireland sign the Solemn League and Covenant in Belfast City Hall, pledging resistance to Home Rule for Ireland. Sir Edward Carson (see 9th February, 20th March, 22nd October and 8th December) was the first to sign, followed by almost 500,000 signatories.

29th September:

1725 The birth of Sir Robert Clive, later 1st Baron Clive of Plassey, in Shropshire (see 22nd November).

1758 The birth of Horatio Nelson, later Admiral, Lord Nelson (see 21st October) in Burnham Thorpe, Norfolk. He was the sixth of eleven children of the Reverend Edmund Nelson and his wife Catherine.

1829 The world's first professional Police Force, the Metropolitan Police Force, is founded by the then Home Secretary Sir Robert Peel (see 5th

February and 2ⁿᵈ July) in London under the provision of the Metropolitan Police Act 1829.

1885 The first electric tramway in Britain is opened in Blackpool, using the conduit system. It was initially operated by the Blackpool Electric Tramway Company and then later by the Blackpool Corporation.

1923 Palestine and Transjordan are incorporated into the British Mandate for Palestine issued by the League of Nations to Great Britain the same day. The territories were inclusive of former elements of the Ottoman Empire (see 25ᵗʰ April and 14ᵗʰ May).

1938 The Munich Agreement is signed between Britain, France, Italy and Germany. The agreement ceded the Sudetenland in north and north-western Czechoslovakia to Germany (see 8ᵗʰ May, 3ʳᵈ September and 30ᵗʰ September). The leaders of the four countries who signed the agreement were Neville Chamberlain (see 18ᵗʰ March and 9ᵗʰ November), Eduoard Daladier, Adolf Hitler and Benito Mussolini. The agreement was popular in Britain as at the time there was no appetite for another war.

30ᵗʰ September:

1673 The marriage by proxy of King James VII (James II of England, see 5ᵗʰ September and 14ᵗʰ October) and his second wife Mary of Modena (see 21ˢᵗ November) in Modena in Italy.

1772 The death of James Brindley in Turnhrst Hall, Stoke on Trent. Born in Derbyshire in 1716, he became a millwright after his apprenticeship and set up business in Leek in Staffordshire. In 1759 he was commissioned as a consultant engineer on the Bridgwater Canal which was completed in 1761. His next work was the Trent and Mersey Canal. Though he never lived to see it completed, he did complete other canal works and built numerous mills. He is perhaps one of the most well-known engineers of the eighteenth century.

1832 The birth of Frederick Sleigh Roberts in Cawnpore, British India (see 14ᵗʰ November).

1840 The Foundation Stone for Nelson's Column, designed by William Railton, is laid in Trafalgar Square at the start of a three-year building programme. The column itself is just over 169 feet high with the granite statue of Nelson atop (see 21ˢᵗ October and 3ʳᵈ November).

1888 Elizabeth Stride becomes the third victim of Jack the Ripper. She is found at one o'clock in the morning in Dutfield's Yard in Henrique's Street, in the Whitechapel area of London. Forty-five minutes later Catherine Eddowes becomes the fourth victim of Jack the Ripper, her body being found in Mitre Square in Whitechapel (see 31ˢᵗ August, 8ᵗʰ September and 9ᵗʰ November).

1928 Alexander Fleming officially announces the discovery of penicillin (see 11ᵗʰ March and 6ᵗʰ August).

1938 On his return to Britain from Germany after signing the infamous Munich Pact Agreement with the German Chancellor, Adolf Hitler, the Prime

Minister Neville Chamberlain (see 18th March and 9th November), delivers his 'Peace in our time' speech at Heston Airfield where he landed (see 8th May, 3rd September and 29th September).

2014 Two RAF Tornados fighters, flying from RAF Akrotiri in Cyprus, carry out two attacks on specific ISIS targets in north-west Iraq following agreement in Parliament for British forces to operate over Iraqi territory. Both Tornados returned safely (see 26th September and 2nd December).

OCTOBER

1st October:

1207 The birth of Henry III at Winchester Castle (see 17th May, 28th October and 16th November).

1795 The death of Robert Bakewell, farmer and pioneer agriculturalist and stock-breeder. Born in 1725 near in Leicestershire, the son of a farmer, he travelled Europe as a young man and learned about farming methods until he took over the family farm in 1760. He set aside large areas of his farm to experiment with ideas on irrigation, drainage and crops amongst others. His great achievement and innovation was in segregating his livestock into males and females and only allowing selective breeding to breed in or breed out desirable or undesirable characteristics. His work on in breeding is still practiced world wide and contributed to a huge increase in the quality of this nation's and the worlds livestock.

1838 The issuing of the Simla Manifesto by George Eden, Lord Auckland, setting out the necessary reasons for intervention in Afghanistan and thus the start of the First Afghan War (1839-1842). The intervention was primarily in support of Shah Shuja's army with the intention of him retaking the throne that was once his (see 6th January and 13th January).

1838 The death of Charles Tennant in Glasgow (see 3rd May). Born in Alloway in 1768, he was a renowned chemist; he discovered bleaching powder in 1799 along with Charles Macintosh. Despite initial business difficulties, in 1800 he founded a chemical works in Glasgow and became very wealthy.

1847 The birth of Annie Besant (née Wood) in London (see 20th September).

1918 The city of Damascus in Syria is captured from the Ottoman Turks by the Egyptian Expeditionary Force comprising mainly Australian, British, Indian and New Zealand units. The surrender was received by Major Olden and the main force entered the city unopposed (see 30th October).

1932 The British Union of Fascists is formed by Sir Oswald Mosley (see 16th November and 3rd December) after disbanding the New Party (see 29th February). Vehemently anti-communist and protectionist, the party (BUF) proposed a reduced House of Commons and the replacing the House of Lords with an elected body. Undeneiably right wing, the party was Britain's first openly Fascist party.

2006 The Employment Equality (Age) Act becomes law making it illegal to discriminate against someone in the work place due to their age.

2009 The Supreme Court is sworn in, including the swearing in of eleven Justices. For the first time, the Judiciary is separated from Parliament and the Lords and is the last Court of appeal, except for criminal cases in Scotland.

2nd October:

1263 The battle of Largs between the Kingdoms of Scotland under Alexander III (see 19th March and 4th September) and Norway under Magnus VI. The Norwegians had control of much of north-western Scotland and were attempting to engage the Scots to secure their realm when they were surprised by their enemy. The Norwegians were superior in number but were attacked by the Scots before they could properly prepare for battle. After a relatively brief fight, the Norwegians force broke and many were slaughtered by the Scots in the ensuing pursuit (see 2nd July).

1452 The birth of Richard III at Fotheringay Castle (see 4th February, 6th July and 22nd August). He was the son of Richard Plantagenet, 3rd Duke of York, and a great-grandson of Edward III (see 21st June and 13th November).

1710 The siege of Port Royal ends when the capital of the French colony of Acadia surrenders to forces led by General Francis Nicholson after eight days of siege. The French forces were allowed to leave with full honours and following its capture, Acadia was renamed Nova Scotia and its capital, Port Royal was renamed Annapolis Royal after Queen Anne, which was confirmed at the Treaty of Utrecht in 1713 (see 31st March).

1713 The birth of Allan Ramsay in Edinburgh (see 10th August).

1780 The murder of Major John Andre (see 2nd May) in Tappen Connecticut, British North America. A British Officer, he was hanged by the rebel American colonists after he was captured on the 23rd September 1780 behind enemy lines in disguise whilst attempting to help the Loyalist Benedict Arnold (see 3rd January and 14th June) surrender West Point to our forces. In 1821, at the request of the Duke of York, his remains were removed from where they were buried under the gallows and reburied in Hero's Corner in Westminster Abbey.

1852 The birth of William Ramsay (see 23rd July) in Glasgow.

3rd October:

1940 Former Prime Minister Neville Chamberlain (see 18th March and 9th November) resigns from Winston Churchill's (see 24th January and 30th November) coalition government (see 10th May) due to ill health.

1952 Tea rationing finally ends (see 9ᵗʰ July) after twelve years. The tea ration had been set at 2oz per person over nine-years-old per week (see 8ᵗʰ January, 5ᵗʰ February, 9ᵗʰ February, 4ᵗʰ July and 9ᵗʰ September).

1952 Britain detonates its first Atomic bomb in the Bay of Trimouille Island, part of the Monte Bello islands, Western Australia, under the code name Operation Hurricane. The nuclear bomb was a 25-kiloton weapon and was detonated within the hull of an old River-class frigate, HMS Plym, which was anchored off Trimouille Island. We therefore become the world's third nuclear power despite obstructions from the United States (see 26ᵗʰ February, 3ʳᵈ March and 15ᵗʰ May).

1980 The Housing Act (1980) comes into force. Often referred to as the 'Right to Buy', it gave the legal right to thousands of council house tenants to purchase the house in which they were living. It had a dramatic affect on home ownership and is seen as one of the defining events in Margaret Thatcher's years as Prime Minister (see 8ᵗʰ April and 13ᵗʰ October).

4ᵗʰ October:

1626 The birth of Richard Cromwell in Huntingdon (see 25ᵗʰ May, 12ᵗʰ July and 3ʳᵈ September).

1694 The birth of George Murray at Huntingtower near Perth (see 11ᵗʰ October).

1716 The birth of James Lind in Edinburgh (see 13ᵗʰ July).

1809 Spencer Percival (see 11ᵗʰ May and 1ˢᵗ November) is appointed Prime Minister by George III (see 29ᵗʰ January and 24ᵗʰ May).

1821 The death of John Rennie (see 7ᵗʰ June) in London. A civil engineer, he was responsible for many canals, bridges and docks throughout Britain, including East India Docks and some in Liverpool, London and Hull. Born in East Lothian, he worked for Andrew Meikle (see 27ᵗʰ November) from an early age. As a young man he moved to Birmingham and then onto London where, in 1791, he set up his own engineering business. After this, he worked on the Lancaster Canal, the Kent and Avon Canal and then improving the drainage in the Fens. He also worked on numerous bridges, docks and other engineering works across the country. He is buried in St. Paul's Cathedral.

1936 The 'Battle' of Cable Street in the east end of London. Oswald Moseley (see 16ᵗʰ November and 3ʳᵈ December) attempted to march his supporters and members of the British Union of Fascists through the strongly Jewish area of London. The clash was between the Metropolitan Police and anti-fascist demonstrators, made up of Jewish groups and a mixed grouping of socialist, Communist and anarchist agitators who did not want the march to continue. The mob erected barricades in several places and when the Police attempted to remove them so the march could continue, the demonstrators attacked. In the end, while running battles were fought between the police and the rioters, Oswald Moseley and his supporters were redirected to Hyde Park.

1948 The death of Sir Arthur Whitten Brown (see 23rd July). Along with Sir John William Alcock (see 5th November and 18th December), they became the first aviators to complete a non-stop trans-Atlantic flight (see 15th June). Born in Glasgow of American parents, he joined the Manchester Regiment during the Great War before joining the Royal flying Corps. On the trans-Atlantic flight he was the navigator. He served as Lieutenant-Colonel of the Home Guard at the start of the Second World War after which he rejoined the RAF and served in the Training Command. His only son died during the war on a raid with the RAF in the Netherlands in 1944.

5th October:

1805 The death of Charles Cornwallis, 1st Marques Cornwallis (see 31st December) in Ghazipur, India. He was one of the leading Commanders during the American Colonial rebellion and led our forces to some notable victories. However, he was eventually forced to surrender at Yorktown when he became surrounded (see 19th October) by the rebels. Following the independence of the American colonies in 1783 (see 3rd September), he was from 1786 to 1793 the Governor General of India and in 1798 he led government forces as Lord Lieutenant of Ireland in the successful campaign to suppress the Irish Rebellion of that year.

1813 The battle of the Thames in Canada results in defeat for our forces and the death of the pro-British Shawnee tribal confederacy leader Tecumseh. Our troops, numbering around 600 with about 1,000 Indian allies commanded by Tecumseh, were outnumbered by over 3,500 Americans. In the ensuing fight, many of our troops were taken prisoner and Tecumseh was killed, destroying the Indian alliance (see 24th December).

1930 H.M. Airship R101 crashes in France on its maiden flight. There are 48 deaths and only 8 survivors, although one of the survivors dies later in hospital. First flown in a series of trial flights in 1929, it was one of two airships built (R100 being the other and both were designed in part by Barnes Wallis) as part of the Government's drive to develop the use of civil airships to provide long distance routes across the Empire. The crash effectively ended Britain's airship industry with the scrapping later of R100.

1936 The start of the Jarrow march on London. Around 200 men from the north-east town of Jarrow begin their 300-mile march to London. Their main demand was to have a steel works built to provide jobs, but they also wanted to highlight the deprivation in the impoverished areas that they came from. The petition, signed by 11,000 local people from the Jarrow area, was carried with the marchers (see 31st October) in a wooden casket.

6th October:

1175 The Treaty of Windsor is signed at Windsor between Henry II (see 5th March and 6th July) of England and Rory O'Connor, King of Connaught.

In signing the treaty, Rory was granted a kingship as long as he swore loyalty to the English King and paid tribute to him as his overlord (see 6ᵗʰ December and 8ᵗʰ December).

1536 William Tyndale is tried, convicted and then executed by strangulation near Brussels; his body was then burned at the stake although there is a possibility that he may have partially revived as he was being burned. Born in Gloucestershire, he studied at Oxford. He was the leading bible translator and martyr of his time. In 1524 he travelled to Wittenberg where he may have commenced translating the New Testament into the English language. By 1526 an entire New Testament was complete and copies were being smuggled into England. In 1530 he published his opposition to Henry VIII's (see 28ᵗʰ January and 28ᵗʰ June) divorce from Catherine of Aragon in favour of Anne Boleyn. He therefore published the first ever bible translation in English.

1762 The city of Manila in the Philippines is finally captured from the Spanish by troops, led by Colonel William Draper and Vice-Admiral Samuel Cornish, less than two weeks after the arrival of our fleet. The battle was part of the Seven Years' War (1756-1763) and the citadel and port were surrendered by the Spanish Governor immediately upon the fall of the city (see 10ᵗʰ February).

1769 Captain James Cook (see 14ᵗʰ February and 27ᵗʰ October), on his first voyage of discovery, reaches New Zealand (see 6ᵗʰ February, 1ˢᵗ July and 26ᵗʰ September) on board HMS Endeavour, becoming the only European since Abel Tasman to reach the country. The expedition was a joint venture between the Royal Navy and the Royal Society (see 29ᵗʰ April).

1783 The birth of Thomas Attwood (see 9ᵗʰ March) in Halesowen.

1891 The death of Charles Stewart Parnell in Hove (see 27ᵗʰ June). A leading Irish Nationalist, he is known for leading the campaign for Home Rule. Born in County Wicklow, his family were Anglo-Irish Protestants. He was educated at Cambridge and in 1875 was elected to Parliament as a representative of the Home Rule League. In 1879 he was elected President of the National Land League and soon rallied support for a boycott for which he was imprisoned and the League suppressed. Despite rising levels of violence, he always condemned acts of violence and championed politics as the way to Home Rule. Following his involvement in a rather public divorce scandal, his political career faded. He is buried in Dublin.

1892 The death of Alfred Tennyson, 1ˢᵗ Baron Tennyson (see 6ᵗʰ August and 19ᵗʰ November). The son of a rector, he was educated at Trinity College, Cambridge. He was Poet Laureate from 1850 and his most well-known poem is 'The Charge of the Light Brigade', as well as others such as 'The Lady of Shallot', 'Ulysses' and 'The Kraken'. He was a favourite of Queen Victoria, who granted him a Baronetcy in 1884 and he was buried in Westminster Abbey.

1951 The British High Commissioner for Malaya, Sir Henry Lovell Goldsworthy Gurney, is assassinated by communist insurgents (see 27ᵗʰ June) of the Malayan Communist Party. He died protecting his wife and their driver. Born in Cornwall, he served during the Great War before joining the Colonial Service (see 18th June and 31st August).

1953 British forces are despatched to British Guiana to quell possible communist unrest after a pro-communist party, the People's Progressive Party, gained a majority of seats in the election. The British Governor suspended the constitution due to the Marxist threat posed by the reforms planned by the new government.

7th October:

1573 The birth of William Laud (see 10th January) in Reading, Berkshire.

1763 By the Royal Proclamation of King George III (see 29th January and 24th May), the government prohibits the settling by colonists on any land west of the Appalachian Mountains in British North America. Following the recent victory over France and the acquisition of the French Colonies, the government decided to consolidate and secure its territories to improve relations with the native inhabitants of the possessions and to regulate the fur trade.

1796 The death of Thomas Reid in Glasgow (see 26th April). A philosopher, he was a leading figure in the Scottish Enlightenment and the founder of the Scottish School of Common Sense. He studied divinity and completed his theological training in 1731. In 1754 he published his first major work, 'An Inquiry into the Human Mind on the Principles of Common Sense', shortly after which he became Professor at Glasgow University. He resigned his post in 1781 in order to devote more time to writing and publishing his essays and work.

1904 The death of Isabella Bishop (née Bird, see 15th October). She was a traveller and author, well-known for writing numerous books about her travels, the more famous being those about her travels in Asia. She was the first woman fellow of the Royal Geographical Society. In 1901 she rode 1,000 miles in from Morocco and the Atlas Mountains.

1919 The death of Alfred Deakin in Melbourne, Victoria, Australia (see 3rd August). An Australian politician, he was the leading member of the Australian Federation Movement and later, the second Prime Minister of Australia. Born in Melbourne, he was elected to Parliament in 1879 as a Liberal. A staunch Imperialist, from the late 1880s he became deeply involved in the cause of Australian federation and in 1903 he became the second Prime Minister for the first of his three terms in office. Due to failing health, he retired from politics in 1913.

1959 A fire on Southend Pier traps 300 people who are eventually all rescued by boat.

2001 British and American forces, using fighter aircraft and cruise missiles, commence the aerial bombardment of Taliban and al-Qaeda targets and positions in Afghanistan as a prelude to the ultimate invasion of the Taliban-controlled country (see 26th October).

8th October:

1754 The death of Henry Fielding in Lisbon, Portugal (see 22nd April). A novelist and dramatist, he was the author of 'Tom Jones' and was the political scourge of the Prime Minister Robert Walpole (see 18th March and 26th August). As a journalist, he became editor of 'The Champion' and wrote a number of novels. He was also largely responsible for forming the Bow Street Runners in 1749 that were in reality the forerunners of the first modern Police force.

1856 Chinese officials board a Chinese-owned and British Hong Kong registered boat named the Arrow and arrested twelve members of her crew. This is recognised as the main catalyst in the Second Opium War 1856-1860 (see 3rd July, 29th August, 23 October and 24th October).

1924 The Labour administration, under Prime Minister Ramsay MacDonald (see 12th October and 9th November), loses a vote of confidence (see 29th October).

1931 The death of General Sir John Monash (see 27th June) in Melbourne, Australia. The son of German-Jewish émigrés, he spent the years before the Great War as a civil engineer. At the outbreak of war, he was appointed the Commander of the 4th Infantry Brigade of the AIF when it went to Egypt prior to its part in the Dardanelles campaign (see 19th February and 25th April). Despite the failure of the Dardanelles campaign, his involvement was without criticisms. He was appointed to Command the Australian 3rd Division in 1917, taking part in many key offensives. He was noted for his meticulous planning and care for the soldiers under his command. In 1918 he became commander of the Australian Corps. On the 12th August 1918 he was knighted by George V (see 20th January and 3rd June) on the battlefield, the first time for 200 years that such an honour had been bestowed in this way. After the war he returned to civilian life. He is the greatest Australian General and one of the greatest officers of the Empire's history and though recognised at the time, he is now unfortunately not given the recognition he deserves outside of Australia.

1967 The death of Clement Richard Attlee (see 3rd January) in Westminster Hospital in London. He became Labour's post-war Prime Minister in a landslide victory in the 1945 election (see 26th July), ousting the war time Prime Minister, Winston Churchill (see 24th January and 30th November). The son of a London solicitor, he became a Barrister in 1906 and joined the Independent Labour Party in 1908. At the outbreak of the Great War he joined the army and served at Gallipoli and in Mesopotamia, where he was badly wounded. After recovering in England, he served on the Western Front until the end of the war. He became an MP in the 1922 General Election and became leader of the Labour Party in 1935. After becoming Prime Minister, he led the country through some of the biggest reforms in our history, the creation of the Welfare State (see 5th July), the nationalisation of the Coal mines (see 1st January), the Railways (see 1st January) as well as the electricity, steel and gas industries and also the beginning of the decline of the Empire.

9th October:

1651 The Navigation Act is passed by the 'Rump' Parliament. The act stated that goods could only be imported into the colonies and territories of England (and later Great Britain after 1701) on English (later British) ships or on ships from the country in which they were produced.

1799 HMS Lutine runs onto a sandbank in a gale and sinks off the coast of Holland. Originally a French frigate, launched in 1779 and captured in 1793 after the siege of Toulon, she entered service for the Royal Navy. The ship's bell is later salvaged and given to the ship's insurers at Lloyds of London. Known as the Lutine bell, it has been rung ever since every time a ship is lost.

1864 The birth of Reginald Edward Harry Dyer (see 23rd July) in Muree, British India.

1942 The Statute of Westminster Adoption Act (1942) receives Royal Assent in the Australian Parliament. By doing so, the Australian Parliament adopted the Statute of Westminster 1931 (see 11th December) passed by the British Parliament and formally recognised their independence as a separate sovereign state (see 26th January). The act was viewed as taking effect from 3rd September 1939 due to the continuing conflict in the Second World War.

1959 The General Election is held. The Conservatives win under Harold Macmillan (see 10th February and 29th December). The Conservatives win 365 seats, Labour 258 and the Liberals 6 seats.

2014 In a by-election in Clacton, the United Kingdom Independence Party wins its first Parliamentary seat as Douglas Carswell, the former Conservative MP for the constituency, is re-elected as the UKIP MP. He had resigned his seat, triggered a by-election, left the Conservative Party and stood as the UKIP candidate.

10th October:

1731 The birth of Henry Cavendish, the grandson of both the Duke of Devonshire and the Duke of Kent, in Nice, France (see 24th February). He was to become well-known as an aristocratic and eccentric scientist.

1903 The Women's Social and Political Union is formed by Emmeline Pankhurst (see 14th June and 14th July) and her three daughters as a way to campaign for women's rights. However, their campaign was not for universal suffrage but for votes for women on the same basis as men (see 6th February and 14th December).

291

1957 Windscale Nuclear Power Station is damaged as a fire breaks out in its main reactor that raged out of control for three days until heroically brought under control by staff at the site. An amount of nuclear contamination was released due to the fire.

1969 The Government announces the disbandment of the Ulster Special Constabulary's 'B' Specials, which is due to take place in 1970. Formed in the 1920s, the Ulster Special Constabulary was an organisation of volunteers who worked alongside the RUC, usually for one evening per week (see 31st July, 12th August and 14th August).

1974 The General election is held. The Labour Party under Harold Wilson (see 11th March and 24th May) win but with a majority of only three seats (see 15th October). Enoch Powell (see 8th February and 16th June) won a seat in Parliament representing South Down in Northern Ireland as a member of the Ulster Unionist Party.

11th October:

1521 Pope Leo X grants Henry VIII (see 28th January and 28th June) the title 'Defender of the Faith' for his pamphlet defending Catholicism.

1727 George II is crowned at Westminster Abbey (see 25th October and 30th October). For the coronation, George Frideric Handel composed four coronation anthems. One of them, 'Zadok the Priest', has been played at every coronation since.

1760 The death of Lord George Murray (see 4th October) in Medemblik, Holland. He was the key military mind in the Jacobite camp during the rising of 1745 and had also taken part in the risings of 1715 and 1719, after which he was pardoned in 1726. He was responsible for the victories at Prestonpans in 1745 (see 21st September) and at Falkirk in 1746 (see 17th January). He also opposed the plans for the Battle of Culloden (see 16th April) for tactical reasons but still led the right wing during the battle due to his loyalty and his personal conviction. Following the Jacobite rout, he led his men in an efficient and orderly withdrawal from the field. He escaped to the continent in December 1745. Sadly he was often ignored by Prince Charles Stewart (see 31st January and 31st December) in favour of other advisers, much to the Prince's later regret.

1797 The Battle of Camperdown off the Dutch Coast during the French Revolutionary Wars. Our fleet of 24 ships under Admiral Adam Duncan beat the Dutch fleet of the Batavian Republic under Vice Admiral de Winter consisting of 25 ships. Eleven of the Dutch ships were taken as prizes with the loss of 220 killed and 812 wounded, while the Dutch suffered 540 killed and 620 wounded.

1865 The beginning of the Jamaican Insurrection in Morant Bay, Jamaica. Between 200 and 300 men and women, led by Paul Bogle, enter the town of Morant and march to the court house where a black islander had be arrested days before for trespass. The local militia, inexperienced and nervous, opened fire killing several people, which caused the protesters to riot and take control of the town (see 6th August).

1872 The birth of Emily Wilding Davison (see 4th June and 8th June) in Blackheath, south-east London.

1889 The death of James Prescott Joule in Sale near Manchester (see 24th December). He was a leading Victorian physicist and was responsible for sharing in the development of the law of the conservation of energy. In 1840 he stated the law that heat is produced in an electrical conductor, later called Joule's Law. The international unit of energy, the Joule, is named after him.

1899 President Kruger of the South African Republic declares war on Britain and our Empire. Later that night, Boer forces attack a train and the Railway siding at Kraaipan in what was the start of the Second Boer War (1899-1902) and called the battle of Kraaipan. At the time it was known as the South African War and was between our Empire and the two Boer Republics of the 'Orange Free State' and the 'South African Republic' (see 31st May).

1929 The death of Reginald Brabazon, 12th Earl of Meath (see 31st July), in London. A Conservative in the House of Lords, Lord Brabazon, was an ardent imperialist and was the foremost proponent of Empire Day in Great Britain (see 24th May) and was instrumental in Empire Day being officially recognised by our government in 1916.

1982 The Mary Rose, the Flag Ship of Henry VIIIs Royal Navy (see 28th January and 28th June) is raised after 437 years under water (see 19th July).

12th October:

1537 The birth of Edward VI at Hampton Court Palace (see 6th July).

1702 The Battle of Vigo Bay, off the coast of Spain is fought as part of the War of the Spanish Succession (1702-1714). Our forces, who are led by Admiral Sir George Rooke, defeat the French and Spanish fleets. Of the eighteen or so French ships in the engagement, none escaped. Five were captured by the English, one by our allies the Dutch and the rest were destroyed. All the Spanish ships were destroyed.

1866 The birth of James Ramsay MacDonald (see 22nd January and 9th November) in Lossiemouth in Morayshire.

1915 Nurse Edith Cavell (see 4th December) is shot by a German firing squad after being accused of spying and aiding in the escape of Allied prisoners of war. A British nurse, she moved to Brussels in 1907 to nurse and became a nursing trainer. Later, when the Great War broke out, she returned to Brussels and worked for the Red Cross. It was whilst working as a nurse that she began to help many British, Belgian and French troops to evade capture and escape to Holland and ultimately Britain. She openly acknowledged her actions to the German Courts Martial and, despite protestations, she was convicted of treason and shot.

1984 The Brighton Hotel bomb blast and attempted murder of the Prime Minister, Margaret Thatcher (see 8th April and 13th October), by the terrorist group the IRA. The Prime Minister and her Cabinet had been staying at the Grand Hotel for the Conservative Party Conference when the bomb detonated at 2.54am. Five people were killed, including a Conservative MP, the wife of another and the wife of the President of the Board of Trade was permanently disabled.

2007 The Armed Forces Memorial at Alrewas, near Lichfield in Staffordshire is dedicated by Her Majesty the Queen (see 21st April). It bears all the names of over 16,000 service personnel who have died since the end of the Second World War in the service of this country and in accidents whilst training. It was opened to the public on the 29th October 2007 and is a perpetual memorial with names being added as our servicemen and women continue to pay the ultimate sacrifice.

13th October:

1005 The date given for the birth of Edward the Confessor (see 5th January), the son of Aethelred the Unready and Emma of Normandy.

1399 The coronation of Henry IV at Westminster Abbey (see 20th March and 4th April).

1812 The Battle of Queenston Heights (see 18th June, 16th August and 24th December). American forces, in an attempt to invade Upper Canada, crossed the Niagara River from Lewiston to Queenston. After an initial spell of success, when General Issac Brock was mortally wounded and the Americans captured Queenston, reinforcements arrived. The British skirted around the invaders position and took them by complete surprise, swiftly forcing an American capitulation.

1845 The death of Elizabeth Fry (see 21st May). Born in Norwich, she married Joseph Fry (a Quaker) on the 19th August 1800. She is most well-known for campaigning for prison reform and a keen interest in the condition of the poor. She started training nurses in Guy's Hospital in London and later she formed the 'Fry Nurses', some of whom went with Florence Nightingale to the Crimea War, 1853-1856.

1860 The city of Peking is surrendered to British and French forces by the Chinese only minutes before a bombardment of the city was due to commence, thus effectively ending the Second Opium War, 1856-1860 (see 20th May, 18th October and 24th October).

1862 The birth of Mary Henrietta Kingsley in Islington in London (see 3rd June).

1884 Greenwich is adopted as the universal time meridian of longitude from which all world times are calculated and known as Greenwich Mean Time (GMT). It was voted as the universal Meridian of longitude at a convention in Washington D.C. in the USA.

1915 The Battle for Loos culminates with the Battle for the Hohenzollern Redoubt near Auchy-les-Mines in France. The Hohenzollern Redoubt was a German fortification well defended that formed a defensive circuit of a former mining complex called Fosse 8. The 46th (North Midland) Division's objective was to attack the Redoubt at a point called 'The Dump'. In the attack, the Division suffered huge casualties that were only overshadowed by the losses on the first day of the Battle of the Somme in 1916 (see 1st July). On this one day, fourteen men from the town of Stone in Staffordshire lost their lives with many more becoming wounded. Though the Division failed to achieve their objective, the men of the North Midlands showed the utmost bravery and gallantry whilst under the most deadly and constant enemy fire.

1925 The birth of Margaret Thatcher (nee Roberts) in Grantham, Lincolnshire (see 11th February, 4th May and 22nd November).

14th October:

1066 The battle of Hastings (originally known as the Battle of Senlac Hill) and the death of King Harold. Invading Norman forces, led by William, Duke of Normandy, were almost beaten by the Anglo-Saxons, led by King Harold Godwinson. However, as the battle seemed decided, the Normans, feigning a retreat, caused the English lines to break in pursuit, after which they were quickly defeated and Harold killed. His loyal retainers gathered around his body and fought valiantly to the last man. The defeat of King Harold marks the end of Anglo-Saxon rule and the start of the Norman occupation of England (see 28th September).

1633 The birth of the future James VII (James II in England, see 5th September, 11th December and 23rd December) and Grandfather of Prince Charles Edward Stewart ('Bonnie Prince Charlie', see 31st January and 31th December) in St. James's Palace.

1644 The birth of William Penn in London (see 30th July).

1747 The Second Battle of Cape Finisterre during the War of the Austrian Succession, 1740-1748. A fleet of fourteen ships, led by Rear-Admiral Edward Hawke (see 16th October), engaged eight French ships escorting a large fleet of merchant ships in the most decisive naval victory of the war. Of the eight French warships, six were captured and seven merchant ships were also taken. The victory resulted in the French fear of our Navy and caused them to avoid conflict with the Royal Navy for the rest of the war.

1758 The death of General James Francis Edward Keith (see 11th June) at the Battle of Hochkirk leading his troops. He was buried nearby but later his body was moved to Staunsdorf Cemetery in Berlin. Born in Inverugie Castle, he trained for a legal career. He took part in two Jacobite risings, the first in 1715 where he showed his ability as a military leader, but ultimate defeat forced him to escape to the Continent. He supported the second rising in 1719 but that also ended in defeat and continued exile on the Continent. After a brief spell in the Spanish army, he went to Prussia where he served with great distinction in the Prussian army and in particular in the Seven Years' War (1756-1763). He was eventually promoted to Field Marshall by his friend, Frederick the Great, and was killed at the Battle of Hochkirk leading the rear guard against the Austrian army.

1899 The beginning of the siege of Kimberley in Cape Colony during the South African War (1899-1902). Boer forces quickly moved to besiege the town which was ill-prepared for defence. However, under the excellent leadership of Colonel Robert Kekewich with the assistance of Cecil Rhodes (see 26th March and 5th July), the inhabitants held out for 124 days until finally relieved by Major General Sir John French (see 15th February).

1899 The start of the siege of Mafeking (see 17th May). President Kruger of the South African Republic declared war on the 11th October and in the following days Boer forces began to move into position around the strategic town. The siege would last 217 days in total and would sap many Boer resources and much manpower as the 1,500 townspeople and the garrison, under the leadership of Robert Baden-Powell (see 8th January and 22nd February), withstood shelling, sniping and near starvation.

1913 Our country's worst Pit Disaster at Senghenydd, near Caerphilly in Glamorgan, South Wales, occurs, killing over 400 miners.

1939 The Battleship HMS Royal Oak is torpedoed and sunk by a U-Boat, U-47 in Scapa Flow whilst at anchor with a total of 833 of the crew killed. The sight of the attack is now a recognised war grave. Though it made no tactical or numerical difference to the Royal Navy's superiority during the war, it was the first battleship sunk in the war and was a considerable blow to morale.

1969 The 10 Shilling note is withdrawn from currency and the 50 pence coin is introduced in preparation for decimalisation (see 15th February).

15th October:

1686 The birth of Allan Ramsey in Lanarkshire (see 7th January).

1702 The death of Frances Teresa Stuart, Duchess of Richmond and Lennox (see 8th July). Born in 1647, she was raised in France after her Royalist parents went into exile following the death of Charles I (see 30th January and 19th November). She became known as 'La Belle Stuart' for her beauty and for refusing to become a mistress of Charles II (see 6th February and 29th May). More importantly, she was chosen as the model for the now familiar figure of 'Britannia' that adorned our coinage until decimalisation in 1971. Her image still remains on our present 50 pence piece, minted until 2008 and still in circulation.

1815 Napoleon Bonaparte, former Emperor of France, defeated twice by Great Britain and our Allies, begins his exile on the island of Saint Helena. He would die there six years later. At the time, Saint Helena was a possession of the East India Company and for the period of his exile the island was heavily garrisoned by British troops and the surrounding waters were patrolled by the Royal Navy to successfully prevent another escape. His body was buried on the island where it remained until 1840 when it was returned to the French (see 30th May, 9th June, 18th June and 20th November).

1832 The birth of Isabella Bird, later Bishop, in Yorkshire (see 7th October).

1964 The general election is held and the Labour Party, under Harold Wilson (see 11th March and 24th May), wins, but with only a small majority (see 10th October).

2012 Monday: In Edinburgh, Prime Minister David Cameron and Scottish First Minister Alex Salmond sign an agreement setting out the terms for an independence referendum in Scotland. They agreed that the referendum would be a simple 'yes' or 'no' question and that it must take place before the end of 2014 (see 1st May and 15th October).

16th October:

1774 The death of Robert Fergusson (see 5th September) in Edinburgh. One of Scotland's most gifted poets, he is most well-known for his works, 'Auld Reekie' and 'The Knight of the Cape'. Following a fall and a severe head injury, his mental state deteriorated and he committed suicide in the Old Darien House, Edinburgh's only public asylum.

1781 The death of Admiral Edward Hawke (see 21st February) in Sunbury on Thames. One of the greatest Admirals of his time and of our country, he is remembered for leading the fleet at the Battle of Cape Finisterre in 1747 (see 14th October) and the Battle of Quiberon Bay in 1759 (see 20th November). He served during the Seven Years' War (1756-1763) during which he was responsible for the almost constant blockade of the French coast. He later served as First Lord of the Admiralty between 1766 and 1771.

1797 The birth of James Thomas Brudenell (see 28th March) in Buckinghamshire.

1834 The original Houses of Parliament, the Palace of Westminster is almost totally destroyed by fire. Only Westminster Hall, the Crypt of St. Stephen's Chapel and the Jewel Tower survived the flames. The fire had begun due to the over enthusiastic burning of tally sticks which caused a chimney flue to overheat, starting the fire which spread rapidly across the medieval complex of buildings (see 27th April).

1854 The birth of Oscar Wilde in Dublin (see 30th November).

1900 The General Election and the Conservative Party win under the Marquis of Salisbury (see 3rd February and 22nd August).

17th October:

1346 The Battle of Neville's Cross. The English totally defeat the Scots after they had invaded England following pressure from their French allies, who had been defeated by the English some two months earlier at the battle of Crècy in 1346 (see 26th August). King David II (Robert the Bruce's only surviving son) of Scotland was captured and spent the next eleven years in captivity

1725 The birth of John Wilkes (see 29th December) in London, the son of Israel Wilkes a malt distiller (see 19th January).

1777 The Battle of Saratoga ends in defeat for our forces as General John Burgoyne, surrounded and unable to hold out until relief forces arrived, surrenders to the colonial rebels, led by Horatio Gates and the then rebel but later Loyalist Benedict Arnold (see 3rd January and 14th June) who was wounded during the battle (see 3rd September).

1868 The death of Laura Secord (see 13th September) in Chippewa, in the Colony of Canada. Born Laura Ingersoll, it was in June 1813, after the Americans had invaded part of Canada, she overheard the occupying Americans discussing a plan to attack the British forces at Beaver Dams. As a result, she set out at night and walked about 18 miles to warn the British of the impending attack. Because of her legendary patriotic actions, the British and Indian troops were able to surprise and capture most of the Americans in the battle of Beaver Dams in 1813 (see 24th June).

1873 The death of Admiral Sir Robert John Le Mesurier McClure (see 28th January) in London. An experienced naval officer, he served with Admiral Sir John Franklin (see 16th April and 11th June) on his first expedition. It was whilst on one of the expeditions searching for the missing Admiral Franklin that in 1854 he became the first person to pass through the North West Passage by means of both boat and sledge.

1956 Britain's and also the world's first full scale Nuclear Power Station is opened at Calder Hall in Cumberland by Queen Elizabeth II (see 21st April). At 12.16pm she pulled the lever that caused electricity generated from the plant to flow into the national grid.

18th October:

1171 Henry II (see 4th March and 6th July) lands in Waterford in Ireland supported by a huge fleet and army to assert his influence over the warring Irish Kings who had requested Norman-English support for their differing arguments. He quickly established control which marked the beginning of English and later British influence in Ireland (see 1st January and 1st July). His intervention in Ireland was primarily due to the fact that the majority of the minor Irish nobles and kings were happy to see Henry II and his support for their stance against the Norman-English incursions and occupation.

1216 The death of King John "*Lackland*" in Newark Castle. Born in 1166 in Oxford, he was the youngest son of Henry II (see 4th March and 6th July) and the brother of Richard I (see 6th April and 8th September). In 1193, when Richard was imprisoned in Germany, John attempted to take control of England but failed. Reconciliation followed and on Richard's death, John became King. War quickly broke out with France and John lost many of his French possessions (see 27th July). To pay for the war he resorted to heavy taxation which caused his Barons to rebel and launch a civil war. The Barons holding London compelled John to agree terms and ultimately sealed the Magna Carta at Runnymede in 1215 (see 15th June). However, he reneged on his agreement and the civil war continued, ending only with his death.

1748 The Treaty of Aix-la-Chapell is signed bringing an end to the War of the Austrian Succession (1740-1748). Though both Britain and France were the driving forces behind the treaty, neither side was actually happy with the agreement. Both countries gave up territories to each other. However, it brought peace to Europe, if not to other areas of competition around the world between Britain and France.

1860 Effectively ending the Second Opium War (1856-1860), British and French troops enter the so-called Forbidden City in Peking, having defeated the Chinese forces. After extensive looting, the city is put to the torch. This was primarily in retaliation for the kidnapping, torture and murder of some of the British envoys. Our forces were led by Lord Elgin in this humiliation for the Qing dynasty (see 20th May, 13th October and 24th October).

1865 The death of Henry John Temple, Lord Palmerston, in London (see 20th October). One of the most well-known Prime Ministers of his day, he served twice in that capacity. He served for almost 60 years in some position in government and served during the time that the Empire was at its height. He was instrumental in many foreign interventions and is widely-remembered for what became known as his 'Civis Romanus sum' speech in 1850, where he declared that any British subject anywhere in the world should expect the protection of the British Empire, comparing the reach and protection of the Empire to that of Rome's.

1871 The death of Charles Babbage (see 14th June and 26th December). A mathematician, he is known as the leading pioneer of computing. In the 1820s he worked on his 'Difference Engine', a machine he designed to carry out mathematical calculations. A six wheeled model, he soon worked on a bigger and better version he called his 'Difference Engine 2'. This led him to develop his Analytical Engine which he designed to perform any mathematical calculation using punched cards to instruct it as well as a memory to store information. He worked closely with fellow mathematician Ada Lovelace (see 27th November and 10th December).

1922 The foundation of the British Broadcasting Company, later the British Broadcasting Corporation or the B.B.C. (see 2nd November). The General Post Office and a number of private communications companies agreed to form a consortium to experiment with radio services (see 14th November).

1963 Harold Macmillan resigns following a period of ill health and believing his condition to be far worse than it was (see 10th February and 29th December). He was succeeded as Prime Minister by Sir Alex Douglas-Home.

19th October:

1745 The death of Jonathan Swift in Dublin. Author of 'Gulliver's Travels' (see 30th November), he was a poet, essayist, priest and pamphleteer. Born in 1667 and educated in Dublin, he later became the Dean of St. Patrick's Cathedral in Dublin. He moved to England but after some years he returned to Ireland. It was in 1726, returning to England, that his most famous work 'Gulliver's Travels' was published, which was an instant success. In 1742 he suffered a stroke, dying from its effects three years later. He is buried in St. Patrick's Cathedral in Dublin.

1781 Lord Charles Cornwallis (see 5th October and 31st December), along with his force of 8,000 troops, surrenders to rebel forces under the command of George Washington at Yorktown after a three-week siege. Although not the end of the conflict, as it would continue for another two years, the surrender effectively handed ultimate victory to the rebel colonists. Our forces lost around 500 casualties to about 50 American rebels and some 200 French (see 19th April, 3rd September and 5th September).

1875 The death of Charles Wheatstone in Paris (see 6th February). A physicist and inventor, he is known for the invention of the concertina in 1829 and in 1837 he patented the electric telegraph. He also invented a sound magnifier that he called by the name 'microphone'. He also had numerous other inventions, mostly in connection with the application of electricity. He was Professor of Experimental Philosophy at King's College London and his pioneering contribution to world communications is often forgotten.

1914 The start of the first Battle of Ypres in Belgium. Our forces, under Field Marshal Sir John French, had fallen back from Antwerp and arrived in the city in an attempt to defend it from the advancing Imperial German forces under General Erich von Falkenhayn as the enemy tried to punch their way through the allied lines (see 31st July).

1926 The sixth Imperial Conference begins in London. It was attended by the Prime Ministers of Great Britain, Australia, Canada, Newfoundland, New Zealand, South Africa and the President of the Executive Council of the Irish Free State (see 22nd November). Discussed at the conference and accepted was the Balfour Declaration which stated that all Dominions enjoyed equal status within the Empire with a common allegiance to the Crown.

1937 The death of Ernest Rutherford (see 30th August) in Cambridge. He is famous for discovering that atoms have a nucleus and is regarded as the father of nuclear physics. In 1908 he was awarded the Nobel Prize for Chemistry and in 1914 he was knighted. From 1917 he continued with his work in physics, becoming an early pioneer of nuclear physics. The unit of radioactivity, the 'Rutherford' his named after him. He was buried in Westminster abbey.

2010 Tuesday: The Strategic Defence Review is announced by the Coalition Government. The cuts meant, amongst many things, that the armed forces would have HMS Ark Royal and the Harrier jet scrapped. The two new

Aircraft carriers would go ahead but would have no aeroplanes until 2019. Around 100 tanks were scheduled to go as well as 7,000 soldiers, 5,000 RAF and 5,000 Royal Navy personnel. Sadly, Great Britain becomes a third-rate military country and a sad shadow of our former self (see 5th July, 2nd November and 24th November) following the cuts.

20th October:

1632 The birth of Sir Christopher Wren, architect and scientist (see 25th February). His father was the King's Chaplain and he spent his early life in Windsor Castle and played with the future King Charles II (see 6th February and 29th May).

1714 The Coronation of George I at Westminster Abbey (see 28th May, 11th June and 1st August).

1784 The birth of Henry John Temple, later 3rd Viscount Palmerston (see 18th October) in Park Street, Westminster.

1818 The 49th parallel is established by Britain and the US as the border between Canada and the United States of America (see 15th June) when the London Convention is signed in London by representatives of the United States Government and British representatives. Although not removing all disputes, the agreement was the last major exchange of land between Great Britain and America on the continent.

1827 The Battle of Naverino in the Ionian Sea, off the coast of the Peloponnese Peninsular, then part of the Ottoman Empire. Vice-Admiral Sir Edward Codrington, leading a fleet of British, French and Russian war ships, defeats the joint Ottoman and Egyptian Fleet on behalf of the Greeks who had rebelled against the Ottoman Empire as part of the Greek War of Independence (1821-1832). No allied ships were sunk or captured, although many were badly damaged. The Ottoman fleet however was all but destroyed (see 6th July).

1890 The death of Richard Francis Burton (see 19th March) in Trieste. He was a writer, soldier, Orientalist, diplomat and African explorer who mastered numerous languages and dialects. In 1857, along with John Hanning Speke (see 4th May and 15th September), he set of on an expedition with one of its objectives to discover the source of the Nile. They were the first Europeans to see Lake Tanganyika. Both men quarrelled over whether or not Lake Victoria was the true source. He wrote several works, including noted translations of the 'Kama Sutra', 'The Perfumed Garden' and 'Arabian Nights'.

1899 The Battle of Talana Hill (also known as the Battle of Dundee) during the Boer War (1899-1902). There were around 4,000 of our troops against about 3,000 Boers. The battle was a victory for our forces but only after heavy casualties were sustained in a bitter fight every step of the way to the summit of the hill. We suffered around 250 casualties and the Boers around twice that amount.

1952 A State of Emergency is declared in Kenya Colony by Governor Baring after the first murder by the Mau Mau insurgents. The murdering terrorists would go on to target white settlers and tribal members they viewed as being collaborators. The insurgency by the rebels would continue until 1960 and their ultimate defeat, although the rebellion was effectively crushed by 1956 (see 1st July and 12th December).

21st October: Trafalgar Day.

1422 Henry VI (see 21st May and 6th December) becomes King of France on this day upon the death of his Grandfather Charles VI (see 6th November and 16th December). This was the result of the Treaty of Troyes in 1420 (see 21st May) which was agreed following the French defeat at Agincourt in 1415 (see 25th October). The treaty allowed for the heirs of Henry V (see 31st August) to gain the throne of France in preference to the Dauphin and his heirs (see 13th April). Through this legal treaty, all subsequent British Monarchs are the true Monarchs of France.

1772 The birth of Samuel Taylor Coleridge, author of 'Kubla Khan' and 'Christabel' (see 25th July).

1805 The Battle of Trafalgar, off the Southern coast of Spain and a British victory over the combined Fleet of France and Spain. The Royal Navy had a fleet with twenty seven ships of the line and chased down and joined battle with the joint French and Spanish fleet that contained thirty three ships of the line. In a hard fought battle, the Royal Navy completely annihilated the enemy, capturing or destroying over twenty ships without losing a single ship. It was one of this country's and the world's greatest naval victories that led to our dominance in the world for over 120 years but also sadly saw the death of Admiral Lord Horatio Nelson (see below).

1805 The death of Admiral Lord Horatio Nelson (see 29th September) during the battle of Trafalgar (see above). Born in Norfolk, he joined the Royal Navy when he was twelve years old, becoming a Captain when he was twenty. When the French Revolutionary War broke out he was given command of HMS Agamemnon in 1793. He served in the Mediterranean and lost the use of his eye during the siege of Calvi on Corsica in 1794 (see 12th July and 10th August) and lost his arm later at the battle of Santa Cruz de Tenerife in 1787. He went on to take part in the Battle of Cape St. Vincent in 1797 (see 14th February) and the Battle of the Nile in 1798 (see 1st August). Following his death, his body was preserved in a cask of Brandy and returned to Britain. He was given a state funeral and he was buried in St. Paul's Cathedral (see 9th January).

1809 Nelson's Pillar is opened in Sackville Street in Dublin. Built to honour and commemorate Nelson and his glorious victory at Trafalgar (see above), the column was 121 feet high with a 13 feet stone statue of Admiral Nelson on top. The pillar offered the best view of the city and was very popular with Dubliners (see 30th September and 3rd November).

1897 The death of Philip France Little in Monkstown, Ireland. Born in 1824 on Prince Edward Island, he became the leader of the Liberal Party and then the first Premier of Newfoundland Colony in 1855 (see 31st March and 26th September). He resigned office in 1858 and later moved to Ireland.

1904 The Dogger Bank incident. During the Russo-Japanese War, the Russian Baltic Fleet, passing through the North Sea on its way to the Far East, mistook a fleet of about 30 British trawlers for a Japanese fleet of submarines and battleships. As a result, the Russians somehow thought they were about to come under attack and fired on the trawlers. Before the error was realised, two fishermen were dead and many others badly injured. Another man was to die some months later. As a result, the Royal Navy's Home Fleet was put on full alert and made ready to sail. Though it was resolved diplomatically and compensation paid by the Russians, it nearly led to war.

1960 HMS Dreadnought, Britain's first nuclear powered Submarine, is launched by Elizabeth II (see 21st April) at Vickers Armstrong in Barrow in Furnace. The submarine would remain in service until 1980 and cost over £18 million and had a crew of 113.

1966 The Aberfan disaster occurs when 144 villagers from Aberfan near Merthyr Tydfil in South Wales, 116 of whom were children, were killed by a huge coal slag heap that slid down onto the village, burying the Pantglas Junior School, some houses and a farm. It happened at 9.15 am as the children were beginning their lessons.

22nd October:

1641 The bloody Irish Rebellion begins as Catholic rebels and conspirators seize certain key strongholds but fail to take Dublin and the element of surprise is lost. Thousands of Protestants were massacred as the initial rebellion against the English administration escalated into the widespread and indiscriminate killing of Protestant settlers by Catholic rebels. The rebellion was not fully suppressed until Oliver Cromwell's (see 25th April and 3rd September) intervention in Ireland in 1649 (see 12th August, 15th August and 11th September).

1764 The Battle of Buxar in Bengal, India. Forces under the East India Company (see 31st December), led by Major Hector Munro and totalling around 10,000, defeated the forces of mainly Bengal infantry of between 40,000 and 50,000 men. In defeating the Bengal troops, the Company ultimately secured the rights to collect taxes in that area and to administer the various states (see 16th August).

1844 The birth of Louis Reil in the Red River Colony, in Rupert's Land in British North America (see 16th November).

1877 The Blantyre mining disaster in which 207 miners are killed becomes Scotland's worst mining accident. Two pits in the William Dixon Colliery were the scene of a huge explosion. Following the disaster, a number the miner's widows and orphans were subsequently evicted from their tied homes.

1935 The death of Rt. Hon. Sir Edward Henry Carson (see 9th February) in Kent. Born in Dublin, he was the first person to sign the Ulster Covenant in 1912 in protest against the third Home Rule Bill (see 20th March and 28th September). He was the chief creator of the Ulster Volunteer Force and an ardent British Nationalist. This was a force of some 80,000 Protestants that were brought into being to counter the threat of Home Rule. They formed virtually the entire 36th Ulster Division of our army during the Great War. He served in Herbert Asquith's (see 15th February and 12th September) coalition administration but later resigned and then served under David Lloyd George's (see 17th January and 26th March) government as first Lord of the Admiralty and later as a cabinet minister without portfolio.

23rd October:

1295 The Auld Alliance between the Kingdom of Scotland and France against their mutual enemy England and its King Edward I (see 17th June and 7th July) is signed in Paris (see 26th April). A diplomatic, economic and military alliance, it was drawn up between Phillip IV of France and John Balliol of Scotland (see 25th November). It had benefits to the Scots of allowing huge numbers to serve as mercenaries in the French armies and for better terms of trade for wine for the home market in Scotland.

1642 Sunday, 2pm: the Battle of Edgehill in Warwickshire, the first major battle of the Civil War (see 3rd September) takes place. Though generally an inconclusive result, the Royalist Armies remained in control of the road to London, a definite advantage. Both sides faced each other with between 13,000 and 14,000 men. The Parliamentarians under the Earl of Essex were repeatedly unable to break the Royalist lines and in the end withdrew to Warwick Castle.

1658 The death of Colonel Thomas Pride. An officer in the New Model Army, he is remembered as the leader of the military expulsion and arrest of anti-army MPs from the Long Parliament (see 6th December). He fought with distinction throughout the Civil Wars and loyally served with Oliver Cromwell (see 25th April and 3rd September). He was present at the trial of Charles I (see 30th January and 19th November) as a judge and signed the warrant for his execution. He was knighted by Oliver Cromwell in 1656.

1856 The Royal Navy begins the bombardment of the town of Canton and razes most of the town to the ground (see 3rd July and 8th October) in what was the first engagement of the Second Opium War 1856-1860 (see 24th October).

1869 The death of Edward Smith-Stanley, the 14th Earl of Derby (see 29th March) in Knowsley Hall, Prescot in Lancashire. He held the office of Prime Minster three times and is the longest-serving leader of the Conservative party. He had begun his political life as a Whig but in 1837 he joined the Tory party. During his second term as Prime Minister, his administration was responsible for the transfer of control of the East India Company to the Crown (see 2nd August). His third government was responsible for the Second Reform Bill in 1867.

1921 The death of John Boyd Dunlop (see 5th February) in Dublin, Ireland. A veterinary surgeon and inventor, he is recognised as the inventor and developer of the first pneumatic tyres and established the company that bears his name today, the Dunlop Pneumatic Tyre Company.

1942 The second battle of El Alamein begins with a huge artillery bombardment of Axis lines followed by British and Empire troops advancing across anti-tank mine fields. The enemy positions were heavily defended and the objective was for the advancing infantry to punch a hole in the Axis' defensive line in what was called Operation Lightfoot, the first part of the battle (see 4th November).

24th October:

1360 The Treaty of Bretigny is ratified between England and France (see 8th May), thus ending the first phase of what would later be called the Hundred Years' War (1337-1443). It was ratified in Calais (see 7th January and 17th July) between the eldest sons of the respective Monarchs, Edward (later referred to as the Black Prince see 8th June and 15th June) on behalf of his father, Edward III (see 21st June and 13th November).

1537 The death of Jane Seymour at Hampton Court Palace. Her death was caused by complications following the birth of her son, the future Edward VI (see 6th July and 12th October). The third wife of Henry VIII (see 28th January, 30th May and 28th June), she was born in Wiltshire and first met Henry when serving as a maid to Catherine of Aragon (see 7th January and 16th December). She is the only one of Henry's wives to receive a state funeral and the only one to be buried with him in St. George's Chapel in Windsor Castle.

1860 The Convention of Peking between Qing China and Lord Elgin for the United Kingdom is signed, bringing an end to the Second Opium War, 1856-1860 (see 20th May, 13th October and 18th October). The convention ceded part of Kowloon to Britain.

1945 The United Nations organisation comes into being with Britain as one of the founder members of the original twenty-two nations as all five permanent members of the Security Council ratify the United Nations Charter agreed earlier in the year.

1964 The Colony of Northern Rhodesia, formed in 1911 under British South Africa Company rule, is granted its independence (see 29th October).

2003 The last commercial flight of the Concorde aeroplane takes place, arriving at Heathrow from New York (see 21st January).

25th October: Agincourt Day

1154 The death of King Stephen at Dover Castle. Born in Blois in France around 1097, he was the Grandson of William I through his daughter Adela and also the last Norman King. His reign was noticeable for his weakness and the civil war between his supporters and those of his cousin Matilda, whose son Henry eventually succeeded Stephen upon his death as Henry II (see 26th December).

1400 The death of Geoffrey Chaucer (born 1343). Born probably in London in the early 1340s, his best known work is the 'Canterbury Tales'. Little is known of his early life. He became a diplomat for Edward III (see 21st June and 13th November) and in 1386 he became an MP. Much of his earlier works were translations of earlier French works into English. Later however, he produced many original works in English and it is mainly through his work that the English language of his day became the language of English literature, replacing Latin and French.

1415 St. Crispin's Day and the Battle of Agincourt that spelt total and humiliating defeat for the French and a glorious victory for England. There were 25,000 French against Henry V's (see 31st August) army of just 6,000. From the French army there were 5 Dukes, 90 Counts and 1,500 of the Barons and Knights who were killed during the battle due to the English employing their Archers as their main tactical weapon. Many more were wounded and captured. 'For Harry, England and St. George' (see 31st August and 16th September).

1759 The birth of William Wyndham Grenville in Buckinghamshire (see 12th January).

1760 The death of George II (see 11th October and 30th October) in Kensington Palace of a ruptured aneurism of the aorta. Born in Hanover in 1683, he was created Prince of Wales when his father acceded to the British throne in 1714. He became King in 1727 (see 11th October) and his reign saw this country involved in the War of the Austrian Succession (1740-1748), and the first half of the Seven Years' War (1756-1763), as well as the acquisition of large areas of the India and the glorious victories during the 'Annus Mirabilis' of 1759. He was the last British Monarch to go into battle, when he led his troops at the battle of Dettingen in 1743 (see 16th June) and he was the monarch at the time of the last and greatest Jacobite rising of 1745 (see 16th April and 19th August).

1854 The Battle of Balaclava during the Crimean War (1853-1856). A Russian force attempted to attack the port at Balaclava but was repulsed by our troops, which included the 'Thin Red Line' of the 93rd Highland Regiment against Russian Cavalry, the Charge of the Heavy Brigade and the famous Charge of the Light Brigade in Southern Crimea. Although the outcome of the battle itself was inconclusive, it was nevertheless an excellent example of the courage and steadiness of our forces when faced with a formidable enemy (see 28th March, 30th March, 20th September and 5th November).

1979 The death of Field Marshall Sir Gerald Walter Robert Templer in London (see 11th September). Commissioned into the army in 1916, he fought in both World Wars and during the Second World War became an Intelligence Officer. After the war he was appointed Director of Military Intelligence. In 1951 he was appointed High Commissioner of Malaya by Prime Minister Winston Churchill (see 24th January and 30th November) to deal with the Malayan Emergency (see 18th June and 31st August). He was to develop what was to become the model for counter insurgency and coined the phrase 'the battle for hearts and minds'. He is credited for bringing the Emergency under control.

26th October:

899 The death of Alfred the Great of England at Wantage. He was the only King to bear the title 'Great'. Born in Wantage in Oxfordshire in 849, he became king of the Kingdom of Wessex. In 871 he beat the Danes at the battle of Ashdown (see 8th January) becoming king of the kingdom of Wessex a year later. However, the Danes continued to attack and he had to take refuge in the Somerset marshes to continue a guerrilla campaign from there. He again beat the Danes at the Battle of Edington in 878 before eventually reaching agreement with them. He is credited with dividing the Kingdom into Shires and Hundreds. He assumed Lordship over the Angles and Saxons and several Princes of Wales after the 'Danelaw' was established. He spent most of his life fighting the Danes and Vikings in their continual attempts to invade this country. He was buried in his kingdom's capital, Winchester.

1764 The death of William Hogarth (see 10th November) in London. A leading painter who initially specialised in portraiture for the rich, he is most well-known for his satirical cartoon-like prints of street scenes of everyday life involving the common masses. These included prints entitled, 'Beer Street', 'Gin Lane', and 'The Four Stages of Cruelty'. He also produced a four-piece work entitled 'The Election' covering scenes from the 1754 election in Oxford. He was also well-known for his criticism of political corruption and his anti-war stance, made public in his publication 'The Times'.

1803 The birth of Joseph Hansom (see 29th June) in York.

1813 The battle of Chateauguay in the Provence of Lower Canada. A force of predominantly Canadian militia and their loyal Mohawk warrior allies repelled a larger force of around 4,000 Americans. The Colonial militia were led by a French Canadian, Charles Salaberry (see 27th February and 19th November). Though greatly outnumbering the Canadians, the Americans, led by General Wade Hampton, were forced to retreat in the face of superior Canadian determination and skill. This battle, along with the battle of Crysler's Farm in 1813 (see 11th November), was instrumental in forcing the Americans to abandon their campaign along the St. Lawrence River and their advance on Montreal (see 18th June and 24th December).

1951 Winston Churchill (see 24th January, 5th April, 10th May and 30th November) is elected Prime Minister again following the General Election the previous day. The Conservatives win 321 seats, Labour 295 seats and the Liberals only 6 seats. Clement Attlee's Labour Government loses and Clement Attlee resigns (see 3rd January and 8th October).

2014 In a ceremony at Camp Bastion in the Helmand Province of Afghanistan, the Union Flag is lowered and British forces end their thirteen-year combat mission in the country, handing the camp over to the Afghan security forces. A total of 453 British service personnel lost their lives and many more suffered injury during our presence in the country (see 7th October).

27th October:

1644 The second Battle of Newbury, in Berkshire. Fought during the Civil War (see 3rd September), it was a Parliamentarian victory. Although casualties were fairly even on both sides, they were heavy and the Royalists under the Command of Prince Maurice conducted an orderly and unchallenged withdrawal under the cover of darkness along with the King to Oxford.

1728 The birth of the future Captain James Cook (see 14th February, 29th April and 6th October) in Marton, North Yorkshire, now part of Middlesbrough.

1908 Parliament and the Liberal government passes the Old Age Pensions Act allowing for the first ever non-contributory pension payments to people over the age of 70 (see 1st January).

1931 Tuesday: the General Election and the Conservatives under Stanley Baldwin (see 3rd August and 14th December) win an absolute majority with a landslide victory and a majority of 324 seats. However, Ramsey MacDonald (see 12th October and 9th November) remained Prime Minister, after having been expelled by the Labour Party for forming a National Government with the Conservatives before the election. The Conservatives campaigned on a protectionist agenda.

1967 The controversial Abortion Act is passed by parliament (see 27th April) after a heated debate and free vote. The act legalised abortions up to 28 weeks gestation by registered practitioners and allowed the services to be carried out free under the National Health Service.

2014 The last British combat troops leave Camp Bastion in the Helmand Province of Afghanistan bringing an end to the thirteen-year combat mission in the country. The last man out, an Officer with the RAF, carried the Union flag lowered the previous day as they were air-lifted to Kandahar on their journey back to Britain (see 26th October). A total of 453 British service personnel lost their lives and many more suffered injury during our presence in the country (see 7th October).

28th October:

1216 The first Coronation of the nine-year-old Henry III at Gloucester Cathedral (see 1st October and 16th November). The coronation was a hurried affair due to the recent civil wars and was to emphasise his royal power and authority (see 17th May).

1704 The death of John Locke (see 29th August) in Essex. A philosopher, he was one of the leading figures of the Enlightenment and was well-known for his influence upon other philosophers as well as the American colonial rebels. He was opposed to authoritarianism and believed in the individuals need to use reason in the search for truth. In his life he wrote a number of important and influential works, including 'Two Treatises of Government', 'Letters Concerning Toleration' and 'Some Thoughts Concerning Education' and he was an early advocate of the separation of Church and State.

1792 The death of John Smeaton near Leeds (see 8th June). The son of a lawyer, he began an education in law but decided to leave law and turn to his interest in engineering. As an engineer, he was responsible for canals, bridges and, in particular, lighthouses. He was elected as a Fellow of the Royal Society in 1753. Often referred to as the 'father of civil engineering', he designed the third Eddystone Lighthouse (see 2nd December) and founded the Society of Civil Engineers in 1771 and coined the term 'Civil Engineers' in order to distinguish them from the Military Engineers.

1971 Britain successfully launches its own satellite into a polar orbit at 04:09 GMT. The 'Prospero' (built by the British Aircraft Corporation) satellite was launched from Woomera in Australia on Britain's own rocket, the Black Arrow (see 5th June and 28th June).

1971 Thursday: The House of Commons backs Edward Heath (see 9th July and 17th July), the Conservative Prime Minister, by a majority of 112 votes, in his desire for Britain to apply to join the European Economic Market (the E.E.C., see 1st January, 30th January, 7th February, 23rd June and 27th November).

1998 The death of Thomas Harold 'Tommy' Flowers (see 22nd December) in London. A technical computing engineer, he is one of the unknown heroes of the Second World War. Born in London, in 1926 he joined the General Post Office in the Telecommunications section and later moved into their research section. It was here as an engineer, and in particular during the Second World War, that he worked with Alan Turin (see 7th June and 23rd June) and designed and created Colossus, the world's first programmable electronic computer. Despite much more work on electronic exchanges, following the war, nothing of his efforts was used by the G.P.O. Due to the secrecy of his work, his role during the war went unrecognised for most of his life.

29th October:

1618 Sir Walter Raleigh, Lord Lieutenant of Cornwall, is beheaded at Whitehall in London. A soldier, Member of Parliament and adventurer, he was at one time a favourite of Elizabeth I (see 24th March and 7th September). Born in Devon around 1552, he spent some time in Ireland as a Landlord and attempted the colonization of Virginia which ended in failure at Ranoake Island. He secretly married Elizabeth 'Bess' Throckmorton and fell out of favour with Queen Elizabeth on discovery of the marriage. He eventually regained favour and took part in many exploits, including the raid on Cadiz in 1596, and became Governor of Jersey. After Elizabeth I's death, he fell out of favour and was accused of involvement in the main plot for which his death sentence was not initially carried out.

1656 The birth of Edmond Halley in Haggerston, Shoreditch, and now part of London (see 14th January).

1704 The birth of John Byng (see 14th March), later an Admiral in the Royal Navy.

1740 The birth of James Boswell in Edinburgh (see 19th May). A writer, friend and the most famous biographer of Samuel Johnson (see 7th September and 13th December).

1889 The British South Africa Company is incorporated by Royal Charter granted today. Founded by Cecil Rhodes, (see 26th March and 5th July) who was also a Director of the company, it was modeled on the East India Company (see 31st December). Its charter was for an initial twenty-five years. The Company was to acquire and administer and police territory, profiting from mineral and other natural resources whilst developing settlements on behalf of the British government but free from governmental interference (see 24th October).

1924 The General Election and the Conservatives under Stanley Baldwin (see 3rd August and 14th December) are re-elected with a landslide victory. Labour under Ramsey McDonald (see 12th October and 9th November) loses with a loss of 40 seats and the Liberals under Herbert Henry Asquith (see 15th February and 12th September) losing 118 seats. Sir Oswald Mosley (see 16th November and 3rd December) loses his seat.

30th October:

1485 The Coronation of Henry VII in Westminster Abbey (see 28th January and 21st April).

1683 The birth of George II in Herrenhausen Palace in Hanover, modern Germany (see 11th October and 25th October). The son of George I (see 28th May and 11th June) and Sophia of Celle, he was the last Monarch to be born outside of Great Britain.

1757 The death of Admiral Edward Vernon also known as 'Old Grog' (see 12th November). He joined the Navy in 1700 and is remembered for his great and heroic victory at Porto Bello in the War of Jerkin's Ear in 1739 (see 21st November). He also became a Member of Parliament. His most enduring legacy was his 1740 order to have his ship's rum ration watered down and fruit juice added, unintentionally improving his crew's health. This mixture was apparently nicknamed 'grog' after his own nickname 'Old Grog', derived from the coat he constantly wore, made from grogram.

1823 The death of Edmund Cartwright (see 24th April). A Clergyman from Nottingham, he is remembered for inventing the power loom, one of the key moments in the progress of the industrial revolution. Following a visit in 1784 to Richard Arkwright's (see 3rd August and 23rd December) cotton mill in Derbyshire, Edmund was encouraged to develop a mechanised weaving machine. Undeterred by initial scepticism from associates, he patented his first machine in 1785, making improvements in subsequent designs. Unfortunately, he never made any real money from his invention, despite his contribution to the Industrial Revolution. In 1809 the Government awarded him £10,000 as recognition for his work on the power loom.

1909 Lord Brabazon of Tara becomes the first Briton to fly over 1 mile in a British-built aeroplane (see 8th February, 30th April, 2nd May and 17th May). In a Short Biplane No. 2, he flew a circular mile, winning £1,000 in prize money from the Daily Mail newspaper.

1918 The Armistice of Mudros is signed on the Aegean island of Lemnos, bringing an end to the conflict in the Middle East during the First World War (see 10th August and 11th November). It was signed aboard HMS Agamemnon between Admiral Gough-Calthorpe for Britain and her Allies and Rauf Bey for the Ottoman Empire. Under the Armistice, the Ottomans were to open up the Dardanelles and the Bosporus to allied ships, surrender all their forts, and demobilize its army and vacate all its Arab possessions. The treaty affectively brought an end to the Ottoman Empire. HMS Agamemnon was to be the last surviving pre-dreadnought battleship of the Royal Navy (see 24th July).

1923 The death of Andrew Bonar Law in London (see 16th September). Born in the Colony of New Brunswick, he is the only Prime Minister to have been born outside of the British Isles. His mother died in 1861 and in 1870 he moved to Helensburgh in Scotland to live with his mother's sister. He entered Parliament in 1900 and in 1911 he became leader of the Conservative party, succeeding Arthur Balfour (see 19th March and 25th July). Following David Lloyd George's resignation in 1922 (see 17th January and 26th March), he became Prime Minister. His term in office lasted only 209 days, the shortest in the twentieth century (see 22nd May). Within six months of his resignation he was dead from cancer. His ashes were interred in Westminster Abbey.

1925 John Logie Baird (see 14th June and 14th August) transmits the first television pictures.

1979 The death of Sir Barnes Neville Wallis in Surrey (see 26th September), the inventor of the famous 'bouncing bomb' that was used to such devastating affect in the 'Dam Busters' raid of World War Two (see 16th May). Born in Ripley in Yorkshire, he became an aviation engineer and worked for Vickers. It was here that he worked on the Airship R100 before becoming Assistant Chief Designer at the outbreak of war. Having developed his idea of a drum shaped 'bouncing bomb', he revealed his invention to the Air Ministry and it was accepted. He also designed the 12,000lb Tallboy bomb and later still, the 10-ton Grandslam bomb. Following the war, he worked for the British Aircraft Corporation until his retirement in 1971. He was made a Fellow of the Royal Society in 1954 and he was knighted in 1968.

1990 A pilot hole connecting the two halves of the Channel tunnel breaks through, connecting Britain and France for the first time (see 1st December).

31st October:

1620 The birth of John Evelyn (see 27th February) in Wooton in Surrey. He would later become the well-known diarist and writer.

1795 The birth of John Keats in London (see 23rd February).

1828 The birth of Joseph Wilson Swan (see 27th May) in Sunderland.

1831 Monday: three days of riots in Bristol over the Reform Act are finally brought to an end. They started as protests against the failure of the Reform Act to be passed in the House of Lords. Over the weekend from Saturday to Monday, around 100 houses were burned and it was only brought under control by the arrival of a detachment of Dragoons who attacked and then killed and wounded several hundred protesters.

1860 The death of Admiral Sir Thomas Cochrane, 10th Earl of Dundonald, in Kensington, London (see 14th December). He was one of our finest and most successful naval heroes and nicknamed the 'Sea Wolf' by the French. He had a dazzling career during the Napoleonic Wars and became a Radical MP. He was tried and convicted of fraud for his role in the Great Stock Exchange Fraud of 1814, resulting in his expulsion from Parliament and the Navy. He then went on to serve in the Chilean Navy, the Brazilian Navy and the Greek Navy during their respective wars of independence. After more heroic exploits with these navies, he was later re-instated into the Royal Navy and promoted a number of times.

1936 The two hundred strong group of unemployed men on the Jarrow March arrive in London carrying the 11,000 name petition with them. The men were demanding jobs and also highlighting the extreme poverty and deprivation in their home town and surrounding area. The Prime Minister Stanley Baldwin refused to see them and there was very little debate or recognition in Parliament at the time (see 5th October).

1956 Royal Air Force and Fleet Air Arm aircraft, along with the French Air Force, bomb selected targets in Egypt at the start of Operation Musketeer, commonly referred to as the Suez Crisis. The main targets are military bases and air fields in order to gain air superiority in readiness for the land forces. The intervention would continue for less than a week. Economic threats and pressure from the United States mounted because Britain acted without consulting them and risked damaging their interests. This pressure from a supposed ally forced a ceasefire and the withdrawal of our forces (see 26th August, 5th November, 25th November and 23rd December).

NOVEMBER

1st November:

866 Viking forces seize control of York from the Northumbrians at the start of their invasion of Anglo-Saxon England. Referred to by the Norsemen as Jorvik, it would become the centre of the 'Danelaw' (see 8th June and 13th November).

1762 The birth of Spencer Percival in London, later a Conservative MP and the only Prime Minister to be assassinated. He is shot just outside the House of Commons (see 11th May).

1765 The Stamp Act of 1764 is enacted in the American Colonies (see 17th March, 22nd March and 5th September). The Act required a paid tax stamp on the majority of printed materials of paper and parchment. This was to help pay for the troops used in the Colonies during the Seven Years' War (1756-1763) to defend the colonists, in particular from the French. However, it caused outrage within the Colonies and also within many political circles in Britain (see 23rd August).

1856 The British Governor General in India, Viscount Charles John Canning (see 17th June and 14th December), declares war on Persia following the Persian seizure of the city of Herat after political encouragement from Russia (see 4th March).

1858 Viscount Charles John Canning (see 17th June and 14th December), Governor General of India, becomes the first Viceroy of British India following the transfer of all responsibility for the governance of India from the East India Company to the Crown (see 2nd August and 31st December).

1914 The Battle of Coronel off the coast of Chile, the first major naval engagement of the Great War and a defeat for our country (see 28th August). Admiral Christopher Craddock of the West Indies Squadron intercepted the Fleet of five ships of Admiral Von Spee and decided to fight the much stronger German ships, SMS Scharnhorst, SMS Gneisenau, SMS Desden, SMS Leipzig and SMS Numberg. He ordered the smaller Otranto to escape and stopped to fight with his Flagship HMS Good Hope, HMS Monmouth and HMS Glasgow. It was a one-sided battle, ending with the death of Admiral Craddock (see 2nd July) and the loss of both his Flagship HMS Good Hope and HMS Monmouth and the loss of all the crew of both ships of around 1,600 Officers and men (see 8th December). HMS Glasgow managed to escape although severely damaged. This was our first naval defeat for over one hundred years. Admiral Cradock had joined the Royal Navy in 1875 and had served during the occupation of Cyprus in 1878, served on the Royal Yacht and in various actions in China in 1900.

2nd November:

1698 The first expedition of about 1,200 mainly Scottish settlers makes landfall at the bay of Darien in South America. They call their new colony New Caledonia. To begin with the settlers constructed a small canal and erected Fort St. Andrew and then later began to construct what was to be the beginning of the capital, New Edinburgh. Unfortunately, just seven months after landing, around 400 settlers were dead, the majority of the rest were disease-ridden and emaciated and the venture was already doomed.

1899 The siege of Ladysmith by Boer forces begins when they cut the railway line south of the town and surround it. The garrison was led by General Sir George White (see 28th February).

1899 The first Australian troops (see 1st March) to serve outside of Australia arrive in Cape Town. They are the New South Wales Lancers and are the first of several contingents to be despatched to fight the Boers in the South African War of 1899-1902 (see 31st May, 11th October and 22nd November).

1917 The proclamation of the Balfour Declaration. In a letter from the Foreign Secretary Arthur Balfour to the British Zionist leader Lord Rothschild, it was stated that our government supported a plan for the partitioning of the Ottoman Empire after the Great War and Britain's support for the Zionist desire for a Jewish homeland in Palestine as well as a provision to safeguard the area's non-Jewish residents.

1936 The BBC begins its first regular television broadcasts and also the world's first high definition television service (see 18th October and 14th November) from its Alexandra Palace television station.

1950 The death of George Bernard Shaw (see 26th July) in Hertfordshire. He was a playwright, most well-known for his play 'Pygmalion' published in 1938. Born in Dublin, he moved to London in 1876 where he began to write and attempted a career in journalism. He became more aware of social reform and joined the Social Democratic Federation, and in 1884 he joined the Fabian Society followed by the Socialist League a year later. He concentrated on the Fabian Society and produced numerous pamphlets about social reform and women's rights. He was strongly in favour of a political movement to further socialism through a political party and supported the formation of the Labour Party. When the Great War broke out, he openly opposed Britain's involvement in the conflict. He continued writing plays between the wars and was awarded the Nobel Prize for Literature in 1925. He was also opposed to the country's involvement in the Second World War.

2010 Two military co-operation treaties with France are signed in London by the Prime Minister David Cameron and French President Nicolas Sarkosy. The treaties formed the agreement for shared military and tactical resources and one on nuclear testing (see 13th January, 19th October and 24th November).

3rd November:

1534 The Act of Supremacy is passed by Parliament legally recognising the Monarch, Henry VIII (see 28th January and 28th June), as the Head of the Church of England and thereby severing the influence of Rome over the King.

1749 The birth of Daniel Rutherford in Edinburgh (see 15th November).

1779 The birth of Hugh Gough (see 2nd March) in County Limerick, Ireland.

1839 The 'Newport Rising' begins. Around 5,000 Chartists and workers begin their demonstration by marching from across the Gwent valleys through the night in torrential rain to converge on the town of Newport in Wales led by amongst others John Frost (see 4th November).

1843 The statue of Admiral Horatio Nelson is placed on top of the Column in Trafalgar Square (see 30th September and 21st October). The statue, measuring 18 feet and 1 inch high, is made from three pieces of sandstone designed by Edward Hodges Bailey.

1914 The town of Great Yarmouth is bombarded by a Battle Cruiser Squadron of the German Imperial Navy. In the early morning, the Germans encountered British vessels that had moved to engage them. During part of the battle, the Germans fired a number of shells at Yarmouth but they fell short, hitting the beach without casualties. This was the first attack on the British mainland of the Great War (see 24th January, 31st May, 1st November, 8th December and 16th December).

1975 Elizabeth II (see 6th February and 21st April) opens the first North Sea oil pipeline in Scotland.

4th November:

1470 The probable date for the birth of Edward V in Sanctuary in Westminster (see 25th June). He was the son of the Yorkist Edward IV (see 9th April and 28th April) and Elizabeth Woodville.

1650 The birth of William 'of Orange' (later William III of England and William II of Scotland) in The Hague (see 8th March). He was the only child of William II, Prince of Orange.

1702 The death of Admiral John Benbow in Port Royal, Kingston in the Colony of Jamaica (see 10th March). He entered the Royal Navy in 1658 and served during the Nine Years' War (1688–1697). Though appointed Master Attendant at Chatham Dockyard in 1690, he was recalled to active service a number of times. He was appointed Commander in Chief West Indies in November 1701 during the War of the Spanish Succession (1701-1714). On 24th August 1702 his leg was shattered by chain shot whilst engaging a French Squadron and it was from these wounds that he died. He was buried in St. Andrew's Church in Kingston.

1839 The 'Newport Rising' concludes as around 5,000 Chartists and workers who had marched through the night in torrential rain to Newport in Wales begin to demonstrate, led by John Frost. They marched on the Westgate Hotel where the local authorities, who were well prepared and expecting trouble, ordered the soldiers to open fire. Although exact details are sketchy, at least 22 of the protesters were killed and around fifty were wounded. The leaders, including John Frost, were arrested, tried and a sentence of execution was commuted to being transported for life (see 3rd November).

1898 French forces, under the command of Major Marchand, are ordered to leave the fort at Fashoda on the Nile by their government. The French had occupied the fort in July in an attempt to deny the British any claim on the area with the hope of forcing Britain to abandon Egypt. However, a flotilla of gun boats and troops under the command of Lord Herbert Kitchener (see 5th June and 24th June) arrived at the fort (see 18th September), which massively outnumbered the meagre French troops. The French, fearful of growing German strength and therefore wishing good relations with Great Britain, ordered Marchand to leave, which he did in disgust.

1918 The death of Wilfred Edward Salter Owen M.C. (see 18th March). A poet soldier of the Great War, he was probably the most well-known and influential of the war poets. A teaching assistant, he worked for a couple of years before the war as a language tutor in France. Enlisting in 1915, he received a commission into the Manchester Regiment and arrived at the Western Front in 1917. Suffering from shell shock, he returned to Britain and there met Siegfried Sassoon who became a major influence on his work. In August 1918 he returned to the front and was awarded the Military Cross two months later. He was killed in action attempting to cross the Sambre-Oise Canal in France whilst leading his men. The telegram bearing the news of his death arrived at his parent's house on Armistice Day, as the church bells were ringing in celebration of the end of the war.

1942 British and Empire troops under General Bernard Montgomery (see 24th March and 17th November) are victorious at the culmination of the hard-fought and brutal Second battle of El Alamein as General Erwin Rommel orders his Afrika Korps forces into a full retreat. This was one of the most important battles of the whole war and saw the Axis powers in retreat for the first time (see 23rd October) since the start of the war.

1990 The death of Colonel Archibald David Stirling (see 15th November) in London. An officer in the Scots Guards, he is famous for being the creator of the Special Air Service (SAS) pioneering the role of special units of the armed forces. He and his men were extremely successful despite initial doubts by the authorities, destroying hundreds of enemy aircraft in airfields deep behind enemy lines. Eventually captured, he took part and masterminded several escape attempts, always ending in his own recapture. He was eventually sent to Colditz Prison Camp. He was awarded the

Distinguished Service Order (DSO) and he was knighted in 1990, shortly before his death.

5th November:

1605 The Gunpowder Plot is officially uncovered. Thomas Catesby, Guy Fawkes (see 31st January) and many of their co-conspirators are discovered and arrested (see 30th January and 8th November) at the Houses of Parliament (Guy Fawkes), their terrorist target, and at other addresses in the country over the following days. As Catholics, the conspirators had intended to blow up the Houses of Parliament whilst King James VI (James I of England, see 27th March and 19th June) was present for the State Opening of Parliament. They then planned to install a puppet Monarchy sympathetic to Catholicism, probably Princess Elizabeth, the daughter of James VI, and ultimately return England to the Catholic faith.

1688 William 'of Orange' lands at Brixham near Torbay in Devon with around 15,000 troops at the start of what would later be called the 'Glorious Revolution' and the ultimate removal of James VII (James II of England, see 5th September and 14th October) as the last Catholic Monarch (see 13th February, 8th March and 4th November).

1854 The Battle of Inkerman during the Crimean War (1853-1856). The Allies, 7,500 British under Lord Raglan and 8,200 French, were greatly outnumbered by the 42,000 Russians. The battle took place as the Russians attempted to assault and then dislodge the Allies in an attempt to bring an end to the siege of nearby Sevastapol. However, the Allies stood firm despite some of the most savage fighting of the war. The 68th Foot (Durham Light Infantry) attacked the Russian forces that outnumbered them by five to one. Their Commanding Officer, Sir George Cathcart, is killed in the advance and the Durhams are reduced to half their strength but the Russians waver in the face of our troops determination and in the end the Durhams carry the day. The Imperial Russian Army withdrew in defeat. Our casualties were 2,357, the French suffered 929 and the Russians suffered over 12,000 casualties. This battle came later to be known as 'the Soldier's Battle' because of the thick fog on the battle field, causing contact to be lost between the armies, meaning that groups of battalion size or less engaged in brutal fighting, cut off from each other. The conduct of our forces was to show the Victorian soldiers as the greatest in the world and that as a force and as individuals, they would never give way (see 28th March, 30th March, 20th September and 25th October).

1879 The death of James Clerk Maxwell (see 13th June) in Cambridge. He was a mathematician and physicist and is developed the electromagnetic theory. During the 1860s and 1870s he worked on confirming Faraday's work on electromagnetism and published his theory on electromagnetic fields. His work did more for the advancement of physics than any other scientist.

1892 The birth of John William Alcock in Old Trafford in Stretford near Manchester (see 15th June and 18th December).

1950 The battle of Pakchon during the Korean War (1950-1953) between British and Australian troops from the UN 27th British Commonwealth Brigade and Chinese troops of their 117th Division. The Chinese and North Korean troops attacked across the Pakchon-Sinanju road but met stiff resistance in defence by the 3rd Battalion Royal Australian Regiment, 1st Argyll and Sutherland Highlanders and the 1st Middlesex Regiment. The Chinese offensive was stopped primarily by the Australians who then launched a counter attack, capturing a key position (see 27th July) and beating off subsequent Communist counter-arracks.

1956 A total of 668 British Paratroops of the 3rd Battalion the Parachute Regiment, flying in from Cyprus parachute onto El Gamal Airfield in Port Said in Egypt. They are shot at by rebel militia on the ground as they descend and there are a few casualties sustained (see 26th August, 31st October, 6th November, 25th November and 23rd December). The immediate area is quickly secured in readiness for incoming support and opposition is suppressed before the Para's move into the city of Port Said itself. This is the beginning of the Suez land campaign, code named 'Operation Musketeer', in which a coordinated assault by British, French and Israeli forces begins with the aim of securing the Suez Canal.

1971 The final launch of Britain's 'Blue Streak' ballistic missile at the Woomera test range in Australia (see 28th June). The missile was designed and built primarily by de Havilland to replace the V Bomber and allow this country the capability to deliver an independent nuclear deterrent. It was first launched in 1964 (see 5th June). Unfortunately, due to increasing costs and a lack of determination by the government, the military aspect of the project was cancelled. The technology was then used to develop the 'Black Arrow' satellite launch system (see 28th October).

6th November:

1429 The Coronation of Henry VI at Westminster Abbey (see 13th April, 21st May, 6th December and 16th December).

1913 The death of William Henry Preece in Penrhos, Caernarvon (see 15th February). He was an electrical engineer and inventor known for his work on telegraphy and early radio. Born in Caernarvon, he studied in London under Michael Faraday. He worked for the General Post Office and in 1892 became their Engineer in Chief. It was whilst at the Post Office that he conducted his experiments with and improvements on telegraphy and early radio transmission using Morse code.

1917 The town of Passchendaele in Belgium is captured by our forces, thus ending the third battle of Ypres. Fighting had begun in the July and the village was finally carried by the heroic 1st and 2nd Canadian Divisions (see 26th July). The casualties for this battle are estimated to be well over 200,000.

1944 Walter Edward Guinness, Lord Moyne, Resident Minister of State for the Middle East is murdered by Jewish terrorists in Cairo, Egypt. Both terrorists involved in the cold-blooded murder were tried and executed for their crime. Lord Moyne had arrived home in his car with a couple of assistants when they were attacked, the driver being murdered also (see 25th April, 14th May and 29th September).

1956 British troops, mainly from the Parachute Regiment, take control of Port Said and the Suez area with French forces in support further to the south. However, following disgraceful political threats and economic blackmail by the United States, Britain's alleged ally, a ceasefire is declared unilaterally by Anthony Eden after only one day of land-based military operations (see 31st October, 5th November, 25th November and 23rd December).

1999 In a national referendum, the Australian people vote to keep the Monarchy as the nation's constitutional Head of State (see 1st January). Out of those voting, 43.13% voted 'yes' to a Republic and 54.87% voted 'no', and to keep the Monarchy.

2002 The Commonwealth Memorial Gates at the end of Constitution Hill in London is unveiled by Queen Elizabeth II (see 21st April). The War Memorial commemorates members of the armed forces of the British Empire from Africa, the Caribbean and British India who served in both world wars (see 1st February, 18th July, 19th July and 11th November). The memorial honours the over five million men and women who served and remembers the almost 1.7 million of that number who died in the service of the Empire. 'Our future is greater than our past' (Ben Okri).

7th November:

1687 The birth of William Stukeley in Holbeach, Lincolnshire (see 3rd March).

1731 The birth of Robert Rogers in the Province of Massachusetts Bay (see 18th May).

1783 The last execution at Tyburn tree in London takes place when John Austen, a Highwayman, is hanged.

1805 The birth of Thomas Brassey in Buerton, Cheshire (see 8th December).

1908 HMS Collingwood, a St. Vincent class Dreadnought battleship (see 10th February and 11th February) and the world's largest battleship to date is launched in Devonport.

1913 The death of Alfred Russell Wallace (see 8th January) in Broadstone in Dorset. Born in Usk, Monmouthshire, he moved to England as a young man. He became a naturalist, explorer and anthropologist. He is widely known for surveying the Amazon basin where he devised the Wallace Line. He is also credited with independently formulating the theory of natural selection, unrelated to Charles Darwin (see 12th February and 19th April) but they jointly published their work in 1858. Although famous in his life time, he has since become eclipsed by Darwin. He was also very interested and known for his socialism and spiritualism as well as his biogeography.

2002 The government of Gibraltar holds a referendum on whether or not to share British sovereignty with Spain. The result was an overwhelming rejection of the idea with over 98% voting 'no' (see 7th February, 31st March, 24th July and 10th September).

8th November:

1605 Holbeche House in Staffordshire, where a large group of Catholic Gunpowder conspirators are hiding is surrounded by troops and a gun battle ensues as the traitors attempt to make a last stand against the High Sheriff of Worcester and around 200 of his men. Outnumbered in the storming of the house, several conspirators are killed, others wounded and the survivors arrested (see 30th January, 31st January and 5th November).

1674 The death of John Milton from gout (see 9th December). He was one of the country's greatest writers and poets as well as an exponent of the Commonwealth (see 19th May), famous for his best known work, 'Paradise Lost'. In 1649 he published 'Eikonoklastes' in defence of the murder of Charles I (see 30th January and 19th November). Following the Civil War, he served in the Commonwealth government and even after the Restoration (see 29th May) he remained a defender of English Republic and Commonwealth.

1745 Charles Edward Louis John Casimir Severino Maria Stuart ('Bonnie Prince Charlie', see 31st January and 31st December) crosses into England from Scotland on his way to London in his bid to reclaim the Crown for his father and the Stewart cause. After crossing into England with around 6,000 men, he made towards Carlisle to begin besieging the town (see 16th April).

1847 The birth of Abraham 'Bram' Stoker in Dublin, Ireland (see 20th April)

1861 The 'Trent Affair' takes place when the USS San Jacinto, an American ship from the Northern Union government's navy stops the British Mail Ship Trent and illegally arrests two Confederate diplomats, James Murray Mason and John Slidell, on their way to Britain, causing a major diplomatic incident between the United States and Great Britain. This was the closest that Britain has come to actual military conflict with the United States since the war of 1812 (see 18th June and 24th December).

1965 The Murder (Abolition of the Death Penalty) Act 1965 receives Royal Assent, officially abolishing the death penalty in the United Kingdom. It meant that all those at the time under sentence of death were commuted to life imprisonment. Also, crimes that would have received a death penalty would, from then on, receive a mandatory life sentence.

2009 Remembrance Sunday and the first one to be conducted without the presence of a veteran from the Great War anywhere in the country (see 25th July and 11th November).

9th November:

1729 The Treaty of Seville is signed between Great Britain and Spain bringing an end to hostilities in the Anglo-Spanish War (1727-1729). The treaty guaranteed British control was maintained over Port Mahon and the rest of the island of Minorca and Gibraltar (see 11th August).

1837 The British philanthropist Moses Montefiore becomes the first Jew to be awarded a knighthood in Britain, allowing him to sit in the House of Lords.

1841 The birth of Prince Albert Edward, the future Edward VII at Buckingham Palace (see 6th May), the eldest son of Queen Victoria (see 22nd January and 24th May) and Prince Albert.

1888 Mary Jane Kelly becomes the fifth and final victim of Jack the Ripper (see 31st August, 8th September and 30th September). Her mutilated remains are found in the single room she rented at 13 Miller's Court in the Whitechapel area of London.

1907 The Cullinan diamond, the largest diamond ever found (see 26th January), is presented to King Edward VII (see 1841 above and 6th May) on his birthday by the Transvaal Colony (see 31st May).

1908 Britain elects its first woman Mayor when Elizabeth Garrett Anderson (see 9th June and 17th December) becomes Mayor of Aldeburgh in eastern England (see 28th September).

1937 The death of James Ramsay MacDonald (see 12th October) aboard the liner Reina del Pacifico in the Atlantic whilst on holiday. The illegitimate son of a farm labourer, he became the first Labour Prime Minister in 1924 (see 22nd January) with a minority government, serving twice in that capacity. Born in Lossiemouth, in 1866, he became a journalist and joined the Independent Labour Party in 1893 and became its leader in 1911. In 1924 he became the first Labour Prime Minister, though supported by the Liberals, and his term only lasted a year. In 1929 he returned to office but had to form a National Government, this time supported by the Conservatives. He was still Prime Minister following the 1931 General Election (see 27th October) but again in a National Government with the Conservatives holding the majority. He continued in office until his health deteriorated and he resigned in favour of Stanley Baldwin in 1935 (see 7th June).

1940 The death of Arthur Neville Chamberlain (see 18th March) from cancer in Highfield Park, Reading. He became Prime Minister in 1937 (see 28th May) and resigned in 1940 (see 10th May). He is best known for his failed appeasement policy with the Germans and his signing of the Munich Agreement with Adolf Hitler. He was also instrumental in the creation of the Special Operations Executive (SOE). Despite criticism of his pre-war approach to the Germans following his death, he was well-respected as a politician by his contemporaries and was admired for his work as Minister of Health.

10th November:

1697 The birth of William Hogarth (see 26th October) in Smithfield, London, the son of Richard Hogarth, a Latin teacher.

1735 The birth of Granville Sharp in Durham (see 6th July), the son of the Archdeacon of Northumberland.

1810 The birth of George Jennings (see 17th April) in Eling in Hampshire.

1813 The battle of Nivelle, near the River Nivelle in France, during the Peninsular War. A combined British, Portuguese and Spanish force, numbering around 80,000 and led by the Marquess of Wellington (see 1st May and 14th September), attacked and routed a retreating French force of around 60,000 men led by Marshall Soult, capturing forts and ground as they advanced deep into France as the French infantry fled.

1848 The birth of Surendranath Banerjee in Calcutta (see 6th August).

1871 Henry Morton Stanley (see 28th January and 10th May), a journalist for the New York Herald, finds the explorer and missionary Doctor David Livingstone (see 19th March and 1st May) at a village called Ujiji near Lake Tanganyika and famously greets him with the words 'Doctor Livingstone, I presume?'.

1944 The Prime Minister Winston Churchill (see 24th January and 30th November) announces to Parliament that this country had been under rocket attack by the German V2 rockets for a number of weeks (see 8th September).

1958 Donald Campbell (see 4th January and 23rd March) breaks the World Water Speed Record again, travelling at 248mph (see 17th July and 3rd September) in his Bluebird K7 on Coniston Water.

11th November: Armistice Day.

1813 The battle of Chrysler's Farm in Canada during the War of 1812 (see 18th June and 24th December). American forces, progressing along the St. Lawrence River towards Montreal, are routed by a force of Canadian militia and British regulars half their size. Although both sides suffered a proportionately similar level of casualties, the Americans were deterred from progressing further into Canadian territory, abandoning their St. Lawrence Campaign and spending the winter on the American side of the river (see 26th October).

1918 The Armistice is signed, ending hostilities in the Great War. The British, French and Germans signed the armistice at 5.10 am aboard a railway carriage in the French forest of Compiegne. The guns then fell silent at 11am, signalling the end of the conflict (see 4th August).

1919 The first commemoration of the Armistice is led by King George V (see 20th January and 3rd June), the Royal Family, Prime Minister David Lloyd-George (see 17th January and 26th March) and Lord Haig (see 28th January and 19th June). May the sacrifice of so many, over so many years for our country never be forgotten (see 8th November.)

1920 The permanent stone Cenotaph Memorial in Whitehall, London and designed by Edward Lutyens (see 1st January and 29th March), is unveiled by King George V (see 20th January and 3rd June) in the presence of the body of the Unknown Soldier (see 18th July and 19th July).

1920 The body the Unknown Soldier is buried in its tomb in Westminster Abbey. In the week following the burial, an estimated 1,250,000 people visited the tomb and it is still one of the most visited graves in the world.

1940 The beginning of the Battle of Taranto (see 12th November) in southern Italy. Known as Operation Judgement, 21 torpedo carrying Swordfish biplanes of the Fleet Air Arm took off from HMS Illustrious and attacked the Italian Fleet in the harbour of Taranto.

1965 Ian Smith, Prime Minister of the colony of Southern Rhodesia (see 8th April and 20th November), illegally declares a Unilateral Declaration of Independence (U.D.I.) from Great Britain, whilst still recognising the Queen as the Head of State and without withdrawing from the Commonwealth. The so-called state of independence is never recognised by our government (see 18th April and 11th December).

12th November:

1595 Admiral Sir John Hawkins, naval hero, merchant and slave trader, credited with introducing the first potato into England sometime in 1563 or 1565, dies of the 'bloody flux' at Puerto Rico. Born 1532 in Plymouth, he was the cousin of Sir Francis Drake (see 27th January) and helped to fight of the Spanish Armada (see 29th July), thus saving England and becoming one of the Navy's great heroes. He is also famous for relieving much gold from the Spanish enemy as well as making a large profit from participation in the slave trade.

1660 John Bunyan is arrested for preaching without a licence (see 18th February, 31st August and 30th November). He had joined the Parliamentary army as a young man and had become a Puritan Preacher. He was to spend the next twelve years in prison.

1684 The birth of Admiral Edward Vernon (see 30th October and 21st November).

1859 The launch of HMS Victoria, the last first-rate three-deck battle ship of the line built for the Royal Navy. She was the largest of all wooden vessels ever to be commissioned and was never used in battle (see 29th December). She was sold for scrap in 1893.

1893 The Durand Line Treaty is signed between representatives of Afghanistan and British India. The agreement prepares the way for a joint undertaking to establish in writing and mapping out the border between the north of British India (see 8th August and 15th August) and Afghanistan.

1925 The submarine M1 sinks without a trace 35 miles south-east of Plymouth. All 69 of her crew were lost. She was the most advanced submarine of her time and was armed with a large gun, capable of hitting a target over twenty miles away.

1940 The conclusion of the Battle of Taranto which started the previous evening (see 11th November). Known as Operation Judgement, 21 torpedo carrying Swordfish biplanes of the Fleet Air Arm took off from HMS Illustrious and attacked the Italian Fleet in the harbour of Taranto. It was the first time a fleet was destroyed by aeroplanes launched from a sea-going ship. The Italian battleship Conte di Carour was sunk and two battleships, Littorio and the Caio Duilio, and a heavy cruiser were all badly damaged. Unfortunately, two planes were lost with two crew killed and two captured. The following day the Italians moved the remainder of their fleet to Naples and Britain and our Allies gained dominance in the Mediterranean.

1944 The culmination of Operation Catechism and the sinking of the German battleship SMS Tirpitz by RAF bombers. A total of thirty two Lancaster bombers from 9 and 617 Squadrons dropped 29 'Tall Boy' bombs at the ship with two direct hits and one a near miss. A fire broke out and caused an ammunition magazine to ignite, causing a large explosion. The ship then capsized very quickly. Those killed are variously put at between 1,000 and just over 1,250 (see 22nd September).

13th November:

1002 The St. Brice's day massacre occurs as Ethelred the Unready orders all Danes in England to be killed. Following several years of repeated Viking attacks, Ethelred was advised that they were receiving help from Danes in England and so decided to issue the order for the Danish deaths (see 8th June and 1st November).

1312 The birth of Edward III at Windsor Castle (see 21st June). His proclamation as King followed him becoming Keeper of the Realm.

1715 The battle of Sheriffmuir between the government forces of the Hanoverian King George I (see 28th May and 11th June) led by John Campbell, 2nd Duke of Argyll and the Jacobite forces led by John Erskine, the Earl of Mar. Though the government forces were seriously outnumbered, the battle was inconclusive and the Jacobite advance had been halted. As a result, enough damage was done to the Jacobite cause to cause morale to fall and the Spanish and French allies to withdraw (see 22nd December).

1761 The birth of John Moore (see 16th January) in Glasgow, the future General of the Peninsular War.

1850 The birth of Robert Louis Stevenson (see 3rd December) in Edinburgh.

1887 Bloody Sunday. A demonstration in Trafalgar Square in London against coercion in Ireland and unemployment, organised by leading Radical politicians and public figures in defiance of the authorities erupts into riots. There were around 10,000 demonstrators and perhaps three times as many spectators. There were up to 2,000 police officers as well as around 400 troops stationed to halt the protest and arrest the ring leaders. The violence was brutally suppressed and though there were many people injured, including many Police Officers, there was only one fatality.

1941 The aircraft carrier HMS Ark Royal is torpedoed on its way to Malta by a German U-Boat, U-81, and sinks the following day (see 13th April and 14th November). She was the first Aircraft Carrier to have her hangars and flight deck as a designed and constructed integral part of the super structure.

14th November:

1501 The marriage of Prince Arthur (see 2nd April), the eldest son of Henry VIII (see 28th January and 28th June), and Catharine of Aragon (see 7th January and 16th December) is held at St. Paul's Cathedral (see 11th June).

1687 At 10pm the actress Eleanor 'Nell' Gwynn dies at the age of 37 in Pall Mall, Westminster in London (see 2nd February). The most famous of all of Charles II's (see 6th February and 29th May) mistresses, she suffered two strokes, one in March then a second in May that confined her to her bed. She was just 37 years old when she died.

1751 The battle of Arcot between East India Company soldiers under Captain Robert Clive (see 25th September and 22nd November) and forces of Raza Sahib, the Nawab of Arcot with the aid of some troops of the French East India Company sent by Joseph François Dupleix. Clive had taken the town and had held out with just 500 men against a force of over 7,000. During the siege by French forces, which lasted fifty-six days until the battle, the small force withstood repeated attacks, including the use of elephants with minimal losses. The failure to take Arcot was the beginning of the end for French colonial ambitions in India.

1770 James Bruce (see 27th April and 14th December), the Scottish explorer, reportedly discovers the source of the Blue Nile in north-west Ethiopia. His account was at first doubted by many back in Britain. However, his descriptions of his African travels proved to be largely correct.

1914 The death of field Marshal Sir Frederick Sleigh Roberts in St. Omer, France (see 30th September). He was probably one of the greatest military commanders of the 19th Century. Born in Cawnpore in British India in 1832, he entered military service for the East India Company in 1851. He saw active service during the Indian Mutiny in 1857 (see 10th May), the Abyssinian Expedition 1868, the Second Afghan War 1878-1880 and the Second Boer War 1899-1902 during which conflicts he was involved in many battles. Highly respected and capable, he died from pneumonia whilst visiting Indian troops in France. He was buried in St. Paul's Cathedral.

1922 The British Broadcasting Corporation, the forerunner of the British Broadcasting Company (BBC), begins broadcasting daily from the Strand in London (see 18th October and 2nd November).

1935 The General Election and victory for the National Government under the Conservative Prime Minister Stanley Baldwin (see 3rd August and 14th December).

1940 The German Luftwaffe bomb Coventry in its heaviest raid on the city during the war and level most of the buildings. The Cathedral, dating from the 14th century, was hit a number of times before being consumed by fire (see 13th March, 14th March, 30th March, 24thApril, 7th September and 29th December).

1941 The aircraft carrier HMS Ark Royal sinks after being torpedoed on its way to Malta by a German U-Boat, U-81 (see 13th November). She was the first Aircraft Carrier of her kind in that the hangars (of which she had two) and the flight deck were integral to the design and not constructed add-ons (see 13th April and 2nd December).

1977 The first national Fire Fighters strike. Over 10,000 soldiers are called upon to help cover those refusing to work.

15th November:

1708 The birth of William Pitt the Elder (see 11th May), later the Earl of Chatham, at Bromley in Kent. He was to become one of the greatest Whig Prime Ministers. He was known as the 'Great Commoner' and was the father of William Pitt the Younger (see 23rd January and 28th May).

1738 The birth of Frederick William Herschel (see 25th August) in Hanover, in the Electorate of Hanover (see 13th March).

1819 The death of Daniel Rutherford (see 3rd November). He is best known as the man who was responsible for the isolation of nitrogen in 1772 which he called 'noxious air' or 'phlogisticated air'. During this work he was a student of Joseph Black (see 16th April and 6th December) and the pair worked together on the discovery.

1897 The birth of Aneurin 'Nye' Bevan in Tredegar in Wales (see 6th July).

1899 Winston Churchill (see 24th January and 30th November) is captured by Boer forces near Frere. He was a war correspondent at the time for the paper *The Morning Post*. He had been on an armoured train that had been attacked by Boer rebels. He led a gallant defence of the train by around 50 soldiers but was forced to surrender after being overwhelmed by the Boer commandoes.

1915 The birth of Archibald David Stirling (see 4th November) near Stirling.

1985 The Anglo-Irish agreement is signed at Hillsborough Castle by Margaret Thatcher (see 8th April and 13th October) and the Irish Prime Minister Garrett FitzGerald. The agreement gave Ireland an advisory role in the running of Northern Ireland and guaranteed that Northern Ireland would remain British as long as the majority of its people did not want unification with the Republic of Ireland.

16th November:

1272 The death of Henry III at the Palace of Westminster (see 1st October). A son of King John (see 18th October), he became King at the age of nine when his father died. During his troubled reign there were many quarrels with the Nobles led by Simon de Montfort who rebelled and won a number of victories. He is buried in Westminster Abbey, which he largely rebuilt during his reign (see 17th May and 28th October).

1745 The City of Carlisle surrenders to the Jacobite forces.

1776 Our forces, led by Admiral William Howe, attack and capture Fort Washington, the last rebel stronghold on Manhattan Island. The rebels, around 3,000 strong and under the command of 'Colonel' Robert Magaw, put up a mixed resistance. The defences on the south and west collapsed easily but the rebels on the north put up a fight, but after a heroic attack by Hessian troops, the Fort was carried and the garrison surrendered (see 19th April and 3rd September).

1857 The second relief of Lucknow during the Indian Mutiny. The relief column, led by General Sir Colin Campbell, finally reach the besieged garrison in the Residency after battling their way through in heavy fighting, much of it hand to hand. Unfortunately, due to the poor position and the heavy casualties, General Campbell decided that the position was not tenable and chose evacuation and abandoned Lucknow to the rebels. During the siege and relief operation, 24 Victoria Crosses were won by our forces (see 10th May, 25th September and 6th December).

1885 The execution of Louis Riel (see 22nd October) by hanging for treason following the Metis Rebellion. A Politician, he founded the Province of Manitoba and was the leader of the Metis Peoples. Following the establishment of the Provisional Government of the Red River Settlement, there was growing antagonism towards representatives of the Confederated Government (see 1st July) and resistance began to spread before breaking out into open rebellion in 1869. Riel is remembered for the murder of Thomas Scott, a representative of the government in 1870. He was tried and executed in Regina, Northwest Territories in Canada.

1896 The birth of Oswald Ernald Mosley at Rolleston Hall near Burton on Trent (see 3rd December).

17th November:

1292 The Scottish Auditors announce their decision before Edward I (see 17th June and 7th July) of England, and John Balliol (see 25th November) is proclaimed King of Scotland in the Great Hall at Berwick Castle. It was from this point that England started to increase its influence over Scotland (see 27th April, 10th July and 30th November).

1558 The death of Queen Mary I (see 18th February) in St. James' Palace and the accession of her Protestant sister, Queen Elizabeth I, Good Queen Bess and Gloriana, one of our Greatest monarchs (see 24th March and 7th September). Mary was the daughter of Henry VIII (see 28th January and 28th June) and the Spanish Catherine of Aragon. With the death of her half-brother Edward VI (see 6th July and 12th October), Mary should have become Queen in July 1553. However, Edward named Lady Jane Grey (see 12th February) as his successor in contradiction of the Act of Succession proclaimed by his father, Henry VIII. However, Mary had the popular support and Lady Jane Grey was swiftly deposed and Mary recognised as Queen. From the moment of her accession, she was determined to re-introduce Catholicism into England. In 1554 she married Prince Philip of Spain (see 25th July) which greatly upset many Protestants within England and raised fears of greater papal influence within the country. Then in 1557, war was declared on France in alliance with Spain, a war which England lost and which became a financial burden, resulting in the loss of Calais (see 7th January). The anniversary of this day was celebrated as Accession Day during the reign of Elizabeth I and for many years thereafter.

1858 The death of Robert Owen in Newtown, Montgomeryshire (see 14th May). A social reformer, he was a founder member of the cooperative movement. Born in 1771 in Newtown, as a young man he gained work in the mills in Manchester. After marrying a Glaswegian girl, he moved to Lanark and purchased the New Lanark mills where he worked to improve the living and working conditions of his employees and their families. The success of his mills received recognition across the world. He was a great advocate of social reform and proposed ideas of small communities working together for the good of one another which ultimately led to his involvement with the cooperative movement.

1887 The birth of Bernard Montgomery DSO, also known as 'Monty', later Field Marshall and Viscount Montgomery of Alamein in London. He served in the Great War and was badly wounded in October 1914 (see 24th March).

1925 The birth of Colin Campbell Mitchell (see 20th July) in London.

18th November:

1477 William Caxton (died in 1492) produced the *Dictes or Sayengis of the Philosophres*, the very first dated book printed on a printing press in England.

1814 The death of William Jessop near Ripley in Derbyshire (see 23rd January). A civil engineer, he is best known for his work on numerous canals, railways and harbours throughout the country. As a young man he worked for and was the assistant of John Smeaton. His importance is often forgotten but he worked with some of the most well-known and successful engineers and was involved in some of the more well-known works around Britain.

1884 The Imperial Federation League is formed in London, with branches being formed later in Australia, Barbados, British Guiana, Canada and New Zealand. Its objective was to promote Imperial Federation across the Empire and in particular between the Dominions, in a similar way to Canadian Confederation in 1867 (see 1st July). An Imperial Parliament in London was also proposed with responsibility for Foreign Affairs and defence, with the local parliaments handling home affairs (see 11th December). The League was instrumental in calling for and establishing the first Imperial Conference in London in 1887 (see 4th April).

1916 The Battle of the Ancre in which the last action and last day of the first Battle of the Somme concludes. The final push, primarily by members of battalions of the Highland Light Infantry, attack Frankfurt and Munich trenches in atrocious conditions. Despite gallant attempts, the forces failed to take and hold the objectives. The Canadian 4th Division was more successful on the right flank. The total British casualties for the battle since July were over 350,000 dead and wounded (see 1st July) and the total casualties for the Empire was 410,000.

1916 The death of John 'Jack' Lorimer on the last day of the Battle of the Somme (see 1916 above and 9th March). His parents separated when he was around seven years old and he was brought up by his uncle James Lorimer in Glasgow. Working for Glasgow Tramways, he volunteered in September 1914 when war broke out. He joined the 15th battalion the Highland Light Infantry and was promoted to Corporal. On the 18th November, as a stretcher bearer, he was helping a wounded comrade when he was injured by shrapnel from a shell bursting over head. Evacuated to a Casualty Clearing Station, he died of his wounds later that day.

19th November:

1600 The birth of the future Charles I in Dunfermline Castle (see 30th January), the son of James VI of Scotland (see 27th March and 19th June) and Anne of Denmark.

1778 The birth of Charles-Michel de Salaberry in Chambly, Lower Canada (see 27th February and 26th October).

1794 The Jay Treaty between Great Britain and the United States of America is signed (see 29th February). The treaty sought to end much post-war tension that had existed since the Treaty of Paris in 1783 (see 3rd September) that involved, amongst other things, trade, the boundary with Canada and the impressment of American citizens by the Royal Navy.

1798 The death of the traitor Theobald Wolfe Tone in prison in Dublin (see 20th June). A founding member of the United Irishmen in 1791 and a leading Irish rebel, he died from his injures after attempting to commit suicide following his capture by the Royal Navy. He was born in Dublin and after studying law, founded the United Irishmen and became a leading Republican campaigner. In 1798 he helped lead a French Invasion force in Ireland during the Irish Rebellion (see 24th May, 21st June, 22nd August and 8th September). Following his capture aboard a French ship, he was tried and sentenced to hanging but in an act of cowardice attempted suicide.

1850 Alfred Tennyson (see 6th August and 6th October) is appointed Poet Laureate following the death of William Wordsworth (see 7th April and 23rd April). He would remain Poet Laureate until his own death in 1892.

1924 Sir Lee Oliver Fitzmaurice Stack, Governor General of Sudan, is shot and murdered by several Egyptians whilst driving through the streets of Cairo (see 8th April and 2nd September).

1941 The Light Cruiser HMAS Sydney engages the German Auxiliary Cruiser Kormoran (which was disguised as a trawler) off the coast of Western Australia resulting in the destruction of both vessels. All 645 of Sydney's crew were killed. The majority of the German crew survived and were picked up by other Australian ships. The actual circumstances of Sydney's destruction remain controversial to this day. Sydney had spotted the Kormoran and had intercepted her, initially believing the German ship to be a Dutch merchant vessel. Once she was within range she was attacked without warning by the enemy and within in an hour, the crippled Sydney had disengaged and sailed away ablaze, only to sink during the night with the loss of all hands.

20th November:

1759 The Battle of Quiberon Bay during the Seven Years' War (1756-1763). The Royal Navy, led by Admiral Sir Edward Hawke (see 16th October) and his Western Squadron chased and finally destroyed the French fleet led by Admiral Conflans. The planned invasion of Britain by the French was thus thwarted, also ending the last hopes of a Jacobite challenge to the British throne. Our Fleet lost two ships, the *Essex* and the *Resolution* and 300 or 400 men and the French lost five ships and 2,500 men, most of who drowned (see 18th August).

1765 The birth of Thomas Francis Fremantle (see 19th December) in Buckinghamshire.

1815 The Treaty of Paris (see 10th February) following Napoleon's return and his subsequent defeat at Waterloo (see 18th June) is signed by Great Britain, Prussia, Russia and Austria on the one side and France on the other. The treaty, written in French, the language of diplomacy at the time, was in fact four different treaties between defeated France and each of the four countries from the alliance. France was ordered to pay around 700 million Francs over five years and to allow an army of occupation of around 150,000 men, maintained by France on its soil for a maximum of five years. It also guaranteed the neutrality of Switzerland in perpetuity (see 30th May, 9th June and 15th October).

1917 The first day of the Battle of Cambrai in Northern France during the Great War. The objective was for British forces to break through the German

Siegfried defensive line and attack and take the town of Cambrai. The first day of the battle is remembered as the first time a large number of tanks were used in close conjunction with artillery and infantry forces (see 28th July and 15th September). A total of 476 tanks were used in a massive surprise attack on the German lines, breaking through and pushing on successfully to Cambrai, covering around 5 miles on the first day. Upon news of the success being received in Britain, Church bells were rung throughout the country.

1935 The death of Admiral of the Fleet John Rushworth Jellicoe, Earl of Scapa (see 5th December), in London. He entered the Navy in 1872 and saw service in the Egyptian War of 1882 and led the Naval Brigade during the Boxer Rebellion (1899-1901). He is famous for being the Admiral who led the Royal Navy's Grand Fleet during the Great War, in particular at the Battle of Jutland in 1916 (see 31st May). At the end of 1916 he became First Sea Lord but was dismissed in 1917. He later became Governor of New Zealand (see 26th September).

2007 The death of Ian Douglas Smith in Cape Town, South Africa (see 8th April). He was Prime Minister of the Colony of Southern Rhodesia, whose government issued the Unilateral Declaration of Independence from Britain in 1965 (see 11th November). Born in the small town of Selukwe in Southern Rhodesia, the son of a Scottish settler, he joined the Southern Rhodesian Air Force during the Second World War, later transferring to the RAF. During the war he was injured in an aeroplane crash and was shot down, serving both in the Middle East and over Europe. In 1948 he was elected to the Southern Rhodesian Assembly. He became Prime Minister of Southern Rhodesia in 1964 and just over a year later, issued the Unilateral Declaration of Independence from Britain over the proposed increased participation of blacks in the democratic process in Rhodesia. Following increased guerrilla activity, he eventually agreed to elections and a black majority government in 1978.

21st November:

1673 The marriage of James VII (James II of England see 5th September and 14th October) to his second wife Mary of Modena at Dover (see 30th September). She was our country's only Italian Queen.

1695 The death of Henry Purcell at Dean's Yard in Westminster. Born in Westminster in 1659, he is one of the greatest British composers of the baroque style and received Royal appointments for music from three successive British monarchs, Charles II (see 6th February and 29th May), James VII (James II of England see 5th September and 14th October) and William of Orange (see 8th March and 4th November) and Mary (see 30th April and 28th December) and he composed music in a wide variety of styles. He is buried in Westminster Abbey.

1739 Porto Bello is captured from Spain by Admiral Sir Edward Vernon (see 30th October and 12th November) with just six ships. Porto Bello was a major Spanish Naval Base and settlement on the Spanish Main and after just 24 hours of siege it surrendered. It was occupied for around three weeks before its fortress and main buildings were destroyed. This was a spectacular triumph throughout the Empire and brought an end to major Spanish raids on Colonial shipping in the area.

1878 The start of the Second Afghan War (1878-1880) as 40,000 of our troops cross the border from India into Afghanistan in three places following the expiry of an ultimatum the previous day. Russia had sent a diplomatic mission to Kabul with the desire to influence the Afghans. To counter this threat, the government had sent a diplomatic mission to Afghanistan that was then refused entry to the country. An ultimatum was issued to the Afghans which expired the previous day on the 20th November 1878 (see 1st September).

1918 The German High Seas Fleet, under Admiral von Reuter, surrenders all seventy ships to the Grand Fleet off the Firth of Forth. The surrender was to Admiral David Beatty (see 17th January and 11th March) and the vessels hauled down their colours at sunset (see 11th November).

1920 Fourteen British Intelligence operatives, known as the 'Cairo Gang', are murdered by the IRA in a series of attacks across Dublin that came to be known as 'Bloody Sunday' (see 24th April, 29th April, 6th December and 8th December).

1953 The so called archaeological find known as the Piltdown man that was 'discovered' in 1911 and declared as the missing link and indicating that mans earliest origins were in Britain, is finally exposed as a fake by British scientists.

22nd November:

1594 The death of Sir Martin Frobisher on the way home to Plymouth from the Port of Brest after an operation on a gun shot wound failed. He was one of the leading seamen of his day and the continual scourge of the Spanish. Though the Spanish claimed he was a pirate, Frobisher always attacked the French, without let up. In 1576 he was in command of an expedition to find the North West passage to Cathay. Failing to discover the passage, he eventually came across Baffin Island in what would later become Canada (see 1st July) before returning to England. In 1558 he accompanied Sir Francis Drake (see 27th January) on his voyage to the West Indies and in 1588 he was one of three commanders, along with Sir Francs Drake and Sir John Hawkins (see 12th November), to lead the English fleet to victory against the Spanish Armada (see 29th July).

1718 Edward Teach, known as Blackbeard, is killed in a fight with a Royal Navy boarding party off the coast of the Colony of North Carolina. Born in Bristol in 1680, he was probably one of the most well-known of pirates operating mainly in the Caribbean and the Atlantic shore line of the American Colonies. He terrorised the coast of the Colonies and around May

1718 audaciously blockaded Charlestown, South Carolina. His brief flag ship was 'Queen Anne's Revenge', originally a British built cargo ship which was eventually run aground by Blackbeard. He shortly afterward accepted a pardon from the Governor of North Carolina.

1774 The death of Sir Robert Clive, 1st Baron of Plassey (see 29th September), at his home in Berkeley Square in London. At the age of 18 in 1744 he had sailed to India to work as a clerk for the East India Company in Madras. After avoiding being taken prisoner when the French captured the city in 1746, he joined the East India Company Army later in the year. He was promoted and recaptured Calcutta from rebels in 1757 (see 2nd January) and became the MP for Shrewsbury and Governor of the Bengal Presidency. He is best remembered for his victory at the Battle of Plassey in 1757 (see 23rd June), which ultimately led to British rule over the many divided kingdoms of India and the true foundation of our Great Empire. His death is still a mystery and it is believed he may have committed suicide, as he had attempted it before, although this is still conjecture.

1819 The birth of Mary Anne Evans (see 22nd December) in Nuneaton, Warwickshire. As a novelist and poet, she would later be remembered by her pen name, George Eliot.

1869 The 'Cutty Sark' is launched in Dunbarton. An iconic ship, she was one of the last of the great tea clippers that would later become a museum to the age of sail. Built right at the end of the 'age of sail', she spent less than ten years transporting tea between China and London before seeking out other cargo, finally transporting wool from Australia to Britain.

1899 In a skirmish near the town of Belmont in South Africa during the South African War of 1899-1902 (see 31st May and 11th October), the New South Wales Lancers (see 2nd November) engage the enemy, becoming the first troops from the colonies of Australia to fight outside of Australia (see 1st March).

1926 The conclusion of the sixth Imperial Conference in London (see 4th April and 19th October). In attendance were the Prime Ministers of Great Britain, Australia, Canada, Newfoundland, New Zealand, South Africa and the President of the Executive Council of the Irish Free State. The conference ended with the Balfour Declaration which stated that all Dominions enjoyed equal status within the Empire and shared a common allegiance to the Crown.

1944 The death of Sir Arthur Stanley Eddington (see 28th December) in Cambridge. The son of Quaker parents, he was one of the leading astrophysicists of the 20th century and is famous for the 'Eddington Limit', indicating the natural limit to the luminance of stars which was named in his honour. He also played a key role in the announcement to the world of Einstein's theory of relativity and he led an expedition to Africa in 1919 that resulted in the first evidence of Einstein's theory that gravity will bend the path of light as it passes near to a star.

1990 Margaret Thatcher announces that she is to resign after eleven years as Prime Minister (see 8th April and 13th October). Having been challenged for the leadership of the Conservative party by Michael Heseltine, she went on to win the first ballot. However, he had attracted enough votes to force a second ballot and after consulting her Cabinet, she decided to resign. She was the first woman to lead a political party (see 11th February) and the first female Prime Minister (see 4th May), winning three General Elections. She was also the Prime Minister at the time of the Falklands War (see 14th June) and the defeat of the Argentineans in 1982.

23rd November:

1499 Perkin Warbeck, pretender to the English throne, is executed in the Tower of London. Believed to have been born in Flanders in the 1470s, he came to Ireland in 1491 and was mistaken for the Earl of Warwick but Warbeck then insisted he was Richard, Duke of York. After much travelling and several conspiracies and attempted rebellions he was imprisoned by Henry VII (see 28th January and 21st April). He attempted to escape and so to prevent the possibility of another rebellion, Henry VII had Warbeck executed.

1853 The first four Pillar Boxes are used for the first time, on the Island of Jersey and become an instant success. They were originally envisaged by Sir Anthony Trollope (see 24th April and 6th December), who at the time was the Surveyor to the Secretary to the Post Office, Sir Rowland Hill. Over the coming century and a half they would become one of the most iconic images of this county.

1887 The birth of Henry Gwyn Jeffreys Moseley in Weymouth, Dorset (see 10th August).

1899 For the first time, troops from New Zealand (see 1st July) are deployed overseas when the first of their soldiers arrive in South Africa (see 18 December) in support of the Empire's campaigns against the Boers in the South African War (see 31st May and 12th October).

1910 Dr Hawley Harvey Crippen is hanged in Pentonville Prison in London for the murder of his wife. An American, he was the first person to be arrested with the aid of wireless communication. The notification for his arrest had been sent whilst he was on board the SS Montrose and he was apprehended when it arrived in Canada (see 31st July).

1963, Saturday, 5.15pm: The very first episode of the science fiction series Doctor Who is broadcast, called 'An unearthly child'. William Hartnell stared as the Doctor, Carole Ann Ford as the Doctor's granddaughter Susan Foreman, Jacqueline Hill as Barbara Wright and William Russell as Ian Chesterton, both of whom were Susan Foreman's teachers. Verity Lambert was the producer. The programme went on to become the most popular and longest running science fiction series in the world and has become an important element in British popular culture.

24th November:

1542 The Battle of Solway Moss just inside England. A force of 3,000 English troops led by Sir Thomas Wharton defeat up to 18,000 Scots soldiers. Moving out from Carlisle, the English cornered the Scots army on English territory just south of the river Esk as they attempted to invade England but were distracted by burning and pillaging. The Scots were engaged by the English in a brief battle that resulted in very few casualties on either side but around 1,200 Scots were taken prisoner, including many nobles, the result of which amounted to a crushing and humiliating defeat for the Scots and their King James V (see 10th April and 14th December).

1572 The death of John Knox, the leading light in the Scottish Protestant Reformation. Influenced by George Wishart, he turned to Protestantism. Captured by the French at St. Andrew's Castle, he was eventually released in 1549 and went to England. Here he championed the cause of Protestantism but had to flee from Mary I (see 18th February and 17th November) and her drive to restore Catholicism to her realm. Later upsetting Elizabeth I (see 24th March and 7th September) in a pamphlet against women holding power, he was unable to return to England. However, he returned to Scotland in 1557 where he led a Protestant, anti-French Calvinistic movement and eventually opposed the rule of Mary Queen of Scots (see 8th February and 8th December). Following the death of Mary and his increased age, his influence began to wane. He was buried in St. Giles's Churchyard in Edinburgh.

1848 The death of William Lamb, Viscount Lord Melbourne (see 15th March), in Hertfordshire. A Whig Statesman, he served as Home Secretary and Prime Minister (1834 and 1835 until 1841) and was the mentor and favourite of the young Queen Victoria (see 22nd January and 24th May) when she first ascended the throne. His various terms in differing government offices were notable for a number of reforming changes, though he himself showed little interest in the working classes. He entered parliament in 1806 and as Home Secretary was responsible for the suppression of the Tolpuddle Martyrs in 1834. As Prime Minister, his ministries were notable for his ability to form a loose partnership between disparate political parties.

1857 The death of Major General Sir Henry Havelock (see 5th April) from dysentery in the city of Lucknow, India, whilst leading the besieged forces within the city. Born in Bishopwearmouth in County Durham, he was a leading military commander and the hero of the first relief of Lucknow during the Indian Mutiny and also for the relief of the city of Cawnpore. He served during the Burmese War (1824-1826), the First Afghan War (1839 1842) and the First Sikh War (1845-1846). One of the great Victorian heroes of Empire, he is buried in Lucknow and has a statue in his honour in Trafalgar Square.

1859 The historic book 'On the Origin of Species by Means of Natural Selection' by Charles Darwin (see 12th February and 19th April) is published and the initial edition was rapidly sold out (see 27th December).

2005 New Licensing Laws come into force allowing, for the first time since original licensing laws were introduced, twenty-four hour drinking in establishments that have successfully applied for a licence.

2010 The last Harrier fighter jet to take off from an Aircraft carrier departs from HMS Ark Royal. The planes were from 800 Naval Air Squadron and this signalled the beginning of a period of around nine years where our country will have no sea-based air power. Both HMS Ark Royal and the Harrier jets were to be scrapped in 2011 as a result of the Strategic Defence Review (see 19th October and 2nd November).

25th November:

1120 William Adelin, only son of Henry I (see 1st December) by his wife, Matilda of Scotland, dies when his ship, the 'White Ship', sinks in the Channel on the way back from Normandy. As he had no issue, his death led to a succession crisis with Henry I declaring his daughter Matilda as heir. However, the Barons rebelled on Henry's death and chose instead Henry's nephew, Stephen of Blois, as his successor (see 25th October).

1314 The death of John Balliol in Picardy, France (see 30th November). As a descendant of King David I of Scotland (see 24th May), he was a contender for the Scottish crown and was chosen by the Scottish Auditors in 1292 (see 17th November) and was crowned 13 days later at Scone (see 30th November). Undermined by Edward I (see 17th June and 7th July), whom he had recognised as his overlord, the Scottish Nobles rebelled and sought an alliance with France (see 23rd October). In retaliation, Edward I invaded Scotland and finally defeated the Scots at the battle of Dunbar in 1296 (see 27th April). He abdicated following the defeat (see 10th July), was imprisoned in England then sent into exile, finally living in France.

1758 Fort Duquesne is captured from the French after it is abandoned by its garrison. General John Forbes led an expedition to capture the key Fort in French America and as his troops approached the fort, the French garrison, their supplies cut by the Royal Navy, destroyed it and abandoned the remains the following day. As General Forbes was ill, the first troops in to capture the remains of the fort were led by Colonel George Washington as commander of the Virginia Regiment (see 11th February and 14th December). Next to the site, Fort Pitt was constructed, ultimately giving its name to the city of Pittsburgh.

1837 The battle of Saint-Charles decides the fate of the rebellion of Lower Canada. The rebellion had broken out as pro-republican colonials of French decent turned to violence in an attempt to break away from British colonial authority. Around 250 rebels took up positions behind barricades and prepared to resist. Under covering fire, the Royal Scots moved forward with fixed bayonets on the rebel's positions. Around 150 rebels died and only seven Government troops perished. The majority of the rebel survivors surrendered (see 7th December).

1875 Britain buys the controlling stock of 176,000 shares in the Suez Canal for £4,000,000, the idea being promoted by the Prime Minister

Benjamin Disraeli (see 26th August, 31st October, 5th November and 23rd December).

1940 The first flight of the famous de Havilland Mosquito takes place at the de Havilland airfield at Hatfield. A fast, two-manned twin engine bomber, it saw much active service and its most famous raid was Operation Jericho, the bombing raid on the Amiens prison in occupied France in 1944 (see 18th February). Altogether there were over 7,700 built.

1947 The Statute of Westminster Adoption Act (1947) receives Royal Assent in the New Zealand Parliament. By doing so, New Zealand adopted the Statute of Westminster 1931 (see 11th December) passed by the British Parliament and formally recognised their independence as a separate sovereign state (see 6th February, 1st July and 26th September).

26th November:

1703 Strong hurricane-like winds sweep across the country in what would become known as the 'Great Storm', resulting in the deaths of as many as 8,000 people and the destruction of thousands of houses and property.

1810 The birth of William George Armstrong in Newcastle upon Tyne (see 27th December).

1836 The death of John Loudon McAdam (see 21st September), Scottish engineer and pioneering road builder whose influence is still felt today. He was the inventor of a new road surface that was called 'macadamisation', using tar to hold the road stones together. After further development, it formed into what we now know as 'tarmac'.

1867 Because of a loophole in the law, where the 1867 Reform Act did not specify that the voting franchise extended to property owners and tenants worth £10 or more had to be male, Lily Maxwell becomes the first woman to vote in a Parliamentary election. She cast her vote for the Liberal Jacob Bright in a Manchester by-election.

1917 The death of Sir Leander Starr Jamieson (see 2nd January, 9th February and 29th December) in Edinburgh. Known for his friendship with Cecil Rhodes (see 26th March and 5th July) and his leadership of the Jamieson Raid in 1899, he was a colonial politician and Imperialist. Born in Edinburgh, he studied medicine in London before moving to South Africa where he met and befriended Cecil Rhodes. Following the Jameson raid, he was imprisoned for a few months in Britain before returning to South Africa where he was elected to Parliament in 1900 and became Prime Minister of Cape Colony between 1904 and 1908. He formed the Unionist Party in 1910 but retired to England in 1912 due to poor health. He was buried in Rhodesia near Cecil Rhodes.

1922 Howard Carter (see 2nd March and 9th May) and Lord Carnarvon (see 5th April and 26th June) enter Tutankhamen's Tomb in Egypt for the first time. The tomb had been discovered some days before but Howard Carter had waited until his partner and sponsor Lord Carnarvon could arrive from Britain for the first entry to the tomb.

1955 Following a series of brutal terrorist attacks on administrative buildings and staff by the terrorist group EOKA, a state of emergency is declared in the Colony of Cyprus by the Governor General Sir John Harding (see 16th August).

1968 The Race Relations Act (1968) comes into force, making it illegal for people to be discriminated against because of their race in areas such as employment, services and housing.

27th November:

1811 The death of Andrew Meikle in East Lothian. Born in 1719 he became a civil engineer, famous for inventing the threshing machine around the year 1786. His invention was used to remove the outer husks from grains of wheat and is regarded as a key moment in the emergence of the Agricultural Revolution.

1852 The death of Augusta Ada King, Countess of Lovelace (née Byron and known as Ada Lovelace), in London (see 10th December). A writer, she is remembered for her work with Charles Babbage (see 18th October and 26th December) on his Difference Engine. During the 1840's she translated works for Charles Babbage and produced notes for his Analytical Machine. She is therefore often referred to as the first computer programmer. Born Augusta Ada Byron, she was the daughter of the poet Lord Byron, who died when she was very young.

1914 Edith Smith, the first Policewoman, goes on duty at Grantham in Lincolnshire. She left the force in 1918 after working seven days a week. She died later that year from an overdose of morphia.

1941 The siege of Tobruk in the Italian Colony of Libya is finally lifted after almost eight months. The Australians and later British garrisons and reinforcements came under constant attack by German and Italian troops commanded by General Irwin Rommel as the city was a key strongpoint along the Libyan coast (see 23rd October and 4th November).

1944 An explosion at 21 Maintenance Unit, RAF Fauld in Staffordshire, kills around seventy people and becomes the largest explosion on British soil. The site stored large amounts of ordinance and it was around 4,000 tons of these explosives, including much high explosive that detonated. Much of the site was obliterated and a nearby farm, large reservoir and gypsum works disappeared. The resulting crater was around four hundred feet deep and debris was scattered over 1,400 yards from the explosion.

1967 Britain's attempt at entry into The European Economic Community was refused a second time by the member states after France, led by De Gaulle, again vetoed the attempt. France and De Gaulle in particular were afraid of our economy, of our country's links with its colonies, its dependencies, the United States and the Commonwealth, despite its own overseas possessions (see 1st January, 30th January, 7th February, 23rd June and 28th October).

28th November:

1291 The death of Eleanor of Castile, the wife of Edward I (see 7th June and 11th July), at Harby near Lincoln. Edward followed the funeral procession to Westminster Abbey for burial. To honour his wife, Edward had a series of stone memorial crosses erected at the different places her body had rested on its way to London. The twelve sites where the Eleanor Crosses were erected were: Lincoln, Grantham, Stamford, Geddington, Hardingstone, Stony Stratford, Woburn, Dunstable, St Albans, Waltham (now Waltham Cross), Westcheap (now Cheapside) and Charing (now Charing Cross).

1757 The birth of William Blake (see 12th August) in Westminster in London, the son of a draper. He would later write the words to the famous hymn 'Jerusalem'.

1893 In the general election in New Zealand, women vote for the first time anywhere within the Empire. The Electoral Act 1893 had received Royal Assent only 10 weeks before (see 19th September) and on polling day 82% of those women registered to vote took part compared to 70% of registered men.

1905 Sinn Fein is founded in Dublin by Arthur Griffith when he presents his 'Sinn Fein policy' to fellow Irish Nationalists (see 24th April, 29th April, 28th June, 6th December and 8th December).

1919 American born Lady Nancy Wicher Astor is elected as the first Lady Member of Parliament for the Plymouth constituency as a Unionist (Conservative) MP (see 2nd May, 19th May and 1st December).

1943 The Tehran Conference begins between our Prime Minister Winston Churchill (see 24th January and 30th November), the American President Franklin D. Roosevelt and the Soviet Prime Minister, Joseph Stalin, at the Soviet Embassy in Tehran. This was the first conference to be held between the 'Big Three' at which Stalin attended. The conference was convened to discuss the invasion of France and relations with and the fate of a number of other countries as well as the second front in Western Europe (see 4th February and 17th July).

29th November:

1530 The death of Cardinal Thomas Wolsey. He was born around 1475 in Ipswich in Suffolk and went to Oxford, becoming ordained around 1498. A Roman Catholic at a time before the Reformation, he was rapidly promoted under Henry VIII, becoming Lord Chancellor. He became one of the most powerful men in England and was responsible for arranging the Field of the Cloth of Gold where Henry VIII met the French King Francis I. However, he failed to secure from the Pope an annulment of Henry VIII's marriage to

Catherine of Aragon and for this he was deposed. He was arrested for treason in the city of York. However, on his way south to face trial he died.

1682 The death of Prince Rupert of the Rhine in Westminster (see 17th December). The Nephew of Charles I (see 30th January and 19th November) and cousin of Charles II (see 6th February and 29th May), he was a leading General in the Civil War. Born in Prague in the Kingdom of Bohemia, he became a soldier at an early age and fought in many battles and campaigns in Europe. At the age of 23 he was appointed commander of the Royalist Cavalry by Charles I during the Civil War. Following the end of the Civil War, he went into exile and had a variety of military roles. After the Restoration (see 29th May) he became a Commander in the Royal Navy during the Third Anglo-Dutch War (1672-1674) and the first Governor of the Hudson Bay Company (see 2nd May).

1745 The city of Manchester is entered by Jacobite forces. However, despite receiving little support, they managed to raise a Regiment of around 300 men that went on to garrison Carlisle Castle on the withdrawal back to Scotland as the main forces retreated to the Highlands (see 16th April and 19th August).

1899 For the first time, Canadian troops are deployed overseas when their troop ship, the Sardinian, docks at Cape Town in South Africa before the 1,050 men boarded trains to their billets in Belmont (see 18th February) in support of the Empire's campaigns against the Boers in the South African War (see 31st May and 12th October).

30th November: St. Andrew's day, Patron Saint of Scotland.

1292 John Balliol (see 25th November) is crowned King of Scotland at Scone (see 17th November). Though King of Scotland, he swore fealty to Edward I of England (see 17th June and 7th July) as his and Scotland's overlord (see 27th April and 10th July).

1628 The baptism of John Bunyan in Elstow in Bedfordshire, a few days after his birth (see 31st August and 12th November).

1667 The birth of Jonathan Swift in Dublin. He was to write 'Gulliver's Travels' (see 19th October).

1874 The birth of Winston Leonard Spencer Churchill (see 24th January and 15th November) in Blenheim Palace, Oxfordshire, the son of Lord Randolph Churchill and the American Jennie Jerome.

1900 The death of Oscar Wilde, poet and playwright, from meningitis in a squalid hotel room in Paris (see 16th October). His more well-known works include, 'The Ballad of Reading Gaol', 'Lady Windermere's Fan', 'An Ideal Husband', 'The Importance of being Earnest' and 'A Woman of No Importance'. In 1884 he married Constance Lloyd and had two sons before beginning an affair with Sir Alfred Douglas for which he was later tried and convicted of gross indecency. He received a prison sentence, serving two years hard labour before being released with his health and reputation in ruins.

1936 The Crystal Palace, designed by Joseph Paxton, burns down in Sydenham Hill. Made of cast-iron and glass, it was originally built in Hyde Park to house the Great Exhibition of 1851 (see 1st May) but after the Exhibition, it was moved and enlarged to Sydenham in 1854 (see 12th May).

1944 The launch of HMS Vanguard, the last Royal Navy Dreadnaught and the last battleship to be launched in the world (see 7th June). The ship was built by John Brown and Company in Clydebank, Glasgow. The ship never saw action or fired her guns in anger. She was decommissioned and sold for scrap in 1960 (see 10th February).

1966 The Colony of Barbados is granted its independence. It was claimed for England in 1625, having been a Portuguese territory and remained an extremely important possession, becoming a Crown Colony in 1652.

1996 The Stone of Destiny arrives in Edinburgh castle after having spent over six centuries in England. The government had decided that the stone should remain in Scotland between the coronations of monarchs (see 25th February and 25th December).

DECEMBER

1st December:

1135 The death of Henry I at Saint-Denis-en-Lyons in France. Legend states that he died from food poisoning due to eating a 'surfeit of lampreys'. His body was returned to England and he was buried at Reading Abbey. During his lifetime he was known for his scholarly interests and knowledge of Latin and for his reorganisation of the court and judicial systems.

1884 The death of George Birkbeck in London (see 10th January). After qualifying as a Physician, he was appointed to Anderson's College in Glasgow where he gave free lectures to the poor people. In 1824 he founded the Mechanic's Institute in London for the furtherance of adult education. The institute was later renamed Birkbeck College in his honour.

1919 Lady Nancy Astor takes her seat in the House of Commons as the first elected female MP (see 2nd May and 19th May). She was elected as the Unionist (Conservative) MP for Plymouth (see 28th November).

1942 The Beveridge Report is published, laying the foundation for the Welfare State, including State Benefits and the National Health Service (see 5th July). The report was the culmination of a detailed investigation by the Parliamentary Committee for Social Insurance and Allied Services; it was revolutionary in its proposals for welfare reform. Its Chairman, Sir William Beveridge (see 5th March and 16th March), identified five 'Great Evils' that needed addressing: 'want, disease, ignorance, squalor and idleness'. This was an explanation of his repeated stance on the 'abolition of want' and his report on welfare reform was designed to address these issues.

1990 Workers on the Channel Tunnel project meet for the first time as both ends of the tunnel finally meet, breaking through from the French side. Workers Graham Fagg and Frenchman Philippe Cozette are the first to make contact and walk through from opposite sides (see 30th October).

2nd December:

1697 The opening and consecration of the new St. Paul's Cathedral is carried out by the conducting of the first service by the Bishop of London, Henry Compton. Designed by Sir Christopher Wren (see 25th February and 20th October), it is the current Cathedral and replaced the earlier Cathedral destroyed in the Great Fire of London (see 2nd September and 6th September).

1755 The second Eddystone Lighthouse burns down. An accident, the result of a storm, its destruction allows the civil engineer John Smeaton (see 8th June and 28th October) to build his famous lighthouse on the same site.

1917 The launch of HMS Argus, the world's first purpose-built 'flush deck' aircraft carrier. Prior to her construction, aircraft carriers had split decks, either side of the superstructure (see 13th April, 13th November and 14th November).

3rd December:

1745 The 'Battle' of Stone, one of biggest battles never to have been fought on British soil is avoided. The Duke of Cumberland's government forces were encamped at Stone in Staffordshire in expectation of the arrival of the Jacobite forces. They spent the night in battle order immediately north of the town. However, the Jacobite army moved south east towards Derby thus avoiding Cumberland's troops and the battle. Had the two armies engaged one another, it could have been as decisive as the battle at Culloden (see 16th April), fought the following year.

1795 The birth of Rowland Hill in Kidderminster (see 10th January and 27th August).

1810 The island of Mauritius is surrendered by the French to our Fleet under the command of Vice Admiral Sir Albemarle Bertie. Under the terms of surrender, the French inhabitants were allowed to keep their possessions and property and to continue using their language whilst the island remained British.

1894 The death of Robert Louis Stevenson (see 13th November) in Vailima in Samoa. His most famous works include the books 'Treasure Island' (1883), 'Kidnapped' (1886) and 'The Strange Case of Dr Jekyll and Mr Hyde' (1886). He suffered from ill health throughout his life, left studying law to pursue his writing and travelled widely. In 1888 he moved with his wife to Samoa, where the locals referred to him as 'The Teller of Tales' and where he would die six years later aged just 44.

1925 The Locarno Pact, negotiated in Locarno, Switzerland, is finally signed in London between Great Britain, Germany, France, Belgium and Italy. The treaty set out that Germany, France and Belgium agreed not to attack one another and both Britain and Italy agreeing to act as guarantors. The overall idea of the treaty was the normalisation of relations with the former aggressor Germany (see 3rd September).

1944 The Local Defence Volunteers, or Home Guard, is officially stood down in a parade in Hyde Park before their Colonel in Chief King George VI (see 14th May). At its peak, the LDV had nearly 2 million members and over 1,200 men had been killed on duty or died from wounds received during the war. Initially raised for the protection of the country due to the threat of invasion, it developed into a civil defence force, guarding key buildings, liaising with the Police and Fire Service during and after air raids, etc.

1945 Captain Eric Melrose 'Winkle' Brown becomes the first person to take off from and then land a jet aircraft on an aircraft carrier. He landed his de Havilland Sea Vampire on the deck of H.M.S. Ocean (see 21st January and 14th July).

1980 The death of Sir Oswald Ernald Mosley (sees 16th November). Founder of the British Union of Fascists (see 1st October), he is best known as the leading figure for several decades in British Fascism. He was married twice, firstly to Lady Cynthia (Cimmie) Curzon, who later died, and then to Diana Guinness (née Mitford). He served during the Great War, where he was wounded and in 1918 he was elected to Parliament as the Conservative MP for Harrow. This lasted until 1924 when he crossed the floor to join the Labour Party. In 1931 he formed the New Party which was the beginning of his association with the far right and Fascism. During the Second World War he was interned, along with his wife and other Fascist associates, for activities 'likely to endanger the realm under Defence Regulation 18B'. After the war, he left Britain in 1949 and lived for a short while in Ireland before moving to France. He attempted to get elected to the Commons a couple of times but was unsuccessful. He was cremated in Paris.

4th December:

1154 Nicholas Breakspear, the only Englishman and Briton to be elected Pope, is elected as Pope Adrian IV (see 1st September).

1214 The death of William the Lion, King of Scotland, in Stirling. In 1174 he invaded England which was then ruled by Henry II (see 4th March and 6th July), in support of Henry's rebellious son. He was captured at Alnwick and wasn't released until agreeing to pay homage to Henry as his feudal Lord. It wasn't until 1189 and the reign of Richard I (see 6th April and 8th September) of England that Scotland became independent of English influence. In 1178 William founded Arbroath Abbey and it was here that he was buried (see 6th April). He was succeeded by his son as Alexander II (see 6th July and 24th August).

1732 The death of John Gay (see 30th June). A poet and dramatist, his most well-known work is the 'Beggars Opera', first performed on 29th January 1728. In it he caricatured the then Prime Minister, Robert Walpole, (see 18th March and 26th August) which caused attempts to ban his subsequent work. He was influenced by his friend Alexander Pope (see 21st May and 30th May) and was buried in Westminster Abbey.

1795 The birth of Thomas Carlyle in Ecclefechan (see 5th February), Dumfries and Galloway.

1798 The Prime Minister, William Pitt the Younger (see 23rd January and 28th May), announces the introduction of Income Tax to help pay for the war with France.

1829 The practice of Suttee, the burning to death of widows on their husbands' funerals pyre is formally banned in the Bengal Presidency of the East India Company (see 31st December) by the Governor, Lord William Bentnick. The ban was extended the following year to both the Madras and Bombay Presidencies.

1865 The birth of Edith Cavell near Norwich (see 12th October).

1893 The Shangani Patrol, led by Major Allan Wilson, is surrounded and all are killed in an ambush in the Colony of Rhodesia during the First Matabele War (1893-1894). The patrol consisted of thirty-seven soldiers employed by the British South African Company. Whilst on patrol they were ambushed by over 2,000 Matabele warriors and after Major Wilson had ordered three men to break out, they made their stand. The patrol managed to kill around five hundred warriors before being overwhelmed and massacred.

1924 The official opening of the Gateway of India on the waterfront in Bombay. Originally designed to commemorate the arrival of the King Emperor George V (see 20th January and 3rd June) and Queen Mary in 1911 for the Delhi Durbar (see 12th December), it was not completed until thirteen years later. Built from yellow basalt and concrete, the arch is eighty-five feet high and was used as the ceremonial entrance to the city of Bombay and India for Viceroys and Governors. It was through the archway that the last British troops marched as they left India for the last time in 1948 (see 28th February).

1961 The female contraceptive, better known as 'the pill', becomes available on the National Health Service.

5th December:

1859 The birth of John Rushworth Jellicoe (see 20th November) in Southampton.

1916 Herbert Henry Asquith resigns as Prime Minister (see 15th February and 12th September). Following an unsuccessful start to the Great War and a growing lack of support from the press, he decided to step down (see 5th April).

1922 The Irish Free State Constitution Act receives Royal Assent. The purpose of the act was to ratify the Anglo-Irish Treaty of 1921 (see 6th December) and to enact into United Kingdom law the Constitution of the Irish Free State, a Dominion within the Empire (see 8th December).

1958 The M6 Preston by-pass is opened and is Britain's first stretch of motorway. It was 8 miles long and cost just under £3 million. At the time of its opening there was no speed limit on the motorway (see 22nd December).

1973 The death of Sir Robert Alexander Watson-Watt (see 13th April) in Inverness. A descendant of James Watt, he is credited with being the inventor of Radio Detection and Ranging, or RADAR (previously known as Radio Direction Finding or RDF). His contribution to the safety of this country and our Airmen was immeasurable and has never been fully recognised.

6th December:

1421 The birth of Henry VI in Windsor Castle (see 21st May, 6th November and 16th December).

1608 The birth of the future General George Monck (see 3rd January) at The Manor House, Great Potheridge, near Torrington in Devon.

1648 The so-called Pride's Purge begins at the Houses of Parliament. Troops under the command of Colonel Thomas Pride (see 23rd October) seal off the buildings and as the MPs arrived, they were checked against a list in his possession and all those who opposed or did not support the Grandees in the New Model Army were either barred from entering or were arrested. The remainder of the members were referred to as the 'Rump Parliament' (see 14th February, 20th April, 19th May and 16th December).

1732 The birth of Warren Hastings in Churchill in Oxfordshire (see 22nd August).

1799 The death of Joseph Black in Edinburgh (see 16th April). He is buried in Greyfriars. He is best known for having discovered 'black air', what we now call Carbon Dioxide. Born in France to an Irish father, he was appointed to Glasgow University in 1757 and in 1761 developed the theory of latent heat, marking the beginning of the study of thermodynamics.

1857 Our troops relieve Cawnpore during the Indian Mutiny after rebel forces besieged the town. The forces at Cawnpore were led by Brigadier Windham who both held off the rebels but also led attacks on their positions until they could be relieved by General Sir Colin Campbell's larger forces (see 10th May, 25th September and 16th November).

1882 The death of Anthony Trollope (see 24th April) in London. He was one of the most prolific and successful authors of his time. He was born in London but had a very unsettled childhood, spending a short time in Belgium. In 1841 he took a job as a postal clerk in Ireland where he later married and it was whilst working for the postal service that he started his writing in earnest. Whilst spending time in England, still working for the Post Office in the 1850s, he began his work on his most famous work in the 'Barchester

Chronicles'. It was whilst working for the Post Office that he recommended the installation and use of post boxes (see 23rd November). He spent some time in Australia visiting his son before settling in West Sussex.

1884 The Representation of the People Act (Third Reform Act) receives Royal Assent today. The electorate was widened further, with all men who rented a property for £10 per year or who were in possession of land with a value of £10 or more were eligible to vote (see 7th June and 15th August).

1916 David Lloyd George (see 17th January and 26th March) becomes the Liberal Prime Minister in a Coalition Government with the Conservatives after ousting his colleague Herbert Asquith (see 15th February and 12th September) and splitting the Liberal Party.

1921 The Anglo-Irish Treaty is signed, between our government and the *de facto* Irish Government, agreeing to bring into being the Irish Free State as an autonomous Dominion within the Empire with George V (see 20th January and 3rd June) as Head of State, represented by a Governor General exactly one year to the day later (see 1922 below, 12th April and 25th May).

1922 The Dominion of the Irish Free State comes into being (see 1921 above) and is granted its independence (see 12th April, 18th April and 8th December) within the Empire.

1923 The General Election is held and the Conservatives win the most seats but briefly form a minority government (see 22nd January). Oswald Mosley (see 16th November and 3rd December) is elected as an Independent Member of Parliament.

7th December:

1549 The execution of Robert Kett, yeoman farmer and the leader of the Norfolk rising (see 20th June and 7th July). He joined the rebellion after it had begun and for a month had some considerable success, including capturing the city of Norfolk, but was defeated in battle at Dussindale in 1549 (see 27th August). He was tortured, tried and sentenced to being hanged in chains from Norwich castle walls until he died days later. His body was left in situ until it had completely rotted away.

1817 The death of Vice-Admiral William Bligh (see 28th April and 9th September) in Bond Street, London. He was most famous for being the Captain of the 'Bounty', on which Fletcher Christian led the famous mutiny. After being set adrift with 18 of his loyal crew, they rowed a full 3,618 nautical miles in 47 days to the island of Timor and rescue. He was exonerated on his return to England.

1837 The battle of Montgomery's Tavern during the Upper Canada Rebellion. Around 400 ill-disciplined rebels of French decent, led by William Lyon Mckenzie (see 12th March and 28th August), had seized the tavern and were approached by around 1,000 loyal militia led by Colonel FitzGibbon. After a brief exchange of fire, the rebels fled and the city of Toronto was secured (see 25th November).

1839 The birth of Redvers Henry Buller (see 2nd June) in Crediton, Devon.

1893 The completion of the Manchester Ship Canal. The first full journey takes place as the thirty-six mile long canal stretched from the Mersey into Manchester. Construction of the canal had begun on 1887 with the hope of increased trade with the Port of Manchester.

1941 Pearl Harbour in Hawaii is bombed by the Japanese. Though not directly affecting our country, troops or Empire, the attack quickly pushed the previously timid United States to enter World War Two (see 8th December) on the side of the already battle-hardened allies.

8th December:

1542 The birth of Mary Stuart, the future Mary Queen of Scots at Linlithgow Palace, West Lothian (see 8th February). She was the daughter of James V of Scotland (see 10th April and 14th December) and Mary of Guise and was the great-niece of Henry VIII of England (see 28th January and 28th June). She became Queen of Scots when she was only 6 days old (see 9th March, 13th May, 15th May, 29th July and 9th September).

1826 The birth of John Brown in Crathie, Aberdeenshire (see 27th March).

1870 The death of Thomas Brassey (see 7th November). A civil engineer, he was a good friend of George Stephenson (see 9th June and 12th August) and became the leading railway builder of his time. Besides being responsible for many of the major railways around Britain, about a sixth of the network, he was also responsible for many projects as far apart as France and Canada.

1903 The death of Herbert Spencer in Brighton (see 27th April). A biologist, philosopher and sociologist, he became a Railway engineer in 1841. He produced many philosophical writings and became one of the founders of sociology. He expounded the importance of the individual and opposition to war and connected evolutionary Darwinism to society and social interaction.

1914 The Battle of the Falklands. This was a decisive victory for our forces and very much to avenge the humiliating defeat at the Battle of Coronel the month before (see 1st November). The Royal Navy inflicted a huge amount of casualties. A total of 1871 Germans were killed, including the German Admiral von Spee. The enemy also lost four ships, the Scharnhorst, Gneisnau, Numberg and the Leipzig.

1922 Northern Ireland, under the Irish Free State Constitution Act of 1922, declared their opt out of the newly formed Dominion of the Irish Free State (see 18th April, 25th May and 6th December) and remain loyally part of the United Kingdom (see 30th March).

1941 In the early hours of the morning, Japan begins its invasion of British Malaya as Japanese troops begin coming ashore in North-East Malaya. Simultaneously, Japanese aircraft begin bombing the Colony of Hong Kong (see 25th December). Great Britain, along with the Dominion of

Australia, the Dominion of New Zealand and our Allies, declare war on Imperial Japan following their unprovoked attack on the Colonies of Malaya and Hong Kong, defended by Australian, British and Indian troops. The attacks happened just eight hours after the attack on the American naval base at Pearl Harbour (see 15th August, 2nd September and 7th December).

9th December:

1608 The birth of John Milton, the future poet and exponent of the Commonwealth (see 8th November).

1814 The death of Joseph Bramah in Pimlico (see 13th April). A locksmith and inventor, he is known for inventing a hydraulic machine press, a safety lock and a beer machine. The screw propeller was one of his more long lived suggestions and he was instrumental in the standardising of screw threads and machine parts for industry.

1868 William Ewart Gladstone is elected Prime Minister, the first of four occasions for the Whig MP (see 19th May and 29th December).

1917 The capture of the city of Jerusalem by our forces from the Turks, marking the virtual end of the Ottoman Empire. The Turkish forces in the city surrendered to the Egyptian Expeditionary Force, commanded by General Sir Edmund Allenby after almost a month of fighting around the city (see 23rd April and 14th May).

10th December:

1815 The birth of Augusta Ada Lovelace or, as she is commonly referred to, Ada Lovelace (see 27th November). The daughter of the poet Lord Byron, she never knew him as he died when she was just eight years old.

1834 Sir Robert Peel becomes Prime Minister for the first time after the collapse of Earl Grey's government (see 5th February and 2nd July). It was following his appointment that he published the Tamworth Manifesto which laid the foundation for the modern Conservative party.

1891 The birth of Harold Alexander (see 16th June) in London.

1899 Our forces, led by Lieutenant General William Forbes Gatacre, are defeated at the Battle of Stromberg during the Boer War (1899-1902). This is the start of what became known as 'Black Week' for the British Army (see 11th December, 15th December and 16th December). In what should have been a straightforward battle, some of our troops advanced on the Boer kopje and were also shelled inadvertently by our artillery. In the end our troops retired, leaving over 600 to be surrounded and ultimately surrender.

1928 The death of Charles Rennie Mackintosh (see 7th June) in London. An architect and designer, he was the leading light of Art Nouveau in Great Britain. As an artist, he worked with many different mediums. He was responsible for many buildings; his most well-known creations being the Royal Highland Fusiliers Museum in Sauchiehall Street, the 'Lighthouse' in

Glasgow, Glasgow School of Art and the Willow Tea Rooms. Born in Glasgow, he spent most of his life in the city, with short periods spent elsewhere, such as France, for a few years in 1923, returning to England when he was diagnosed with cancer.

1936 Edward VIII (see 28th May and 23rd June) signs the Instrument of Abdication (see 11th December), allowing him to marry the American divorcee Wallis Simpson and his brother to succeed him as George VI (see 6th February and 14th December).

1941 The sinking of the battle cruiser HMS Repulse and the battleship HMS Prince of Wales, north of Singapore, off the coast of Malaya, by Japanese torpedo planes. Both ships were the first Royal Navy ships sunk by aircraft only during the Second World War. They were two key ships of Force Z that was tasked with deterring or intercepting any possible Japanese landing off the coast of Malaya (see 31st January, 15th February, 15th August, 17th September and 8th December).

1963 The Aden Emergency begins following a terrorist grenade attack against the British High Commissioner resulting in one death and numerous injuries (see 19th January, 20th June and 5th July).

11th December:

1282 Llywelyn ap Gryffydd, the last Prince of what could be described as an independent Wales, is killed in battle against the armies of Edward I (see 17th June and 7th July) at the battle of Orewin Bridge, thus effectively ending the Welsh rebellion. Llywelyn's brother David was then subsequently executed for his part in the rebellion. The day after the battle, Llywelyn's body was recognised and decapitated, his head being taken to London for display (see 3rd March).

1688 James VII (James II of England, see 5th September and 14th October) attempts to leave Britain for France following the landing of William, Prince of Orange (see 5th November and 23rd December), but is captured before he is able to do so.

1894 At a meeting at the Westminster Palace Hotel, the origins of the British Navy League were established. The League's role was primarily to promote public interest in the Royal Navy and to expand recognition of this country's reliance on the service as its protector and guardian (see 31st May).

1899 The Battle of Magersfontein, near Kimberley in the Cape Colony, which was another loss for our forces against the Boer rebels (see 10th December, 15th December and 16th December). Our forces, led by Lieutenant General Methuen, were moving to relieve Kimberley, which was being besieged by the Boers, when they came across a force of Boers.

1931 The Statute of Westminster gains Royal Assent. The Statute gave legislative equality within the Empire to the six Dominions of the British Commonwealth and the United Kingdom (see 28th April). The Dominions were the Dominion of Australia (see 26th January and 9th October), the

Dominion of Canada (see 1st July), the Dominion of the Irish Free State (see 6th December), the Dominion of Newfoundland (see 26th September), the Dominion of New Zealand (see 6th February) and the Union of South Africa (see 31st May).

1936 Edward VIII's (see 28th May and 23rd June) abdication is confirmed with the Declaration of the Abdication Act (see 10th December). In the evening, he made a radio broadcast to the nation to explain his actions and then left the country for Austria. His brother, Prince Albert, Duke of York, immediately succeeded to the throne as George VI (see 6th February and 14th December).

1975 As part of the ongoing Third Cod War (1975-1976) with Iceland, three unarmed British vessels are attacked by an Icelandic gun boat. Two Fisheries Support Vessels, the Star Aquarius and the Star Polaris, were in distress and taking water and were being assisted by the British tug Lloydsman when they came under fire from the gun boat Thor. Although within Icelandic territorial waters, international law allowed them to receive assistance and the Icelandic vessel should have done accordingly. The Lloydsman moved between the two Support Vessels and the gun boat when they came under fire in order to protect them, when there was a collision. The Thor was badly damaged but the Lloydsman was unscathed (see 7th January).

1979 The Rhodesian government, unrecognised by Great Britain, votes itself out of power, handing authority back to Britain until elections can be held (see 18th April and 11th November).

12th December:

1724 The birth of Samuel Hood (see 27th January) at Butleigh in Somerset.

1731 The birth of Erasmus Darwin in Elston near Nottingham (see 18th April).

1781 The Second Battle of Ushant in the Bay of Biscay during the American Colonial Rebellion (see 3rd September) and a victory for the Royal Navy. Our Squadron of twelve ships under Admiral Kempenfelt attacked a French convoy of over twenty transports and nineteen ships of the line. The escort ships were scattered in the fray and over a dozen French transports were captured.

1889 The death of Robert Browning (see 7th May) in Venice, Italy. He was a major Victorian poet and playwright. Born in Camberwell in London, he was primarily educated at home, though attended the University of London for a year. He began to write in the 1830s and despite some initial positive reviews, he received much criticism. In 1846 he married Elizabeth Barrett, after which the couple moved to Italy. It was during this period and following her death that his work received critical acclaim right up until his death. He is buried in Westminster Abbey.

1901 Gugliemo Marconi sends the very first trans-Atlantic wireless message to Newfoundland from Poldhu on the Cornish coast.

1911 The Delhi Durbar and the proclamation of George V as Emperor of India (see 20th January and 3rd June). As part of the ceremony, the King Emperor declared that the capital of India would move from Calcutta to the newly-created city of New Delhi (see 4th December and 15th December).

1963 The Colony of Kenya, established in 1920 from the East Africa Protectorate, is granted its independence (see 1st July and 20th October).

1975 The six day Balcombe Street siege ends with the arrest of four IRA terrorists and the release of their two hostages. The four terrorists had been responsible for a number of murders and terrorist actions in London during the year when they were spotted and chased by Police Officers. Unable to evade the Police, they forced their way into the flat, taking the two residents hostage. The terrorists gave up when they believed that the SAS were about to be used to end the siege (see 31st July and 14th August).

13th December:

1721 The death of Alexander Selkirk, probably from yellow fever, aboard the ship Weymouth. He was buried at sea off the west coast of Africa. Born in 1676 in Fife, he was the son of a cobbler. He went to sea as a privateer against the Spanish off the Spanish Main. In 1704 he was on a privateering expedition when he demanded to be put ashore on an isolated island as he was in fear of the ship sinking. His stay would last for over four years (see 2nd February). In 1712 he returned to Scotland and published his story the following year. Six years later Daniel Defoe published 'Robinson Crusoe', his fictionalised account of Selkirk's story. In 1720 he joined the Royal Navy, only to die the following year.

1778 Our troops, numbering around 5,000 under General Grant, land on the French Colony of St. Lucia in the West Indies (see 18th December and 28th December).

1784 The death of Doctor Samuel Johnson at the age of 75 (see 7th September). Born in Lichfield where he was educated, he spent some time at Oxford. He moved to London in 1737 where he worked as a journalist. Probably the most famous of this country's writers, he is best known for his Dictionary. Commissioned for the work in 1747, the first proper dictionary of the English language was finally published in 1755 (see 15th April). A writer, playwright, wit and an ardent tea-drinker, he is perhaps one of the greatest literary geniuses of our country. In 1773, he and his friend James Boswell (see 19th May and 29th October) spent three months touring the Highlands of Scotland about which they both wrote. He was buried in Westminster Abbey.

1939 The battle of the River Plate in the South Atlantic Ocean. This was the first major naval engagement of the Second World War (see 8th May and 3rd September). The German pocket battleship Graff Spee was engaged by HMS Exeter, HMS Achilles and HMS Ajax. During the initial battle, HMS

Exeter was badly damaged and put out of action. However, the Germans were pursued into the estuary of the River Plate. The German ship entered Montevideo harbour and after some indecision, she was finally scuttled by her crew on the 17th December 1939 when her captain realised that the Royal Navy had his ship cornered.

14th December:

1542 King James V of Scotland (see 10th April) dies in Falkland Palace shortly after his defeat at the battle of Solway Moss (see 24th November). His six-day-old daughter Mary becomes Queen (see 8th February and 8th December). The son of James IV (see 17th March and 9th September) and Margaret Tudor, James had himself acceded to the throne when he was just one year old after his father's death at the battle of Flodden (see 9th September). During his childhood, Scotland was ruled by a series of Regents, his mother being the first.

1730 The birth of James Bruce at Kinnaird House, Larbert near Stirling (see 27th April and 14th November).

1775 The birth of Thomas Cochrane in Annsfield near Hamilton (see 31st October).

1780 The death of Ignatius Sancho in London. It is believed that he was born in 1729 onboard a slave ship off the coast of Africa and that as a young man he was sent to England and worked in the household of three sisters. He came under the influence and care of the Montagu family where he learned to read and write well. Gout affected him badly and the Montagus provided money for him to establish himself as a shopkeeper in London. It was because of his property rights as a shopkeeper that allowed him to become the first known black person to vote, doing so in the 1780 General Election. He is best known for the numerous letters that he exchanged with many people across Britain. He wrote against the slave trade in the Colonies and the treatment of blacks in Britain (see 1st August and 28th August).

1799 The death of George Washington (see 11th February) in Virginia. A farmer and initially a Loyalist, he later rebelled and turned traitor against King and Country and agreed to lead the 'Continental Army' in their rebellion against Great Britain. Prior to this treachery, he had loyally entered service in the Virginia Militia in 1753 and fought in the Seven Years' War (1756-1763), taking part in the Braddock Expedition in 1755 (see 9th July). Following the granting of independence to the rebel colonies (see 3rd September), he was to become their first President. However, he was vindictive and exceptionally harsh towards those Loyalists who remained in the newly independent rebel colony, in stark contradiction to the stated aims of the rebels at the outset of their rebellion.

1861 The death of Prince Albert at Windsor Castle (see 26th August), the Prince Consort to Queen Victoria (see 22nd January and 24th May). Born in Schloss Rosenau in Bavaria, his father was the Duke of Saxe-Coburg-Gotha.

Victoria was his cousin and they married in 1840 (see 10th February). At first he was unpopular but overtime became his wife's secretary and advisor. In 1857 he became Prince Consort to the Queen. He was the driving force and creator of the Great Exhibition of 1851 (see 1st May). He died of typhoid and the Queen never recovered, spending the rest of her life in mourning for the loss of her husband.

1862 The death of Charles John Canning, 1st Earl Canning (see 17th June) in London. He was born in 1812 and entered parliament in 1836. He was the last Governor General of India under the East India Company and the first Viceroy of British India (see 1st November). As Governor General throughout the Mutiny, he was known as 'Clemency Canning' due to a perceived soft approach to the punishment of traitorous Sepoys and their supporters.

1895 The birth of George VI (see 6th February) in Sandringham, Norfolk. Formally known as Prince Albert, the Duke of York, he was known as 'Bertie' to his family and friends.

1896 The opening of the Glasgow District Subway, a twin circular railway line entirely underground and originally a cable railway, later becoming electrified (see 9th January and 15th December).

1918 The General Election polling begins and for the first time, women over the age of 30 are eligible to vote. All women over 30 who were householders, wives of householders or resident in houses with an annual rent of £5 or above were granted the vote under the Representation of the People Act 1918, earlier in the year (see 6th February and 12th May).

1919 Oswald Moseley (see 16th November and 3rd December) is elected for the first time to Parliament as a Unionist MP (see 28th February, 29th February, 10th March, 27th March and 20th May).

1947 The death of Stanley Baldwin (see 3rd August) at Stourport on Severn. A Conservative, he was Prime Minister three times. His first administration was short-lived after calling a General Election six months into his Premiership. After the short-lived failure of the first Labour administration, he was again Prime Minister. This term of office saw some noticeable achievements, including the Locarno Pact in 1925 (see 3rd December), increased pensions and the extension of the voting franchise. His second term also saw him stand firm against the General Strike in 1926 (see 4th May, 11th May and 12th May). He was deeply involved in the National Government in the 1930s. He was initially somewhat hesitant about re-arming the country in the 1930s following Hitler's rise to power, much to Winston Churchill's annoyance. However, he later changed his view point. He supported Neville Chamberlain and the Munich Agreement of 1938 and was Prime Minister during the abdication crisis.

1970 The death of Viscount William Slim (see 6th August) in London. A career soldier, he joined the army during World War One as a private but received a commission not long after. During the Second World War he was promoted to General. After one or two set backs, he was instrumental in reorganising the Army and then leading our forces to victory against the

Japanese in Asia and regaining all the Colonies previously lost to them (see 15th August). He was one of the greatest Generals of his time.

2006 Thursday: Tony Blair (see 1st May) becomes the first serving Prime Minister to be interviewed by the Police. He is interviewed for over two hours at 10 Downing Street over the 'Cash for Honours' scandal.

15th December:

1857 The death of Sir George Cayley (see 27th December) in Brompton, Yorkshire. Often referred to as the 'Father of Aerodynamics', he invented and built the first human carrying glider which flew in 1853. He also discovered and classified the four aerodynamic forces of mechanical flight: weight, lift, drag and thrust.

1899 The Battle of Colenso on the Tugela River, Natal. Our forces suffered a bloody defeat for our troops in the Transvaal. Led by General Sir Redvers Buller (see 2nd June and 7th December), we suffered 1,200 casualties against the Boers supposed total of 29 casualties in a running battle along the banks of the Tugela River in Northern Natal (see 10th December, 11th December and 16th December).

1906 The opening of the Piccadilly Line on the London Underground (see 9th January and 14th December).

1911 George V (see 20th January and 3rd June) and Queen Mary lay the foundation stone for the new Indian city of New Delhi (see 4th December and 12th December). The city was designed primarily by Sir Edwin Lutyens (see 1st January and 29th March) and Sir Herbert Baker to become the new capital of India, replacing the previous capital of Calcutta.

16th December:

1431 Henry VI, at only ten years old is crowned the rightful King of France in the Cathedral of Notre Dame in Paris by Cardinal Beaufort (see 13th April, 21st May, 21st October, 6th November and 6th December).

1485 The birth of Catherine of Aragon in Madrid (see 7th January, 2nd April, 11th June and 14th November), the daughter of King Ferdinand and Queen Isabella of Spain.

1653 Oliver Cromwell (see 25th April and 3rd September) is sworn in as 'Lord Protector'; the head of state for life of the 'Commonwealth of England, Scotland and Ireland' (see 20th April and 7th May).

1689 The 'Bill of Rights' is passed by parliament, establishing the supremacy of parliament over the Monarchy. It restricted the powers of the monarchy, confirmed certain basic rights on the subjects of the Crown and the requirement of the Crown to seek the consent of the people as represented by Parliament (see 15th June) and is still in effect to this day.

1773 The so called 'Boston Tea Party' is carried out by rebel colonists protesting against the taxes introduced by Parliament. Three East Indiamen were blocked into Boston harbour and a group of rebels, thinly disguised as native Indians, boarded the vessels and emptied around 350 casks of tea into the waters of the harbour. This criminal act is often thought of as the event that sparked the American colonial rebellion (see 10th May).

1775 The birth of Jane Austen in Steventon, Hampshire (see 18th July).

1899 The end of 'Black Week' for our Army (see 11th December). This was a week during the Boer War (1899-1902) which was one of the worst weeks in our Military history. From the 10th December to this day, our forces suffered three unexpected and devastating defeats at the hands of the Boer Commando in the battles of Stormberg (see 10th December), Magersfontein (see 11th December) and Colenso (see 15th December). Though a dreadful humiliation, the setbacks allowed the government and the military to reassess the strategies and approach to the conflict (see 31st May).

1914 In the early hours of the morning, the High Seas Fleet of the German Imperial Navy bombarded the towns of Scarborough, Hartlepool and Whitby, causing close to 150 casualties. This was the first attack on mainland Great Britain that caused casualties (see 24th January, 31st May, 1st November, 3rd November and 8th December).

17th December:

1538 Henry VIII, King of England and France and Lord of Ireland is officially excommunicated by Pope Paul III from the Roman Catholic Church (see 28th June and 28th January).

1619 The birth of Prince Rupert of the Rhine in Prague in the Kingdom of Bohemia (see 29th November). His mother was Elizabeth, the sister of Charles I (see 30th January and 19th November) and is often referred to as 'The Winter Queen'.

1778 The birth of Humphrey Davy in Penzance, Cornwall (see 29th May).

1857 The death of Rear-Admiral Sir Francis Beaufort (see 27th May) in Sussex. An officer in the Royal Navy, he is remembered as the creator of the Beaufort scale for measuring the force of wind. He joined the British East India Company (see 31st December) on merchant ships and served during the Napoleonic Wars, fighting in the 'Glorious First of June' in 1794 (see 1st June). After being badly wounded, he returned to serve in the Royal Navy. It was during his many travels on different ships that led him to devise the means of measuring wind speed that was named after him. He was appointed the Hydrographer of the Royal Navy, was a member of the Royal Observatory, the Royal Society and helped form the Royal Geographic Society.

1907 The death of Sir William Thomson, 1st Baron Kelvin (see 26th June) in Largs, Scotland. He was a mathematical physicist and engineer at Glasgow University and is most well-known for developing the Kelvin scale of absolute temperature measurement. Born in Belfast in 1824, he moved to Glasgow in 1832 when his father became Professor of Mathematics. He studied at Cambridge and at Glasgow University and became Professor of Natural Philosophy there in 1846. It was there that he helped develop the second law of Thermodynamics and also invented the absolute temperature scale, which bears his name. During 1857-1858 he was chief consultant for the laying of the first trans-Atlantic telegraph cable. He is buried in Westminster Abbey.

1917 The death of Elizabeth Garrett Anderson, the first female Doctor (see 9th June, 28th September and 9th November) to qualify in Britain. She initially studied as a nurse at the Middlesex Hospital. In 1865, after discovering that the rules did not specify that applicants had to be male, she sat the Society of Apothecaries examination and passed, being granted a certificate to practice as a Doctor, which she did in London. She had an active role in medicine and in 1908 she became the first female Mayor in England. A prominent member of the Suffragette movement, she was the sister of Millicent Fawcett. She worked towards the creation of the New Hospital for Women and the London School of Medicine for Women.

18th December:

1745 The Battle of Clifton in Cumbria. The last battle fought on English soil following the Jacobite Army's retreat from Derby. The Jacobite rear guard fought a well-disciplined retreat through the village but ultimately had to retire having suffered 12 deaths. The Government forces suffered a similar amount of casualties. Regarded by some as little more than a skirmish, it was nonetheless the last action upon English soil (see 16th April, 19th August and 3rd December).

1778 French reinforcements of around 9,000 men land on the former French Colony of St. Lucia in the West Indies in an attempt to retake the island. In the ensuing battle, the battle hardened troops of our forces repel repeated advances, inflicting a humiliating defeat upon the French and causing a large amount of casualties (see 13th December and 28th December).

1793 The combined British and Spanish Fleet under the command of Vice Admiral Lord Hood (see 27th January and 12th December) and Admiral Juan de Langara abandon the Port of Toulon after being under siege by French Republican forces. Earlier in the day, the huge arsenal had been blown up by British and Spanish troops and forty-two French ships had been set alight. Then, as many French Royalists as possible were taken aboard the ships (see 28th August) before the fleets departed.

1834 Prime Minister Robert Peel (see 5th February and 2nd July) publishes his famous Tamworth Manifesto. As the MP for Tamworth, the manifesto was an address to his constituency. However, as was the custom, it was also published for the wider population and is generally recognised as the beginning of the modern Conservative Party.

1845 The battle of Mudki in the Punjab forming part of the First Sikh War (1845-1846). A hard-won British victory by British regulars and troops of the East India Company against the Khalsa, the rebellious Sikh army. Our forces of British and Bengal Native Regiments, commanded by Major General Sir Hugh Gough and General Sir Henry Hardinge suffered 872 men killed and wounded, 414 of which were from the British regiments (see 28th January, 10th February and 21st December).

1892 The death of Sir Richard Owen in London (see 20th July). A biologist and Palaeontologist, he is best remembered for his opposition to Charles Darwin's (see 12th February and 19th April) theory on the evolution of species and for inventing the word 'Dinosauria' in 1842, meaning terrible reptile for what we now call Dinosaurs. Born in Lancaster, he attended Edinburgh University and studied medicine in London. In 1856 he began working at the British Museum and eventually oversaw the moving of the natural history section to what would become the Natural History Museum in Kensington. He wrote and published a vast amount of papers and books on various aspects of his field of science. A controversial figure in the world of science during the latter part of his career, he became an open critic of Darwin. Although agreeing with the theory of evolution, he differed considerably from Darwin on the causes and development of the process.

1899 At the battle of Jasfontein in the South African War (see 31st May and 11th October), troops from New Zealand (see 1st July) are deployed in battle for the first time outside of New Zealand when they engage Boer forces (see 23rd November).

1919 The death of Captain Sir John William Alcock near Rouen in France (see 5th November). Along with Arthur Whitten Brown (see 23rd July and 4th October), he became one of the first two men to fly non-stop across the Atlantic Ocean (see 15th June). Born in Old Trafford, he joined the Royal Naval Air Service during the Great War and was awarded the Distinguished Service Cross. He died in France when his plane crashed in fog. He is buried in Manchester.

2012 Queen Elizabeth II (see 21st April) becomes the first Monarch since 1781 to attend a cabinet meeting of her ministers. Her attendance at the cabinet meeting, chaired by the Prime Minister David Cameron at 10 Downing Street, was part of the celebrations for her Diamond Jubilee (see 6th February, 3rd June and 4th June).

2012 During a visit to the Foreign Office by Queen Elizabeth II (see 21st April), Foreign Secretary William Hague announces that 169,000 square miles of the British Antarctic Territory will be named Queen Elizabeth Land in honour of the Queen and in celebration of her Diamond Jubilee. It is roughly a third of our territory in the Antarctic and is twice the size of the United Kingdom (see 6th February, 3rd June and 4th June).

2013 The Bank of England announced that in 2016 the first plastic £5 notes will be issued, bearing the image of Sir Winston Churchill (see 24th January and 30th November).

19th December:

1154 The coronation of Henry II *'Curtmantle'* at Westminster Abbey (see 4th March and 6th July).

1783 William Pitt the younger (see 23rd January and 28th May) becomes the youngest Prime Minister at 24 years old (see 10th May) following the collapse of the Fox-North Coalition and accepting the offer to form a government by King George III (see 29th January and 24th May).

1819 The death of Vice-Admiral Sir Thomas Francis Fremantle (see 20th November) in Naples. A successful naval officer, he was a contemporary and friend of Admiral Lord Horatio Nelson (see 29th September and 21st October) and was involved in actions during the French Revolutionary War as well as in a number of well-known fleet actions including the battle of Tenerife in 1797 (see 22nd July to 25th July), the battle of Copenhagen 1807 (see 2nd September, 5th September and 7th September) and the glorious battle of Trafalgar in 1805 (see 21st October).

1922 The death of Clementina Black (see 27th July). A trade unionist and novelist, she also campaigned for women's suffrage. Educated at home, she became friends with Eleanor Marx, daughter of Karl Marx and became involved with the Women's Protective and Provident League. She wrote two books that were important for the understanding of women in industry and their conditions in the early twentieth century, 'Sweated Industry and the Minimum Wage' (1907) and 'Married Women's Work' (1915). She was an advocate of the National Union of Women's Suffrage and helped to organise the suffrage petition of 1909.

1932 The BBC's Empire Service is broadcast for the first time. This was the first time the BBC had broadcast outside of Britain and its aim was to unite the English-speaking populations of the huge Empire (see 5th February, 23rd April and 25th December).

20th December:

1856 The birth of Reginald Theodore Blomfield (see 27th December) in Devon, the son of a Curate.

1915 The last Australian and New Zealand ANZAC force troops are evacuated from Gallipoli (see 25th April). Both Suvla Bay and Anzac Cove were evacuated, taking the last men off in the early hours. There were no casualties in the entire evacuation except two men wounded at Suvla Bay. Despite the courage and heroic actions of the allied troops and in particular the ANZAC force, the overall Dardanelles campaign was a disaster for the Empire (see 30th October).

1942 Imperial Japanese aircraft carry out their first bombing mission on the city of Calcutta. Eight aircraft in total bombed the city but caused relatively little damage. However, the attack caused a huge impact on morale as over a million people panicked and fled the city (see 15th August and 10th December).

1955 Cardiff is declared the capital city of Wales (see 3rd March).

2007 Queen Elizabeth II (see 21st April) becomes our oldest ever Monarch at 5pm today. She surpasses Queen Victoria (see 22nd January and 24th May) who was our oldest Monarch up until this point.

21st December:

1620 The first landing parties go ashore from the ship The Mayflower, carrying the first English Puritans, to form a permanent settlement that would later be called Plymouth Bay in the future Plymouth Colony. Some exploratory and foraging parties had gone ashore in the days before, but this was the first proper and permanent landing (see 10th April, 26th April, 13th May, 14th May and 3rd September).

1803 The birth of Joseph Whitworth in Stockport (see 22nd January).

1804 The birth of Benjamin Disraeli (see 19th April), later Conservative Prime Minister and Lord Beaconsfield, in London.

1845 The battle of Ferozeshah in the Punjab as part of the First Sikh War of 1845-1846 (see 28th January, 10th February, 9th March and 18th December). A force of around 18,000 men from the British regular army and the Bengal Presidency under Generals Sir Hugh Gough and Sir Henry Hardinge faced the Sikh Khalsa of around 30,000 in the fortified town of Ferozeshah. After some intense and ferocious hand to hand fighting, elements of our forces forced themselves into the Sikh camp and took control before night fell. Having suffered huge casualties and being low on ammunition, our forces withdrew the following day and abandoned Ferozeshah.

1962 During an emergency meeting in Nassau in the Bahamas, the Prime Minister Harold Macmillan (see 10th February and 29th December) and President Kennedy of the United States of America announce that America will sell the Polaris missile system to Great Britain as part of the Nassau Agreement (see 22nd December). It was agreed that Britain would build the nuclear submarines and the warheads for the Polaris missiles (see 26th February, 15th May, 19th August and 3rd October).

1988 A Pan Am jet (Pan Am Flight 103) is destroyed by a bomb on board at 31,000 feet over the village of Lockerbie in Scotland and the wreckage crashes onto houses in the village killing all 243 passengers and 16 crew as well as 11 people in the town.

22nd December:

1715 James Frances Edward Stewart or the Jacobite James III, known as the 'Old Pretender' (see 1st January and 10th June) and son of the deposed James II (see 5th September and 14th October), lands at Peterhead in a failed attempt to reclaim the British crown (see 23rd March, 6th September and 13th November).

1727 James Wolfe is born at Westerham in Kent, the eldest son of General Edward Wolfe. He was to become famous for the capture of Quebec (see 13th September).

1767 The death of John Newbery (born 1713). A well-known publisher of his day, he is credited with being the first publisher to make a success of publishing children's books. One of the more famous people whose works he published was Samuel Johnson (see 7th September and 13th December). The Newbery Medal, awarded in America for contributions towards American children's literature is named in his honour.

1879 The Battle of Kabul during the Second Afghan War (1878-1880). Our forces, numbering only 7,000 British and Indian troops, were led by Major General Sir Frederick Roberts (see 30th September and 14th November) against around 50,000 Afghan tribesmen and soldiers. Our forces took over and defended the Sherpur Military encampment against the enemy. From dawn until after midday our troops repulsed numerous attacks on their positions before using the artillery to persuade the Afghans to disperse. Our casualties were said to be 33 dead and the Afghans suffering around 3,000, most of whom were killed.

1880 The death of Mary Anne Evans, better known by her pen name George Eliot (see 22nd November), in Chelsea, London. A novelist and poet, she was one of the most famous of the Victorian writers. Her mother died when she was fifteen, forcing her to leave school to help in her father's business. Settling in London after her father's death, she contributed to and later edited the 'Westminster Review'. She met then lived with then married George Henry Lewes, scandalising Victorian society. Lewes was the encouragement she needed in her writing and her better known works included 'The Mill on the Floss' (1860), 'Middlemarch' (1871-1872) and 'Daniel Daronda' (1876). She was buried in Highgate Cemetery in London.

1905 The birth of Thomas 'Tommy' Flowers (see 28th October) in London.

1962 The Nassau Agreement is concluded with a formal Treaty between the Prime Minister Harold Macmillan (see 10th February and 29th December) and President Kennedy of the United States. Signed in Nassau in the Bahamas, it was the culmination of several days of heated discussions between the UK and America. The agreement maintained Britain's right to an independent nuclear deterrent and the progression of the Polaris programme (see 21st December), despite American reluctance (see 26th February, 15th May, 19th August and 3rd October).

1965 The 70 mph maximum speed limit is applied for the first time on all dual carriage ways and motorways. Prior to this there had been no limits (see 31st January, 18th March and 5th December) except 30mph in built up areas.

23rd December:

1688 James VII (James II of England see 5th September and 14th October) finally makes his escape from captivity near the coast and goes into exile in France (see 11th December).

1732 The birth of Richard Arkwright (see 3rd August) in Preston, Lancashire.

1834 The death of the Reverend Robert Thomas Malthus (see 13th February) in Bath. A leading scholar in economics, he became well-known for his theories on population and its increase or decrease due to influence from differing factors. His principle work, 'An Essay on the Principle of Population' (1798), explained that eventually populations become checked by natural factors such as disease and famine.

1919 The Government of India Act received Royal Assent. The Act expanded the level of participation in Indian government by Indians themselves and allowed for elected representatives of the people a definite share in governance of the Colony (see 10th May, 2nd August and 15th August)

1956 The last of our troops leave Port Said in Egypt following betrayal by the United States of America and the United Nations. Over 600 Egyptian insurgents had died in the conflict, with British and French casualties amounting to 26 dead. Of those 26 killed, 22 were British with 129 wounded (see 5th November and 6th November). Despite the operation being a military success, our supposed closest ally and one with which we possess a supposed 'special relationship' had seen the campaign as being against their own interests. America had given our government ultimatums and thinly-veiled threats both politically and economically to pressure our government into the climb down. A total disregard by our allies for the sacrifice of our troops lives. May our troops' heroism and our betrayal never be forgotten (see 26th August and 31st October).

24th December:

1167 The supposed birth of the future King John 'Lackland' at Beaumont Palace, Oxford (see 27th May and 18th October), the youngest son of Henry II (see 4th March and 6th July).

1650 Edinburgh Castle surrenders to parliamentarian troops under Oliver Cromwell (see 25th April and 3rd September). The castle's Governor, Sir Walter Dundas surrendered the castle despite having plenty of supplies and the potential to hold out for many more months.

1814 The Treaty of Ghent is signed between Britain and America in the recently freed Austrian Netherlands, thus ending the 1812 to 1815 war between the British and Americans (see 18th June). The Treaty was ratified by our government on 27th December and by the American government on 16th February 1815. The Treaty guaranteed the return of all lands captured by both sides to their pre-war status. This was the first time the United States of America had declared war on another country. However, for America, this was nothing less than a complete humiliation as their original objectives of the conquest of our territories in North America and the Caribbean were thwarted and our objective of the pre-war status quo was resoundingly achieved. The war had bankrupted America, destroyed her trade and caused their President to flee the capital and the White House, which was subsequently burned by our glorious and heroic forces, in a humiliating panic (see 24th August).

1818 The birth of James Prescott Joule in Salford, Lancashire (see 11th October), the son of Benjamin Joule, a wealthy and successful brewer.

1863 The death of William Makepeace Thackeray (see 18th July) in London. A famous satirist, he is remembered for his novel 'Vanity Fair', published in 1847-1848. Born in Calcutta, his father died when he was four years old. After studying at Cambridge, he left after two years without a degree. He travelled to Germany for a while and returned to London to eventually begin work as a journalist. He also contributed to 'The Times', the 'Morning Chronicle' and 'Punch'. Other novels included 'The History of Henry Esmond', 'Newcomes' and 'The Virginians'.

1872 The death of William John Maquorn Rankine in Glasgow (see 5th July). An engineer and physicist, he was one of the founding fathers of the science of thermodynamics. Born in Edinburgh, he trained as a civil engineer and in 1843 his early work was published on metal fatigue on railway axles. In 1859 he described the thermodynamic cycle of pressure and temperature and his method of measurement was called the Rankine cycle. He published a number of other papers and manuals on applied mechanics, steam engines and civil engineering.

1914 The first German air raid on Britain. A Zeppelin drops a bomb in the grounds of St. James's Rectory in Dover (see 19th January, 31st May and 7th June).

1914 The death of John Muir in Los Angeles, California, America (see 21st April). A naturalist, he was an early advocate of the preservation of the American wilderness and many places across the United States were preserved in whole or in part due to his activities and work. Born in Dunbar, the family emigrated to the United States in 1849. He travelled across the United States and Canada conducting botanical and geological studies. In the 1870s he embarked completely on his conservation work and followed this as a prolific writer on the subject, publishing many articles and books.

25th December:

1066 William the Conqueror is crowned King in Westminster Abbey (see 9th September and 14th October). This is the first documented coronation held at the Abbey.

1642 The birth of Sir Isaac Newton in Woolsthorpe, Lincolnshire, three months after the death of his father (see 20th March).

1914 The 'Christmas truce' between some elements of our British Expeditionary Force and those of the Imperial German Army takes place on the Western Front (see 4th August and 11th November). Breaking out in several places across the front, the 'truces' were small and spontaneous acts of friendship between enemies that have since become almost mythical in their telling.

1932 King George V (see 20th January and 3rd June) makes the first Royal Christmas Day broadcast to the Empire on radio. The speech was written by Rudyard Kipling and was transmitted from the King's small office in Sandringham House to inaugurate the BBC Empire Service (see 23rd April and 19th December).

1942 The Governor of the Colony of Hong Kong, Sir Mark Young, surrenders to the Japanese in the Peninsular Hotel in Hong Kong (see 20th January and 1st July) after 18 days of brutal fighting (see 15th February, 15th August, 2nd September and 8th December), bringing an end to the battle of Hong Kong. During the defence of the Colony over 2,100 troops were killed with well over 10,000 subsequently taken prisoner. This is the only time a Crown Colony has surrendered to any invading force.

1950 The Stone of Destiny is stolen from Westminster Abbey where it has lain for over 650 years. Four Scottish students took the stone, which was in fact in two parts and ultimately left them at Arbroath Abbey. Used for centuries to crown Scottish Monarchs, the stone was captured in 1296 by the forces of Edward I (see 17th June and 7th July) and taken to Westminster where it was contained within a wooden chair. Since then almost all Monarchs have been crowned upon the coronation chair that contains the stone (see 25th February and 30th November).

1957 Queen Elizabeth II (see 21st April) gives the first Christmas Queen's speech that is televised. This was her sixth broadcast and was recorded at Sandringham House as in previous years.

26th December:

1135 The Coronation of King Stephen at Westminster Abbey (see 25th October).

1776 The Battle of Trenton and defeat for our forces against the rebel colonists in America. The treacherous rebel leader, George Washington (see 11th February and 14th December), led his troops across the Delaware River to surprise the mainly German Hessian troops that were garrisoned in the town of Trenton. Taken by surprise, the Hessians lost around 20 killed, 100 wounded and 1,000 taken prisoner. The rebels suffered about four casualties. This victory gave the rebels new hope and galvanised their troops to continue with the rebellion that had until this point began to falter (see 3rd September).

1791 The Constitutional Act of 1791 comes into effect, creating the two Canadian Provinces of Upper Canada and Lower Canada. The reorganisation was necessary to accommodate the changed situation in the Canadian Colonies following the influx of thousands of United Empire Loyalists from the rebellious American colonies during and after the American rebellion (see

3rd September). Upper Canada was predominately English-speaking and culturally British and Lower Canada was able to retain the French language, French institutions and the Roman Catholic Church whilst remaining a British Colony.

1791 The birth of Charles Babbage (see 14th June and 18th October), probably in London.

1797 The death of John Wilkes, MP for Aylesbury (see 19th January and 17th October). Elected as MP for Aylesbury in 1757, he became an outspoken opponent of George III (see 29th January and 24th May) and his Prime Minister and attacked him and his administration in his periodical, 'The North Briton'. An outspoken radical, he was charged with seditious libel in 1764 but escaped to France before being arrested. However, after five years he returned, stood again for parliament and though elected, was imprisoned on similar charges. In 1774 he became Mayor of London (see 10th May). His popularity with the masses waned somewhat in the last 15 years of his life, especially after his involvement in leading troops defending the Bank of England during the Gordon Riots in 1780.

1871 Boxing Day is officially recognised as a Bank Holiday following the passing of the Bank Holidays Act 1871 (see 1st January and 1st May).

1887 The birth of Arthur Ernest Percival in Aspenden in the county of Hertfordshire (see 31st January and 15th February).

1943 The Battle of North Cape where Royal Navy forces, consisting of several ships, attack and sink the solitary German Battleship Scharnhorst off the Norwegian coast. Following a high-speed chase, the German ship was shelled from the chasing ships, led by the Battleship HMS Duke of York, and was eventually finished off with a mixture of shell and torpedoes, leaving only 36 survivors of a crew of nearly 2,000 men. The Scharnhorst was the last operational German battleship and with her sinking, there ended any real threat from the German Navy, and the Royal Navy continued to hold its superiority.

27th December:

1647 The Treaty of Engagement is signed by Charles I (see 30th January and 19th November) and three Scottish Commissioners the following day at Carisbrooke Castle on the Isle of Wight. The treaty was between Charles I and moderate Scots Royalists and covenanters, agreeing to restore Charles as long as he agreed to establish the Presbyterian Church in England for a three year term and agreeing to the terms of the Solemn League and Covenant as well as closer links with the Westminster Parliament.

1773 The birth of George Cayley in Scarborough, Yorkshire (see 15th December).

1831 Charles Darwin sets sail in the ship HMS Beagle (see 12th February and 19th April) for a five year expedition. The purpose of the expedition was to conduct surveys off the coast of South America and then on to Australia and to produce much more accurate nautical charts. Darwin was on board as the resident geologist with the aim of collecting specimens to study and bring back to Britain (see 24th November).

1900 The death of William George Armstrong (see 26th November) in Northumberland. An industrialist, he was the founder of the Armstrong Whitworth Company. During the Crimean War (1853-1856) he pursued a career in arms development and designed the Armstrong guns, a series of breech loading, rifled field and heavy guns. The company later diversified and was also responsible for the design and construction of gun boats and battle ships. He worked for the War Department and received a Baronetcy for his service to the Crown.

1942 The death of Reginald Theodore Blomfield (see 20th December) in London. A popular architect of the late Victorian and Edwardian era, his heyday involved the design and construction of many country houses as well as many restoration projects. However, after the First World War, he is best remembered for the design of the Cross of Sacrifice that is present in most Commonwealth War Cemeteries around the world. Other memorials he designed include the Menin Gate in Ypres, the RAF Memorial in London and the Brandhoek Military Cemetery in Belgium.

28th December:

1065 The consecration of Westminster Abbey in London. The Abbey was founded by Edward the Confessor and was built under his direction (see 5th January and 25th December).

1694 The death of Queen Mary II (see 30th April), the daughter of James VII (James II in England, see 5th September and 14th October) and the wife of William of Orange (see 8th March), in Kensington Palace from smallpox. She came to the throne with her husband following the 'Glorious Revolution' in 1688, which saw her father ousted in a relatively quiet 'revolution' against the Catholic Stewart Monarchy. She insisted that she and William rule as joint monarchs. They were responsible for a number of acts of legislation that began to curtail the power of the Monarch and thus help ensure that there would be no similar constitutional crisis.

1734 The death of the legendary Rob Roy MacGregor (see 7th March) in his house in Balquhidder. A supporter of the Stuart cause, he and his clan fought against the Government of William of Orange and was at the battle of Glen Shiel in 1719 (see 10th June). He was declared an outlaw and was evicted from his house after arguments over debts to his creditors. After continuing his feud with the Duke of Montrose, he was captured and imprisoned before being pardoned and released.

1778 The French garrison on their former Colony of St. Lucia surrender to our troops under General Grant after an attempt by the French to reinforce them was defeated and the island was abandoned (see 13th December and 18th December).

1879 The collapse of the Tay Railway Bridge in Scotland. The bridge crossed the Firth of Tay between Dundee and Wormit and was at the time the longest rail bridge in the world. The central section collapsed during a violent storm whilst a train was crossing it, resulting in the deaths of all 75 people on board.

1882 The birth of Arthur Stanley Eddington (see 22nd November) in Kendal.

1885 The first session of the Indian National Congress convenes in Bombay. The Indian National Congress was founded by British and Indian members of the Theosophical Society, inspired and led by Allan Octavian Hume (see 6th June and 31st July). The Congress in its first couple of decades, though advocating a greater say for Indians in the running of British India, nonetheless swore loyalty to the Crown (see 1st January, 1st May, 22nd June, 18th July and 15th August).

29th December:

1170 The Archbishop of Canterbury, Thomas Beckett, is murdered at the altar of Canterbury Cathedral by four of Henry II's Knights (see 5th March and 6th July). The son of a successful London merchant, he worked for the Archbishop of Canterbury. When the Archbishop died in 1161, Henry appointed Thomas Archbishop. However, though friends, Thomas began to support the church in its disputes with the King. In 1164 he fled to France as the King became more and more displeased with Thomas's stand for the church. He eventually returned in 1170. The knights, who had believed that Henry had wanted Thomas dead, stormed into the Cathedral and confronted Thomas before striking him with a sword.

1766 The birth of Charles MacIntosh (see 25th July) in Glasgow.

1809 The birth of William Ewart Gladstone in Liverpool (see 19th May and 9th December).

1813 The birth of Alexander Parkes in Birmingham (see 29th June).

1837 The 'Caroline affair'. A Royal Navy Captain and Canadian Loyalists cross the Niagara River into American waters and capture the American steamer Caroline, which was being used by Canadian rebels, and tow it into Canadian waters. It is abandoned and set alight and then sent over the Niagara Falls. In the capture of the vessel, an American was killed. The Canadian rebels were seeking shelter in American waters and were receiving supplies from their American sympathisers. This led to strained relations between the Americans and us that looked as if war was looming. However, the situation was resolved in the end by the US President's understanding and actions to prevent further support for Canadian rebels.

1860 The launch of HMS Warrior, the world's first iron-hulled, armour-plated warship. Powered by both steam and sail, she was the largest and fastest battleship of her time. Although she never saw battle, she was built in response to the French building their iron-clad battle ship, la Gloire. She was twice the size of the new French ship and outmanoeuvred her in every way, thus showing the world the continued dominance of the Royal Navy.

1895 The Jameson raid into Transvaal begins. Led by Doctor Leander Starr Jameson (see 9th February and 26th November), around 600 mainly mounted police and volunteers crossed the border with Transvaal and headed for Johannesburg. Their goal was to trigger an uprising of the 'Uitlanders', non Boer settlers, mainly British expatriate or of British descent. They would then seize Johannesburg and the gold mines with the possibility of the area becoming at least more pro-British. However, after meeting stiff resistance and the failure of the Uitlanders to rise against the Boers, the raiders surrendered to the Boers (see 2nd January) with 16 dead.

1940 In the single most destructive night of the Blitz, German bombers drop over 10,000 high-explosive and incendiary bombs on the city of London. The attack caused a huge firestorm that came to be referred to as the Second Great Fire of London. Following the order from Prime Minister Winston Churchill (see 24th January and 30th November) to save St. Paul's Cathedral at all costs, Firemen and volunteers successfully put up a heroic fight to save the building that became an icon of defiance to Nazi Germany (see 13th March, 14th March, 30th March, 7th September and 14th November).

1986 The death of Harold Macmillan (see 10th February), former Prime Minister, in Stockton on Tees. Born in London, he attended Oxford University and served during the Great War as a Captain in the Grenadier Guards, being wounded three times. He was elected to parliament in 1924. He succeeded Anthony Eden (see 14th January and 12th June) as Prime Minister in 1957 following his resignation after the Suez Crisis in 1956 (see 31st October, 5th November, 6th November, 25th November and 23rd December). He won the General election of 1959. During his second term in office, Britain's application to join the EU was vetoed by France and in 1962, in an attempt to restore confidence in his administration, he purged the cabinet in the infamous 'the night of the long knives' (see 13th July). Following the Profumo Scandal, he resigned from office in 1963 (see 18th October).

30th December:

1460 The Battle of Wakefield during what would later be called the 'Wars of the Roses' (1455-1485) and the death in Battle of Richard Duke of York and his son, Edmund, Earl of Rutland. After leaving the safety of Sandal Castle, the Yorkists sallied forth to attack a number of the Lancastrians. However, it was a trap and they quickly became surrounded and around 3,000 men were killed, including the senior Yorkists in the army. The heads of the Duke of York and the Earl of Rutland were displayed over the walls of York.

1865 The birth of Rudyard Kipling, poet and author (see 18th January), in Bombay, India.

1885 The Battle of Gennis in Upper Egypt (present day Sudan). Our forces were led by Major General Evelyn Wood and Herbert Smith-Dorien was present (later a Brigadier General during the Great War). The battle was little more than a skirmish and our forces were victorious. It is now most remembered as the last time British soldiers were to wear their scarlet tunics into battle. From that point onwards they would wear khaki uniforms in combat, thus presenting a less visible target to the enemy.

31st December:

1384 The death of John Wycliffe in Lutterworth in Leicestershire from the effects of a stroke a few days before. Born about 1330 in Yorkshire, he was a theologian and a philosopher who is remembered for contributing to the first Bible written in the English language, translating many books from Latin into English himself. A university teacher at Oxford, he also called for the reform of the Catholic Church and spoke out against many of the basic doctrines and traditions of the church including its power over the secular, the right of each individual to interpret the bible for themselves and belief in transubstantiation. His followers came to be known as Lollards.

1600 The founding of the Honourable East India Company (popularly known as 'John Company' to its employees) by the granting of a Royal Charter to the Directors of the company by Elizabeth I (see 24th March and 7th September). The charter allowed the company to challenge the Dutch and Portuguese for control over the spice trade in the East Indies. The company, in the form of a consortium of London merchants, was given the monopoly over trade between Britain and lands in the east and also eventually led to the growth of the tea industry. This is one of the key events that would lead to the emergence of our Empire (see 1st January) and the company itself was to last for over 250 years (see 2nd August). Its headquarters were situated in the grand building in Leddenhall Street in London and it would be from here that India would initially be ruled. The Company, in effect a private commercial enterprise, had its own army and naval vessels and used these to secure trading opportunities across the east and in particular in India.

1691 The death of Robert Boyle (see 25th January) in London. A scientist with a particular interest in chemistry, he is famous for devising Boyle's Law. In 1866 he moved to Oxford and there, along with Robert Hooke, he invented the vacuum chamber or air pump. Always keen to observe things and see how they reacted and behaved, he began to conduct the first true scientific experiments. He introduced many of the familiar scientific tests, including the litmus test. Boyle's law states that if the volume of a gas is decreased, then the pressure will increase proportionally. In 1660, along with eleven other like-minded men, he founded the Royal Society.

1695 The Window Tax is introduced. It was brought in by William III 'of Orange' (see 8th March and 4th November) to help pay for his military campaigns in Ireland and Europe, with the result that many house owners would brick up some of the windows of their properties to avoid paying the tax.

1720 The birth of Charles Edward Louis John Casimir Severino Maria Stuart, commonly referred to as 'Bonnie Prince Charlie' (see 31st January), in the Palazzo Muti in Rome. He was the son of James Francis Edward Stuart (see 1st January and 10th June), who in turn was the son of the former King James VI (James II of England see 5th September and 14th October) who was ousted in the so-called Glorious Revolution of 1688.

1738 The birth of Charles Cornwallis (see 5th October) in London.

1775 The Battle of Quebec in the Province of Quebec. American Colonial rebels, led by Benedict Arnold (see 14th January and 14th June) and the traitorous Irishman, the so called 'Brigadier' Richard Montgomery, and their French allies are beaten back and defeated by our forces after they had attempted to lay siege to Quebec and to capture it. Our troops, consisting of British regulars and Canadian Volunteers, were led by General Guy Carleton and Lieutenant Colonel Allan Maclean a former Jacobite Rebel in the '45. We suffered 20 casualties and the rebels around 500 men. The victory safeguarded our possessions, Provinces and territories in North America from involvement in the American colonist's rebellion (see 3rd September).

1857 Queen Victoria (see 22nd January and 24th May), following a request from the Legislative Assembly of the Province of Canada (see 10th February) to choose a site for the Colony's capital, officially chooses the frontier town of Ottawa (see 1st July).

1912 The birth of John Dutton Frost (see 21st May) in Poona, India.

1964 Donald Campbell (see 4th January and 23rd March) sets a new Water Speed Record at 276.33 mph in his Bluebird K7 on Lake Dumbleyung in Western Australia. In setting this record, he became the only person to achieve the 'double' (see 17th July), holding both the Land Speed Record and the Water Speed Record in the same year.

2006 The United Kingdom makes a payment of about £45.5m ($83m) to the United States, making it the last of the payments to pay off the loans from the Second World War. Despite Britain's solitary stand against tyranny until America's reluctant entry into the war, her supposed ally was able to profit very well from Britain's desperate lone stand and need for support from her ally (see 2nd January).

The events from our ancient history that have no precise dates. Many of the years below are approximate.

BC

450,000 The Palaeolithic Age or Old Stone Age starts. The earliest known traces left by the inhabitants of this country appear, interspersed with long gaps in known habitation.

250,000 The first appearance of early forms of modern man.

60,000 Neanderthal man begin to inhabit the southern parts of Britain.

40,000 The first Homo sapiens begin to appear.

30,000 The disappearance of the Neanderthals about this time. This occurred either violently, through disease or by interbreeding with Homo sapiens. There is much speculation and debate about how this happened but the reasons could be a mixture of some or all of the above.

10,000 The ice caps begin to retreat and the Mesolithic or Middle Stone Age commences and the resettlement of our Isles begins.

8,000 Rising sea levels begin to form the English Channel and the North Sea starts to form as water begins to cover the area between Britain and Europe now called Doggerland, thus cutting the British Isles off from Europe.

7,000 Farming is introduced to the British Isles.

4,500 The start of the Neolithic or the New Stone Age.

2750 Stonehenge is begun.

2300 The start of the Bronze Age.

1900 The 'Beaker' folk begin to arrive in Britain.

1300 Stonehenge is completed.

1200 The Later Bronze Age begins.

800 The first waves of what are referred to as 'Celtic' settlers begin to arrive from Northern Europe.

700 The start of the Iron Age.

55 Julius Caesar makes his and Rome's first contact with Britain.

54 Julius Caesar makes his and Rome's second contact with Britain.

AD

43 The Romans invade Britain led by General Aulus Plautius on behalf of the Emperor Claudius, landing in the Kent area. This is the start of about 360 years of occupation (see 406 AD).

60/61 The Iceni tribe begin a revolt led by their Queen Boudicea against the Roman occupation. They killed thousands of Romans and destroyed the cities of Camulodunum (Colchester), Verulamian (St. Albans) and also Londinium (London), burning them all to the ground.

61 Anglesey is conquered by the Romans. The Druids, religious leaders of the Celtic peoples of this island, are wiped out.

83/84 The Battle of Mons Gropius. The Romans defeat the Picts somewhere in Scotland. The site is generally believed to be near Aberdeen.

123 Hadrian's Wall is completed. It runs for 74 miles across Northern Britain from the East to the West coast and is for the most part 10 feet wide and 30 feet high.

143 The Antonine Wall, built under orders from the Emperor Antonius Pius and stretching forty miles between the Firth of Clyde and the Firth of Forth, is completed. This was to be the furthest outpost of the Roman Empire.

163 The Romans withdraw to Hadrian's Wall and use this as the final frontier of the North of their Empire.

406 The last of the Roman Legions leave Britain, never to return.

440 to 450 The arrival of the first Angles, Saxon and Jute settlers in England from Northern Europe. Some may have come to England in the preceding couple of decades, serving as Mercenaries to some of the local Roman-British tribes and some may have then settled in this country. From this time on, the British are pushed further and further back to Scotland, Wales and Cornwall.

c500 The Battle of Badon between Britons and Anglo-Saxons. The exact date and place remain unknown but it was a major battle that the Britons won, slowing the Anglo-Saxon advance for decades.

878 May Battle of Edington, the greatest of all English battles, when Alfred the Great defeats a great Danish army under Guthrum. Guthrum was captured and agreed to be baptized.

1348-1350 The Black Death spreads rapidly across England from some of the port cities. Over a quarter of the population were to succumb to the disease.

1526 February: William Tyndale's English translation of the Bible arrives in England.

Chapter 3

The Colonies, Dominions and Protectorates of our Empire: with information on their acquisition and dates of their independence from Sovereign rule and protection or their present status

Since the Empire had its first beginnings over 400 years ago, there have been a number of differing classifications of primarily English and then, after 1707, British influence, with Dominions, Colonies, Protectorates and Territories amongst others. Over the centuries, their positions within the Empire have often changed as they merged with other colonies, changed their status or eventually became self-governing and ultimately independent. These changes can often cause considerable confusion. However, listed below are as many of our Empire's interests as possible, listed with their Empire names. Because of these difficulties, the list cannot claim to be an exhaustive catalogue of our Empire. The countries are initially recorded as they were named at the time immediately prior to their independence or change of status. So, for example, Sri Lanka is here recorded as Ceylon and the United States of America is not recorded at all, as the original thirteen colonies were not recognised officially under this one name until they gained independence in 1783. However, some post-colonial names are given in brackets only if the colonial name has since become forgotten. Also, where countries became independent from each other after their break with the Empire, then only their Empire name is given. Pakistan is not recorded and also Bangladesh for example, as it was part of Pakistan at the time of that country's independence and therefore did not exist. Also, some of those listed below merged with other Colonies or Protectorates and existed under another name or title. Though many of these countries formed the present day Commonwealth, we are here dealing with our glorious Empire and its spheres of influence.

The Different classifications of British Colonies and Territories:

Colonies: Are countries that are ruled directly by Britain or its representatives, who are usually called Governors or Residents. This classification ceased in 1981 with the introduction of the British Nationality Act, when all Colonies were reclassified as Dependent Territories.

Condominium: A territory where Britain agrees to jointly share Dominion over a designated area with another country.

Crown Dependency: This applies to the Bailiwick of Jersey, the Bailiwick of Guernsey and the Isle of Man. They are not part of the United Kingdom but owe allegiance to the Crown.

Dependent Territories: This classification replaced Crown Colonies in 1981. This continued until they were replaced by the classification 'Overseas Territories' in 2002.

Dominions: Autonomous, self-governing communities within the British Empire that were formally Colonies or a group of merged Colonies.

Mandated Territories: The responsibility for control of a Mandate was given to Great Britain by either the League of Nations or its successor the United Nations.

Overseas Territories: Dependent states whose citizens retain British citizen status but are not part of the United Kingdom. This is has been a classification in use since 2002. Prior to this they were called Dependent Territories. Their citizens are automatically credited with British citizenship. They are: Anguilla, Bermuda, British Antarctic Territory, British Indian Ocean Territory, British Virgin Islands, Cayman Islands, Falkland Islands, Gibraltar, Montserrat, Pitcairn Islands, Saint Helena, Ascension Island and Tristan da Cunha, South Georgia and the South Sandwich Islands, Sovereign Base Areas Akrotiri and Dhekelia and Turk and Caicos Islands.

Proprietary Provinces: These were primarily administrations in Colonial North America. The status was granted to an individual or a small group of investors led by an individual instead of a Company.

Protectorates: These are states that form a partnership with Britain and where Britain retains power over defence and business in return for an agreement to protect the state.

Presidency: Established by the British East India Company in Bengal, Bombay and Madras.

Provinces: These are independent areas of a Federated Colony or Dominion, such as South Australia in the Dominion of Australia.

Sovereign Base Areas: These are primarily Military bases that remain in our possession after the countries in which they are situated become independent from Britain and the Empire. The Treaty Ports of Berehaven, Queenstown and Lough Swilly in Southern Ireland were Treaty Ports that remained British following the Anglo-Irish Treaty of 1921. They were given to Ireland in 1938. The Sovereign Base Areas Akrotiri and Dhekelia, on the island of Cyprus, are the last two such areas.

Trading Posts: These were very often small towns with their harbours in a foreign country that were allowed to be run by the local ruler as a form of outpost of this country. They were often the first foothold in what would later become a full colony.

Treaty Ports: These are virtually the same as the Sovereign Base Areas above but also include numerous ports that were acquired by Britain on the coast of China in the 19th century. The main ones were Hong Kong (prior to becoming a Colony), Amoy, Canton, Fuchow, Ningpo and Shanghai.

The Possessions:

Aden Colony: The area became a Crown Colony on 1st April 1937 after being a territory of the Bombay Presidency of British India. The colony merged with the Aden Protectorate and became the Federation of South Arabia, a Protectorate, on the 18th January 1963.

Aden Protectorate: The Protectorate consisted of nine tribal areas that came under British protection from 1874. The Protectorate covered the area surrounding the separate Aden Colony, which consisted of the Port City of Aden and the immediate surrounding area. The Protectorate merged with the Colony of Aden and became the Federation of South Arabia, a Protectorate on 18th January 1963.

Andaman and Nicobar Islands: These islands originally came under British rule during the Napoleonic wars. They became a Colony in 1858 and were used primarily as a Penal Colony up until the Second World War. They were granted their independence in 1947.

Anguilla: The Island situated in the Caribbean, a British possession since 1650, became a Colony in 1663. It became part of the Leeward Islands Colony in 1871 until 1958. It remains a British Overseas Territory.

Antigua: Situated in the Caribbean, it came under British rule in 1633. For a long period it was part of the Leeward Islands Colony. It gained internal autonomy in 1967 and became independent within the Commonwealth on 1st November 1981.

Aruba: An island in the Caribbean Sea, it was taken from the Dutch in 1799 and remained British until 1802. It was returned only to be taken back into British control between 1804 and 1816.

Ascension Island: Situated in the southern Atlantic Ocean, it was first occupied by the Navy in 1815 as a base and it became a dependency in 1922. It is now part of a single territorial group, along with St. Helena and Tristan da Cunha under the Sovereignty of the Crown governed by a Governor based on St. Helena. As part of Saint Helena, Ascension Island and Tristan da Cunha, it remains a part of a British Overseas Territory

Australia, Dominion of: The separate Australian States united and formed the Commonwealth of Australia on 1st January 1901 and became a Dominion of Great Britain within the Empire by the Federation of the six

Colonies: New South Wales, Queensland, South Australia, Tasmania, Victoria and Western Australia.

Bahamas: Situated in the Caribbean, the Island became a Colony in 1717. It became independent on 10th July 1973.

Bahrain: Situated in the Persian Gulf, it became a Protectorate in 1868 until its independence in 1971.

Banda Islands: Situated in the Indonesian sea. The main Island as well as Run and Ai were in and out of British and Dutch control from 1603 until they were given fully to the Dutch at the Treaty of Breda in 1667 in exchange for Manhattan Island.

Bantam: This trading post at the southern tip of Sumatra was established in 1601 and lasted until 1620 when, under agreement, the East India Company closed it down and moved its trade to Batavia. However, after they fell out with the Dutch they moved back to Bantam in 1628. It was finally closed down after the local Sultan sided with the Dutch in 1682.

Barbados: The Island became a Crown Colony in 1652. The Colony became independent on 30th November 1962.

Barbuda: On 9th January 1685 a lease was granted from Charles II. For a long period it was part of the Leeward Islands Colony, until 1960. It became independent within the Commonwealth on 1st November 1981.

Basutoland: It became a Protectorate in 1868 and then it was annexed by Cape Colony in 1871. It returned to Crown rule in 1884 and became independent on 4th October 1966.

Batavia: The trading post was shared with the Dutch between 1620 and 1628 when the representatives of the East India Company left after a disagreement with the Dutch. It was taken from the Dutch in 1811 and handed back in 1816.

Bay Islands Colony: These islands off the coast of South America were gained in 1643 from the Dutch and were dependent on the Colony of Jamaica. They were finally incorporated into British Honduras in 1860.

Bechuanaland: It became a Protectorate on 31st March 1885, being administered from Cape Colony by a Resident Commissioner. The northern half became independent as Botswana on 30th September 1966.

Bencoolen (Bengkulu): Established by the British East India Company in 1685 as a trading post. It was ceded to the Dutch in 1824 in exchange for Malacca.

The Bengal Presidency: Was first established in 1690 in Calcutta in Bengal. In 1765 the Bengal Presidency was formally declared and Calcutta became its capital.

Berbice: Captured from the Dutch and the French and occupied several times on and off. It was ceded to Britain finally in 1814 and became a Colony. In 1831 it united with Demerara and Essequibo to form the Colony of British Guiana.

Berehaven: A Treaty Port in Southern Ireland that remained British following the Anglo-Irish Treaty of 1921. It was given to Ireland in 1938.

Bermuda: An island in the Atlantic Ocean, it was originally granted to the Colony of Virginia by Royal Charter in 1612. Its importance grew following the American rebellion. It remains a British Overseas Territory.

Bight of Benin: It was established as a Protectorate on 1st February 1852. In 1861 it merged with the bight of Biafra.

Bight of Biafra: (see British Nigeria). It was established on 6th June 1849. In 1861 it merged with the Bight of Benin.

Bombay Presidency: Originally acquired as part of Catherine of Braganza's dowry on her marriage to Charles II in 1661, it became the paramount East India Company's possession in India in 1687.

Bonaire: An island in the Caribbean Sea, it was taken from the Dutch in 1807 and remained British until 1816.

Bourbon: As the Isle Bonaparte, this island in the Indian Ocean was captured from the French in 1810 and renamed Bourbon, its older French name and in honour of the deposed French Royal family. Under the terms of the Treaty of Vienna 1815, it was returned to the French that same year.

British Antarctic Territory: This area was registered in 1908, formally created a Territory in 1962 and was administered from the Falkland Islands by a High Commissioner until 1989 when it has since been administered from London. It contains Graham Land, the South Orkney Islands and the South Shetland Islands. It remains a British Overseas Territory.

British Central African Protectorate: It was created in 1891 and lasted until 6th July 1907 when it became the Nyasaland Protectorate.

British Columbia: It was a Colony from 1858 until it merged with Vancouver Island in 1866 to form the United Colonies of Vancouver Island and British Columbia.

British East Africa Protectorate: From 1885 it covered most of the future Colony of Kenya and from 1902 the Protectorate included the area that would be the future Colony of Uganda. On 23rd July 1920 it became the Colony of Kenya.

British Guiana: Formed by the Union of the three Colonies of Berbice, Demerara and Essequibo in 1831. It gained independence on 26th May 1966.

British Honduras: Located on the east coast of Central America, it was a Crown Colony from 1862. It gained independence on 21st September 1981 as Belize.

British Indian Ocean Territory: A collection of six large atolls and numerous islands, its biggest island is Diego Garcia which contains a joint British and US Air base. The area was ceded to Britain by France at the Treaty of Paris in 1814. It remains a British Overseas Territory.

British Kaffraria: The original settled area near Cape Colony was annexed to the Cape in 1835. In 1860 it became a separate Crown Colony and in 1866 it was incorporated into Cape Colony.

British Leeward Islands: These islands were a Colony from 1833 until 1960. The Colony consisted of the islands of Antigua, Barbuda, the British

Virgin Islands, Montserrat, Saint Kitts, Nevis, Anguilla and until 1940 Dominica. See Leeward Islands Colony.

British New Guinea: annexed in 1884 and declared a protectorate, it was later declared a Colony in 1886. The Colony was transferred to the Dominion of Australia in 1906 and renamed the Territory of Papua.

British North Borneo: See North Borneo.

British Somaliland: Situated on the north east coast of Africa, it became a Protectorate in 1884 and was administered from British India. It became independent on 26th June 1960.

British Togoland: It was first formed in 1916 by the partition of the German Colony of Togoland. In 1922 it was granted as a League of Nations Mandated territory, administered by Great Britain. It became part of the Gold Coast Colony in 1956.

British Virgin Islands: Situated in the Caribbean Sea, the fifty or so islands have been in British possession since the 1600s. In 1872 they became part of the Leeward Islands until 1956. They became a Colony in 1960 and autonomous in 1967. They remain a British Overseas Territory.

British Western Pacific Territories: A Colonial group of islands, they became a collective Protectorate in 1877. The protectorate came to an end in 1976. Between these two dates the Protectorate consisted, at differing times, of the islands of Canton and Enderbury Islands, Cook Islands, Fiji, Gilbert and Ellice Islands, Nauru, New Hebrides, Savage Island, Pitcairn Islands, Solomon Islands, Tonga and Union Islands.

Brunei, Sultanate of: The Sultanate came under British influence over a long period, finally becoming a Protectorate in 1888. It gained its independence on the 1st January 1984.

Burma: It came under British protection in 1824. On 1st January 1886 it came under the authority of British India. It became independent on 4th January 1948

Bushire: Situated in Persia, it became a trading and naval base for the East India Company in 1763 and later for the Royal Navy, with the agreement of the Persian Sultan. It was occupied between 1856 and 1857 during the Anglo-Persian War. In 1948 the British Residency was finally closed.

Calcutta: Situated in Bengal, it was declared a Presidency town in 1699 by the East India Company. In 1765 the Bengal Presidency was formally declared and Calcutta became its capital.

Canada, Province of: It was formed in 1841 from the union of Upper Canada and Lower Canada. It lasted until 1st July 1867 when it joined the Canadian Confederation as two separate Provinces, Ontario and Quebec.

Canada, Dominion of: It came into existence on the 1st July 1867 from the confederation of the Colonies of New Brunswick, Nova Scotia, Ontario and Quebec.

Canton and Enderbury Islands: These islands in the central Pacific Ocean were a British and American Condominium from 1939 to 1979, when they gained their independence.

Cape Breton Island: In 1631 it was granted to Robert Gordon by Royal Charter but was eventually settled by the French. It was ceded in 1763 under the Treaty of Paris, after having been captured from the French in 1745. Up until 1784 it was part of Nova Scotia. In 1784 it became a separate Colony. It was merged with Nova Scotia in 1820.

Cape Colony: It was annexed from the Dutch permanently in 1806, then as 'The Cape of Good Hope'. It became a Colony in 1814. It became part of the Union of South Africa on 31st May 1910 and was given Dominion status.

Cape of Good Hope, the: Captured from the Dutch in 1806, it became Cape Colony at the Anglo-Dutch Treaty of 1814 (see Cape Colony).

Carleton Island: Situated in the St. Lawrence River in New York, it was still a British possession after the American rebellion and then independence in 1783. However, it was captured in 1812 during the war with America and ceded to them at the Treaty of Ghent in 1814.

Carolina, Province of: It was formed in 1663 by Charter from Charles II. Following disputes between the Proprietors, the Colony finally split in 1712 into the two separate Colonies of North Carolina and South Carolina.

Cayman Islands: Comprising three islands in the Caribbean Sea, they were ceded to England in 1670 and governed with Jamaica until Jamaica's independence in 1962. They remain a British Overseas Territory.

Ceylon: The Island was ceded to Britain on 25th March 1802 under the Treaty of Amiens. Following the First Kandyan wars of 1803, the whole island came under British rule. It gained independence on 4th February 1948.

Christmas Island (Indian Ocean): Named on Christmas Day 1643 it was declared part of the British Dominion in 1888. Sovereignty was transferred to Australia in 1958.

Christmas Island (Pacific Ocean): Discovered by Captain Cook in 1777, it was claimed by the Americans in 1857. In 1888 it was annexed by the Crown. They became independent in 1979.

Connecticut Colony: Became a Colony in 1662 when united with New Haven Colony. It was one of the 13 rebellious Colonies that were granted independence on 3rd September 1783 at the Treaty of Paris.

Cook Islands: The Islands became a protectorate in 1888 and responsibility for its Protectorate status was handed over to New Zealand in 1901.

Cuba: The Island was captured from the Spanish in 1762. However, it was exchanged in 1763 for Florida and handed back to the Spanish.

Cyprus: The Island came under British control from 4th June 1878 and gained independence on 16th August 1960.

Demerara: A long standing Colony, in 1814 it was ceded to Britain by the Dutch and united with Essequibo to form the Demerara-Essequibo Colony.

Demerara-Essequibo: Formed in 1814 by the uniting of the two separate colonies of Demerara and Essequibo when they were ceded to Britain by the Dutch. In 1831 it was united with the Colony of Berbice to form British Guiana.

Dindings: This group of small Islands were ceded to Britain in 1874. It is a settlement within the Straits Settlements.

Diamond Rock: A small island off the coast of the French Colony of Martinique, it was captured from the French in 1803 and officially designated HMS Diamond Rock. It was garrisoned by 120 and a few officers. For 17 months it harassed shipping coming and going from the port Fort-de-France on Martinique before being captured by the French in June 1815.

Dominica: Captured from the French in 1761 and ceded to Britain at the Treaty of Paris in 1763. Despite a number of attacks and occupations, the island remained British. For a long time it was part of the British Leeward Islands Colony. The island became independent on 3rd November 1978.

Dubai: The town itself became a protectorate in 1892 and remained so until 1971.

East Florida: It was taken from the Spanish as part of the Seven Years' War and was confirmed officially at the Treaty of Paris in 1763. At the Treaty of Paris of 1783 it was handed back to Spain.

East Jersey: The Colony of New Jersey was divided between in 1672 and 1702 into the Proprietary Provinces of East Jersey and West Jersey. East Jersey was a Scottish enterprise. East Jersey and West Jersey joined together again in 1702 to form New Jersey, now a Crown Colony.

Egypt: An expeditionary force was landed in 1882 to prop up the struggling Khedive. It was formally declared a Protectorate in 1914. Independence was declared by the British Government on 28th February 1922. However, Britain retained control of the important Suez Canal area until 1956.

Essequibo: Originally a Dutch colony, it was occupied on and off several times until it became a Colony in 1814. It was united with the Colony of Demerara in 1831 to form the Colony of Demerara-Essequibo.

Falkland Islands: In the South Atlantic Ocean, they were originally claimed in 1592 and were argued over through the seventeenth and eighteenth centuries. They became a Protectorate in 1833 during which they were a naval station until 1840 when the islands officially became a Colony. They remain a British Overseas Territory.

Federal Colony of the Leeward Islands: The Leeward Islands were Federated and reformed in 1871 until 1956 The main islands during these periods were Antigua, Anguilla, Barbuda, British Virgin Islands, Dominica (until 1940), St. Christopher (St. Kitts) and Montserrat. See the individual Islands for more details.

Federated Malay States: Established in 1895, it was a federation of the four protectorate States of Negeri Sembilan, Pehang, Perak and Selangor. It existed until 1946 when it formed part of the Malayan Union.

Federation of Malaya: It replaced the Malay Union in 1948. It consisted of the two Settlements of Malacca and Prince of Wales Island (Penang) and the nine Protectorate Malay States of Johore, Kedah, Kelantan, Negeri Sembilan, Pehang, Perak, Perlis, Selangor and Terengganu and continued until independence in 1957.

Federation of Rhodesia and Nyasaland: This was a semi-independent territory and though it was a Federal realm of the Crown, it was not a Colony or a Dominion. It consisted of Northern Rhodesia, Southern Rhodesia and Nyasaland from 1953 until 31st December 1963 when Northern Rhodesia and Nyasaland gained their independence.

Federation of South Arabia: Formed on 4th April 1962, it merged with Aden Colony and the Aden Protectorate in 1963. It became independent on 30th November 1967.

Fernando Po: An Island of the west coast of Africa, it was leased from the Spanish for use as a base for the Royal Navy from 1827 until 1855 when it was finally handed back.

Fiji: The islands became a Colony in 1874 after requests for annexation due to lawlessness. The Colony was granted independence on 10th October 1970.

Freetown: This was established in 1787 on the west coast of Africa as a refuge for freed slaves from across the Empire. The city became a Colony in 1887 and the interior of the country a Protectorate. It joined with the interior of the country to become an independent state on 27th April 1961.

Gambia: On the west coast of Africa. After much conflict with France it was granted to Britain under the Treaty of Paris in 1783. In 1888 it became a separate Colonial administration from Sierra Leone and became a Crown Colony in 1889. It was the last of our West African Colonies to gain independence, which it gained on 18th February 1965.

Georgia, Province of: The charter for the Colony was granted in 1732. It became a Crown colony in 1755. It was one of the 13 rebellious Colonies that were granted independence on 3rd September 1783 at the Treaty of Paris.

Gibraltar: Captured from the Spanish in 1704, it was ceded to Britain in 1713 at the Treaty of Utrecht. It remains a British Overseas Territory.

Gilbert and Ellis Islands: Both islands jointly formed the one protectorate from 1892. In 1916 they became a Colony within the British Western Pacific Territories Protectorate until 1971. By 1976 both had become separate independent nations.

Gold Coast, Colony of: On the west coast of Africa, British rule started in 1821 until independence on 6th March 1957.

Goree: An island off the coast of Senegal, it was regularly fought over by the British and Dutch and then the British and French. It was captured from the French in 1758 and held until 1763 when it was handed back under the Treaty of Paris of the same year. It was briefly taken again in 1779 and finally it was in our hands from 1800 until 1817.

Grenada: Situated in the West Indies, it became a Crown Colony in 1877 and gained independence on 7th February 1974.

Guadeloupe: A group of islands in the Caribbean and originally seized from the French in 1794 and again in 1810, it remained a possession until 1813 when it was ceded to Sweden.

Guernsey, Bailiwick of: It is a Crown Dependency. As the main island in the Bailiwick of Guernsey, its authority covers smaller islands such as Alderney, Sark, Brecqhou, Herm, Jethu and Lihou.

Havana: The city was captured from the Spanish in 1762. It was returned to them in 1763 as part of the Treaty of Paris.

Hawaii: The Islands were originally called the Sandwich Islands after they were discovered and named by Captain Cook in 1778. The local term the 'Hawaii Islands' was used more commonly from the 1840s. The islands became a Protectorate in 1794, then a Colony in 1843. On the death of its King, it very quickly became influenced by America from 1893.

Heligoland: An island in the North Sea, it was seized from Denmark in 1807 and then ceded to Germany in exchange for Zanzibar in 1890.

Hong Kong: It was ceded to Britain at the Treaty of Nanking in 1842. It became a Crown Colony as a whole from 1898 with its capital the City of Victoria. It was returned to the Republic of China in 1997.

India: From the first arrival of merchants and traders in 1608, India became one of the most influential possessions within the Empire. The incorporation of India within the Empire took place incrementally over many years before the whole area, including present day Afghanistan, Bangladesh, Burma, Pakistan and Sri Lanka, were all under the control or influence of Britain. This was done solely under the administration of the East India Company until its interests were taken over by the crown in 1858. Prior to British rule and then independence, there had been no united single state of India due to political, religious, ethnic and cultural differences. India was granted independence on 15th August 1947.

Ionian Islands: The islands were taken from the French in 1797 and formally annexed in 1814. It became a Protectorate until 1864 when they were handed over to Greece.

Ireland: Henry II arrived in 1171 after being granted the island by the Pope. English influence spread continually to form effective English rule. It was united with Great Britain in 1801. The 26 southern counties were granted Dominion status on 6th December 1922 (see the Irish Free State).

Irish Free State: It came into being on 6th December 1922 and was a Dominion within the Empire. It lasted until 1937 when it called itself Eire and in 1948 it was granted independence after declaring itself a Republic and left the Commonwealth.

Isle of Man: The Island is a Crown Dependency. It was brought under greater control of the government in 1765.

Jarvis Island: Located in the South Pacific Ocean. It was annexed in 1889 by the Government for phosphate from Guano. The island was reclaimed by the United States in 1935.

Jamaica: It became a British possession in 1655. It gained full independence on 6th August 1962.

Jersey, Bailiwick of: It is a Crown Dependency. It is also the largest of the Channel Islands.

Johor: A small state in the Malay Peninsula. It became a Protectorate in 1885. It later accepted an Advisor in 1904 and joined the Malay Union in 1946.

Kedah: A small state in the Malay Peninsula, it became a Protectorate in 1909 after agreement with Siam and then became part of the Malay Union in 1946.

Keeling Islands: Situated in the Indian Ocean. Following ownership by a British family, it was annexed by Britain in 1857. In 1867 the islands were placed under the Straits Settlements Colony. In 1955 the islands were handed over to Australia for administration.

Kelantan: A small state in the Malay Peninsula, it became a Protectorate in 1909 after agreement with Siam. It then became part of the Malay Union in 1946.

Kenya Colony: It became a Protectorate under the Imperial British East Africa Company (see British East Africa Protectorate) in 1887. It became a Colony in 1920 and became independent on 12th December 1963.

Kiribati: (See Gilbert and Ellis Islands)

Kuwait: Became a Protectorate in 1899 but was rather neutral during the First World War. It was granted independence on 19th June 1961.

Labuan: It was ceded to Britain by the Sultan of Brunei in 1846 and it became a Colony in 1848. It became part of North Borneo in 1890.

Lagos: There has been British influence via the Royal Navy since 1851. A Royal Naval base was established in 1861 and it grew as a result as a colony. In 1914 it was incorporated into the newly formed Colony of Nigeria.

Leeward Islands Colony: This was a collection of different Islands that varied over the years. The Colony existed between 1671 and 1816 when it was dissolved then again between 1833 and 1871 when it became the Federal Colony of the Leeward Islands. The main islands during these periods were Antigua, Anguilla, Barbuda, British Virgin Islands, Dominica, St. Christopher

(St. Kitts) and Montserrat. See the British Leeward islands and the individual Islands for more details.

Lough Swilly: A Treaty Port in Southern Ireland that remained British following the Anglo-Irish Treaty of 1921. It was given to Ireland in 1938.

Lower Canada: It was a Province from 1791 to 1841, mainly covering the former French possessions, including New France, when it merged with Upper Canada to form the Province of Canada.

Lower Colonies on the Delaware: After being captured from the Dutch in 1664 it became a British Colony. It was one of the 13 rebellious Colonies that were granted independence on 3rd September 1783 at the Treaty of Paris

Madras Presidency: in existence since 1659 and centred around Fort St. George, it was finally declared one of three Presidencies in 1785, the core of British India.

Maine, Province of: settled in the early 1600s, there was a Charter from 1639. In 1652 it was taken under the administration of the Province of Massachusetts Bay and being finally incorporated within that Colony in 1692

Malacca: It was ceded to Britain in 1824. In 1826 it became administered under the Straits Settlements.

Malaya, Federation of: It was formed in 1948. It became independent as part of the Commonwealth on 31st August 1957.

Malayan Union: A Crown Colony, it was formed on 1st April 1946. It consisted of the Federated Malay States and the Straits Settlements after Singapore became a separate Crown Colony. After protests from Nationalists it was dissolved on 31st January 1948.

Malta: It was surrendered by the French garrison in 1800, ceded to the Empire at the Treaty of Paris in 1814 and then became a Dominion within the Empire. It became independent on 21st September 1964.

Maldive Islands: Became a Protectorate in 1887. They gained independence on 26th July 1965.

Manila: The city was captured from the Spanish in 1762. It was returned to them in 1763 after the Treaty of Paris of the same year.

Manitoba: Created from the Northwest Territories and the Red River Colony, it became federated into Canada as a Province in 1870.

Marie-Galante: An island in the Caribbean Sea, it was taken from the French in 1759 during the Seven Years' War. It was returned at the Treaty of Paris in 1763.

Martinique: The French colony was captured in 1762 during the seven Years' War but returned in 1783 under the Treaty of Paris. It was captured again in 1794 by a Fleet under Admiral Sir John Jervis. It was returned in 1802 only to be captured again in 1809 and handed back in 1814 and finally captured yet again but briefly in 1815.

Maryland, Province of: It was granted a Royal Charter from Charles I in 1632. It was one of the 13 rebellious Colonies that were granted independence on 3rd September 1783 at the Treaty of Paris.

Mashonaland: It became a Protectorate of the British South African Company in 1893. In 1923 it became part of Southern Rhodesia.

Massachusetts Bay Colony: 1629 to 1692 when it merged with Plymouth Colony to form the Province of Massachusetts Bay.

Massachusetts Bay, Province of: It became a Colony by Royal Charter in 1692. It was one of the 13 rebellious Colonies that were granted independence on 3rd September 1783 at the Treaty of Paris.

Matabeleland: It was declared a Protectorate in 1891. It was annexed to the Bechuanaland Protectorate in 1911.

Mauritius: The Island was surrendered to Britain by the French garrison on 3rd December 1810 and remained a Colony. It became independent on 12th March 1968.

Mesopotamia, British Mandate of: The area was entrusted to Britain by the League of Nations in the 1920 Treaty of Sevres. Mesopotamia became independent in October 1932 on its entry into the League of Nations as Iraq.

Minorca: This Mediterranean island came into our possession in 1708 following the War of the Spanish Succession until 1756. After that it went in and out of our possession until it was finally ceded to Spain at the Treaty of Amiens in 1803 after being occupied by us for the last time since 1798.

Montserrat: The Island, part of the Leeward Islands in the West Indies came under British control in 1632. It remains a British Overseas Territory.

Mosquito Coast: Situated in South America, it first became a Protectorate in 1655. However in 1860 the Protectorate was given over to Honduras.

Natal Colony: Annexed on 4th May 1843. It became part of the Dominion of the Union of South Africa on 31st May 1910.

Nauru (Pleasant Island): Situated in the South Pacific, the League of Nations mandated the island jointly to Great Britain, Australia and New Zealand. The United Nations reiterated the mandate in 1947. It became independent in 1968.

Negeri Sembilan: An island state in the Malay Peninsula, it became a Protectorate with a British Resident in 1874. It became a state within the Federated Malay States in 1895.

Nepal: It became a Protectorate in 1816 after a minor war. It supported Britain during the Indian Mutiny in 1857 and gained complete independence in 1923.

Nevis: This Island was colonised by settlers from nearby Saint Kitts in 1628. In 1882 the Island was unified with nearby Saint Kitts.

New Albion: This area off the West coast of modern day America was discovered in 1579 by Francis Drake and claimed for Elizabeth I. Its exact whereabouts remain a mystery and no colony was established.

New Brunswick: It was created in 1784 when it separated from Nova Scotia. It became a part of the Federation of Canada in 1867.

New Caledonia: This was a very brief Scottish Colony established in 1698 and then again in 1699 on the East Coast of South America in the Bay of Darien on what is now the Isthmus of Panama. Following threats from Spain and no support from England, it was abandoned in 1699, less than a year after being founded. Both sets of Colonists had lost the majority of their members to disease. The Colony was abandoned in 1700.

New England, Dominion of: This was an administrative union of the colonies of the New England area. The colonies included were the Massachusetts Bay Colony, Plymouth Colony, Province of New Hampshire and the Province of Maine and ran from 1686 until 1689 when it was dissolved and the colonies were reverted to their previous forms of colonial government.

Newfoundland: Claimed in 1583 for Britain. It was granted responsible government status in 1854. Became a Dominion on 26th September 1907 and joined Canada on 31st March 1949.

New Hampshire, Province of: Became a separate Colony in 1679 when it separated from the Colony of Massachusetts. It was one of the 13 rebellious Colonies that were granted independence on 3rd September 1783 at the Treaty of Paris.

New Haven Colony: Was a Colony from 1637 until 1662 when it merged with Connecticut Colony.

New Hebrides: These islands in the South Pacific were a Condominium run jointly with France from 1906 until 1980 when it gained its independence.

New Jersey, Province of: It became a colony in 1664 after being seized from the Dutch. It divided in 1676 into East Jersey and West Jersey. They merged again in 1702 to form a Crown Colony. It was one of the 13 rebellious Colonies that were granted independence on 3rd September 1783 at the Treaty of Paris.

New South Wales: It started as a Colony in 1788. It became part of the Dominion of Australia in 1901.

New York, Province of: The Duke of York was granted a charter in 1664. It was one of the 13 rebel Colonies that were granted independence on 3rd September 1783 at the Treaty of Paris.

New Zealand: British Sovereignty was declared in 1840. On 26th September 1907 it becomes a Dominion within the Empire. It became independent on 25th November 1947.

Niger Coast Protectorate: It was formed in 1893 from the Oil Rivers Protectorate. It merged with territories of the Royal Niger Company to form Southern Nigeria Protectorate in 1900 (see the Oil Rivers Protectorate).

Nigeria: Formed by the merger of Northern Nigeria and the Southern Nigeria Protectorate in 1914. It gained its independence on 1st October 1960.

North Borneo: It became a Protectorate under the North Borneo Company from 1882 to 1946 during which time it joined the Straights Settlements in 1906. It then became a Crown Colony in 1946 until its independence in 1963.

North Carolina, Province of: From 1663 it was originally part of the Province of Carolina; South Carolina split from the South to form a separate Colony in 1712. It was one of the 13 rebel Colonies that were granted independence on 3rd September 1783 at the Treaty of Paris.

North Eastern Rhodesia: Formed in 1891 and administered under charter by the British South African Company as a Protectorate. In 1911 it amalgamated with North Western Rhodesia to form Northern Rhodesia.

Northern Nigeria: Formed as a colony in 1900, it merged with Southern Nigeria in 1914.

Northern Rhodesia: Formed in 1911 by the amalgamation of North Western Rhodesia and North Eastern Rhodesia and became independent on 24th October 1964.

North Western Rhodesia: Formed in 1891 and administered under charter by the British South African Company as a Protectorate. In 1911 in amalgamated with North Eastern Rhodesia to form Northern Rhodesia.

North-Western Territory (Northwest Territories): From early 1700s under British influence. From it several Provinces were to be formed. On 15th July 1870 it became part of the Dominion of Canada.

Nova Scotia: Captured as Acadia from the French and renamed Nova Scotia, it was ceded to Britain in 1713 at the Treaty of Utrecht. It achieved Responsible Government in 1848. It entered Canadian Confederation in 1867.

Nyasaland Protectorate: Created from the former British Central African Protectorate on 6th July 1907. Between 1953 and 1963 it was part of the Federation of Rhodesia and Nyasaland. It became independent on 6th July 1964.

Oil Rivers Protectorate: Formed in 1881, it became a Protectorate in 1885. In 1893 it became the Niger Coast Protectorate.

Oman: It became a Protectorate in 1800 and gained complete independence in 1970.

Orange River Colony: It came into existence on 28th May 1900 when the former Boer Republic of the Orange Free State came under British rule. It gained self government in 1907 and became part of the Union of South Africa in 1910.

Orange River Sovereignty: Situated in southern Africa between the Orange and Vaal rivers, it was briefly, between 1848 and 1854, an unofficial sovereign colony. However, a lack of interest from Britain resulted in a Royal proclamation renouncing all dominion over the area and it became independent as the Republic of the Orange Free State (see Orange River Colony).

Palestine: It became a UN mandated territory under British administration in 1920. It became independent in 1948.

Pehang: An island state in the Malay Peninsula it became a Protectorate with a British Resident in 1887. It became a state within the Federated Malay States in 1895.

Pennsylvania, Province of: It was a Proprietary Colony granted to William Penn on 4th March 1681 by Charles II. It was one of the 13 rebellious Colonies that were eventually granted independence on 3rd September 1783 at the Treaty of Paris.

Perak: A small state in the Malay Peninsula, it became a Protectorate with a British Resident in 1874. It became a state within the Federated Malay States in 1895.

Perlis: A small state in the Malay Peninsula, it became a Protectorate in 1909 after agreement with Siam. It later formed part of the Malay Union in 1946.

Phoenix Islands Settlement Scheme: From 1938 an attempt was made to colonise the three islands in this group, Gardner, Hull and Sydney, situated in the western Pacific Ocean. It was not successful and in 1963 almost all the settlers were evacuated. The islands are now part of Kiribati.

Pitcairn Islands: A group of four main islands situated in the South Pacific Ocean, Pitcairn became a Colony in 1838. The islands of Ducie, Henderson and Oeno were annexed to Pitcairn in 1902.They remain a British Overseas Territory.

Plymouth Colony: One of the earliest Colonies in North America, it was formed in 1620 and lasted until 1692 when, by Royal Charter, it merged with the Massachusetts Bay Colony to form the Province of Massachusetts Bay.

Port Edward: See Wei-hai-wei.

Prince Edward Island (originally called St. Johns Island until 1798): It was obtained from France in the Treaty of Paris of 1763. It changed its name in 1798 to Prince Edward Island. It received self government in 1851. It joined the Federation of Canada in 1873 as part of the Dominion.

Prince of Wales Island (Penang): It became a Protectorate in 1786. In 1800 the Province of Wellesley was added to the Protectorate. In 1826 it became part of the Straits Settlements.

Prince Rupert's Land: In 1670 Charles II granted a trading charter to the Hudson Bay Trading Company for a huge area in present day Canada. It was sold to the Canadian government in 1869, finally joining the newly-formed Dominion of Canada in 1870.

Protectorate of South Arabia: It came into being on 18th January 1963 from the states that did not join the Federation of South Arabia, including part of the Protectorate of Aden. It became independent with the Federation of South Arabia on 30th November 1967.

Province of Wellesley: It was ceded to Britain in 1798 and in 1800 it was merged with Prince of Wales Island (Penang).

Qatar: The country came under our influence from 1878 with its break from Bahrain. It became an official Protectorate in 1916 and gained its independence in 1971.

Quebec, Province of: Originally the French Colony of New France, it was captured from the French in 1759. It was officially ceded to Britain in 1763 at the Treaty of Paris when it became the Province of Quebec.

Queensland: Formed in 1859 after separating from New South Wales, it became part of the Dominion of Australia in 1901.

Queenstown: A Treaty Port in Southern Ireland that remained British following the Anglo-Irish Treaty of 1921. It was given to Ireland in 1938.

Red River Colony: Set up in 1811 but not very successful. In 1870 it formed the basis of Manitoba following the Manitoba Act of 1870.

Rhode Island and Providence Plantations, Colony of: It was granted a charter in 1663 by Charles II. It was one of the 13 rebellious Colonies that were eventually granted independence on 3rd September 1783 at the Treaty of Paris.

Roanoke Colony: An island Colony along the coast of modern North Carolina. It was first settled in 1584 but the Colony failed. Another attempt was made in 1587 but between then and 1590 the colonists mysteriously disappeared, including the first colonist born in the Colonies of North America, Virginia Dare.

Rodrigues: The Island was captured from the French in 1809 and then used as a spring board to capture the French colony of Mauritius. It became a Colony in 1814 and was administered under the Colony of Mauritius; it became independent with Mauritius in 1968.

Run: The Island was first reached by English sailors in 1603. In 1616 the island was claimed for Britain but in 1620 the Dutch captured it. Attempts to retake it failed and at the Treaty of Breda it was formally exchanged for the area that would later become New York.

Rupert's Land: A huge area in present day Canada that was granted to the Hudson Bay Company by Royal Charter from Charles II in 1670. It was sold to the newly-formed Dominion of Canada in 1870.

St. Christopher: See St. Kitts and Nevis.

Saint Eustatius: A small island Dutch Colony in the Caribbean, it was captured from them on 3rd February 1781. Unfortunately, it was recaptured by the French, allies of the Dutch just ten months later.

Saint Helena: The British East India Company received a charter from Richard Cromwell in 1657 for the Island and garrisoned it the following year. Part of a single territorial group, along with Ascension Island and Tristan da Cunha, who are dependencies of St. Helena under the Sovereignty of the Crown governed by a Governor based on St. Helena. It remains part of a British Overseas Territory.

Saint Helena, Ascension Island and Tristan da Cunha: Situated in the Southern Atlantic, it was formed in 2009 and is comprised of Saint Helena and its two former dependencies, Ascension Island and Tristan da Cunha. It remains a British Overseas Territory.

Saint John's Island (see Prince Edward Island): Obtained by Britain in the Treaty of Paris 1763 and changed its name to Prince Edward Island in 1798.

Saint Kitts: Became a Colony in 1624, sharing half the Island with the French. In 1713 the island was unified and in 1882 it was unified with the Island of Nevis.

Saint Kitts and Nevis: was formed in 1882 and became independent on 19th September 1983.

Saint Kitts-Nevis-Anguilla: This was formed in 1958. In 1980 Anguilla separated from Saint Kitts and Nevis.

Saint Lucia: The islands were first taken over from the French in 1663. It changed hands numerous times until Britain finally took complete and permanent control in 1814. It became self governing in 1967 and then gained its independence on 22nd February 1979.

Saint Martin: Originally captured from the Dutch in 1690 and held until 1699. It would pass between Britain and France on a number of occasions. It was finally retaken in 1810 and eventually returned to France in 1816 after their defeat in the Napoleonic wars.

Saint Vincent and the Grenadines: An Island chain in the West Indies. It was regained for Britain in the Treaty of Paris in 1783 and became independent on 27th October 1979.

Sandwich Islands: These islands were discovered by Captain James Cook in 1778. They became a Protectorate in 1794, then a Colony in 1843. During the 1840s, the islands began to be called by their local name, the Hawaiian Islands. On the death of its King, it very quickly became influenced by America from 1893.

Sarawak: Situated in South East Asia, it became a Protectorate in 1888 under the Brook Rajah. It came under Crown rule as a Colony in 1946 and became independent in 1963.

Saybrook Colony: Situated on the East Coast of North America, it was founded in 1635 and lasted until 1644 when it merged with Connecticut Colony.

Selangor: An island state in the Malay Peninsula, it became a Protectorate with a British Resident in 1874. It became a state within the Federated Malay States in 1895.

Senegal: The colony was originally captured from the French in 1758 and returned to them in 1783 following the Treaty of Paris. It was retaken in 1809 due to the Napoleonic wars and then returned in 1816.

Senegambia: Situated on the west coast of Africa. It was created in 1758 with the loose collection of British interests in the Senegal area and the

Gambia. It lasted until 1779 when the French captured Saint Louis and it officially ended as an administration in 1783 with the Treaty of Paris.

Seychelles: Came under our control in 1812 and formalised at the Treaty of Paris in 1814. It became a Crown Colony in 1814 and then became independent on 29th June 1976.

Sierra Leone: On the west coast of Africa. In 1787 we established a refuge in Sierra Leone for freed slaves, known as the city of Freetown; in 1896 the interior of the country became a Protectorate. It became independent on 27th April 1961.

Singapore: It was under British influence since 1819. It became a Crown Colony in 1867, gaining its independence on 31st August 1963.

Solomon Islands Protectorate: Britain declared a Protectorate over the islands in 1893 with other islands added to the Protectorate in subsequent years. They gained their independence in 1978.

South Africa, Dominion of: The Dominion came into existence on 31st May 1910 as the Union of South Africa from the amalgamation of the Cape Colony and the Natal Colony as well as the two former Boer republics of the Orange River Colony (previously Orange Free State) and the Transvaal Colony (previously Transvaal). It became a republic on 31st May 1961.

South Australia: The Colony was proclaimed in 1836. It became part of the Dominion of Australia in 1901.

South Carolina, Province of: From 1663 it was originally part of the province of Carolina, South Carolina split from the North to form a separate Colony in 1712. It was one of the 13 rebel Colonies that were granted independence on 3rd September 1783 at the Treaty of Paris.

Southern Nigeria Protectorate: Formed in 1900 from the Niger Coast Protectorate and the territories and interests of the Royal Niger Company. It merged with Northern Nigeria in 1914.

Southern Rhodesia: It became a Colony in 1895. U.D.I. was declared on 11th November 1965 and following a period as a Republic, it was again briefly under British rule for about three months until independence on 17th April 1980.

South Georgia and the South Sandwich Islands: Formed in 1985 after being part of the Falkland Island Dependencies. It remains a British Overseas Territory.

Sovereign Base Areas Akrotiri and Dhekelia: The bases, on the island of Cyprus, acquired this status on the independence of Cyprus on 16th August 1960. They remain a British Overseas Territory.

Straits Settlements: It was a collection of smaller Colonies and Protectorates that were brought under the collective administration of the Straits Settlements in 1826 and became a collective Colony in 1867. These were the Dindings, Malacca, Prince of Wales Island (Penang), Province of Wellesley and Singapore. It was dissolved in 1946.

Sudan: From 1899 it was administered by an Anglo-Egyptian authority as a Condominium. Despite many attempts by Egypt and some Sudanese to unite Egypt and Sudan, it gained its independence on 1st January 1956.

Suez Canal Zone: This was part of British Egypt until Egyptian independence in 1922 when it became a British Military Protected Area. This continued until British withdrawal in 1956.

Swan River Colony: It was founded in 1829 and lasted until 1832 when it became known as Western Australia.

Swaziland: This land-locked country in Southern Africa became a Protectorate during the Boer War and gained its independence in 1963.

Tanganyika Territory: Formerly a German colonial territory, it is situated on the eastern central African coast. It was gained by Britain during the First World War and after the Great War it was granted to Britain in 1919 under a United Nations Mandate. It became independent on 9th December 1961.

Tangier: This port was part of a dowry that accompanied Catherine of Braganza in 1662 when she married Charles II. Following a lengthy siege by Moroccans, the town was finally evacuated in 1684 and destroyed.

Tasmania: It was first settled in 1803 and became a separate Colony from New South Wales in 1825. It became part of the Dominion of Australia in 1901.

Terengganu: A small state in the Malay Peninsula, it became a Protectorate in 1909 after agreement with Siam and then later formed part of the Malay Union in 1946.

Tobago: It became a Colony in 1814 and in 1882 it was united with Trinidad to become the Crown Colony of Trinidad and Tobago.

Tonga: The islands became a Protectorate in 1900, forming part of the British Western Pacific Territories from 1901 until 1952. It gained its independence in 1970.

Transjordan: It became a UN Mandated Territory under British administration in 1921. It was technically part of the British Mandated Territory of Palestine but was usually administered separately. It became independent in 1946.

Transvaal Colony: It came into existence in 1877 when it became part of the Empire. It regained its independence in 1881 as a Boer republic. Following the Boer War it again became part of the Empire in 1902 and then became part of the Union of South Africa in 1910.

Trinidad: The Island was surrendered by the Spanish in 1797. It was then united with the island of Tobago in 1882 to form Trinidad and Tobago.

Trinidad and Tobago: In 1882 Trinidad and Tobago were united to form a Crown Colony. On 31st August 1962 it gained its independence.

Tristan da Cunha: Annexed to Cape Colony in 1816 it became a dependency of Saint Helena in 1938. In 2009 it became part of a single territorial group, the British Overseas Territory of Saint Helena, Ascension Island and Tristan da Cunha. It remains part of a British Overseas Territory.

Trucial Oman: Also sometimes referred to as the Trucial States, this was a disparate grouping of sheikdoms that became a collective Protectorate in 1892 due in large part to their opposition to the Ottoman Empire. The states covered by the Treaty were Abu Dhabi, Ajman, Sharjah, Ajman, Umm al-Quwain, Ras al-Khaimah and Fujairah. The treaty came to an end in 1971.

Turk and Caicos Islands: In 1799 the Islands were incorporated into the Empire and administered from the Bahamas. They were then part of the Colony of Jamaica from 1873 and in 1962 at Jamaican independence they became a separate Colony. The islands are a British Overseas Territory.

Uganda: Placed under the charter of the British East Africa Company in 1888 and then became a Protectorate in 1902. It gained independence on 9th October 1962.

United Colonies of Vancouver Island and British Columbia: Created in 1866 when British Columbia and Vancouver Island merged. It became part of the Dominion of Canada in 1871.

Upper Canada: It was a Province from 1791 to 1841 when it merged with Lower Canada to form the Province of Canada.

Vancouver Island: Became a Colony in 1849 to 1866 when it merged with British Columbia to form the United Colonies of Vancouver Island and British Columbia.

Victoria: It was first settled in 1800 and became a separate Colony from New South Wales in 1851. It became part of the Dominion of Australia in 1901.

Virginia, Colony of: It became a Colony in 1607. It was one of the 13 rebel Colonies that were granted independence on 3rd September 1783 at the Treaty of Paris.

Walvis Bay: On the South West coast of Africa, the port and bay were acquired in 1840 and then annexed and administered by Cape Colony in 1878.

Wei-hai-wei: Sometimes known as Port Edward, the port area on the mainland of North East China was leased to Britain in 1898 and used as a port and Naval base until its return to China in 1930.

West Florida: It was taken from the Spanish as a result of the Seven Years' War and this was confirmed officially at the Treaty of Paris in 1763. At the Treaty of Paris in 1783 it was handed back to Spain.

West Jersey: The Colony of New Jersey was divided between in 1672 and 1702 into the Proprietary Provinces of East Jersey and West Jersey. West Jersey was an English enterprise. East Jersey and West Jersey joined together again in 1702 to form New Jersey, now a Crown Colony.

Western Australia: It was created in 1832 when the Swan River Colony was renamed Western Australia and the lands of the entire Western part of Australia were included in the Colony. It joined the Dominion of Australia in 1901.

West Indies Federation: Created in 1958, the Federation was comprised of the ten territories of Antigua, Barbuda, Barbados, Dominica, Grenada, Jamaica, Montserrat, St. Kitts-Nevis-Anguilla, Saint Lucia, Saint Vincent and Trinidad and Tobago. The Federation lasted until its collapse in 1962 with the withdrawal of Jamaica.

Zanzibar: An island off the east coast of Africa, it became a Protectorate on 4th November 1890 and gained its independence on 19th December 1963.

Zululand: It became a Protectorate in 1879, being finally annexed in 1887 and governed as a separate Colony until; in 1897 it was merged with Natal Colony.

The Thirteen Colonies as they were known at the time of their rebellion against Great Britain in an attempt to form an independent United States of America:

Connecticut Colony
Lower Colonies on the Delaware
Province of Georgia
Province of Maryland
Province of Massachusetts Bay
Province of New Hampshire
Province of New Jersey
Province of New York
Province of North Carolina
Province of Pennsylvania
Colony of Rhode Island and Providence Plantations
Province of South Carolina
Colony and Dominion of Virginia

The Colonies and Provinces that later became the Dominion of Canada:

New Brunswick: Federated on 1st July 1867
Nova Scotia: Federated on 1st July 1867
Ontario: Federated on 1st July 1867
Quebec: Federated on 1st July 1867

North Western Territory joined the federation in June 1870
Prince Rupert's Land in joined the federation in June 1870

British Columbia and Vancouver Island united to form the United Colonies of Vancouver Island and British Columbia in 1866 then as the United Colonies of Vancouver Island and British Columbia they joined the federation on 21st July 1873.

Prince Edward Island joined the federation on 1st July 1873

Founding Colonies of the Dominion of Australia:

New South Wales 26th January 1788
Tasmania (Van Diemen's Island) 1825
South Australia (from New South Wales) 1836
Victoria (from New South Wales) 1851
Queensland (from New South Wales) 1859
Western Australia (1832)

Founding Colonies of the Dominion of South Africa:

Cape Colony: 31st May 1910.
Natal Colony: 31st May 1910.
Orange River Colony: 31st May 1910.
Transvaal Colony: 31st May 1910.

India, the Raj:

The British influence in the Indian sub-continent began in the early 17th Century with the establishments of trading ports by English merchants and entrepreneurs. Over the years the influence, mainly through the East India Company, increased as British interests moved further inland. Over this period of British contact and influence, the various provinces and states that came within our sphere of influence fluctuated. However, up until the unification of India under British rule India had been a splintered society. Below is a list of some of the provinces and kingdoms and their dates of establishment, annexation or formal influence:

Madras Presidency was established in 1640.
Bombay Presidency was established in 1687.
Bengal Presidency was established in 1690.
Eastern Bengal and Assam was incorporated in 1825.
Coorg was annexed in 1834 under British protection.
Punjab Province ceded in 1846 and annexed in 1849.
Oudh Province was annexed in 1856.

By **1938**, at the height of the Empire, there were eleven provinces in British India:
Sind

North West Frontier
Punjab
United Provinces
Bihar
Bengal
Assam
Orissa
Central provinces
Madras
Bombay

British Overseas Territories:

These are the fourteen dependent territories whose citizens retain British citizen status but are not part of the United Kingdom. This has been the classification in use since 2002. Prior to this they were called Dependent Territories. Their citizens are automatically credited with British citizenship. The total combined population of the Territories is around 260,000. The Territories are:

Anguilla: The Island situated in the Caribbean, a British possession since 1650, became a Colony in 1663. It became part of the Leeward Islands Colony in 1871 until 1958. Its capital is The Valley.

Bermuda: An island in the Atlantic Ocean, it was originally granted to the Colony of Virginia by Royal Charter in 1612. Its importance grew following the American rebellion. Its capital is the town of Hamilton.

British Antarctic Territory: This area was registered in 1908, formally created a Territory in 1962 and was administered from the Falkland Islands by a High Commissioner until 1989 when it has since been administered from London. It contains Graham Land, the South Orkney Islands and the South Shetland Islands.

British Indian Ocean Territory: A collection of six large atolls and numerous islands, its biggest island is Diego Garcia which contains a joint British and US Air base. The area was ceded to Britain by France at the Treaty of Paris in 1814.

British Virgin Islands: Situated in the Caribbean Sea, the fifty or so islands have been in British possession since the 1600's. In 1872 they became part of the Leeward Islands until 1956. They became a Colony in 1960 and autonomous in 1967. The capital town, situated on the island of Tortola is Road Town.

Cayman Islands: Comprising three islands in the Caribbean Sea, they were ceded to England in 1670 and governed with Jamaica until Jamaica's independence in 1962. The islands' capital is George Town.

Falkland Islands: In the South Atlantic Ocean, they were originally claimed in 1592 and were argued over through the seventeenth and eighteenth centuries. They became a Protectorate in 1833 during which they were a naval station until 1840 when the islands officially became a Colony. The islands capital is Stanley.

Gibraltar: Captured from the Spanish in 1704, it was ceded to Britain in 1713 at the Treaty of Utrecht.

Montserrat: The Island, part of the Leeward Islands in the West Indies came under British control in 1632. Its capital prior to its destruction by a volcanic eruption was Plymouth.

Pitcairn Islands: A group of four main islands situated in the South Pacific Ocean, Pitcairn became a Colony in 1838. The islands of Ducie, Henderson and Oeno were annexed to Pitcairn in 1902. Adamstown is the only settlement on the only inhabited island.

Saint Helena, Ascension Island and Tristan da Cunha: The British East India Company received a charter from Richard Cromwell in 1657 for the Island and garrisoned it the following year. Part of a single territorial group, along with Ascension Island and Tristan da Cunha, who are dependencies of St. Helena under the Sovereignty of the Crown governed by a Governor based in Jamestown on the island of St. Helena.

South Georgia and the South Sandwich Islands: Formed in 1985 after being part of the Falkland Island Dependencies.

Sovereign Base Areas Akrotiri and Dhekelia: The bases, on the island of Cyprus, acquired this status on the granting of independence to Cyprus on 16th August 1960.

Turk and Caicos Islands: In 1799 the Islands were incorporated into the Empire and administered from The Bahamas. They were then part of the Colony of Jamaica from 1873 and in 1962 with the granting of Jamaican independence they became a separate Colony. The capital, Cockburn Town, is located on the largest island, Grand Turk Island.

The Commonwealth Realms

The sixteen realms are sovereign states within the Commonwealth of Nations that currently have Elizabeth II as the reigning constitutional monarch. Next to each Commonwealth Realm is the Queen's full title within that Realm.

Antigua and Barbuda: Her Majesty Elizabeth the Second, by the Grace of God, Queen of Antigua and Barbuda and of Her other Realms and Territories, Head of the Commonwealth.

Australia: Her Majesty Elizabeth the Second, by the Grace of God, Queen of Australia and Her other Realms and Territories, Head of the Commonwealth.

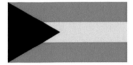

The Bahamas: Her Majesty Elizabeth the Second, by the Grace of God, Queen of the Commonwealth, of the Bahamas and of Her other Realms and Territories, Head of the Commonwealth.

Barbados: Her Majesty Elizabeth the Second, by the Grace of God, Queen of Barbados and of Her other Realms and Territories, Head of the Commonwealth.

Belize: Her Majesty Elizabeth the Second, by the Grace of God, Queen of Belize and of Her Other Realms and Territories, Head of the Commonwealth.

Canada: Her Majesty Elizabeth the Second, by the Grace of God of the United Kingdom, Canada and Her other Realms and Territories Queen, Head of the Commonwealth, Defender of the Faith.

In French: Sa Majesté Elizabeth Deux, par la grâce de Dieu Reine du Royaume-Uni, du Canada et de ses autres royaumes et territoires, Chef du Commonwealth, Défenseur de la Foi.

Grenada: Her Majesty Elizabeth the Second, by the Grace of God, Queen of the United Kingdom of Great Britain and Northern Ireland and of Grenada and Her other Realms and Territories, Head of the Commonwealth.

Jamaica: Her Majesty Elizabeth the Second, by the Grace of God, Queen of Jamaica and of Her other Realms and Territories, Head of the Commonwealth.

New Zealand: Her Majesty Elizabeth the Second, by the Grace of God, Queen of New Zealand and Her Other Realms and Territories, Head of the Commonwealth, Defender of the Faith.

Papua New Guinea: Her Majesty Elizabeth the Second, Queen of Papua New Guinea and of Her other Realms and Territories, Head of the Commonwealth.

Saint Kitts and Nevis: Her Majesty Elizabeth the Second, by the Grace of God, Queen of Saint Christopher and Nevis and of Her other Realms and Territories, Head of the Commonwealth.

Saint Lucia: Her Majesty Elizabeth the Second, by the Grace of God, Queen of Saint Lucia and of Her other Realms and Territories, Head of the Commonwealth.

Saint Vincent and the Grenadines: Her Majesty Elizabeth the Second, by the Grace of God, Queen of Saint Vincent and the Grenadines and of Her other Realms and Territories, Head of the Commonwealth.

Solomon Islands: Her Majesty Elizabeth the Second, by the Grace of God, Queen of Solomon Islands and of Her other Realms and Territories, Head of the Commonwealth.

Tuvalu: Her Majesty Elizabeth the Second, by the Grace of God, Queen of Tuvalu and of Her other Realms and Territories, Head of the Commonwealth.

The United Kingdom of Great Britain and Northern Ireland: Her Majesty Elizabeth the Second, by the Grace of God of the United Kingdom of Great Britain and Northern Ireland, and of Her other Realms and Territories Queen, Head of the Commonwealth, Defender of the Faith.

Chapter 4

National Days of Celebration and also Commemoration

1st January:

Act of Union Day: The union of the Kingdom of Great Britain and the Kingdom of Ireland to form the Kingdom of Great Britain and Ireland.

1st March:
St. David's Day: Patron Saint of Wales.

17th March:
St. Patrick's Day: Patron Saint of Ireland

23rd April:
St. George's Day: Patron Saint of England.

1st May:
Act of Union Day: The union of the English and Scottish parliaments in 1707 to form Great Britain.

8th May:
V.E. Day: Victory in Europe Day in 1945.

24th May:
Empire Day: The birth of Queen Victoria and the celebration of the greatness of Empire.

6th June:
D Day: The Normandy landings in 1944.

18th June:

Waterloo Day: The battle of Waterloo in 1815 and the defeat of Napoleon and France.

15th August:
V.J. Day: Victory over Japan day and the end of the Second World War.

15th September:
Battle of Britain Day: The battle of Britain in 1940.

21st October:
Trafalgar Day: The battle of Trafalgar in 1805

25th October:
Agincourt Day: The battle of Agincourt in 1415

11th November:
Armistice Day: The Armistice is signed in 1918 bringing fighting in the Great War to an end.

30th November:
St. Andrew's Day: Patron Saint of Scotland.

Chapter 5

Monarchs of Britain and our Empire with the years of their reigns

Anglo Saxon Kings of Wessex and all England.

Egbert
802 – 839
Ethelwulf
839 – 855
Ethelbald
855 – 860
Ethelbert
860 – 865
Ethelred I
865 – 871
Alfred the Great, King of Wessex
871 – 899
Edward the Elder
899 – 924
Athelstan, King of all England.
924 – 939
Edmund I 'The Magnificent'
939 – 946
Edred
946 – 955
Crowned 16th August 946
Edwy
955 – 959
Edgar
959 – 975
Edward II 'The Martyr'
975 – 979
Ethelred II 'The Unready'

979 – 1013 and 1014 -1016
Sweyn (Viking)
1013 – 1014
Edmund II 'Ironside'
April to November 1016
Canute the Great (Viking)
1016 – 1035
Harold Harefoot (Viking)
1035 – 1040
Hardicanute
1040 – 1042
Edward III 'The Confessor'
1042 – 1066
Harold II
January to 14th October 1066

Rulers of all England

Harold Godwinsson
1066
Edgar the Aetheling
1066 (never crowned)

House of Normandy

William I
1066 – 1087
William II
1087 – 1100
Henry I
1100 – 1135

House of Blois

Stephen
1135 – 1154

House of Plantagenet

Henry II
1154 – 1189
Richard I
1189 – 1199
John
1199 – 1216

Henry III
1216 – 1272
Edward I
1272 – 1307
Edward II
1307 – 1327
Edward III
1327 – 1377
Richard II
1377 – 1399

House of Lancaster

Henry IV
1399 – 1413
Henry V
1413 – 1422
Henry VI (King of France 1422 – 1453)
1422 – 1461

House of York

Edward IV
1461 – 1470

House of Lancaster (restored)

Henry VI
1470 – 1471

House of York (restored)

Edward IV
1471 – 1483
Edward V
April – June 1483
Richard III
1483 – 1485

House of Tudor

Henry VII
1485 – 1509
Henry VIII
1509 – 1547

Edward VI
1547 – 1553
Mary I
1553 – 1558
Elizabeth I
1558 – 1603

Rulers of Scotland

House of Alpin

Kenneth I
843 – (13 February) 858
Donald I
858 – (13 April) 862
Constantine I
862 – 878
Aedh
878 – 879
Eochaid
879 – 889
Donald II
889 – 900
Constantine II
900 – 942
Malcolm I
942 - 954
Indulf
954 – 962
Dubh/Duff
962 – 966
Cuilen/Colin
966 – 971
Kenneth II
971 – 995
Constantine III
995 – 997
Kenneth III
997 – (25 March) 1005
Malcolm II
1005 – 1034

House of Dunkeld

Duncan I

1034 – 1040
Macbeth
1040 – 1057
Lulach (the Fool)
1057 – 1058
Malcolm III
1058 – 1093
Donald Bane
1093 – 1094
Duncan II
1094
Donald Bane
1094 – 1097
Edgar
1097 – 1107
Alexander I
1107 – 1124
David I
1124 – 1153
Malcolm IV
1153 – 1165
William I
1165 – 1214
Alexander II
1214 – 1249
Alexander III
1249 – 1286
Margaret
1286 – 1290

The First Interregnum:
Following the death of Margaret, the 'Maid of Norway' 1290 – 1292
John Balliol (an appointee of Edward I of England)
1292 – 1296
The Second Interregnum:
Edward I of England proclaims himself 'King of Scotland'. The resultant struggle for independence was led initially by William Wallace 1296 – 1306.

House of Bruce
Robert I (The Bruce)
1306 – 1329
David II
1329 – 1371
House of Stewart
Robert II

1371 – 1390
Robert II
1390 – 1406
James I
1406 - 1437
James II
1437 - 1460
James III
1460 - 1488
James IV
1488 - 1513
James V
1513 – 1542
Mary I
1542 – 1567
James VI (James I of England and Great Britain)
1567 – 1625

Monarchs of Great Britain and the Empire

Stewart
James I (James VI of Scotland)
1603 – 1625
Charles I
1625 – 1649

British Interregnum: the term Commonwealth is often used to cover the entire period, including the Protectorate years.

The Commonwealth (Council of State)
1649 – 1653
Protectorate
Protectorate with Oliver Cromwell as Lord Protector
1653 – 1658
Protectorate with Richard Cromwell as Lord Protector
1658 – 1659
The Commonwealth (Council of State)
1659 – 1660

Stewart (continued)
Charles II
1649 – 1685
James II (James VII of Scotland)
1685 – 1688
William III and Mary II

1689 – 1694
William III
1694 – 1702
Anne
1702 – 1714

Hanover

George I
1714 – 1727
George II
1727 – 1760
George III
1760 – 1820
George IV
1820 – 1830
William IV
1830 – 1837
Victoria (**Queen Empress**)
1837 – 1901
Edward VII (**King Emperor**)
1901 – 1910

Windsor
George V (**King Emperor**)
1910 – 1936
Edward VIII (**King Emperor**)
1936
George VI (**King Emperor until 1950**)
1936 – 1952
Elizabeth II
1952 –

The Welsh Princes
Whilst they were not Monarchs like their English and Welsh counterparts, they were Princes, those recognised by history as princes of a majority of the area now called Wales.

Dafydd ap Llyweln (son of Llywelyn an Ionwerth Llywelyn the Great)
1240 – 1246
Llywelyn ap Gruffudd
1267 – 1282
Dafydd ap Gruffudd
1282 – 1283

Madog ap Llywely – led a nationwide rebellion against the English under Edward I.
1294 – 1295
Owain Glyndwr – the last to rebel against the English under Henry IV.
1400 – 1409.

The Jacobite Claimants to the throne of Great Britain and Ireland.

James VII
1685 – 1701
James VIII
1701 – 1766
Charles III
1766 – 1788
Henry IX
1788 – 1807

Chapter 6

Prime Ministers

The dates of their entering and leaving office do not always correspond to the dates of General Elections, as some became Prime Minister following the incumbent's resignation.

18th Century

Sir Robert Walpole (W) 1721 – 1742
Earl of Wilmington (W) 1742 – 1743
Henry Pelham (W) 1743 – 1754
Duke of Newcastle (W) 1754 – 1756
Duke of Devonshire (W) 1756 – 1757
Duke of Newcastle (W) 1757 – 1762
Earl of Bute (T) 1762 – 1763
George Grenville (W) 1763 – 1765
Marquess of Rockingham (W) 1765 – 1766
Earl of Chatham (W) 1766 – 1767
Duke of Grafton (W) 1767 – 1770
Lord North (T) 1770 – 1782
Marquess of Rockingham (W) 1782
Earl of Shelburne (W) 1782 – 1783
Duke of Portland (Cln) 1783
William Pitt (T) 1783 – 1801

19th Century

Henry Addington (T) 1801 – 1804
William Pitt (T) 10th May 1804 – 1806
Lord Grenville (W) 1806 – 1807
Duke of Portland (T) 1807 – 1809
Spencer Percival (T) 1809 – 1812
Earl of Liverpool (T) 1812 – 1827
George Canning (T) 1827

Viscount Goderich (T) 1827 – 1828
Duke of Wellington (T) 1828 – 1830
Earl Grey (W) 1830 – 1834
Viscount Melbourne (W) 1834
Sir Robert Peel (T) 1834 – 1835
Viscount Melbourne (W) 1835 – 1841
Sir Robert Peel (T) 1841 – 1846
Lord John Russell (W) 1846 – 1852
Earl of Derby (T) 1852
Earl of Aberdeen (P) 1852 – 1855
Viscount Palmerston (L) 1855 – 1858
Earl of Derby (C) 1858 – 1859
Viscount Palmerston (L) 1859 – 1865
Earl Russell (L) 1865 – 1866
Earl of Derby (C) 1866 – 1868
Benjamin Disraeli (C) 1868
William Gladstone (W) 1868 – 1874
Benjamin Disraeli (C) 1874 – 1880
William Gladstone (W) 1880 – 1885
Marquess of Salisbury (C) 1885 – 1886
William Gladstone (Lib) 1886
Marquess of Salisbury (C) 1886 – 1892
William Gladstone (Lib) 1892 – 1894
Earl of Rosebery (L) 1894 – 1895
Marquess of Salisbury (C) 1895 – 1902

20th Century

Arthur Balfour (C) 1902 – 1905
Sir Henry Campbell-Bannerman (Lib) 1905 – 1908
Herbert Asquith (Lib) 1908 – 1915
Herbert Asquith, Liberal (Cln) 1915 – 1916
David Lloyd-George, Liberal (Cln) 1916 – 1922
Andrew Bonar Law (C) 1922 – 1923
Stanley Baldwin (C) 1923 – 1924
James Ramsey MacDonald (Labour) - 1924
Stanley Baldwin (C) 1924 – 1929
James Ramsey MacDonald Labour (National Gov) 1929 - 1931
James Ramsey MacDonald, Labour (National Gov) 1931 – 1935
Stanley Baldwin, Conservative (National Gov) 1935 – 1937
Neville Chamberlain, Conservative (National Gov) 1937 – 1940
Winston Churchill, Conservative (National Gov) 1940 – 1945
Clement Attlee (Lab) 1945 – 1951
Sir Winston Churchill (C) 1951 – 1955
Sir Anthony Eden (C) 1955 – 1957

Harold Macmillan (C) 1957 – 1963
Sir Alec Douglas-Home (C) 1963 – 1964
Harold Wilson (Lab) 1964 – 1970
Edward Heath (C) 1970 – 1974
Harold Wilson (Lab) 1974 – 1976
James Callaghan (Lab) 1976 – 1979
Margaret Thatcher (C) 1979 – 1983
Margaret Thatcher (C) 1983 – 1987
Margaret Thatcher (C) 1987 – 1991
John Major (C) 1991 – 1997
Tony Blair (Lab) 1997 – 2001

21st Century

Tony Blair (Lab) 2001 – 2005
Tony Blair (Lab) 2005 – 2007
Gordon Brown (Lab) 2007 – 2010
David Cameron, Conservative (Cln) 2010 –2015
David Cameron (C) 2015-1016
Theresa May (C) 2016-

Key

C - Conservative
W - Whig
Lib - Liberal
Lab - Labour
T – Tory
Cln – Coalition
National Gov – National Government

Chapter 7

General Elections of the 20th and 21st centuries

Thursday 7th May 2015 Conservative (David Cameron)
Thursday 6th May 2010 *Hung Parliament* Conservative/Liberal Democrat coalition (David Cameron).
Thursday 5th May 2005 Labour (Tony Blair)
Thursday 7th June 2001 Labour (Tony Blair)
Thursday 1st May 1997 Labour (Tony Blair)
Thursday 9th April 1992 Conservative (John Major)
Thursday 11th June 1987 Conservative (Margaret Thatcher)
9th June 1983 Conservative (Margaret Thatcher)
3rd May 1979 Conservative (Margaret Thatcher)
10th October 1974 Labour (James Callaghan)
28th February 1974 Labour (Harold Wilson)
19th June 1970 Conservative (Edward Heath)
31st March 1966 Labour (Harold Wilson)
15th October 1964 Labour (Harold Wilson)
8th October 1959 Conservative (Harold Macmillan)
26th May 1955 Conservative (Anthony Eden)
25th October 1951 Conservative (Winston Churchill)
23rd February 1950 Labour (Clement Atlee)
5th July 1945 Labour (Clement Atlee)
14th November 1935 Conservative (Stanley Baldwin)
Tuesday 27th October 1931 Conservative (Ramsey MacDonald National Gov)
30th May 1929 Labour (Ramsey MacDonald)
29th October 1924 Conservative (Stanley Baldwin)
6th December 1923 Labour (Ramsey MacDonald)
15th November 1922 Conservative (Andrew Bonner-Law)
14th December 1918 Coalition
3rd December – 19th December 1910 Liberal
15th January – 10 February 1910 Liberal
12th January - 8th February 1906 Liberal
25th September – 24th October 1900 'Khaki election' Conservative (Marquess of Salisbury)

Chapter 8

The Imperial system of currency and measurements

The Imperial system of measurements was used in this country and throughout the Empire for centuries. Except for currency, the weights and measurements were first defined as we recognise them today in the Weights and Measures Act 1824 and then altered and reduced a number of times since. It officially came to an end in 1971 with the introduction of decimalization. However, we still use this system for distances on road signs, in many homes and measuring beer in pubs, and the majority of people still use these measurements throughout our day to day lives.

Currency:

This is the currency in use throughout our Imperial history and the majority of the 20th century. There were many other coins in use throughout our history but they were withdrawn at varying times long before the start of the 20th Century.

(1 Anna = 1 Half farthing) ceased in 1869.
2 Farthings = 1 Half penny
2 Half pennies = 1 Penny

(3 pennies = 1 Three penny piece
6 pennies = 1 six penny piece)
12 Pennies = 1 Shilling (1/)
2 Shillings = 1 Florin
2 ½ Shillings = ½ Crown (2/6d)
5 Shillings = 1 Crown
4 Crowns (20 shillings or 240 pennies) = 1 Pound
1 Pound = 1 Sovereign.
21 Shillings = 1 Guinea

The symbols for the currency were £ a pound, s for shilling and d for a penny. As an example, half a crown, or two shillings and six pence, would be simply written as 2/6d or more simply 2/6, as above.

Length

1 inch is divided into 16ths.
12 inches = 1 foot
3 feet (36 inches) = 1 yard
1760 yards (5280 feet) = 1 mile
1 Furlong = 660 feet, 220 yards or 1/8 mile.
League = 5280 yards or 3 miles.
Acre = 4840 square yards (43560 square feet).

Weight (Mass)

16 ounces = 1 pound (lb)
14 pounds = 1 Stone
1 Quarter = 2 Stone
1 hundredweight = 4 quarters or 8 stone
1 ton = 20 hundredweight or 2240 pounds

Weight (Volume)

Wet

5 fluid ounces = 1 gill
1 gill = 5oz
20 fluid ounces = 1 pint
1 pint = 4 gills/20oz
1 gallon = 8 pints

Weight (Volume)
Dry

1 peck = 2 gallons
1 kenning or bucket = 2 peks/4 gallons

Temperature

Fahrenheit

32 degrees is freezing point
98.6 degrees is the average body temperature
212 degrees is boiling point

Nautical

1 Fathom = 6 feet
1 Knot = 1 nautical mile
1 Nautical mile = (6080 feet pre 1970)
1 League = 3 nautical miles

Chapter 9

Our National Songs

God Save the Queen

God save our gracious Queen,
Long live our noble Queen,
God save the Queen.
Send her victorious,
Happy and glorious,
Long to reign over us;
God save the Queen.

O Lord our God arise,
Scatter her enemies,
And make them fall;
Confound their politics,
Frustrate their knavish tricks,
On thee our hopes we fix,
God save us all!

Thy choicest gifts in store
On her be pleased to pour;
Long may she reign;
May she defend our laws,
And ever give us cause,
To sing with heart and voice,
God save the Queen!

Not in this land alone,
But be God's mercies known,
From shore to shore!
Lord make the nations see,
That men should brothers be,
And form one family,

The wide world over.

From every latent foe,
From the assassins blow,
God save the Queen!
O'er her thine arm extend,
For Britain's sake defend,
Our mother, prince and friend,
God save the Queen!

Lord grant that Marshall Wade
May by thy mighty aid
Victory bring.
May he sedition hush,
And like a torrent rush,
Rebellious Scots to crush
God save the Queen!

Flower of Scotland

O Flower of Scotland,
When will we see your like again
That fought and died for
Your wee bit hill and glen.
And stood against him,
Proud Edward's army,
And sent him homeward
Tae think again.

The hills are bare now,
And autumn leaves lie thick and still
O'er land that is lost now,
Which those so dearly held
That stood against him,
Proud Edward's army
And sent him homeward
Tae think again.

Those days are past now
And in the past they must remain
But we can still rise now
And be the nation again!
That stood against him
Proud Edward's army

And sent him homeward
Tae think again.

O Flower of Scotland,
When will we see your like again
That fought and died for
Your wee bit hill and glen.
And stood against him,
Proud Edward's army,
And sent him homeward
Tae think again

Hearts of Oak

Come cheer up my Lads,
'Tis to glory we steer,
To add something more
To this wonderful year
To honour we call you
As free men, not slaves
For who are so free
As the sons of the waves

Hearts of oak are our ships
Jolly Tars are our men
We always are ready
Steady, boys, steady
We'll fight and we'll conquer
Again and again

Our worthy forefathers
Let's give them a cheer
To climates unknown
Did courageously steer
Through oceans to deserts
For freedom they came
And dying, bequeathed us
Their freedom and fame

Hearts of oak are our ships
Hearts of oak are our men
We always are ready
Steady, boys, steady
We'll fight and we'll conquer

Again and again

Music by: **Dr William Boyce** 1759
Words by: **David Garrick** 1759

Jerusalem

And did those feet in ancient time
Walk upon England's mountain green?
And was the Holy Lamb of God
On England's pleasant pastures seen?
And did the countenance divine
Shine forth upon those clouded hills?
And was Jerusalem builded here,
Among those dark satanic mills?

Bring me my bow of burning gold,
Bring me my arrows of desire;
Bring me my spear! O clouds unfold!
Bring me my chariot of fire!
I will not cease from mental fight,
Nor shall my sword sleep in my hand
Till we have built Jerusalem
In England's green and pleasant land.

Music by: **Charles Hubert Hastings Parry**
Words by: **William Blake.**

Land of Hope and Glory

Dear Land of Hope, thy hope is crowned.
God make thee mightier yet!
On Sov'ran brows, beloved, renowned,
Once more thy crown is set.
Thine equal laws, by Freedom gained,
Have ruled thee well and long;
By Freedom gained, by Truth maintained,
Thine Empire Shall be strong.

Land of Hope and Glory, Mother of the Free,
How shall we extol thee, who are born of thee?

Wider still and wider shall thy bounds be set;
God, who made thee mighty, make thee mightier yet.

Thy fame is ancient as the days,
As Ocean large and wide:
A pride that dares, and heeds not praise,
A stern and silent pride:
Not that false joy that dreams content
With what our sires have won
The blood a hero sire hath spent
Still nerves a hero son.

Land of Hope and Glory, Mother of the Free,
How shall we extol thee, who are born of thee?
Wider still and wider shall thy bounds be set;
God, who made thee mighty, make thee mightier yet.

Music by: **Edward Elgar**
Words by: **Arthur C Benson** 1902

Rule Britannia

When Britain first, at heavens command,
Arose from out the azure main,
Arose from, arose from out the azure main;
This was the charter, the charter of the Land
And Guardian Angels sang this strain:

Rule Britannia, Britannia rule the waves!
Britons never, ever shall be slaves.
Rule Britannia, Britannia rule the waves!
Britons never, ever shall be slaves.

The nations, not so blest as thee,
Must, in their turns, to tyrants fall,
Must, in their turns, to tyrants fall,
While thou shalt flourish great and free,
The dread and envy of them all.

Rule Britannia, Britannia rule the waves!
Britons never, ever shall be slaves.
Rule Britannia, Britannia rule the waves!
Britons never, ever shall be slaves.

Still more majestic shalt thou arise,
More dreadful from each foreign stroke;
More dreadful, dreadful from each foreign stroke.
As the loud blast, the blast that tears the skies
Serves but to root the native oak.

Rule Britannia, Britannia rule the waves!
Britons never, ever shall be slaves.
Rule Britannia, Britannia rule the waves!
Britons never, ever shall be slaves.

Thee haughty tyrants ne'er shall tame;
All their attempts to bend thee down;

Rule Britannia, Britannia rule the waves!
Britons never, ever shall be slaves.
Rule Britannia, Britannia rule the waves!
Britons never, ever shall be slaves.

The Muses still with Freedom found
Shall

Rule Britannia, Britannia rule the waves!
Britons never, ever shall be slaves.
Rule Britannia, Britannia rule the waves!
Britons never, ever shall be slaves.

Words by: **James Thomson**.
Music by: **Dr Thomas Arne**

I Vow to Thee My Country

I Vow to Thee My Country all earthly things above,
Entire and whole and perfect, the service of my love;
The love that asks no question, the love that stands the test,
That lays upon the alter dearest and the best;
The love that never falters, the love that pays the price,
The love that makes undaunted the final sacrifice.

And there's another country, I've heard of long ago,
Most dear to them that love her, most great to them that know;
We may not count her armies; we may not see her King,

Her fortress is a faithful heart, her pride is suffering;
And soul by soul and silently her shining bounds increase,
And her ways are ways of gentleness and all her paths are peace.

Words by: **Cecil A Spring-Rice** (1918)
Music by: **Gustav Holst**

Land of My Fathers

The land of my father's is dear to me
Land of poets and singers, and people of stature
Her brave warriors, fine patriots
Shed their blood for freedom
Chorus:
Land! Land! I am true to my land!
As long as the sea serves as a wall for this pure, dear land
May the language endure forever.
Old land of the mountains, paradise of the poets,
Every valley, every cliff a beauty guards;
Through love of my country, enchanting voices will be
Her streams and rivers to me.
Chorus:
Though the enemy have trampled my country underfoot,
The old language of the Welsh knows no retreat,
The spirit is not hindered by the treacherous hand
Nor silenced the sweet harp of my land.

Words by: **Evan James** 1856

Chapter 10

British Counties prior to 1974

On the 1st April 1974 the Local Government Act (1972) for England and Wales came into force. The Act abolished the existing local government structure of administrative counties. Listed are the counties of the three Kingdoms and the one Principality that constituted this Great Country before the Act came into force.

England: 39 Counties

Bedfordshire
Berkshire
Buckinghamshire
Cambridgeshire
Cheshire
Cornwall
Cumberland
Derbyshire
Devon
Dorset
County Durham
Essex
Gloucestershire
Hampshire
Herefordshire
Hertfordshire
Huntingdonshire
Kent
Lancashire
Leicestershire
Lincolnshire
Middlesex
Norfolk
Northamptonshire

Northumberland
Nottinghamshire
Oxfordshire
Rutland
Shropshire
Somerset
Staffordshire
Suffolk
Surrey
Sussex
Warwickshire
Westmorland
Wiltshire
Worcestershire
Yorkshire

Scotland: 33 Counties

Aberdeenshire
Angus (Forfarshire)
Argyll
Ayrshire
Banffshire
Berwickshire
Buteshire
Caithness
Clackmannanshire
Dumfriesshire
Dunbartonshire
East Lothian
Fife
Inverness-shire
Kincardineshire
Kinross-shire
Kirkcudbrightshire
Lanarkshire
Midlothian
Morayshire
Nairnshire
Orkney Islands
Peeblesshire
Perthshire
Renfrewshire
Ross & Cromarty
Roxburghshire

Selkirkshire
Shetland Islands
Stirlingshire
Sutherland
West Lothian
Wigtownshire

Wales: 13 Counties

Anglesey
Breconshire
Caernarvonshire
Cardiganshire
Carmarthenshire
Denbighshire
Flintshire
Glamorgan
Merionethshire
Monmouthshire
Montgomeryshire
Pembrokeshire
Radnorshire

Northern Ireland: 6 Counties of Ulster

County Antrim
County Armagh
County Down
County Fermanagh
County Londonderry
County Tyrone

Chapter 11

Remembrance Day

The Exhortation

They shall grow not old, as we that are left grow old:
Age shall not weary them, nor the years condemn.
At the going down of the sun and in the morning
We will remember them

Response: We will remember them.

From 'The Fallen'
Laurence Binyon (1869-1943)
1914

The Kohima Epitaph

When you go home tell them of us and say -
For your tomorrow we gave our today.

John Maxwell Edmonds (1875-1958)
1916

The End